THE CAMBRIDGE HANDBOOK OF ARTIFICIAL INTELLIGENCE

The technology and application of artificial intelligence (AI) throughout society continues to grow at unprecedented rates, which raises numerous legal questions that to date have been largely unexamined. Although AI now plays a role in almost all areas of society, the need for a better understanding of its impact, from legal and ethical perspectives, is pressing, and regulatory proposals are urgently needed. This book responds to these needs, identifying the issues raised by AI and providing practical recommendations for regulatory, technical, and theoretical frameworks aimed at making AI compatible with existing legal rules, principles, and democratic values. An international roster of authors including professors of specialized areas of law, technologists, and practitioners bring their expertise to the interdisciplinary nature of AI.

LARRY A. DIMATTEO is Huber Hurst Professor of Contract Law at the Warrington College of Business and Levin College of Law, University of Florida. He was the University of Florida's 2012 Teacher-Scholar of the Year and is the former Editor-in-Chief of the *American Business Law Journal*. He is the author, coauthor, or coeditor of more than 150 publications, including 15 books. His books include *The Cambridge Handbook of Judicial Control of Arbitral Awards* (edited; Cambridge University Press, 2020); *The Cambridge Handbook of Smart Contracts, Blockchain Technology and Digital Platforms* (edited; Cambridge University Press, 2019); *Comparative Contract Law: British and American Perspectives* (edited; Oxford University Press, 2nd ed., 2021); and *International Sales Law: Principles, Contracts and Practice* (edited; Beck, Hart, & Nomos, 2016).

CRISTINA PONCIBÒ is Professor of Comparative Private Law at the Law Department of the University of Turin, Collegio Carlo Alberto Affiliate and a faculty member at Georgetown Law Center for Transnational Legal Studies, London. She is also a fellow of the Transatlantic Technology Law Forum (Stanford Law School and Vienna School of Law). Her most recent books include *Contracting and Contract Law in the Age of Artificial Intelligence* (edited; Hart, 2022) and *The Cambridge Handbook of Smart Contracts, Blockchain Technology and Digital Platforms* (edited; Cambridge University Press, 2019). She is the scientific director of the Master's in International Trade Law at the University of Turin, ITC-ILO, in cooperation with Unicitral and Unidroit. In her career, she has been a Marie Curie Intra-European fellow (Université Panthéon-Assas) and a Max Weber fellow (European University Institute).

MICHEL CANNARSA is Dean of Law at Lyon Catholic University, France. His areas of research are international and European law, commercial law, comparative law, consumer law, law of obligations, and legal translation. His recent works have focused on the interaction between law and technology, contract, and products liability law, including *The Cambridge Handbook of Smart Contracts, Blockchain Technology and Digital Platforms* (Cambridge University Press, 2019); "Interpretation of Contracts and Smart Contracts," *European Review Private Law* (2018); "Remedies and Damages," in *Chinese Contract Law: Civil and Common Law Perspectives* (DiMatteo and Lei, eds., Cambridge University Press, 2017); and *La responsabilité du fait des produits défectueux: étude comparative* (Giuffrè, 2005). He is a fellow of the European Law Institute.

The Cambridge Handbook of Artificial Intelligence

GLOBAL PERSPECTIVES ON LAW AND ETHICS

Edited by

LARRY A. DIMATTEO

University of Florida

CRISTINA PONCIBÒ

University of Turin

MICHEL CANNARSA

Lyon Catholic University

CAMBRIDGE
UNIVERSITY PRESS

CAMBRIDGE
UNIVERSITY PRESS

University Printing House, Cambridge CB2 8BS, United Kingdom

One Liberty Plaza, 20th Floor, New York, NY 10006, USA

477 Williamstown Road, Port Melbourne, VIC 3207, Australia

314–321, 3rd Floor, Plot 3, Splendor Forum, Jasola District Centre, New Delhi – 110025, India

103 Penang Road, #05-06/07, Visioncrest Commercial, Singapore 238467

Cambridge University Press is part of the University of Cambridge.

It furthers the University's mission by disseminating knowledge in the pursuit of education, learning, and research at the highest international levels of excellence.

www.cambridge.org
Information on this title: www.cambridge.org/9781316512807
DOI: 10.1017/9781009072168

First published 2022

A catalogue record for this publication is available from the British Library.

ISBN 978-1-316-51280-7 Hardback

Contents

Figures

Contributors

Pınar Çağlayan Aksoy is an associate professor of Civil Law at Bilkent University Faculty of Law, Ankara. She received her LLB degree from Bilkent University Faculty of Law and her LLM and PhD from Ankara University Faculty of Law. She is a member of Blockchain Turkey Platform, Istanbul Blockchain Women Society, and the University of Zurich Blockchain Center. As a member of the European Law Institute, she acts as a member of the Consultative Committee for the project titled "Blockchain Technology and Smart Contracts." Her current research deals with contract law, tort law as well as the legal implications of the newly emerging technologies, especially artificial intelligence and distributed ledger technology. Çağlayan Aksoy has authored and edited books and published articles on international sales law, comparative contract law as well as tort law.

Sam Boro practices in Washington, DC, where he counsels clients including banks, fintech companies, financial services firms, and credit card companies on payments processing, consumer protection, business operations, government investigations, and regulatory compliance. His primary focus is technology transactions and privacy law in such industries as artificial intelligence, machine learning, payments, blockchain, digital assets, and fintech.

Michel Cannarsa is Dean of Law at Lyon Catholic University. His areas of research are international and European law, commercial law, comparative law, consumer law, law of obligations, and legal translation. His recent works have focused on the interaction between law and technology, contract, and products liability law, including *The Cambridge Handbook of Smart Contracts, Blockchain Technology and Digital Platforms* (Cambridge University Press, 2019); "Interpretation of Contracts and Smart Contracts: Smart Interpretation or Interpretation of Smart Contracts?," *European Review Private Law* (2018); "Remedies and Damages," in *Chinese Contract Law, Civil and Common Law Perspectives* (DiMatteo and Lei, eds.; Cambridge University Press, 2017); and *La responsabilité du fait des produits défectueux: étude comparative* (Giuffrè, 2005). He is a fellow of the European Law Institute.

Giuseppe Colangelo is Jean Monnet Professor of European Innovation Policy and Associate Professor of Law and Economics at the University of Basilicata, and a Transatlantic Technology Law Forum fellow at Stanford University Law School. He is Adjunct Professor of Markets, Regulations, and Law and of Competition and Markets of Innovation at Luiss and Scientific Coordinator of the Research Network for Digital Ecosystem, Economic Policy, and Innovation (Deep-In). His research areas include antitrust, intellectual property, market regulation, digital platforms, and law and economics.

Joshua P. Davis is a professor at the University of San Francisco, School of Law and the director of the Center for Law and Ethics. He has published dozens of articles and book chapters on various topics including artificial intelligence, ethics, and law; jurisprudence; jurisprudence and legal ethics; class action doctrine; private antitrust enforcement; civil procedure; and free speech doctrine. He has testified before Congress on federal civil procedure. He also served as the Reporter for the California Supreme Court Advisory Task Force on Multijurisdictional Practice and the Committee on Multijurisdictional Practice, drafting rules on multijurisdictional practice that were codified at California Supreme Court Rules 964–967. His publications have been cited by federal trial and appellate courts.

Larry A. DiMatteo is the Huber Hurst Professor of Contract Law at the Warrington College of Business and Levin College of Law at the University of Florida. He was the University of Florida's 2012 Teacher-Scholar of the Year; former Editor-in-Chief of the *American Business Law Journal*; and a 2012 Fulbright Scholar (University of Sofia). He is the author, coauthor, or coeditor of more than 150 publications, including 15 books. His books include *The Cambridge Handbook of Judicial Control of Arbitral Awards* (coedited; Cambridge University Press, 2020); *The Cambridge Handbook of Smart Contracts, Blockchain Technology and Digital Platforms* (coedited; Cambridge University Press, 2020); *Chinese Contract Law: Civil and Common Law Perspectives* (coedited; Cambridge University Press, 2017); *Comparative Contract Law: British and American Perspectives* (coedited with Hogg; Oxford University Press, 2016); *International Sales Law: Principles, Contracts and Practice* (coedited with Janssen, Schulze, and Magnus; Beck, Hart, & Nomos, 2nd ed., 2021); and *Global Challenge of International Sales Law* (edited; Cambridge University Press, 2014).

Luigi Distefano is an associate with Finnegan Europe LLP. With more than ten years of intellectual property experience, Distefano has gained a wide spectrum of technical expertise, particularly in the fields of telecommunications, AI, cryptography, optical devices, computer graphics, cybersecurity, and quantum computing. He is a UK and European patent attorney whose practice focuses on patent prosecution, portfolio development and management, drafting, client counseling, and oppositions and appeals before the European Patent Office. He specializes in the fields of electronic and mechanical engineering and in prosecuting computer-implemented inventions in Europe.

Mateja Durovic is a reader in Contract and Commercial Law and Deputy Director of the Centre for Technology, Ethics, Law and Society at King's College London. Durovic holds PhD and LLM degrees from the European University Institute (EUI), an LLM degree from the University of Cambridge, and an LLB degree from the University of Belgrade. He was a postdoctoral research associate at the EUI, as well as being visiting scholar at Stanford Law School and the Max Planck Institute of Private International and Comparative Law. Durovic has worked for the Legal Service of the European Commission, as well as being a consultant for the European Commission, BEUC, and the United Nations. His work has been published in leading law journals and prominent publishers, such as Oxford University Press and Hart Publishing. He is a member of the European Law Institute, Society of Legal Scholars, and Society for European Contract Law.

Martin Ebers is an associate professor of IT Law at the University of Tartu and permanent research fellow at the Humboldt University of Berlin. He is the cofounder and president of the Robotics & AI Law Society. In addition to research and teaching, he has been active in the field of legal consulting for many years. His main areas of expertise and research are IT law, liability and insurance law, and European and comparative law. In 2020, he published the books *Algorithms and Law* (Cambridge University Press) and *Rechtshandbuch Künstliche Intelligenz und Robotik* (C. H. Beck).

Mark Fenwick is Professor of International Business Law at the Faculty of Law, Kyushu University. His primary research interests are white-collar and corporate crime, as well as technology and law. Recent publications include *Legal Tech, Smart Contracts & Blockchain* (coedited with Corrales and Haapio; Springer, 2019), *Robotics: AI and the Future of Law* (coedited; Springer, 2018); and *International Business Law: Emerging Fields of Regulation* (coauthored with Corrales and Forgo; Hart, 2018). He has a master's and PhD from the Faculty of Law, University of Cambridge, and has been a visiting professor at the University of Cambridge, Chulalongkorn University, Duke University, the University of Hong Kong, Shanghai University of Finance & Economics, National University of Singapore, Tilburg University, and Vietnam National University. He has also conducted research for the EU, the OECD, and the World Bank.

Nicholas Fox is a partner at Finnegan Europe LLP. He practices intellectual property law with a focus on electronics, telecoms, and software patent litigation. With degrees in mathematics and computer science, Fox has technical experience in the areas of electronics and software. The subject matter of his work ranges from image processing and voice recognition to telecoms and e-commerce. He is a qualified solicitor and qualified as a European and Chartered British patent attorney, with full rights to appear in proceedings in the English High Courts. He has also been admitted as an attorney in New York.

Florence G'sell is a professor of Private and Comparative Law at the University of Lorraine and a lecturer at Sciences Po. She holds the Digital, Governance, and Sovereignty Chair at the Sciences Po School of Public Affairs. She has researched in the areas of causation in tort law and the evolution of the judicial system and legal professions. In recent years, her publications have mainly focused on technology. She recently edited the book *Law and Big Data* (Dalloz, 2020) and published *Justice Numérique* (Dalloz, 2021).

Robert A. Heverly is an associate professor of Law at Albany Law School and an affiliated fellow with the Information Society Project at Yale Law School. He holds a JD from Albany Law School and an LLM from Yale Law School. He has served as the director of the LLM in Information, Technology, and Intellectual Property at the University of East Anglia. Heverly's research areas are in technology, law, and society, including drones, robots, AI, and human augmentation. He has held the position of Chair of the American Association of Law Schools' Internet and Computer Law Section and was the Reporter for the Uniform Law Commission's "Uniform Tort Law Relating to Drones Act."

Charlyn L. Ho is a partner at Perkins Coie, Washington, DC. She provides counsel to clients on legal issues related to technology and privacy, including those affecting e-commerce sites, mobile devices and applications, AI/machine learning, virtual reality, mixed reality and augmented reality platforms, cloud services, enterprise software, cryptocurrency platforms, and Internet of Things devices. Ho provides strategic advice and counseling to all types of technology companies throughout their life cycle, from start-ups to established enterprises. She previously served as an active-duty Navy Supply Corps officer and was responsible for negotiating contracts for nuclear-powered aircraft carrier refueling and overhaul projects, such as replacing spent nuclear fuel in nuclear-powered ships.

Geraint Howells is Executive Dean and Established Professor at the University of Galway, and Visiting Professor at the University of Manchester. He was previously Professor of Commercial Law and Associate Dean for Internationalisation for Humanities at the University of Manchester and Chair Professor of Commercial Law and Dean of the Law School at City University of Hong Kong, as well as having held chairs at Sheffield, Lancaster, and Manchester, and being head of law schools at Lancaster and Manchester. Howells is a barrister at Gough Square Chambers, London and a former president of the International Association of Consumer Law.

Coimbra Jackson practices in Washington, DC, where she is an associate in the Technology Transactions & Privacy Law practice. Jackson advises clients on issues relating to technology-related transactions. Her clients include sophisticated and emerging companies offering cloud-based services, Internet of Things products and devices, consumer products, and telecommunications. Jackson has counseled on legal issues arising from artificial intelligence and machine-learning products, including issues related to privacy and machine-learning product liability. She is currently engaged in work focused on combating bias in artificial intelligence and machine learning in consumer-facing services.

André Janssen is Chair Professor at the University of Radboud (Nijmegen) and holds the Francqui-chair at the Catholic University Leuven. He previously held positions at the Universities of Münster, Turin and City University of Hong Kong. He has published more than 170 books and articles in the field of private, European and comparative law and artificial intelligence and law. His latest books are *International Sales Law: Contract, Principles & Practice* (coedited with DiMatteo, Magnus, and Schulze; Beck, Hart, & Nomos, 2nd ed., 2021) and the *Cambridge Handbook of Lawyering in the Digital Age* (coedited with L. DiMatteo, P. Ortolani, F. de Elizalde, M. Cannarsa and M. Durovic, CUP, 2021). He is the chief editor of the *European Review of Private Law* and a member of the editorial board of the *International Arbitration Law Review*.

Jonas Knetsch is a professor of Civil and Comparative Law at the Sorbonne Law School at the University Paris 1 Panthéon-Sorbonne. Before his PhD in Comparative Tort Law, he graduated from the University Panthéon-Assas (Paris 2) and from the University of Cologne. He previously held professorships at the University of Reunion Island and at the Jean Monnet University of Saint-Étienne. Knetsch has published extensively in tort and insurance law as well as in private international and comparative law. He is a fellow of the European Centre of Tort and Insurance Law and has an associate membership of the International Academy of Comparative Law.

Pascal D. König is a research associate at the chair of Political Science with a focus on Policy Analysis and Political Economy at TU Kaiserslautern, Germany. His research mainly deals with policies regarding digital technologies, political communication, and party competition. Recent work has appeared in Comparative Political Studies, Big Data & Society, and Regulation & Governance.

Tobias D. Krafft is a PhD candidate at the chair "Algorithm Accountability" of Prof. Katharina A. Zweig at the TU Kaiserslautern. He is an expert in black box analysis and regulatory approaches for algorithmic decision systems. As holder of the Weizenbaumpreis 2017 of the Forum Informatiker für Frieden und gesellschaftliche Verantwortung, his research interests range from the (pure) analysis of algorithmic decision systems to discourse on their use in the social context.

Migle Laukyte is a tenure track professor in Cyberlaw and Cyber Rights at the University Pompeu Fabra in Barcelona. Previously she was a visiting professor at the Human Rights Institute "Bartolomé de las Casas" at the Universidad Carlos III de Madrid and CONEX-Marie Curie fellow at ALLIES (Artificially Intelligent Entities: Their Legal Status in the Future), specifically drafting a project for a model of legal personhood for AI. She earned her PhD at the Bologna University School of Law and was a Max Weber postdoctoral fellow at the

European University Institute. Her research interests are legal, ethical, and philosophical questions related to AI, robotics, and other disruptive technologies. Her recent publications include "The Intelligent Machine: A New Metaphor through which to Understand Both Corporations and AI," *AI and Society* (2020) and "Robots: Regulations, Rights and Remedies," in *Legal Regulations, Implications and Issues Surrounding Digital Data* (Jackson and Shelly, eds.; IGI Global, 2020).

Christian E. Mammen is an intellectual property (IP) litigation partner with Womble Bond Dickinson in Palo Alto, CA. He holds a JD from Cornell Law School and a DPhil in legal philosophy from Oxford University. Mammen has practiced in San Francisco and Silicon Valley for over twenty years and has held visiting faculty positions at Oxford University, UC Berkeley Law School, and UC Hastings College of the Law. He sits on the Berkeley Center for Law & Technology Advisory Board, the Silicon Valley Advanced Patent Law Institute Steering Committee, Law 360's 2020–2022 Intellectual Property Editorial Advisory Board, and the Intellectual Property Owners Association's AI and Emerging Technologies Committee. He is also a cofounder of the Oxford Entrepreneurs Network.

Marc Martin is a partner at Perkins Coie, Washington, DC. He is the chair of the Communications Industry Group and specializes in the areas of regulatory, transactional, and strategic advice to technology, media, and telecom companies, entrepreneurs, investors, and enterprise customers. Martin structures and negotiates agreements in the areas of technology and content licensing, supply chain procurement, mobile apps, and distribution platforms.

John O. McGinnis is the George Dix Professor in Constitutional Law at the Northwestern Pritzker School of Law. He is a graduate of Harvard College and Harvard Law School where he was an editor of the *Harvard Law Review*. He also has an MA degree from Balliol College, Oxford, in Philosophy and Theology. McGinnis clerked on the US Court of Appeals for the District of Columbia. From 1987 to 1991, he was the deputy assistant attorney general in the Office of Legal Counsel at the Department of Justice. He is the author of *Accelerating Democracy: Transforming Government through Technology* (Princeton University Press, 2013) and *Originalism and the Good Constitution* (with Rappaport; Harvard University Press, 2013). He is a past winner of the Paul Bator award given by the Federalist Society to an outstanding academic under forty.

Francesco Mezzanotte is an associate professor at Roma Tre. He is the author of more than fifty publications, including "Risk Allocation and Liability Regimes in the IoT," in *Digital Revolution: New Challenges for Law* (Schulze and De Franceschi, eds.; Beck/Nomos, 2019) and "Access to Data: The Role of Consent and the Licensing Scheme," in *Trading Data in the Digital Economy: Legal Concepts and Tools* (Lohsse, Schulze, and Staudenmayer, eds.; Hart/Nomos, 2017).

Eliza Mik holds a PhD in Contract Law from the University of Sydney. She has taught courses in contract law and in the law of e-commerce at the Singapore Management University and the University of Melbourne, as well as courses in fintech and blockchain at Bocconi University in Milan. Her research focuses on distributed ledger technologies and smart contracts, particularly the challenges of expressing agreements in code as well as domain-specific programming languages. She is also involved in multiple projects relating to the legal implications of automation, the deployment of "intelligent agents" in transactional environments, as well as the burgeoning area of LegalTech. Mik holds multiple academic affiliations, including with the

Tilburg Institute for Law, Society, and Technology, the Center for AI and Data Governance in Singapore, and the Nanjing University of Science and Technology. Before joining academia, she worked in-house at several software companies, internet start-ups, and telecommunication providers in Australia, Poland, Malaysia, and in the United Arab Emirates where she advised on technology procurement, payment systems, and software licensing.

Marjolaine Monot-Fouletier is Professor of Public Law, Director of the Law Clinics, and Head of the Legal, Political, and Social Sciences Research Center at the Faculty of Law of Lyon Catholic University. She holds a PhD in Law (1999) and a habilitation to conduct research from the University Paris-Cité (2019). Her research focus is in the areas of administrative law, administrative property law, and new technologies law. Monot-Fouletier has published over twenty scientific articles, as well as a manual on administrative property law. She is a contributor to the *Encyclopedia of Jurisclasseur* and is a member of the European Law Institute.

Yelena Morozova is an associate with Finnegan Europe LLP. She is an experienced patent attorney with a background in computer science and technical expertise especially in the areas of information technology and software, and telecommunications. Her experience includes patent drafting and prosecution of patent and design applications internationally, developing and implementing intellectual property strategies tailored to business plans, worldwide patent portfolio management, freedom-to-operate searches and infringement, and validity advice. Morozova is a qualified patent attorney in the United States and Europe.

Florian Möslein is Director of the Institute for Law and Regulation of Digitalisation and Professor of Law at the Philipps-University Marburg. Möslein holds academic degrees from the University of Munich, University of Paris-Assas (*licence en droit*), and University of London (LLM in International Business Law). His current research focus is on regulatory theory, corporate sustainability, and the legal challenges of the digital age. He previously held academic positions at the Universities of Berlin, St. Gallen, and Bremen, and visiting fellowships at the European University Institute, NYU, Stanford, Berkeley, University of Sydney, CEU San Pablo, and Aarhus. Möslein has over eighty publications including three monographs and seven edited books.

Christy Ng is a legal technologist who has advised on a range of documentation and innovation initiatives within the derivatives industry and fintech space. She is a consultant with D2 Legal Technology LLP and its Hong Kong subsidiary where she works on projects relating to legal data for machine learning and digitalization of financial services. She has worked with banks, investment firms, asset managers, and law firms in both an external and in-house capacity. Through her experience she has gained unique insight into the current state of and upcoming trends in the financial industry from a documentation and Legal-Tech perspective. Ng is an author of *The LegalTech Book* (Wiley, 2020).

Frank Pasquale is a professor at the Brooklyn Law School. He is a noted expert on the law of AI, algorithms, and machine learning. He is a prolific and nationally regarded scholar whose work focuses on how information is used across a number of areas. His wide-ranging expertise encompasses the study of the rapidity of technological advances and the unintended consequences of the interaction of privacy law, intellectual property, and antitrust laws. His recent works include *New Laws of Robotics* (Harvard University Press, 2020); *The Oxford Handbook of Ethics of AI* (Oxford University Press, 2020); and *The Black Box Society: The Secret Algorithms That Control Money and Information* (Harvard University Press, 2015). Pasquale is an affiliate fellow at Yale University's Information Society Project and a member of the American Law Institute. He is the author of seventy articles and chapters, including "Data-Informed Duties in AI Development," *Columbia Law Review* (2019).

Cristina Poncibò is Professor of Comparative Private Law at the Law Department of the University of Turin, Collegio Carlo Alberto Affiliate and a faculty member at Georgetown Law (Center for Transnational Legal Studies, London). She is also a fellow of the Transatlantic Technology Law Forum (Stanford Law School and Vienna School of Law). Her most recent books include *Contracting and Contract Law in the Age of Artificial Intelligence* (edited; Hart, 2022) and *The Cambridge Handbook of Smart Contracts, Blockchain Technology and Digital Platforms* (edited; Cambridge University Press, 2019). She is the scientific director of the Master's in International Trade Law at the University of Turin, ITC-ILO, in cooperation with Unicitral and Unidroit. In her career, she has been a Marie Curie Intra-European fellow (Université Panthéon-Assas) and a Max Weber fellow (European University Institute).

Wolfgang Schulz is Chair for Media Law and Public Law and is the director of the Hans-Bredow-Institut for Media Research at the University of Hamburg. He is also the director at the Alexander von Humboldt Institute for Internet and Society in Berlin. Schulz is a member of the Committee of Experts on Internet Intermediaries (MSI-NET) and serves on the advisory board of the Law & Technology Centre of Hong Kong University. He is coauthor of *Human Rights and Encryption* (UNESCO, 2016) and *Regulated Self-Regulation as a Form of Modern Government* (Indiana University Press, 2004).

Indra Spiecker genannt Döhmann is Professor of Public Law, Information Law, Environmental Law, and Legal Theory at Goethe University Frankfurt am Main, where she heads the Data Protection Research Unit. She received her PhD from the University of Bonn and completed her habilitation at the University of Osnabrück and received an LLM from Georgetown University. She is member of the Competence Center on IT-Security (KASTEL) at the Karlsruhe Institute of Technology. She is the copublisher of the *European Data Protection Law Journal* and the coeditor of *Computer und Recht* (*Computer and Law*). In 2016, as first lawyer, she was appointed a member of the German Academy of Technical Sciences of the Union of German Academies of Sciences and Humanities. She regularly advises state and private institutions on regulatory matters of digitalization.

Gerald Spindler is Professor of Civil, Commercial, Business, Multimedia, and Telecommunications Law at the University of Göttingen. He studied Law and Economics at Frankfurt am Main. He received research fellowships in Frankfurt, where he was conferred a Comparative Law PhD. His habilitation focused on "Organisational Duties of Companies," for which he received his *venia legendi* for Civil Law, Commercial and Economic Law, International Private Law, Comparative Law, and Labor Law. Spindler is Vice-Chairman of the German Society of Law and Information Science and has advised the German and European legislators on various questions concerning the information society and corporate law.

Eric Tjong Tjin Tai is Professor of Private Law at Tilburg University. He obtained degrees in Computer Science from Delft University of Technology, and in Philosophy and in Law from the University of Amsterdam. Tjong Tjin Tai worked for eight years as a lawyer prior to taking up a position at Tilburg University. His research covers digitalization and private law, service contracts, procedural law, and methodology. He publishes extensively in leading Dutch and European law journals and has authored several books. His current research focuses on the interaction of IT and human labor in organizations and its consequences for private law, as well as the changes to private law in dealing with new technologies.

Divya Taneja is an associate at Perkins Coie, Seattle, WA, where her practice focuses on technology, media, and intellectual property transactions and counseling across a variety of industries. Taneja has negotiated software license agreements, SaaS agreements, data-sharing agreements, nondisclosure agreements, master services agreements, and other technology-related agreements. She has counseled clients on data privacy and cybersecurity matters, including advising on breach response, drafting privacy policies and procedures, preparing incident response plans, and analyzing compliance with applicable privacy laws and regulations. She is an information privacy professional certified by the International Association of Privacy Professionals.

Susan Y. Tull is a partner in Finnegan's office in Washington, DC, where she specializes in all phases and forums of patent litigation and client counseling. Her patent litigation, appeals, and postgrant proceedings practices focus on technologies related to consumer products, software, AI and machine learning, medical devices, automotive, and other mechanical and electrical systems. Tull has researched and written extensively on patenting AI and software technologies.

Christian Twigg-Flesner is Professor of International Commercial Law at the University of Warwick. Previously, he was associated with the University of Hull, Nottingham Trent University, and Sheffield University. He is a fellow of the European Law Institute, an associate academic fellow of the Honourable Society of the Inner Temple, and coeditor of the *Journal of Consumer Policy*. He has been a senior international fellow at the University of Bayreuth. His research interests are in the areas of international, English, and European commercial, consumer, and contract law, with a particular focus on the implications of digitalization. He has published many articles and book chapters on EU consumer and contract law. His authored or coauthored books include *Rethinking EU Consumer Law* (Routledge, 2017) and *The Europeanisation of Contract Law* (Routledge, 2013). He edited the *Elgar Research Handbook on EU Consumer and Contract Law* (Edward Elgar, 2016) and the *Cambridge Companion to European Union Private Law* (Cambridge University Press, 2010).

Jonathon Watson is a postdoctoral research fellow at King's College London in the National Research Centre on Privacy, Harm Reduction and Adversarial Influence Online. He completed his undergraduate studies in English and German Laws (LLB) at the University of Liverpool and his Dr. iur., LLM at the University of Münster.

D. Sean West is an associate at Perkins Coie, Seattle, WA, where he counsels clients on issues related to intellectual property, commercial transactions, privacy, e-commerce, the Internet of Things, AI, and consumer protection. West works with clients, ranging from start-ups to large public companies, in a variety of industries, including hardware, software, e-commerce, luxury goods, standard bodies, digital media, and the Internet.

Stefan Wrbka is Professor of Business Law at the University of Applied Sciences for Management and Communication, Vienna. Previously, he was an associate professor at Kyushu University. Wrbka earned a Mag. iur. from the University of Vienna, an LLM at Kyushu University, and a PhD (Dr. iur.) from the University of Vienna. Prior to entering academia, he was an in-house counsel at the global headquarters of Red Bull. He is the author or coauthor of more than seventy publications in English, German, and Japanese including *International Business Law: Emerging Fields of Regulation* (Bloomsbury, 2018) and author of

European Consumer to Access Revisited (Cambridge University Press, 2015). He was a coeditor of *The Shifting Meaning of Legal Certainty in Comparative and Transnational Law* (Springer, 2017) and *Flexibility in Modern Business Law: A Comparative Assessment* (Springer, 2016).

Katharina A. Zweig is a professor at the TU Kaiserslautern and head of the Algorithm Accountability Lab. She was a member of the Enquete Commission on Artificial Intelligence for the consultation of the German Parliament (2018–2020); and is on the ITA Advisory Board of the Federal Ministry of Education and Research. She founded a new field of studies called Socioinformatics and her bestselling German book is currently translated and will published under the title "Awkward Intelligence" at the end of the year 2022.

Foreword

There was a time when, as a general rule, lawyers took little interest in technology and, coming from the opposite direction, technologists took little interest in the law. From a lawyering perspective, technology seemed to be neither particularly salient nor significant. Even legal scholars who were interested in setting the law "in context" would not normally highlight technology as an important part of the context. Of course, there were exceptions to this general rule: There were individuals who developed niche interests in particular technologies (such as computing); the imagination of tort lawyers was sometimes stirred by new technologies and their applications (famously so in the case of Warren and Brandeis[1]); and intellectual property lawyers needed to be aware of the changing technological background. However, this was all destined to change and to do so in two disruptive phases.[2]

First, developments in biotechnologies and, at much the same time, in information and communication technologies (ICTs) became salient as a challenge for lawyers – particularly for legislators and regulators.[3] To be sure, some lawyers continued to downplay the significance of these developments,[4] but the challenges were both real and significant. Lawmakers and regulators were expected to make the right interventions at the right time, always balancing the interest in supporting and incentivizing beneficial innovation with the interest in protecting individuals against unacceptable risk, guarding against systemic risk, and respecting a community's fundamental values.[5] While biotechnologies (particularly modern genetics) provoked new questions about respect for human life, human rights, and human dignity,[6] ICTs presented major challenges for national regulators who sought to impose their own rules on the transnational

[1] Samuel D. Warren and Louis D. Brandeis, "The Right to Privacy" (1890) 5 *Harvard Law Review* 193.

[2] See Roger Brownsword, *Law, Technology and Society: Re-imagining the Regulatory Environment* (Abingdon: Routledge, 2019) and "Law Disrupted, Law Re-imagined, Law Re-invented" (2019) 1 *Technology and Regulation* 10.

[3] Also, for patent examiners: see Roger Brownsword and Morag Goodwin, *Law and the Technologies of the Twenty-First Century* (Cambridge: Cambridge University Press, 2012), Ch. 1; and Aurora Plomer and Paul Torremans (eds.), *Embryonic Stem Cell Patents: European Law and Ethics* (Oxford: Oxford University Press, 2009).

[4] Compare Frank H. Easterbrook, "Cyberspace and the Law of the Horse" (1996) *University of Chicago Legal Forum* 207.

[5] Compare Brownsword and Goodwin, Law and the Technologies (n. 3) and Roger Brownsword, 'Legal Regulation of Technology: Supporting Innovation, Managing Risk and Respecting Values' in Todd Pittinsky (ed.), *Handbook of Science, Technology and Society* (New York: Cambridge University Press, 2019), 109.

[6] See Deryck Beyleveld and Roger Brownsword, *Human Dignity in Bioethics and Biolaw* (Oxford: Oxford University Press, 2001); and Roger Brownsword, *Rights, Regulation and the Technological Revolution* (Oxford: Oxford University Press, 2008).

online environment that was ushered in by the Internet.[7] Moreover, whether the developments were in biotechnologies or in ICTs, they were coming too thick and too fast for legislators who wanted to enact hard-wired and sustainable legal frameworks. In short, whatever benefits these technologies promised to bring with them, from a legal point of view they were a problem and the challenges that they presented simply could not be ignored.

Secondly, much more recently, developments in AI and machine learning as well as in the use of the blockchain, together with a raft of developments in surveillance, identifying, tracking, and monitoring technologies, have given the legal and regulatory salience of technology a major boost. To some extent, these technological developments are still seen as a problem. Currently, we have lively debates about how to regulate AI, big data, profiling, cryptoassets, facial recognition technologies, deepfakes and so on. Like genetic manipulation and online transactions and content before them, the latest technologies are, so to speak, "out there" as regulatory targets challenging lawyers to find acceptable, effective, and agile ways of governing them. However, the twist – and it is potentially a huge twist – is that we now see these same technologies as tools that can be applied by lawyers and regulators for the smarter performance of legal and regulatory functions, such as the more efficient delivery of legal services.[8] Viewed in this new light, the salience and significance of technology is, distinctively, that it presents lawyers and regulators with fresh options: LawTech (or LegalTech) and RegTech are opportunities. If law is to be fit for purpose, it is not enough that we have the right rules in place and the right kind of people undertaking legal functions; we also need to be thinking about how new tools might be deployed to complement, or even to supplant, our reliance on persons and our reliance on rules and standards.[9]

To see the bigger picture of the relationship between law and technology, we would need to supplement our initial sketch in several respects: We would need to fill in how technologists now view tools for law; we would need to add in the way in which ethicists have related to, and do now relate to, both law and technology (the law/ethics/technology triad); we would need to underline what is being "decentered" as technology moves into the foreground (sidelining public governance, challenging public participation, taking humans and rules out of the loop, and putting the emphasis of governance on ex ante risk management and prevention rather than ex post punishment, correction, and compensation);[10] and we would need to consider whether concepts like justice, trust, authority, and respect continue to be meaningful once governance is turned over to machines, or by machines that are under some degree of human control.[11]

It is against this background of disruption and transformation that this timely Cambridge handbook offers a view of the landscape of lawyering in our digital age, a view that is wide-ranging (covering the impact of AI on the legal profession; alternative dispute resolution; consumers and small claims, and in relation to public law; and the interface between, on the one side, legal ethics and societal values and, on the other, AI) and, importantly, a view that is deep, detailed, and reflective. From the many cues for further discussion given in this impressive

[7] Seminally, see David R. Johnson and David Post, 'Law and Borders – The Rise of Law in Cyberspace' (1996) 48 *Stanford Law Review* 1367.

[8] For critical assessment, see, e.g., Karen Yeung and Martin Lodge (eds.), *Algorithmic Regulation* (Oxford: Oxford University Press, 2019); and Simon Deakin and Christopher Markou (eds.), *Is Law Computable?* (Oxford: Hart, 2020).

[9] Compare Brownsword, Law, Technology and Society (n. 2) and Roger Brownsword, *Law 3.0: Rules, Regulation and Technology* (Abingdon: Routledge, 2020).

[10] For the decentering of law, see Roger Brownsword, *Rethinking Law, Regulation and Technology* (Cheltenham: Edward Elgar, 2022), Ch. 1.

[11] See, further, Roger Brownsword and Han Somsen, 'Law, Innovation and Technology: Fast Forward to 2021' (2021) 13 *Law, Innovation and Technology* 1.

book, let me pick up on one of the concluding remarks which is to the effect that, in addition to disrupting the practice of law, AI "will have a major impact on legal education and legal ethics" – how right that surely is.

To start with the disruption of law schools, there have been numerous silver linings stemming from COVID. It might have led to "greener" policies and practices, and it has acted as an accelerator for the use of digital technologies in the delivery of legal education and in the undertaking of legal research. However, the disruption that is now contemplated is not so much in *how* we teach or research the law, it is in *what* we teach and *what* we research (as well as with whom we research).

In the law schools, it is axiomatic that our mission is to train students "to think like lawyers." When lawyers had no interest in technology, thinking like a lawyer was inward-looking, doctrinal, and guided by general principles. By the time that lawyers saw technology as a challenge, thinking like a lawyer needed to become more "regulatory," more policy-orientated, and more outward-looking (with a view to learning from economics, sociology, and philosophy), but, generally, the law schools persisted with their habitual doctrinal approach and treated regulatory scholarship as marginal to legal education. Now that we are in the age of digital law, it makes no sense to resist thinking that is both regulatory and interested in developing technical solutions. To think like a lawyer now has to be a three-dimensional exercise (engaging with general legal principles, with regulatory approaches, and with technological solutions to regulatory challenges). Moreover, thinking like a lawyer has to be guided by an overarching understanding of the importance of the critical infrastructures on which human communities are predicated – an appreciation of which holds the key to whether the modality, the process, and the substance of governance is legitimate.[12] Precisely how law schools should rewrite their curriculum to reflect this rethinking of what it is to think like a lawyer, of what it is to have the relevant legal skills, is now the big question.[13]

No less a challenge is presented by the future of legal research. Once upon a time, the agenda for legal research was almost entirely doctrinal. Researchers took the coherence and integrity of legal doctrine (and, similarly, of adjudication) as the benchmark and had no difficulty in uncovering the many tensions and contradictions that were often flagged by the leading cases. For regulatory scholarship, the agenda was rather different, but it was dominated by instrumental concerns, by identifying which regulatory interventions worked and which did not (and why). As I have said, this kind of legal scholarship invited collaboration with other disciplines, but not usually with science and technology. Today, the agenda is moving on. In just the way that the handbook proposes and, indeed, exemplifies, lawyers need to figure out how to engage with the technological dimension of legal thinking and this particular modality of governance. Whether or not the legal scholars of tomorrow also need to become data scientists or some other kind of technologist is a moot question but, in any event, if they are to engage with governance by technologies, lawyers will surely need to be involved in a much wider range of interdisciplinary collaborations. Crucially, lawyers need to be in the vanguard in developing our intelligence about how best to discharge legal and regulatory functions. To be sure, as questions about AI

[12] See further Brownsword, *Law, Technology and Society* (n. 2), and *Rethinking Law* (n. 10).

[13] See, e.g., Brownsword, *Rethinking Law* (n. 10), Chs. 14 and 15; Mark Fenwick, Wulf A. Kaal, and Erik P. M. Vermeulen, 'Legal Education in the Blockchain Revolution' (2017) 20 *Vanderbilt Journal of Entertainment and Technology Law* 351; Julian Webb, 'Information Technology and the Future of Legal Education: A Provocation' (2019) 7 *Griffith Journal of Law and Human Dignity* 72; Mark Findlay, *Globalisation, Populism, Pandemics and the Law* (Cheltenham: Edward Elgar, 2021) esp. at 146; and William N. Lucy, 'Law School 2061' (2021) 84 *Modern Law Review* (2022) 85 Mod. L. Rev. 1468.

soon reveal, digital law brings with it a good deal of uncertainty – we know that there are things that we do not know about governance by technologies and we know that there are major challenges in operating under conditions of uncertainty but, before we despair, we should at least gather up and synthesize the things that we do know. Lacking a hub that gathers such intelligence, nationally and internationally, is a major weakness in our institutional arrangements.[14]

These comments take me to a few words about ethics. The story of the relationship between law and ethics is a bit like that of law and technology. Initially, law has no interest in ethics as an external reference point; ethics at this stage has been internalized in various doctrines (such as general principles that require good faith or reasonable endeavors, or that provide relief against unconscionable conduct). However, at the same time that law comes to see technology as a challenge, it begins to take an interest in external (particularly professional medical and health care) ethics but, in order to improve the chances of regulatory interventions being treated as acceptable, a broader range of community ethics needs to be taken into account. In the present phase, when law sees technology as an opportunity, we find that some regulators are very ready to be guided by expert ethics groups (the case of AI applications in the EU is a striking example) but we also find that technologists and tech enterprises are keen to shape ethical thinking. The external ethification of law, the relationship between tech-generated codes and the law, and the relationship between local ethics and cosmopolitan standards are urgent topics for research.[15] In the bigger picture, the drivers behind LawTech and RegTech are efficiency, convenience, and workability and, while these are relevant considerations, it is important that ethics operates as a counterpoint to a discourse that is largely instrumental.[16]

Finally, I am confident that one thing that reviewers will say is that all lawyers should read this handbook. Not only is the handbook a valuable guide to where we stand in the evolution of the relationship between law and technology, it is an essential preparation for the turbulence that will be experienced as new technologies and novel applications create new tools that insinuate themselves into every corner of the practice of law.

Roger Brownsword

Professor Roger Brownsword is a professor of Law at King's College London. He was the founding director of King's College Centre for Technology, Ethics, and Law in Society in 2007. He is the founding general editor of *Law, Innovation and Technology* as well as being on the editorial board of the *Modern Law Review*, the *International Journal of Law and Information Technology*, and the *Journal of Law and the Biosciences*.

[14] See, further, Brownsword, *Rethinking Law* (n. 10), Chs. 10 and 11.

[15] On the last-mentioned, see Roger Brownsword, 'Migrants, State Responsibilities, and Human Dignity' (2021) 34 *Ratio Juris* 6.

[16] Compare, e.g., Ethan Katsh and Orna Rabinovich-Einy, *Digital Justice* (Oxford: Oxford University Press, 2017); and Benjamin H. Barton and Stephanos Bibas, *Justice Rebooted* (New York: Encounter Books, 2017).

Preface

Due to the acceleration of technology, books dealing with issues involved with the subject quickly become obsolete. This book attempts to avoid this outcome by discussing the current and future states of artificial intelligence (AI). It provides commentary on existing AI systems, focusing on its enhancing and disruptive effects on the current state of law. It also provides insight regarding the function of law in a future of advanced AI or superintelligence. Finally, it will discuss the dimensions of human intelligence and artificial intelligence from both legal, societal, and ethical perspectives.

This book comprises a collection of chapters focused on the role of law and ethics in the development and application of AI. It should be noted that all the editors equally contributed to this book project. The topics selected for the book seek to present a range of perspectives on the rise of AI and to theorize about how best to plan for the future. The book is broad in scope, discussing numerous areas of laws and uses of AI. Some of the broad issues discussed include definition and operation of AI systems, benefits and pitfalls of AI, preventing AI bias, security and privacy of personal data, issues posed by physical manifestations of AI, risks and threats of the interconnectivity of AI to the Internet of Things, developing public policy relating to AI, benefits and threats of the future development of "superintelligence," ethical standards and guidelines for AI, and whether AI should be granted personhood. More specific to practitioners is the discussion of AI's impact on the practice of law, on the negotiation and performance of contracts, as well as on corporate governance, and tort theory's application to AI from European and American perspectives. Other areas covered include application of agency law to AI agents, liability for harm caused by AI systems (autonomous vehicles), AI's interrelationship with competition law, use and regulation of robo-judges, patentability of AI, and AI as inventor or creator.

We are grateful for the work and patience of our numerous contributors. Due to the pandemic the project was postponed several times. It is only through the honoring of their commitments that this book was made possible. We are also indebted to the University of Torino, University of Florida, and Lyon Catholic University for their support. Special thanks to the commissioning and editorial staff at Cambridge University Press, especially Matt Gallaway.

PART I

AI: Development and Trends

1

Artificial Intelligence

The Promise of Disruption

Larry A. DiMatteo

1.1 INTRODUCTION

Disruption – societal and economic – has been a part of humankind from the beginning of time. One example is the transition from a mostly agrarian economy to the industrial age toward the end of the nineteenth century. Over time stalwart career paths were made obsolete. The need for blacksmiths gradually diminished, while the demand for welders arose. The technological age is just another example although the disruption of employable skills and ways of doing business has been amplified due to the recent acceleration of technological development. Advanced artificial intelligence (AI) or superintelligence promises much greater disruption. Although disruption of the status quo is viewed in a derogatory sense, mainly by those anchored in the status quo, taken from the broader view of the betterment of humankind disruption has been a positive force in the macro sense. However, advancement or disruption does not come without costs – the industrial age put the world on the path toward the existential threat of climate change. Nevertheless, this was not an inevitable pathway. If the wealthier nations had the political will, aided by technological breakthroughs, then the environment crisis could have been avoided or diminished.

The world is close to reaching another inflection point: the so-called existential threat of superintelligence with the potential of replacing human control and decision-making with its creation. Before that point, AI and other technologies have caused major disruption in the economy and employment, and this disruption will only accelerate in the future. The pivotal issue is not whether advanced AI is preventable. It is not. Even if it can be delayed there are strong utilitarian and deontological arguments that favor the encouragement of AI development. The focus should be on mitigating the negative effects of disruption and using smart design to prevent AI from ever becoming an existential threat to humankind. Professor John O. McGinnis makes an eloquent argument along these lines in his chapter entitled: "The Folly of Regulating against AI's Existential Threat" (Chapter 27).

Artificial intelligence is currently used in many areas of society – economic, big data, and government activities. It has shown its many benefits in medicine, industry, consumer marketing, and so forth. The acceleration of technology has made it obvious that AI will continue to get smarter with greater abilities to make decisions previously made by humans. The AI of the future will be characterized by greater degrees of autonomy in searching big data, accelerated machine learning, and physical robots. This brings up the issue of – despite the benefits of AI – what threats does AI pose to society and democratic institutions?[1]

Movers in society, law, design, and technology need to work together to avoid the pitfalls of future advanced AI or superintelligence. Automation has been a core factor in creating more efficient and wealthier economies. However, automation coupled with AI has led to the fear that AI decision-making, which lacks human involvement, will threaten our way of life. A truly autonomous AI system may make decisions not wanted or expected. Some have suggested that the fear of AI as an existential threat is misplaced because it will never be able to replicate the human mind. Nobel Laureate Daniel Kahneman notes that AI is only able to master System 2 thinking, which entails deliberative, rational thinking, but not System 1 thinking, consisting of intuitive and creative thinking, which will remain the domain of human beings.[2] This may be true but there is still the threat that unregulated, unmonitored autonomous systems will sometime in the future coopt the ability of humans to intervene with System 1 thinking.

This chapter sketches out the many issues related to advanced AI and its governance. It reviews the legal and ethical dimensions of that governance. Due to the acceleration of technology, the legal response will lag behind, but at some point, law will have to become forward-thinking in order to anticipate and prevent the dangers that future AI presents. For now, a few rules of thumb can be noted. AI decision-making must not be totally autonomous and must allow for human intervention. Current legal and ethical concepts, such as agency, autonomy, fairness, contract, property, intellectual property (IP), and trust, will be flexible enough to regulate abuse in the early stages of development. At some point in time specialized regulation will need to be created. Specialized regulation will include the use of technological design to ensure compliance with the law. At the ethical level, society should make normative assessments of when the pure efficiency of technological advancement is outweighed by the quality of human life and community. In the end, any solutions to future dangers presented by superintelligence must be an interdisciplinarity process that includes the input of policy makers, technologists, ethicists, and lawyers.[3]

It is clear that human beings will have an ongoing role to play in supervising AI from ethical and legal perspectives. AI will need to be monitored to prevent it from overshadowing the human element. AI will know the world differently than the way humans do; it does not possess first-person experiences that humans have developed over millennia through evolutionary processes. To lose that element would be to lose a vital piece of our humanity.

This book takes a broad view of the current and future uses of AI. It is structured along a number of topical areas. The areas chosen for study show the broad impact of AI, but remain only a selective sampling of the areas, now and in the future, that AI will impact. This introductory chapter discusses AI from a broader societal view through the perspectives of law, ethics, and public policy.

[1] This future threat was symbolized by the computer HAL in Stanley Kubrick's 1968 movie *2001: A Space Odyssey*. HAL represents humans' greatest achievement, which evolves to threaten the destruction of its human overlords.

[2] Daniel Kahneman, *Thinking, Fast and Slow* (New York: Farrar, Straus & Giroux, 2011). For a fuller discussion of the application of Kahneman's theory of thinking see Joshua Davis, "AI, Ethics and Law: A Possible Way Forward," Chapter 21, pp. 306–307.

[3] "Interdisciplinary teams are necessary for AI and application design to bring together technical developers with experts who can account for the societal, ethical and economic impacts of the AI system under design." HUB4NGI, "Responsible AI – Key Themes, Concerns & Recommendations for European Research and Innovation" (June 2018), www.ngi.eu. Permission of Steve Taylor (S.J.Taylor@soton.ac.uk).

The most positive understanding of the value of AI is to see it as a public good: "One area of great optimism about AI and machine learning is their potential to improve people's lives by helping to solve some of the world's greatest challenges and inefficiencies."[4] However, many things introduced to advance the public good work for and against that good. As such, if good is used as the basis of power the illicit use of that power is likely to follow. Something promoted for the public good will still need to be regulated. The key is that regulation must be focused on the overreach of the power that is AI, while not retarding its development. The right kind of regulation works hand in hand with the expansive use of AI. The more any misuse of AI can be prevented (or punished) the greater will be the trust in its development as a safe means to cure the many problems the world faces (e.g., climate change, poverty, equal opportunity, pandemics, and scarcity of resources).

Despite the many benefits that AI promises its development must be placed within a broader landscape of public policy. Automation, for example, is disruptive of the current employment needs of companies by making current skills sets obsolete. A forward-looking industrial policy, which includes the transitioning of workers into the skill sets created by AI, will need to be created. Foreseeable disruption without planning and mitigation will unleash the demons of human nature. The consequences of disruption caused by AI can be lessened by public policies and programs that sit outside of AI innovation.

The ethical implications of replacing human decision-making with AI decision-making must also be forward thinking. There are elements that need to be incorporated into the process of AI development – transparency, human intervention, and skills training. In the area of transparency, understanding the process of AI decision-making is vital to any interests that are impacted by such decisions: "Transparency concerns focus not only on the data and algorithms involved, but also on the potential to have some form of explanation for any AI-based determination." However, the ability to understand advanced AI systems, as well as predicting their behavior, is problematic. Therefore, the second element of ethical AI requires the design of AI that allows for human intervention to monitor and overturn AI decision-making. Finally, technical skills must be accompanied by ethical and legal skills in the design and use of AI. Technological progress of what is possible needs to be done in a framework of "putting good intentions into practice by doing the technical work needed to prevent unacceptable outcomes."[5]

There are many questions being debated about the use of advanced AI, both specific and broad in nature. More specifically, what are the implications that AI systems pose for privacy, security, and protection of personal and sensitive data? What are the ethical implications of AI's use in dealing with consumers? Should AI be granted personhood? More broadly, how should ethical standards and guidelines be developed for AI? How should public policy be constructed relating to AI? What are the benefits and threats of the future development of superintelligence?

This chapter will analyze current soft law instruments and literature to determine the ways society may minimize the risks of superintelligence becoming an existential threat to humanity.[6] Types of regulations to be considered include targeted statutory law, self-regulation, and

[4] National Science and Technology Council, "Preparing for the Future of Artificial Intelligence" (October 2016), 2.

[5] National Science and Technology Council, "Preparing for the Future," 3.

[6] The idea of a robot takeover has been the grist for many sci-fi movies. Some of the doomsday scenarios pose such questions as, "What if one day machines decided that humans were just a waste of resources and started a robocalypse? Or, will artificial general intelligence be humanity's last invention?" See Doomsday Now, "Robot Takeover," https://doomsdaynow.com/robot-takeover/.

standardization.[7] In some ways an analogy can be drawn between the development of advanced AI and the cloning of human beings. Despite the perceived benefits of cloning, such as growing human organ replacements, cloning of human beings has been universally condemned for medical, safety, and ethical reasons. The biggest concern is that it would lead to the creation of "better human beings" violating principles of equality and human dignity. In the same way, the growth of superintelligence threatens the autonomy and dignity of human beings. This chapter will explore the ways that can be used to prevent this from happening.

Section 1.2 explores the nature of law – how it evolves and how this evolution lags behind real-world developments. This lag is generally beneficial because it allows new things to develop more quickly and incentivizes innovation. However, in the age of the acceleration of technology[8] legal gradualism poses a problem in managing the development of advanced AI and fortuitously mapping out impermissible AI systems and applications. Section 1.3 will review the types of principles offered by soft law instruments to encourage the responsible development and use of AI. Section 1.4 discusses the genesis of a European approach to the development of trustworthy AI. Section 1.5 reviews the coverage of the book.

1.2 NATURE OF LAW

The relationship between law and society can be framed a binary one. On the one hand, law needs to respond to developments in society or face becoming obsolete. In this way law is purely reactive in nature. On the other hand, law can be a positive force in the development of society by placing normative limits on social development or what Karl Llewellyn called the "marking off of the impermissible."[9] In this way, law plays a proactive role in shaping how society evolves.

The evolution of law is reactive in nature resulting in a lag between real-world developments and their regulation. The virtue of "lag" is that premature regulation of something new may stifle its development and discourage innovation. The history of the Internet is an example of determining when the best time is to regulate a new technology. There were two points of view regarding the regulation of the Internet – the libertarian view that it should not be regulated in order to allow for it to continue to develop unimpeded and the traditionalist view that the newness of the Internet and unknown dangers posed by such technology required targeted law to prevent abuse. In this case, the libertarian view won out leading to the central role the Internet now plays in daily life. In recent years serious consideration has been given to enact laws, such as the EU General Data Protection Regulation (GDPR), to manage the threat that social media companies and big data, enabled by the Internet, present to human autonomy and dignity. This is the issue now presented by AI: Should it be regulated or not and, if so, when

7 Standards provide requirements, specifications, and guidelines to be applied to ensure that AI meets its technical and ethical objectives. Standards can address issues in the areas of software engineering (security, monitoring), performance (accuracy, reliability, scalability), safety (control systems, regulatory compliance), interoperability (data, interfaces), security (confidentiality, cybersecurity), privacy (control of information, transmission), traceability (testing, curation of data), and so forth. See National Science and Technology Council, "The National Artificial Intelligence Research and Development Strategic Plan" (October 2016), 32–33.

8 Thomas Friedman states that: "Technology is now accelerating at a pace the average human cannot keep up with." MIT News, "Thomas Friedman Examines Impact of Global Accelerations" (October 2, 2018), https://news.mit.edu/2018/thomas-friedman-impact-global-accelerations-1003#:~:text=%E2%80%9CTechnology%20is%20now%20accelerating%20at%20a%20pace%20the,added%2C%20emphasizing%20a%20key%20theme%20of%20his%20talk. See also Thomas Friedman, *Thank You for Being Late: An Optimist's Guide to Thriving in the Age of Accelerations* (New York: Farrar, Straus & Giroux, 2016).

9 Karl N. Llewellyn, "Book Review," *Harvard Law Review* 52 (1939): 700, 704.

should it be regulated and how? In this case, the threats to society are on a larger scale in that the creation of better autonomous systems that will lead to a major shift from human decision-making to machine decision-making. The lure of autonomous AI decision-making is that it is more accurate and efficient. The era of big data makes automated processes a necessity.

The reactive nature of law through the ages has generally been a positive feature mainly because of the gradual nature of change. Today, the acceleration and complexity of technology renders law enfeebled in the face of modernity. This presents the problem that if law continues to lag behind the technological advancement of superintelligence (independent decision-making with the ability of human intervention) and super-superintelligence (the loss of the ability of humans to intervene) any regulation will prove to be futile. This is seen in what has been called the alignment problem[10] of advanced AI in which the autonomous system something that it "believes" is in the best interest of its human benefactor and instead the decision is not the one that the human being would have made. Stated differently, AI makes a value judgment that is not aligned with the values or expectations of the human parties. This is akin to the agency problem found in corporate law where director–officer–employee interests may diverge with the interests of the corporation and its shareholders.[11]

Law to be effective will have to be proactive. An analogy can be seen in evolutionary biology where Stephen Jay Gould contested evolutionary theory as a slow, gradual process by showing that the fossil records indicate times of evolutionary "jumps" or "punctuated equilibria."[12] In the area of AI, the law will at some point of development of AI need to jump ahead in order to prevent future dangers from occurring. Hopefully, the "angst of futuristic surrender to an AI and robotically controlled world" will provide the motivation for proactive regulation.[13]

The regulation of future, unknown technological developments seems to be an impossible task, but in fact a plausible regulatory framework can be envisioned to regulate perceived future threats. The precautionary principle used in environmental protection is a case in point. Principle 15 of the United Nations' Rio Declaration on Environment and Development states: "In order to protect the environment, the precautionary approach shall be widely applied by States according to their capabilities. Where there are threats of serious or irreversible damage, lack of full scientific certainty shall not be used as a reason for postponing cost-effective measures to prevent environmental degradation."[14] Stated more simply, the precautionary principle means that an action should not be taken if the consequences are uncertain and potentially dangerous. Thus, if the consequences of a technological advancement pose potential dangers to human dignity, human rights, or democratic processes then it should be prohibited despite its perceived benefits. This is a rejection of the notion that the benefit of AI is an unassailable truth.

[10] Peter McBurney and Simon Parsons, "Talking about Doing," in Katie Atkinson, Henry Prakken, and Adam Wyner (eds.), *From Knowledge Representation to Argumentation in AI: Law and Policy Making* (London: College Publications, 2013), 151–166.

[11] See Patrick McColgan, "Agency Theory and Corporate Governance: A Review of the Literature from a UK Perspective" (May 22, 2001), https://pdfs.semanticscholar.org/79c5/2954af851c95a27cb1fb702c23feaae86ca1.pdf.

[12] Stephen Jay Gould and Niles Eldredge, "Punctuated Equilibria: The Tempo and Mode of Evolution Reconsidered," *Paleobiology* 3 (1977): 115–151.

[13] This danger is known as known as "'singularity,' whereby superintelligent machines take over and permanently alter human existence through enslavement or eradication." Mike Thomas, "The Future of Artificial Intelligence," https://builtin.com/artificial-intelligence/artificial-intelligence-future (updated April 20, 2020).

[14] Report of the United Nations Conference on Environment and Development, A/CONF.151/26 (Vol. I) August 12, 1992, www.un.org/en/development/desa/population/migration/generalassembly/docs/globalcompact/A_CONF.151_26_Vol.I_Declaration.pdf.

Big data and analytics have shown that the harvesting of personal data can produce high profits. This type of monetary incentive will result in the amoral exploitation of AI. An analogy is seen in blockchain technology, which provides a secure, efficient, and anonymous vehicle for transferring information, but in the wrong hands it can be used to illegally launder money. Just as clandestine laboratories may seek to illegally clone a human being, incredulous enterprises may seek to develop types of AI and applications prohibited by future law. The pervasiveness and depth of regulation and monitoring will be pivotal in stemming such illicit activities. The rest of the chapter will analyze a basket of regulations that can be used to prevent the exploitation of AI.

1.3 RESPONSIBLE AI

Dianna Wallis sees the speed of technological development and the complexity of the issues it presents as a call to arms. She asserts that "the sooner we start as a society discussing the issues now presented by advanced technologies, such as AI and superintelligence, the more it is likely that national and international legal systems can develop a holistic approach to the appropriate use and ethical safeguards related to such technologies."[15] This approach requires law and policy makers to be proactive. Instead of waiting until AI poses a threat to democracy and endangers society, "AI needs to be guided by a deliberative political process, to determine how fast and how far such technology should go."[16] The impact of AI programs on democratic processes has been seen in recent elections and noted by the Council of Europe: "AI-based technologies used in online media can contribute to advancing misinformation and hate speech, create 'echo chambers' and 'filter bubbles' which lead individuals into a state of intellectual isolation."[17]

1.3.1 *Landscape of AI, Society, Law, and Ethics*

AI is already in use in many sectors of society touching large companies, government operations, and the consumer marketplace. Figure 1.1 shows one view of an increasingly complex relationship between AI and its stakeholders. It focuses on six themes that need to be considered in creating responsible AI: (1) regulation and control, (2) transparency, (3) responsibility, (4) design, (5) ethics, and (6) socioeconomic impact.[18]

In the area of ethics, society must develop a framework of applied ethics for AI. This includes the selection of existing ethical norms and new norms that adhere to the use of AI. Transparency relates directly to information and education. AI or the humans implementing AI systems must be required to disclose the nature of the processes being used, the personal information being processed, and how decisions are made. Regulation and control require that humans remain in control of autonomous systems including the ability to intervene to change an AI decision. The

[15] Diana Wallis, "Visions of the Future," in Larry DiMatteo, Michel Cannarsa, and Cristina Poncibò (eds.), *Cambridge Handbook on Smart Contracts, Blockchain Technology and Digital Platforms* (New York: Cambridge University Press, 2020), 363–364.

[16] Wallis, "Visions of the Future," 368.

[17] Council of Europe, Report of Committee on Political Affairs and Democracy, "Need for Democratic Governance of Artificial Intelligence," Doc. 15150 (September 24, 2020), 9–10.

[18] See also, Jessica Fjeld, Nele Achten, Hannah Hilligoss, Adam Nagy, and Madhulika Srikumar, "Principled Artificial Intelligence: Mapping Consensus in Ethical and Rights-Based Approaches to Principles for AI," Berkman Klein Center Research Paper No. 2020-1 (January 15, 2020), https://cyber.harvard.edu/publication/2020/principled-ai. This study provides a meta-analysis of thirty-six AI principles documents and finds eight prominent themes in order of emphasis: privacy, accountability, safety and security, transparency and explainability, fairness and nondiscrimination, human control of technology, professional responsibility, and promotion of human values.

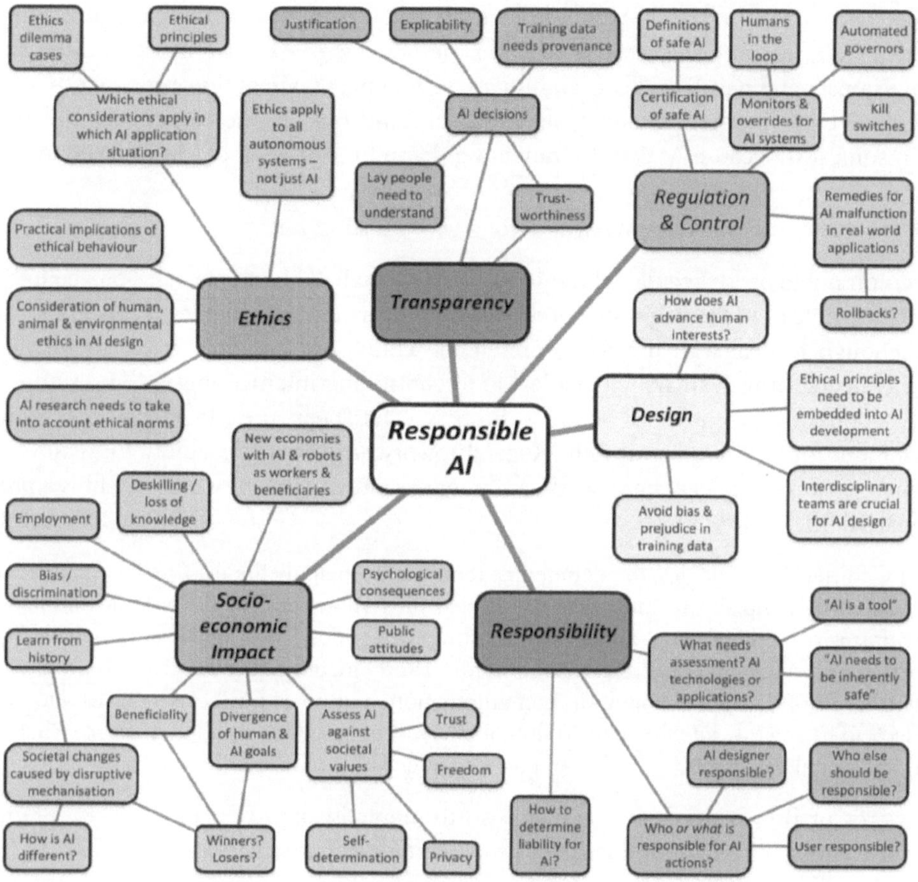

FIGURE 1.1 "Responsible AI" (six main themes)[19]

larger issue is a determination of what is safe AI and the areas where the use of AI is considered inappropriate. This type of assessment must be done through interdisciplinary dialogue as the issues involved cut across the fields of law, computer science, ethics, and technology. It manifests the urgency to turn future conversations on these questions into a "liquid network,"[20] an interdisciplinary space expanding and generating a reliable flow of knowledge.[21]

Design may consist of the use of technology to manage and monitor itself. AI systems must be designed to act ethically and ensure personal information is protected by design. Also, great precaution must be taken so that AI does not replicate the biases of its human programmers. Responsibility is the determination of which of the stakeholders – programmers, creators, owner-users – should be allocated liability if the AI system fails or causes harm.[22] Finally, due diligence

[19] HUB4NGI, "Responsible AI."

[20] Steven Johnson, *Where Good Ideas Come From* (New York: Penguin Group, 2010), 45.

[21] Barbara Pasa and Larry A. DiMatteo, "Observations on the Impact of Technology on Contract Law," in Larry A. DiMatteo, Michel Cannarsa, and Cristina Poncibò (eds.), *Cambridge Handbook on Smart Contracts, Blockchain Technology and Digital Platforms* (New York: Cambridge University Press, 2020), 338, 347.

[22] An example would be how does current product liability law apply to AI systems? See Irina Carnat, "The Notion of Defectiveness Applied to Autonomous Vehicles: The Need for New Liability Bases for Artificial Intelligence," *Trento Student Law Review* 2 (2020): 15 (notes five levels of vehicle autonomy; concludes that the American risk-utility and European consumer expectation approaches to product liability is ill-suited to AI; a better approach would include the development of harmonized technical standards to be applied in the development of autonomous vehicles).

on the socioeconomic impact of AI should be undertaken before its creation and throughout its life cycle. The question to be asked is whether the benefits of AI outweigh its socioeconomic disruptive impact and negative effects on human well-being, which range over concerns of trust, privacy, democratic values, psychological impact in and outside the workplace, and human rights. In sum, just because AI can do something doesn't mean it should be allowed to.

1.3.2 *What Is Wrong with Existing Law?*

The decision not to overly regulate the Internet with specialized bodies of rules proved to be the right decision at least in the beginning of the era of information. Existing legal constructs proved flexible enough to deal with the issues presented. Traditional contract, tort, and intellectual property concepts proved amazingly malleable in controlling internet abuses. For example, the oldest of common law causes of action – trespass – has been used to litigate the improper encroachment on a party's bandwidth. Roger Brownsword refers this ability to fit novel real-world change to existing legal frameworks as the coherentist approach where the fit is a product of manipulation:

> Faced with new technologies, the coherentist tendency is to apply the existing legal framework (the traditional template) to innovations that bear on transactions, or to try to accommodate novel forms of contracting within the existing categories. We need only recall Lord Wilberforce's much-cited catalogue of the heroic efforts made by the courts – confronted by modern forms of transport, various kinds of automation, and novel business practices – to force "the facts to fit uneasily into the marked slots of offer, acceptance and consideration" or whatever other traditional categories of the law of contract might be applicable.[23]

In the words of Brownsword, the regulatory-instrumentalist approach provides an alternative approach. It looks at policy not doctrine as they pertain to particular communities and fundamental values. The difference in approaches is shown in this question: "Even if transactions are largely automated, are there not still Rule of Law concerns implying that there will be some limits on the permitted use and characteristics of [the technology]?"[24] In the end, a combination of both approaches may be needed. Existing legal constructs should be retained and applied to new technologies, but that application should be based on an overt discussion of how best and for what purposes should those constructs be applied. Regulatory instrumentalism will be needed when the peripheral use of existing constructs meets their limitations or borders and more specialized new laws will be needed to align a new technology, such as advanced AI, to community values. This is the point when the benefits of technocracy and efficiency must yield to core values of democracy and human dignity.

1.3.3 *Escaping the Law*

With the advancement of AI and machine learning, a paradigmatic shift, sometime in the future, may be in store, where code will be seen as having the effect of law ("code

[23] Roger Brownsword, "Smart Transactional Technologies, Legal Disruption and the Case for Network Contracts," in Larry A. DiMatteo, Michel Cannarsa, and Cristina Poncibò (eds.), *Cambridge Handbook on Smart Contracts, Blockchain Technology and Digital Platforms* (New York: Cambridge University Press, 2020), 313, 322, quoting Lord Wilberforce in *New Zealand Shipping Co Ltd.* v *A. M. Satterthwaite and Co Ltd.*: The Eurymedon [1975] AC 154, 167.

[24] Brownsword, "Smart Transactional Technologies," 332.

is law").[25] Lawrence Lessig has argued that coders and software programmers, by making a choice about the working and structure of IT networks and the applications that run on them, create the rules under which the systems are governed. The coders therefore act as quasi-legislators. In other words, "code is law" is a form of private sector regulation whereby technology is used to enforce the governing rules.[26] This may be true as a technological fait accompli, but it may not be legal or ethically just. For example, an illegal term cannot be made legal simply by placing a contract on a blockchain. Even though the term will be self-executing, and the contracting parties may have little recourse, these characteristics do not magically make the term legal.

The above example is seen as an attempt to escape the law and the court system. The future of AI will provide a similar scenario but in a more potent form. Will democratic and communal values be lost to technological decision-making? Democracy is not the most efficient of governing systems often infected by waste and corruption. In order to prevent such infections, it may be tempting to turn over governmental activities to AI that will be able to make incorruptible and efficient decisions. In this scenario, AI will rise above the law. This would lead to a diminishment in human value and dignity. AI systems lack the human empathy and judgment so vital to human governance. As stated earlier, the threat is that the advancement of AI may proceed to a point where human intervention is no longer possible. In the short term, responsible AI must be developed and monitored in order to protect basic human values. In the long term, further development of truly autonomous AI systems may have to be prohibited.[27]

1.4 REGULATING AI: AREAS OF CONCERN

The depth of the legal, ethical, and policy literature on AI is enormous. For this reason, this section will focus on the initiatives undertaken by the European Union and the Council of Europe. Many of the issues discussed above are recognized in these documents and some solutions are offered. In many cases, however, no specific solution is offered but a pathway to future regulation is given. In 2017, the European Economic and Social Committee (EESC) identified that the most important AI "societal impact domains include: safety; ethics; laws and regulation; democracy; transparency; privacy; work; education and equality."[28] The European Union and the Council of Europe have recognized the need to work toward a regulatory-ethical scheme to deal with future advances in AI. The European Commission, in June 2018, established the High-Level Expert Group on Artificial

[25] Jia Wang and Lei Chen, "Regulating Smart Contracts and Digital Perspectives: A Chinese Perspective," in Larry A. DiMatteo, Michel Cannarsa, and Cristina Poncibò (eds.), *Cambridge Handbook on Smart Contracts, Blockchain Technology and Digital Platforms* (New York: Cambridge University Press, 2020), 183, 194.

[26] Lawrence Lessig, *Code and Other Laws of Cyberspace* (New York: Basic Books, 1999).

[27] See Dirk Helbing et al., "Will Democracy Survive Big Data and Artificial Intelligence?" in Dirk Helbing (ed.), *Towards Digital Enlightenment* (London: Springer, 2019), 73–98; Steven Livingston and Matthias Risse, "The Future Impact of Artificial Intelligence on Humans and Human Rights," *Ethics & International Affairs* 33 (2019): 141–158.

[28] EESC Opinion on AI and society (INT/806, 2017). It should be noted that the EU's major concern in the beginning was to encourage the development of AI. In communications of April 25, 2018 and December 7, 2018, the European Commission set out its vision for AI, which supports "ethical, secure and cutting-edge AI made in Europe." "Three pillars underpin the Commission's vision: (i) increasing public and private investments in AI to boost its uptake, (ii) preparing for socio-economic changes, and (iii) ensuring an appropriate ethical and legal framework to strengthen European values." COM(2018)237 and COM(2018)795.

Intelligence,[29] which began work on "Ethics Guidelines on Trustworthy AI" (*Trustworthy AI*).[30] Subsequently, in 2020, the Council of Europe (COE) Ad hoc Committee on Artificial Intelligence (CAHAI) published "Towards a Regulation of AI Systems" (*Towards Regulation*).[31] These documents discuss the "impact of AI on human rights, democracy and rule of law; development of soft law documents and other ethical-legal frameworks; and drafting of principles and providing key regulatory guidelines for a future legal framework."[32] These documents will be discussed below. The following three sections explore the principles needed to guide the future regulation of AI, AI's threats to human rights, and the elements of trustworthy AI.

1.4.1 *Future Regulation of AI*

Towards Regulation ferrets out a number of ethical themes and related issues:

1. Justice is mainly expressed in terms of fairness and prevention (or mitigation) of algorithmic biases that can lead to discrimination; fair access to the benefits of AI (designing AI systems especially when compiling the training datasets).
2. Nonmaleficence and privacy: misuse via cyberwarfare and malicious hacking (privacy by design frameworks).
3. Responsibility and accountability: includes AI developers, designers, and the entire industry sector.
4. Beneficence: AI should benefit "everyone," "humanity," and "society at large."
5. Freedom and autonomy: freedom from technological experimentation, manipulation, or surveillance (pursuing transparent and explainable AI, raising AI literacy, ensuring informed consent).[33]
6. Trustworthiness: control should not be delegated to AI (processes to monitor and evaluate the integrity of AI systems).
7. Dignity: prerogative of humans but not of robots; protection and promotion of human rights; not just data subjects but human subjects.[34]

Towards Regulation incorporates an Israeli Study[35] and Ethics Report.[36] The Study notes that due to the increasing complexity of AI systems "it is difficult to anticipate and validate their behavior in advance."[37] The Ethics Report enunciates six ethical principles central to creating public policy relating to AI:

[29] https://ec.europa.eu/digital-single-market/en/high-level-expert-group-artificial-intelligence.

[30] European Commission, "Ethics Guidelines on Trustworthy AI" (First Draft, December 2018), April 8, 2019, https://ec.europa.eu/digital-single-market/en/news/ethics-guidelines-trustworthy-ai.

[31] COE CAHAI, "Towards Regulation of AI Systems," DGI (2020), 16.

[32] COE CAHAI, "Towards Regulation," 7.

[33] An analogy can be drawn to the GDPR's "right to be forgotten."

[34] COE CAHAI, "Towards Regulation," 53–55.

[35] Isaac Ben-Israel, Eviatar Matania, and Leehe Friedman, "Harnessing Innovation: Israeli Perspectives on AI Ethics and Governance," Report for CAHAI, https://sectech.tau.ac.il/sites/sectech.tau.ac.il/files/CAHAI%20-%20Israeli%20Chapter.pdf; COE CAHAI, "Towards Regulation," 120.

[36] *The National Initiative for Secured Intelligent Systems to Empower the National Security and Techno-Scientific Resilience: A National Strategy for Israel*, Special Report to the Prime Minister, eds. Isaac Ben-Israel, Eviatar Matania, and Leehe Friedman (in Hebrew) (September 2020), 32.

[37] COE CAHAI, "Towards Regulation," 130.

1. Fairness: striving for substantial equality, prevention of biases and discrimination (in information, in the process, and in the product), and avoidance of widening socioeconomic and educational gaps.
2. Accountability: incorporates the principles of transparency (information about the process and related decision-making); Explainability: being able to explain on the level of individual users, as well as on a collective level if the system affects groups; Ethical and legal responsibility: determining the responsibilities for setting reasonable measures to prevent the risk of harm.
3. Protecting human rights: preventing harm to life; Privacy: preventing damage to privacy due to collecting, analyzing, and processing information; Autonomy: maintaining the individual's ability to make intelligent decisions; Civil and political rights: right to elect, freedom of speech, and freedom of religion.
4. Cyber and information security: maintaining the systems in working order, protecting the information, and preventing misuse by a malicious actor.
5. Safety: preventing danger to individuals and to society.
6. Maintaining a competitive market and rules of conduct that facilitate competition.

The Ethics Report[38] then proposes the following model, to match different regulatory approaches based on the risk level associated with a particular activity. Thus, for example, high-risk activities are better addressed by legislation and self-regulation ex ante, than by post hoc judicial intervention. At the other end, low-risk activities do not necessarily require dedicated legislation, and can be addressed through standards and self-regulation. This model, of course, is not meant to apply in a rigid fashion. Rather, it presents a framework that enables policy makers and regulators to gauge the appropriate means of regulating an activity, factoring in a multitude of variables. The Report notes that the question of "who regulates" is no less important: regulation by a central AI body enables the development of consistent policies; however, there is a risk of overregulation and chilling innovation if a regulation is adopted across the board. Conversely, regulation could be left to different sector-based bodies, which would allow for greater experimentation, at the expense of uniformity of rules.[39]

1.4.2 *Impact of AI on Human Rights*

The Council of Europe and Commissioner for Human Rights issued a Recommendation involving steps to protect human rights from AI.[40] The Recommendation notes that the threat of AI to human rights is the central concern going forward. It suggests that public authorities perform human rights impact assessments "prior to the acquisition and/or development of [an AI] system" and that assessment must determine "whether an AI system remains under meaningful human control throughout the AI system's lifecycle."[41] The Recommendation also urges that "AI actors take effective action to prevent and/or mitigate the harms posed by their AI systems."[42] Furthermore, AI systems must not be "complex to the degree it does not allow for

[38] K. Nahon, A. Ashkenazi, R. Gilad Bachrach, D. Ken-Dror Feldman, A. Keren and T. Shwartz Altshuler, "Working Group on Artificial Intelligence Ethics & Regulation Report," in *The National Initiative for Secured Intelligent Systems*, 172.

[39] COE CAHAI, "Towards Regulation," 139.

[40] Council of Europe (COE) and Commissioner for Human Rights (CHR), "Unboxing Artificial Intelligence: 10 Steps to Protect Human Rights" (Recommendation) (May 2019).

[41] COE and CHR, "Recommendation," 7.

[42] COE and CHR, "Recommendation," 9.

human review and scrutiny"[43] and independent oversight should be required at the "administrative, judicial, quasi-judicial and/or parliamentary levels."[44] The Recommendation also prohibits the use of "AI systems that discriminate or lead to discriminatory outcomes," which includes "transparency and accessibility of information of the training data used in the development of an AI system."[45] In the area of data protection and privacy, it states that the "use of facial recognition technology should be strictly regulated."[46] The most meaningful protection, which would largely mitigate the fears of an AI takeover, is that "AI systems must always remain under human control, even in circumstances where machine learning or similar techniques allow for the AI system to make decisions independently."[47] Finally, at a societal level, governments should promote AI literacy through "robust awareness raising, training, and education efforts" and developers and appliers of AI should be required to gain knowledge of human rights law.[48]

1.4.3 *Trustworthy AI and Regulation by Design*

The High-Level Expert Group on Artificial Intelligence guide for creating *Trustworthy AI* focuses on three general areas of responsible AI – lawful AI, such as conformity with the GDPR; ethical AI, which is especially important when hard law rules are inexistent; and robust AI. Robust AI is a relatively vague concept that requires AI to "perform in a safe, secure and reliable manner, and safeguards should be foreseen to prevent any unintended adverse impacts."[49] The idea of designing safeguards to prevent any unintended adverse impacts is vital in principle, but as a general statement it is specious and without meaningful content. Finally, the study lists seven requirements for trustworthy AI: (1) human agency and oversight, (2) technical robustness and safety, (3) privacy and data governance, (4) transparency, (5) diversity, nondiscrimination, and fairness, (6) environmental and societal well-being, and (7) accountability.[50]

The High-Level Expert Group on Artificial Intelligence, discussed above, recognizes the technical component in the development of trustworthy or responsible AI. One element is the development of "whitelist" rules (acceptable or required behaviors or states) that the system should always follow and "blacklist" rules (restrictions on behaviors or states that the system should never transgress). This would be given to AI developers a priori in order to design systems that do not violate the prohibitions and incorporate the required safeguards.[51] An important component of any regulation of AI will be ex ante. Instead of waiting for problems to surface, regulation by design attempts to prevent the problems from occurring in the first place. Early examples of this coopting of technology for regulatory purposes are privacy-by-design and security-by-design. For example, the requirements of the GDPR should be incorporated into the design of an AI system. Thus, law and ethical principles would be used to standardize AI development.

[43] COE and CHR, "Recommendation," 10.
[44] COE and CHR, "Recommendation," 10.
[45] COE and CHR, "Recommendation," 11.
[46] COE and CHR, "Recommendation," 13.
[47] COE and CHR, "Recommendation," 13–14.
[48] COE and CHR, "Recommendation," 14.
[49] European Commission's High-Level Expert Group on Artificial Intelligence, "Ethics Guidelines for Trustworthy AI" (2019), 6–7.
[50] European Commission, "Trustworthy AI," 2.
[51] European Commission, "Trustworthy AI," 14 and 21.

The US Government has advanced a strategic AI development plan.[52] It is characterized as a three-level structure. At the bottom are foundational values or principles that cut across all areas of AI innovation and applications, and include: (1) ethical, legal, and societal implications; (2) safety and security; (3) standards and benchmarks; (4) datasets and environments; and (5) capable AI workforce. Based on these foundational values, basic research and development focuses on two general areas: long-term investments and human–AI collaborations. Under the former category research is focused on data analytics, perception, theoretical limitations, general AI, scalable AI, human-like AI, robotics, and hardware. In the area of human–AI collaboration, the focus is targeted at human-aware AI, human augmentation, natural language processing, interfaces, and visualizations. Finally, in the application of AI, the plan recognizes the fields or sectors of agriculture, communications, education, finance, government services, law, logistics, manufacturing, marketing, medicine, science and engineering, transportation, and security. This strategy is well thought out but implementation of it will be problematic since it is based on collaboration across public-private entities, industries, and academic disciplines.

Regulation by design would not only consist of implementing existing law and ethical principles but would include a development process that anticipates future problems that may have negative ethical and socioeconomic impact. A component of regulation by design includes the allocation of responsibility. Currently, responsibility and potential liability can be easily allocated to the humans who develop and apply AI systems. This is because AI systems today are "closer to intelligent tools than sentient artificial beings."[53] However, "should the current predictions of superintelligence become realistic prospects, human responsibility alone" may not be sufficient. Instead, interdisciplinary assessments will be needed to determine where moral and legal responsibility lies when "AI participates in human-machine networks."[54]

1.4.4 *Glance into the Future*

The current and short-term progeny of AI in commerce and government has reduced costs to businesses and consumers and has effectuated more egalitarian benefits such as greater access to justice. Thus, the fear of the dangers attributed to AI have been inflated. There remains a large chasm between today's AI and that in the foreseeable future and the creation of artificial general intelligence – "a notional future AI system that exhibits apparently intelligent behavior at least as advanced as a person across the full range of cognitive tasks."[55] Even though superintelligence may be decades away, it is important that humankind begin forming an "environment (human) protection" impact study on how best to ensure that superintelligence works to enhance human existence and preserve human dignity.

The above notion of due diligence begins with the current understanding of AI and its applications. Today's regulators need to use the new technologies of today – machine learning, autonomous vehicles and systems, and AI decision-making – to develop frameworks and human capital necessary to deal with the AI of the future. Such frameworks will need to account for numerous factors, such as the quality and costs of certain technologies, as well as security, weaponization, privacy, safety and control, workforce, and fairness and justice concerns. The future regulator will be a technologist knowledgeable of the workings of AI, as well as being

[52] National Science and Technology Council, "AI Strategic Plan," 16.
[53] HUB4NGI, "Responsible AI."
[54] HUB4NGI, "Responsible AI."
[55] National Science and Technology Council, "Preparing for the Future," 7.

steeped in the understanding of the primary importance of democratic institutions and human dignity.

1.5 SCOPE OF COVERAGE

This section describes the book's coverage of a broad selection of topical areas with their own unique issues and problems. It provides a truly interdisciplinary and global perspective of the law and ethics of AI. The author group is a cosmopolitan mix of legal scholars, legal practitioners, and technologists in a variety of countries including Austria, China, Estonia, France, Germany, Italy, Japan, Netherlands, Spain, Switzerland, Turkey, United Kingdom, and United States.

The book is unique due to its breadth of coverage. It is divided into seven parts: Development and Trends; Contracting and Corporate Law; AI and Liability; AI and Physical Manifestations; AI and Intellectual Property Law; Ethical Framework for AI; and Future of AI. Part I introduces the key elements of AI and lays the foundation for the understanding of subsequent chapters. It includes an examination of the potential of AI to make law more efficient and less biased. It also examines the dangers of AI relating to its regulation, liability of entities that use AI, the replication of bias, and threats to democratic institutions. Chapter 2 is written by law and political scientists, as well as technologists who explain the various types of AI from machine learning to AI decision-making. Finally, the impact of AI and technology on the practice of law will be explored.

Part II consists of a series of chapters covering the application of AI to contracting and company law. In the area of contracting, the impact of AI on the negotiation, drafting, and formation of contracts, as well as in the performance of contracts, will be discussed. The final chapter of the part examines the role of AI in corporate decision-making and the board directors' duty of disclosure to shareholders.

Part III examines the issues of liability related to the creation and implementation of AI, including: a comparative analysis of the application of existing tort theories and potential liabilities from the European and American perspectives; an analysis of the question of liability relating to AI decision-making, data protection, and privacy; and an analysis of the application of agency law to AI systems.

Part IV focuses on the physical manifestations of AI, such as self-driving cars, other types of autonomous systems including robots, and the interconnectivity of AI to the Internet of Things. The scholars ask what happens if there are algorithmic errors that cause harm and who is liable for damages? The conclusion is that a new liability regime will be needed to allocate liability between the creators of the AI-controlled manifestations and those who sell or implement the AI system.

Part V examines the intersection of AI and intellectual property law. Key issues to be discussed include the patentability of AI from European and American perspectives; whether AI should be recognized as the creator of intellectual property; and whether AI-generated artistic works should be recognized under copyright law.

Part VI distinguishes between the ethical and unethical uses of AI. Given that regulation often lags behind technological developments, ethics will play an important part in setting limits for AI applications. The focus is on the relationship of AI to consumers in the areas of data privacy and security and the implications of AI for consumer law in general. The topics analyzed include whether AI should be recognized under the law as an artificial being, much like corporations; that is, should advanced AI be given legal status? Also studied are the implications of AI for legal and judicial ethics. How do current ethical standards apply to the lawyer's use of AI? The final chapter theorizes that the best approach is moving beyond traditional approaches to ethics to a model of standardizing ethical AI.

The final part, Part VII, anticipates the future of AI as a disruptive force in such areas as the role of AI in the judicial system, public policy, legality and regulation of AI, and the ability of competition law to prevent AI collusion. The penultimate chapter ("The Folly of Regulating against AI's Existential Threat") ponders the future of AI. It takes a costs-benefits approach to the potential existential danger of advanced AI and suggests the appropriate government policy toward this accelerating technology. The final chapter summarizes the major findings and recommendations of the book.

Some of the more specific perspectives captured in the analysis include small and large business, government officials and regulators, legal practitioners and educators, ethicists, consumers, and citizens. Cross-chapter analyses cover the use of AI in government decision-making; legal practice (negotiation, drafting, and performance of contracts, as well as company law); ethical use of AI; and legal liability for AI including in tort law, data protection and privacy, and in agency law. Part VII also examines the issue of the liability for AI decision-making, liability for physical manifestations of AI, such as self-driving cars, other autonomous systems, robotics, and harm related to interconnectivity. The symbiotic relationship between AI and intellectual property law is explored including AI as inventor, patentability of AI, and protection of AI-generated works under copyright law.

From a broader perspective, there is the issue of "just because something can be done or achieved does that mean it should be done?" The normative element of autonomous systems and advanced AI are discussed in relationship to consumers, ethical frameworks, AI as a legal person, and control of AI through standardization. In Chapter 27, Professor John O. McGinnis leaves the reader with a positive and hopeful view of the development of advanced AI. He notes that AI as an existential threat to democracy and humanity is mostly speculative, but not certain. In the end, rationality warrants the encouragement of AI research because of the benefits it holds for humankind. AI is not the case for the application of a precautionary principle to prevent unexpected harm. It is simply a product of human creativity that can be harnessed for the greater good. Governments through funding and facilitative regulations or standardization should play a key role in this harnessing.

2

Essence of AI

What Is AI?

Pascal D. König, Tobias D. Krafft, Wolfgang Schulz, and Katharina A. Zweig

2.1 INTRODUCTION

As artificial intelligence (AI) systems increasingly become more widespread in society, many people regularly interact with them as a normal part of their everyday lives. The increasing prevalence of and seeming familiarity with everyday applications that employ AI may, however, easily betray its complexity. Diagnoses of the role of AI in society in public and scholarly discourse regularly depict AI as a uniform, monolithic phenomenon – almost like a force of nature that drives societal change. This is palpable, for instance, in statements that posit that AI will transform all aspects of social and economic life. However, while it is true that a certain set of technological advances largely rooted in computer science are responsible for an entire array of innovations in various domains, speaking of AI as a single technical entity conceals how elusive and multifaceted the term is.

Not only is there no commonly accepted definition of AI, but what the term refers to will, at the very least, depend on whether one is talking about AI as (a) a scientific field, (b) a technology or method, or (c) concrete applications of AI systems. The description of AI below will refer to each of these aspects and will partly show a certain overlap that is hard to avoid when talking about AI. We will use this categorization in the text for greater clarity.

A closer look at concrete implementations of AI quickly reveals a considerable diversity in its technical features, purposes, and scope. This means that the term AI is used differently by different people and may refer to many different things. Obviously, when it comes to confronting ethical, legal, and regulatory questions that are tied to the use of AI systems and their consequences, it is important to have a clear understanding of what one is dealing with. Adequate regulatory responses in particular may be hindered by a disconnect between policy actors and AI researchers in how they understand AI.[1] From a regulatory and policy perspective, it is therefore important to have an understanding of AI that captures aspects relevant to societal intervention while being aware of AI's current and future technical capabilities. Yet it is equally important to recognize that any attempt to get to the essence of AI needs to acknowledge that there is no common understanding of its definition and that it is used for multiple interwoven but separate concepts by different people. The present chapter thus aims to offer an answer to the question "what is AI?" that takes into account these considerations. It describes what makes

[1] P. M. Krafft, M. Young, M. Katell, K. Huang, and G. Bugingo, "Defining AI in policy versus practice," *Proceedings of the AAAI/ACM Conference on AI, Ethics, and Society* (New York: ACM, 2020), pp. 72–78.

AI so hard to pin down and points to those aspects that are essential for understanding the specific ethical and legal consequences of using AI systems.

The next section will first provide a brief history of the field of AI to illustrate the roots of this term's complexity and to put more recent developments in perspective. It highlights what is special about the more recent advances, which have caused a surge in societal and political interest in AI as a technology. In a second step, we identify core elements of a definition of AI. By describing the difficulties and challenges of trying to find a single, unifying definition, we show why AI can only meaningfully be understood as a complex, inherently multifaceted term. Third, we offer a concise account of how concrete implementations of modern AI commonly work (Sections 2.3 and 2.4). Going beyond the technical dimension, we also discuss the embeddedness of AI systems and show in what sense they need to be understood as part of larger socio-technical systems. Finally, we synthesize those features of AI that have direct consequences for legal concepts in Section 2.5.

2.2 AI PAST AND PRESENT

A historical perspective on the scientific discipline of AI is helpful for understanding what makes the term so difficult to define. Throughout history as a scientific field, AI has been marked by a high degree of diversity. Not only are there different strands that are interested in different capabilities known from human cognition, such as perception, representation, or reasoning, but there is also a pluralism in the approaches to implementing AI, if not "an anarchy of methods."[2] Although new approaches have been devised over time there is also a discernible continuity in the evolution of the field of AI, with current approaches being rooted in decades-old developments and partly revitalizing the dreams of the field's founders.

The term AI was coined in the Dartmouth workshop organized by the mathematician John McCarthy in the year 1956. While this date is commonly seen as the birth of the field of AI research, the basis for this research had been formed through scientific breakthroughs, especially in the preceding three decades. Important theoretical foundations had been laid for theoretical computer science with contributions that, somewhat ironically, showed the limitations of computation. With his incompleteness theorems, Kurt Gödel[3] pointed to the limits of provability in formal axiomatic theories, showing that there are statements in higher-order logic that are true but not provable. And Alan Turing[4] demonstrated the so-called halting problem with proof that no program can determine, for all other programs and any given input, whether they will finish in finite time.

It was also Turing who discussed the possibility of creating AI and proposed an empirical test as a sufficient condition for such intelligence that mimics human intelligence.[5] His test was supposed to determine whether a machine, in conversation with a person, can trick that person into believing the machine is a human. This "Turing Test" profoundly influenced the field of AI, but its attempt to provide an operational definition of intelligence and its explicit comparison

[2] J. Lehman, J. Clune, and S. Risi, "An anarchy of methods: Current trends in how intelligence is abstracted in AI" (2014) 29 *IEEE Intelligent Systems* 56–62.

[3] K. Gödel, "Über formal unentscheidbare Sätze der Principia Mathematica und verwandter Systeme I" (1931) 38 *Monatshefte für Mathematik und Physik* 173–98.

[4] A. M. Turing, "On computable numbers, with an application to the Entscheidungsproblem" (1937) s2–42 *Proceedings of the London Mathematical Society* 230–65.

[5] A. M. Turing, "Computing machinery and intelligence" (1950) 54 *Mind* 433–60.

of machine with human intelligence may have also distracted from or hindered further developments for some time.[6]

The human mind and its intellectual capacity were the clear point of reference in early work on AI, which was primarily interested in problems of math, logic, and language use. Despite the limited means of that time, AI research was guided by the big question of how to create human-like intelligence, and overwhelming optimism marked the spirit of that age. In 1967, Marvin Minsky, a pioneer of AI research and co-organizer of the Dartmouth workshop, made the overly ambitious prediction that "within a generation, I am convinced, few compartments of intellect will remain outside the machine's realm – the problem of creating 'artificial intelligence' will be substantially solved."[7]

These expectations were formulated against the backdrop of remarkable advances since the early 1940s. McCullough and Pitts formulated the foundations of neutral networks in 1943, showing that neurons, that is, input-processing cells or nodes, could perform Boolean operations and, therefore, serve for computation in general.[8] The implementation of their approach, however, was limited by the hardware of that time. Research on neural networks was later carried forward by Marvin Minsky with the computational implementation of a neural net in 1951, and by Frank Rosenblatt, who created the perceptron, consisting of two layers of neurons that generate yes/no answers to data inputs, in 1958. What made perceptrons a promising advance was that they could be trained to make classifications through feeding them input data for which the class membership of objects is known. Hence, neural networks could be used for machine learning as these networks could adapt their internal structure based on processed inputs. The fact that computers could be programmed to learn and thus do more than perform functions that were explicitly programmed by humans was also impressively demonstrated with the checker player developed by Arthur Samuel – a program that learned to choose the best move from annotated checkers games and was able to beat advanced players of the game.[9]

Despite these successes, the expectations of what was achievable in AI were exaggerated at the time. The perceptrons were plagued by computational limitations and these were only overcome later, that is, only after a disillusionment with AI developments that led to a marked decrease in funding for AI research.[10] Despite the resulting so-called AI winter of the 1970s, important developments continued and built upon previous advances.

An important step forward was the creation of expert systems as a concrete application of AI. These systems encoded human expert knowledge and used inference to solve real-world problems, for example to arrive at a medical diagnosis based on patient information and medical knowledge. Expert systems continued the top-down approach – also called "Good Old-Fashioned AI" – of the 1950s with methods rooted in logic-based reasoning while aiming at the creation of provable applications. This strand of AI development hit another wall as the process of representing the relevant knowledge required major efforts and because the limited ability of expert systems to grasp degrees of certainty collided with the complexity of the real world.[11]

[6] B. Whitby, "The Turing Test: AI's biggest blind alley?" in P. Millican and A. Clark (eds.), *Machines and Thought: The Legacy of Alan Turing* (Oxford: Oxford University Press, 1996), pp. 53–62.
[7] M. Minsky, *Computation: Finite and Infinite Machines* (Upper Saddle River, NJ: Prentice-Hall, 1967), p. 2.
[8] S. Franklin, "History, motivations, and core themes," in K. Frankish and W. M. Ramsey (eds.), *The Cambridge Handbook of Artificial Intelligence* (Cambridge: Cambridge University Press, 2014), pp. 15–33 and pp. 16–17.
[9] A. L. Samuel, "Some studies in machine learning using the game of checkers" (1959) 3 *IBM Journal of Research and Development* 210–29.
[10] Franklin, "History, motivations, and core themes," 19.
[11] E. Alpaydin, *Machine Learning: The New AI* (Cambridge, MA: MIT Press, 2016), p. 51.

At the same time, the foundations for overcoming the limits of prevailing logic-based deductive approaches had already been laid, with techniques for coping with uncertainty and imprecision emerging in the mid- to late 1980s. Further, the study of neural networks was revitalized with the use of the backpropagation algorithm by Paul John Werbos.[12] These developments together led to an overarching shift in AI research as there was a concomitant move away from the ambitious goal of creating forms of general and human-like intelligence and toward devising solutions for narrowly defined problems. This led to a productive diversification in AI research, relying on a broad range of methods.

A major shift occurred with a greater reliance on bottom-up or "soft" or "scruffy" (versus neat) approaches. These became possible with the combination of several conditions. Theoretical advances and refined methods, the increased computational power and the availability of larger amounts of machine-readable data from all kinds of sensory inputs are important requirements for AI applications based on inductive rather than deductive methods.[13] The task of language translation is an instructive example in this regard. Considerable progress in this area has been achieved through refraining from attempts to formulate explicit and universal grammatical rules to provide a correct translation for any given case. Instead, by harnessing massive amounts of data in the form of human translations, machine learning can be used to find regularities that allow for predicting a correct and useful translation for a given input.[14]

This inductive and data-driven solution has proven to be very useful in various domains, such as speech recognition and complex games, and has helped to deal with research problems in other disciplines, such as physics and engineering.[15] As a result, machine learning has become the dominant paradigm in AI, with the result that, simply put, comparatively more weight is placed on data for creating AI applications whereas relatively less weight is placed on algorithms.[16] This has led to solutions to problems that were long thought to be far out of reach, such as in speech recognition or language translation. Nonetheless, the foundations of more recent successful approaches, as prominently displayed with the superhuman performance of the Go-playing system AlphaGo, had already been laid between the 1940s and the 1970s. The history of advances in the field of AI, as illustrated in Figure 2.1, is thus marked by more continuity than may appear, given the variable public attention to the field over the years.

It may seem that in the current state of AI, the engineering of AI solutions to concrete problems has superseded the endeavor of creating more general forms of intelligence. However, both strands prevail and partly complement each other in moving toward a more general approach.[17] The prospects for realizing such more comprehensive forms of AI are closely tied to the challenge of achieving embedded or embodied AI, meaning systems that maintain relations with their environment and exhibit some sort of situational awareness.[18] This will also be crucial for intelligent AI systems to be able to navigate a world that has been shaped by

[12] P. J. Werbos, *The Roots of Backpropagation: From Ordered Derivatives to Neural Networks and Political Forecasting* (Hoboken, NJ: Wiley, 1974).

[13] Franklin, "History, motivations, and core themes," 21–24.

[14] T. Poibeau, *Machine Translation* (Cambridge, MA: MIT Press, 2017).

[15] See, e.g., J. Schmidt, M. R. G. Marques, S. Botti, and M. A. L. Marques, "Recent advances and applications of machine learning in solid-state materials science" (2019) 5 *npj Computational Materials* 1–36.

[16] S. J. Russell and P. Norvig, *Artificial Intelligence: A Modern Approach*, 3rd ed. (London: Pearson, 2016), p. 27.

[17] Franklin, "History, motivations, and core themes," 30–31.

[18] S. Franklin, "Autonomous agents as embodied AI" (1997) 28 *Cybernetics and Systems* 499–520; Y. Maruyama, "The conditions of artificial general intelligence: Logic, autonomy, resilience, integrity, morality, emotion, embodiment, and embeddedness," in B. Goertzel, A. I. Panov, A. Potapov, and R. Yampolskiy (eds.), *Artificial General Intelligence* (Cham: Springer International Publishing, 2020), pp. 242–51.

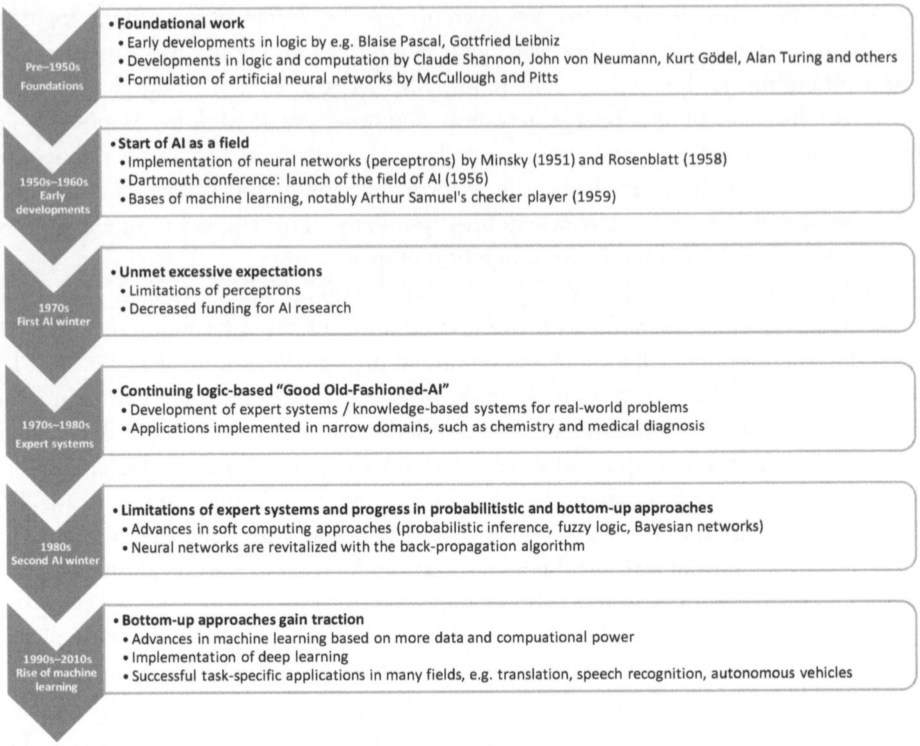

FIGURE 2.1 Timeline of major developments in AI research and applications

humans and that requires competent language use, a commonsense understanding of this world as well as the abilities to engage in cumulative learning and devise abstract plans of action.[19]

Some have also voiced concerns that the limitations of current approaches that have led to recent successes may already have been reached and that a new AI winter is imminent.[20] Ultimately, the idea of an AI winter may be misleading because, as the history of AI shows, there have been ongoing developments that have advanced the field. Yet, this evolution is largely detached from the ebb and flow of public attention to AI. The heightened attention has been accompanied by a stylized depiction of the technology and very high expectations regarding its potential, partly fueled by the marketing efforts of tech companies benefiting from a public belief in the potential of AI.

It is therefore highly possible that a recent optimistic outlook will again give way to disenchantment. The risk in that case is "that the backlash is excessive, the disappointment too negative, and potentially valuable solutions are thrown out with the water of the illusions."[21] However, even if the overblown expectations of AI – the dangers as much as the promises – do not materialize, the applications that already exist today and those that can be expected in the coming years are certain to create ethical, legal, and regulatory challenges.

[19] S. J. Russell, *Human Compatible: AI and the Problem of Control* (London: Penguin Books, 2020), pp. 78–92.

[20] T. Nield, "Is another AI winter coming? And, has deep learning already hit its limitations?" (February 8, 2019), https://medium.com/hackernoon/is-another-ai-winter-coming-ac552669e58c; S. Shead, "Researchers: Are we on the cusp of an 'AI winter'?" (January 12, 2020), www.bbc.com/news/technology-51064369.

[21] L. Floridi, "AI and Its New Winter: From Myths to Realities," (2020) 33 *Philosophy & Technology* 1–3 at 2.

2.3 AI AS A MULTIFACETED CONCEPT

AI is notoriously difficult to define. It has repeatedly been remarked that no consensus has been achieved in the field of AI research on how AI should be understood.[22] There are several reasons why it is difficult to arrive at a unifying definition. First, there are many subfields of AI research that foreground different capabilities commonly linked to intelligence such as reasoning, planning, vision, and natural language processing. This disciplinary heterogeneity of AI research is further increased with ties to other disciplines like neuroscience, biology, and cognitive sciences. Cutting across the various research problems are a multitude of AI approaches and methods, like logic programming, probabilistic reasoning, and various forms of machine learning, through which researchers and developers aim to implement forms of AI. In light of this heterogeneity of AI as a discipline, it is hardly surprising that achieving a single and shared definition has been untenable: "Many definitions of AI are disliked by researchers, not because they are wrong, but because they are not useful."[23]

The limited usefulness of a unifying definition of AI at least for some strands of the field is also rooted in a second reason that stems from the intelligence part of AI. Historically, AI research has been informed by an anthropocentric notion of intelligence. Human intelligence as the point of reference is present in several definitions of AI. For instance, AI has been called "the art of creating machines that perform functions that require intelligence when performed by people"[24] and "the study of how to make computers do things at which, at the moment, people are better."[25] Similarly, the Merriam Webster dictionary describes AI as "the capability of a machine to imitate intelligent human behavior."[26] Indeed, the aim of achieving a likeness between minds and machines was already prevalent among pioneers of AI research, such as Wiener,[27] Turing,[28] and von Neumann.[29]

While human intelligence provides a useful standard of comparison, it is ultimately of limited use. Not only do existing applications of AI already show super-human performance with regard to specific tasks, such as playing and winning at chess, but also, they do not have to function like the human mind, nor do they need to exhibit self-awareness and consciousness to perform tasks that would otherwise require intelligence when done by humans. Furthermore, there can be forms of nonhuman intelligence, as is found in some animals but also in certain phenomena of collective behavior, such as swarm intelligence.[30] Important distinctions can thus be made between a human versus a more general rational standard and between behavioral versus thought-based definitions of intelligence.[31] However, even within these categories it is possible to conceive of intelligence differently, for example in terms of capabilities, functions, or

[22] Krafft et al., "Defining AI in Policy versus Practice"; P. Wang, "On defining artificial intelligence" (2019) 10 *Journal of Artificial General Intelligence* 1–37.
[23] Wang, "On defining artificial intelligence," 5.
[24] R. Kurzweil, *The Age of Intelligent Machines* (Cambridge, MA: MIT Press, 1990), p. 117.
[25] E. Rich and K. Knight, *Artificial Intelligence*, 2nd ed. (New York: McGraw-Hill, 1991), p. 3.
[26] Merriam Webster, "Artificial intelligence" (2020).
[27] N. Wiener, *Cybernetics, or Control and Communication in the Animal and the Machine* (Hoboken, NJ: Wiley, 1948).
[28] Turing, "Computing machinery and intelligence."
[29] J. von Neumann, *The Computer and the Brain* (New Haven, CT: Yale University Press, 1958).
[30] D. R. Hofstadter, *Gödel, Escher, Bach: An Eternal Golden Braid*, 20th anniversary ed. (New York: Basic Books, 1999); A. Winfield, "Intelligence is not one thing," in D. Monett, C. W. P. Lewis, and K. R. Thórisson (eds.), *Journal of Artificial Intelligence*: Special Issue "On Defining Artificial Intelligence" – Commentaries and Author's Response (2020), pp. 97–100.
[31] Russell and Norvig, *Artificial Intelligence*, pp. 2–5.

principles.[32] In sum, there is, as Moore has noted, "no general theory of intelligence or learning that unites the discipline."[33]

Nonetheless, there seems to be a widespread acceptance of the general technical understanding of intelligence, understood as "the computational part of the ability to achieve goals in the world. Varying kinds and degrees of intelligence occur in people, many animals and some machines."[34] It should be noted that in this definition, intelligence does not necessarily comprise adaptivity, which is often deemed an aspect of intelligence more generally and also forms part of other definitions of AI.[35] As Winfield states, intelligence, as the capability to find and select the most appropriate course of action, should be analytically distinguished from adaptation, as the ability to acquire new strategies for action selection and new actions.[36] At the same time, intelligence may comprise adaptivity in the sense that the most appropriate decision in a given situation may lie exactly in trying out a novel course of action.[37]

Consensus on a general technical understanding of intelligence in AI would have limited usefulness of a unifying definition in that AI as a technology is subject to changing perceptions. The field of AI itself is continuously evolving, making AI a moving target.[38] Also, technological implementations of AI and their perceptions are of a malleable nature, an idea that is encapsulated in the so-called AI-effect.[39] This "effect" refers to the fact that if a machine can solve a given cognitive problem, it is no longer considered AI. Applications that were once seen as sophisticated become normalized and lose their aura of a remarkable achievement.

When it comes to realizing AI as technology, this can also take vastly different forms. An important distinction in this regard is between manually derived decision rules (e.g., in expert systems) and rules "learned" by an AI system – with the latter introducing further complexity and novel problems, as explained further below. A second central distinction is that between general and narrow AI. The discipline of AI has since its very origins been aiming at the realization of a demanding notion of general intelligence that, comparable to human intelligence, amounts to an ability to deal with a wide range of tasks and to adapt to novel tasks by acquiring adequate problem-solving capabilities. However, while the aim of creating a "General Problem Solver"[40] has informed AI research since its incipiency, only a small fraction of AI research and applications is dedicated to this goal of creating a *general* (or "*strong*") AI. Rather, the majority of efforts are directed at developing solutions that fall under *narrow* (or "*weak*") AI, which serves to deal with narrowly defined tasks by achieving a certain goal or a set of goals.

32 Wang, "On defining artificial intelligence."

33 J. Moore, "The Dartmouth College Artificial Intelligence Conference: The next fifty years" (2006) 27 *AI Magazine* 87–91 at 88.

34 J. McCarthy, "What is artificial intelligence: Basic questions" (2007), p. 2, http://jmc.stanford.edu/artificial-intelligence/what-is-ai/index.html.

35 R. J. Sternberg, "The concept of intelligence and its role in lifelong learning and success" (1997) 52 *American Psychologist* 1030–37 has proposed a general definition of intelligence as "comprising the mental abilities necessary for adaptation to, as well as selection and shaping of any environmental context" (1031).

36 Winfield, "Intelligence is not one thing," 99.

37 On this, see, e.g., Russell and Norvig, *Artificial Intelligence*.

38 A. Bertolini, *Artificial Intelligence and Civil Liability*, Study commissioned by the European Parliament's Policy Department for citizens' rights and constitutional affairs at the request of the JURI Committee, 2018, PE 608.848, p. 15.

39 P. McCorduck, *Machines Who Think: A Personal Inquiry into the History and Prospects of Artificial Intelligence*, 25th anniversary updated ed. (Natick, MA: A.K. Peters, 2004).

40 G. W. Ernst and A. Newell, "Some issues of representation in a general problem solver," *Proceedings of the April 18–20, 1967, Spring Joint Computer Conference – AFIPS'67* (Atlantic City, NJ: ACM Press, 1967), p. 583.

Examples of such narrow AI are the spam filter for one's email inbox, optical character recognition for turning images into text, facial recognition software, or a system designed to play (and win at) the board game Go. Although the development of narrow AI is highly fragmented and removed from the intricate and holistic task of creating a general intelligence, it is precisely the focus on specific tasks that has led to major advances.[41] And these are the applications that already have major real-world impacts and are creating legal and regulatory challenges.

AI in its narrow form is a multiplicity of concrete realizations of AI systems that comprise applications ranging from a single executed program over computer networks to robots. They may perform such different functions as speech recognition, assisting people in the organization of everyday life, or autonomously moving objects (e.g., shipping containers) from one place to another. Their complexity is highly varied. Some AI systems achieve an objective in a way that is heavily determined by human inputs, whereas others require minimal human input to achieve a predefined goal as they learn and update their decision model. What they learn exactly and which objective they achieve, in turn, depends on the concrete setting in which AI systems are deployed.

AI both as a field and as a technology with its concrete realization are extremely heterogeneous. Not only does this make formulating a coherent and agreed-upon definition of AI very difficult, but also a unifying definition is not very helpful because definitions depend on the purpose for which they are created – an aspect that is furthermore tied to disciplinary perspectives. However, with an eye on the trove of new legal questions, it is helpful to take AI as denoting the set of digital artifacts (hardware and software, possibly combined) that contains at least one learning or learned component, that is, a component that is able to change its behavior based on presented data and the patterns induced from that data. This induction of patterns that are turned into behavior can either be finished by the time the artifact is used ("learned component") or be ongoing ("learning component").

2.4 IMPLEMENTING AND EVALUATING AI

At the heart of modern AI lies the concept of agents that are situated in an environment and interact with that environment while showing a certain degree of autonomy.[42] Such an agent senses the environment through perceptual inputs (percepts) and acts upon these inputs in pursuit of certain goals. In doing so, the agent may affect its environment via actuators of some sort and thereby also influence what perceptions it will receive later.[43] This notion of an agent is illustrated in Figure 2.2. Key to the agent's behavior is its agent program, which maps any perceptions it receives to actions and effectively realizes cognitive-like functions of information processing (e.g., recognition or reasoning). This program can be rather simplistic and work akin to a reflex that only considers the most recent inputs, or act according to a fixed program that also takes into account earlier inputs. In principle, it may also perform complex and open learning processes based on an internal representation of the state of the environment and through modeling the expected performance resulting from different actions or action

[41] Wang, "On defining artificial intelligence," 14.

[42] Franklin, "History, motivations, and core themes," 28–29.

[43] S. Franklin and A. Graesser, "Is it an agent, or just a program?: A taxonomy for autonomous agents," in J. P. Müller, M. J. Wooldridge, and N. R. Jennings (eds.), *Intelligent Agents III: Agent Theories, Architectures, and Languages* (Berlin; Heidelberg: Springer International Publishing, 1997), pp. 21–35.

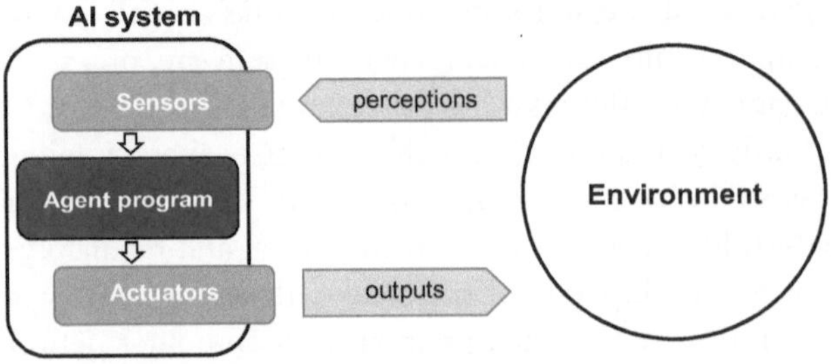

FIGURE 2.2 AI systems understood according to the agent concept

sequences. However, for now, these systems are deemed to be unsafe and are unlikely to be deployed in the real world in the near future.[44]

Concrete applications of AI systems modeled on agents can operate in very different environments. Accordingly, their sensors and the kind of actions they perform can be of vastly different natures depending on where they are implemented. They might interact with a physical environment, which is clearly the case for the object recognition systems in autonomous vehicles. Or, alternatively, they are software agents that are designed to interact with the physical world in a specific way, as do chatbots that operate as text-based or voice-controlled conversational agents. Others may be entirely simulated in a virtual environment and even interact with other virtual agents, which is the case, for example, for AI as part of computer games or simulations.

Some AI systems may operate less as agents interacting with an environment and more as tools that people can use to better manage their own environment. For instance, a system designed for facial recognition may process inputs to produce some sort of classification as an output only when prompted to do so. And what happens with this output may be entirely up to human decision-makers. Nonetheless, such an AI system can still be understood in terms of the agent model because this kind of system depends on receiving inputs that it processes while optimizing a predefined goal with its classifications. Also, while outputs produced by a facial recognition system are different from actuators that allow, for example, a robot to act on its environment, the classification results of the facial recognition system can still have an effect on human actions that, in turn, can feed back into the system.

The complexity of the relationship between an agent and its environment can vary considerably. For instance, an environment that is fully observable, static, and characterized by discrete states, like the positions of figures among the fields of a chess board, is more manageable, ceteris paribus, than environments for which this is not the case.[45] In fact, notably successful applications of AI, possibly even surpassing human capabilities, have occurred in settings marked by a

[44] The notion of general AI is also linked to debates about the future development of AI in relation to human intelligence. Some have discussed a control problem that could ensue if an AI system surpasses human intelligence in a way that allows the system to alter the course of its own development and that is no longer intelligible to its human creators. The creation of highly intelligent machines may thus lead to an "intelligence explosion" – I. J. Good, "Speculations concerning the first ultraintelligent machine" (1966) 6 *Advances in Computers* 31–88 – in which machines create other, more intelligent machines, thereby setting AI on its own evolutionary trajectory. In this extreme scenario, humans could lose control over AI (N. Bostrom, *Superintelligence: Paths, Dangers, Strategies* [Oxford: Oxford University Press, 2014]). While it is generally unpredictable, when human-like or superhuman AI becomes a reality is inherently unpredictable. It will most likely take at least several more decades as various major conceptual breakthroughs are still required. Russell, *Human Compatible*, pp. 77–78.

[45] Russell and Norvig, *Artificial Intelligence*, pp. 41–46.

rather simple environment. The superhuman capabilities of game-playing AI systems, for instance, are achieved in a setting that is easily formalizable with discrete, observable states and involving simple and known rule sets. This is not the case in the real world, where the situation quickly becomes much more complex.

For any given environment, AI can show a certain quality of performance in dealing with some tasks. This performance is tied to the objective that an agent is supposed to realize. It must be incorporated into its agent program, which is commonly done via performance measures in the form of a utility or cost function that is to be maximized or minimized, respectively. For example, an image recognition software designed to distinguish military from civilian aircraft could be trained for this task with a learning algorithm that minimizes the number of false classifications. Note, however, that different classification errors could be given different "costs." One might want to give missing a military aircraft greater weight than the error for classifying an image as a military aircraft although it is a civilian plane. Considerations of this sort must be explicitly expressed in the cost or utility function of an AI system. Such cost functions form measures of the performance quality of an AI system.

There is no single correct performance measure for a given application; this is a question of human judgment. Depending on the purpose of an application, the realized goals of an AI device may also include fairness in how decisions are made, as is the case in risk assessments in the criminal justice context – where different demographic groups may incur different classification errors. Again, as with the overall performance measure, there is no one correct way of assessing the fairness of an AI system and different fairness measures are, under common conditions, incompatible with each other.[46]

There are two sides to assessing the performance of an AI agent. On the one hand, the creators of an AI system have an idea of what the desirable goals and performances are in dealing with a given task. On the other hand, whether an AI system can match this performance standard also depends on constraints in the form of the actions that the agent can perform and the information that it has. This means that an AI system may work well when assessed against what it can achieve even when it does not achieve a predefined performance goal. In other words, an agent may show a poor performance when held against external human standards but still perform optimally within its own limitations of possible actions and knowledge. This distinction is encapsulated in the notion of a rational agent, understood as an agent that selects an action that is expected to maximize its objectives given the knowledge that the agent has – meaning that it optimizes its expected performance.[47]

A key element in producing such a rational agent that maximizes a performance measure is a learning capability that allows the agent not just to update its representation of the environment but also to assess its performance achieved with certain actions. Based on an internal evaluation of its performance, a learning agent can change its rules for generating outputs – and thus for interacting with its environment. Hence, the learning component of an agent is separate from and can influence the part of the agent program that is responsible for selecting actions.[48]

[46] J. Kleinberg, J. Ludwig, S. Mullainathan, and A. Rambachan, "Algorithmic fairness" (2018) 108 *AEA Papers and Proceedings* 22–27.

[47] Russell and Norvig, *Artificial Intelligence*, pp. 36–38.

[48] Russell and Norvig, *Artificial Intelligence*. AI system creators may also add further complexity to a system by giving them an ability of learning to learn, that is, of *meta-learning* that allows an AI system to evaluate its own learning process and to modify and improve its learning mechanism. On this, see S. Hochreiter, A. S. Younger, and P. R. Conwell, "Learning to learn using gradient descent," in G. Dorffner, H. Bischof, and K. Hornik (eds.), *Artificial Neural Networks – ICANN 2001* (Berlin; Heidelberg: Springer International Publishing, 2001), pp. 87–94.

As the learning capabilities of an AI system become more sophisticated, they can become more independent of prior knowledge and human inputs, but they will also become harder to understand and their outputs and actions harder to explain. However, regardless of the learning method implemented in AI applications, they are still based on human design choices. Certain assumptions and expectations are necessarily incorporated into an AI system: For instance, so-called unsupervised learning seems to leave the learning process entirely to the machine without specifying what known targets (e.g., object classes) the system is supposed to find. However, unsupervised learning procedures also require a definition of what should be optimized exactly, and the choice of such relevant criteria will affect the operations of a learning system – and thus determine to some degree what kind of patterns a system will find. This is an important consideration in the design and evaluation of AI systems, pointing to the relevance of adopting a wider perspective that sees the development of AI systems and their implementation as socially embedded. Hence, understanding how AI operates in practice demands that one sees them as a part of larger socio-technical systems.

2.4 AI AS PARTS OF SOCIO-TECHNICAL SYSTEMS

AI systems often only form a technical component that is embedded in a social process. Together, they make up a more comprehensive socio-technical system, and the impacts of a given AI system always depend on this larger context in which they are implemented. The technical specification of an AI system does not predetermine the impact that it will have and the risks that it entails when it is implemented. A given technological solution, such as a lip-reading device, may well be harmless or even vastly beneficial in one setting, for example, for deaf persons, but cause profound ethical and regulatory problems as part of a public video surveillance system[49] – meaning that when an AI application is transposed from one setting to a different setting it may have radically different social consequences. The way in which an AI system operates and the outputs it produces will already depend on the kind of data from which the system is trained. The data that the system is fed reflects a specific representation of the reality and environment in which it operates. This means that problems of data quality due, for example, to missing data, noise, errors, or a lack of representativeness for the domain of interest, can heavily impair the quality of the AI system's performance. And a system that performs well after having been trained with data from one setting may not work well in other settings.

It is thus important to conceive of AI systems as socio-technical systems that cannot be properly understood and assessed without considering the concrete context in which they are deployed.[50] Beyond the general technical functionality of an AI system, one has to consider (a) the concrete objective or set of objectives realized in the given setting and (b) the environment in which the system is supposed to operate, including which parts of the environment the system can "perceive." In an even broader perspective, one can also look at the larger environment in which the system is embedded, which includes the actors responsible for the design, implementation, and operation of an AI system. The fact that there are different roles involved in these processes means that depending on the concrete constellation, the stakes, interests, and the

[49] Bertolini, *Artificial Intelligence and Civil Liability*, p. 9.

[50] D. G. Johnson and M. Verdicchio, "Reframing AI discourse" (2017) 27 *Minds and Machines* 575–90; K. A. Zweig, *Ein Algorithmus hat kein Taktgefühl: wo Künstliche Intelligenz sich irrt, warum uns das betrifft und was wir dagegen tun können* (Munich: Heyne Verlag, 2019); K. Zweig, W. Neuser, V. Pipek, M. Rohde, and I. Scholtes (eds.), *Socioinformatics: The Social Impact of Interactions between Humans and IT* (Berlin: Springer International Publishing, 2014).

distribution of responsibilities behind a developed and operated AI system may differ.[51] Hence, while AI might be seen as a risky technology, the specific risks of AI applications stem from a combination of purpose- and context-specific as well as technical aspects.

There are concrete risks that are tied to the functionality of an AI application operating in a given environment, but which are not inherent to the AI system. For instance, AI that is used for pattern recognition in medical diagnoses to inform treatment decisions involves very different stakes than, for example, a recommendation system on a video streaming platform. Similarly, where an AI application performs a function (e.g., object recognition) based on which an entity can physically interact with an environment, such as with a self-driving car, the potential harm can be serious. The possible adverse consequences and the scale of this impact will depend on where and how AI is implemented.[52] The stakes in a given context of implementation also have direct consequences for the evaluation of an AI system's performance.

When developing an AI system, there are two ways of looking at its performance. On the one hand, developers of a system may merely register how an application performs based on conventional metrics that quantify, for example, how many errors a system makes. In an image recognition task, various developed systems may perform differently in terms of how many images they classify correctly. On the other hand, the situation is entirely different if the outputs produced by an AI system inform or lead to decisions with real-world consequences: The costs of erring may vary greatly, which renders the standard of performance, by which an AI system is assessed, crucial. This is a question of calibration and of aligning the design of an AI system with the concrete goals and values it is supposed to achieve in a real-world context.[53] Which objectives an AI system achieves will furthermore depend on who is developing it and for what purposes. An application may therefore be very closely aligned with the goals of those whom it serves, but it may well create societal or public risks, such as market abuse or interfering with public will formation.[54]

2.5 CONSEQUENCES OF AI CORE CHARACTERISTICS WITH LEGAL IMPORTANCE

Viewing AI systems as a part of larger socio-technical systems highlights the fact that the risks associated with the implementation of these systems largely do not depend on the technologies described above as "AI." Indeed, the vast majority of issues discussed under the heading "AI and Law" refer, at least on closer inspection, to old and well-known legally relevant consequences. For instance, the categorization of people based on AI systems triggers risks for human rights, for example the principle of equality, that already exist with "traditional" algorithms that may lead to unfair discrimination, while problems of diversity created by news recommender systems[55] are similarly not restricted to uses of AI.

[51] M. Ananny and K. Crawford, "Seeing without knowing: Limitations of the transparency ideal and its application to algorithmic accountability" (2018) 20 *New Media & Society* 973–89; K. A. Zweig, G. Wenzelburger, and T. D. Krafft, "On chances and risks of security related algorithmic decision making systems" (2018) 3 *European Journal for Security Research* 181–203.

[52] T. D. Krafft, K. A. Zweig, and P. D. König, "How to regulate algorithmic decision-making: A framework of regulatory requirements for different applications" (2020) *Regulation & Governance* (online first).

[53] Russell and Norvig, *Artificial Intelligence*.

[54] F. Saurwein, N. Just, and M. Latzer, "Governance of algorithms: Options and limitations" (2015) 17 *info* 35–49.

[55] W. Benedek and M. C. Kettemann, *Freedom of Expression and the Internet*, updated and revised 2nd ed. (Strasbourg: Council of Europe, 2020).

Besides such consequences and risks that are rooted in the purpose and the context of an AI application, further risks and legally relevant issues arise from the core characteristics of AI systems themselves. In the following we focus on this second basket of issues and discuss essential features of AI that have implications for legal studies and for legal practice. These issues result directly from the definition of AI formulated above as sets of digital artifacts that contain at least one learning or learned component that can change an AI system's behavior based on processed input data.

2.5.1 *Opacity and Intelligibility*

A major challenge that can arise with the implementation of AI systems is a lack of transparency. While the opacity of these systems can be intentional or exist due to a lack of literacy and expertise needed to understand how a system produces outputs – a problem that can, however, be overcome – there is also an inherent opacity due to the complexity of the systems.[56] This latter kind of opacity differs categorically from the opacity of "traditional" technological systems. An AI system may remain unintelligible as it acquires rules and representations of reality that are not readily interpretable to humans. Specifically, AI applications can engage in complex learning processes that are high-dimensional, unconstrained, and/or nonlinear,[57] but this also means that they do not have an internal statistical model that would be intelligible to humans: "Machine optimizations based on training data do not naturally accord with human semantic explanations."[58] An application for image recognition, for instance, may learn that certain regions and patterns in an image are predictive of the image falling into the category "cat." Yet this may happen in ways that humans would not deem relevant because the algorithm likely identifies segments that do not correspond to familiar and interpretable features like ears or a nose.[59] Hence, while the implementation of AI systems may deliver a task performance that exceeds human capabilities, they do not furnish information about how exactly they arrive at decisions or behavior.[60]

This is the other side of bottom-up data-driven machine learning approaches to solving cognitive tasks, because "such unforeseeable behavior was intended by the AI's designers, even if a specific unforeseen act was not."[61] The AI system is supposed to provide useful outputs by building its own decision model, but does not have to be understandable to humans to be effective.[62] From a pragmatic perspective, an AI system may well be highly useful, for example for predicting whether a person will pay back a loan, but this value might only be based on correlations and does not necessarily correspond to causal theories about what constitutes relevant and plausible relationships. Consequently, such applications cannot help humans to

[56] J. Burrell, "How the machine 'thinks': Understanding opacity in machine learning algorithms" (2016) 3 *Big Data & Society* 1–12.

[57] The same AI system may learn different decision-rules depending on the sequence in which inputs are provided.

[58] Burrell, "How the machine 'thinks,'" 10.

[59] K. Sokol and P. Flach, "Explainability fact sheets: A framework for systematic assessment of explainable approaches," in *Proceedings of the 2020 Conference on Fairness, Accountability, and Transparency* (Barcelona: ACM, 2020), pp. 56–67.

[60] W. Samek and K.-R. Müller, "Towards explainable artificial intelligence," in W. Samek, G. Montavon, A. Vedaldi, L. K. Hansen, and K.-R. Müller (eds.), *Explainable AI: Interpreting, Explaining and Visualizing Deep Learning* (Cham: Springer International Publishing, 2019), pp. 5–22.

[61] M. U. Scherer, "Regulating artificial intelligence systems: Risks, challenges, competencies, and strategies," (2016) 29 *Harvard Journal of Law & Technology* 354–400 at 366.

[62] A. Matthias, "The responsibility gap: Ascribing responsibility for the actions of learning automata," (2004) 6 *Ethics and Information Technology* 175–83 at 179.

guide their own decision-making – or to gain new insights themselves – and there is a potential problem of opacity of decision-making that may be critical in certain sensitive decision domains, such as medical diagnoses or crime prediction. Without a proper understanding of an AI system, it may perform well on a given task, but it may do so unwittingly due to a spurious correlation resulting from "clever Hans" predictors. For instance, a system might be capable of reliably distinguishing wolves from huskies in images, but only because of the presence of snow in those instances in which a husky is shown.[63] Understanding how a system works is therefore important, not least to identify misbehavior by an AI system. However, forms of AI that inherently defy human interpretation make it impossible to gain a true causal understanding of how a system translates inputs into outputs – which has led to calls for only inherently interpretable models to be used in high-stakes decisions.[64]

There is a problem of explainability regarding the outputs of certain AI systems. It is important to note that there is a technical side to this problem that is partly decoupled from legal considerations. The explainability of AI has long been a research topic in computer science, but it has remained detached from legal demands for transparency in decision-making[65] – indicating a need for more interdisciplinary work. Approaches developed in computer science to achieve explainability aim to achieve a general understanding of the decision model through post-hoc modeling and reconstruction of its behavior. The goal is to build a model that approximates how an AI system behaves.[66] This, however, amounts to building a model on top of another model and adds a further layer of complexity. While this approach may serve to find regularities in the behavior of an AI system, it does not amount to an actual explanation of how it arrives at its outputs based on known causal factors.[67]

This technical problem of explainability is not per se relevant from a legal perspective. Even if – with great effort due to the complexity of the system – one could trace how an output was produced, the information that, for example, a specific neuron in a neural network flipped and determined the outcome, is not relevant for legal purposes. Rather, what is needed from a legal perspective is a form of transparency that entails providing information that makes a difference in the legal system, such as giving the person who was subject to a decision based on an AI system an informational basis on which to judge whether the decision met the standards the law requires for these kinds of decisions.

Legal discussions have addressed the issue of the explainability of AI,[68] but have often remained on an abstract level and lacked nuance in some regards. First, the idea that AI is generally not explainable informs large parts of legal discourse – which may in part be due to the industry drawing attention to a general issue of explainability. The possibility of explainability, however, depends on the application in question, and computer science may even devise ways to make the more complex systems explainable. Second, general calls for explainability and

[63] Samek and Müller, "Towards explainable artificial intelligence."

[64] C. Rudin, "Stop explaining black box machine learning models for high stakes decisions and use interpretable models instead" (2019) 1 *Nature Machine Intelligence* 206–15.

[65] R. Goebel, A. Chander, K. Holzinger, F. Lecue, and A. Zeynep, "Explainable AI: The new 42?" in 2nd International Cross-Domain Conference for Machine Learning and Knowledge Extraction (CD-MAKE), August 2018, Hamburg, Germany, pp. 295–303.

[66] Samek and Müller, "Towards explainable artificial intelligence."

[67] Rudin, "Stop explaining black box machine learning models for high stakes decisions."

[68] L. Edwards and M. Veale, "Slave to the algorithm: Why a right to an explanation is probably not the remedy you are looking for" (2017) 16 *Duke Law & Technology Review* 18–84; M. E. Kaminski and G. Malgieri, "Algorithmic impact assessments under the GDPR: Producing multi-layered explanations" (2020) (online first) *International Data Privacy Law* 1–20.

transparency as abstract concepts are not helpful, as they distract from the question of what kind of information satisfies a legal transparency requirement. Specifically, from a legal perspective it is required to stipulate (1) what goal transparency is expected to achieve, (2) what exactly needs to be understood to reach this goal, and (3) who needs to gain this understanding (end-user, evaluator, regulator, or others) to make the regulatory concept work. The answers to those questions vary considerably depending on the legal context, though.

There is also disagreement over what degree of transparency is guaranteed by existing regulation. The extent to which the GDPR (art. 22 read in connection with recital 71) provides a "right to explanation" of decisions made by automated systems is heavily debated.[69] If it entails such a right, the goal would be to give data subjects sufficient knowledge to evaluate whether the decision was wrong and provide the subject with the necessary information to take legal action in case the decision was erroneous.[70] This is the yardstick to measure whether a decision based on an AI system meets the standards of explainability under the GDPR (assuming there is such a right enshrined in the GDPR). For other fields of regulation, the requirements might be different.

Existing regulation already has a significant impact on how AI systems are developed and implemented. That is also true with respect to explainability. Specifically, to avoid liability problems, the actors involved, such as developers and managers, may be legally compelled to use explainable machine learning models.[71] There are design choices that influence what can be traced and explained and various instruments and provisions for screening AI systems already exist – meaning that "explainable AI" is not something that may only be achieved in the distant future but could be established much earlier. Furthermore, recent regulatory attempts go well beyond existing regulation and emphasize the demand for explainable AI. The legislative proposal for the EU Digital Services Act (published December 2020) entails, inter alia, the right of the EU Commission to order platforms to provide "explanations relating to its databases and algorithms."

2.5.2 *Agency and Autonomy*

The presence of learning or learned components that can change an AI system's behavior based on processed input data can lend AI applications a certain degree of independence and unpredictability. An AI application can arrive at behaviors that were unintended or even unforeseen by those who developed the application. Again, context matters in this regard because an AI system may show an unanticipated behavior when placed in and interacting with an environment. One example is the experimental chatbot that Microsoft launched on social media. The bot was intended to learn to converse with users – and indeed performed within the predefined technical parameters – but ended up frequently uttering chauvinist remarks and racial slurs that it had picked up from users.[72]

69 Edwards and Veale, "Slave to the algorithm"; G. Malgieri and G. Comandé, "Why a right to legibility of automated decision-making exists in the General Data Protection Regulation" (2017) 7 *International Data Privacy Law* 243–65; S. Wachter, B. Mittelstadt, and L. Floridi, "Why a right to explanation of automated decision-making does not exist in the General Data Protection Regulation" (2017) 7 *International Data Privacy Law* 76–99.

70 S. Dreyer and W. Schulz, *The General Data Protection Regulation and Automated Decision-Making: Will It Deliver?* (Gütersloh: Bertelsmann Stiftung, 2019).

71 P. Hacker, R. Krestel, S. Grundmann, and F. Naumann, "Explainable AI under contract and tort law: Legal incentives and technical challenges" (2020) 28 *Artificial Intelligence and Law* 415–39.

72 G. Neff and P. Nagy, "Talking to bots: Symbiotic agency and the case of Tay" (2016) 10 *International Journal of Communication* 4915–31.

The malleability and openness of an AI system's behavior leads to a kind of "autonomy" of technical systems in such a way that the decision architecture in a given socio-technical system can change significantly from a legal perspective. Autonomy should therefore not be confused with human autonomy in this context; it refers to the fact that machines – based on AI – take over more tasks than before. In this respect it may be more appropriate to speak of degrees of automation than of degrees of autonomy. As the "division of work" between humans and machines changes, this raises fundamental questions of responsibility, accountability, and liability.[73] Again, the questions and adequate answers are not universally valid, but vary significantly depending on the legal system and the field of law.

Regarding the liability of creators and operators of AI systems, an old thought experiment may become reality: A technical system, for example a robot, can become so autonomous that under the given liability regime the operator (or creator) does not have enough control to establish liability for harm caused by the robot.[74] Scholars convincingly argue that the human rights of the victims demand a change of the liability regime in that case.[75] However, the level of automation based on AI transforms this hypothetical scenario to a real challenge for liability systems. The possible impact of existing regimes of liability, responsibility, and accountability on the development of AI, and, vice versa, the pressure put on those regimes by the implementations of AI systems creates a new field of legal research of significant complexity.[76]

The new level of automation also provokes a second question, one which is by no means new but may now become pressing. Is there a need to give AI systems the status of a legal personality and to grant them rights?[77] In part, this question follows on from the discussion of the liability gap (see Chapter 9). On the one hand, the liability gap could be closed by simply attributing all responsibility to the developers of AI systems, which would create strong incentives not to introduce technology over which they may lose control. If, on the other hand, a legal personality for AI were introduced, the AI system itself, and not the creator or operator, could be held liable.

It is useful to differentiate according to different legal perspectives. At the level of constitutional law, the question invites a very fundamental discussion of the constitution's conception of humankind and the nature of the human being. From a civil law perspective, the main question is whether and how a liability fund can be assigned to the legal personality. Only then does the construction make sense from the perspective of civil law, as was previously the case with the construction of legal personality for companies.[78]

2.5.3 *New Types of Errors?*

The implementation of AI systems can also seemingly introduce new kinds of errors for which new rules may be needed. Law is designed to help humans to coordinate their behavior and to influence that behavior in the public interest. The legal rules are designed to account for human error wherever possible. Traffic signs, for example, are designed in terms of size and positioning to control drivers' behavior as effectively as possible. The different ways in which AI systems

[73] MSI-AUT, *Responsibility and AI*. Council of Europe study DGI(2019)05 (Council of Europe, 2019).

[74] Matthias, "The responsibility gap."

[75] MSI-AUT, *Responsibility and AI*.

[76] MSI-AUT, *Responsibility and AI*.

[77] J. Turner, *Robot Rules: Regulating Artificial Intelligence* (Berlin: Springer International Publishing, 2019).

[78] A. Karanasiou and D. Pinotsis, "Towards a legal definition of machine intelligence: The argument for artificial personhood in the age of deep learning," in *Proceedings of the 16th Edition of the International Conference on Artificial Intelligence and Law* (London: ACM, 2017), pp. 119–28.

receive and process information can therefore become a problem as automation increases. To illustrate this point, we will briefly look at two examples.

First, there are multiple examples of how AI-based systems can "misinterpret" symbols (like traffic signs) due to wrong pixels that humans cannot detect. And these glitches in AI systems could also be used by malicious actors to manipulate them.[79] Second, there are phenomena like "catastrophic forgetting" that could trigger problems that other technologies do not evoke. Catastrophic forgetting refers to the tendency of an artificial neural network to forget previously learned information completely and abruptly upon learning new information.[80] As these examples illustrate, there are further aspects of the technology of AI itself, specifically novel kinds of errors, than can trigger legal questions. This may create a need for regulation that aims at securing the integrity of existing systems of human interaction or guaranteeing that a certain level of decision quality is reached.

2.6 CONCLUSION

AI is a complex, multifaceted concept and is therefore hard to define because AI can refer to technological artifacts, certain methods, or a scientific field that is split into many subfields and that is continuously changing and evolving. From a legal perspective, one can, however, concentrate on the concrete implementations of AI systems, as these are the applications that create ethical, legal, and regulatory challenges. Such AI systems can be grasped with the concept of agents that interact with an environment by processing inputs and producing outputs, which occurs based on an agent program that has been acquired from previous data inputs. AI systems can therefore be seen as digital artifacts that require hardware and software components and that contain at least one learning or learned component, that is, a component that is able to change the system's behavior based on presented data and the processing of this data.

These AI systems need to be understood as parts of larger socio-technical systems, which means that the impacts, stakes, and risks of these applications depend on the concrete setting in which they are deployed. The specific risks involved, for example unfair discrimination, will often be well known and stem from the social context rather than from the technology. There are, however, also core features of the technology itself that have legally relevant consequences. These are primarily challenges resulting from, first, an inherent opacity of certain kinds of AI systems that involve more complex forms of learning and, second, a significant degree of independence and unpredictability due to the learning component and complexity of AI systems.

Finally, the discussion above also shows that bringing a legal perspective to AI demands an interdisciplinary understanding that is sensitive to how certain concepts are used differently and how they highlight different aspects as relevant. This is palpable, for example, in discussions about explainable and transparent AI, where concepts such as transparency have different meanings in computer science and in the law. Being aware of these semantic gaps will be important to bridge the disciplines in ways that allow for jointly and productively addressing novel challenges that arise with the adoption of AI.

[79] M. Sharif, S. Bhagavatula, L. Bauer, and M. K. Reiter, "Accessorize to a crime: Real and stealthy attacks on state-of-the-art face recognition," in *Proceedings of the 2016 ACM SIGSAC Conference on Computer and Communications Security* (Vienna: ACM, 2016), pp. 1528–40.

[80] R. French, "Catastrophic forgetting in connectionist networks" (1999) 3 *Trends in Cognitive Sciences* 128–35.

3

AI in the Legal Profession

Christy Ng

3.1 INTRODUCTION

Artificial intelligence (AI) is often referred to as one of the great disruptive platforms of the twenty-first century that will fundamentally change the way we live and work. It can be described as a once-in-a-lifetime event in the sense that AI is replacing our cognitive process in doing a job in its significant entirety, and doing it dramatically better, no matter which industry it is deployed in and the nature of the task. In the context of the legal industry, the obvious examples of AI that are seen in the market are automation in case flow management, contract review and legal research. These are tasks that take up increasing lawyer-hours that contain many repetitive elements to them, taking time away from the more complex transactions and cases that lawyers deal with on a regular basis. The idea behind this first wave of AI application is to free up the headspace and time that lawyers use to complete these secondary tasks so that they can focus on the task of "lawyering," that is, identifying the relevant law, applying the law to the facts and advising the clients on their options and best way forward. There has been less thought leadership and progress made in the deployment of AI to these more substantive functions of being a lawyer in itself. This chapter identifies this as the second wave of AI application in the legal services. Although there are commercial incentives to each wave of AI application, this chapter posits that there are challenges that hinder the progress and potential of the second wave. These are the difficulties in structuring legal data as a precondition to training AI for optimized outcomes, namely, the lack of linguistic and machine-readability standards and the confinement of AI training to the proprietary datasets of each organization, limiting the purpose for which it can be used. In this chapter we will discuss the potential of AI technologies in the provision of legal services and the more advanced AI use-cases in the legal industry. Next, the chapter will address the obstacles standing in the way of the second and third waves of AI application and potential solutions that involve the development of machine-readability and linguistic standards for structured legal data, using Logical English in over-the-counter (OTC) derivative documentation as a key example. Finally, we will discuss the way forward for lawyers as managers of the robo-lawyer technologies, positing that this will involve big legal data analytics as an informative tool to enhance legal thinking. This will be the third wave of AI application with potential exponential value creation and regulatory risk enhancements for institutions and market players that can harness it.

3.2 OPTIMIZING THE SECOND WAVE: THE POTENTIAL OF AI IN THE LEGAL SERVICES

First, we must define exactly what we mean by "AI." Providing a definition of AI is a counter-intuitive task because the best way to grasp what AI is, is to ask whether or not the technology is something that traditional programming methods can do. If traditional programming can achieve it, it is not AI. AI includes a broad family of technologies such as, but not limited to, deep learning, machine learning, neural networks, natural language processing and big data analytics.

AI, in the form of machine learning, has been around since the 1950s with scientists, mathematicians and philosophers planting the seeds for discussion on whether or not machines could use available information to reason in order to problem-solve and make decisions. The most notable thinker on this subject was Alan Turing, whose 1950 paper on "Computing Machinery and Intelligence" laid down the approach to testing and building machine intelligence.[1] He made a proposal, now known as "The Turing Test," given the increasingly posed question of whether machines can think, which he thought was rather meaningless. According to Turing, the question ought to be replaced with what he called "an imitation game." The basic idea of the Turing Test is to have a human assessor to judge natural language conversations between a human and a machine. The assessor would be aware that one of the two participants is a machine, the other a human – but cannot see either participant. If the assessor cannot reliably tell the machine from the human, the machine is said to have passed the Turing Test – effectively a yardstick to determine whether a computer was able to imitate human intelligence. Since then, various forms of machine learning started to flourish after the mass-market accessibility of computers in the 1990s rendered computing experiments less expensive. Computer scientists could then produce proofs of concept to secure the funding required to develop machine intelligence further.

From 2010 onward, breakthroughs in our understanding and application of deep learning garnered the interest of the media, and initiatives from market participants of all industries to explore how AI could be implemented in their fields. Fast forward to the present day, strategic thinking and creativity can be demonstrated by one of the most advanced AI programs in the world, AlphaGo Zero, which was created by DeepMind's developers and has since been acquired by Google to be deployed to mass commercial use.[2] DeepMind's developers trained AlphaGo Zero to learn to play the game of Go by programming it to play millions of matches against itself, with the aim to avoid losing. Through this process of reinforcement learning, AlphaGo Zero was able to come up with moves that the best human Go players had not conceived of previously,[3] and achieved superhuman performance, winning 100–0 against the previous model AlphaGo, which had already beaten expert Go players.[4] Just like a human being, AlphaGo Zero learned new moves and strategies each time it played a match and was able to substantially improve its performance by learning from previous games.[5] Its algorithms

[1] Turing, A. M. (1950) Computing machinery and intelligence. *Mind* 59(236), pp. 433–460.

[2] Gannes, L. (2014) Exclusive: Google to buy artificial intelligence startup DeepMind for $400M. Available from www.vox.com/2014/1/26/11622732/exclusive-google-to-buy-artificial-intelligence-startup-deepmind-for (accessed April 10, 2021).

[3] Hassabis, D. and Silver, D. (2017) AlphaGo Zero: Starting from scratch. Available from https://deepmind.com/blog/article/alphago-zero-starting-scratch (accessed on April 11, 2021).

[4] Silver, D. et al. (2017) Mastering the game of Go without human knowledge. Available from https://deepmind.com/research/publications/mastering-game-go-without-human-knowledge (accessed on March 28, 2021).

[5] Ibid., p. 1.

allow the program to learn *without human data, guidance, or domain knowledge beyond the rules of the game.*[6] Today, Google uses DeepMind's algorithms for intelligent image search, speech recognition, fraud and spam detection, translation and much more.[7] This is just the tip of the iceberg.[8] Other companies claim to have other AI learning techniques, including one that can be idea-learning without supervision and with less time and less data to train.[9] DeepMind has since developed improved algorithms such as AlphaZero that uses a deep neural network and the basic rules of the game to develop *its own unique and creative way to play*,[10] and MuZero, which matches the improved performance of AlphaZero *without being told the rules of any game to plan winning strategies in unknown domains.*[11] Unlike humans who are limited to the computing power of their brains, AI does not have hardware limitations due to the fact that any AI program can be plugged into any number of machines, including networks of machines. As for software limitations, this is a matter of training the machines according to what the programs want to accomplish, using the increasingly advanced techniques developed by data and computer scientists.

This case study of DeepMind's algorithms shows how AI can be idea-learning and generate original ideas in new domains. The ramifications for legal application are significant. Techniques such as those deployed in AlphaGo indicate that AI may not need any hard knowledge of the law or contextual understanding in order to generate ideas pertaining to the rules of the law it can be taught. If AI could be programmed using similar techniques to generate independent ideas and identify the likely outcomes as a result of those rules it is fed, this is not unlike the substantive functions of identifying and applying the law. What is left then, is for lawyers to sanity-check the outputs of the AI program, make recommendations and advise, taking into consideration the social, commercial and circumstantial context of the clients' position. The most effective lawyers will then differentiate themselves at this hour by proving themselves to be adept managers of these robo-lawyer technologies and by the quality of advice that they can give, based on the insights they can glean from the outputs of the AI. They will need to draw inferences and make decisions as is the case now, however, the difference is that the material they will be doing this from will be significantly enhanced by AI for higher-level thinking. This is where the role of lawyers will evolve to take more center-stage in decisions on business direction and strategy.

3.3 STAGES OF EACH WAVE IN THE LEGAL INDUSTRY

How do these projections pertain to the current state of the legal industry? The answer is twofold. Firstly, currently the global legal industry is generally focused on the first wave of AI application, and is still in the process of fully harnessing the simple first-wave AI tools. While there are a handful of companies working on technologies that could fall into the second and

6 Silver et al, *supra* note 4 at p. 1.

7 Reese, H. (2016) Google DeepMind: A cheat sheet. Available from www.techrepublic.com/article/google-deepmind-the-smart-persons-guide/ (accessed on April 10, 2021).

8 There are numerous other advanced AI techniques such as digital reasoning and scaled interference, which are beyond the scope of this chapter.

9 Gamalon (n.d.) Idea learning defined. Available from https://content.gamalon.com/white-paper-idea-learning-defined (accessed on April 21, 2021).

10 Hassabis, D. (2017) AlphaZero: Creative player. Available from https://deepmind.com/research/case-studies/alphago-the-story-so-far#alphazero (accessed on April 20, 2021).

11 Schrittwieser, J. (2020) MuZero: Mastering Go, chess, shogi and Atari without rules. Available from https://deepmind.com/blog/article/muzero-mastering-go-chess-shogi-and-atari-without-rules (accessed April 28, 2021).

third wave, advanced AI techniques have not yet been fully explored. The position is largely the same around the world, with different countries leading in the investment of various different types of legaltech and London being the hub of focus for the development of the legal technologies. The focus of the first wave is to solve the large-scale inefficiencies bogging down the legal profession by creating reliable automation tools to simplify paperwork and case management to free up lawyers' legal minds to focus on solving substantive legal problems. Examples of first-wave AI application in the legal industry include cloud-based tools for intelligent storage of documents for easier search,[12] a computer program for expansive searches at regulatory registers at a faster pace than humans[13] and natural language-processing engines for faster contract review.[14]

There are dozens of vendors creating AI technologies that use machine learning to help with aspects of case management such as workflow automation,[15] e-discovery tools[16] and data extraction.[17] Examples of second-wave technologies include AI tools to enhance a lawyer's abilities, creating a robot lawyer,[18] AI software scan technology to interpret contracts for commercial risk[19] and AI technology trained to think like a lawyer and read documents to draw out key due diligence findings.[20] There are also vendors working on third-wave AI, such as prediction analysis tools in big data analytics to help with intelligent search and prediction of litigation outcomes using aggregated data from court decisions,[21] which are particularly relevant to civil litigation practices. The advantages of the first wave are to transform the way that lawyer-hours are spent so that performance can be enhanced.

Secondly, the current trends of the legaltech sectors in the United Kingdom, parts of Europe and United States indicate that the whole of the legal profession is moving toward the second wave of AI application. As more and more developers create new AI techniques and traditional legal service providers integrate AI technologies into their platforms, there will be a requirement for digital systems (that are ever more pervasive) to consume legal data in structured form, since unstructured data is generally not suitable for deep learning. The higher quality the data, the better the output of the systems. A layman's understanding of structured data versus unstructured data typically refers to the difference between any kind of unorganized free text and image such as a Reddit post on memes versus information organized in a table or relational database, making

12 Everlaw is the world's most advanced e-discovery software, www.everlaw.com (accessed on April 13, 2021).

13 Hill, C. (2017) In brief: Linklaters wins legal technology team of the year award. Available from https://legaltechnology.com/in-brief-linklaters-wins-legal-technology-team-of-the-year-award/ (accessed on April 1, 2021).

14 ThoughtRiver (n.d.) Automated contract review & negotiation. Available from www.thoughtriver.com (accessed on April 15, 2021).

15 For a list of companies with technologies for managing legal workflows, see: Artificial Lawyer (n.d.) Decision automation. Available from www.artificiallawyer.com/al-100-directory/workflow-automation/ (accessed on April 5, 2021).

16 Boyes Turner LLP (2020) e-Discovery and artificial intelligence. Available from www.lexology.com/library/detail.aspx?g=fee65cee-02e4-469c-b352-3e89486b7873 (accessed on April 19, 2021).

17 Artificial Lawyer (n.d.) Collaboration + legal data platforms. Available from www.artificiallawyer.com/al-100-directory/collaboration-legal-data-platforms/ (accessed on April 17, 2021).

18 Ross Intelligence (n.d.) About us. Available from www.rossintelligence.com/about-us (accessed on April, 17 2021).

19 *Supra* note 14; ThoughtRiver's legaltech solutions are both first and second wave in nature.

20 Luminance (n.d.) Use cases. Available from www.luminance.com/product/diligence/use-cases.html (accessed on April 18, 2021).

21 Lex Machina (n.d.) Lex Machina provides Legal Analytics® to law firms and companies, enabling them to craft successful strategies, win cases, and close business. Available from https://lexmachina.com/about/ (accessed on April 18, 2021).

the information easy to break down into parts and categorize in its own code. Structuring legal data takes this a step further in the sense that the information must be organized in a way that reflects legal reasoning, with the difficult aim of making legalese machine-readable so that clear rules can be extracted by any AI program for downstream users.

The process of structuring legal data can involve various tasks, such as reducing fuzzy logic[22] and defining legal terms from the indeterminate and ambiguous,[23] to physically reorganizing the information in the contracts, such as data entry in Excel spreadsheets, for further propagation as a precondition for further technological implementation. However, before advanced forms of idea-learning and generating AI can be applied to the substantive tasks of the second wave, there are certain hurdles to structuring legal data and the use of that data for AI implementation that have to be addressed.

3.4 BEYOND THE FIRST WAVE: HINDRANCES TO FURTHER AI APPLICATION

Currently, each organization develops its own standards for structuring its legal data and relies on its own proprietary data to train its AI for its own purposes. While this model works superficially to enable the use of AI for bespoke outcomes, it conversely creates the problem of inaccurate filtering out of unstructured information and cognitive biases in legalese for machine-readability. Other headaches involved in applying in-house standards from scratch include the technical difficulties of quantifying degrees of uncertainties and legal grey areas in machine-readable language.

Most lawyers are not trained in computer science, statistics or data science, and will need the input of quantitative domain experts to translate jargon and obscure legal rules to accurate, consumable computer language for machine learning. If the industry settles on the use of arbitrary standards for convenience, then the AI programs will be limited to providing mediocre recommendations and rudimentary outcomes. The second issue pertains to the nature of AI training to certain subsets of high-quality internal data in each organization. When training AI, organizations have to use the best quality legal data that they have the resources to structure. Whilst this is not in itself an issue for firms looking to achieve bespoke, inward-focused objectives (such as scouring their own records, know-how and previously made decisions), for outward-facing objectives such as aligning client work to market standards and analyzing their work to compare to wider trends, these AI programs trained on internal proprietary data will not be able to deliver directly relevant outputs. It is uncertain if it is even possible for transfer learning to be accurately performed, such as, adapting machine learning algorithms trained on one set of data to achieve the same purposes it was trained for accurately on another set of data from another source.[24] As such, for these more outward-related objectives that involve aggregated data from different sources, we will have to address this with big legal data analytics, the third wave of AI application.

[22] Fuzzy logic aims to facilitate the transition from natural language to numerical expressions. See Philipps, L. and Sartor, G. (1999) Introduction: From legal theories to neural networks and fuzzy reasoning. *Artificial Intelligence and Law* 7(2–3), pp. 115–128.

[23] Ibid.

[24] Williams, J., Tadesse, A., Sam, T., Sun, H., and Montanez, G. D. (2020) Limits of Transfer Learning. Accepted for presentation at the Sixth International Conference on Machine Learning, Optimization, and Data Science (LOD 2020), July 19–23, 2020, Cornell University, pp. 1–18.

3.5 DEVELOPMENT OF STANDARDS FOR STRUCTURING LEGAL DATA

As a prerequisite for optimized results in advanced AI applications to legal practice, legal data has to be structured effectively. Certain sectors are more advanced in the recognition of this need, such as the OTC derivatives[25] and securities lending industries.[26] Both of these markets are moving toward increasing standardization of the relationship-level legal documentation governing their underlying transactions, known as International Swaps and Derivatives Association (ISDA) Master Agreements and Global Master Securities Lending Agreement (GMSLA) respectively, to counter the systemic risk to the global financial industry posed by the inherently risky nature of derivative and securities financing trades that are not centrally cleared or exchanged, all in the backdrop of increasing commercial pressures to execute the documents in parallel to the fast pace of market movements, and the regulatory governance lessons learnt in the aftermath of the 2008 financial crisis.[27]

Among the key aims to standardize and structure the legal data in the ISDA Master Agreements is the need to better manage and keep track of the credit-related legal clauses that allow the parties to terminate either the agreement or certain transactions well before the faultless party will be exposed to the fallout of certain bankruptcy events, cross-default and the deteriorating creditworthiness of the counterparty or its affiliates. The ISDA Master Agreement contains a preprint that is effectively untouched and contains boilerplate terms that reduce the number of deal points to negotiate[28] and the definitions of the terms. The schedule is highly negotiated and contains bespoke amendments to the boilerplate terms. The schedule is subject to ongoing efforts by the ISDA to continuously simplify and streamline with legal data specialists and technology vendors.

On the challenge of structuring the legal data in the ISDA Master Agreements, D2 Legal Technology (D2LT) has worked with Professor Robert Kowalski to explore the use of his Logical English system to structure legal data in a way uniquely well suited for legal documents. In Robert Kowalski and Akber Datoo's paper on "Logical English Meets Legal English for Swaps and Derivatives,"[29] the authors informally introduce Kowalski's syntactic sugar for logic programs known as "Logical English" or "LE." LE consists of sentences that all have the same standard form, either as rules of the form *conclusion **if** conditions* or as unconditional sentences of the form *conclusion.*[30] LE is a controlled natural language that is computer-executable and readable by English speakers without special training, although users will have to familiarize themselves with the rules of the computational logic. Using the ISDA Master Agreements as an example, the paper applies LE to the automatic early termination clauses to demonstrate how LE can be used in lieu of conventional legal English for expressing legal concepts. As an alternative to conventional computer languages, it is especially well suited for structuring legal

[25] ISDA (n.d.) ISDA Clause Library Project memo. Available from www.isda.org/a/DZdEE/ISDA-Clause-Library-Project-Memo.pdf (accessed on April 30, 2021).

[26] ISLA (n.d.) Legal Clause Library & legal data standards. Available from www.islaemea.org/wp-content/uploads/2021/02/D2LT-ISLA_Legal_Clause_Library__Legal_Data_Standards_White_Paper.pdf (accessed on April 30, 2021).

[27] D2 Legal Technology created industry clause taxonomies and libraries for both industry trade associations (ISDA and ISLA), which enumerate the business outcomes for each clause contained in the master agreements, paving the way to common standard data representations of them, and use by AI tools and smart contracts.

[28] Choi, S. J. and Gulati, G. M. (2005) Contract as statute. *Michigan Law Review* 104, pp. 1129–1142, at p. 1139.

[29] Datoo, A. and Kowalski, R. (2021) Logical English meets legal English for swaps and derivatives. Available from www.doc.ic.ac.uk/~rak/papers/Logical%20English%20meets%20Legal%20English.pdf (accessed on April 15, 2021).

[30] Ibid., p. 1.

data as it is a general-purpose computer language inspired in part with the language of law in consideration.

The benefits of using LE for lawyers is that they can structure legalese in a way that is similar to natural language and is compatible with the logic of legal reasoning. This also allows lawyers to ensure their AI is being trained on data that meets the standards of machine-readability and cuts down on the inconsistencies of natural language. LE also affords lawyers the linguistic parameters to quantify more indeterminate boundaries of legal principles. The risks of an undisciplined approach include a failure to filter out cognitive bias and the creation of data exhaust that the computers cannot read. Where lawyers are dealing with real-world application to client work and data, the first stepping-stone to ensure that there are no human oversights in the structuring of the data and the training of the AI is imperative, otherwise the commercial value of that process is compromised. In order for the industry to advance in its implementation of AI, the use of logic systems like LE should be used to impose standards in structuring legal data to avoid arbitrariness and inaccuracies. At the moment, the legal profession is behind in the development of standards to structure legal data to the requirements of AI consumption, with each organization using its own scattershot approaches with varying effectiveness.

3.6 LOOKING AHEAD: BIG LEGAL DATA ANALYTICS AS AN INFORMATIVE TOOL

Big data in law involves large-scale data analysis and predictive technologies to generate legal directives and recommendations tailored to the client or regulated entity.[31] In this chapter, we seek to refine the use of big data in law as a comparative tool for users to assess the outputs of the second-wave AI programs against the practices of the peer group and market behaviors in the available aggregated data. This data can be pulled from anywhere, including but not limited to centralized servers, databases, courtroom records, anonymized trade reports and information from publicly accessible government depositories. It also does not have to be limited to strictly legal documents, but documents that lawyers consider having relevant legal bearing, such as term sheets, and prospectuses[32] in the context of the financial services. Due to the algorithmic and acontextual nature of big data, the use of big data should not be used to replace legal thinking,[33] but rather to inform lawyers of how the recommendations of their AI programs compare against the market, and to flag up points in these recommendations and in the lawyers' analyses that differ from the market norm. Trends that are picked up by big data serve as points of reference for lawyers to investigate in order to adjust their legal advice and make decisions that would influence business strategy.

What big legal data can offer is a holistic view of market player achievements so that lawyers can differentiate businesses' legal strategies and try to keep ahead. It can also provide a tool for lawyers to align their legal advice to the market standard, where necessary. For other downstream users such as stakeholders in risk, liquidity and capital, this allows them the benefit of having lawyers that can better inform them on the legal position relative to the rest of the market. For regulators, big data can change the way they manage the data and information they have access to, allowing regulators a tool to view market behavior from an empirical perspective and

[31] Devins, C., Felin, T., Kauffman, S., and Koppl, R. (2017) The law and big data. *Cornell Journal of Law & Public Policy* 27(2), pp. 357–413, at p. 358.

[32] The analysis on capacity to enter into derivative trades is not always limited to strictly legal contracts but also in prospectuses and ancillary trading authorization documents.

[33] Devins et al, *supra* note 31 at p. 388.

address holes in the regulatory frameworks based on existing and predicted trends. Harnessing big legal data is a starting point for regulators to make forecasts about problematic market practices for further legislation. A common complaint by critics is that regulation is always imposed after the fact, rather than in a preemptive manner to maintain market integrity. Using big legal data analysis, regulators can have tools that are data-driven and theory-agnostic to better inform and add support to decisions that have legal impact on market participants.

3.7 CONCLUSION

Much ado has been made over which technologies will usher in the next disruptive event. However, as demonstrated in the chapter, the legal marketplace is diverse enough to accommodate, and is in need of, different approaches to harnessing AI and different types of AI technologies. As all the markets embrace different types of AI technologies, the role of lawyers will transform from purely that of traditional legal practitioners to that of legal decision-makers directing business strategy and managers of the emerging robo-lawyer technologies.

To be effective robo-tech managers ushering in the various AI waves, lawyers should ask themselves whether or not they have deployed the technology with intentionality, and be mindful not to write off any new AI approaches and technologies due to an initial unfamiliarity with how it aligns with traditional legal practice. It would be a lost opportunity to explore new methods that could spearhead the legal profession's growing importance in the sectors that lawyers operate in and serve.

The legal industry must look toward how lawyers can always be the managers of the AI that is commonly said to replace them, and reframe these technologies as tools that emphasise the value of the human legal decision-maker, who can give AI-enhanced advice with an understanding of the virtues and theories behind judicial decisions and the context of the task in mind. To set the stage for this, the legal industry must develop computational and linguistic standards for structuring legal data. As illustrated in this chapter, the future potential of advanced AI techniques, its utility and commercial value in the legal profession have barely been scratched. Part of that future will be the use of big legal data analytics to show how the data collected relates to itself and the insights within that data for lawyers to make more well-informed and strategic decisions.

PART II

AI: Contracting and Corporate Law

4

AI in Negotiating and Entering into Contracts

Eliza Mik

4.1 INTRODUCTION

This chapter retains a safe working distance from the usual hype surrounding artificial intelligence (AI) as well as from theories seeking to replicate human intelligence or intention. Taking into account the current state of the art, it explores whether a difference in the degree to which AI can augment or optimize human performance in the contracting process necessitates an adaptation of the law. After all, much of legal scholarship seems to have been seduced by technological progress, the popular assumption being that a change in technology necessitates a change in the law. The chapter distinguishes between entering into contracts, defined as a mechanistic form of transacting that involves unilaterally imposed terms and fixed prices, and negotiating contracts, which involves a more complex multi-attribute decision-making process. The starting hypothesis is that AI cannot negotiate contracts because the negotiation requires understanding and the ability to reason about the mental states of the other party. Nonetheless, even the less complex process of entering into contracts by means (or with the assistance) of AI may expose latent problems in existing legal principles. Abstracting from futuristic visions of "intelligent machines gone mad," it is necessary to confront the purported absence of human intention in the transacting process and examine the legal implications, if any, of interposing one or two AI devices between the contracting parties. If no humans are present at the time of contract formation, can we still speak of states of mind? While the complexity of an algorithm must not be regarded as a proxy for intelligence or intention, it must be acknowledged that more sophisticated information systems are prone to emergent behavior, including entering into unplanned or commercially unfavorable transactions.

In 1960, the father of cybernetics, Norbert Wiener, stated that it was "now generally admitted, over a limited range of operation, machines act far more rapidly than human beings and are far more precise in performing the details of their operations. This being the case, even when machines do not in any way transcend men's intelligence, they very well may, and often do, transcend men in the performance of tasks."[1] This quote forms a perfect backdrop for the discussion below as it abstracts from intelligence and, adopting a pragmatic approach, focuses on optimizing performance. After all, in 2022 it is clear that in a commercial setting, machines are generally not designed to mimic human intelligence but to improve human decision-making.[2]

[1] N. Wiener, "Some Moral and Technical Consequences of Automation" (1960) 131(3410) *Science* 1355.
[2] J. G. Brookshear and D. Brylow, *Computer Science* (13th ed., London: Pearson, 2020), p. 597.

Entering into contracts clearly falls within the latter category. Contracts can be formed in many ways. In most instances, one party agrees to the standard terms imposed by the other. No actual negotiations take place; there is no bargaining or haggling over the terms. The choice is binary: agree or not. Such a situation can hardly be described as negotiation as it is generally assumed that the term denotes the *process* of reaching agreement. *Imposing* terms differs from *proposing* terms and gradually working out the differences concerning the transactional details. Absent a fixed definition of the term, we can assume that "negotiation" denotes various forms of entering into contracts that do not involve such impositions. In setting the limits as to what AI can or cannot do, we must also assume that some terms can be expressed in numbers or formulae, such as prices or delivery dates, while others require an actual understanding of natural language and the law, such as clauses dealing with risk allocation. While both types of terms can be the subject of negotiations, we must realistically assume that only the former are amenable to "automated negotiations," that is, those that can be captured in numbers or algorithms. Moreover, we can also assume that "actual negotiations" involve, or *require*, a broad range of uniquely human skills, such as an understanding of the other party's motivations or emotions. Without such understanding, it is unlikely that negotiating parties can apply pressure, make concessions or engage in a myriad of subtle manipulations that aim to secure the best deal possible. At the current state of the art, no AI can negotiate complex *legal* terms, draft clauses that allocate the risks of breach or reason about the mental states of the other party. We must acknowledge, however, that AI can surpass humans in those aspects of the contracting process that involve (or require) a real-time analysis of vast amounts of transaction parameters such as prices, delivery terms, product selections, etc.

Irrespective of whether the contract is the product of protracted negotiations or of the simple acceptance of an offer, we can assume that it involves a series of decisions, which vary in number and complexity. They may concern the simple question whether to enter into the contract or relate to virtually every detail of the transaction – from the choice of the contracting party and the description of the product or services to be provided to the manner of price calculation. Contracting is decision-making. It is here where we see the direct relevance of AI in the process of entering into contracts. Unfortunately, sensationalistic headlines about the "dawn of the AI economy" tend to overshadow the simple fact that humans have relied on various decision aids for centuries – and that AI is only a more advanced form of such a decision aid or, to put it more bluntly, a tool we use to optimize the transacting process. Once described in such unimaginative terms the discussion loses its sheen of novelty while, at the same time, promoting a more commonsensical approach to the problems at hand. The latter are predominantly related to the purported absence of human intention at the time of contract formation and to the inevitable dangers accompanying all computer programs – that of emergent, unplanned or unpredictable operations.

One observation before proceeding: The use of AI in the process of entering into contracts must be distinguished from its much simpler predecessor, namely electronic negotiation systems.[3] The latter term refers to systems facilitating commercial communications, such as the structured exchange of electronic messages or electronic auction models.[4] Although such systems increasingly rely on AI, they are limited to the support of human negotiators and cannot

[3] M. Bichler, G. Kersten and S. Strecker, "Towards a Structured Design of Electronic Negotiations" (2003) 12 *Group Decision and Negotiation* 311.

[4] M. Schoop, A. Jertila and T. List, "Negoisst: A Negotiation Support System for Electronic Business-to-Business Negotiations in E-Commerce" (2003) 47(3) *Data & Knowledge Engineering* 371.

negotiate *instead* of humans[5] – unless we understand the term "negotiate" in the narrowest possible sense.[6]

4.1.1 Problem Delineation

This chapter does not succumb to the temptation to contemplate the personhood of AI. The grant of legal personhood is a normative choice, not the result of fulfilling any technical criteria.[7] Similarly, we need not discuss theories seeking to validate contracts formed by means of (or with!) computers by relying on principles of agency law. For an agency relationship to exist, there need to be two persons.[8] If one is not a person, one cannot be an agent. The same principle applies in English and in American law. This chapter does not indulge in theoretical and philosophical issues surrounding AI.[9] Instead, it adopts a pragmatic approach grounded in commercial practice. After all, AI (under various labels) has already permeated the home and the marketplace. This is commonly known as the "AI effect": Once a program becomes sufficiently complex to perform a task that was considered to require AI it is discarded as not being "really" intelligent.[10] The trend is to set new goals, or tests, of (artificial) intelligence whenever a previously unattainable goal (winning at chess or Go) is achieved.[11] As soon as AI successfully solves a problem, it is relegated to "complex computation."[12] This illustrates not only the conceptual vicinity of intelligence and computation but also the fact that we might have been surrounded by "intelligent" computer systems for a very long time. One could thus argue that our fascination with AI is unjustified and that the (purported) legal problems in the area of contract law can be regarded as a delayed (and redundant!) reaction to something that has been part of commerce for over two decades. After all, Amazon's website has been powered by technologies that, technically speaking, can be considered AI from the early 2000s. Yet, we do not attempt to retrospectively question the validity of the transactions formed thereon.

We must also not get seduced by headlines about the "revolutionary" progress in AI, particularly in the context of games, automated translation or image recognition. A famous example concerns the game of Go. When Google's AlphaGo program was pitted against professional Go player Lee Sedol in March 2016, it made the famous move 37 – a move that was not only unprecedented but indicative of human intuition.[13] AlphaGo won four out of five games against Sedol, creating a media frenzy and an avalanche of predictions as to what AI *will*

[5] G. Dobrijević, "Bargaining Chip: Artificial Intelligence in Negotiation," in B. Christiansen and T. Škrinjarić (eds.), *Handbook of Research on Applied AI for International Business and Marketing Applications* (Hershey, PA: IGI Global, 2021), p. 256.

[6] C. M. Jonker et al., "Negotiating Agents" (2012) 33(3) *AI Magazine* 79.

[7] B. Brozek and M. Jakubiec, "On the Legal Responsibility of Autonomous Machines" (2017) 25 *Artificial Intelligence Law* 293; J. Bryson, T. D. Grant and M. Diamantis, "Of, for and by the People: The Legal Lacuna of Synthetic Persons" (2017) 25 *Artificial Intelligence Law* 273.

[8] E. Peel, *The Law of Contract* (13th ed., London: Sweet & Maxwell, 2011), p. 603.

[9] For interesting considerations of the attribution of agency, morality and intentionality to artificial entities see: G. Teubner, "Rights of Non-humans? Electronic Agents and Animals as New Actors in Politics and Law" (2006) 33 *Journal of Law & Society* 497; L. Floridi and J. Sanders, "On the Morality of Artificial Agents" (2004) 14(3) *Minds and Machines* 349.

[10] See generally: S. J. Russell and P. Norvig, *Artificial Intelligence: A Modern Approach* (3rd ed., London: Pearson, 2016), p. 18.

[11] M. Campbell, A. J. Hoane and F.-H. Hsu, "Deep Blue" (2002) 134 *Artificial Intelligence* 57.

[12] Interestingly, Herbert Simon, a pioneer in "artificial intelligence," suggested naming the field "complex information processing."

[13] D. Silver et al., "Mastering the Game of Go with Deep Neural Networks and Tree Search" (2016) 529 *Nature* 484; D. Silver et al., "Mastering the Game of Go without Human Knowledge" (2017) 550 *Nature* 354.

soon be able to do. We must remember that even the most sophisticated game-playing algorithm cannot do anything but play a single type of game. A program that plays Go or pilots fighter planes is of no use when it comes to forming contracts. Lastly, we must not forget that when speaking of AI, we are speaking of computer programs. Consequently, while acknowledging the complexity and multitude of technologies that fall under the ambit of AI, I use the term interchangeably with "computer" or "computer program."

This chapter focuses on contractual intention and on the "unintended" operations of computer programs.

4.2 WHERE IS INTENTION?

It is frequently observed that contracts formed with the assistance of computers or – to be more in tune with the popular narrative – contracts formed "by" computers lack the requisite intention. Intention is a purely human phenomenon, and computers, irrespective of their sophistication, cannot intend anything. If there are no humans involved in the contracting process, intention is absent, and the validity of the resulting contract can be questioned. Although such theories form a common thread in most literature on automated transacting and AI,[14] they derive from a limited understanding of the fundamental principles of contract law. They may also derive from the fact that the majority of law and technology literature addresses aspects of AI in the context of public law and, without much analysis, subsumes issues of private law under the generalized assumption that "the use of AI in the transacting process requires an adaptation of the law," or similar. Arguably, were we to address AI in the context of competition law, the absence of human intent or knowledge may lead to doctrinal difficulties.[15] The same cannot be said, however, if we analyze AI in the context of contract law. The deployment of AI in various commercial processes may create problems in one area of law but leave others unaffected. Leaving aside such uninformed generalizations, we must appreciate that contract law has successfully "survived" more than a hundred years of drastic technological changes, including the introduction of the telephone, vending machines and, more recently, the Internet. The resilience of contract law is largely attributable to the broad and technology-neutral formulation of its core principles.[16] When it comes to contract formation, the principles are surprisingly straightforward: The parties must intend to be bound and they must exchange consideration. Intention must be manifested, and such manifestation can occur in any form or manner, excluding silence. In some instances, we may deploy the offer and acceptance model to establish the precise time when the contract was formed. Consideration, in turn, requires an exchange of performances or promises to perform. While there are many practical challenges in applying these principles, we must remember that nothing more than intention and consideration is required.

4.2.1 *Back to Basics*

How then, should we address the purported absence of *human* intention in contracts that were formed with the assistance of or "by" AI? To fully address this question, we must revisit the

[14] T. Allen and R. Widdison, "Can Computers Make Contracts?" (1996) 9 *Harvard Journal of Law & Technology* 25.
[15] M. S. Gal and N. Elkin-Koren, "Algorithmic Consumers" (2017) 30 *Harvard Journal of Law & Technology* 309.
[16] See generally: E. Mik, "The Resilience of Contract Law in Light of Technological Change," in M. Furmston (ed.), *The Future of Contract Law* (Abingdon: Routledge, 2020), p. 112.

basics – and it is the *legal* basics that are frequently forgotten when it comes to discussions of technological progress. Technicalities aside, we must recall that the main function of contract law is to facilitate bargains and that, to this end, it generally disregards the actual, subjective intention of the transacting parties.[17] Instead of focusing on the presence of actual intention, it focuses on observable behaviors that can be considered as communicating intention: If the parties *seem* to engage in transacting behavior then contract law will *infer* that both parties had the requisite legal intention.[18] Legal consequences are ascribed to *outward manifestations* of intention, for example statements or acts, not to the mental states underlying such statements or acts.[19] "A contract has, strictly speaking, nothing to do with the actual intent of the parties. A contract is an obligation attached by the mere force of law to certain acts of the parties, usually words."[20] According to Farnsworth, establishing intention "does not invite a tour through [the plaintiff's] cranium, with [the plaintiff] as the guide."[21] "Purely mental imaginings and reservations, however real they are to the actor or however serious the consequences to which they might in due course lead, have no status in this world of interaction. . . . [A] contract cannot be held hostage to the vagaries of the private intention."[22] Similar quotes abound in treatises and in cases. The point is simple: Contractual intention is the product of circumstances in which a particular act or utterance occurred. It is evaluated objectively, from the perspective of a reasonable addressee.[23] This approach, commonly referred to as the objective theory of contract, protects commercial certainty[24] and the expectations of those to whom such words and behavior are directed.[25] Arguably, commercial transactions between strangers would not be "as numerous and common as they are,"[26] were it not possible to rely on appearances of agreement. In mass-market transactions appearances are everything, as neither the origin of a statement nor the "thinking process" behind a particular decision can be leisurely investigated. Any theory that would require such an investigation would paralyze commercial dealings. Common textbook references to the "meeting of minds" can be regarded as a historical convention rather than as a legal prerequisite of validity.

The skeptical reader must be reminded that the objective theory of contract rests on the assumption that manifested intention *is* the actual intention. Why would one make an offer to sell something at a particular price if one did not intend to do so? What is particularly important in the present context is that the origins of a statement are irrelevant because they are not apparent from its contents. Contract law does not inquire *how* or *why* a statement came into being or investigate the underlying decision-making process. It only inquires whether the reasonable addressee of such statement would think the other party intends to contract on the

17 S. Waddams, *Principle and Policy in Contract Law: Competing or Complementary Concepts?* (Cambridge: Cambridge University Press, 2011).

18 R. Craswell, "Offer, Acceptance and Efficient Reliance" (1996) 48 *Stanford Law Review* 481, 482.

19 Furmston, at p. 42.

20 R. A. Lord, *Williston on Contracts* (4th ed., New York: Lawyers Cooperative Publishing, 2003–2020), Vol. 1, §4.1. See also O. W. Holmes, *The Common Law*, M. De W. Howe (ed.) (Boston: Little Brown & Co, 1963), p. 242 (the law "must go by externals").

21 E. A. Farnsworth, *Contracts* (4th ed., New York: Wolters Kluwer, 2004), §3.6, p. 115.

22 E. Weinrib, *The Idea of Private Law* (Cambridge, MA: Harvard University Press, 1995), p. 104.

23 J. M. Perillo, "The Origins of the Objective Theory of Contract Formation and Interpretation" (2000) 69 *Fordham Law Review* 427.

24 R. Barnett, "A Consent Theory of Contract" (1986) 86 *Columbia Law Review* 269, 306; H. Beale, ed., *Chitty on Contracts* (31st ed., Oxford: Sweet & Maxwell, 2012) at paras. 1-027 to 1-029; C. Fried, *Contract as Promise: The Theory of Contractual Obligation* (Harvard, MA: Harvard University Press, 1982).

25 A. Robertson, "The Limits of Voluntariness in Contract" (2005) 29 *Melbourne University Law Review* 180, 203.

26 J. Raz, "Promises in Morality and Law" (1982) 95 *Harvard Law Review* 916.

terms provided.[27] In other words, it focuses on the perception of the addressee of a statement, not on the mind of its maker. The objective theory of contract examines the output of the decision-making process, not the decision-making process itself. It is therefore legally inconsequential whether a person relied on an AI device in making their decision to enter into a contract or whether such decision is the product of purely mental processes.

4.2.2 *Intention and Intelligence: A Question of Appearances*

Intelligence is not a premise of a valid contract. Intention is. Theoretically then, questions of intelligence are unrelated to questions of intention. Nonetheless, we can draw some parallels between the objective theory of contract and the goals of AI research. Intelligence, just like contractual intention, is judged by outward behavior. Historically, a large part of AI research has focused not so much on achieving but on imitating intelligence. The famous Turing Test, originally known as the "Imitation Game," is commonly understood as serving to establish whether an AI has reached human-level intelligence. It is often forgotten that the test is not based on any technical criteria but, exclusively, the perceptions of those who interact with the program.[28] To recall: The test participants are placed in separate rooms and interact by means of typed communications. They evaluate whether the other party is human (or... *intelligent?*) exclusively on the basis of the contents of such indirect communications. The test does not seek to determine whether an AI has achieved actual intelligence but only whether a person interacting with the AI *perceives* it as intelligent or, to be more precise – as human. Moreover, Turing does not ask whether machines can think but "are there imaginable digital computers which would do well in the imitation game?"[29] In other words, if the computer acts sufficiently human-like to be indistinguishable from humans then, physical embodiment aside, it is unimportant whether it *actually* thinks or whether it is *actually* intelligent. Humanity, intelligence and the ability to think are, if we follow Turing, all a question of appearances. Similarly, as long as there are appearances of contractual intention, it is irrelevant whether such intention is actually present. Outward behavior constitutes a proxy for intelligence *and* for intention. This reliance on appearances is even more pronounced in an earlier version of Turing's Imitation Game, which involved three chess players. Player A played chess as they normally would, while player B, being a proxy for a computer program, followed a written set of rules. Player C had to determine which of the other players was human. According to Turing, Player C "may find it quite difficult to tell which he is playing."[30] From C's perspective, it makes no difference who (*or what!*) moves the pieces on the chessboard.[31] From C's perspective, it makes no difference *why* the other player moved the knight to c6. Did the opponent use their brain, copy the moves from a sheet of paper or rely on a chess computer? At the risk of oversimplifying a complex topic, we could say that both the objective theory of contract and Turing's Imitation Game adopt a behaviorist approach to intention and to intelligence, respectively. If I received a message that *looks like* it was sent by a human, I will assume that I am communicating with a human. If the message contains an offer, I will assume that its sender intends to contract on the terms provided. If a person *looks* like they want to enter into a contract on particular terms, the person *will be*

27 P. Atiyah, *Essays on Contract* (Oxford: Oxford University Press, 1990), p. 21.

28 A. M. Turing, "Computing Machinery and Intelligence" (1950) 236 *Mind* 433, 436.

29 M. Mitchell, *Artificial Intelligence: A Guide for Thinking Humans* (London: Penguin, 2019), p. 46.

30 A. M. Turing, *Intelligent Machinery: A Report by A. M. Turing* (National Physical Laboratory, 1948), p. 20.

31 For a broader discussion see: D. Proudfoot, "The Turing Test – From Every Angle," in J. Copeland et al., *The Turing Guide* (Oxford: Oxford University Press, 2017), p. 290.

regarded as intending to form such a contract. The objective theory of contract seems to work particularly well when parties transact at a distance and use methods of remote communication. In online commerce and in the Turing Test, the presence of intention and intelligence is evaluated solely on the basis of the contents of messages.

4.2.3 *Implications of Objectivity*

Extrapolating from the fact that contractual intention is evaluated objectively and that such objectivity rests on appearances and not on the presence of the actual intention of a person making a statement, we can make two broader interrelated observations.

First, we can suspect that a statement generated by an AI may be indistinguishable from a statement made by a human. A reasonable (and extremely perceptive!) addressee may be unable to differentiate between a statement made by a human stockbroker and a statement generated by a trading algorithm. The statements will look identical. This difficulty, if not inability, to distinguish human from nonhuman statements is particularly pertinent in e-commerce, where all communications occur at a distance by means of email or through a web interface. For example, Amazon's side of the transaction is virtually devoid of human participation. The entire contracting process is automated: starting from product recommendation and price determination to order processing and product delivery. The contents displayed on Amazon's website are selected and presented in a specific manner by a myriad of computer programs that operate in the background. Needless to say, many of those programs – or Amazon's e-commerce engine as a whole - qualify as AI.[32] The person interacting with Amazon *through its website* is, however, unable to determine whether the contents displayed thereon have been generated by a group of laborious employees or by a myriad of algorithms operating in (or "on"?) one of Amazon's data centers. Consequently, once contracts are made online, the only indication that a particular statement was of "artificial origin" may be the exceptional speed of the other party's response – but not its contents. We must acknowledge that many less advanced chatbots are primitive and annoying, leaving no doubt that "their" statements are generated by a nonintelligent and nonhuman entity. Nonetheless, if we adhere to the objective theory of contract and rely exclusively on appearances of intention, then it simply does not matter how a statement came into being or how it was communicated. If the contents of a message make commercial sense it does not matter how they came into being.

Second, the fact that an addressee may be unable to determine the origins of (or the decision-making process behind) a statement leads to an even more interesting point. In many instances, a statement that is communicated by a human has in fact been generated with the assistance of or "by" a computer. Historically, commercial decisions have often involved the use of abacuses and calculators. After all, most humans are incapable of complex calculations. Humans can use a calculator to, well, calculate the price and subsequently communicate such a price as part of the offer. While we cannot equate an abacus with an AI in terms of computational capabilities, we must acknowledge that humans have been using various technologies to aid them in decision-making and that such decisions often concern the commercial terms of a transaction. Progressively, such decision-support technologies have increased in sophistication and complexity – both with regards to processing speed and with regards to the amount of data they are

[32] L. Chen, A. Mislove and C. Wilson, "An Empirical Analysis of Algorithmic Pricing on Amazon Marketplace" (2016) *Proc. 25th International Conference on World Wide Web* 1339; B. Smith and G. Linden, "Two Decades of Recommender Systems at Amazon.com" (2017) 21(3) *IEEE Internet Computing* 12.

capable of analyzing, as vividly illustrated in the context of algorithmic trading.[33] Analyzing thousands of data points, computers may determine the shortest delivery route as well as the delivery date. They may also suggest the best price at which to purchase a particular stock or, on a broader level, assist in making investment decisions or devising entire investment strategies. Consequently, when a human trader relies on a trading algorithm to decide whether to buy certain shares at a particular price, we cannot confidently state that, say, their offer to buy such stock was made by them or "by" their trading program. In fact, when the program is used as a decision aid it may be difficult to state whether a particular decision was made by a human or by a computer program. After all, the human trader only repeats what the AI has "advised" them to do. Every day millions of decisions are based on predictions made by computers.[34] From doctors and traders to lawyers and judges, many professionals use decision-support software in the performance of their duties. Their liability remains unaffected even if they rely on such software entirely and "only" communicate the computer-generated decision to their customers.[35] Should there be a *legal* difference depending on the sophistication of the decision aid? Should there be a *legal* difference depending on the degree to which a human has relied on an AI in making a decision? Does it matter whether the aforementioned trader relies on a program to determine the optimal price of a stock but communicates the resulting offer themself or whether they let the program determine the price *and* communicate the offer?

The above paragraphs suffer from a latent linguistic shortcoming. It is unclear whether we should use scare quotes round the preposition "by" in sentences like "the statement was generated by an AI." Of course, in legal terms, the statement is always attributable to some natural or corporate person because the AI is not a separate legal entity. It is, after all, a computer program. The point is that from a purely technical perspective, the AI has produced a certain output and that this output is relied on by a human to enter into a contract. The question whether the decision is made "by" a human or "by" the AI must be relegated to future debates.

4.3 AN INTERLUDE ON AUTOMATION

Given the apparent complexities of establishing "who" makes a decision when AI is used as a decision aid, it is useful to further elaborate on the automation of tasks associated with the processing of information. After all, while not synonymous, in many instances the terms AI and automation are difficult to distinguish. Automation is a technology-neutral term and AI can be regarded as one of the technologies that can be used to automate certain types of tasks or processes. And so, according to a seminal paper by Raja, Sheridan and Wickens we can automate four classes of functions: 1) information acquisition; 2) information analysis; 3) decision and action selection; 4) action implementation.[36] Within each class, automation can be applied on different levels from low to high, that is, from fully manual to fully automatic. What is important in the context of deploying AI in the contracting process is that humans may decide

[33] E. Budish et al., "The High-Frequency Trading Arms Race: Frequent Batch Auctions as a Market Design Response" (2015) 130 *The Quarterly Journal of Economics* 1547.

[34] J. Kleinberg et al., "Human Decisions and Machine Predictions" (2018) 133 *The Quarterly Journal of Economics* 237; C.-F. Tsai and J.-W. Wu, "Using Neural Network Ensembles for Bankruptcy Prediction and Credit Scoring" (2008) 34 *Expert Systems with Applications* 2639; Y. Deng et al., "Deep Direct Reinforcement Learning for Financial Signal Representation and Trading" (2017) 28 *IEEE Transactions on Neural Networks and Learning Systems* 653.

[35] See, e.g., D. A. Waterman and M. A. Peterson, *Models of Legal Decisionmaking: Research Design and Methods* (Santa Monica, CA: Rand Corp., 1981), pp. 13–14.

[36] P. Raja, T. B. Sheridan and C. D. Wickens, "A Model for Types and Levels of Human Interaction with Automation" (2000) 30 *IEEE Transactions on Systems, Man, and Cybernetics* 286, 288.

to delegate only some or all of the above functions to a computer. It is, after all, possible to automate different aspects of the contracting process: from acquiring and analyzing information, to suggesting decisions or even implementing such decisions. In some industries, such as stock trading, by trading programs convert market information directly into buying decisions.[37] Similarly, Gal and Elkin-Koren observe that in the context of e-commerce software can be deployed at all stages of consumer transactions – including the formation and performance of a contract.[38] A computer can suggest a decision (or range of decisions) with a human selecting among different alternatives and implementing the chosen decision by performing the required action, such as selecting a particular product or making an offer at a specified price. A computer can also be programmed to select and directly implement decisions. In the latter instance, we speak of decision selection and action implementation. The concept of "action implementation" seems particularly relevant in our context as it demonstrates the futility of differentiating between statements that are generated by computers *but* communicated by humans and statements that are generated *and* communicated by computers. According to Raja, Sheridan and Wickens, "[a]ction implementation refers to the actual execution of the action choice. Automation of this stage involves different levels of machine execution of the choice of action, and typically replaces the hand or voice of the human."[39]

The broader point is that, technically, the AI can be involved in the first three stages of information acquisition, analysis and action selection with the human "only" implementing the decision that was recommended by the AI. It can also be involved in all four stages and include action implementation. In the latter instance, the AI does not only "make" or "generate" the decision but also communicates it to the other party. The unconvinced reader can be reminded of supermarket employees who do not make any decisions with regards to the goods sold but only implement data-driven decisions made upstream, by the supermarket management. The latter has most likely made such decisions with the assistance of computer programs... Moreover, to continue this mundane example, the same product can often be bought via an automated checkout or from a website. From the perspective of contract law there is, however, no difference.

4.4 PROGRAMMING INTENTION

We have established that intention is evaluated objectively and that the mental or technical origins of a statement may not be apparent from its contents. Still, we need to dispel any remaining doubts concerning the presence of human intention when a contract is formed automatically, without direct human participation. The key word in the preceding sentence is "direct." If a computer does something, it does so because it was programmed to do so.[40] Consequently, if a person programs a computer to do "x," the person must be deemed to intend "x."[41] The purported lack of intention at the time of contract formation derives from the inevitable interval between the act of programming and the execution of the program. By

[37] M. A. Goldstein, P. Kumar and F. C. Graves, "Computerized and High-Frequency Trading" (2014) 49 *The Financial Review* 177, 180.

[38] Gal and Elkin-Koren, at 318.

[39] Raja, Sheridan and Wickens, at 289.

[40] N. M. Richards and W. D. Smart, "How Should the Law Think About Robots?" in R. Calo, A. M. Froomkin and I. Kerr (eds.), *Robot Law* (Cheltenham: Edward Elgar, 2016), p. 3.

[41] For a more extensive version of this argument see: E. Mik, "From Automation to Autonomy: A Non-existent Problem in Contract Law" (2020) 36 *Journal of Contract Law* 1.

definition, computer programs execute instructions not when they are programmed but at a certain point in the future when, for example, certain conditions are met, and the program is actually run. Admittedly, at the time of contract formation, there is no direct human involvement. The latter can, however, always be found at an earlier moment. Contract law does not require that the statements made by the contracting parties be perfectly synchronized.[42] Parties need not be present at the same place, at the same time. This is confirmed by the validity of contracts made at a distance by means of traditional communications, such as the post. In the case of vending machines, which are regarded as offers made to the world at large,[43] the offeror's intention persists as long as the machine is held out. Although every day millions of contracts are entered into by means of vending machines, there is no single case denying the legal validity of such contracts on the ground that the offeror was not present or did not intend to contract. The same argument could be made with regards to practically all e-commerce websites, such as Amazon.com, which can be regarded as an advanced form of vending machines. Extrapolating from these examples it can be said that the intention of the person who programmed an AI to enter into contracts persists as long as the AI is allowed to operate in a transactional environment.

Every contract that derives from its programming must be regarded as intended. To clarify: The computer is not programmed to intend anything. The computer is programmed to generate and/or communicate statements that represent the intention of the programmer or, in broader terms, fulfill the commercial aims of the person who deploys the program. Such statements can take the form of websites, emails or messages "made by" chatbots. The specific means of communication seems of secondary relevance; what matters is that the contents of the message, as well as its very existence, derive from a prior decision to program a computer in a particular manner. We must remember that computers always realize the goals of their "human masters."[44] In the words of Stephen Wolfram: "I see technology as taking human goals and making them automatically executable by machines. Human goals of the past have entailed moving object from here to there, using a forklift rather than our own hands. Now the work we can do automatically ... is mental rather than physical."[45]

The "human masters" can either explicitly program each individual step to be followed to achieve such a goal or program the system to achieve the goal by creating its own instructions.[46] Turing emphasized that it "is impossible to produce a set of rules purporting to describe what a man should do in every conceivable set of circumstances."[47] Consequently, it may be more advantageous to program the computer to develop its own rules on the basis of data obtained from its operating environment.[48] For example, "a reinforcement learning agent trained to maximize long-term profit can learn short-term trading strategies based on its past actions and concomitant feedback from the market."[49] Consequently, the verb "program" must be interpreted broadly as encompassing not just fixed instructions but also instructions that permit or

[42] *Kennedy* v. *Lee* 36 Eng. Rep. 170 (Ch 1817); J. M. Perillo, "The Origins of the Objective Theory of Contract Formation and Interpretation" (2000) 69 *Fordham Law Review* 427, 439–40.

[43] *Thornton* v. *Shoe Lane Parking Ltd* [1971] 2 QB 163; *Carlill* v. *Carbolic Smoke Ball Co* [1893] 1 QB 256 at 262; *Lefkowitz* v. *Great Minneapolis Surplus Store* 86 NW 2d 689 (Minn. 1957); *Lexmead (Basingstoke) Ltd* v. *Lewis* [1982] AC 225.

[44] N. Wiener, "Some Moral and Technical Consequences of Automation" (1960) 131 *Science* 1355.

[45] S. Wolfram, "Artificial Intelligence and the Future of Civilization," in J. Brockman (ed.), *Possible Minds: 25 Ways of Looking at AI* (London: Penguin Press, 2019), p. 268.

[46] N. Bostrom, *Superintelligence* (Oxford: Oxford University Press, 2014), p. 169.

[47] Turing, "Computing Machinery and Intelligence," at 29, 452.

[48] D. Lehr and P. Ohm, "Playing with the Data: What Legal Scholars Should Learn about Machine Learning" (2017) 51 *University of California Davis Law Review* 653.

[49] Rahwan, I. et al., "Machine Behaviour" (2019) 568(7753) *Nature* 477.

require the program to develop "on its own." Even in the case of supervised machine learning, "most of the automation comes after humans have designed and built the system."[50] What bears repeating is that computers do not make their "own" decisions but execute earlier human decisions or manifest human decision in pursuance of human goals.[51] The output of their operations, such as entering into contracts on certain terms, always derives from prior programming. This approach is unequivocally adopted by the Uniform Electronic Transactions Act: "When machines are involved, the requisite intention flows from the programming and the use of the machine."[52]

In practice, the person who creates a program is not the same person who deployed the program for their commercial benefit. With the exception of such e-commerce giants as Google, Amazon or Facebook, who develop most of their software in-house, we can assume that most businesses purchase, license or commission the development of computer programs that will assist them in transacting. Nonetheless, for the purposes of establishing intention in the contract between the customer and the online business, the relationship between those who write the program and those who use the program must be regarded as one. After all, those who decide to use a particular program must be deemed to know what it does (at least theoretically) and also provide the actual transaction parameters that the program will execute. Moreover, from the perspective of the party who interacts with the program, it does not matter whether the other party who deploys the program created it themself, whether they procured its creation or simply licensed it from a commercial provider.

4.5 EMERGENCE, PREDICTABILITY AND "EXPLAINABILITY"

It appears that the objective theory of contract can seamlessly accommodate the deployment of AI in the contracting process. Unfortunately, the story does not end here. While computers "only" execute prior human instructions and reproduce actions they have been programmed to do, the processing capabilities and sophistication of many programs has led to "the tantalizing prospect of original action."[53] Some AIs may exhibit emergent behaviors – behaviors that are impossible to predict, understand or retrospectively explain, even by those who have programmed or trained them.[54] On a more mundane level, some of the AI's operations may be the result of programming errors. For the sake of doctrinal and technical correctness, we should differentiate between those operations of the AI that cannot be explained, those that were unplanned or unpredictable and those that simply derived from malfunctions. At the same time, we must acknowledge that from the perspective of the reasonable addressee, the person interacting with the AI, such distinctions may be irrelevant as the output will look identical.

[50] See generally: M. Zalnieriute, L. Bennett Moses and G. Williams, "The Rule of Law and Automation of Government Decision-Making" (2019) 82 *Modern Law Review* 425.

[51] M. du Sautoy, *The Creativity Code* (New York: Forth Estate, 2019), p. 114.

[52] UETA section 14 and comment 1.

[53] R. Calo, "Robotics and the Lessons of Cyberlaw" (2015) 103 *California Law Review* 513, 532.

[54] P. Voosen, "The AI Detectives" (2017) 357 *Science* 22; Y. Bathaee, "The Artificial Intelligence Black Box and the Failure of Intent and Causation" (2018) 31 *Harvard Journal of Law & Technology* 889; T. Zarsky, "The Trouble with Algorithmic Decisions: An Analytic Road Map to Examine Efficiency and Fairness in Automated and Opaque Decision Making" (2016) 41 *Science, Technology and Human Values* 118, 121; S. Wachter, B. Mittelstadt and L. Floridi, "Why a Right to Explanation of Automated Decision-Making Does Not Exist in the General Data Protection Regulation" (2017) 7 *International Data Privacy Law* 76.

4.5.1 *Explainability*

The inability to explain or understand the output or operation leading to such output has resulted in the creation of a new research area labeled explainable AI (or "xAI"), which aims to make algorithmic decision aids more understandable and accountable.[55] On one hand, it seems absurd to create an entire new field of research to understand our own creations! On the other, the very creation of such a field confirms that humans have been using technologies as decision aids for a long time or to a greater degree than we might have initially assumed. What is important in the present context is that contract law does not require that the statements made by the contracting parties be understandable or explainable. As indicated, contract law generally disregards the decision-making process leading to a statement.[56] Contractual intention, manifested as a decision to contract on specific terms, need not be explainable or understandable. Neither the maker of a statement nor its addressee need to be able to understand or explain its contents or existence. After all, the exact mental origins of most of our decisions cannot be understood or explained retrospectively either...[57] More importantly, anything that the AI "does" can be traced to the design choices of the human programmer.[58] The programmer will, for example, select "the value of a learning rate parameter, the acquisition of the representation of knowledge and state, or the wiring of a convolutional neural network."[59] This selection will, in turn, determine or influence the kinds of behaviors that the algorithm exhibits and, ultimately, the output it produces. The programmer may choose to expose the AI to arbitrary data or even to let the AI gather its own data. "The choice of which algorithms to use, what feedback to provide them and on which data to train them are also, at present, human decisions."[60] According to Kroll, the inability to explain the system's operations does not derive from its technical complexity but from a choice to design and use the system in a particular way – a "choice is made by the system's designers, operators and controllers."[61] It is not a technical inevitability.

4.5.2 *Predictability*

The complexity of certain programs may lead to situations where their operations result in the conclusion of contracts that are commercially unfavorable. Such would be the case when a website offers goods far below their market price or when a trading algorithm purchases a large amount of stock at an unreasonably high price. Those who deploy programs to automate parts or the entirety of the transacting process may argue that a particular transaction (speak: contract!) was unpredictable and hence unintended. *Un*surprisingly (pun intended!) such persons may

55 B. Mittelstadt, C. Russell and S. Wachter, "Explaining Explanations in AI," in *Proceedings of the Conference on Fairness, Accountability, and Transparency* (New York: Association for Computing Machinery, 2019), p. 280; J. Burrell, "How the Machine 'Thinks': Understanding Opacity in Machine Learning Algorithms" (2016) 3 *Big Data & Society* 1.

56 With the possible exception of vitiating factors, where the decision-making process of the "exploited" party might be scrutinized.

57 K. Burns and A. Bechara, "Decision-Making and Free Will: A Neuroscience Perspective" (2007) 25 *Behavioral Sciences and the Law* 2, 26; cf. N. A. Farahany, "A Neurological Foundation for Freedom" (2011) 11 *Stanford Technology Law Review* 1, 29.

58 A. Etzioni and O. Etzioni, "Keeping AI Legal" (2016) 19(1) *Vanderbilt Journal of Entertainment and Technology Law* 133, 137–8.

59 Rahwan et al., at 480.

60 Ibid.

61 J. A. Kroll, "The Fallacy of Inscrutability" (2018) 376 *Philosophical Transactions of the Royal Society* 2133, 2135.

attempt to avoid being bound by such "unintended contracts," constructing arguments along the lines of "I cannot be held liable for some unpredictable computer operations!" Admittedly, such attempts will be made only if such transactions produce losses, not when they result in commercial gains. I must clarify that although problems of predictability are generally associated with systems based on machine learning, they concern software in general – including relatively simple rule-based programs that do not iteratively modify their operations based on prior experiences or incoming data.

The inability to predict the operations of computer programs *in general* derives from the fundamental impossibility of ensuring that a computer program always fulfills certain properties or always produces a certain output without actually running such a program.[62] Translated into the current discussion, we are extremely limited in our ability to verify that a program will always do what it is supposed to do. Unless an AI is tested in specific circumstances, we cannot predict how it will execute in such circumstances. In other words, we cannot predict what a program will do given a set of inputs unless it has been tested for this very set of inputs. It is, however, practically impossible to test a program for all possible inputs and determine how it will behave in *all* circumstances.[63] It may also be extremely difficult, if not impossible, to retrospectively determine whether particular output is, in fact, the product of emergent behavior or derives from a programming error. Consequently, it is technically impossible to prevent "unintended transactions." This problem becomes even more prominent in the case of machine learning, especially if the program operates in a complex environment.[64]

Those who rely on AI in the transacting process are not allowed to disavow certain contracts on the ground that they are the product of emergent, erroneous, unpredictable or unplanned operations.[65] From the addressee of a statement produced by the AI, emergent operations may be impossible to distinguish from operations that are the product of programming errors or other malfunctions. Ultimately, what matters is commercial certainty. As long as the statement lies within the realms of commercial possibility, the AI's "human master" is bound by it. The only exception concerns situations where a reasonable addressee of a statement knows or should know that such a statement does not represent the actual intention of its maker. If, for example, an offer is commercially absurd, the offeree is deemed to know that it cannot represent the offeror's true intention. Although the objective theory of contract relies on appearances, it does not apply when a reasonable addressee knows or should know that such appearances do not represent reality. A classic example is an offer to sell a high-end printer for S$67, while its market price exceeded S$2,600,[66] or the exchange of cryptocurrencies at 150 times the market rate.[67]

5.6 CONCLUSION

I could devote hundreds of pages to examples of technological advancements that culminate in the uncanny ability of certain programs to evolve and to produce unplanned or unexplainable

[62] See generally: J. A. Kroll et al., "Accountable Algorithms" (2016) 165 *University of Pennsylvania Law Review* 633.
[63] Kroll et al., at 633, 650.
[64] Burrell.
[65] B. Bodo et al., "Tackling the Algorithmic Control Crisis: The Technical, Legal, and Ethical Challenges of Research into Algorithmic Agents" (2017) 19 *Yale Journal of Law and Technology* 133; H. Nissenbaum, "Accountability in a Computerized Society" (1996) 2 *Science and Engineering Ethics* 1, 25.
[66] In the famous case of *Chwee Kin Keong* v. *Digilandmall.com Pte Ltd* [2004] SGHC 71 the erroneous price of the printers (S$67 instead of S$2,500) resulted from an accidental uploading of training data by an employee not from an erroneous computation.
[67] *B2C2 Ltd* v. *Quoine Pte Ltd* [2020] SGCA (I) 2.

output. Such descriptions, combined with the use of arcane terms such as "convolutional neural networks" or "deep learning," may lead us to believe that in contracts that have been concluded with the assistance of such technologies, the human decision-making process (aka: *intention*!) blurs into the distance, to a point where it disappears and renders the whole transaction doctrinally questionable. In reality, a program that contains the instructions for all future contracts is used to manifest human intention. Every transaction that derives from such a program must be regarded as intended. The complexity of the program or the specific technology underlying the decision aid used by the human is irrelevant.

Once we realize how AI is deployed in practice and acknowledge that many of our commercial decisions are based on the automation of cognitive tasks, we may develop a more balanced and less sensationalistic perspective regarding the role of AI in the contracting process. AI informs decisions made by judges, doctors, lawyers, pilots, regulators and managers in virtually every industry. We have been observing an increasing reliance on computers in every aspect of commerce. Humans have been using technology as decision aids for hundreds of years. The fact that our abacuses and pocket calculators have gradually morphed into self-learning supercomputers is technologically (and philosophically!) exciting but of little, if any, significance in the context of contract law. At present, the law of contract does not distinguish between statements produced "by" or "with the assistance of" computers and statements made in a traditional manner. To complicate matters, statements produced by a computer are often indistinguishable from statements produced by the human brain. The question is not what the maker of a statement intended or how they reached a decision that culminated in a particular statement. The question is what the reasonable addressee was led to believe. Legal differentiations based on how a statement came into being seem arbitrary and find no doctrinal support.

Some confusion will persist, largely due to the unavoidably anthropomorphic undertones of such expressions like "made by computers." As described above, such expressions must not be read verbatim but constitute linguistic shortcuts. Somewhat confusingly, they can be regarded as factually correct in the sense that the computer program actually performs the computations that led to the decision and to the legally relevant statement manifesting such a decision.

5

AI and Contract Performance

André Janssen

5.1 INTRODUCTION

The use of technical aids to fulfil contracts has been common practice in business for a long time. Examples include vending machines, which make traditional human-to-human sales obsolete, and automated ordering systems in the field of e-commerce.[1] Automation was and is often the key for entrepreneurs to survive in the long term. Private law, and especially contract law, has so far found satisfactory solutions for automation driven by technical systems. This applies to both common and civil law.

Newer AI systems are now increasingly conquering the market. They are capable of learning and outcomes can no longer be precisely predicted, unlike purely technical automation. The autonomy inherent in AI systems brings legal challenges. The reason is that it is no longer possible to predict whether and how explanations and actions emanating from AI systems originate and whether they are attributable to the AI system or its operators (users). The core research question of this chapter is whether the operator of AI systems is contractually liable for the damage caused by its malfunctioning. Is contract law sufficiently prepared for the use of AI systems for contract performance? This will be illustrated using the common law, the United Nations Convention on Contracts for the International Sale of Goods (CISG), and the German Civil Code (BGB). Which of these laws and legal systems are better equipped for the challenges posed by emerging AI systems? Will changes in contract law be needed to accommodate issues specific to AI?

Increasingly, AI systems are being used in the various phases of contracting. These systems differ from conventional software used for automation because of their reactivity and the proactivity of their behaviour.[2] They can learn and adapt their behaviour to different sets of circumstances. Unlike conventional software, the behaviour of AI systems can no longer be accurately predicted or explained because they have a considerable degree of autonomy.[3] This distinguishes them from automated systems based on conventional software, such as digital

[1] C. Wendehorst and J. Grinzinger, 'Vertragsrechtliche Fragestellungen beim Einsatz intelligenter Agenten' in M. Ebers, C. Heinze, T. Krügel and B. Steinrötter (eds.), *Künstliche Intelligenz und Robotik: Rechtshandbuch* (Munich: C. H. Beck, 2000), p. 141.

[2] Ibid., pp. 141 et seq.

[3] G. Spindler, 'Haftung für autonome Systeme – ein Update' in S. Beck, C. Kusche, and B. Valeruis (eds.), *Digitalisation, Automation, AI and Law* (Baden-Baden: Nomos, 2020), p. 257; G. Teubner, 'Digitale Rechtssubjekte? Zum privatrechtlichen Status autonomer Softwareagenten' (2018) 218 *Archiv für die civilistische Praxis (AcP)*, 164.

measuring devices or industrial robots.[4] AI systems are increasingly able to make autonomous and not just automated decisions, detached from any human influence. From a legal point of view, it is no longer possible to exactly say whether and how declarations and actions emanating from AI systems originate from the operators.[5]

A secondary question is under what conditions can the operator be held liable? Ultimately, the topic leads to the broader question of whether contract law, based on an anthropocentric view, still leads to appropriate solutions or whether legal systems need to revise existing contract law to be 'AI-ready'.

To answer these questions several legal frameworks will used to flesh out issues relating to the application of law to AI systems. As noted above, the common law, CISG, and BGB have been selected for this analysis. Given the differences across common and civil legal systems, the laws selected for study are merely intended to serve as examples, to flesh out problems and to offer conceivable solutions.

Section 5.2 discusses the scope of the analysis being undertaken. Section 5.3 explores defining AI in the context of contract law and the phenomenon of contractual performance by AI systems. Section 5.4 examines the remedial scheme of contract law in civil and common law, and their application to breach of contract caused by AI systems. Section 5.5 summarizes the analysis and provides an outlook into the future of the contractual liability for breach of contract caused by AI systems.

5.2 SCOPE OF THE CONTRIBUTIONS: CONTRACT PERFORMANCE BY AI SYSTEMS

AI systems can impact the different phasing of contracting – the *pre-contractual phase* (such as algorithmic pricing), the *conclusion (formation) of the contract* through unilateral and bilateral use of AI systems or software agents (machine-to-machine communication or human-to-machine communication), or the *contract performance* by AI systems. This chapter focuses on the latter phase.

In the case of contract performance by AI systems, a distinction must be made between two situations. There are the cases in which one or more contracting parties are supported by AI systems, but the actual performance of the contract itself is still carried out by humans (so-called human in loop-scenarios). The more interesting scenario for this contribution is where contract performance is directly carried out by AI systems. The AI system used for contract performance can either be proprietary (internally developed by a company) or owned by third-party creators of AI systems.

This chapter does not deal with a whole series of topics. Some of these topics are dealt with elsewhere in this book – questions of contract negotiation and contract formation through AI are discussed by Eliza Mik (Chapter 4),[6] Eric Tjong Tjin Tai discusses liability for AI decision-making (Chapter 9),[7] Fenwick and Wrbka deal with AI personhood

[4] F.-U. Pieper, 'Vertragsschluss mit KI, Anfechtung und Schadensersatz' in M. Kaularz and T. Braegelmann (eds.), *Rechtshandbuch Artificial Intelligence und Machine Learning* (Munich: C. H. Beck, 2020), p. 239.

[5] Ibid., p. 242.

[6] For a German perspective see D. Effer-Uhe, 'Erklärungen autonomer Softwareagenten in der Rechtsgeschäftslehre' (2021) *Recht Digital (RDi)*, 169 et seq.; Wendehorst and Grinzinger, 'Vertragsrechtliche Fragestellungen beim Einsatz intelligenter Agenten', pp. 149 et seq.

[7] See on this from a German perspective also J. Eichelberger, 'Zivilrechtliche Haftung für KI und smarter Roboter' in M. Ebers, C. Heinze, T. Krügel, and B. Steinrötter (eds.), *Künstliche Intelligenz und Robotik: Rechtshandbuch* (Munich: C. H. Beck, 2020), pp. 174 et seq.

(Chapter 20),[8] and Pınar Çaglayan Aksoy examines AI and agency law (Chapter 11). Finally, the topic of smart contracting and contract performance is not dealt with here.[9] This is because smart contracts do not require AI.

5.3 DEFINING AI IN THE CONTEXT OF CONTRACTING

The possible fields of application of AI systems are numerous and the methods underlying their applications diverse. A general definition of AI is inherently broad. Essentially, the term AI refers to technologies that emulate human cognitive abilities.[10] AI is characterized by it receiving data, which it then processes, evaluates it regarding a goal specified by a natural person, and adjusts its functioning accordingly.[11] AI applications are based on the use of algorithms, which represent mathematical instructions for solving problems. Translated into programming language, an algorithm can be used as a software solution. The new development is referred to as 'adaptive' software and machine learning, which can be implemented.[12] Due to this non-determinability or opacity, AI decision-making processes can sometimes be difficult or impossible to understand, even for programmers. This is referred to as the 'black box' problem.[13]

A distinction is currently made between 'strong AI' and 'weak AI'.[14] They are distinguished by weak AI's ability to independently set goals that go beyond its human-created specifications, whereby strong AI does not yet exist in practice. AI can be purely software-based in a virtual environment (pure software) or integrated into hardware (robot).[15] It is important to keep in mind that in tort law, and more specifically in product liability law, the variation between the two can make a significant difference.

[8] See also S. M. Mayinger, *Die künstliche Person* (Frankfurt am Main: Fachmedien Recht und Wirtschaft in Deutscher Fachverlag, 2017); T. Allen and R. Widdison, 'Can Computers Make Contracts?' (1996) 9 *Harvard Journal of Law & Technology*, 41 et seq.

[9] For contributions on smart contracts see L. DiMatteo, M. Cannarsa, and C. Poncibò (eds.), *Cambridge Handbook of Smart Contracts, Blockchain Technology, and Digital Platforms* (Cambridge: Cambridge University Press, 2020); A. J. Casey and A. Niblett, 'Self-Driving Contracts' (2017) 43 *Journal of Corporation Law* 1 et seq.; M. Durovic and A. Janssen, 'The Formation of Blockchain-based Smart Contracts in the Light of Contract Law' (2018) *European Review of Private Law (ERPL)*, 753 et seq.; E. Mik, 'Smart Contracts: Terminology, Technical Limitations and Real World Complexity' (2017) 10 *Journal of Law, Innovation and Technology (JLIT)*, 269 et seq.; R. O'Shields, 'Smart Contracts: Legal Agreements for the Blockchain' (2017) 21 *North Carolina Banking Institute*, 177 et seq.; M. Raskin, 'The Law and Legality of Smart Contracts' (2017) 1 *Georgetown Technology Review*, 305 et seq.; J. M. Sklaroff, 'Smart Contracts and the Cost of Inflexibility' (2017) 166 *University Pennsylvania Law Review*, 263 et seq.; K. Werbach and N. Cornell, 'Contracts Ex Machina' (2017) 67 *Duke Law Journal*, 313 et seq.

[10] J. Grinzinger, 'Der Einsatz Künstlicher Intelligenz in Vertragsverhältnissen' in E. Beyer et al. (eds.), *Privatrecht 2050: Blick in die digitale Zukunft* (Baden-Baden: Nomos, 2020), p. 152 (with further references); Wendehorst and Grinzinger, 'Vertragsrechtliche Fragestellungen beim Einsatz intelligenter Agenten', p. 141.

[11] Grinzinger, 'Der Einsatz Künstlicher Intelligenz in Vertragsverhältnissen', pp. 152 et seq. (with further references).

[12] Wendehorst and Grinzinger, 'Vertragsrechtliche Fragestellungen beim Einsatz intelligenter Agenten', p. 142; H. Zech, 'Künstliche Intelligenz und Haftungsfragen' (2019) 2 *Zeitschrift für die gesamte Privatrechtswissenschaft (ZfPW)*, 199 et seq.

[13] Wendehorst and Grinzinger, 'Vertragsrechtliche Fragestellungen beim Einsatz intelligenter Agenten', p. 142.

[14] Grinzinger, 'Der Einsatz Künstlicher Intelligenz in Vertragsverhältnissen', pp. 153 et seq.

[15] Terms used for the phenomenon of AI include: 'autonomous system', 'robots', 'software agent', 'intelligent agent', or 'autonomous agent'. See, e.g., J. Grapentin, *Vertragsschluss und vertragliches Verschulden beim Einsatz von Künstlicher Intelligenz und Softwareagenten* (Baden-Baden: Nomos, 2018), p. 31 (AI and software agent terms). See also P. Hacker, 'Verhaltens- und Wissenszurechnung beim Einsatz von Künstlicher Intelligenz' (2018) *Rechtswissenschaft (RW)*, 245; Wendehorst and Grinzinger, 'Vertragsrechtliche Fragestellungen beim Einsatz intelligenter Agenten', p. 141.

5.3.1 *Examples of Contract Performance by AI Systems*

In the context of contract performance, the discussion about the practical possibilities of use focus often on AI systems that are integrated into hardware (a robot). In the literature, for example, one finds the examples of 'painting robots',[16] 'cleaning robots',[17] or 'care robots'.[18] Robotic AI includes drones equipped with AI to inspect wind turbines. The drone automatically flies a predefined flight pattern and photographs the wind turbines from several angles. The resulting photos are evaluated by AI and summarized automatically in a report. Based on the associated images, irregularities are highlighted and recommendations for action are automatically given.[19] However, the drone's AI only makes recommendations for action with the final decision to repair being made by a human. The AEROARMS project (AErial RObotic system integrating multiple ARMS and advanced manipulation capabilities for inspection and maintenance) goes a decisive step further.[20] In large refineries operating tens of thousands of kilometres of pipes, this project offers a solution to prevent corrosion and accidents. The AEROARMS drones use advanced AI and can fly to the most elevated structures, map them, calculate pipe wall thickness using ultrasonic sensors, deploy non-destructive test sensors, and in contrast to the previously mentioned example they can even perform important maintenance tasks themselves. These examples illustrate the use of AI systems to undertake contract performance. The situations in which malfunctioning AI systems can cause damage during contract performance are diverse.

5.4 DAMAGES FOR BREACH OF CONTRACT CAUSED BY AI SYSTEMS UNDER COMMON AND CIVIL LAW

5.4.1 *Liability for Breach of Contract: General Remarks*

Again, the core question is whether the operator of AI systems used to perform a contract can be held liable for damages. For a better understanding of the issue of liability for breach, a few words on contractual liability in common law and civil law are useful. One of the fundamental differences between common and civil laws is the different requirements for awarding damages in contract law.[21] While the common law assumes strict liability of the contracting party in breach of contract (existence of a breach is sufficient), the civil law legal systems also require fault (intent or negligence).[22] The CISG is a legal hybrid and cannot be assigned to either

[16] M. Foerster, 'Automatisierung und Verantwortung im Privatrecht' (2019) *Zeitschrift für die gesamte Privatrechtswissenschaft (ZfPW)*, 430.

[17] Hacker, 'Verhaltens- und Wissenszurechnung beim Einsatz von Künstlicher Intelligenz', 248.

[18] S. Klingbeil, 'Schuldnerhaftung für Roboterversagen' (2019) *Juristenzeitung (JZ)*, 718 et seq.

[19] See 'So revolutionieren Drohnen und KI die Inspektion von Windenergieanlagen', available at www.funk-gruppe.de/de/leistungen/funk-beyond-insurance/so-revolutionieren-drohnen-und-ki-die-inspektion-von-windenergieanlagen.

[20] See 'AErial RObotic System Integrating Multiple ARMS and Advanced Manipulation Capabilities for Inspection and Maintenance', available at https://cordis.europa.eu/article/id/251211-ai-powered-drones-for-difficult-maintenance-tasks/de.

[21] See K. Zweigert and H. Kötz, *Einführung in die Rechtsvergleichung* (Tübingen: Mohr Siebeck, 3rd ed., 1996), pp. 501 et seq.

[22] The two major EU laws on contract law, the Sale of Goods Directive 2019/771 and the Digital Content Directive 2019/770, will do little to change the common law/civil law divide in Europe. First, the UK is no longer obliged to implement the Directives. Second, the regulation of damages for a breach of contract remains the domain of national law.

common or civil law.[23] For a better understanding of contract laws relationship to AI systems, the notion of the common law/civil law divide will be retained.

5.4.2 *Strict Liability Approach: Common Law and CISG*

5.4.2.1 **Common Law's Remoteness Test**

In the common law the existence of a breach of contract is sufficient to bring a claim for damages.[24] The problem with this strict liability approach is that

> if all of the risks of a breach of contract were placed upon a defaulting promisor, regardless of the unusual nature of the risks, a crushing burden may be imposed upon him. ... [F]airness demands that some equitable division of risks flowing from nonperformance occur so that the reasonable expectations of the promisee may be fulfilled without simultaneously placing an undue burden upon the defaulting promisor.[25]

The common law's response to potential injustice is the 'remoteness test' recognized in the seminal 1854 case of *Hadley* v. *Baxendale*,[26] which limited damages to those that were foreseeable at the time of the conclusion of the contract.[27] The loss must be foreseeable not merely as being possible, but as being not unlikely – the parties must have considered it as a *probable* consequence of breach.[28] In determining foreseeability of damages common law courts focus on the implied knowledge of the parties relating to the *ordinary course of things* and *actual knowledge of special circumstances* outside the ordinary course of things, such as information communicated from one party to the other party.[29]

The limitation on collectable damages is not well-suited for damages caused by AI systems. First, in a technical sense AI's ability to predict outcomes is something different than human foreseeability. Second, from the human creator and operator foreseeability is clouded given the unpredictability of machine learning, especially due to the multitude of possible uses and circumstances directed at the AI. For example, if an AI-directed inspection and maintenance drone comes to an erroneous conclusion that a certain pipe vital to the operation of a manufacturing plant does not need repair or if the repair is carried out incorrectly, is the operator or creator liable for the resulting damages (loss of profits due to a production stoppage)? The most plausible answer is that the damages were foreseeable when the AI was created or implemented. Here, the contracting parties are likely to know what happens in the *ordinary course of things*, namely that depending on the circumstances unrepaired or defectively repaired pipes can lead to a loss of profits resulting from the production stoppage. Of course, the seller operator also must have known (communication) or should have known (circumstances) that the stoppage was a likely consequence of the AI system's failure.

[23] On the legal nature of the CISG as a legal hybrid, see A. Janssen and N. Ahuja, 'Bridging the Gap: The CISG as a Successful Legal Hybrid between Common and Civil Law?' in Francisco de Elizalde (ed.), *Uniform Rules for European Contract Law? A Critical Assessment?* (Oxford: Hart, 2018), pp. 137 et seq.

[24] If the party in breach of the contract is liable for the damage caused by the AI system, it may have a right of redress against the producer of the AI system. Any such right is hindered by problems of proof and limitation periods.

[25] J. E. Murray, *Murray on Contracts* (New York: LexisNexis, 5th ed., 2011), p. 763.

[26] (1854) 9 Exch 341.

[27] Murray, *Murray on Contracts*, pp. 763 et seq.

[28] Ibid., p. 766.

[29] See N. Andrews, *Contract Law* (Cambridge: Cambridge University Press, 2nd ed., 2015), pp. 500 et seq.; Murray, 'Murray on Contracts', pp. 763 et seq.

5.4.2.2 *Contractual Deviation from the Strict Liability and Force Majeure Clauses*

Due to the strict liability for contract breach in common law, contracting parties often negotiate contractual clauses to limit or exclude liability for damages caused by breach. The validity of such clauses depends on the facts of the case at hand, such as whether the transaction is a commercial (B2B) or consumer (B2C) contract, whether clauses were negotiated or standard terms, and so forth. This, in turn, depends largely on the strength of the respective contractual position.

A few words are needed relating to the role of force majeure clauses, despite the existence of the doctrines of objective impossibility and frustration of purpose. The general strictness of these common law's exemption or excuse doctrines are eased or tightened through a broadening or narrowing of exemption by force majeure clauses. An example of such a clause is the ICC Force Majeure Clause 2020. Under this clause, a malfunctioning AI system would not regularly constitute a force majeure event.[30] Given the newness of AI technology it is difficult to carry the burden of proving the *unforeseeability* of the malfunctioning of an AI system. It can be argued that the malfunctioning of AI systems is always foreseeable in the legal sense. Finally, such malfunction is not captured by any of the recognized categories of force majeure, such as war, civil unrest, natural disasters, government intervention, and so forth.

5.4.2.3 *CISG: Strict Liability Approach*

5.4.2.3.1 REMOTENESS TEST Although the CISG is a legal hybrid, it follows the common law approach in assessing strict liability for breach of contract.[31] A breach of contract is considered sufficient for a claim of damages (see Art. 45(1)(b) CISG and Art. 61(1)(b) CISG). Like the common law, the CISG is also concerned to limit the potentially harsh consequences of strict liability by adopting a version of the foreseeability (remoteness) standard. Art. 74 s. 2 CISG[32] states that damages are limited to the losses that the breaching party 'foresaw or ought to have

[30] See ICC Force Majeure Clause 2020 (short version):

1. 'Force Majeure' means the occurrence of an event or circumstance that prevents or impedes a party from performing one or more of its contractual obligations under the contract, if and to the extent that that party proves: [a] that such impediment is beyond its reasonable control; and [b] that it could not reasonably have been foreseen at the time of the conclusion of the contract; and [c] that the effects of the impediment could not reasonably have been avoided or overcome by the affected party.
2. In the absence of proof to the contrary, the following events affecting a party shall be presumed to fulfil conditions (a) and (b) under paragraph 1 of this Clause: (i) war (whether declared or not), hostilities, invasion, act of foreign enemies, extensive military mobilisation; (ii) civil war, riot, rebellion and revolution, military or usurped power, insurrection, act of terrorism, sabotage or piracy; (iii) currency and trade restriction, embargo, sanction; (iv) act of authority whether lawful or unlawful, compliance with any law or governmental order, expropriation, seizure of works, requisition, nationalisation; (v) plague, epidemic, natural disaster or extreme natural event; (vi) explosion, fire, destruction of equipment, prolonged break-down of transport, telecommunication, information system or energy; (vii) general labour disturbance such as boycott, strike and lock-out, go-slow, occupation of factories and premises.

The contract may be terminated by either party if the duration of the impediment exceeds 120 days.

[31] The liability of the party in breach of the contract is however limited to the extent that the breach was caused by the first party's act or omission (see Art. 80 CISG).

[32] Art. 74 CISG:

Damages for breach of contract by one party consist of a sum equal to the loss, including loss of profit, suffered by the other party because of the breach. Such damages may not exceed the loss which the party in breach foresaw or ought to have foreseen at the time of the conclusion of the contract, in the light of the facts and matters of which he then knew or ought to have known, as a possible consequence of the breach of contract.

foreseen at the time of the conclusion of the contract . . ., as a possible consequence of the breach of contract'. This contrasts with the *Hadley* v. *Baxendale* rule as one that limits damages to the *probable* consequences of a breach. Therefore, the foreseeability of damages is broader under the CISG (than the *Hadley* v. *Baxendale* rule about *possible* consequences vs. *probable* consequences). This means that under the CISG an operator is less likely to escape liability for a defective AI system. Only rarely will it be possible to argue that damages were not foreseeable as a *possible* consequence.

5.4.2.3.2 CISG ARTICLE 79 CISG AND THE STRICT LIABILITY REGIME The CISG exemption rule is found in Art. 79.[33] Although less detailed than the ICC Force Majeure Clause 2020, the main content is essentially the same:

> (1) A party is not liable for a failure to perform any of his obligations if he proves that the failure was due to an impediment beyond his control and that he could not reasonably be expected to have taken the impediment into account at the time of the conclusion of the contract or to have avoided or overcome it or its consequences.

As with the ICC Clause, an invocation of force majeure in the use of malfunctioning AI systems for contract performance is likely to fail due to the lack of unforeseeability. Given current Art. 79 case law, its use in the cases of malfunctioning AI systems would be narrowly construed anyway and is unlikely to play much or a role.

Also, under the CISG the principle of party autonomy (Art. 6 CISG), as in the common and civil laws, allow for the broadening of exemption from liability through contract clauses. Thus, liability for AI malfunctioning is likely to be limited by such clauses under current contract law. For the CISG, this would only apply to commercial contracts.[34]

5.4.2.3.3 INTERIM RESULT The use of AI systems in contract performance will not necessitate a revision of the common law or the CISG. Unlike civil law, common law does not require a finding of fault. The common law and the CISG's strict liability principle, as well as its damages and exemption rules work without any restriction when AI systems are used to perform contracts. However, a malfunctioning AI system will almost never constitute a force majeure event. Thus, no paradigm shift in applying contract rules to AI systems is necessary. The promisor

[33] Article 79 CISG:

(1) A party is not liable for a failure to perform any of his obligations if he proves that the failure was due to an impediment beyond his control and that he could not reasonably be expected to have taken the impediment into account at the time of the conclusion of the contract or to have avoided or overcome it or its consequences.
(2) If the party's failure is due to the failure by a third person whom he has engaged to perform the whole or a part of the contract, that party is exempt from liability only if:
    (a) he is exempt under the preceding paragraph; and
    (b) the person whom he has so engaged would be so exempt if the provisions of that paragraph were applied to him.
(3) The exemption provided by this article has effect for the period during which the impediment exists.
(4) The party who fails to perform must give notice to the other party of the impediment and its effect on his ability to perform. If the notice is not received by the other party within a reasonable time after the party who fails to perform knew or ought to have known of the impediment, he is liable for damages resulting from such non-receipt.
(5) Nothing in this article prevents either party from exercising any right other than to claim damages under this Convention.

[34] Art. 2(a) CISG.

and that the same time operator of the AI remains liable whether the contract is performed by human or AI systems.

5.4.3 *Fault Liability Approach of German Civil Law*

In contrast to common law, the German civil law (BGB) adopts a fault liability approach to compensation for breach. The core provision on damages for a breach of contract (breach of duty) is found in section 280 (going forward all section references are to the BGB). Section 280(1) reads: 'If the obligor breaches a duty arising from the obligation, the obligee may demand damages for the damage caused thereby.'[35] Hence, the obligor must have breached a duty arising from that obligation (*Pflichtverletzung*). An obligation is not exclusively, but regularly created by a contract according to section 311(1), according to which '[i]n order to create an obligation by legal transaction ..., a contract between the parties is necessary ....'[36] Under section 280 the type or severity of the breach of duty is irrelevant. It can be a breach of main performance obligations (*Hauptleistungspflichten*), but also of secondary obligations (*Nebenleistungspflichten*) such as duties of protection and care (*Schutz- und Obhutspflichten*). When AI systems are used to perform a contract, there may be a breach of both main performance obligations (cargo drone drops the goods to be delivered over the sea) and secondary obligations in the form of duties of protection (cargo drone damages other property).[37]

In contrast to common law systems, the obligor is only liable for damages under German law if it is also responsible for a breach of duty as required by section 280(1) s. 2, which in turn is determined by the sections 276–278 (these sections describe the German remoteness test or objektive Zurechnung, which limit liability to a foreseeable extent). According to section 276 (1),[38] the obligor is responsible for intent and negligence (*Vorsatz und Fahrlässigkeit*). Section 276(2) states that '[a] person acts negligently if he fails to exercise reasonable care'. However, the obligor may be responsible not only for their own fault, but also for the fault of others. According to section 278,[39] 'the obligor is responsible for fault on the part of his legal representative, and of persons whom he uses to perform his obligation, to the same extent as for fault on his own part'.

Section 280(1) 2 states that the obligor must prove that they are not responsible for a breach of duty. The obligor's fault is thus presumed to be to their detriment (*Verschuldensvermutung*).[40] This is a shift in the burden of proof from claimants to respondents in a dispute. The obligee

[35] See, in English, R. Schulze, 'Section 280 of the German Civil Code' in C. Dannemann and R. Schulze, *German Civil Code, Volume 1: Books 1–3* (Munich: C. H. Beck, 2020), pp. 408 et seq. (English version).

[36] Although under German law there are quasi-contractual or statutory obligations from which rights and obligations can arise.

[37] A. Leupold and A. Wiesner, 'Teil 9.6.4 Zivilrechtliche Haftung bei Einsatz von Robotern und Künstlicher Intelligenz' in A. Leupold, A. Wiebe, and S. Glossner (eds.), *IT-Recht* (Munich: C. H. Beck, 4th ed., 2021), no. 31.

[38] Section 276 BGB (responsibility of the obligor):

(1) The obligor is responsible for intention and negligence, if a higher or lower degree of liability is neither laid down nor to be inferred from the other subject matter of the obligation, including but not limited to the giving of a guarantee or the assumption of a procurement risk.
The provisions of sections 827 and 828 apply with the necessary modifications.

(2) A person acts negligently if he fails to exercise reasonable care.

(3) The obligor may not be released in advance from liability for intention.

[39] Section 278 BGB (responsibility of the obligor for third parties): 'The obligor is responsible for fault on the part of his legal representative, and of persons whom he uses to perform his obligation, to the same extent as for fault on his own part.' The provision of section 276(3) does not apply.

[40] This presumption of fault was introduced into the revised BGB in 2002 by the reform of the law of obligations (*Schuldrechtsreform*).

needs to prove the breach of duty and the damage based on it within the scope of section 280(1), but not the fault of the obligor. Rather, the obligor must show and prove in court that it is not *at* fault for a breach of duty. Contractual changes to the fault rule are possible in principle (such as the waiver of the presumption of fault according to section 280(1) s. 2) but any such contractual change is subject to legal restrictions such as section 305's et seq. regulation of standard business terms.

5.4.3.1 *Liability of Operator When Using Malfunctioning AI Systems for Contract Performance*

If the obligor uses an AI system to perform a contract, that subsequently causes harm to the other party, is it liable for damages? According to German law, this liability could arise due to the user's own culpable breach of duty according to section 280 in conjunction with section 276. Liability based on the attribution of the behaviour of the AI system is also conceivable.[41] The operator's liability for '*third-party* culpable breach of duty' (namely of the AI system) would be based on section 280 BGB in conjunction with section 278.

Regarding the liability of the user of malfunctioning AI systems for contract performance due to their own culpable breach of duty, it is unclear which duties of care need to be fulfilled. However, there is agreement that the use of AI systems for contract performance as such is not regarded as a culpable breach of duty.[42] Replacing an employee with an AI system is therefore permissible under private law and in principle does not entail any liability on the part of the operators of AI systems. However, the situation is different if the operator selects an AI system that is unsuitable for the contractual purpose.[43] The operator's failure to update the AI system can also be regarded as a culpable breach of duty, which can give rise to liability for damages.[44] The operator can also be required to test the AI system before it is used. Failure to do so may be a culpable breach of duty giving rise to liability.[45]

Apart from the above instances, there is no presumption that an operator of an AI system has committed a culpable breach of duty under section 280 in conjunction with section 276 BGB. This is because of the high degree of autonomy and the resulting unpredictability of the actions of AI systems. Constant monitoring of AI systems by operators is implausible because that would run counter to the purpose of using AI.[46] It should also be considered that AI systems will

[41] An idea of some scholars is to introduce vicarious liability of the operator or creator of AI systems. See G. Wagner, 'Verantwortlichkeit im Zeichen digitaler Techniken' (2020) *Versicherungsrecht (VersR)*, 734 et seq.; Zech, 'Künstliche Intelligenz und Haftungsfragen', 214 et seq.

[42] Grinzinger, 'Der Einsatz Künstlicher Intelligenz in Vertragsverhältnissen', p. 175; J. P. Günther, *Roboter und rechtliche Verantwortung* (Munich: Utzverlag, 2016), p. 69; J. Hanisch, *Haftung für Automation* (Göttingen: Cuvillier Verlag, 2010), p. 22; Wendehorst and Grinzinger, 'Vertragsrechtliche Fragestellungen beim Einsatz intelligenter Agenten', p. 167.

[43] Foerster, 'Automatisierung und Verantwortung im Privatrecht', 431; Grinzinger, 'Der Einsatz Künstlicher Intelligenz in Vertragsverhältnissen', p. 175; T. Schulz, *Verantwortlichkeit bei autonom agierenden Systemen* (Baden-Baden: Nomos, 2015), p. 137; Wendehorst and Grinzinger, 'Vertragsrechtliche Fragestellungen beim Einsatz intelligenter Agenten', p. 168.

[44] B. Raue, 'Haftung für unsichere Software' (2017) *Neue Juristische Wochenschrift (NJW)*, 1841, 1842; Wendehorst and Grinzinger, 'Vertragsrechtliche Fragestellungen beim Einsatz intelligenter Agenten', p. 167.

[45] Leupold and Wiesner, 'Teil 9.6.4 Zivilrechtliche Haftung bei Einsatz von Robotern und Künstlicher Intelligenz', no. 33.

[46] Grinzinger, 'Der Einsatz Künstlicher Intelligenz in Vertragsverhältnissen', p. 175; Schulz, 'Verantwortlichkeit bei autonom agierenden Systemen', p. 137; Wendehorst and Grinzinger, 'Vertragsrechtliche Fragestellungen beim Einsatz intelligenter Agenten', p. 167; S. Horner and M. Kaulartz, 'Haftung 4.0 Verschiebung des Sorgfaltsmaßstabs bei Herstellung und Nutzung autonomer Systeme' (2016) *Computerrecht (CR)*, 9 (critical of a limitation of the duty to monitor AI systems).

increasingly monitor themselves. Consequently, operators will only be obliged to monitor the monitoring function of AI.[47] Another obligation would be a duty to ease using an AI system that repeatedly malfunctions.[48]

5.4.3.2 *Liability for Malfunctioning AI Systems Not Due to Operator's Culpability*

It is apparent that the operator of AI systems used for contract performance will only rarely be accused of a culpable breach of duty and if sued will often be able to rebut the presumption of fault under section 280(1) paragraph 2. Thus, the best contractual claim would in theory be under section 278. The purpose of section 278 is the attribution of *third-party* culpable breaches of duty to the obligor.[49] As previously mentioned, the obligor is responsible for fault on the part of their legal representative (*gesetzlicher Vertreter*) and of persons whom she uses to perform obligation (*Erfüllungsgehilfe* or 'contractual assistant'). The provision regulates not only the attribution of the fault of the contractual assistant or legal representative, but also when the status as contractual assistant is not clearly expressed. A contractual assistant is according to the German Supreme Court a person who acts with the knowledge and intention of the principal within the scope of the principal's rights and duties as their auxiliary person.[50] The legal relationship between the obligor and the contractual assistant is irrelevant. The only decisive factor is the actual performance of an obligation incumbent on the obligor. It is not necessary that the contractual assistant is an employee of the obligor or is bound by her instructions. An independent company commissioned by the obligor can also be a contractual assistant.

Section 278 exemplifies the basic problem of civil law (at least in the form of the German law) and its application to the use of AI systems for the performance of contracts. The provision assumes human actors and uses the 'fault' of the contractual assistant as the basis for the obligor's liability. German law continues to apply an anthropocentric image. Since AI systems have no legal personhood (yet), they cannot be a 'person' in the sense of section 278, and therefore lack the capacity to be at fault. Even if AI was recognized as a legal person there would remain the problem that the category of 'fault' is a profoundly human one. In short, section 278 is not relevant for AI systems used for contract performance, and AI systems cannot be contractual assistants under it. An attribution of the behaviour of the AI to the operator cannot take place.

If the traditional attribution provisions of the BGB are irrelevant for the use of AI systems, this will have serious consequences for the entire liability structure. By using AI systems for contract performance, the user could escape contractual liability. The consequence would release operators of AI systems from liability unless a culpable breach of duty can be proven. Thus, liability shifts away from the operator of AI systems to the creator of the systems, since the duties of care such for monitoring the AI system would largely shift to the latter compared to non-autonomous systems, where the duty to monitor is with the operator.[51] Under tort law, the injured party would have to make a claim against the creator of the AI system and not its contractual partner.

[47] Horner and Kaulartz, 'Haftung 4.0 Verschiebung des Sorgfaltsmaßstabs bei Herstellung und Nutzung autonomer Systeme', 9.

[48] Wendehorst and Grinzinger, 'Vertragsrechtliche Fragestellungen beim Einsatz intelligenter Agenten', p. 168; Leupold and Wiesner, 'Teil 9.6.4 Zivilrechtliche Haftung bei Einsatz von Robotern und Künstlicher Intelligenz', no. 33 (with further monitoring obligations).

[49] See R. Schulze, 'Section 278 of the German Civil Code' in C. Dannemann and R. Schulze, *German Civil Code, Volume 1: Books 1–3* (Munich: C. H. Beck, 2020), pp. 406 et seq. (English version).

[50] BGHZ 13, 111, 113; R. Schulze, 'Section 278 of the German Civil Code', p. 407.

[51] Horner and Kaulartz, 'Haftung 4.0 Verschiebung des Sorgfaltsmaßstabs bei Herstellung und Nutzung autonomer Systeme', 9.

5.4.3.3 *Future of Contractual Liability for the Operator of Malfunctioning AI Systems*

The question now for German law is how it will deal with the above challenge. In doing so, two aspects of the problem must be examined. First, is there currently a *liability gap* due to the emergence of AI systems, which makes an equalization of AI systems and human contractual assistants in contract performance necessary (attribution to the obligor/operator)? And secondly, if such a need exists, would the *de lege lata* (law as it is) or *de lege ferenda* (law as it should be) solution be preferred? The next few sections illustrate the main themes of each solution.

5.4.3.3.1 FIRST VIEW: THERE IS NO LIABILITY GAP Some scholars argue that there is no liability gap due to the emergence of AI systems for contract performance but only a shift in liability.[52] It is primarily the creator of the AI system that is liable and not the operator of the AI system. This is justified because effectiveness of autonomous AI systems come within the duty of care of its creator. The duties of operators decrease significantly in comparison with their duties when using non-autonomous systems. Under this view, the injured party would simply make a claim against the creators of AI systems.[53]

This above argument is not completely convincing in that the shifting of liability does not mean a liability gap does not exist. Let us assume that a client commissions a contractor to inspect and repair defective pipes at its factory using an AI done. Due to a malfunction in the drone's AI system, the drone fails to make a proper inspection. This in turn ultimately leads to a production stoppage at the client's plant. By all accounts, the drone's AI was properly designed, worked perfectly in prior cases, and was regularly monitored by both the operator and the creator of the AI system. The operator would in this scenario would not be seen as committing a culpable breach of duty. In the absence of the applicability of section 278 BGB to AI systems, she would not be liable to the plant owner under either contract or tort law. The producer of the drone also would not be contractually liable under current German law for the damages incurred by the plant owner. Contractual liability is excluded since there is no contract between the producer and the injured party.

The general tort law, found in section 823(1) BGB,[54] would also not be applicable. It provides that liability for damages is only given if a person intentionally or negligently injures the life, body, health, freedom, property, or another right of another person. A claim in tort would be thwarted because the producer of the drone never physically harmed the owner's property,[55] did not breach any duty of care, and section 823(1) does not recognize claims for pure economic loss.

[52] Spindler, 'Haftung für autonome Systeme – ein Update', pp. 269 et seq.; B. Heiderhoff and K. Gramsch, 'Klassische Haftungsregimes und autonome Systeme – genügt "functional equivalence" oder bedarf es eigenständiger Maßstäbe?' (2020) *Zeitschrift für Wirtschaftsrecht (ZIP)*, 1943.

[53] See, e.g., Leupold and Wiesner, 'Teil 9.6.4 Zivilrechtliche Haftung bei Einsatz von Robotern und Künstlicher Intelligenz', no. 34; Spindler, 'Haftung für autonome Systeme – ein Update', p. 269.

[54] Section 823 (liability in damages):

(1) A person who, intentionally or negligently, unlawfully injures the life, body, health, freedom, property, or another right of another person is liable to make compensation to the other party for the damage arising from this.

(2) The same duty is held by a person who commits a breach of a statute that is intended to protect another person. If, according to the contents of the statute, it may also be breached without fault, then liability to compensation only exists in the case of fault.

[55] However, the situation would be different if the faulty AI of the drone had also led to a faulty repair. In this case, one could assume an infringement of property within the meaning of section 823(1).

The producer of the drone is also not liable under the German Product Liability Act as the Act does not recognize claims for pure economic loss.[56] This example shows that under the current legal regime, a party who suffers a loss due to a malfunctioning AI system may not always have recourse to collect damages. Therefore, despite the shift of the duty of care from the operator to the producer of the AI systems, a liability gap in some cases will prevent the injured party from receiving full compensation for its damages.

5.4.3.3.2 SECOND VIEW: EXISTING LIABILITY GAP CAN BE ELIMINATED *DE LEGE LATA* Other scholars have acknowledged the existence of a liability gap. They consider this gap and the resulting release of the obligor's (operator) liability to be inequitable. Gunter Teubner summarizes the problem as follows: 'It is the principle of equal treatment that requires liability here. For if a human were to be used for the performance of the contract, the principal would be liable for his breaches of duty according to § 278 BGB, so he cannot [should not] be exempt from liability if a software agent is used for the identical task.'[57]

The more far-reaching the autonomy of AI systems, the less justifiable the unequal treatment in the use of AI in contrast to human contractual assistants seems.[58] It is unfair to exempt the operators of AI systems because harm caused by such systems attributed to the operators' sphere of control.[59] As a result, the denial of liability leads to an unjustifiable privileging of operators using AI systems instead of humans.

One *de lege lata* solution, as previously noted, would be to apply section 278 analogously to AI systems to prevent a liability gap.[60] However, this solution has met with considerable resistance from scholars.[61] For example, the necessary regulatory gap and comparable interests for the assumption of an analogy are denied, since AI systems are not comparable to human assistants. Even if AI systems are equipped with decision-making discretion, it is argued that they will always act within a pre-programmed framework, which speaks against the analogy.[62] Furthermore, an analogous application of section 278 is difficult because most autonomous

[56] Implementation of Directive 85/374/EEC. Section 1(1) Product Liability Act Liability states:

> In such case as a defect in a product causes a person's death, injury to his body or damage to his health, or damage to an item of property, the producer of the product has an obligation to compensate the injured person for the resulting damage. In case of damage to an item of property, this shall only apply if the damage was caused to an item of property other than the defective product and this other item of property is of a type ordinarily intended for private use or consumption and was used by the injured person mainly for his own private use or consumption.

[57] G. Teubner, 'Digitale Rechtssubjekte? Zum privatrechtlichen Status autonomer Softwareagenten', 188 ('Es ist der Gleichbehandlungsgrundsatz, der hier die Haftung verlangt. Denn würde ein Mensch für die Vertragsdurchführung herangezogen, so haftete der Prinzipal nach § 278 BGB für dessen Pflichtverletzungen, er kann aber nicht von der Haftung befreit sein, wenn für die identische Aufgabe ein Softwareagent herangezogen wird'). See also, the EC Expert Group on Liability and New Technologies – New Technologies Formation, 'Report on Liability for Artificial Intelligence and other Emerging Digital Technologies, available at https://op.europa.eu/en/publication-detail/-/publication/1c5e30be-1197-11ea-8c1f-01aa75ed71a1/language-en, p. 3 ('A person using a technology which has a certain degree of autonomy should not be less accountable for ensuing harm than if said harm had been caused by a human auxiliary.')

[58] Wendehorst and Grinzinger, 'Vertragsrechtliche Fragestellungen beim Einsatz intelligenter Agenten', p. 169.

[59] Klingbeil, 'Schuldnerhaftung für Roboterversagen', 719.

[60] Grinzinger, 'Der Einsatz Künstlicher Intelligenz in Vertragsverhältnissen', p. 175; Wendehorst and Grinzinger, 'Vertragsrechtliche Fragestellungen beim Einsatz intelligenter Agenten', pp. 168 et seq.

[61] Grapentin, 'Vertragsschluss und vertragliches Verschulden beim Einsatz von Künstlicher Intelligenz und Softwareagenten', p. 131; Heiderhoff and Gramsch, 'Klassische Haftungsregimes und autonome Systeme – genügt "functional equivalence" oder bedarf es eigenständiger Maßstäbe?'; Leupold and Wiesner, 'Teil 9.6.4 Zivilrechtliche Haftung bei Einsatz von Robotern und Künstlicher Intelligenz', no. 34; Pieper, 'Vertragsschluss mit KI, Anfechtung und Schadensersatz', pp. 264 et seq.

[62] Leupold and Wiesner, 'Teil 9.6.4 Zivilrechtliche Haftung bei Einsatz von Robotern und Künstlicher Intelligenz', no. 34.

systems are no longer comprehensible and cannot be thought of as human behaviour.[63] Furthermore, the AI system cannot be at fault because it lacks the capacity for insight and judgement. One recommendation is to dispense with this requirement altogether and create a 'digital assistant liability' (*digitale Assistenzhaftung*).[64] The fear of such an approach is that it would lead to a strict liability regime unknown to German law, due to a lack of culpability.[65]

Because of the difficulty of placing operator liability into existing legal structures, some argue for the creation of uniform standards of due diligence for AI systems (as a sort of robot or AI culpability).[66] A comparison with the standard of care applicable to the operator using human assistants could be used to set a standard for AI systems to determine a 'culpable breach of duty'. If the capabilities of the AI system exceed those of the human user, the standard of care could instead be determined by comparing the AI system with the comparable systems available on the market.[67]

5.4.3.3.3 THIRD VIEW: EXISTING LIABILITY GAP CAN ONLY BE ELIMINATED *DE LEGE FERENDA* Due to the problems identified, but also due to the fundamental changes that an analogous application of section 278 BGB to AI systems would bring about, the most plausible conclusion is that the liability gap cannot be meaningfully closed *de lege lata*.[68] The most far-reaching idea would be to grant advanced AI systems a limited legal personhood *de lege ferenda*.[69] This is intended to solve the problems of fault, liability, and responsibility, as well as attributability under section 278. Such a solution would have to be enacted by the legislature.

The idea of creating a parallel standard for AI systems that corresponds to section 278 has the greatest future potential in the long term.[70] This would result in uniform liability of the obligor (operator) when using AI systems or human contractual assistants with as few changes to the overall system as possible. But a new regulation of this order would face the same scrutiny as a *de lege lata* interpretation of section 278.[71] Should the principle of fault of section 278 be waived for AI systems? Should German law embrace a strict liability principle for AI? Should one compare the conduct of AI systems with the standard of care applicable to humans to establish a 'culpable breach of duty'? Should a standard of care specific to AI systems be adopted based on the capabilities of comparable systems? The problem, however, is that for certain AI systems there is no comparable other AI system.

[63] M. Kuhn, *Rechtshandlungen mittels EDV und Telekommunikation* (Munich: C. H. Beck, 1991), p. 282; A. Wiebe, *Die elektronische Willenserklärung* (Tübingen: Mohr Siebeck, 2002), p. 188.

[64] For example, Teubner, 'Digitale Rechtssubjekte? Zum privatrechtlichen Status autonomer Softwareagenten', 192.

[65] M. Kuhn, *Rechtshandlungen mittels EDV und Telekommunikation*, p. 282; A. Wiebe, *Die elektronische Willenserklärung*, pp. 188 et seq.

[66] Grinzinger, 'Der Einsatz Künstlicher Intelligenz in Vertragsverhältnissen', p. 177; Wendehorst and Grinzinger, 'Vertragsrechtliche Fragestellungen beim Einsatz intelligenter Agenten', p. 170.

[67] Wendehorst and Grinzinger, 'Vertragsrechtliche Fragestellungen beim Einsatz intelligenter Agenten', p. 170.

[68] For example, Klingbeil, 'Schuldnerhaftung für Roboterversagen', 719 et seq.; H. Köhler, 'The Problem of Automated Legal Transactions' (1982) 182 *Archiv für die civilistische Praxis (AcP)*, 168.

[69] See Günther, 'Roboter und rechtliche Verantwortung', pp. 251 et seq.; A. Matthias, *Automaten als Träger von Rechten* (Berlin: Logos-Verlag, 2008), pp. 83 et seq.; Spindler, 'Haftung für autonome Systeme – ein Update', p. 274; Wagner, 'Verantwortlichkeit im Zeichen digitaler Techniken', 737 et seq.

[70] See in this regard in detail Klingbeil, 'Schuldnerhaftung für Roboterversagen', 723 et seq.

[71] See Section 5.4.3.3.2.

5.4.3.4 *Interim Result*

Unlike common law, AI systems used for contract performance present significant challenges for civil law. The German law must clarify whether and under what conditions the operator of AI systems is liable for its own culpable breaches of duty. Under current law, the increasing autonomy of AI systems reduces the level of the operators' duty of care (the monitoring obligation), while that of the creator of the AI system correspondingly increases.

An even greater challenge is the liability for third-party culpable breaches of duty because of the use of AI systems for contract performance. This is where civil law in the form of section 278 BGB reaches its limits. An AI system is neither a 'person' in the sense of section 278, nor is the principle of fault appropriate for the conduct of AI systems. If one assumes a liability gap, the question arises as to how this gap can be eliminated. The gap is not likely to be filled by an expanded *de lege lata* interpretation of section 278. This leaves the solution in the hands of the legislature to change the BGB. Any such change would need to reassess the fault requirement and adopt a strict liability regime for AI systems in contract law.

5.5 CONCLUSION

The core issue examined in this chapter was whether the operator of an AI system is contractually liable for the damage caused by a malfunctioning AI system. A larger issue is how AI will impact existing contract law in the future. The common law and the CISG are well equipped to determine breach and allocate liability for AI systems used to perform contracts. The principles of contractual liability for damages in common law function regardless of whether the obligor fulfils or attempts to fulfil the contract itself, through human agents or through AI systems. The liability for AI systems under strict liability centres on the obligor, as is otherwise the case, and can be applied without restriction to AI systems. Common law is 'blind' in a positive sense to whether humans or AI systems are breaching the contract. Common law can therefore proceed cautiously in adjusting its rules in the face of new technological developments.

The civil law basic construct, illustrated by the BGB, is fault liability. With the increasing autonomy of AI, the duties of care of the operator of AI systems (especially the monitoring duties) are reduced. The operator may therefore rebut the presumption of fault found in section 280(1) s. 2 BGB and thus escape liability. This causes a shift of liability from the operator to the creator of AI systems, whose duties of care intensify with the increasing autonomy of their systems.

The greatest challenge for civil law is the doubtful applicability of provisions regulating the attribution of AI conduct to the operator as a 'third-party culpable breach of duty'. This is because norms found in section 278 are exclusively addressed to human fault. This chapter argues that the inapplicability of the norms for third-party culpable breaches can lead to liability gaps when AI systems are used to perform contracts. In contrast to common law, it makes a significant difference in civil law whether the obligor performs or attempts to perform the contract through humans or AI systems. One way of filling the liability gap is through analogous application of the attribution provisions found in section 278 or by the *de lege ferenda* creation of comparable provision for AI systems.

No matter which solution one prefers, one comes to fundamental questions for civil law: Is the fault principle simply inappropriate for AI systems and should not apply to them? This would create a strict contractual liability regime for AI systems. On the other hand, legislators could undertake the difficult task of developing a fault standard for AI systems. Whatever the various civil law systems decide, they are currently at a crossroads: do they chose continuity by leaving the existing liability regime untouched, resulting in possible liability gaps, or do they disrupt the current law by adopting contractual strict liability for AI behaviour?[72]

[72] There are other possible ways to close the liability gap, such as the tortious strict liability of the users and/or the creators of the AI systems.

6

AI and Corporate Law

Florian Möslein

6.1 INTRODUCTION

With the recent proposal of the European Commission for a so-called Artificial Intelligence Act, this technology becomes a regulatory subject in its own right.[1] While the Commission proposal primarily adopts a market-oriented approach,[2] artificial intelligence (AI) also plays an increasingly important role in the internal decision-making of corporations. The technology promises increased efficiency, especially for business decisions that are made on the basis of extensive and complex data. AI makes it possible, for instance, to analyse data from customer relationships or production processes on a massive scale, and to prepare it for decision-making processes, such as in the context of algorithmic marketing, algorithmic market research or algorithmic controlling.[3] Automated decision-making in corporations thus promises key entrepreneurial advantages and efficiency gains. However, automated decision-making also represents the crucial regulatory challenge of this technology.[4]

Entrepreneurial decisions are legally embedded by the rules of corporate law that, along with the articles of association, define a governance framework of competencies and procedures that corporate decision-makers must follow. These rules stipulate, for example, whether the board of directors or the shareholders' meeting is competent to decide on certain issues, and in what form the respective decision needs to be taken (convening requirements, collegial decisions or majority requirements).[5] Such decision-making rules are indispensable because corporate law deals with complex long-term cooperative relationships between a large number of actors (so-called relational legal relationships): unlike in simple exchange contracts, operational questions in such relationships typically cannot be decided completely in advance, at the time when the

[1] Proposal for a Regulation of the European Parliament and of the Council Regulation laying down harmonized rules on artificial intelligence (Artificial Intelligence Act), COM(2021), 206 final.

[2] Although the proposed regulation is not strictly limited to market transactions, its prevailing market orientation already becomes apparent in the rank order of its Art. 1 (a), according to which the regulation lays down 'harmonised rules for the placing on the market, the putting into service and the use of artificial intelligence systems ("AI systems") in the Union'.

[3] Cf. Peter Gentsch, *Künstliche Intelligenz für Sales, Marketing und Service* (Heidelberg: Springer, 2018), pp. 63–77.

[4] Bitkom e.V./DFKI, 'Künstliche Intelligenz – Wirtschaftliche Bedeutung, gesellschaftliche Herausforderungen, menschliche Verantwortung', 2017, p. 58 et seq., available at www.dfki.de/fileadmin/user_upload/import/9744_171012-KI-Gipfelpapier-online.pdf.

[5] See, e.g., Markus Ruffner, *Die ökonomischen Grundlagen eines Rechts der Publikumsgesellschaft* (Zurich: Schulthss, 2000), p. 164.

(corporate) contract is concluded.[6] If AI is therefore increasingly used in corporate decision-making, the question arises as to whether and under what conditions such technology-based decision-making is in accordance with the legal requirements of corporate law.

For reasons of brevity and relevance, however, the general topic of 'AI in corporate law' needs to be narrowed down in several respects, namely with regard to legal systems, legal forms, decision-making bodies and the intensity of the use of technology:[7] firstly, corporate law is still predominantly a matter of domestic law, even though numerous legal aspects in this field have been harmonized within the European Union and standardization is also occurring at the global level, in particular by means of the OECD principles on corporate governance. This chapter does not focus on a single national legal system, but aims to provide a principle-based view that takes functional commonalities of corporate laws – the 'anatomy of corporate law' – as a theoretical basis.[8] For the purpose of clarification, however, provisions of specific national legal systems will serve as examples.

Secondly, the focus is not on corporations in general and corporate law as a whole, but exclusively on public limited companies and, therefore, on the law of stock corporations. However, the use of AI is by no means irrelevant in other legal forms. Yet, at present, the use of AI is particularly widespread in larger companies, which are typically incorporated as stock corporations due to their capital requirements.[9] The volumes of data that make the use of such technology worthwhile are usually generated in corporations of a larger size.

Thirdly, the focus is not on all possible decision-making bodies of stock corporations, but exclusively on the management board. As a result of its management power, the board of directors is equipped with the primary decision-making authority on entrepreneurial matters; it is responsible not only for the day-to-day management of the company, but also for many strategic business decisions.[10] These decisions are particularly complex and require a broad database that is potentially easier to manage with the help of AI. In quantitative terms, too, the decisions to be made by the board of directors are particularly numerous because they also involve issues relating to day-to-day management. Accordingly, the primary use of AI is in the decisions of the board of directors, even though its role in annual general meeting decisions or, if applicable, in decisions by the supervisory board or independent directors is equally conceivable.

Fourthly, and finally, this chapter does not focus on the rather futuristic situation in which AI completely replaces human board members (so-called AI company directors or robots in the boardroom),[11] but rather concentrates on the arguably much more realistic scenario in which

[6] On relational contracts see the path-breaking work of Ian R. Macneil, 'Contracts: Adjustment of Long-Term Economic Relations under Classical, Neoclassical and Relational Contract Law', (1978) 72 *Northwestern University Law Review* 854; on (stock) corporations as relational contracts, Ruffner, *supra* n. 5, at p. 162 et seq., with further references.

[7] For a more comprehensive account, see Florian Möslein, 'KI und Gesellschaftsrecht', in Martin Ebers et al. (eds.), *Rechtshandbuch Künstliche Intelligenz und Robotik* (Munich: C. H. Beck, 2020), § 13.

[8] Cf. Reinier Kraakman et al. (eds.), *The Anatomy of Corporate Law: A Comparative and Functional Approach* (Oxford: Oxford University Press, 3rd ed., 2017).

[9] According to a recent study, AI is used primarily in companies 'that employ more than 500 people (83%) and/or generate up to one billion euros in revenue (72%)'; see PwC, 'Künstliche Intelligenz in Unternehmen', 2018, p. 8, available at www.pwc.de/de/digitale-transformation/kuenstliche-intelligenz/studie-kuenstliche-intelligenz-in-unternehmen.pdf.

[10] For more details, see John Armour, Luca Enriques, Henry Hansmann and Reinier Kraakman, 'The Basic Governance Structure', in Kraakman et al. (eds.), *supra* n. 8, p. 49, at 50 et seq.; cf. also Florian Möslein, *Grenzen unternehmerischer Leitungsmacht im marktoffenen Verband* (Berlin: de Gruyter, 2007), pp. 23–50.

[11] This was the title of the algorithm that was used under the name VITAL (abbreviation for 'Validating Investment Tool for Advancing Life Sciences') in the much-cited example case of the venture capital company Deep Knowledge

technology merely supports the – human – board members, for example, by preparing relevant data material and submitting decision proposals. Accordingly, this chapter does not discuss questions regarding the independent legal capacity of AI or its capacity as a corporate body,[12] but merely the possibilities of AI in supporting human board decisions.

6.2 DELEGATION OF DECISION-MAKING TASKS

Board members cannot perform every task themselves, but require a wide range of support. To this end, they delegate tasks. Traditionally, this delegation has been made to subordinate employees or to external parties. However, decision-making tasks can increasingly also be delegated to AI, in that the sifting and evaluation of data material as well as the selection of decision options can be completed through software-based technologies. Accordingly, it must be considered whether there is an authority – or even an obligation? – to delegate respective decisions to AI or, more generally, to technological devices and algorithms.[13] So far, case law and jurisprudence have barely dealt with delegation to algorithms. The academic debate, however, is gaining momentum.[14] From a doctrinal perspective, it must be considered how the conventional principles for delegation to subordinate employees and external parties can be applied when delegating to algorithms.

6.2.1 *Authority to Delegate*

Delegation is regarded as an essential tool of effective leadership because the management task would hardly be manageable without delegation.[15] However, there are various limits to the directors' power of delegation. These limits can be derived from the principle of comprehensive management responsibility under stock corporation law. Thus, tasks that the law expressly assigns to the management board or that count as original management tasks are usually deemed impermissible to delegate. In contrast, preparatory and executive measures may be delegated to subordinate levels of the company, provided that the management board only takes final decisions in a well-considered manner and on its own responsibility.[16] US corporate law, for

Ventures from Hong Kong (but which in reality also only had a supporting function), in more detail: Florian Möslein, 'Robots in the Boardroom: Artificial Intelligence in Corporate Law', in Woodrow Barfield and Ugo Pagallo (eds.), *Research Handbook on the Law of Artificial Intelligence* (Cheltenham: Edward Elgar, 2018), p. 649, at 649 et seq.

[12] On this question, from a comparative law perspective: Shawn Bayern, Thomas Burri, Thomas D. Grant, Daniel M. Häusermann, Florian Möslein and Richard Williams, 'Gesellschaftsrecht und autonome Systeme im Rechtsvergleich', *Aktuelle Juristische Praxis (AJP)* 2 (2017) 192; Shawn Bayern, Thomas Burri, Thomas D. Grant, Daniel M. Häusermann, Florian Möslein and Richard Williams, 'Company Law and Autonomous Systems: A Blueprint for Lawyers, Entrepreneurs, and Regulators', (2017) 9 *Hastings Science and Technology Law Journal* 135.

[13] For an extensive discussion, based on German law, see Florian Möslein, 'Digitalisierung im Gesellschaftsrecht', *Zeitschrift für Wirtschaftsrecht (ZIP)* 2018, 204, at 208–212; with respect to Italian law cf. Maria Lillà Montagnani, *Il ruolo dell'intelligenza artificiale nel funzionamento del consiglio di amministrazione delle società per azioni* (Milan: EGEA, 2021).

[14] See, e.g., Martin Ebers, 'Regulating AI and Robotics', in Martin Ebers and Susana Navas (eds.), *Algorithms and Law* (Cambridge: Cambridge University Press, 2020), p. 37, at 51; Jacob Turner, *Robot Rules: Regulating Artificial Intelligence* (Cham: Palgrave Macmillan, 2019), pp. 181–183; Georgios Zekos, *Economics and Law of Artificial Intelligence* (Heidelberg: Springer, 2021), pp. 119–132.

[15] In this sense, e.g., Stefan Grundmann, *European Company Law* (Antwerpen/Oxford: Intersentia, 2nd ed., 2012), p. 267 ('In all countries, tasks are of course split in reality'); cf. also Holger Fleischer, 'Zur Leitungsaufgabe des Vorstands im Aktienrecht', *ZIP* 2003, 1, at 7 et seq.

[16] Similar with respect to German law, e.g., Fleischer, *supra* n. 15, at 6.

instance, does not allow directors 'to delegate duties which lie at the heart of the management of the corporation'.[17]

Most corporate laws do not define more precisely what those core decisions include. In a ruling on partnerships, however, the German Federal Court of Justice formulated quite specific requirements. In a comparatively generous manner, the court did not object to the fact that a third party who had been extensively entrusted with management tasks was neither subject to individual instructions with regard to the performance of these tasks nor subject to dismissal at any time.[18] It was considered to be sufficient that the management of such business had been determined by guidelines and was able to be monitored by means of comprehensive rights to information, inspection and control.[19] According to this case law, a delegate's own decision-making discretion is acceptable as long as their discretion is subject to predefined guidelines, compliance with which is systematically monitored. Although the ruling concerned a partnership, the same principles are supposed to apply to corporations.[20] The difference is, however, that corporations are managed by employed board members. In general, employees tend to be more inclined to delegate than partners who are themselves exposed to the entrepreneurial risks of incorrect decisions. Nonetheless, it was held to be permissible, for example, to transfer the entirety of the data processing tasks to another corporation, provided only that it had been ensured that the quality of the data processing and the flow of information were of the same standard as if the company had its own IT systems.[21]

If these legal principles are applied to the use of algorithms in corporate decision-making, it would equally seem necessary to require that human managers remain in control of the process and retain the final decision-making authority. Conversely, a legally binding commitment to mandatorily obey the decisions of the AI device would not be compatible with the responsibility of the board to run the company. Beyond that, however, it is difficult to draw the line between merely advisory use of the technology, which is supposed to be always permissible and legally unproblematic, and improper delegation to AI with binding effect.[22]

Computer technologies are capable of exerting a decisive influence on the decision-making capabilities of people, even if they do not force decisions (so-called *persuasive technologies*).[23] For this reason, the use of such technologies should always be considered to constitute a delegation. Nevertheless, the intensity of the legal requirements depends on the question of how much decision-making power human business managers retain legally or even in practice. Moreover, an important difference to the classic cases of delegation is that it is more difficult to bind AI with legal or contractual constraints than employees or third parties. Guidelines or recall clauses, such as those contained in operating agreements, are not usable when delegating to

[17] *Chapin* v. *Benwood*, Del.Ch., 402 A 2d 1205, 1210 (1979), aff'd sub nom. *Harrison* v. *Chapin*, Del.Supr., 415 A 2d 1068 (1980).

[18] Bundesgerichtshof (BGH), *Neue Juristische Wochenschrift (NJW)* 1982, 1817 ('Holiday Inn'); see also BGH, *NJW* 1962, 738.

[19] See again BGH, *NJW* 1982, 1817 (1818).

[20] In this direction, for example Fleischer, *supra* n. 15, at 9 f.; see also Florian Möslein, 'Aktienrechtliche Leitungsverantwortung beim Einsatz künstlicher Intelligenz', in Markus Kaulartz and Tom Braegelmann (eds.), *Rechtshandbuch Artificial Intelligence und Machine Learning* (Munich: Beck, 2020), p. 509, at 512 (with further references in n. 19).

[21] Landgericht (LG) Darmstadt, *ZIP* 1986, 1389, at 1391 et seq.

[22] See, however, Dirk Zetzsche, 'Corporate Technologies – Zur Digitalisierung im Aktienrecht', *Die Aktiengesellschaft (AG)* 2019, 1, at 7.

[23] Brian Jeffrey Fogg, *Persuasive Technology: Using Computers to Change What We Think and Do* (San Francisco: Morgan Kauffmann, 2003); see also the research agenda of the Persuasive Technology Lab at Stanford University, http://captology.stanford.edu/.

technologies. Delegation to AI is only technically controllable and manageable; its technical code provides the framework within which it operates (code is law).[24] The standards of AI decision-making therefore depend on programming and learning algorithms, not on legal rules. Board members who intend to delegate decisions to algorithms must therefore have a certain degree of knowledge of the applied technology in order to understand the inherent logic of the algorithm's decision-making. It is only by doing so that they can retain their own ultimate decision-making power.[25] Similarly to autonomous vehicles, such basic understanding is a prerequisite for being able to intervene whenever necessary with corrective action.

Specific legal challenges can potentially arise from the self-learning character of AI. Due to the way in which self-learning systems develop in order to detect and automatically correct errors, their results are neither programmable nor predictable. As is well known, such systems are a kind of 'black box'.[26] This specific feature inevitably makes such systems less controllable and thus less explainable. Consequently, the management board, for example, can hardly provide meaningful information about the decision-making process of their systems. However, the board is typically required to do so, for instance under German law vis-à-vis the supervisory board (sec. 90 of the German Stock Corporation Act).[27] At a minimum, the board should be able to provide information on core parameters within the meaning of Article 13 (2) (f) of the General Data Protection Regulation (GDPR). On the other hand, the self-learning capacity is a core precondition of the ability of technological devices to permanently develop and improve their decisions or recommendations. It would therefore seem implausible to require board members to completely refrain from using such technologies, despite their potential risks. However, the management board has a duty to adequately control the risks inherent in the respective technology, for example, in the form of a shutdown device.[28] Under some corporate laws, delegation may well be subject to lower requirements if the articles of association expressly provide for such a possibility. In that case, delegation undoubtedly corresponds to the intention of the shareholders.[29] In addition, if the statutory object of the company can only be achieved by means of algorithm-based decision-making, for example, in the case of suppliers of robo-advice,[30] the admissibility of such delegation is without question from the outset. Even then, however, a minimum degree of technological competence is required, as well as the preservation of the ultimate decision-making authority.

6.2.2 *Duty to Delegate*

Conversely, the question arises as to whether directors not only have authority to delegate decisions to AI, but whether they have a duty to do so. Such a duty to delegate calls for a closer

[24] The much-cited formulation relates to Lawrence Lessig, 'Code Is Law – On Liberty in Cyberspace', *Harvard Magazine*, Jan./Feb. 2000, available at https://harvardmagazine.com/2000/01/code-is-law-html; see also Lawrence Lessig, *Code and Other Laws of Cyberspace* (New York: Basic Books, 1999), at p. 89.

[25] More generally on governance duties in times of digital change, Michael Hilb, 'Towards an Integrated Framework for Governance of Digitalization', in Michael Hilb (ed.), *Governance of Digitalization* (Berne: Haupt, 2017), p. 11, at 20.

[26] Lutz Strohn, 'Die Rolle des Aufsichtsrats beim Einsatz von Künstlicher Intelligenz', *Zeitschrift für das gesamte Handelsrecht und Wirtschaftsrecht (ZHR)* 182 (2018), 374.

[27] On these risks, cf. again Strohn, *supra* n. 26, at 374.

[28] Sec. 91 (2) of the German Stock Corporation Act (AktG) serves as a legal basis for such a requirement; see Zetzsche, *supra* n. 22, at 7 et seq.

[29] In contrast to other jurisdictions, however, German corporate law does not require such clauses in the Articles of Association; see Möslein, *supra* n. 10, at 35 et seq. (with numerous comparative law references).

[30] See again Zetzsche, *supra* n. 22, at 7.

consideration if algorithmic decisions are in fact superior to human decisions, for example, because they provide forecasting decisions under uncertainty, rather than discretionary value judgments.[31] Such superiority is likely to be all the more pronounced the larger the volumes of data and the more complex and computationally intensive the decisions in question.[32] If management boards were obliged under a specific corporate law to make the best conceivable decision in each and every case, they would undoubtedly be subject to a duty of delegation under these conditions. As is well known, however, the management board of a corporation enjoys, for good reasons, broad entrepreneurial discretion. However, boards of directors must make their decisions on the basis of adequate information.

The well-known business judgment rule expressly provides that members of the management board exceed their entrepreneurial discretion if they cannot reasonably assume to have acted on the basis of such information.[33] However, one cannot derive an absolute duty to make algorithm-based decisions from this duty to obtain information. It is generally accepted that not 'all available sources of information' have to be exhausted.[34] Instead, the board of directors may well weigh up the costs and benefits of obtaining information in a specific decision-making situation. However, unlike the business decision itself, this weighing is subject to judicial review.[35] The more affordable and accurate algorithms are, but also the more widespread their use in corporate practice, the more difficult it is to justify not taking advantage of them. The development of a corporate law duty to make appropriate use of algorithms is therefore foreseeable,[36] even if its validity, scope and intensity still need to be clarified.[37] Beyond that, a proper duty to delegate can apply where sector-specific provisions require, for example, obligations to 'maintain information technology systems adequate to deal with the complexity, variety and type of services and activities performed'.[38] Obligations of this kind apply predominantly in the financial sector and are enshrined in both European and national law.[39]

[31] Ajay Agrawal, Joshua Gans and Avi Goldfarb, 'Exploring the Impact of Artificial Intelligence: Prediction versus Judgment', (2019) 47 *Information Economics and Policy*, 1; see also Daniel Kahneman, *Thinking Fast and Slow* (London: Penguin, 2011), at pp. 222–233.

[32] For more details, see the contributions in Nikos Karacapilidis (ed.), *Mastering Data-Intensive Collaboration and Decision Making* (Heidelberg: Springer, 2015).

[33] In detail, Stephen A. Radin, *The Business Judgment Rule* (Alphen aan den Rijn: Wolters Kluwer, 6th ed., 2019); for German law, cf. Sec. 93 (1) Sentence 2 AktG.

[34] In this sense, however, BGH, *NJW* 2008, 3361, at 3362 (with respect to the GmbH: duty to exhaust all available sources of information of a factual and legal nature); different though is BGH, *Neue Zeitschrift für Gesellschaftsrecht (NZG)* 2011, 549 para. 19 (with reference to the current wording of section 93(1) sentence 2 AktG). Critical of this case law: Andreas Cahn, 'Aufsichtsrat und Business Judgment Rule', *Wertpapier-Mitteilungen (WM)* 2013, 1293, at 1298; Holger Fleischer, 'Aktuelle Entwicklungen der Managerhaftung', *NJW* 2009, 2337, at 2339.

[35] Similar, e.g., Gregor Bachmann, 'Reformbedarf bei der Business Judgment Rule?', *ZHR* 177 (2013), 1, at 11.

[36] Similar, Andrew McAfee and Erik Brynjolfsson, 'Big Data: The Management Revolution', (2012) 90 *Harvard Business Review*, issue 10, 3; see also Roland Müller, 'Digitalization Decisions at the Board Level', in Hilb, *supra* n. 25, p 43, at 50: 'additional tasks of information governance'.

[37] Clearly more reserved, Zetzsche, *supra* n. 22, at 9; on the other hand, however, see Möslein, *supra* n. 13, at 209 et seq.; similar, e.g., Gerald Spindler, 'Gesellschaftsrecht und Digitalisierung', *Zeitschrift für Gesellschaftsrecht (ZGR)* 2018, 17, at 43.

[38] Cf., for instance: Art. 26 (6) Regulation (EU) No. 648/2021 on OTC derivatives, central counterparties and trade repositories (with respect to central counterparties).

[39] See, e.g., Section 25a of the German Banking Act (KWG) in conjunction with the requirements of the German supervisory authority's administrative circular letter on risk management (*Mindestanforderungen an das Risikomanagement, MaRisk*); in more detail, Möslein, *supra* n. 7, para. 33.

6.3 LIABILITY FOR DELEGATED DECISIONS

This section examines the issue of liability for delegated, but erroneous decisions. The liability issue is more complicated than it may appear. First, a design is needed for directors' duties relative to the implementation of AI systems. Second, a standard of care is needed to apply to such decisions.

6.3.1 *Preliminary Considerations*

Insofar as delegation is permissible or even obligatory according to the aforementioned principles, the question arises as to who is liable for delegated decisions if the decision in question, delegated to AI, subsequently proves to be erroneous.[40] Two different categories of erroneous algorithmic decisions can be distinguished. On the one hand, decisions can prove to be economically disadvantageous. For example, an algorithm may have recommended that the board of directors invest in a certain company that subsequently turns out to be a disadvantageous investment, for instance because the company in question proves to be less valuable than expected due to the non-existence of key patents.[41] After such an economically detrimental decision, shareholders are faced with the question of whether the board of directors – or the algorithm itself – can be held liable for the losses incurred. On the other hand, decisions can also prove to be incorrect because their content violates certain (legal) rules. Examples include algorithms that systematically discriminate on the basis of ethnic origin, religious affiliation or gender, such as in the selection of applicants or in credit scoring.[42] Irrespective of whether the decision in question is economically disadvantageous, it already appears to be flawed because it violates certain requirements, in this case those of European non-discrimination rules. In this second category, too, the question of legal remedies arises. However, such remedies are unlikely to be filed by shareholders, but will rather be initiated by those affected in the specific case, such as the unsuccessful (credit) applicant.[43]

If delegated decisions turn out to be wrong in one way or another, the question arises as to who is liable for this incorrect decision. The algorithm itself cannot be considered a liable party, because (or insofar as) AI devices have no legal capacity. The European Parliament's Committee on Legal Affairs may well have proposed a particular legal status for sophisticated AI devices so that these may have 'specific rights and obligations, including that of making good any damage they may cause, and applying electronic personality to cases where robots make smart autonomous decisions or otherwise interact with third parties independently', but this proposal has only been made in a draft report.[44] In most – if not all – jurisdictions, such a status does not comply with the current law, unless the software devices are not embedded in some sort

[40] More generally on the responsibility of AI, Dimitrios Linardatos, 'Künstliche Intelligenz und Verantwortung', *ZIP* 2019, 504, at 506.

[41] See also Möslein, *supra* n. 7, paras. 22 and 35.

[42] For the example of credit scoring in more detail: Katja Langenbucher, 'Responsible A.I.-based Credit Scoring: A Legal Framework', (2020) 31 *European Business Law Review*, 527.

[43] Moreover, these legal consequences are not necessarily directed at compensation for financial losses in the form of damages, but also at other forms of subsequent redress, such as compensation; see Möslein, *supra* n. 20, at 515, with further references at n. 43.

[44] European Parliament Committee on Legal Affairs, 'Draft report with recommendations to the Commission on Civil Law Rules on Robotics (2015/2103 (INL))', of 31 May 2016, p. 12.

of legal housing (for example, by taking advantage of LLC statutes).[45] However, it seems conceivable that the misjudgement of the algorithm could be attributed to the management board that delegated this decision. An analogous application of legal provisions on the personal liability of agents (for instance, § 278 BGB in German law) to the failure of machines and electronic data processing systems is sometimes advocated.[46]

However, the situation is different from the delegation to human agents, in particular because AI devices cannot act culpably. Moreover, because these devices do not act as agents of the management board but exclusively within the scope of duties of the stock corporation, such an analogy would not help to attribute liability to the board anyway. The company, not the management board, is the principal.[47] Accordingly, only the liability of the management board for its own faults can possibly arise. The respective breach of duty may relate to the fact that the delegation is defective, for example, because tasks are transferred that are not legitimately transferable, such as inalienable management tasks.[48] However, such personal liability may also be based on the fact that the selection, instruction or supervision of the delegates was careless.[49] In general, the duty to supervise requires the management board to provide ongoing monitoring and to ensure that the delegated tasks are properly performed.[50]

6.3.2 *Designing AI-Specific Directors' Duties*

The liability of board members who delegate investment decisions to AI therefore depends largely on the scope and intensity of that duty of supervision. Case law sometimes refers briefly to circumstances of an individual case,[51] which is rightly criticized as an empty formula.[52] Even the statutory provision of Section 91(2) of the German Stock Corporation Act (AktG), which obliges the management board to take appropriate measures, in particular to set up a monitoring system, in order to identify developments that could jeopardize the continued existence of the company in a timely manner, does not provide more than a vague indication as to the liability of board members.[53] At the very least, it establishes an obligation to adequately counter risks that are inherent in technology.[54] A more precise outline of the program of duties, however, requires the development of specific individual duties that must be followed when delegating entrepreneurial decision-making tasks to algorithms. These duties are aimed at certain organizational precautions that prevent erroneous algorithmic or AI decisions.[55] Since AI is a new technical

[45] Extensively on such possibility: Shawn Bayern, *Autonomous Organizations* (Cambridge: Cambridge University Press, 2021); see also references *supra*, n. 12.

[46] In detail on the situation under German law (and with further references): Möslein, *supra* n. 20, at 515.

[47] Cf. BGH, *NJW* 1994, 1801.

[48] In more detail, with regard to German law: Meinrad Dreher, 'Nicht delegierbare Geschäftsleiterpflichten', in Stefan Grundmann et al. (eds.), *Festschrift für Klaus J. Hopt* (Berlin: de Gruyter, 2010), p. 517, at 534 et seq.

[49] Holger Fleischer, 'Überwachungspflicht der Vorstandsmitglieder', in Holger Fleischer (ed.), *Handbuch des Vorstandsrechts* (Munich: Beck, 2006), § 8 para. 28.

[50] Dreher, *supra* n. 48, at 536 et seq.

[51] Cf. for example, BGH, *Neue Zeitschrift für Strafrecht (NStZ)* 1986, 34.

[52] Jean Nicolas Druey, 'Wo hört das Prüfen auf?', in Ernst A. Kramer and Hans-Georg Koppensteiner (eds.), *Festschrift für Hans-Georg Koppensteiner* (Vienna: LexisNexis, 2001), p. 3, at 8.

[53] See Linardatos, *supra* n. 40, at 507.

[54] Zetzsche, *supra* n. 22, at 7 et seq.

[55] In general, for a more developed view, Holger Fleischer, 'Vorstandsverantwortlichkeit und Fehlverhalten von Unternehmensangehörigen – Von der Einzelüberwachung zur Errichtung einer Compliance-Organisation', AG 2003, 291, at 293–295.

phenomenon, such specific obligations are not yet standardized in positive law. The corporate digital responsibility of the management board still needs to be defined.[56]

In view of this regulatory gap, various legal and extra-legal sources could possibly serve as guidelines for the future design of corporate law rules. First and foremost, the European Commission has recently published a proposal for a regulation laying down harmonized rules on AI (the so-called Artificial Intelligence Act).[57] However, this proposal follows a predominantly market-based approach and does not focus on the internal use of AI devices by companies. Therefore, it will only very indirectly affect the corporate directors' standard of care and their relationship to shareholders in general. Moreover, the proposal has not yet been adopted.

However, there are already legal rules in force that concern algorithmic decisions, albeit in other contexts. In particular, the rules on algorithmic trading enshrined in Art. 17 of the EU Directive 2014/65/EU on markets in financial instruments and amending Directive 2002/92/EC and Directive 2011/61/EU on markets in financial instruments (MiFID II) provide for a number of obligations that must be fulfilled by investment firms that engage in algorithmic trading.[58] In particular, these firms are required to have in place effective systems and risk controls suitable to the business they operate to ensure that their trading systems are resilient and have sufficient capacity, are subject to appropriate trading thresholds and limits, and prevent the sending of erroneous orders or the systems otherwise functioning in a way that may create or contribute to a disorderly market. Because decisions made by algorithms are at issue both in algorithmic trading and when the board takes advantage of algorithmic decision-making, and because Art. 17 attributes certain responsibilities to those who operate algorithmic systems in order to protect potentially injured parties, the relevant interests are similar, at least in principle.[59]

Finally, recourse to extra-legal but generally accepted rules of conduct could also serve as a yardstick for the design of future legal rules. In view of the novelty of the technology, however, the period for the development of a market standard is relatively short. Nevertheless, an extremely dynamic norm-building process has already begun. This process relates to so-called ethical issues that the use of AI raises. The development of these rules of conduct can be observed at very different regulatory levels. The most prominent example is the OECD Council Recommendation on Artificial Intelligence, dated 22 May 2019.[60] With this text, the relevant principles have received formal recognition by a wide range of governments worldwide.[61] At the European level, the EU Commission's Communication on 'Building Trust in Human-Centred Artificial Intelligence[62] supports key requirements of the Ethics Guidelines published by a group of high-level experts appointed by the Commission in its preliminary finalized version on 8 April

[56] In detail, Florian Möslein, 'Corporate Digital Responsibility – Eine aktienrechtliche Skizze', in Stefan Grundmann, Hanno Merkt and Peter O. Mülbert (eds.), *Festschrift für Klaus J. Hopt* (Berlin: de Gruyter, 2020), p. 805.

[57] Reference *supra*, n. 1.

[58] See also Florian Möslein, 'Regulating Robotic Conduct: On ESMA's New Guidelines and Beyond', in Nikita Aggarwal, Horst Eidenmüller, Luca Enriques, Jennifer Payne and Kristen van Zwieten (eds.), *Law and Autonomous Systems* (Munich/Oxford: C. H. Beck/Hart, 2019), p. 45.

[59] In more detail, Möslein, *supra* n. 7, para. 39; similar with regard to robo-advice, Florian Möslein and Arne Lordt, 'Rechtsfragen des Robo-Advice', *ZIP* 2017, 793, at 803.

[60] The OECD Recommendation (Recommendation of the Council on Artificial Intelligence) is available at www.oecd .org/going-digital/ai/principles/.

[61] In addition to the thirty-six member states, six other states have already signed so far; with the Osaka Final Declaration, the recommendations also received the support of all G20 member states – see G20 Ministerial Statement on Trade and Digital Economy of 9 June 2019, p. 3 et seq. and Annex.

[62] COM(2019) 168 final.

2019,[63] after intensive discussion.[64] On this basis, the high-level expert group has recently presented an assessment list for Trustworthy Artificial Intelligence (ALTAI).[65]

From these different sources – future and existing legal rules as well as extra-legal guidelines – a number of common principles can be derived. These principles can contribute to the creation of entrepreneurial standards for corporate digital responsibility.[66] The first group of principles concerns the controllability and mastery of the technology used. The rules on algorithmic trading, for example, require that the technical systems in question be designed in a stable manner, that they contain precautions against misuse and that entities using such systems understand and master the respective algorithms.[67] Similarly, the European principles on AI emphasize, on the one hand, the primacy of human agency and oversight[68] and, on the other hand, the need for the human actors responsible for the technical system to ensure its technical robustness and safety.[69] Comparable requirements can be found in the OECD principles.[70] According to these principles, board members who delegate tasks to AI must familiarize themselves with the functionality and risks of the information technology used and, if necessary, test its validity in a risk-protected area.

In addition, organizational or operator obligations can be developed, as they apply similarly to other technologies, such as nuclear energy.[71] In individual cases, however, it is often difficult to decide what degree of the decision-making autonomy of AI is compatible with these basic principles: Do entrepreneurial decisions require human supervision in every individual case? Is this only the case above a certain threshold defined in financial terms, for example, or is it sufficient if the basic corporate strategy is decided by humans? The European Commission at least suggests that overall control by humans shall suffice in principle.[72]

Secondly, the technical processes must be disclosed so that they can be verified and traced in retrospect. The rules on algorithmic trading stipulate corresponding disclosure responsibilities. In addition to standard logging and documentation obligations, the EU Commission and the OECD principles require that the algorithmic decision-making processes need to be explainable to the persons involved in a comprehensible manner.[73] They even suggest an accountability obligation for AI systems,[74] which also demands verifiability for AI systems, for instance by assessments of internal and external auditors.[75] In particular, the principles call for the

[63] Available at https://digital-strategy.ec.europa.eu/en/library/ethics-guidelines-trustworthy-ai; based on European Commission Communication, Artificial Intelligence for Europe, COM(2018) 237 final, p. 14 et seq.

[64] Over 500 comments were received during the consultation process. The first draft version of the guidelines is available at https://digital-strategy.ec.europa.eu/en/library/draft-ethics-guidelines-trustworthy-ai.

[65] The assessment list is available at https://digital-strategy.ec.europa.eu/en/library/assessment-list-trustworthy-artificial-intelligence-altai-self-assessment.

[66] For a map that illustrates the variety of different (mainly US-based) AI principles, elaborated by the Berkman Klein Center for Internet and Society at Harvard University, see https://ai-hr.cyber.harvard.edu.

[67] More closely Möslein, *supra* n. 58, at 47.

[68] COM(2019) 168 final, at 4 (key requirement I).

[69] COM(2019) 168 final, at 4 et seq. (key requirement II).

[70] OECD Recommendation, *supra* n. 60, at 1.2 and 1.4.

[71] Extensively on this sort of obligations, e.g., Gerald Spindler, *Unternehmensorganisationspflichten* (Cologne: Heymanns, 2001) at pp. 17–41.

[72] COM(2019) 168 final, at 4 (stressing in n. 13 that 'human intervention in every decision cycle of the system' is 'in many cases . . . neither possible nor desirable').

[73] COM(2019) 168 final, at 5 (key requirement IV); OECD Recommendation, *supra* n. 60, at 1.3. In general, on the requirement for the explainability of algorithms, Joshua A. Kroll, Joanna Huey, Solon Barocas, et al., 'Accountable Algorithms', (2017) 165 *University of Pennsylvania Law Review* 633.

[74] COM(2019) 168 final, at 6 (key requirement VII); OECD Recommendation, *supra* n. 60, at 1.5.

[75] COM(2019) 168 final, 6.

identification, assessment, documentation and minimization of potential negative impacts of AI systems.[76] This accountability is intended to ensure the enforceability of the other obligations through effective procedural instruments, explicitly by easily 'accessible mechanisms ... that ensure adequate redress', according to the EU Commission's communication.[77]

Thirdly, various requirements that serve to safeguard specific individual rights are more closely related to substantive law. While the OECD principles list 'freedom, dignity and autonomy, privacy and data protection, non-discrimination and equality ... and internationally recognised labour rights',[78] the EU Commission concentrates on 'privacy and data governance' and 'diversity, non-discrimination and fairness'.[79] Conversely, it goes into greater detail when it calls, in addition to data protection, for ensuring the integrity of the data used and regulating the governance and control of access to the data.[80] By calling for diversity, non-discrimination and fairness, the principles also establish an obligation to avoid (unintentional) data-based biases.[81] The principles thus aim at a similar objective to the corporate law principle of equal treatment, which is, however, more narrow in its scope.[82] This example demonstrates that AI-specific and corporate law substantive standards can overlap, but may also possibly collide with each other.

Finally, the AI-specific frameworks of the OECD and the EU postulate public good requirements for AI systems or providers. For example, the OECD principles state that stakeholders should 'proactively engage in responsible stewardship of trustworthy AI in pursuit of beneficial outcomes for people and the planet ... thus invigorating inclusive growth, sustainable development and well-being'.[83] In a similar vein, the Commission calls for the promotion of sustainability and the ecological responsibility of AI systems, as well as consideration of their overall societal and social impacts.[84] As vague as these program phrases are, their potential impact is far-reaching: when AI devices are used in the corporate realm, for example, must the board of directors ensure that sustainability considerations take precedence over the goal of maximizing corporate profits?[85] Such an obligation would result in the use of the corporate purpose as the fundamental yardstick of board decisions. Do AI-specific rules therefore decide, at least within their scope, the almost eternal and still controversial debate between the shareholder or stakeholder value orientation of corporations? If this is the case, these rules would transform corporate law fundamentally, albeit only for corporate decisions that are taken (or supported) by AI devices.

76 See again COM(2019) 168 final, 6.
77 COM(2019) 168 final, 6.
78 OECD Recommendation, *supra* n. 60, at 1.2.a).
79 COM(2019) 168 final, 5 et seq. (key requirement III and V).
80 See COM(2019) 168 final, 5 (key requirement III).
81 COM(2019) 168 final, 5 et seq. (key requirement V).
82 More extensively on the equal treatment of shareholders: Federico M. Mucciarelli, 'Equal Treatment of Shareholders and European Union Law', *European Company and Financial Law Review* 2010, 158; see also Lucian A. Bebchuk, 'Toward Undistorted Choice and Equal Treatment in Corporate Takeovers', (1985) 98 *Harvard Law Review* 1693.
83 OECD Recommendation, *supra* n. 60, at 1.1.
84 COM(2019) 168 final, 6 (key requirement VI).
85 In a similar direction, the EU Commission has recently published a report that it had commissioned from the accounting firm EY on directors' duties and sustainable corporate governance, available at https://op.europa.eu/de/publication-detail/-/publication/e47928a2-d20b-11ea-adf7-01aa75ed71a1/language-en. The report triggered an intensive debate; see, e.g., Florian Möslein and Karsten Engsig Sørensen, 'Sustainable Corporate Governance: A Way Forward', (2021) 18 *European Company Law* 7 (with further references in n. 2–4).

6.3.3 *Standard of Care?*

The close-knit network of substantive duties that can be developed from these various sources raises above all the question of the intensity of the applicable standard of care. After all, the board of directors enjoys broad entrepreneurial discretion in its decisions pursuant to the business judgment rule. As a consequence, corporate directors' decisions are typically not subject to judicial review.[86] In particular, directors enjoy organizational discretion and are therefore in principle free to delegate decisions, including to algorithms.[87] However, this discretion is likely to be limited by the normative framework: under German stock corporation law, for instance, the duty to act in accordance with the law is considered to be one of the cardinal duties of every corporate director.[88] Other jurisdictions impose a similar obligation on directors, although under a variety of names (e.g., *duty of obedience*, *duty of legality* or *duty to act lawfully*), and with parameters that often appear 'somewhat undefined'.[89] In particular, it is disputed whether this duty of legality is strictly limited to statutory requirements or whether, conversely, it also applies in the case of duties that are not standardized in positive law but, for example, embody ethical standards of conduct. Some argue in favour of a duty of board members to comply with generally accepted principles of business ethics,[90] whereas others call for restraint on the basis that modern private law only allows moral evaluations to shape civil law assessment in a restricted and indirect manner via statutory general clauses.[91]

The boundary line between legal requirements that the board must, due to the duty of legality, strictly comply with, and ethical and moral values that do not in principle limit its organizational discretion, however, comes under scrutiny in the case of AI-specific duties. The reason lies in the aforementioned differences within the normative foundations of these duties.[92] The specific duties can either be derived from specifically tailored, but not directly applicable, legal rules, but they can also be based on other sources that are not of a legal nature. Some duties can also be derived from various, heterogenous sources. The duty to control the technological devices, for instance, can be based both on an analogy to the rules on algorithmic trading (as enshrined in section 80(2) sentence 3 of the German Securities Trading Act (WpHG), for example), but can also be derived from the AI guidelines of the OECD and the European Commission. In view of this overlapping of different norms, the seemingly clear distinction between a strict duty of legality and broad entrepreneurial discretion becomes blurred. The intensity of the obligation nevertheless varies depending on the respective norms from which it was derived, albeit rather gradually: it is stricter the more the obligation in question is enshrined within laws, and the more explicitly it is formulated. In the case of requirements that are expressed solely in the legally non-binding guidelines, it is correspondingly low, for example,

86 Cf. text *supra*, at n. 33.

87 See *supra* at Section 6.2.1.

88 In this sense, e.g., Fleischer, *supra* n. 34, at 2337; see also BGH, *NJW* 2012, 3439, 3441; Landgericht Stuttgart, NZG 2018, 665, at 676.

89 Patrick O'Malley, *Directors Duties and Corporate Anti-Corruption Compliance: The 'Good Steward' in US and UK Law and Practice* (Cheltenham: Edward Elgar, 2021), at p. 131; see also Alan R. Palmiter, 'Duty of Obedience: The Forgotten Duty', (2011) 55 *New York Law School Law Review* 457.

90 With regard to German law, e.g., Peter Schlechtriem, 'Schadensersatzhaftung der Leitungsorgane. von Kapitalgesellschaften', in Karl Kreuzer (ed.), *Die Haftung der Leitungsorgane von Kapitalgesellschaften* (Baden-Baden: Nomos, 1991), p. 9, at 21.

91 Holger Fleischer, 'Corporate Social Responsibility', AG 2017, 509, at 516.

92 On the difficulty of such distinctions in general: Florian Möslein, 'Genuine Self-Regulation in Germany: Drawing the Line', in Harald Baum, Moritz Bälz and Marc Dernauer (eds.), *Self-Regulation in Private Law in Japan and Germany* (Cologne: Heymanns, 2018), p. 83.

with regard to the safeguarding of individual rights as well as public welfare obligations. In contrast to unwritten principles of business ethics, however, even these obligations are comparatively strongly juridified: they are not only laid down in writing, but also have a supranational, in part global claim and enjoy multilateral backing from state governments.[93] In view of the current highly dynamic development of standards, it is not possible to predict for the time being which set of rules will become a normative guiding principle for responsible corporate boards – and what standard of care will ultimately apply.

6.4 FUTURE PERSPECTIVES

Due to digital transformation, dealing with AI will become a core corporate task. In a digital world, the duties of corporate directors also include corporate digital responsibility, and in particular, the responsible handling of AI.[94] This responsibility requires not only that directors recognize the potential of innovative business models, but also optimized processes, and new types of products and services for their own companies. It also includes their responsibility for the corporate use of digital tools, in particular AI: corporate digital responsibility will therefore form a key component of corporate liability in the future.[95] The intersection of digital responsibility and corporate law can be exemplified by the various principles that are common to the aforementioned sets of rules: the principle of the primacy of human agency and oversight, for example, will have an impact on the board's scope for delegation. It will support the legal position that board decisions must never be made entirely by AI, but that the ultimate responsibility for corporate decisions must always remain with the human members of the board.[96]

The principles of technical robustness and safety, as well as the principles on privacy and data governance, will contribute to the shaping of corresponding organizational duties under company law. The transparency requirements, like accountability, will have an impact on the scope of disclosure requirements and conversely on shareholders' rights to information. In this manner, the ethical guidelines on AI will sooner or later develop into a source of legal standards that flesh out and supplement the content of the existing set of corporate law duties. The initial emphasis of the Commission, along with other rule-makers, that its guidelines are 'non-binding and as such do not create any new legal obligations' will not hinder the evolution of new, AI-related legal norms.[97] The recent proposal of the European AI Act demonstrates this development very clearly.

[93] Extensively Florian Möslein, 'Die normative Kraft des Ethischen: Ein Fallbeispiel zur Effektivität von Leitlinien für Künstliche Intelligenz', *Recht Digital (RDi)* 2020, 34.

[94] Möslein, *supra* n. 13, at 204.

[95] See *supra*, reference n. 56.

[96] Cf. Möslein, *supra* n. 13, at 208 et seq.; see also Möslein, *supra* n. 7, paras. 27–39.

[97] COM(2019) 168 final p. 4.

PART III

AI and Liability

7

Are Existing Tort Theories Ready for AI?

An American Perspective

Robert A. Heverly

7.1 INTRODUCTION

What does it mean to ask whether "tort theories" are ready for artificial intelligence (AI)? How will tort system respond to the problems that AI will bring to society? Tort law has a number of systems and structures at its disposal to address the challenges posed by AI technologies. It will not be necessary to significantly alter our understanding of tort law's foundations to be ready for AI.

By looking at tort law's application to airplanes and the Internet, along with proposals for the application of tort law to questions raised by the use of AI, the most plausible argument is that tort law has sufficient flexibility to adjust to the demands of cases involving AI technologies.[1] Issues will certainly arise as AI is more fully integrated into society and will be solved though tort litigation and policymaking without precluding innovative AI development nor exposing the public to wrongs resulting from AI use.

The objective here is not to determine how tort law *should* apply to AI, or to argue for a specific set of doctrines that are best placed to address the problems that AI will pose to society and the legal system. The focus here is making the argument that the tort system has the tools to handle questions of harm caused by potential uses of AI in society. This chapter presents a review of some of the tort law options applicable to the malfeasance caused by AI systems.

7.2 SCHOLARLY PERSPECTIVES

There is a vibrant scholarly and policy discussion[2] surrounding AI, and specifically the application of existing tort law – and other legal[3] – doctrines to AI. The existing scholarship often considers which causes of action or "tort theories" would be most effective in addressing the

[1] See, e.g., F. Patrick Hubbard, "Allocating the Risk of Physical Injury from Sophisticated Robots: Efficiency, Fairness, and Innovation" in Ryan Calo, A. Michael Froomkin, and Ian Kerr (eds.), *Robot Law* (Cheltenham: Edward Elgar, 2016), pp. 25–50.

[2] See Iria Giuffrida, "Liability for AI Decision-Making: Some Legal and Ethical Considerations" (2019) 88 *Fordham L. Rev.* 439; Hannah R. Sullivan and Scott J. Schweikart, "Are Current Tort Liability Doctrines Adequate for Addressing Injury Caused by AI?" (2019) 21 *AMA J. Ethics* 160.

[3] See, e.g., Mihalis Diamantis, "The Extended Corporate Mind: When Corporations Use AI to Break the Law" (2020) 97 *N. C. L. Rev.* 893.

concerns raised by AI. Some scholars argue for specific alterations to specific applications, but such arguments are predicated on the conclusion that the tort system will somehow fail in balancing disincentives to innovation against harm and incentives to pursue safe uses of AI.[4] With the accelerated development of AI, some scholars have modified their arguments[5] and new issues have arisen.[6] Some of these contributions examine the question at the comparably narrow level of the use of AI in a particular type of system or technology[7] and do not focus on whether tort law has sufficient flexibility to address questions of liability in the AI age. The discrete issues raised by considering specific technologies – such as self-driving automobiles – provide important analyses without overly broadly theorizing. That said, the tort system does provide a starting point for these issues since it includes generally accepted theoretical and doctrinal propositions.

This chapter begins with a discussion of the larger tort system's relationship to AI liability before applying its principles to specific areas – AI liability in health care, economic settings, and self-driving vehicles. A framework is built on viewing the history of tort law's application to technological change and the cases of structural changes to tort law. For example, tort (and property) law changed in response to the advent of human flight. However, there were no groundbreaking legal changes taken immediately following the Wright Brothers' first flight or in the first years following the start of commercial flight.

Another benchmark is the application of tort law to the Internet. Congress intervened in the legal landscape and set a broad rule against liability in certain cases. The intervention of tort doctrine in the Internet's relative infancy have had long-lasting and unpredictable effects; some of the negative effects were avoidable if tort law had been able to evolve before statutory or regulatory interventions. A review of scholarly arguments advocating for specific application of tort law to discrete uses of AI leads to the conclusion that the tort system, as with the Internet, needs time to evolve to deal with issues of liability related to AI technologies without legislative or policy-based interventions.

After a discussion of tort law's application to new technologies, the foundational basis for the tort system will be examined, before looking at liability questions specific to AI. Again, this analysis weighs against the adoption of systems that are designed to provide certainty but that may have unintended consequences. Corrections can and should be made along the way, but should be made cautiously. Major changes are likely to inhibit AI's ability to improve human existence. Given our more recent experiences in adjusting to technological developments, it becomes apparent that lawyers, judges, and legislators should use the tort system's existing systemic and doctrinal approaches, rather than attempting to develop new or unique structures in response to the problems that AI will pose in our future.

[4] See, e.g., A. Michael Froomkin, Ian Kerr, and Joelle Pineau, "When AIs Outperform Doctors: Confronting the Challenges of a Tort-Induced Over-Reliance on Machine Learning" (2019) 61 *Ariz. L. Rev.* 33 (arguing that tort law may make doctors overreliant on machine learning technologies and proposing responses in law, such as altering the standard of care, requiring a doctor in the process, and providing various "exceptions" to liability in relation to their use).

[5] Curtis Karnow, "Liability for Distributed Artificial Intelligences" (1996) 11 *Berk. Tech. L.J.* 147, reprinted in Curtis Karnow, *Future Codes: Essays in Advanced Computer Technology and the Law* (London: Artech House, 1997), pp. 137–187.

[6] Curtis Karnow, "The Application of Traditional Tort Theory to Embodied Machine Intelligence" in Calo et al., *Robot Law*, pp. 51–77.

[7] See, e.g., Gary E. Marchant and Rachel A. Lindor, "The Coming Collision between Autonomous Vehicles and the Liability System" (2012) 52 *Santa Clara L. Rev.* 1321.

7.3 ARTIFICIAL INTELLIGENCE AND TORT LAW

Defining AI is perhaps more difficult than one might expect. Margaret Boden describes the goals and methodologies of AI as follows: "Artificial intelligence seeks to make computers do the sorts of things that minds can do." This type of reasoning is described as "intelligent." But human intelligence involves a variety of psychological skills. Perception, association, prediction, planning, and motor control enable humans to attain their goals. Intelligence has many dimensions; it is a richly structured space of diverse information-processing capacities. Accordingly, AI uses many different techniques, addressing many different tasks.[8]

Many descriptions discuss the discrete ways in which AI works, but they fail to tell us what AI *is*. One source takes seven pages to define AI's goals and methods, including tables.[9] Such a labored definition is the result of there being no generally accepted definition of AI. One of the better attempts is Nils J. Nilsson's statement: "For me, artificial intelligence is that activity devoted to making machines intelligent, and intelligence is that quality that enables an entity to function appropriately and with foresight in its environment."[10] Ryan Calo uses a similar definition: "There is no straightforward, consensus definition of artificial intelligence. AI is best understood as a set of techniques aimed at approximating some aspect of human or animal cognition using machines."[11] Calo continues, "[AI] is an umbrella term, comprised by many different techniques."[12] Note that the potential for AI to be self-aware or "alive" is not included in these definitions because it is unlikely to exist in the near-term future.

The techniques utilized within the AI umbrella include machine learning, deep learning, computer vision, natural language processing, and robotics and automation, among others. One thing that unifies these techniques is an attempt to make the machines intelligent, and thus, to make the outcomes not subject to specific prediction. This unpredictability means that outcomes may be inappropriate, especially due to AI not processing contextual factors. The task then becomes how to create better outcomes that are more predictable.

AI's inevitable unpredictability raises problems for tort law. In designing technologies that are unpredictable, due to mistakes or errors, the issue is what party is liable for the harm caused. This question has been taken up by a number of commentators who, applying legal doctrine, policy arguments, and other analytical skills, argue in one direction or the other.[13] In more traditional circumstances, assigning liability can be a complex endeavor.[14] Often a detailed analysis is performed to allocate responsibility to one or another actor. Modern tort law provides

[8] Margaret Boden, *AI: Its Nature and Future* (Oxford: Oxford University Press, 2016), p. 1.

[9] John Paul Mueller and Luca Massaron, *Artificial Intelligence for Dummies* (Hoboken, NJ: John Wiley & Sons, 2018), pp. 7–13.

[10] Nils J. Nilsson, *The Quest for Artificial Intelligence: A History of Ideas and Achievements* (Cambridge: Cambridge University Press, 2010), p. 13.

[11] Ryan Calo, "Artificial Intelligence Policy: A Primer and Roadmap" (August 8, 2017), p. 4, https://ssrn.com/abstract=3015350 or http://dx.doi.org/10.2139/ssrn.3015350

[12] Ibid.

[13] See, e.g., W. Nicholson Price, "Medical Malpractice and Black Box Medicine" in I. Glenn Cohen, Holly Fernandez Lynch, Effy Vayena, and Urs Gasser (eds.), *Big Data, Health Law, and Bioethics* (Cambridge: Cambridge University Press, 2018), pp. 295–306; Barbara J. Evans and Frank A. Pasquale, "Product Liability Suits for FDA-Regulated AI/ML Software" in I. Glenn Cohen, Timo Minssen, W. Nicholson Price II, Christopher Robertson, and Carmel Shachar (eds.), *The Future of Medical Device Regulation: Innovation and Protection* (Cambridge: Cambridge University Press, 2022); Marchant and Lindor, "Coming Collision"; Karnow, "Liability for Distributed Artificial Intelligences."

[14] See, e.g., Robert Heverly, "More Is Different: Liability of Compromised Systems in Denial of Service Attacks" (2020) 47 *Fl. St. U.L. Rev.* 531 (arguing that cases involving a singular or few plaintiffs, but many defendants, should be treated differently from cases that involve many plaintiffs but few defendants).

a variety of mechanisms to determine the answer. Many liability issues arise in relation to causation: Where an actor is a factual cause of another's injury, tort law often holds that person liable in damages for that injury. However, the actor may be partially excused under tort law and the actor's or injured party's conduct may also excuse other actors from liability.

The AI situation is different because tort law is based on human action, where humans are expected to act reasonably to avoid causing injury to others. AI is different because it does not have a separate legal existence. It is simply a tool, technique, or technology used by humans. The fact that AI can learn or think in some way is irrelevant because it has yet to be recognized as a person for legal purposes.[15] It has no legal rights and no legal duties, and therefore, it has no legal culpability.

Thus, the focus remains on who is responsible for the technology and which parties are assigned the responsibility for harm caused by an AI system. These issues have been the focus of current legal scholarship. Some of the arguments advocate for the application of established doctrinal rules such as vicarious liability, strict liability, or enhanced liability of those who choose to use a technology. The methods advocated vary, but in the end they all rely on the usefulness or applicability of tort law in general, or its underlying justifications. It is the application to AI of the underlying justifications for tort law that will be examined here. Again, such application will show that no significant changes to the tort system will be needed.

7.4 LAW AND TECHNOLOGY: A FRAMEWORK

The core constructs of law old language: have remained malleable to changes brought by "new" technologies. The addition of seat belts to automobiles did not require a fundamental rethinking of liability in automobile accidents (though it did alter the way in which causation might be argued in specific cases). The question then becomes how do we know when a new technology causes significant tension in the legal system.

Jack Balkin's notion of salience is helpful here. Balkin encourages us not to think about whether something is merely different or new, but rather to think rigorously about technologies and their interaction with the world: "Instead of focusing on novelty, we should focus on salience. What elements of the social world does a new technology make particularly salient that went relatively unnoticed before? What features of human activity or of the human condition does a technological change foreground, emphasize, or problematize?"[16] The consideration of salience provides us with an opportunity to look closely at how and why a particular technology is likely to challenge existing legal understandings rather than just assuming it will challenge law because it is new. This perspective allows for the planning of a strategy for minimizing unnecessary tensions as these situations arise while not automatically assuming they will arise.

By combining the notion of salience with additional observations gleaned from scholarship on the Internet's development, a framework for the analysis of technology's interaction with law can be constructed. Some of the scholarly observations show that (1) technologies not only affect us, but we affect our technologies,[17] (2) we must be aware that technology is observed from

[15] Marchant and Lindor, "Coming Collision."

[16] Jack M. Balkin, "Digital Speech and Democratic Culture: A Theory of Expression for the Information Society" (2004) 79 *N.Y.U. L. Rev.* 1, 2.

[17] Julie Cohen, *Configuring the Networked Self: Law, Code and the Play of Everyday Practice* (New Haven, CT: Yale University Press, 2012).

numerous perspectives such as the user's subjective view or society's objective view,[18] and (3) we need to be cautious in our adoption of metaphors to describe the interactions of new technologies with the world, society, and law.[19]

These principles – salience, embodied perception, perspective, and metaphorical awareness – form a framework for the consideration of technology and law. This framework allows us to consider whether the legal responses to a technology's development are permissive, encouraging the technology to flourish in a relatively lenient legal landscape or precautionary, potentially, slowing development of AI in the interests of controlling perceived negative technological effects.[20] With this framework in mind, the next section considers the foundations of tort law.

7.4.1 *A Short Aside: A Justification for Tort Law*

Existing tort law theory starts with private wrongs. Many theoretical approaches to tort law that try to either explain or justify its doctrinal rules and their application begin at that point. It is regularly debated whether tort law should provide incentives for people to act reasonably – to avoid committing wrongs – so as to prevent harm to others, or whether it should be viewed as a structure to make injured people whole. Wrongs that cause harm are the core interest that tort law is concerned with. Tort law has been and remains focused on harms. Where harm is not a part of the prima facie cause of action, it is often presumed to be present. The foundation of tort in addressing harm has led to competing inconsistent accounts of how tort law is and should be used in relation to those harms. These include theories intended to minimize the costs of injuries, especially in relation to accidents, theories attempting to encourage activities where the benefits of those activities outweigh their costs, theories that argue that harm itself is a sufficient condition to impose liability on those who have caused the harm, and theories based in either corrective justice or civil recourse.

Though some of these theories would eschew the word "harm," focusing instead on what are termed as costs, the former term is broad enough to encompass the second. In other words, costs are a form of harm that justify the invocation of tort law principles to provide a remedy for the harm. Harm, not wrongfulness, is the basic and unifying principle of tort law. Tort law is often defined as the law of civil wrongs, but there are a variety of situations in which no wrong – as that term can be reasonably understood – has occurred. This happens in the area of strict liability when a dangerous activity results in harm. For negligence, it is the unreasonable act combined with harm that results in liability. Focusing on the dangerous activity in strict liability would leave us unable to explain negligence liability, while focusing on unreasonable behavior would leave us unable to explain strict liability. Harm, however, is the unifying factor between the two causes of action, and remains the bedrock justification for activating the tort system.

Intentional torts are unique in that proof of damage or injury are not a part of the prima facie case for battery, assault, false imprisonment, or trespass to land, while proof of some harm is required to make a case for intentional infliction of emotional distress and trespass to chattels. Two other intentional torts – nuisance and conversion – require some degree of harm. In the case of nuisance, it is an unreasonable interference with the use and enjoyment of land and in the case of conversion it is the serious deprivation of possession or control of a chattel. Both of

[18] Orin Kerr, "The Problem of Perspective in Internet Law" (2003) 91 *Georgetown L.J.* 357.

[19] Dan Hunter, "Cyberspace as Place, and the Tragedy of the Digital Anticommons" (2003) 91 *Cal.. L. Rev.* 439.

[20] See Rebecca Crootof and B. J. Ard, "Structuring Techlaw" (2021) 34 *Harv. J. L. & Tech.* 347, https://ssrn.com/abstract=3664124 or http://dx.doi.org/10.2139/ssrn.3664124.

these latter elements or specific types of harm fit the harm model outlined above in this section. That leaves the question of where the harm is found in cases involving battery, assault, false imprisonment, and trespass to land. The harm in these cases is defined by tort law itself to be the commission of the tort itself. Battery, assault, and false imprisonment are dignitary torts, designed to recognize the dignity of individuals and the individual's right to avoid even the threat of certain types of harm. Thus, harm as the commission of the tort itself allows us to retain harm as the unifying element in all torts, even where the element itself is assumed in certain tort causes of action.

If harm is at the core of tort law's interests, the question becomes what should tort law do when harms occur? Here things become more complicated, with a variety of theories vying to explain and justify the form and function of tort law. There is no unifying theory of tort law that commands respect above all others; instead, tort law provides a toolbox of reasoning into which lawyers, courts, and legislators can reach to achieve ends that appear to be just and fair under the circumstances.

Not all harms are compensated by the tort system, nor should they be. Some remedies are found within the domains of contract law, criminal law, or are statutory in nature. Other types of harm may not be recognized at all, especially where the harm is not seen as resulting from the invasion of some protected right or interest. When a cognizable harm occurs and is tied to protected rights and interests the legal system provides some redress or compensation. Jules Coleman et al. describe this as follows: "In such a view, the core concepts of tort law appear to be 'rights,' 'wrongs' and 'redress' and the dual goals of tort theory are to identify the principle that connects the category of wrongs that torts address and to justify the distinctive mode(s) of redress for wrongs that tort law adopts."[21] This is the project in which we are engaged, though with a focus on harms rather than wrongs. Again, not all harms provide a cause of action in tort, such as loss of time spent when waiting at a traffic light when someone does not promptly respond to a light turning green or for the emotional harm caused by losing a game or competition. Not all harms are compensable or fit within the tort system, but where there is a harm that demands redress, courts have often seen fit to create a cause of action that fits the harm.[22]

The fact that all actionable torts have some form of harm associated with them has implications for harm caused by an AI system. Can an AI system commit a wrong? The focus on harm, discussed above in this section, provides a better fit for the concerns that AI will raise for tort law. Section 7.5 discusses the relationship of tort law's focus on harm and how tort law applies to harms caused by AI. The initiation of commercial flight and the Internet will act as case studies of tort law's reaction to new technologies.

7.4.2 *Experience: Tort Law and Technological Advances*

AI is not the first technology to challenge our perceptions and expectations of the law. While much of the scholarship in the law and technology area is focused on the introduction and widespread adoption of the Internet into society, earlier technologies have likewise challenged the law in general and tort law specifically by creating new tensions between established doctrines and their applications.

[21] Jules Coleman, Scott Hershovitz, and Gabriel Mendlow, "Theories of the Common Law of Torts," *Stanford Encyclopedia of Philosophy* (2015). http://plato.stanford.edu/archives/win2015/entries/tort-theories/.

[22] See, e.g., *Eichinwald* v. *Rivello*, 321 F. Supp. 3d 562 (D. Md. 2018) (recognizing a cause of action for intentional infliction of harm).

The advent of air travel brought with it a conflict between the historically recognized *ad coelum* doctrine and the ability of a new industry to be able to operate in the skies over individual pieces of property. The *ad coelum* doctrine was an expression of the right of an owner of surface land to the entirety of the column of space above the land and the space below the land to the center of the earth. If *ad coelum* was law, then airships, balloons, dirigibles, and eventually airplanes were trespassing when they flew through the skies above privately owned property.[23]

The development and expansion of air travel led to a number of interesting propositions. Some commentators suggested that airplanes should only be allowed to fly over public streets and highways. Others suggested that the mass organization of easements for air travel would be required to allow for air travel. These solutions were necessary, so the arguments went, because the tort of trespass to land encompassed "above the land" trespasses, and as such landowners would be entitled under the common law to seek injunctions to stop the flight of such aircraft above their properties.[24]

The solution, however, was a mixture of statutory changes, narrowing of the relevant property and tort doctrines, and utilization of a separate cause of action in nuisance to protect the rights of property owners while allowing the new technology to flourish. The first step was Congress passing legislation claiming navigable airspace for the federal government (public good). Much like navigable waterways, airspace was to be open for navigation as a public resource for the entirety of the nation.

The federal courts, including the Supreme Court,[25] eventually narrowed the application of the *ad coelum* doctrine, holding that the skies were held for use by the public, and that overflights were not trespasses per se, but only those that substantially interfered with the use and enjoyment of underlying parcels. In the latter case, the property owner could bring suit for damages in a claim for aerial trespass. Thus, the question framed initially in the context of trespass was shifted, with the support of legislation, to the domain of aerial trespass. In other words, tort law's doctrines were clarified, and their application modified, to adjust to the cultural, technological, and societal circumstances. These considerations are being reevaluated as society and law seek to integrate another new technology – drones – into the national airspace.

A very different approach was taken by Congress during the advent of the internet era and its expansion during the 1990s. At that point, two apparently conflicting defamation decisions inspired Congress to enact Section 230 of the Communications Decency Act of 1996. In the 1991 *Cubby* v. *Compuserv*[26] decision, a federal district court applied defamation law to the actions of a company that provided online services for users. It reasoned that the provider was akin to a "newsstand" and thus not liable for user defamation unless the provider knew or had reason to know that the content posted was defamatory. In 1995, in *Stratton Oakmont* v. *Prodigy Services*,[27] a New York State court held that defamation law applied to online services through which users posted content. The court also held, however, that where a service provider edits or changes the content posted by its users, it is no longer appropriate to use the newsstand analysis. Instead, it held that one who edits or alters content is a traditional publisher, and is thus liable for defamatory content distributed via its service.

[23] See Stuart Banner, *Who Owns the Sky? The Struggle to Control Airspace from the Wright Brothers On* (Cambridge, MA: Harvard University Press, 2008) (history of the advent of flight and the law).
[24] Ibid.
[25] *United States* v. *Causby*, 328 US 256 (1946).
[26] *Cubby* v. *Compuserv*, 776 F Supp. 135 (SDNY 1991).
[27] *Stratton Oakmont, Inc.* v. *Prodigy Services Co.*, 23 Media L. Rep. 1794 (NY Sup. Ct. 1995).

Commentators and industry representatives argued that the analysis in Stratton Oakmont would either drive online services out, due to the sheer volume of content for which they might be held liable, or would drive such platforms to avoid any kind of actions that would "touch" their users' content, turning the Internet into a completely unregulated forum.[28] The former outcome would stifle internet innovation and the latter would have resulted in the proliferation of defamatory content.

Section 230 immunizes online intermediaries for liability arising from content uploaded by users of their services. The law was designed to counter the argument that without such immunity online service providers would be unable to set standards for content, including altering and removing it, without facing liability as publishers. Section 230 immunity resulted in the internet landscape expanding to include companies like Google, Facebook, Twitter, Instagram, TikTok, and many others.[29]

The §230 immunity impacted the application of the tort system because it was broadly construed by the courts. Internet service providers received immunity not only for claims based in defamation law, but also those arising in negligence,[30] unfair business practices,[31] and public nuisance law.[32] The immunity extended to providers that refused to take any action at all, even when confronted with a court order finding the content to be defamatory[33] and to providers that encouraged content that was defamatory.[34] Recently, there have been calls to narrow the immunity because of the fear that the service providers could remove content and limit free speech.

The history and development of §230 can be contrasted to the development of air travel. What these examples show us is that fixing a problem linked to a new technology is a difficult and complex task. Some legislative involvement in the development of AI may be appropriate, such as by making hard policy choices and implementing overarching frameworks, as was done during the early years of the age of manned flight. Direct legislation concerning liability in the AI sphere may have detrimental effects on individuals and society. The more cautious approach is to allow the common law to form a framework first, and to only intervene once that framework is largely agreed upon within the judicial realm. Recall that §230 was enacted primarily in response to one case. It prevented the common law from evolving in this area. For example, the *Cubby* decision, in which defamation law was applied to online service providers, may have been rejected by subsequent courts. The legislative preemption prevented the development of structure that may have allowed some redress for those harmed by internet content.

7.5 APPROACHES TO PRIVATE AI HARMS

This section analyzes potential tort-based methods for addressing questions of liability for harms caused by the use of AI in a variety of settings. The focus will be on discrete, individual, private harms, not greater or more public-based harms. There are a variety of situations in which AI use may cause harm to individuals. I will discuss two of these here. The first is harm in the health

[28] See, e.g., Robert T. Charles and Jacob H. Zamansky, "Liability for Online Libel after Stratton Oakmont, Inc. v. Prodigy Services Co." (1996) 28 *Conn. L. Rev.* 1173; R. Hayes Johnson Jr., "Defamation in Cyberspace: A Court Takes a Wrong Turn on the Information Superhighway in Stratton Oakmont, Inc. v. Prodigy Services Co." (1996) 49 *Ark. L. Rev.* 589, 594 (gathering industry reactions).

[29] See Eric Goldman, "Why Section 230 Is Better Than the First Amendment" (2019) 95 *Notre Dame L. Rev. Online* 33.

[30] *Doe* v. *MySpace*, 528 F 3d 413 (5th Cir. 2008).

[31] *Gentry* v. *eBay*, 121 Cal. Rptr. 2d 703 (Cal. Ct. App. 2003).

[32] *Dart* v. *Craigslist, Inc.*, 665 F Supp. 2d 961 (ND Ill. 2009).

[33] *Hassell* v. *Bird*, 381 P.3d 231 (Cal. 2016).

[34] *Jones* v. *Dirty World Entertainment, LLC*, 755 F 3d 398 (6th Cir. 2014).

care setting when AI makes a mistake, such as in prescribing particular courses of treatment or in identifying particular diseases or conditions.[35] This scenario illustrates two disparate approaches to tort liability for harm: one which advocates for holding the user (medical professional) responsible for choosing or operating an AI. The other approach advocates for a system based on products liability, an area of law whose existing doctrines create difficulties when it comes to application to software-involved products.[36]

The second is in the area of self-driving or autonomous vehicles, where some scholars have advocated for adopting a modified version of products liability to avoid the harshness that a more traditional products liability approach would have on automobile manufacturers.[37] Others have argued for granting immunity from liability – creating a permissive regime for AI development at the expense of causing individual and uncompensated harms.

These two approaches to AI liability are apparent in the literature. One side advocates for working within the existing tort law system, perhaps with some minimal doctrinal extensions. The second group advocates for at least one, if not more, significant alterations or changes to the existing tort system.[38]

Initially, it might seem as though some scholars are arguing for significant extensions in tort doctrines to cover what are perceived to be challenging facts presented by AI liability scenarios. These may revolve around placing responsibility either on an individual – such as a physician – for choosing and implementing particular AI technology, or on an entity or entities who have made those choices. This might be analogized to an employer-employee liability regime relying on *respondeat superior* to hold the employer liable for the torts of the employee (at least those within the scope of the employee's employment).

One of the difficulties with this approach, however, is that while it is firmly embedded in established tort doctrine, a plaintiff would still have to prove some fault on the part of the AI related technology. As commentators have argued, this can be difficult to do because the decision-making of the A.I. may be held within a "black box." This is further complicated by a general lack of understanding of the workings of AI sufficient to determine the exact reason for a bad outcome.[39] Regardless of these realities, however, there can be little disagreement that the approach is one that fits easily into the torts toolbox: a person has made a choice; one of the outcomes of that choice is harm to another; the original actor is therefore liable for that harm.[40]

The same is generally true of those efforts that would modify tort law in an attempt to apply products liability principles. Barbara Evans and Frank Pasquale, for example, have argued that while courts are generally not inclined to treat software as a product for products liability purposes, the Food and Drug Administration's authority to regulate devices that include machine learning elements means that where AI is part of medical devices it may be subject to strict products liability. As with the argument that users of AI could be held liable for the

35 For cases that involve embodied AI operating surgical equipment, which is another category of AI use not addressed here, see, e.g., *O'Brien* v. *Intuitive Surgical, Inc.*, 10 C 3005 (ND Ill. Jul. 25, 2011) (holding that proof of causation is required where a defect in a surgical robot is alleged).

36 See, e.g., Zach Harned, Matthew P. Lungren, and Pranav Rajpurkar, "Comment, Machine Vision, Medical AI, and Malpractice" (2019) *Harv. J.L. & Tech. Dig.* https://jolt.law.harvard.edu/digest/machine-visionmedical-ai-and-malpractice; Evans and Pasquale, "Product Liability Suits."

37 Marchant and Lindor, "Coming Collision," at 1337.

38 I leave aside here arguments relating to recognizing AI as discrete legal entities, or persons. Such a decision is unlikely to be taken solely within a tort case, as it raises too many significant questions of rights, personhood, autonomy and more to be decided within the narrow confines of tort litigation.

39 See, e.g., Frank Pasquale, *The Black Box Society: The Secret Algorithms That Control Money and Information* (Cambridge, MA: Harvard University Press, 2015); Nicholson Price, "Medical Malpractice and Black Box Medicine."

40 This is an oversimplification, but it tracks the *Restatement (Third) of Torts*, §7(a), which provides: "(a) An actor ordinarily has a duty to exercise reasonable care when the actor's conduct creates a risk of physical harm."

injuries caused by those technologies, this argument would extend tort law incrementally. It would not require a significant shift in tort law principles, nor would it insulate a particular industry from tort law's reach. As such, the argument falls within the ambit of existing tort law, even if the boundaries are subject to dispute.

Arguments, however, that certain technologies should be immunized from tort law's application advocate for a significant shift in tort's principles for the purpose of providing certainty in support of technological innovation. Ryan Calo, one of the first scholars to weigh in on the issues raised by AI and robots, argues Congress should shield manufacturers and distributors of open robotic platforms from suits by consumers related to their personal use of robots, just as it immunizes gun manufacturers from suits based on gun violence or websites that allow users to upload and post.[41] In a similar vein, Gary Marchant and Rachel Lindor argue that some limited form of immunity may be necessary to provide sufficient certainty to incentivize creation of important and worthwhile AI technologies.[42] F. Patrick Hubbard counters that any form of immunity is impractical since it shifts costs to users for any injuries suffered.[43]

Calo specifically references Communication Decency Act §230 as a basis for suggesting a limited liability regime, and while §230 remains a topic of both popular and scholarly attention, immunity in relation to AI technologies has the potential to significantly reshape the development and implementation of AI. Section 230 has itself shown us this, as it has been applied by courts in expansive ways, which have been instrumental in creating the Internet of today, both the good and the bad. Perhaps that is a good thing, but we are not particularly good at predicting the future. Perhaps the negative impacts on AI development will never occur, in which case immunizing such developers from liability is both unnecessary and unfair. The cases have not been heard yet. Any fundamental shift in the workings of the tort system should be based on court precedents. In this way, Calo was right to point to §230 as a precedent for intervention into tort liability questions for technological innovation, but that precedent raises more questions. The question is whether early intervention is the better option or whether waiting to see how liability is determined by the courts is the more prudent way forward.

7.6 CONCLUSION

When we think about the ways in which AI may pose challenges to the determination of liability for harm in tort law – when we ask what is legally salient about harms to individuals – the questions of responsibility and proof come to the forefront. There are many issues that tort law has dealt with over centuries, adjusting its course and creating appropriate precedents. The tort system moves slowly, with only incremental changes to the law being made as necessary to adjust to changing circumstances. Legislatures, both state and federal, step in when courts have taken paths that those bodies believe are counter to the public welfare. Again, while some legislative interventions are significant, others simply direct the courts in the development of appropriate doctrinal rules for addressing the questions before them.

Given the general flexibility inherent in the tort system, and the existing methods of making incremental change, allowing time for the tort system to respond to AI-related harms is the most prudent course. A statutory leap embracing one of the extremes – immunity from liability or strict liability – would preempt that development of tort law and its ability to provide a measured response. Such a leap may provide a degree of certainty, but it would be at the cost of preventing tort law from providing a better solution.

[41] Ryan Calo, "Open Robotics" (2011) 70 *Maryland L. Rev.* 571.

[42] Marchant and Lindor, "Coming Collision," at 1337.

[43] Hubbard, "Allocating the Risk of Injury from Sophisticated Robots."

8

Are Existing Tort Theories Ready for AI?

A Continental European Perspective

Jonas Knetsch

8.1 INTRODUCTION

The rapid development of robotics and intelligent systems raises the issue of how to adapt the legal framework to accidents arising from devices based on artificial intelligence (AI) and machine learning. In the light of the numerous legal studies published in recent years, it is clear that 'tort law and AI' has become one of the hot topics of legal scholarship[1] both in national and comparative contexts. Given the broad interest in compensation and tort law issues, one might even think that the dissemination of autonomous vehicles, drones, medical software, robot-assisted surgery, and other AI-based devices will inevitably lead to a sharp increase in the number of accidents and corresponding compensation claims. It seems almost as if those technologies were not destined to reduce fatality rates in traffic accidents, improve medical treatment, and anticipate cybersecurity threats, but to bring a scourge over humanity. This bias has to be taken into account when analysing tort law issues related to AI[2] if we wish to avoid alarmism or anti-technological panic-mongering.

Like other new technologies, AI-based devices can create the risk of harm to legally protected interests in various fields of application. In this context, the self-learning feature of AI-based products and services represents a genuine paradigm shift, casting doubt on the adequacy of traditional tort law regimes and, more generally, of the legal reasoning used by tort lawyers to date. In particular, the fact that AI products and services are designed to delegate the decision-making process to algorithms is significant when applying tort law regimes that were conceived for the assessment of human behaviour.

Against this background and under the consideration of the shift from human-centred technologies to autonomous systems, the European Parliament provided the Commission with recommendations on how to adjust civil-law rules to the development of robotics and AI.[3]

[1] For an extensive list of references in the English language, see, e.g., Marta Infantino and Weiwei Wang, 'Algorithmic Torts: A Prospective Comparative Overview' (2019) 28 *Transnational Law & Contemporary Problems* 309–62 at n. 17, 25. For literature in the German language, see Martin Sommer, *Haftung für autonome Systeme* (Baden-Baden: Nomos, 2020), pp. 511–68. For a bibliographical overview of French legal literature, see Jean-Sébastien Borghetti, 'How Can Artificial Intelligence Be Defective?' in Sebastian Lohsse, Reiner Schulze, and Dirk Staudenmayer (eds.), *Liability for Artificial Intelligence and the Internet of Things* (Baden-Baden: Nomos, 2019), pp. 63–76.

[2] On cognitive biases in tort law, see, e.g., John E. Montgomery, 'Cognitive Biases and Heuristics in Tort Litigation: A Proposal to Limit Their Effects without Changing the World' (2006) 85 *Nebraska Law Review* 15–51.

[3] Report with recommendations to the Commission on Civil Law Rules on Robotics (2015/2103(INL)); Recommendations to the Commission on a Civil Liability Regime for Artificial Intelligence (2020/2014(INL)).

In July 2019, the then-candidate to the presidency of the European Commission, Ursula von der Leyen, announced a coordinated European approach to the human and ethical implications of AI.[4] Since then, an expert group has published its conclusions on liability for AI.[5] The Commission has also issued an extensive white paper on AI[6] and a specific report on liability and safety issues.[7] In addition to the working papers elaborated on the European level, 'tort law and AI' is also an area of concern for the member state governments. Their responses to the 2020 white paper are valuable sources of information about existing legal adjustments and prospective ideas for legal reform in the EU member states.[8] Most recently, in April 2021, the European Commission published a proposal of an 'Artificial Intelligence Act', which has been subject to doctrinal analysis in the following months.[9]

This chapter aims to explore whether existing tort theories are ready for AI in this rapidly changing political and legal context. In conjunction with another chapter in this book focusing on a common-law perspective (Chapter 7), this contribution will address the situation in continental Europe and, more specifically, in two EU member states, namely France and Germany. Reflecting the author's language skills and legal knowledge, this selection directs attention to two tort law systems that are characterised by different 'tort law cultures'[10] and civil liability regimes.

Before addressing the substantive issues of this topic and taking the discussion further, it is necessary to clarify terminology. Tort lawyers with a civil-law background may not be familiar with the term 'tort theory' as it has a concrete meaning in common-law jurisdictions. Legal scholars from English-speaking countries will associate this term with specific theoretical perspectives on tort law, particularly with the economic and moral fault-based and strict liability approaches.[11] In the United States in particular, the rise of 'law and economics' led to the development, dispute, and refinement of two divergent tort theories in the 1970s and 1980s.[12]

4 Ursula von der Leyen, *Political Guidelines for the Next European Commission 2019–2024* (2019) 13, https://ec.europa.eu/info/sites/default/files/political-guidelines-next-commission_en_0.pdf ('in my first 100 days in office, I will put forward legislation for a coordinated European approach on the human and ethical implications of Artificial Intelligence').

5 Expert Group on Liability and New Technologies, *Liability for Artificial Intelligence and Other Emerging Digital Technologies* (2019), https://op.europa.eu/en/publication-detail/-/publication/1c5e30be-1197-11ea-8c1f-01aa75ed71a1/language-en.

6 White Paper on Artificial Intelligence – A European Approach to Excellence and Trust (COM(2020) 65 final).

7 Report on the Safety and Liability Implications of Artificial Intelligence, the Internet of Things and Robotics (COM (2020) 64 final).

8 See, e.g., the responses of the German Federal Government (*Stellungnahme der Bundesregierung der Bundesrepublik Deutschland zum Weißbuch zur Künstlichen Intelligenz*) or the French Higher Committee for Digital Technology and Postal Services (*Commission Supérieure du Numérique et des Postes*), https://ec.europa.eu/digital-single-market/en/news/white-paper-artificial-intelligence-public-consultation-towards-european-approach-excellence.

9 Proposal for a Regulation of the European Parliament and of the Council Laying Down Harmonised Rules on Artificial Intelligence (Artificial Intelligence Act) and Amending Certain Union Legislative Acts (COM(2021) 206 final). For a detailed assessment of this text, see Chapter 22 on 'Standardizing AI – The Case of the European Commission's Proposal for an Artificial Intelligence Act'.

10 See, in particular, the contributions to the special issue dedicated to 'Cultures of Tort Law in Europe' (2012) 3 *Journal of European Tort Law* 147–264. See also the references listed in n. 14–15.

11 For an overview, see, e.g., Jules Coleman, 'Theories of the Common Law of Torts' in Edward N. Zalta et al. (eds.), *Stanford Encyclopedia of Philosophy* (2015), https://leibniz.stanford.edu/friends/preview/tort-theories; John C. P. Goldberg, 'Twentieth-Century Tort Theory' (2002–2003) 91 *Georgetown Law Journal* 513–83.

12 For pivotal contributions to this debate, see Guido Calabresi, *The Costs of Accidents: A Legal and Economic Analysis* (New Haven, CT: Yale University Press, 1970); Richard Posner, 'A Theory of Negligence' (1972) 1 *Journal of Legal Studies* 29–96; Richard Epstein, 'A Theory of Strict Liability' (1973) 2 *Journal of Legal Studies* 151–204; George Fletcher, 'Fairness and Utility in Tort Theory' (1972) 85 *Harvard Law Review* 537–73; Jules Coleman, 'The Morality of Strict Tort Liability' (1976) 18 *William and Mary Law Review* 259–86; Stephen Perry, 'The Moral Foundations of Tort

In continental Europe, where the 'law and economics' movement enjoys less attention and less academic prestige, the economic analysis of (tort) law is also less known to legal scholars and, what is more, it lacks an equivalent theoretical framework.[13] What comes closest to 'tort theories' in a common-law sense is the debate on the functions of civil liability and the policy considerations that led to a departure from traditional fault-based liability towards more strict liability regimes and no-fault compensation schemes. Yet, even if one admits that there are certain parallels in this context, a tort law scholar from a common-law jurisdiction will likely be surprised by the lack of thorough analysis of tort law from a philosophical point of view in civil-law jurisdictions. In contrast, continental European tort lawyers will likely be puzzled when questioned about existing 'tort theories' in their jurisdictions.

This preliminary finding entails the adjustment of the aim of this research. Given the discrepancy between the methodological approaches in common-law jurisdictions and continental Europe, this contribution will address whether the dogmatic framework of tort law in France and Germany is fit for the challenges arising from AI products and services. Is it able to integrate or even anticipate the policy choices that are to be made by the national and European legislature?

Therefore, this survey will address the civil liability rules applicable to the 'actors' involved in the development, design, and operation of AI-based devices. They can be divided into two groups, the users and the manufacturers. Both can also be held liable under various liability regimes, to which two main sections of this chapter will be dedicated (Sections 8.3 and 8.4). To better understand the policy choices available in France and Germany, however, it is essential to set out the tort law cultures that exist in both countries (Section 8.2). Finally, the chapter outlines the perspective of a compensation scheme for harm caused by AI-based systems that is distinct from tort law (Section 8.5).

8.2 TORT LAW CULTURES IN CONTINENTAL EUROPE

When debating civil liability for AI, we often forget that legal solutions to the compensation of victims are closely connected to national tort law rules and the cultural context in which tort lawyers apply them on a daily basis. The international and European dimension taken by this debate tends to overshadow the fact that tort law traditions are strikingly different from one jurisdiction to another and that in the foreseeable future, there will be no common law of torts in continental Europe. Whether the legislature should introduce new liability rules or not and how these rules should be designed depends mainly on the current tort law practice. Therefore, it is essential to set the scene for the legal debate in France and Germany by briefly presenting their respective tort law cultures.

In 2012, a special issue of the *Journal of European Tort Law* investigated the concept of legal culture and its meaning in comparative tort law. Devoted to different cultures of tort law in Europe, four authors representing England, France, Germany, and Scandinavia explored the attitudes, practices, and values linked to tort law in the relevant countries and region.[14] In his

Law' (1982) 77 *Iowa Law Review* 449–514; Ernest Weinrib, 'Toward a Moral Theory of Negligence Law' (1983) 2 *Law and Philosophy* 37–62. See also John Gardner, 'Tort Law and Its Theory' in John Tasioulas (ed.), *The Cambridge Companion to the Philosophy of Law* (Cambridge: Cambridge University Press, 2020), pp. 352–70.

[13] See the contributions to Klaus Mathis (ed.), *Law and Economics in Europe: Foundations and Applications* (Dordrecht: Springer, 2014).

[14] See Jean-Sébastien Borghetti, 'The Culture of Tort Law in France' (2012) 3 *Journal of European Tort Law* 158–82; Jörg Fedtke, 'The Culture of German Tort Law' (2012) 3 *Journal of European Tort Law* 183–209; Håkan Andersson, 'The

introduction to the national reports, Ken Oliphant suggested that legal culture might embrace five elements in the tort law context. Based on former research,[15] he identified societal attitudes towards tort law, the practice of tort law and the 'lived experience' of tort law, as well as tort law's institutional context, and, finally, the cultural values enshrined in substantive tort law.[16] France and Germany are good examples to illustrate that policy choices have to integrate those parameters since their tort law cultures are, in many respects, each other's opposites.

One of the most distinctive features of French tort law is the breadth of its scope of application. All types of loss or damage, whether pecuniary or non-pecuniary in nature, are deemed compensable, and in principle, there is no restriction of interests protected by the rules of civil liability.[17] The general principle of liability for fault provided for in Articles 1240 and 1241 of the French Civil Code does not distinguish between interests relevant under tort law and those that are not protected. Consequently, French lawyers find it very natural to seek compensation for pure economic loss, non-pecuniary damage, or the loss of a chance (*perte d'une chance*) without even the slightest acknowledgement that in other jurisdictions, those concepts are subject to intense legal debate. Although this broad and, therefore, pro-victim approach in tort law[18] is based upon the wording of Article 1240 Civil Code, it would likely not exist without the generalisation of liability insurance. With the exception of intentional acts, almost every facet of human life or economic activity is eligible for first- or third-party insurance coverage, which is often compulsory,[19] thereby disguising the economic consequences of the victim-oriented stance of French tort law. Using the words of Jean Savatier, 'civil liability, instead of getting to its sources, now only draws on its results; it does not start with the tortfeasor, but with the victim; it has been reversed'.[20]

The contrast with German tort law is striking. As is well known, the central tort law provision of § 823(1) of the German Civil Code (BGB) establishes a list of rights and interests protected under tort law. According to this provision, an extra-contractual compensation claim based on fault (*Verschulden*) is limited to recovery for injury to life, physical integrity, health, personal liberty, property, and other 'absolute rights', which are comparable to property.[21] For the courts, these rights are the starting point when deciding whether to award compensation or not. Unlike in France, the idea of liability without fault (*Gefährdungshaftung*) is recognised only in specific

Tort Law Culture(s) of Scandinavia' (2012) 3 *Journal of European Tort Law* 210–29; Richard Lewis and Annette Morris, 'Tort Law Culture in the United Kingdom: Image and Reality in Personal Injury Compensation' (2012) 3 *Journal of European Tort Law* 230–64.

15 See James L. Gibson and Gregory A. Caldeira, 'The Legal Cultures of Europe' (1996) 30 *Law & Society Review* 55–85; David Nelken, 'Defining and Using the Concept of Legal Culture' in Esin Örücü and David Nelken (eds.), *Comparative Law: A Handbook* (London: Hart, 2007), pp. 109–32. See also Åse B. Grødeland and William L. Miller, *European Legal Cultures in Transition* (Cambridge: Cambridge University Press, 2015), p. 2.

16 Ken Oliphant, 'Cultures of Tort Law in Europe' (2012) 3 *Journal of European Tort Law* 147–57 at 148.

17 On this issue, see also Christophe Quézel-Ambrunaz, 'Fault, Damage and the Equivalence Principle in French Law' (2012) 3 *Journal of European Tort Law* 21–43.

18 For an assessment of this *idéologie de la réparation* ('compensation ideology'), see Loïc Cadiet, 'Les faits et méfaits de l'idéologie de la réparation' in *Le juge entre deux millénaires: Mélanges offerts à Pierre Drai* (Paris: Dalloz, 2000), pp. 495–510.

19 The risk of civil liability related to the personal life of private individuals living in France is covered by the so-called multirisk home insurance scheme (*assurance multirisques habitation*), which is compulsory for tenants and flat owners.

20 René Savatier, *Métamorphoses économiques et sociales du droit privé d'aujourd'hui* (3rd ed.; Paris: Dalloz, 1964), p. 292. See also Yvonne Lambert-Faivre, 'L'évolution de la responsabilité civile d'une dette de responsabilité à une créance d'indemnisation' (1987) *Revue trimestrielle de droit civil* 1–19.

21 For more details, see Basil S. Markesinis, John Bell, and André Janssen, *Markesinis's German Law of Torts* (5th ed.; London: Hart, 2019), p. 29; Gerald Spindler and Oliver Rieckers, *Tort Law in Germany* (3rd ed.; Alphen aan den Rijn: Wolters Kluwer, 2019), p. 38.

and well-defined cases and generally kept outside the BGB to preserve the internal consistency of the almost entirely fault-based law of delict (*Deliktsrecht*).[22] More generally speaking, the idea that, in principle, the loss should lie where it falls (*casus sentit dominum*) is still very much present among German tort law scholars and is often used as a tagline for the presentation of civil liability rules. Following the tradition of Roman law, the 'law of delict' is not defined by its compensatory function (as in France) but instead as a legal instrument reconciling the individual freedom of the (potential) tortfeasor and the (potential) protection of the victim.[23]

Although superficial and incomplete,[24] this brief survey of the significant features of tort law cultures in France and Germany may give an idea of the different states of mind in which tort law experts from both countries address civil liability for AI. While French lawyers will primarily seek to verify that the existing tort law regimes are adequate for the compensation of victims, their German counterparts will tend to use more differentiated policy choices as a basis for their analysis.

From which end do we have to analyse the consistency of existing tort law rules? The compensation of victims and the delimitation of spheres of personal liability are both important aims that are constantly balanced before the legislature and civil courts. However, it is essential to consider the specific sensitivities of national jurisdictions when addressing the liability of the user and the manufacturer of AI-based technologies.

8.3 LIABILITY OF THE USER OF AI-BASED TECHNOLOGIES

8.3.1 *Overview*

Cases in which harm can be attributed to AI-based technology, the injured person's initial response will most likely be to turn against the person who was using the AI during the occurrence of the harm. This may lead to the civil liability of commercial operators who employ AI-enhanced devices in the exercise of their business activity, such as private hospitals using medical robots or banking institutions and insurance companies using AI-based software. As laid out by Spindler,[25] compensation claims made in this context will often lead to contractual liability. In jurisdictions in which there is a *non-cumul* rule,[26] claimants cannot even choose the legal basis of their claim and will thus have to rely on the law of contract to obtain damages. However, depending on the particular circumstances, injured persons may also turn against private parties who use AI in their everyday life for leisure activities, personal travel, or domestic purposes. In those cases, it will be more unlikely that the claimant can invoke contractual liability, but it is not excluded. Nevertheless, the central issue is not so much that of the contractual or extra-contractual basis of the claim, but rather whether the claimant has to establish fault to receive compensation.

[22] Cees van Dam, 'Who Is Afraid of Diversity? Cultural Diversity, European Co-operation, and European Tort Law' (2009) 20 *King's Law Journal* 281–308 at 288. See also Markesinis, Bell, and Janssen, *German Law of Torts*, chapter 7.

[23] See, e.g., Nils Jansen, *Die Struktur des Haftungsrechts* (Tübingen: Mohr Siebeck, 2003), p. 76.

[24] Fedtke, 'The Culture of German Tort Law', 208 ('The culture of German tort law cannot be adequately described in a single article').

[25] Gerald Spindler, 'User Liability and Strict Liability in the Internet of Things and for Robots' in Lohsse et al., *Liability for Artificial Intelligence*, pp. 125–43 at 131.

[26] Which is the case in France. For more details, see Jonas Knetsch, *Tort Law in France* (Alphen aan den Rijn: Wolters Kluwer, 2021), paras. 55–64.

8.3.2 *Fault-Based Liability*

In French and German tort law, liability for fault is generally seen as the cornerstone for civil liability. According to the famous Article 1240 of the French Civil Code, 'any human action whatsoever which causes harm to another creates an obligation in the person by whose fault it was caused to make reparation for it'.[27] In contrast to this broad approach *à la française*, § 823(1) BGB provides that 'a person who, intentionally or negligently, unlawfully injures the life, body, health, freedom, property or another right of another person is liable to make compensation to the other party for the damage arising from this'.[28]

Claimants may well invoke both provisions in the context of AI, and no tort lawyer in France or Germany would be shocked if the courts declared users of AI-based products or services to be responsible for harm caused by misuse or abuse. However, the potential of fault-based liability depends heavily on the degree of autonomy of the device using AI, which means that the more control is shifted from the user to the autonomous system, the less a claimant will be able to establish a wrongful behaviour on behalf of the user. More specifically, one has to examine to what extent the operator's personal judgement was irrelevant in using the technology and which personal duties the user had to comply with at the time of the damage.[29]

While the fault-based liability of users is not yet given broad attention in legal scholarship in the context of AI, this may change in the future as the legislature prepares to clarify what obligations AI users have to meet to escape from civil liability. In Germany, the 2021 Autonomous Driving Act (*Gesetz zum Autonomen Fahren*) seems to foreshadow a sector-based legislative approach for the use of AI-based technologies.[30] This legislative Act establishes a comprehensive legal framework for driverless vehicles by setting out specific duties for a technical supervisor (*technische Aufsicht*) who may be in the vehicle or at a control centre. The breach of one of those duties will thus give rise to the operator's civil liability for negligence.

In Germany fault-based liability is still the undisputed pillar of tort law and may be invoked as such by claimants in any event; this is not the case in French law. Indeed, for victims of traffic accidents, in 1985, the French legislature enacted an extra-strict liability regime that was given an exclusive character. In other words, for traffic accidents in which a motor vehicle is involved, claimants cannot base their claim against its driver or keeper on Article 1240 of the Civil Code, but are instead obliged to invoke the strict liability regime laid out by the so-called *loi Badinter* from 1985.[31] Together with other strict liability regimes, the *loi Badinter* contributed significantly to the marginalisation of fault-based liability, especially in the area of new technologies.[32]

[27] For a more detailed assessment of this provision in English, see Knetsch, *Tort Law in France*, paras. 68–125. See also Bernadette Auzary-Schmaltz, 'Liability in Tort in France before the Code Civil: The Origins of Art. 1382 ff. Code Civil' in Eltjo J. H. Schrage (ed.), *Negligence: The Comparative Legal History of the Law of Torts* (Berlin: Duncker & Humblot, 2001), pp. 309–40; Jean-Sébastien Borghetti, 'The Definition of *la faute* in the *Avant-projet de réforme*' in John Cartwright, Stefan Vogenauer, and Simon Whittaker (eds.), *Reforming the French Law of Obligations* (London: Hart, 2009), pp. 271–88.

[28] In English, see Markesinis, Bell, and Janssen, *German Law of Torts*, chapter 2; Spindler and Rieckers, *Tort Law in Germany*, paras. 69–108.

[29] From a Belgian point of view on this aspect, see Jan De Bruyne and Jochen Tanghe, 'Liability for Damage Caused by Autonomous Vehicles: A Belgian Perspective' (2017) 8 *Journal of European Tort Law* 324–71 at 334.

[30] For an overview in English, see Alexander Kriebitz, Raphael Max and Christoph Lütge, 'The German Act on Autonomous Driving: Why Ethics Still Matters' (2022) 35 *Philosophy & Technology* article 29.

[31] For more details on this regime, see Knetsch, *Tort Law in France*, paras. 174–80 (with further references in English).

[32] On the 'decline' of the concept of fault in French tort law, see Yvonne Flour, 'Faute et responsabilité civile. Déclin ou renaissance?' (1987) *Droits* 29–42. See also the other contributions to the special issue 'Fin de la faute?' (1987) *Droits* 1.

8.3.3 *Strict Liability Regimes*

In response to the rise of technology-related risks, in several jurisdictions, the legislature has introduced civil liability regimes that are unrelated to the compliance of the defendant with existing duties. Even though the concept was already present in Roman law,[33] the importance of strict liability (*Gefährdungshaftung* or *responsabilité sans faute*) has increased significantly throughout the twentieth century, albeit to different extents and depths.

One of the elements defining continental European tort law is the enactment of strict liability regimes for road traffic accidents, making drivers and keepers of motor vehicles liable regardless of their conduct.[34] Over the last few years, several authors have investigated the adequacy of those regimes to address the risks of accidents with autonomous vehicles.[35] At first glance, the idea of driverless cars seems to be in conflict with a liability regime that is based on the identification of a driver. It was therefore important to provide clarification in the case a vehicle without any driver (in the usual sense of this word) is involved in an accident. The German Road Traffic Act made clear that 'a driver is also the person who activates a highly or fully automatic driving function ... and uses it for vehicle control, even if he does not control the vehicle himself within the scope of the intended use of this function'.[36]

However, the broader sentiment among legal scholars in both countries seems to be that, with slight adjustments, the existing rules will be perfectly fit to absorb the accident risk related to autonomous vehicles. In particular, it is argued that the current combination of strict liability and compulsory liability insurance functions has proven reliable and effective and that there is no need for a specific liability regime. Regardless, it would be difficult to draw a line between traditional motor vehicles subject to the existing regime and autonomous vehicles with specific liability rules.[37]

In France, where the idea of strict liability had more impact compared to in Germany, claimants can invoke other regimes to hold users of AI liable for harm caused by autonomous systems. In addition to the product liability regime, the French Conseil d'État has acknowledged strict liability for operators of medical devices used in public hospitals, even though they do not fall under the framework of the 1985 directive.[38] However, it is important to note that this case law has not yet been confirmed by the Court of Cassation for clinics and private practice doctors.[39]

[33] See Jonas Knetsch, 'The Role of Liability without Fault' in Jean-Sébastien Borghetti and Simon Whittaker (eds.), *French Civil Liability in Comparative Perspective* (London: Hart, 2019), pp. 123–42.

[34] See, for example, the collective work of Wolfgang Ernst (ed.), *The Development of Traffic Liability* (Cambridge: Cambridge University Press, 2010).

[35] For an assessment of German law, see, for example, Petra Buck-Heeb et al., 'Haftungsfragen' in Bernd Oppermann and Jutta Stender-Vorwachs (eds.), *Autonomes Fahren – Rechtsfolgen, Rechtsprobleme, technische Grundlagen* (2nd ed.; Munich: C. H. Beck, 2019), chapter 3.1; Rainer Freise, 'Rechtsfragen des automatisierten Fahrens' (2019) *Zeitschrift für Verischerungsrecht* 65–79; as for French law, see Marie Dugué and Jonas Knetsch, 'Responsabilité civile et assurance' in Lionel Andreu (ed.), *Des véhicules autonomes. Une offre de loi* (Paris: Dalloz, 2018), chapter 2; Iolande Vingiano-Viricel, *Véhicule autonome: qui est responsable?* (Paris: LexisNexis, 2019), paras. 51–69; Jean-Sébastien Borghetti, 'L'accident généré par l'intelligence artificielle' (2017) *La Semaine Juridique. Edition générale* (special issue) 23–8.

[36] Regarding this provision in English, see Ulrich Magnus, 'Autonomously Driving Cars and the Law in Germany' (2019) 4 *Insurance Law Journal* 13–24.

[37] Dugué and Knetsch, 'Responsabilité civile et assurance', para 02.06.

[38] See Conseil d'État (CE), 9 July 2003, no. 220437 and, more recently, CE, 12 March 2012, no. 327449; 25 July 2013, no. 339922 and 27 May 2021, no. 433822.

[39] See Court of Cassation, First Civil Chamber (Civ 1), 9 November 1999, no. 98-10010; 12 July 2012, no. 11-17510; 14 November 2018, nos. 17-28529 and 17-27980. See also Civ 1, 26 February 2020, no. 18-26256, commented in Jonas

What is more, outside the area of road traffic accidents and defective medical devices, the French civil courts have acknowledged a general principle of strict liability for 'guardians' (*gardiens*) of things, regardless of whether they are defective and have caused harm to another individual. Even though the rationale of this far-reaching principle is subject to academic debate[40] and some influential voices have called for a restriction of its scope,[41] strict liability for things is still an important part of the French tort law culture.

Its potential for AI-related harm should not, however, be overestimated, since a claimant has to establish the 'active role' (*fait actif*) of the thing; for example, an internal defect, a wrong position, or an abnormal 'behaviour'.[42] Only in cases in which the thing was in motion and has had direct physical contact with the property damaged or the person injured is the 'active role' presumed. In addition to this, for the general principle to be applicable, defendants must qualify as 'guardians' of the thing, which means that they possessed its 'use, direction and control' (*usage, direction et contrôle*).[43] Both requirements, the 'active role' of the thing and its guardianship, should limit the impact of the general principle of liability for things in the context of AI. Nonetheless, there is a strong potential of strict liability regimes for holding users of AI products liable. Due to the generalisation of liability insurance, the financial consequences of the compensation will mostly be borne by insurance companies.

8.3.4 *Impact of Insurance Coverage*

Given the intricate connection between tort law and insurance, it would not be accurate to appreciate the sole consistency of civil liability rules and their appropriateness for AI-induced harm. In France, first- or third-party insurance coverage is widely available and is often compulsory. The ubiquity of liability insurance disguises the economic consequences of the victim-oriented stance of French tort law, shifting the financial burden of compensation from the individual to the community of insured persons, for example vehicle owners in the field of motor insurance, healthcare professionals for medical liability insurance and even larger parts of society when it comes to civil liability related to the life of private individuals.

In this context, it has become commonplace, both in French and German legal scholarship, to point out the decline of individual civil liability[44] and the rise of collective compensation via liability insurance. In numerous cases, the rules of civil liability are no longer a process through which to hold individuals liable for harm caused by them, but serve only to determine the shares

Knetsch and Zoé Jacquemin, 'France' in Ernst Karner and Barbara Steininger (eds.), *European Tort Law 2020* (Berlin: de Gruyter, 2021), paras. 33–39.

40 See Jean-Sébastien Borghetti, 'La responsabilité du fait des choses, un régime qui a fait son temps' (2010) *Revue trimestrielle de droit civil* 1–40 and in response, Philippe Brun, 'De l'intemporalité du principe de responsabilité du fait des choses' (2010) *Revue trimestrielle de droit civil* 487–97. See also the extensive study in English by Edward A. Tomlinson, 'Tort Liability in France for the Act of Things: A Study of Judicial Lawmaking' (1988) 48 *Louisiana Law Review* 1299–1367.

41 One of the reform drafts, elaborated upon by a group of tort law scholars and professionals under the supervision of François Terré, suggests limiting the scope to corporeal things (*choses corporelles*). See the arguments presented by Jean-Sébastien Borghetti, 'Des principaux délits spéciaux' in François Terré (ed.), *Pour une réforme du droit de la responsabilité civile* (Paris: Dalloz, 2011), pp. 163–83 at 173–5.

42 For more details, see Knetsch, *Tort Law in France*, para 170 (with further references).

43 On this issue, see the more detailed presentation by John Bell, Sophie Boyron, and Simon Whittaker (eds.), *Principles on French Law* (2nd ed.; Oxford: Oxford University Press, 2008), pp. 387–8; Eva Steiner, *French Law: A Comparative Approach* (2nd ed.; Oxford: Oxford University Press, 2018), pp. 272–3.

44 See the pivotal monograph of Geneviève Viney, *Le déclin de la responsabilité individuelle* (Paris: LGDJ, 1965, reprint 2013).

of the economic consequences of compensation among insurance companies.[45] In the light of the increased availability of liability insurance coverage, even in jurisdictions where the idea of compulsory insurance is not as present as in France, the compensation of harm caused by AI will likely be handled at an initial stage by the operator's insurance company, before recourse against the manufacturers and, where relevant, their own insurer.

8.4 LIABILITY OF THE MANUFACTURER OF AI-BASED TECHNOLOGIES

One of the major issues raised by continental European tort lawyers addressing the topic of 'AI and tort law' is the appropriateness of the rules governing product liability. It is foreseeable that future legal debate will focus on the liability of manufacturers, as they appear to be those who shall ultimately bear the cost of victim compensation if malfunctioning or programming errors have caused the accident. The product liability rules will therefore be a crucial element, either in the context of the recourse of the operator's insurer, or for direct compensation claims that victims may file against manufacturers.

This has also been recognised by the European Commission, which has set up an expert group on liability and new technologies divided into two teams, one dedicated to the rewriting of the 1985 EC directive ('product liability formation') and the other to the assessment of existing liability regimes in the wake of emerging digital technologies ('new technologies formation').[46] In April 2021, the European Commission proposed a new legislative framework for the regulation of AI.[47] However, the Commission proposal lacks ambitious recommendations regarding civil liability rules.[48]

Pending the advancement of the preparatory work on a European 'Artificial Intelligence Act', the current legal debate in continental Europe concerns the existing rules on liability for defective products and their adequacy with AI-based technologies. It is astonishing that, despite the common European core of product liability rules and the maximal harmonisation character of the 1985 EC directive, several basic questions have not yet yielded an adequate response. In France and Germany, it would even appear that the transposition of the directive has introduced into the existing civil liability system a 'foreign body' that has not yet become completely acculturated to the national tort law.[49] This is because the implementation of a liability regime with a minimum threshold for property damage and specific industry-friendly defences (development risks and regulatory compliance) marked, especially in France, a departure from the deeply rooted pro-victim stance of the existing tort law rules.

Theoretical reflections on the rationale of the European product liability regime may help to better understand its interplay with other civil liability regimes, in particular with fault-based

[45] Among the German tort law scholars, see Hans-Leo Weyers, *Unfallschäden* (Frankfurt: Athenäum Verlag, 1971); Dieter Schäfer, *Soziale Schäden, soziale Kosten und soziale Sicherung* (Berlin: Duncker & Humblot, 1972); Hein Kötz, *Sozialer Wandel im Unfallrecht* (Karlsruhe: C. F. Müller, 1976).

[46] On this expert group, see the detailed information sheet available on the website of the European Commission, https://ec.europa.eu/transparency/regexpert/index.cfm?do=groupDetail.groupDetail&groupID=3592.

[47] Proposal for a Regulation of the European Parliament and of the Council Laying Down Harmonised Rules on Artificial Intelligence (Artificial Intelligence Act) and Amending Certain Union Legislative Acts (COM(2021) 206 final).

[48] The work of the 'new technologies formation' had already been published in the form of a report. See Expert Group on Liability and New Technologies, *Liability for Artificial Intelligence and Other Emerging Digital Technologies* (2019).

[49] See Jonas Knetsch, 'European Tort Law in Western Europe' in Paula Giliker (ed.), *Research Handbook on EU Tort Law* (Cheltenham: Edward Elgar, 2017), pp. 342–58 at 345–9. See also Simon Whittaker, *Liability for Products* (Oxford: Oxford University Press, 2005), p. 452 ('an alien intrusion for a French lawyer').

liability. The analysis of underlying policy choices can also help to clarify central legal concepts such as defectiveness and the insurance background of product liability.

8.4.1 *Product Liability and Fault-Based Liability: A Complicated Relationship*

The starting point to assess the interaction between the European product liability regime and the civil liability rules in the EU member states is Article 13 of the 1985 directive.[50] According to this provision, the directive 'shall not affect any rights which an injured person may have according to the rules of the law of contractual or non-contractual liability or a special liability system existing at the moment when [the directive] is notified'.

The German and French legislatures have transposed this rule in different terms, suggesting that the coordination between European and national tort law cannot be considered to be natural.[51] § 15 of the German Product Liability Act excludes compensation claims regarding physical harm caused by pharmaceutical products from the scope of this act, for which a specific regime exists under the Pharmaceutical Products Act, and further states that 'liability in accordance with other provisions remains unaffected'. On the other hand, Article 1245-17 of the French Civil Code states that 'the provisions of this Title may not affect any rights which an injured person may have according to the rules of contractual or tort liability or of a special liability system' and that 'a producer remains liable for the consequences of his fault or for that of the persons for whom he is responsible'.

The margin of action that both legislatures have themselves recognised for the sake of the transposition reveals that product liability is difficult to classify within existing tort law categories. While it is generally considered as a regime of strict liability,[52] the assessment of the German and French law does not fully confirm this position.

In Germany, product liability is primarily based on the central norm governing fault-based liability, namely § 823 BGB, which comprises the breach of a general duty of care (*Verkehrspflicht*) or a statutory duty (*Schutzgesetz*).[53] The Federal Court of Justice has developed a comprehensive set of case-law rules allowing claimants to claim damages for harm caused by different kinds of defects (manufacturing, design, or product information). In practice, the duties imposed on the manufacturer according to the case law of the German courts are very close, if not converging to the concept of defect under the 1985 directive.

[50] See Jean-Sébastien Borghetti, *La responsabilité du fait des produits: Étude de droit comparé* (Paris: LGDJ, 2004), paras. 523–6. See also, in German, Gerhard Wagner in Franz Jürgen Säcker, Roland Rixecker, Hartmut Oetker, and Bettina Limperg (eds.), *Münchener Kommentar zum BGB* (8th ed., 14 vols.; Munich: C. H. Beck, 2020), vol. 7, under § 15 ProdHaftG, paras. 2–6; Simon Taylor, 'The Harmonisation of European Product Liability Rules: French and English Law' (1999) 48 *International and Comparative Law Quarterly* 419–30.

[51] On the German transposition of the 1985 directive, see Joachim Zekoll, 'The German Products Liability Act' (1989) 37 *American Journal of Comparative Law* 809–18; Stefan Lenze, 'German Product Liability Law: Between European Directives, American Restatements and Common Sense' in Duncan Fairgrieve (ed.), *Product Liability in Comparative Perspective* (Cambridge: Cambridge University Press, 2005), pp. 100–25. On the French transposition, see in English, Whittaker, *Liability for Products*, pp. 531–52; Duncan Fairgrieve, '*L'exception française?* The French Law of Product Liability' in Duncan Fairgrieve (ed.), *Product Liability in Comparative Perspective* (Cambridge: Cambridge University Press, 2005), pp. 84–99; Knetsch, *Tort Law in France*, paras. 181–6 (with further references).

[52] Report from the Commission on the Application of Directive 85/374 on Liability for Defective Products (COM/2000/0893 final). In the French legal literature, see, for example, Geneviève Viney, Patrice Jourdain, and Suzanne Carval, *Les régimes spéciaux et l'assurance de responsabilité* (4th ed.; Paris: LGDJ, 2017) para 14 ('Ce texte pose donc un principe de responsabilité objective …').

[53] In a contractual context, the claimant can also request damages in contract, according to §§ 280–3 BGB. See Lenze, 'German Product Liability', 101–7.

According to § 15(2) of the German Product Liability Act, it is perfectly possible to invoke those judge-made rules (known as *Produzentenhaftung* in contrast to the EU-law-based *Produkthaftung*), despite the existence of a specific European product liability regime and the aim of the European Commission to achieve complete harmonisation between the member states in this field. Even more intriguing is the fact that German authors interpret the case law of the European Court of Justice[54] as allowing such a cumulative approach.[55] Consequently, it is likely that practitioners in Germany tend to be of the opinion that the product liability pales in comparison to the civil liability rules elaborated by the national courts on the basis of the BGB.

The situation under French law is more complex. While there was no specific legislation on product liability until 1998, the courts applied contract law in a highly consumer-friendly way to compensation claims filed against manufacturers or retailers of defective goods.[56] In particular, from 1988 when the deadline for the transposition of the directive expired, the Court of Cassation developed a genuine liability regime based on a strict 'safety obligation' (*obligation de sécurité de résultat*), which allowed buyers of defective products to obtain compensation from the vendor solely on the basis of harm caused by the product. To ensure that this case law was only temporary, the French civil courts explained that it was based on (former) Articles 1147 and 1384(1) of the Civil Code, 'as interpreted in the light of the 1985 EC directive'.[57]

In 2007, the Court of Cassation held that the judge-made product liability regime based upon an *obligation de sécurité* could no longer be invoked against a professional supplier and that even in cases in which the product was put into circulation before 1998, there should be no other liability regime applicable than the one arising from the directive.[58] While this judgment clarified that the temporary liability regime designed to 'bridge' the late transposition of the directive was no longer in force, it failed to explain the relationship between fault-based liability and product liability. In particular, in cases where a defect in the sense of the directive could be analysed as a *faute* under Articles 1240 and 1241 Civil Code, one could wonder if the blocking effect of Article 13 of the directive could bar claimants from invoking the traditional fault-based liability. In contrast to the case law of the German Federal Court of Justice, the French Court of Cassation decided in 2017 that in cases where a lack of information caused harm to a product user, the trial courts had to apply the EU-law-based product liability regime, even though the claimant and the defendant had issued their pleadings on the basis of the fault-based liability.[59]

In the light of this brief survey of two European jurisdictions, it is astonishing that the current debate on 'AI and tort law' does not always take into account the complex interplay of the European product liability regime with domestic civil liability rules, as well as its hybrid character, placing it halfway between strict liability and fault-based liability.[60] Unlike in some

[54] See, Case C-402/03, *Skov Æg* v. *Bilka Lavprisvarehus A/S* [2006] ECR I-199; commented upon by Simon Whittaker (2007) *Zeitschrift für Europäisches Privatrecht* 858–71.

[55] Wagner, *Münchener Kommentar*, paras. 2–5.

[56] For a survey of the development of product liability in French law, see Fairgrieve, '*L'exception française?*', 86–91; Jean-Sébastien Borghetti, 'The Development of Product Liability in France' in Simon Whittaker (ed.), *The Development of Product Liability* (Cambridge: Cambridge University Press, 2010), pp. 87–113.

[57] See, for example, Civ 1, 28 April 1998, no. 96-20421.

[58] Civ 1, 15 May 2007, no. 05-17947. See also Case C-402/03, *Skov Æg* v. *Bilka Lavprisvarehus A/S* [2006] ECR I-199.

[59] Court of Cassation, Mixed division (Ch mixte), 7 July 2017, no. 15-25.651, commented upon by Jean-Sébastien Borghetti, (2017) *Revue des contrats* 594–8.

[60] See also Andreas Spickhoff in Beate Gsell et al. (eds.), *beck-online. Großkommentar BGB* (Munich: C. H. Beck, 2020) under § 15 ProdHaftG, para 11 ('deutliche Verschleifung der verschuldens-unabhängigen und der verschuldens-unabhängigen Haftung in der gerichtlichen Praxis').

common-law jurisdictions,[61] there does not seem to be an extensive political debate on determining the nature of liability rules for AI-based products or services.

8.4.2 *Legal Requirements for Product Liability: Need for Clarification*

When looking into the legal requirements set out by the European product liability regime, it quickly becomes obvious that the current legal framework has become partially obsolete. Pending the reform of the 1985 EC directive, the existing national product liability regimes, based on fault, may thus become more competitive, as their legal basis allows a more flexible approach, giving national courts a greater margin of appreciation. Indeed, two central concepts of the 1985 product liability directive are proving to be difficult to put into practice. Both have been assessed in several publications on the application of product liability to AI. Therefore, this chapter will only make some general remarks on those issues.

At first, the mere legal term 'product' raises vital difficulties when applied to AI-enhanced technologies.[62] Article 2 of the 1985 directive limits its scope of application to movables, commonly understood as referring to corporeal things.[63] Without any doubt, the European product liability regime applies to products in which an AI-based algorithm or even classical software is embedded. However, it is far from certain that so-called stand-alone algorithms are also applicable to those liability rules. The drafters of the directive have not considered this issue, as the development of information technology was in its infancy at the time. While the European Commission made clear that software could be regarded as a 'product' when embedded on a data storage device (such as floppy disks, CDs, memory cards, flash drives, or external hard drives),[64] the prevailing view in the legal literature seems to be that the wording of the directive does not include cloud-based software that is not stored on a physical data device. As highlighted by several authors, AI software is sometimes even more likely to be qualified as a service rather than as a product,[65] thus falling outside the scope of the European product liability regime and into the legislative competences of the member states.[66]

This question is also critical when it comes to the identification of the liable person(s) in case of a defect of the digital content of an AI-enabled product. If the software is embedded in a tangible device, the manufacturer of the product 'as a whole' will be the 'producer' in the sense of article 3 of the Directive. However, if the AI software does not qualify as a product, the injured

61 Ryan Abbott, 'The Reasonable Computer: Disrupting the Paradigm of Tort Liability' (2018) 86 *George Washington Law Review* 1–45 at 9 ('computer-generated torts should be negligence based').

62 See Tiago Sérgio Cabral, 'Liability and Artificial Intelligence in the EU: Assessing the Adequacy of the Current Product Liability Directive' (2020) 27 *Maastricht Journal of European and Comparative Law* 615–35 at 618–21; Gerhard Wagner, 'Robot Liability' in Lohsse et al., *Liability for Artificial Intelligence*, pp. 27–62 at 41–2. For a survey in German see Sommer, *Haftung für autonome Systeme*, pp. 220–4; Gerhard Wagner, 'Produkthaftung für autonome Systeme' (2017) 217 *Archiv für die civilistische Praxis* 709–65 at 713–19.

63 According to this provision, 'for the purpose of this Directive "product" means all movables, with the exception of primary agricultural products and game, even though incorporated into another movable or into an immovable'.

64 Written Question no. 706/88 (5 July 1988) and 'Answer by Lord Cockfield on behalf of the Commission' (15 November 1988), OJ 114/42, 8 May 1989.

65 Cabral, 'Liability and Artificial Intelligence', 620. See also Duncan Fairgrieve et al., 'Product Liability Directive' in Piotr Machnikowski (ed.), *European Product Liability: An Analysis of the State of the Art in the Era of New Technologies* (Cambridge: Intersentia, 2016), pp. 17–108 at 42. See also Karin Alheit, 'The Applicability of the EU Product Liability Directive to Software' (2001) 34 *The Comparative and International Law Journal of Southern Africa* 188–209.

66 Cabral, 'Liability and Artificial Intelligence', 620.

person will have difficulty holding 'the manufacturer of a component part' jointly liable, although it is explicitly referred to in the Directive.[67]

Second, the assessment of a product defect (*défaut du produit*; *Produktfehler*) needs to be revised in the presence of AI-based products or services. If the harm can be attributed to negligence in designing the algorithm,[68] in embedding the software in the finished product (car, robot, etc.) or in giving a comprehensive set of information and warnings to the final user, legal professionals may not have any difficulties handling the concept of defect. However, the most critical issue is the assessment of a defect in case the outcomes of a seemingly well-designed algorithm have led to an accident.

According to Article 6 of the 1985 Directive, a product is defective 'when it does not provide the safety which a person is entitled to expect'. Considering the vagueness of this definition, national courts in the European Union have acknowledged that different elements may lead to the establishment or at least a presumption of a product defect: malfunction of the product, violation of safety standards, balance of the product's risks and benefits, and the comparison of the product with other existing products of the same kind.[69]

So far, neither the courts of the EU member states nor the European Court of Justice have provided any guidelines in the assessment of a product defect when dealing with 'algorithmic' torts.[70] In legal scholarship, the most promising path seems to be a comparative approach that consists of confronting the 'behaviour' of the algorithm with a legal standard. Thus, as outlined by Wagner and Borghetti,[71] it is not obvious which legal standard should be chosen to set the threshold of defectiveness. While a comparison with the behaviour of a reasonable human being does not adequately address the concept of AI, it is as of yet unclear to what extent other algorithms with 'reasonable behaviour' may be taken as references. It may even be possible that, under the guise of the defectiveness test, the legal idea of a 'reasonable robot' subject to anthropomorphic rules of conduct will emerge.

A related issue is the relevance of the risk development defence[72] in AI torts. According to Article 7 of the Directive, 'the producer shall not be liable . . . if he proves: . . . (e) that the state of scientific and technical knowledge at the time when he put the product into circulation was not such as to enable the existence of the defect to be discovered'. As is well-known, this defence has been introduced to enhance the development of new technologies, as producers benefit from an exemption of civil liability if they have complied with state-of-the-art enforced safety. Some authors call for an application of the risk development defence when dealing with harm caused

67 According to Article 3 of the Directive, '"[p]roducer" means the manufacturer of a finished product . . . or the manufacturer of a component part'. Article 5 of the Directive provides that 'where, as a result of the provisions of this Directive, two or more persons are liable for the same damage, they shall be liable jointly and severally . . .'. See also, Article 1245-7 of the French Civil Code; §§ 4(1) and 5 of the German Product Liability Act.

68 For example, an incorrect code line or a negligently designed network security system, making the AI device prone to a cyberattack.

69 See Jean-Sébastien Borghetti, 'How Can Artificial Intelligence Be Defective?' in Lohsse et al., *Liability for Artificial Intelligence*, pp. 63–76 at 66–8; Borghetti, *Responsabilité du fait des produits*, paras. 446–64.

70 The term is borrowed from Infantino and Wang, 'Algorithmic Torts'.

71 Borghetti, 'Defectiveness of Artificial Intelligence', 68–71; Wagner, 'Robot Liability', 42–5. See also Fairgrieve et al., 'Product Liability', 50–61.

72 Also known as the 'later-defect defence' or, with reference to the US product liability rules, 'state of the art defence'. See Cabral, 'Liability and Artificial Intelligence', 624–5; Ulrich Becker and Konrad Rusch, 'Das Problem des Entwicklungsrisikos und der state of the art defense im deutschen, französischen und US-amerikanischen Recht' (2000) *Zeitschrift für Europäisches Privatrecht* 90.

by AI.[73] However, under the European product liability regime, the corridor of action is particularly narrow when it comes to allowing manufacturers to benefit from this ground of exemption. In the past thirty years, national courts as well as the European Court of Justice have been highly reluctant to give a practical dimension to a ground of exemption, which has remained a dead letter since the enactment of the 1985 directive.[74] What is more, it has been argued that AI-based products are not eligible for the development risk defence, as manufacturers of self-learning algorithms are fully aware of the risks that can arise from this technology.[75]

The current European legal framework of product liability is not consistent with the development of AI-enhanced technologies.[76] As long as basic concepts such as 'products' or 'defects' present intractable difficulties, national courts will be tempted to find adequate legal solutions under domestic law on the grounds of fault-based liability rather than under the European regime. The need to reform the 1985 directive and the complex interplay between European and national liability rules in the field of defective products may obscure or interfere with the policy choices that European or national legislature will have to take. In particular, the lawmakers should consider that it is the designer of the algorithm who has the information, expertise, and resources needed to increase the safety of autonomous systems, becoming the 'cheapest cost avoider of accidents' in the sense of law and economics.[77]

8.4.3 *Insurance Background of Product Liability*

In comparison to the reflections on product liability rules, less attention has been paid to the insurance background of the liability of manufacturers.[78] In particular, national and European authorities should consider the introduction of compulsory insurance coverage to guarantee the compensation of injured persons or, in case damages have already been awarded to them by the user's insurance company, to make sure that the cost is shifted to the manufacturer's sphere. For example, in the event of an accident caused by the defective algorithm of a self-driving car, the motor vehicle insurer will try to recover the damages paid to the victim(s) from the manufacturer.

In France and Germany, it is very common for companies that produce goods or provide services to obtain business liability insurance (*Betriebshaftpflichtversicherung* or *assurance multirisques professionnelle*) covering product liability risks, even though there is no general statutory duty to do so.[79] However, the idea to introduce compulsory third-party liability insurance needs

73 See, for example, Spindler, 'User Liability and Strict Liability', 143. For a more nuanced approach, see Cabral, 'Liability and Artificial Intelligence', 624 ('clarification could be relevant to ensure that this defence is not abused in the context').

74 There is little case law on the development risk defence that was accepted by the courts. The French Court of Cassation made it clear that the 'state of scientific and technical knowledge' shall be the most advanced available and that the development risk should be assessed individually for each production lot. On the development risk defence in French law, see also Whittaker, *Liability for Products*, pp. 494–5.

75 Wagner, 'Produkthaftung für autonome Systeme', 750. This is also one of the options mentioned by the most recent consultation organized by the European Commission (see at n. 49).

76 See also Cabral, 'Liability and Artificial Intelligence'; Duncan Fairgrieve and Geraint Howells, 'Rethinking Product Liability: A Missing Element in the European Commission's Third Review of the European Product Liability Directive' (2007) 70 *Modern Law Review* 962–78; Daily Wuyts, 'The Product Liability Directive: More Than Two Decades of Defective Products in Europe' (2014) 5 *Journal of European Tort Law* 1–34.

77 See Wagner, 'Robot Liability', 40–1; Spindler, 'User Liability and Strict Liability', 135; Sommer, *Haftung für autonome Systeme*, p. 229. In the context of autonomous vehicles, see also De Bruyne and Tanghe, 'Liability for Damage', 364.

78 See, however, Georg Borges, 'New Liability Concepts: The Potential of Insurance and Compensation Funds' in Lohsse et al., *Liability for Artificial Intelligence*, pp. 145–63.

79 For a presentation of French law, see Axelle Astegiano-La Rizza, *Les assurances de responsabilité de l'entreprise* (6th ed.; Paris: L'Argus, 2014). For a survey of the legal framework in Germany, see Friedhelm G. Nickel and Anke

to be considered, if the capacity for product liability risks in standard insurance contracts is too low. According to Koch, the insurance contracts subscribed to by German car manufacturers only provide for a capacity 'in the three-digit million range', which may not be sufficient.[80]

Yet, the implementation of compulsory insurance does not resolve the issue of financial guarantees in an international context. For example, a French motor vehicle insurer will have great difficulty in taking recourse against an American manufacturer of a self-driving car or its Indian supplier of AI-enhanced software. To maintain the prospects of success for recourse claims, the EU might consider introducing an obligation for manufacturers of AI devices to provide adequate insurance coverage when applying for access to the single market.[81]

8.5 REPLACEMENT OF TORT LAW WITH A NO-FAULT COMPENSATION SCHEME?

The starting point of this survey was the question concerning the adequacy of existing 'tort theories' to the rise of AI. Faced with this questioning, a French legal academic will undoubtedly think of a phenomenon known as the 'socialisation of risks' (*socialisation des risques*), which is not precisely a tort theory in a common-law sense, but may be compared to a movement of ideas or even a school of thought.

According to this view, French tort law has undergone a profound shift from individual liability to a system of collective compensation through social security, first-party and liability insurance as well as compensation schemes (*fonds d'indemnisation*). While this observation applies to many jurisdictions in which the idea of social welfare is deeply engrained, it is particularly the case in France where social security and private insurance coverage are extremely broad and compensation funds play an important role.[82]

What is more, while the idea of *socialisation des risques* was initially developed to describe, and therefore gain a better understanding of, the interplay of civil liability, social security, and private insurance,[83] over the decades it has become a policy catchword used by legal scholars to claim an even greater departure from individual liability and for a greater conversion to socialised compensation. In the 2000s, this led to the establishment of various compensation funds for victims of 'medical accidents', terror acts, asbestos, defective drugs, crop failures, pesticides, etc.[84] The underlying rationale is that society, as a whole, must show solidarity with its vulnerable members who are affected by predicaments beyond their control. This idea of *solidarité nationale* is not only the political basis of the comprehensive social security system, but

Nickel-Fiedler, *Allgemeine Haftpflichtversicherungsbedingungen. Kommentar zu Teil I unter besonderer Berücksichtigung der Betriebs-Haftpflichtversicherung* (Karlsruhe: VVW, 2012).

80 Robert Koch, 'Herausforderungen für die Haftpflichtversicherung autonomer Systeme und der Sharing Economy' (2020) *Zeitschrift für Versicherungsrecht* 741–55 at 746.

81 Dugué and Knetsch, 'Responsabilité civile et assurance', paras. 02.291–02.296.

82 Knetsch, *Tort Law in France*, paras. 27–28, 199–203; Olivier Moréteau, 'Basic Questions of Tort Law from a French Perspective' in Helmut Koziol (ed.), *Basic Questions of Tort Law from a Comparative Perspective* (Vienna: Jan Sramek Verlag, 2015), pp. 3–95 at paras. 1–3 to 1–13.

83 For a comprehensive assessment of this trend, see Geneviève Viney, *Introduction à la responsabilité* (4th ed.; Paris: LGDJ, 2019), paras. 45–66 (with further references). On this concept in English, see Simon Deakin and Zoe Adams, *Markesinis and Deakin's Tort Law* (8th ed.; Oxford: Oxford University Press, 2019), p. 8; see also Yves-Louis Sage, 'Reinforcing the Rights of the Victim in the French Law on Civil Liability' (1998) 28 *Victoria University of Wellington Law Review* 543–72.

84 See Jonas Knetsch, 'Compensation Funds in France and Germany' in Thierry Vansweevelt and Britt Weyts (eds.), *Compensation Funds in Comparative Perspective* (Cambridge: Intersentia, 2020), pp. 45–66.

also in the process of becoming a genuine legal concept that is invoked by partisans of socialized compensation to claim new compensation schemes.[85]

While no equal to the catchword *solidarité nationale* exists in Germany, the development of liability insurance and social security throughout the twentieth century also had an impact on German tort law. Since the 1970s, the legal doctrine reported the rise of legal tools designed to shift the burden of compensation from individuals to collective entities (*kollektiver Schadensausgleich*), relegating civil liability rules to a mere 'law of recourse action'.[86] However, compared to the situation in France, public authorities did not create specific compensation schemes, such as funds or compensation offices to a similar degree. It is significant that German medical law is still dominated by tort law rules rather than by compensation funds based on the idea of *solidarité nationale*, as is the case in France, even though there is a current legal debate on the opportunity to create a compensation fund for medical malpractice.[87]

In the context of AI-related accidents, the European Parliament suggested creating a compensation scheme separate from the civil liability rules. Indeed, in its 2017 and 2020 recommendations, the European Parliament called on the European Commission to investigate the perspective of a 'general fund for all smart autonomous robots or ... an individual fund for each and every robot category' and to ensure 'that a compensation fund would not only serve the purpose of guaranteeing compensation if the damage caused by a robot was not covered by insurance'.[88] This proposal has also been investigated by legal scholars, not only in the USA,[89] but also in Germany[90] and France.[91]

Although it is an appealing idea to create a compensation fund to ensure that emerging risks related to the use of AI products be shifted to society as a whole, one should not underestimate the legal problems related to compensation schemes. In fact, their adaptability is also their biggest handicap, as the enactment of a compensation fund needs to resolve sensitive political issues, such as the funding of the scheme and its exact scope. It is highly unlikely that the legislature, be it national or European, will agree to a general solution addressing *any* compensation claims related to AI, as the underlying economic context is directly dependent on the type of product used.

Even if it is conceivable to create sector-based compensation funds with specific budgetary solutions, the legislature would have to resolve considerable problems with the definition of their scope, let alone their funding. For example, it would be a complex task to demarcate the exact field of application of a compensation scheme for accidents in which a self-driving car was involved. As there are different levels of autonomy in algorithm-based driving, the legislature would have to arbitrarily set a threshold beyond which a vehicle will be subject to a specific legal

85 On the legal dimension of *solidarité nationale*, see Jonas Knetsch, 'La solidarité nationale, genèse et signification d'une notion juridique' (2014) *Revue française des affaires sociales* 32–43.

86 Weyers, *Unfallschäden*, p. 401. See also Hein Kötz, 'Einführung' in John G. Fleming, Jan Hellner, and Eike von Hippel (eds.), *Haftungsersetzung durch Versicherungsschutz* (Frankfurt: Metzner, 1980), pp. 7–10 at 9 ('a dessication [*Austrocknen*] of tort law').

87 See Gerhard Wagner, 'Bedarf es eines Härtefallfonds für Behandlungsschäden?' (2021) 39 *Medizinrecht* 101–9 (with further references).

88 Report with recommendations to the Commission on Civil Law Rules on Robotics (2015/2103(INL)). See also Recommendations to the Commission on a Civil Liability Regime for Artificial Intelligence (2020/2014(INL)).

89 Tracy Hresko Pearl, 'Compensation at the Crossroads: Autonomous Vehicles & Alternative Victim Compensation Schemes' (2019) 60 *William and Mary Law Review* 1827–91 at 1857–88.

90 Borges, 'New Liability Concepts', 145.

91 See Dugué and Knetsch, 'Responsabilité civile et assurance', para 02.06. See also David Noguéro, 'Assurance et véhicules connectés: Regard de l'universitaire français' (2019) *Dalloz IP/IT* 597–602.

treatment regarding the compensation of accident victims,[92] raising delicate issues of equality before the law. While they first appear to be a 'Swiss army knife' in the field of victim compensation, compensation funds eventually prove not to be an all-purpose answer to all shortcomings of the traditional tort law rules. Indeed, the legislature should use the legal tool of compensation funds sparingly, for example to close gaps in case the AI manufacturer did not subscribe sufficient liability insurance coverage.

8.6 CONCLUDING REMARKS

The aim of this chapter was limited, as it is only intended to provide an outline of current legal developments in the field of 'tort and AI' in the light of continental European tort law. The examples of French and German tort law provide interesting insights into the ways in which legal technique and legal policy are intertwined, without any specific 'tort theories' emerging from the doctrinal analysis. Continental European legal scholarship is more characterised by a 'methodological syncretism', using more than one mindset to provide input on the debate surrounding the compensation of victims of AI-related accidents.

It has likely become obvious to the reader that this chapter did not give an in-depth analysis of all legal problems related to the application of civil liability rules to AI, but instead intended to give a glimpse of the underlying theoretical and policy-related trends on this issue. Other contributions to this book give more insight on specific issues; for example, on product liability.[93]

The comparison of the continental European debate and tort theories from the common-law world has shown that much remains to be done to bring the current civil liability rules in line with the challenges arising from AI. While victims of AI-induced accidents may be able to obtain compensation from users of AI products or their insurers, the real issue at stake is that the rules governing the liability of manufacturers of AI products and algorithms, especially based on the EU product liability regime, are not fit for a widespread use of those technologies.[94]

[92] See, for example, Pearl, 'Compensation at the Crossroads', 1878–9 (according to the author, 'An autonomous vehicle crash fund should only be accessible to Level 4 and 5 vehicle crash victims. The fund should not cover Level 2 and 3 crash victims because driver inattention or error is more likely to cause these incidents than problems with the vehicle itself.').

[93] See, in particular, Chapter 9 on 'Liability for AI Decision-Making' and Chapter 12 on 'Liability for Autonomous Vehicle Accidents'.

[94] In August 2021, the European Commission issued its 108-page proposal of an 'Artificial Intelligence Act', giving additional input to an already extensive series of government reports, white papers, and doctrinal sources (Proposal for a Regulation of the European Parliament and of the Council Laying Down Harmonised Rules on Artificial Intelligence (Artificial Intelligence Act) and Amending Certain Union Legislative Acts (COM(2021) 206 final)). The issue of liability is not directly addressed in this text. However, the possible enactment of specific codes of conduct and transparency obligations suggests that tort law scholars will find new stimulus for the creation of civil liability rules compatible with the rapid progress of AI-enhanced products and services. See, in particular, Chapter 22 on 'Standardizing AI.'

9

Liability for AI Decision-Making

Eric Tjong Tjin Tai

9.1 INTRODUCTION

Since the second AI revolution started around 2009, society has witnessed new and steadily more impressive applications of AI. The growth of practical applications has in turn led to a growing body of literature devoted to the liability issues of AI. The present text is an attempt to assess the current state of the law and to advance the discussion. To do so, in a global legal environment, I will focus less on a single jurisdiction, and more on the analysis of what the issues are and how they are generally resolved or may be resolved in legal systems around the world. I will discuss the available grounds of liability in different jurisdictions.[1] Furthermore, several grounds of liability that are not directly applicable will be investigated as a model for future regulation. The discussion culminates in a justification for liability, and suggestions for approaches to regulating liability.

Given the position of this chapter in this book, the focus is on AI that is deployed within organizations to make decisions. I will not discuss AI that is embedded in a system that physically moves or acts (such as robots or cars). The liability issues regarding robots and autonomous vehicles are dealt with in other chapters.[2] I will concentrate on cases involving economic loss, not on physical injury or property damage as those are typically caused by robots. When there is physical injury and/or property damage there may be numerous specific torts and grounds of liability that may apply, and it is more likely that compensation will be obtained. In a few situations a decision-making system may indirectly cause physical harm, such as AI that gives an incorrect medical diagnosis, or AI that gives a patient an incorrect dose of medicine. Arguably such cases can be regulated in the same way as the cases discussed here, if needed with a higher standard of care or stricter obligations. Finally, I will concentrate on tort liability, because in contractual settings liability is usually restricted by limitation clauses that typically exclude compensation for pure economic loss.

9.1.1 *AI Decision-Making in Organizations*

AI refers to the entire field of artificial intelligence, encompassing many different approaches and insights. In current public debate AI is, however, principally conceived in a narrower sense,

[1] See also Then Foek Erik Tjong Tjin Tai, 'Liability for (Semi-)Autonomous Systems' in Vanessa Mak, Then Foek Eric Tjong Tjin Tai and Anna Berlee (eds.), *Research Handbook in Data Science and Law* (Cheltenham: Elgar Publishing, 2018), pp. 55–82.

[2] See also Susana Navas, 'Robot Machines and Civil Liability' in Martin Ebers and Susana Navas (eds.), *Algorithms and Law* (Cambridge: Cambridge University Press, 2020), pp. 157–173.

as a specific kind of software that derives conclusions from given input. In particular, it involves what technically is called 'deep learning', based on layered neural networks that are trained by massive amounts of data to provide certain outputs on a set of input values. The result is a 'model', a set of numeric values that is used by the software (which embodies the structure or 'topology' of the neural network) to calculate output from a set of input values (which can consist of images, text or other complex data). Such a neural network provides the basis of advanced pattern recognition, not only for images but also for determining patterns in other kinds of data. By ingenious ways of training the neural network and combining it with certain inputs and outputs, the power of AI can be used in many different kinds of applications, such as automated language translation, unmanned vehicles and algorithmic trading. This kind of AI is nowadays also popularly called 'algorithms', even though an algorithm strictly speaking is simply a term for the abstract procedure implemented in a piece of code (such as the Sieve of Eratosthenes for calculating prime numbers).

Considered this way, AI differs from traditional software in that it is not constructed in a determinate way as pure code: it consists of a coded neural network (topology) combined with the values connected with the nodes in the model, and these values have been determined by the model itself during training. The developers have no direct influence on how the AI performs and do not have insight in the decisions it makes. This can be contrasted to more traditional software in the form of a detailed coded algorithm, where the programmer could in theory predict precisely the behaviour of the program by simply following the code. I say, 'in theory', because actually it is also quite hard to predict software behaviour. But in case of undesirable outcomes, it is possible to read the code and pinpoint the source of the problem (a programming mistake, a design error). In the case of AI, the finished neural network operates like a black box that simply provides output in an opaque manner.[3] It is possible to analyse AI to determine how it came to certain mistakes as a consequence of the training data, but the developers do not directly determine the outcomes in the way a programmer of a piece of code does.

When considering AI deployed in organizations, the function of AI is to process input data to generate certain output. Technically the output takes the shape of a set of numeric values that can be interpreted in various ways, depending also on the training set-up. The values may be transformed to provide human-readable form such as text or images,[4] or serve as input for other systems.

The question is now, what does it mean that AI makes decisions? I believe we have to distinguish between making a decision and executing a decision. A traditional car can be used to execute the decision to turn to the right, but it doesn't make the decision itself. In an autonomous vehicle the AI may decide to turn to the right, and then the execution of the decision is the task of the remaining components of the car. The distinguishing element is that the decision is executed without further ado, once decided. Thereby a decision is distinct from mere advice (as provided, for instance, by a navigation system). One can imagine AI producing advice to buy certain stock, but if the decision to buy is left in the hands of the human operator, the AI does not itself make a decision. Consequentially when we speak of AI decision-making we

[3] Martin Ebers, 'Regulating AI and Robotics: Ethical and Legal Challenges' in Ebers and Navas, *Algorithms and Law*, pp. 37–99, pp. 48–50.

[4] The technical process involved may be quite complicated, as in the case of video deep fakes or automatic translation, or relatively straightforward, as in the case of character recognition.

are implicitly also assuming the presence of an automatic mechanism of execution. That mechanism may actually involve humans as well if those humans have been instructed by the organization to simply follow the decision unchallenged.

It can be argued that automata could already decide before the advent of contemporary AI. A vending machine, to take the oft-used example, could decide on whether to accept a coin and eject a soda can, or to reject the coin as being invalid. A factory could have a sensor that automatically opens a safety valve whenever the temperature at a certain point gets too high: the decision process might be implemented with purely mechanical means, but the logic behind it is identical to a digitized process. Such decisions could even have significant consequences if incorrect (see the example of a factory, where a malfunctioning sensor could lead to an explosion). However, the decision process typically was simple (involving a yes/no question) and also had a clearly circumscribed scope (opening a valve or not). These can be handled fairly easily by existing legal instruments.

This comparison highlights that the change with AI is not the notion of automated decision-making in itself, rather it is the extent of possible outcomes (both in number and scope) and the opacity of the decision-making itself. Therein lies the leap that AI has accomplished, whereby AI is now able to operate in the domain we hitherto believed to be exclusively the province of human intelligence, As Weaver states, "[a] fundamental assumption underlying almost all of our laws is that all decisions are made by human intelligence'.[5] That is the reason why a renewed examination of liability law is needed.

Finally, what kind of decisions are we talking about?[6] An important category consists of commercial decisions, in particular algorithmic trading in securities and stock. Another category is business or managerial decisions, such as automated review of resumes and review of employees. Administrative and judicial decisions by the state and by courts, as well as medical diagnoses, are also fields where automation and use of AI is spreading. There is also discussion on using AI in blockchain technology.

Several of these examples are actually on the boundary of the current discussion: they involve AI as a decision-making system that executes its decisions, but could be overridden if so decided. An automated rejection letter can be reviewed if the applicant complains. It could be argued that any implementation of AI should be encapsulated in such a way. In particular the mandatory obligation to review automated decisions in Article 22 GDPR[7] is an expression of this principle. Similarly, the EU Parliament resolution on robotics call for an op-out mechanism or 'kill switch' in the design of AI.[8] Another example is the requirement of having a human operator who can intervene in the operation of an autonomous vehicle.[9] However, it is not a generally accepted principle that AI should always be either shielded from direct interaction with the environment or at least supervised. I will return to this option later in the chapter.

5 John F. Weaver, 'Regulation of Artificial Intelligence in the United States' in Woodrow Barfield and Ugo Pagallo (eds.), *Research Handbook on the Law of Artificial Intelligence* (Cheltenham: Edward Elgar Publishing, 2018), pp. 155–212, p. 159.

6 See also, Ari E. Waldman, 'Algorithmic Legitimacy' in Woodrow Barfield (ed.), *The Cambridge Handbook of the Law of Algorithms* (Cambridge: Cambridge University Press, 2021), pp. 107–120, p. 108; Ruth Janal, 'Extra-Contractual Liability for Wrongs Committed by Autonomous Systems' in Ebers and Navas, *Algorithms and Law*, pp. 174–206, p. 190.

7 General Data Protection Regulation 2016/679, OJ 2016 No. L119/1.

8 European Parliament resolution of 16 February 2017 with recommendations to the Commission on Civil Law Rules on Robotics, 2015/2103(INL), under 'Licence for designers'.

9 Antje von Ungern-Sternberg, 'Autonomous Driving Regulatory Challenges Raised by Artificial Decision-Making and Tragic Choices' in Barfield and Pagallo, *Research Handbook*, pp. 251–278, p. 269.

Incidentally, I am not concerned with accountability for algorithms. That discussion is about decisions that might be defensible if sufficiently motivated.[10] Here the discussion is about liability for *incorrect* decisions by AI, that is, decisions for which there is no proper motivation, only an explanation of how they were reached.

9.1.2 *Which Persons May Be Liable for AI?*

Before we can examine the various grounds of liability, we need to clarify which persons we will focus on as possibly being liable for AI. In the case of fault liability, the tortfeasor must have acted wrongfully, that is, acted in a way different from what legally was required. This would principally point to the developer of the AI and the organization deploying the AI. Furthermore, there may be a distinction between the actual developer and the manufacturer who markets the AI. We can also distinguish between a researcher who has developed the abstract algorithm (for example, suitable for pattern recognition) and the developer who has trained the algorithm with a data set for a specific purpose (such as recognizing persons). We can theorize also about the liability of the supplier of the training data or the researcher who devised a new technique for AI, but these persons seem to have less relevance as they are farther removed from the actual application that caused harm. Arguably it would be the responsibility of either the developer or the organization to take sufficient precautions. Furthermore, these parties may contractually take recourse on relevant related other parties for damages paid if they are themselves found liable.

From the perspective of strict liability, though, there are various persons for which there is reason to hold them liable, by way of their relationship to the AI (Section 9.5).[11] Other forms of strict liability work with notions like owner, keeper, employer and driver. If we translate this to AI, the principal defendant would be the organization that deployed the AI, as that is the organization that can control or supervise that the AI actually makes decisions and has effects in the real world. Furthermore, the developer of the AI controlled how the AI is actually constituted and what it does on its own.

To structure the discussion, I therefore propose that we focus on the developer of the AI and the organization that deploys or operates the AI. We can refer to those parties as *developer* and *operator*. In practice there are many other parties, such as the developer of the software package and the individual employees of the operator who actually work with the AI. But from the point of view of regulating liability most other parties are of lesser importance as they can usually be addressed through the developer or the operator, by means of contracts concluded by those two, or by other forms of strict liability (such as vicarious liability).

9.2 FAULT LIABILITY

9.2.1 *Negligence*

The principal norm for fault liability is negligence, or in civil law systems its equivalent, such as wrongfulness (§ 823 I Bürgerliches Gesetzbuch (BGB)) or fault (Article 1240 of the French Code

[10] See Margot E. Kaminski, 'Understanding Transparency in Algorithmic Accountability' in Barfield, *Cambridge Handbook*, pp. 121–138.

[11] See also, Janal, 'Extra-Contractual Liability', p. 193; Tjong Tjin Tai, 'Liability for (Semi-)Autonomous Systems', sec. 4; Andrew D. Selbst, 'Negligence and AI's Human Users' (2020) 100 *Boston University Law Review* 1315 focuses on the operator.

civil): the notion that someone acts wrongfully by acting in a negligent or careless manner, showing insufficiently care for the interests of others. The standard of care (Section 9.2.2) may be influenced by private regulation, customary law or in another way, and is in concrete cases ultimately decided by the courts.[12] If there are statutory rules that also set a standard of care,[13] these may either be taken into account as well under a general notion of fault (as in Article 1240 Cc) or are considered as an independent tort (breach of statutory duty) or ground of liability (such as in German law, § 823 II BGB).

The common law tort of negligence requires that the defendant had a duty of care, breached that duty, that damage resulted from that breach and the damage is not too remote.[14] The norm of a duty of care, which is assessed by the 'reasonable person' standard, is in theory sufficiently broad to encompass many different activities and to take into consideration the interests of third parties.[15] However, when it comes to AI there is the complication that negligence in principle does not allow recovery of pure economic loss. Even though there is no general exclusionary rule,[16] the case law makes it abundantly clear that there is strong hesitation towards compensating pure economic loss under negligence.[17] The kind of cases that we discuss here typically only involve pure economic loss, therefore negligence is not a suitable basis for a claim for damages. An exception is the liability for negligent misstatement, which can be considered a specific form of negligence where pure economic loss can be recovered. This requires the presence of a special relationship.[18] However, a wrongful *decision* by AI typically does not constitute or lead to a misstatement.

In civil law systems there is a less restrictive attitude. Through the concepts of wrongfulness and fault, a similar 'reasonable person' standard is applied. German law has a fairly complex system whereby pure economic loss is often not recoverable.[19] However, in the cases considered here we are by definition looking at cases where AI decisions caused non-physical harm, and if that is wrongful under German law, the specific ground may be one that does allow recovery of pure economic loss. In particular for certain forms of unfair competition, the violation of the 'Right to an established and operative enterprise' (*Recht am eingerichteten und ausgübten Gewerbebetrieb*)[20] comes to mind, as well as intentional actions under § 826 BGB that cover some of the same area as the English economic torts.

In French law there is no particular restriction to compensation of pure economic loss. If the AI has been developed in a negligent manner, or if the AI is deployed in a way that lacks safety measures or preventive measures, the producer or deployer might be held liable on the basis of

[12] This is given shape in precedents in English law (cf. *Robinson* v. *Chief Constable of West Yorkshire Police (Rev 1)* [2018] UKSC 4), but in civil law systems the doctrinal works also categorize cases on the basis of case law.

[13] Statutes that do not themselves have a private law remedy. If they do, they are self-contained grounds of liability or statutory torts.

[14] James Goudkamp and Donal Nolan, *Winfield & Jolowicz on Tort* (20th ed.; London: Sweet & Maxwell), para. 5-002, Michael A. Jones (ed.), *Clerk & Lindsell on Torts* (23rd ed.; London: Sweet & Maxwell, 2020), para. 7-04.

[15] Selbst, 'Negligence and AI's Human Users' discusses the foreseeability requirement as possibly an obstacle.

[16] Goudkamp and Nolan, *Winfield & Jolowicz on Tort*, paras. 5-048 through 5-056 discusses the 'narrowly confined' situations in which recovery is allowed.

[17] Jones, *Clerk & Lindsell on Torts*, para. 7-103: 'First, whilst the links between negligence and physical damage depend largely on the laws of nature and necessarily limit the type of relationship giving rise to a claim, those between negligence and pure financial loss are primarily human in creation and can form a complex web through which financial losses can ripple out from the one negligent act.'

[18] *Hedley Byrne & Co.* v. *Heller and Partners Ltd* [1964] AC 465; see Jones, *Clerk & Lindsell on Torts*, paras. 7-104ff. and Goudkamp and Nolan, *Winfield & Jolowicz on Tort*, paras. 12-006ff.

[19] Hein Kötz and Gerhard Wagner, *Deliktsrecht* (13th ed.; Munich: Vahlen, 2016), paras. 86–102. In particular for violation of *Verkehrspflichten*, which protect against property damage and personal injury.

[20] Kötz and Wagner, *Deliktsrecht*, paras. 431–434, one of the 'other rights' protected under § 823 I BGB.

the general fault liability of Article 1240 Cc. The only restriction is that damage must be 'certain and direct'; it should not be too remote. For systems that follow the French approach of a general fault-liability provision, there is therefore a fairly solid basis for fault liability.

There is presently very little case law about when a developer or operator of AI may be liable. This can partly be explained by the restrictions regarding pure economic loss. In the absence of case law, we can make a more abstract analysis of possible relevant aspects, inspired partly by specific legislation[21] as models of best practices for limiting risks by AI decision-making.

9.2.2 *Standard of Care for AI*

As the discussion above makes clear, in the absence of specific restrictions to compensation of pure economic loss, the production and deployment of AI may be tested against a standard of care. This begs the question: what standard of care should be applied? What would a reasonable developer or operator do? We can assume (as is currently positive law) that the production and deployment of AI is not in itself wrongful. Hence negligence or another form of fault liability has to be established on specific facts. We can imagine a few specific ways in which a person may show a lower level of care towards others than might be required. These are not intended to be limitative, only to give an indication of what may be expected.

First of all, there are several measures that can be taken by the developer:[22]

- Doing insufficient training with the AI, whereby its results are (foreseeably) too often incorrect. This comprises as well training with insufficient data or insufficiently correct data (data that has been categorized sloppily or has not been checked as to its quality).
- Incorrect structure of the AI (the use of an inappropriate neural network topology that would not allow sufficiently fine-grained decisions, or would result in insufficient layers or nodes).[23]
- Insufficient hardware (too slow hardware for the AI, whereby decisions are incorrect or delayed, which may for example be a problem in high speed financial trading). Note that 'insufficient' depends on the specific purpose for which the AI is deployed. These errors lead to AI that does not function correctly on its own, that is, draws invalid conclusions. This is primarily the responsibility of the developer. The second set of measures is in the operational environment where the AI is put into operation.[24]
- Depending on the information provided by the developer, errors could also be due, for example, to the use of a simplistic linguistic translation program to translate contracts. In that case either the developer would internally be liable, or the user if they did not heed the warnings by the developer. Arguably the victim might sue both or either, on the basis of joint and several liability.
- Insufficient precautionary measures. As it is clearly foreseeable that AI may cause harm – the fact that there is considerable discussion about liability proves this beyond any doubt – we may expect an operator to put precautionary measures into place to limit the possibility of harm and to restrict the extent of harm. Besides the ultimate measure of not allowing AI

[21] For example, Gerald Spindler, 'Control of Algorithms in Financial Markets: The Example of High-Frequency Trading' in Ebers and Navas, *Algorithms and Law*, pp. 207–220.

[22] These are inspired partly by the approach of product liability.

[23] Whether this is the case also depends on the state of the art and existing knowledge.

[24] These are inspired partly by approaches in organizational liability, other forms of negligence, and vicarious liability.

to act directly – which is outside the scope of this chapter – the operator would at least be expected to add a form of supervision that allows detection of irregularities, just like an organization might do with human employees. Financial trading shows several examples (Section 9.4.3): limitations in trading, warning signals when certain indicators show something amiss and human employees monitoring the AI in some way[25] combined with an actual kill switch or interruption mechanism.[26] Other measures are aimed at directly assessing the reliability of the AI by way of audits, demanding explanation of its operation by the developer. Furthermore, a proper organization may require adequately instructing employees to make them aware of the risks involved by AI, and the possibly necessary intervention measures. The complete set of measures resembles the way in which a new machine might be employed, and indeed one might argue that AI should be treated in a similarly circumspect manner bearing in mind the risks that it can cause.

A practical problem is how a victim may in a specific case establish that the operator or deployer actually were negligent. In practice this would simply be litigated in the same way as any other tort case: the victim will argue and attempt to make a prima facie case that the decision was incorrect, and that there is harm that would not have occurred if the correct decision had been made. Then it seems likely that the operator or developer would be asked to explain how that decision came about and what they had done to prevent it or its negative consequences. This would resemble a presumption of negligence, even though it follows simply from an application of the general rules of fault liability.

9.2.3 *Other Forms of Fault Liability*

Besides negligence there are in common law other torts that may on occasion be applicable for harm caused by AI. When the harm is caused intentionally one of the economic torts may apply. Similarly, for intentional actions that violate 'good morals' (*Gute Sitten*) § 826 BGB may provide a ground for liability in German law that allows recovery of pure economic loss. The possibility of intentional harm by AI may seem far-fetched, as in such cases the AI will probably be considered only as an instrument towards realizing that intent, and the actual tortfeasor can directly be held liable as acting wrongfully. However, insofar as intent may also cover cases of gross negligence (which may depend on the jurisdiction), intentional wrongful behaviour is a relevant ground.

Most of the other torts are not relevant to AI. Specific torts generally offer protection against physical injury or property damage, or require intent in a form that precludes application for merely negligent development of AI. An exception is specific statutory regimes that might give rise to liability for breach of a statutory duty. A few specific statutory regimes are discussed in Section 10.6.3. Two torts should be mentioned briefly. First, defamation is a tort that does not require intention, and there is already case law regarding defamation by algorithms

[25] This need not consist of monitoring every single decision, but could for example be done by monitoring the general pattern of trading, the volume or financial exposure, in the hopes that a human might intuitively detect when something is amiss.

[26] The importance of such a mechanism has been underlined even in the absence of AI with several cases of millions of dollars of loss caused by a human error that could not be remedied because the system did not allow it. For example, the Citibank Revlon transfer error of 11 August 2020 (www.reuters.com/article/us-citigroup-revlon-lawsuit-idUSKBN2AG1TJ) and the 2005 J-COM trading error on the Tokyo Stock Exchange (www.jpx.co.jp/english/corporate/news-releases/0063/20150904-01.htm).

(Section 9.4.3).[27] Second, in rare circumstances, the tort of conversion might be applied, in cases where AI has in some way deprived a possessor of their right. An example could be AI deciding to block a car from starting on the grounds that it (mistakenly) believes that the owner missed a payment for the car. To be true, cases like that should usually be resolved under contractual liability, but it is possible that the tort of conversion may also apply in specific circumstances.

For systems following the German system of protected interests, the principal ground would be wrongful conduct, leading to infringement of such an interest. As this implies that the defendant was negligent and thus is blamed for not taking certain precautionary measures, the analysis in Section 9.2.2 applies here as well. In the French system with a single general norm (Article 1240 Cc), that analysis suffices, too.

Furthermore, it is conceivable that in some jurisdictions particularly egregious infringements of fundamental or constitutional rights may provide a ground for liability The European Convention on Human Rights may provide an indirect ground for signatory states. Finally, in the European Union it is possible that the principle of effectiveness may require that a right recognized in EU legislation needs to be protected with a remedy of damages.[28] These approaches are all variants of a certain protection of rights. However, they will usually still require that the infringement occurred *negligently*. Therefore, the remarks on the applicable standard of care can also be used for these grounds.

9.3 STRICT LIABILITY

Insofar as fault liability does not provide sufficient ground, the alternative is to look at strict liability. The main obstacle here is that the existing forms of strict liability rarely apply to AI. An investigation into strict liability is nonetheless useful as it may provide inspiration for how to set up liability for AI. I will therefore quickly sketch the approaches and limitations over the relevant forms of strict liability.[29]

9.3.1 *Standard Applicable to AI*

An issue that has to be resolved for all forms of strict liability is what standard is to be applied to the AI. Strict liability presumes either a tort by the person you are liable for, or a certain undesirable event that is blamed on an object (such as a defective product). That implies a standard for AI. In the literature it is frequently argued (with which I agree) that the standard must be that the AI performs at least as well as could be expected from a human, and possibly may need to perform better if the average AI becomes better than humans.[30] The dual

[27] Seema Ghatnekar Tilak, 'Injury by Algorithms' in Barfield, *Cambridge Handbook*, pp. 459–470; Stavrula Karapapa and Maurizio Borghi, 'Search Engine Liability for Autocomplete Suggestions: Personality, Privacy and the Power of the Algorithm' (2015) 23 *International Journal of Law and Information Technology* 261.

[28] See for various legal issues the ECJ Case 14/83, *Von Colson* v. *Land Nordrhein-Westfalen* [1984] ECR 1891, Case C-203/99, *Veedfald* v. *Århus Amtskommune* [2001] ECR I-3569, Case C-168/00, *Leitner* v. *TUI* [2002] ECR I-2631, Case C-295/04, *Manfredi* v. *Lloyd Adriatico Assicurazioni SpA* [2006] ECR I-6619.

[29] Comparative references and discussion in Janal, 'Extra-Contractual Liability', and Tjong Tjin Tai, 'Liability for (Semi)-Autonomous Systems', sec. 7–8.

[30] Tjong Tjin Tai, 'Liability for (Semi-)Autonomous Systems', sec. 12; Karni Chagal-Feferkorn, 'The Reasonable Algorithm' (2018) *Journal of Law, Technology & Policy* 111; and Jean-Sébastien Borghetti, 'How Can Artificial Intelligence Be Defective?' in Sebastian Lohsse, Reiner Schulze and Dirk Staudenmayer (eds.), *Liability for Artificial Intelligence and the Internet of Things* (Baden Baden: Nomos, 2019), pp. 63–76, argue that the AI should at least decide as a reasonable human. Similarly, Janal, 'Extra-Contractual Liability', p. 192, argues as a minimum for

approaches can be explained by AI's point of comparison: do we consider AI just like another product or movable good (for which the criterion is how a normal product or good should behave) or as a stand-in for a human decision-maker (for which the reasonable person is the standard)? A supporting argument for the standard of the reasonable human decision-maker is that if a decision is delegated to AI it should not lower the standard (as is also seen with non-delegable duties; Section 9.4.2). A lower standard for AI would provide an incentive for businesses to use AI instead of human beings in cases where the business will not directly suffer for wrong decisions, as that would remove liability for the incorrect decisions that the 'reasonable' AI would make. A high standard for AI does need to be complemented with defences such as force majeure or contributory negligence,[31] to keep liability within reasonable bounds.

9.3.2 *Vicarious Liability*

One obvious comparison is with vicarious liability,[32] the liability of an employer for torts committed by employees. If AI is used to make decisions within an organization, the AI performs a task that in the past would have been entrusted to a (human) employee. If the employee makes a mistake causing harm to a third party and was wrongful, the employee would be liable for committing a tort and the employer would be liable on the basis of vicarious liability. Vicarious liability is recognized in practically all jurisdictions.[33]

If we look further into the way vicarious liability is given shape, it is noteworthy that there is a tendency to link the extent of liability to the notion of control. In English law, liability may extend to persons in a relationship akin to employment, for which the control or authority over activities is an important factor.[34] In French law, the Cour de cassation has extended the liability for other persons to cases where a 'guardian' could organize, direct and control the actions of those persons.[35] This was applied to an instituted minor and to members of a sports club, although later case law has been fairly restrictive.[36]

It should be noted, however, that common law does not generally recognize liability for children and mentally disabled persons: common law systems typically require specific statutes for those forms of strict liability. Civil law systems, on the other hand, usually do recognize these forms of strict liability as well. The comparison with vicarious liability shows that there is justification for extending liability to others who autonomously decide and act, if there is some measure of control or authority over those others. That may provide a ratio for adopting strict liability for AI.

the reasonable person standard, supplemented (when AI performs better than humans) with a standard of an average AI (acknowledging that this is difficult to assess).

31 As is usually the case with strict liability. I will not discuss this later on, in order to limit the length of this text.

32 The US doctrine is called *respondeat superior*, on which (applied to AI) see Samir Chopra and Laurence F. White, *A Legal Theory for Autonomous Artificial Agents* (Ann Arbor: University of Michigan Press, 2011), pp. 128–130; Nathan Reitinger, 'Algorithmic Choice and Superior Responsibility' (2015) 51 *Gonzaga Law Review* 79.

33 For English, French and German law see Paula Giliker, *Vicarious Liability in Tort* (Cambridge: Cambridge University Press, 2010) and Cees C. van Dam, *European Tort Law* (2nd ed.; Oxford: Oxford University Press, 2013), pp. 502–516.

34 *Various Claimants* v. *Catholic Child Welfare Society* [2012] UKSC 56, at 47, and the discussion in Goudkamp and Nolan, *Winfield & Jolowicz on Tort*, paras. 21-012 through 21-014.

35 C. Cass. plén. 29 March 1991 (Blieck), D. 1991, Jur. p. 324, note Larroumet, JCP 1991, II, No. 21673, note Ghestin, and C. Cass. 2e, 22 May 1995, JCP 1995.II.22550.

36 Geneviève Viney, Patrice Jourdain and Suzanne Carval, *Traité de droit civil: Les conditions de la responsabilité* (4th ed.; Paris: LGDJ, 2013), pp. 1020–1027.

9.3.3 *Liability for Objects and Dangerous Activities*

Another ground of liability is the liability for objects and activities.[37] Many jurisdictions recognize a form of strict liability for animals and for motorized vehicles.[38] The latter category may apply directly to autonomous vehicles, and liability for animals is often suggested as a model for liability for robots.[39] Its main characteristic is that the owner or keeper of the animal is liable (for vehicles it is the owner and driver). The extent of liability is not always entirely clear: does it involve specific acts of the animal, defects of the car or does it cover any harm caused by the animal or car? Furthermore, the scope of protection may be limited to personal injury and property damage.[40] While a useful model, the actual extent seems to be limited in a way that appears to preclude extension to AI for pure economic loss. Again, this depends on the jurisdiction.

There are also jurisdictions that have a more general strict liability for tangible objects. In French law (and systems influenced by French law)[41] there is a form of liability for all tangible objects, following an extensive interpretation by the Cour de cassation of the introductory part of what nowadays is Article 1242 Cc 2016.[42] The rule is interesting as it requires demarcation of the kinds of events that lead to liability. French law operates with the notion of '*fait de la chose*', an 'act of the object'. This may include an event where the object was passive but showed a perceived deficiency, as in the case of a glass door that broke when someone accidentally tried to run through: that the door was prone to break in such an event was sufficient for liability as it showed that the door had a 'character of abnormality'.[43]

An alternative approach is to look at the liability for dangerous activities that is found in several jurisdictions. A precursor is the § 519–520 US Restatement (Second) of Torts that provides for liability for 'abnormally dangerous' activities. However, this ground is actually only applied in a few restricted categories of cases.[44] Nonetheless, many recent codifications have accepted the liability for dangerous objects and/or activities.[45] This is not the place for an extensive comparative investigation of these provisions. Suffice to say that on the one hand these provisions show an openness to recognize new forms of dangerous activities that could cover AI, but on the other hand tend to restrict application and seem to focus particularly on personal injury and property

[37] For this and the following sections see also the comparative overview of Christoph Oertel, *Objective Haftung in Europa* (Tübingen: Mohr Siebeck, 2010).

[38] A noteworthy exception is England, where the Animals Act 1971 only covers dangerous animals and a few specific instances, and negligence covers motorized vehicles.

[39] Richard Kelley, Enrique Schaerer, Micaela Gomez and Monica Nicolescu, 'Liability in Robotics: An International Perspective on Robots as Animals' (2010) 24 *Advanced Robots* 1861, Peter M. Asaro, 'A Body to Kick, But Still No Soul to Damn: Legal Perspectives on Robotics' in Patrick Lin et al. (eds.), *Robot Ethics: The Ethical and Social Implications of Robotics* (Cambridge, MA: MIT Press, 2012), pp. 169–186, p. 177, Ruth Janal, 'Die deliktische Haftung beim Einsatz von Robotern – Lehren aus der Haftung für Sachen und Gehilfen' in Sabine Gless and Kurt Seelmann (eds.), *Intelligente Agenten und das Recht* (Baden Baden: Nomos, 2016), pp. 139–162, p. 150.

[40] E.g. in German law, s. 7(1) Straßenverkehrsgesetz.

[41] For example, Article 6:173 Dutch BW, Article 1392 of the 2018 Djibouti Code civil.

[42] C. cass (Chambre réunie) 13 February 1930, DP 1930.I.57 (Jand'heur II).

[43] C. cass. (civ.) 24 February 2005, case no. 03-13536.

[44] John C. P. Goldberg and Benjamin C. Zipursky, *The Oxford Introductions to U.S. Law: Torts* (Oxford: Oxford University Press, 2010), pp. 255–263.

[45] For instance, Article 601 of the Vietnamese Bộ Luật (Civil Code 2015), Article 1757 of the Argentine Código Civil y Comercial de la Nación (2015) and Article 1065 of the Russian Civil Code; Erdem Büyüksagis and Willem H. van Boom, 'Strict Liability in Contemporary European Codification: Torn between Objects, Activities, and Their Risks' (2013) 44 *Georgetown Journal of International Law* 609.

damage. They seem to focus on extremely risky activities, such as nuclear plants or chemical plants.[46]

Although AI could theoretically be classified as a dangerous activity, the norm in the jurisdictions that recognize such a form of strict liability is usually limited. AI currently is not considered in general to be so dangerous as to deserve a blanket condemnation as dangerous activity that gives rise to strict liability. Arguably this may be different for the use of AI in social media or in algorithmic trading, having such extensive social effects that they could be considered dangerous.

9.3.4 *Product Liability by Analogy*

Another analogue may be found in product liability.[47] Again this does not apply to AI as here discussed: it generally only applies to tangible objects and electricity. Product liability operates with a useful conceptual distinction between design defects, production defects and information defects. Product liability regimes use specific rules to deal with a complicated supply chain whereby various elements in the chain may be held liable. A limitation of the comparison in this context is that product liability is mainly concerned with consumer products where the buyer is harmed by the product, and not to the typical cases discussed here of AI deployed in a business where its decisions cause harm to third parties. Furthermore, product liability is typically restricted to personal injury and property damage.

9.4 SPECIFIC REGIMES

There are three specific approaches that do not directly fit the division in fault liability and strict liability, and are relevant to the current issue.

9.4.1 *Organizational Liability*

Firstly, the liability for AI might be regulated by looking at the surrounding organization instead of the persons directly responsible for the AI. It is well known that such a duty of care for the organizational structure may achieve a protection similar to, but not limited to, vicarious liability in cases where that does not directly apply. The legal basis is usually found in fault liability, in particular some form of negligence.[48] In the case of AI this approach seems fruitful. It points to the necessity of adding sufficient preventive measures and intervention (see Section 9.2.2).[49]

9.4.2 *Non-delegable Duties*

In specific instances the law may impose so-called non-delegable duties on certain persons. If they do not fulfill their duty (regardless of whether they delegated the actual performance to an

[46] Cf. Oertel, *Objektive Haftung*. Compare *M. C. Mehta* v. *Union of India (UOI)* and Ors. 1987 SCR (1) 819, AIR 1987 965 where strict liability was established for the explosion in a chemical factory.

[47] See among many others, particularly related to robots to which product liability does apply: Gerhard Wagner, 'Robot Liability' in Lohsse et al., *Liability for Artificial Intelligence*, pp. 27–62; Bernard A. Koch, 'Product Liability 2.0 – Mere Update or New Version?' in Lohsse et al., *Liability for Artificial Intelligence*, pp. 99–116; Karni Chagal-Feferkorn, 'When Do Algorithmic Tortfeasors That Caused Damage Warrant Unique Legal Treatment?' in Barfield, *Cambridge Handbook*, pp. 471–492; David C. Vladeck, 'Machines without Principals: Liability Rules and Artificial Intelligence' (2014) 89 *Washington Law Review* 117.

[48] In Germany § 823 I BGB; see Kötz and Wagner, *Deliktsrecht*, pp. 127–129.

[49] This is also mentioned as the principle behind strict liability; see Janal, 'Extra-Contractual Liability', p. 194.

independent contractor) they are held liable as if they performed the duty themselves. In English law this doctrine has only limited application,[50] but the manner of reasoning may seem suitable for application to AI as well. Similarly, in German law there is the doctrine of negligent delegation of *Verkehrspflichten* (*sorgfaltswidriger Delegation von Verkehrspflichten*).[51] Hence in certain cases a negligent fulfilment of an obligation can be attributed to the person who delegated the obligation. Admittedly the notion of *Verkehrspflichten* does not protect against pure economic loss, but the argumentative structure may be applied to AI.

9.4.3 *Result-Oriented Liability*

In specific areas there are forms of liability for AI that bear similarity to non-delegable duties, in that the operator of AI is held liable for undesirable behaviour or results of the AI. A noteworthy example is financial trading. In an excellent analysis of the relevant German and European legislation regarding AI in high-frequency trading Gerald Spindler shows how the rules impose obligations as to the development of AI and the organizational structure in which they are deployed.[52] This includes an obligation to have effective systems and risk controls in place against certain specifically mentioned risks and in general against acting in breach of rules against market abuse. This also requires including emergency systems, to allow employees to control the algorithm on time and to provide adequate limits to the trade.[53] These rules on the one hand mandate specific measures that obviously help to limit negative consequences. On the other hand, some of the obligations point to a result that must be achieved (such as not acting contrary to rules against market abuse).

A justification for this approach is that there is little doubt about liability if someone creates a program in order to do a wrongful act. It is unacceptable that a stock trader could escape liability for price fixing by making a program do it for them. By extension it seems proper that if you use a program to do your trading, you have to ensure that it does not commit prohibited acts. To be true, this could be covered under negligence, but an easier route for regulators would be to institute a form of strict liability: that would provide a strong incentive to develop properly behaved programs. The same applies to AI, even though the developer has less control over the specific decisions of AI.

A second example is the ongoing development to regulating algorithmic supervision of content on social media. Recently there has been a strong push to force social media to take action against undesirable content. Policy makers expected results particularly from employing algorithms besides human moderators. EU regulation is moving towards increasing filter obligations, even though these are formulated rather as fault liability, referring to best efforts and diligence.[54] The proposal for a Digital Services Act[55] contains provisions that would

[50] Goudkamp and Nolan, *Winfield & Jolowicz on Tort*, paras. 21-042 through 21-050, see *Woodland* v. *Essex County Council* [2013] UKSC 66.

[51] Kötz and Wagner, *Deliktsrecht*, para. 281.

[52] Spindler, 'Control of Algorithms'.

[53] German Supervisory Authority, Rundschreiben 6/2014 of 18 December 2013. Some of those rules are also found in similar form in European rules, in particular Article 17 and 48(6) MiFID II Directive 2014/65/EU, OJ 2014 No. L 173/ 349, and Regulation 2017/589, OJ 2017 No. L 87/417.

[54] See regarding copyright filters: Article 17 Directive Copyright in the Digital Single Market 2019/790, OJ 2019 No. L 130/ 92, and the surrounding debate; Karina Grisse, 'After the Storm – Examining the Final Version of Article 17 of the New Directive (EU) 2019/790' (2019) 14 *Journal of Intellectual Property Law and Practice* 887; F. Romero Moreno, '"Upload Filters" and Human Rights: Implementing Article 17 of the Directive on Copyright in the Digital Single Market' (2020) 34 *International Review of Law, Computers & Technology* 153.

[55] 15 December 2020, COM(2020) 825 final.

empower the supervisory authorities to demand information on the development of AI used by online platforms.[56] The rules do not go as far as to impose a result-oriented form of liability for content. However, there is case law whereby search engines were held liable for defamatory search suggestions,[57] which does amount to a liability for a certain result. The difference in approaches can be explained in that algorithmic filters attempt to block content supplied by the primary tortfeasor (hence are a form of secondary liability), while in the case of search engine liability the algorithm itself is the primary agent.

A sectorial approach has definite benefits. It allows for more specific, detailed obligations that are more predictable than a general rule. It also allows the legislator to intervene specifically in areas where the deployment of AI creates huge risks, and allows specific rules to regulate the damage in a way that befits the specific conditions and risks of the sector. Thereby the objections to a general strict liability for AI become less convincing.

Having a result-oriented form of liability has two distinct advantages: it is limited to only those specific results that have to be accomplished per the legislation and therefore is less open to the objection of a boundless liability, and it makes clear to the defendant what is expected (and thereby provides stronger incentives to improve the AI's performance). Indeed, product liability can be conceived as a form of result-oriented liability as it only pertains to products that have to be safe for persons and property.

9.5 JUSTIFYING LIABILITY

Although there is a growing body of literature pleading for some form of liability for AI, as a matter of positive law there are very few grounds for holding someone liable, mostly in civil law systems in the French tradition. Furthermore, there are a few specific statutory regimes where an operator of AI may be held liable when the AI does not meet certain objective standards: a result-oriented form of liability. Given this state of affairs one may wonder why the status quo should be changed at all.[58]

Indeed, there are several reasons why an unrestricted liability for AI decision-making seems unadvisable. For one, AI is developed in a complex chain where software and training models are built on top of each other, where developers benefit from each other's efforts. Liability for AI would, if not carefully limited in some way, end up as a form of strict liability for software that would stifle the development of software, in particular open-source software that is developed and made available for free.[59] In contrast to product liability, it is harder to say whether a certain piece of software is really defective, as it depends on what the software is intended for and the context in which it was developed. A tangible component of a car can be tested on its own to certain circumstances (such as normal temperature range on earth), while the intangible contexts of operation of a piece of Python code are boundless. The supply chain model of product liability appears therefore to be unsuitable to liability for AI and software in general.

[56] See Articles 54 and 57.

[57] Karapapa and Borghi, 'Search Engine Liability'; Tilak, 'Injury by Algorithms'; Janal, 'Extra-Contractual Liability', p. 203.

[58] Tjong Tjin Tai, 'Liability for (Semi-)Autonomous Systems', sec. 11 and 12. For general discussions on justifying strict liability see van Dam, *European Tort Law*, pp. 297–300, Oertel, *Objektive Haftung*, pp. 282–296.

[59] T. F. E. Tjong Tjin Tai, 'Duties of Care and Diligence and Cybercrime', research report Tilburg University, 2015, https://research.tilburguniversity.edu/files/5733322/Tjong_Tjin_Tai_cs_Duties_of_Care_and_Cybercrime_2015.pdf, pp. 84–87 and 167–169 on pros and cons of liability for software, also Michael L. Rustad and Thomas H. Koenig, 'The Tort of Negligent Enablement of Cybercrime' (2005) 20 *Berkeley Technology Law Journal* 1553; Michael D. Scott, 'Tort Liability for Vendors of Insecure Software: Has the Time Finally Come?' (2008) 67 *Maryland Law Review* 425.

Strict liability for AI may also stifle efforts to improve AI within bona fide organizations. Indeed, academic research may likewise be afflicted, as many of the current wave of AI applications find their roots in concepts and tools developed first in academia. If the developer of a specific kind of neural network may be held liable for all applications of that topology, they would surely be advised by their employer to keep their research secret or at least to not make the code available.

There is also an issue from the point of view of the system of tort law. Even for tangible objects there is in many jurisdictions no general form of strict liability. The focus is mainly on particularly dangerous objects and activities, per the US approach, mirrored in other jurisdictions, and/or for explicitly enumerated and identified dangerous objects such as animals and motorized vehicles. It would create an imbalance if strict liability for the even more contested area of intangible objects was to be adopted overall, while liability for tangible objects remained limited to specific categories. Only for specific new activities such as nuclear plants and airplanes have specific statutes or rules been established. Even then the liability was often limited, either in amount or in the kind of damage, whereby pure economic loss was often left out.[60] This does not support an extension to AI. At best it would support a similar piecemeal, sector-based and limited approach.

If we look, however, to the other side, there is a pressing need for some form of liability for AI decision-making. First of all, the extent of deployment of AI is growing at an ever-increasing pace, and its ramifications are felt everywhere. In the absence of any form of third-party accountability there is no incentive for organizations to improve the operation of AI. Indeed, there may be an incentive to accelerate the replacement of human decision-making to AI: an organization is vicariously liable for decisions by its employees, but not if these same decisions are made by AI, even if the AI is worse at these decisions than humans are. Hence there is a perverse incentive in liability law. In economic parlance: the use of AI creates externalities that should be internalized again by means of liability, in order for businesses to have the proper incentives to improve AI. It is well established that strict liability may provide a positive incentive to remove externalities and to improve the operation and safety of certain risk factors in business. Liability for animals, dangerous activities and the like is justified partly from that perspective. A supporting ratio is the consideration that businesses in principle profit from the employment of humans and objects and should therefore also bear the costs of the harm caused by those same resources. An added argument is that the operator of AI deliberately chose to employ the AI, bringing this risk into the world. The social impact of wide-scale deployment of AI is such that it can no longer be ignored by liability law.

9.6 HOW TO SET UP LIABILITY FOR AI

At this point we can conclude that there are strong arguments for imposing at least a limited form of liability for AI decision-making. The proposed regime, however, is not a simple strict liability but rather a combination of several approaches that support and strengthen each other. Incidentally, there are also other useful measures outside of liability.[61]

60 See the extensive discussion in Oertel, *Objektive Haftung*, and treaties such as the Paris Convention on Third Party Liability in the Field of Nuclear Energy (1960) and the Convention on damage caused by foreign aircraft to third parties on the surface (1952).

61 Mario Martini, 'Regulating Algorithms: How to Demystify the Alchemy of Code?' in Ebers and Navas, *Algorithms and Law*, pp. 100–135; Tjong Tjin Tai, 'Liability for (Semi-)Autonomous Systems', sec. 11.

First of all, a sectorial approach is preferable.[62] AI is too diverse, and its consequences are too diverse as well, to warrant a single approach. One might argue for a limited form of liability for AI overall, but the specific details and expectations will need to be adapted for areas where the consequences of malfunctioning AI are more serious than in mundane cases. A case in point is the regulation for algorithmic trading.

Secondly, it seems advisable to focus on the operator of the AI, the person who deploys AI. They can control the entire environment in which AI functions, and as we have seen, it is primarily in that environment that security measures and controls can be set up. The operator should in theory contract with the developer to arrange for appropriate measures during the development phase. To strengthen the position of the operator, a restricted form of AI product liability could be drafted whereby AI that was knowingly created for a specific purpose with a risk of major harm would be subject to a regime of liability where the developer could be held liable. The developer would be required to be more careful in development, training and selection of data, testing of the AI and restricted in the kind of contractual limitation clauses allowed towards the operator. Furthermore, the victim might be allowed a direct claim on the developer in such cases.

Thirdly, for the specific organization of liability a general form of strict liability seems too broad. However, for areas where there is a particularly pressing need for liability (due to the amount of harm and the need for incentives) a specific result-oriented liability or strict liability regime may be imposed. One should realize, however, that the difference with fault liability is not as large as it may appear. Fault liability can also be used with a presumption of fault, whereby the wrongful decision presumes a lack of care by the operator that can be rebutted by pointing out complete compliance with all the detailed precautionary measures and furthermore a sufficiently convincing explanation of how the decision occurred without any lack of care on the part of the operator. An even more restricted form would simply be that the wrongful decision suggests a presumption of negligence that can be rebutted, but that is already the state of the law in fault liability and does not require any change. In any case, negligence will be needed as a general fallback option. For the detailed kind of care (including precautionary measures) that may be expected, I refer to the discussion in Section 9.2.2. Such obligations could be spelled out in specific statutes, but even in the absence of a detailed written rule, the courts could assume such obligations as part of unwritten law, best practices or custom. If such an obligation were to be violated that would give reason to presume a causal connection between the negligent act and the wrongful decision.

In the fourth place, a change that has to be made is a broadening of the kinds of harm that are compensated. It is imperative that pure economic loss can also be recovered, otherwise any form of liability is toothless.[63] To assuage the fear of boundless liability, the aforementioned sectorial approach could be used to limit liability to particularly sensitive sectors. Furthermore, it is conceivable that specific legislation is drawn up to limit the amount of damages that can be awarded, following the example or regulation in other areas of new technology (airplanes, nuclear plants or space). There is reason to allow recovery for pure economic loss in the specific case of AI decision-making, as that has become so important. One might consider an approach similar to how English law has accepted an exceptional form of negligence in *Hedley Byrne*: one

[62] Ebers, 'Regulating AI', p. 93.

[63] The proposal of the European Parliament for regulating liability for AI is restricted in this respect, requiring serious immaterial harm as a precondition for compensating economic loss (art. 3(i) Proposal as annex to the Report with recommendations to the Commission on a civil liability regime for artificial intelligence, 2020/2014(INL)). In several other respects the proposal is similar to the approach advocated here.

could conceive of a kind of negligent deployment of AI decision-making, conditional on the presence of a special relationship between operator and victim that would warrant additional protection to the victim.

The above suggestions could also be used as an example of how contractual liability could be arranged. Insofar as pure economic loss may be compensated on the basis of breach of contract, the suggestions show how risk may be distributed (which excuses are to be accepted; when non-performance may be attributed). Alternatively, it could give inspiration to contract lawyers as to the kind of warranties and security measures they would want to put in a contract or service-level agreement.

10

AI and Data Protection

Indra Spiecker and Genannt Döhmann

10.1 INTRODUCTION

The regulatory framework of artificial intelligence (AI) can derive from a variety of regulatory needs and it can use a variety of tools. It may focus on the specific purposes for which AI is used, such as in diagnosis of cancer, in the calculation of a score to assess creditworthiness or in the personalization in online marketing. It may concentrate on the methods of learning employed, such as whether it is using a theory of mind approach. It may regulate the design of AI by requiring transparency. It may address certain consequences of the use of AI, such as the liability in a shared AI–human interaction. The choices for regulatory impact are manifold, as this book illustrates.

This chapter concentrates on regulation affecting prerequisites of AI on the one hand – that is the regulation of data used to train, develop, improve and control AI – and the use of AI in regard to certain data on the other hand. In short, this chapter deals with the regulatory aspects deriving from data protection and privacy regulation. This aspect is still much unknown and little researched.[1] The chapter will look at the implications of AI on data protection and vice versa on the basis of the presently most comprehensive regulatory approach in data protection law, the EU General Data Protection Regulation (GDPR).[2] The EU has recently presented an AI regulation bill by which it intends to regulate the use of AI in some decision situations.[3] Part of these regulatory efforts would also be a certain limitation of data use, such as standards of quality, objectivity or correctness of the data used to train AI. Some of these standards can also be found within the GDPR, in particular derived from the rights of the data subject. Therefore, a future EU AI regulation may have certain overlaps with the GDPR. Nevertheless, many of the (personal) data-relevant aspects are not addressed within the AI regulation so that the GDPR provisions will remain applicable and remain a guiding regulatory tool.

The chapter first develops why the data protection law, the GDPR, has any impact on AI at all (Section 10.2). It then gives an overview of selected data protection principles and provisions that have to be adhered to in the particular context of AI (Section 10.3). This section – due to the

[1] The commentary of C. Kuner, L. Bygrave and C. Docksey (eds.), *The EU General Data Protection Regulation* (Oxford University Press, 2018) offers three (!) listings in the index, the commentary of S. Simitis, G. Hornung and I. Spiecker genannt Döhmann (eds.), *Datenschutzrecht DSGVO mit BDSG* (Baden-Baden: Nomos Verlagsgesellschaft, 2019) offers at least seven and distinguishes more than one aspect.

[2] J. Albrecht in Simitis et al., *Datenschutzrecht*, mn. 205.

[3] Proposal for a Regulation Laying Down Harmonised Rules on Artificial Intelligence (Intelligence Act), SEC(2021) 167 final – SWD(2021) 84 final – SWD(2021) 85 final.

limitations of this chapter – concentrates on the principle of purpose limitation and the principle of lawfulness of data processing. In it, the chapter describes several problematic areas, among them risk assessment, the prohibition of automated decision-making and the application of data subjects' rights (arts. 11–20 GDPR). The conclusion and outlook show where data protection should draw the attention of AI developers and users (Section 10.4).

10.2 AI AND CORE ELEMENTS OF DATA PROTECTION LAW

Data protection law is in its origin and core a technology law: it aims at regulating potential risks arising out of the use of an emerging technology where the consequences and dangers of this technology are not yet fully known. This purpose is connected to the term of 'data processing' that art. 4(2) GDPR defines as 'any operation or set of operations which is performed on personal data or sets of personal data'. The provision further gives examples of typical data processing, that is, 'collection, recording, organization, structuring, storage, adaptation or alteration, retrieval, consultation, use, disclosure by transmission, dissemination or otherwise making available, alignment or combination, restriction, erasure or destruction'. This list clarifies, in reaction to the somewhat disputed interpretation of a similar provision in the predecessor of the GDPR, the EU Data Protection Directive.[4]

Although the first computers were designed in the middle of the previous century, the development of automated data processing has not reached a point where an assessment of its potential, its risks and chances can be performed easily. This is due to the tremendous growth of digitalization that has led to a large variety of services and products that have been built upon it. AI is one of the latest developments in computer science. It is expected to revolutionize the use of algorithmic systems.[5] Considering these further advances of information technology, data protection law still adheres to the principle of precaution as a technology law with preventive measures, although the GDPR also includes some instruments closer to a risk-based-approach.[6]

10.2.1 Use of Data Protection Law in Development and Use of AI

The GDPR as the leading data protection regulatory regime does not explicitly address AI as a specific way of data processing. No special AI provisions exist within data protection law if art. 22 GDPR is left aside. However, AI is based on personal data, and it is used for the processing of personal data. Data protection law applies typically when personal data is processed – art. 2(1) and art. 4(1) GDPR. Thus, AI only falls under any data protection regulatory regime in such cases. In order to assess this, one needs to understand the functioning of AI in general.

Dynamic AI systems typically include two stages, the training and then the development stage. Both stages are closely linked to (personal) data. Within the first stage of AI, training data is used in order to make the algorithmic system function generally. In simpler models, the development stage consists of a repeated training stage. More refined systems continuously alter existing systems according to the underlying values and structures. This in particular is useful when an

[4] Directive 95/46/EC on the protection of individuals with regard to the processing of personal data and on the free movement of such data.

[5] E. Alpaydin, *Machine Learning: The New AI* (Boston: MIT Press, 2016), p. xii, preface.

[6] I. Spiecker genannt Döhmann, 'Data Protection: The More the Merrier – A Dynamic Approach Learning from Prior Mis-governance' in A. Peukert (ed.), *Global Digitality* (London: Hart, in press); I. Spiecker genannt Döhmann and G. Hornung in Simitis et al., *Datenschutzrecht*, mn. 242, art. 35 mn. 20; B. Buchner 'Rechtmäßigkeit der Datenverarbeitung unter der DS-GVO' (2016) 3 *Datenschutz und Datensicherheit (DuD)* 155, at 157.

adaption of the model is taking place, especially if fast-changing environmental factors, dependencies and trends have to be integrated. When in use, AI according to its programming continuously makes use of the data acquired in the course of its task and potentially also other available data in order to adjust the decision-making process continuously. It evaluates and processes it according to the normative standards laid down. So, data protection law has to be adhered to continuously, if personal data is involved. This will be very likely the case, considering the fact that a set of data including any small amount of personal data will trigger the application of the GDPR for all of the data if not separated from the rest.[7]

However, application of the GDPR extends beyond the well-established control of (personal) data. This is often not well acknowledged. Data protection law has always aimed at reducing risks from information power asymmetry as such.[8] It is thus not only interested in the data itself as its regulatory impact but also in the decisions arising out of the use of it. The use of the data for particular purposes or the assessment of the consequences of the processing of data are typical testing grounds within data protection law. Art. 22 GDPR, which this chapter will only briefly discuss, is the most obvious illustration of this overall goal of data protection law to protect beyond the immediate control rights. According to the provision, fully automated decision-making, typically for AI applications, falls under a right to objection by the data subject exposed to this decision. Also, many other provisions within the GDPR also directly apply to the use of AI. The focus of this chapter will be on these more general principles, but also some specific provisions will be discussed.

10.2.2 *Principles within the GDPR and Their Functionality*

AI and its implications are not yet fully understood. Its unrestricted use is thus in general questionable.[9] Even if a future EU AI regulation addressed certain aspects of AI use, the data processing aspects remain within the regulatory framework of the GDPR. The AI regulation is not meant to exclude applicability of the GDPR.[10] Thus, any AI development and use has to adhere to the principles laid down within the GDPR. Only the most relevant ones for AI will be analysed here.

The GDPR names a number of principles that protect informational self-determination and prevent exploitation of informational power asymmetries, in particular in art. 5(1) GDPR such as lawfulness, transparency and fairness of data processing (art. 5(1)(a) GDPR), data minimization (art. 5(1)(c) GDPR), purpose limitation (art. 5(1)(b) GDPR), accuracy (art. 5(1)(d) GDPR, storage limitation (art. 5(1)(e) GDPR), integrity and confidentiality (art. 5(1)(f) GDPR) or accountability (art. 5(2) GDPR). These (and the other) principles govern the interpretation of more specific provisions. However, they also include abstract rules for any data processing. Thus, any data processing not only has to take into account specific provisions in regard to procedure and content of data processing but also test whether the abstract principles are fulfilled.

[7] See Case C-131/12 *Google Spain SL* v. *AEPD* and Mario Costeja González [2014] EU:C:2014:317.

[8] Spiecker gen. Döhmann, 'Data Protection'; I. Spiecker genannt Döhmann and G. Hornung in Simitis et al., *Datenschutzrecht*, mn. 25; M. Rost, 'Künstliche Intelligenz Normative und operative Anforderungen des Datenschutzes' (2018) 9 *DuD* 558, at 560; A. Freiherr von dem Bussche, 'The Right to Erasure in the EU Data Protection Law' (2020) 6 *EDPL* 473, at 474.

[9] See T. Hoeren and M. Niehoff, 'KI und Datenschutz – Begründungserfordernisse automatisierter Entscheidung' (2018) 1 *Rechtswissenschaft* 47, at 58; C. Conrad, 'Kann die Künstliche Intelligenz den Menschen entschlüsseln? – Neue Forderungen zum Datenschutz' (2018) 9 *DuD* 541, at 545.

[10] A. Ebert and I. Spiecker genannt Döhmann, 'Die EU als Trendsetter weltweiter KI-Regulierung: Der Kommissionsentwurf für eine KI-Verordnung der EU' (2021) 40 *NVwZ* 1188.

Naturally, this testing is of high legal uncertainty and needs further clarification, especially through the courts. In any case, any interpretation of specifications of the general principles has to take into account the meaning of the principles as such,[11] in particular since they are often founded in EU constitutional law such as, but not limited to, the EU Charter of Human Rights. Thus, they are an important interpretative guideline for specific provisions.

10.3 PRINCIPLE OF PURPOSE LIMITATION AND LAWFULNESS

10.3.1 *Data Processing for Training, Learning and Controlling Purposes*

One of the most relevant – potentially also most relevant – element of EU data protection law for AI use consists of the purpose limitation as stated in art. 5(1)(b) GDPR. It is very closely connected to the principle of lawfulness of data processing, art. 5(1)(a) and art. 6(1) GDPR that will be covered subsequently.

The principle of purpose limitation and purpose precision, art. 5(1)(b) GDPR has in essence two meanings. First, the purpose limitation binds the data controller to a purpose – the original purpose for which the data was first processed under their control. This allows self-control and self-governance. At the same time, this also allows legal certainty, as any processing for the original purpose is still covered by the original legitimation of art. 6(1) GDPR. It also restricts the use of data: it is not legal under the GDPR to process data without a purpose and outside of the purposes for which the data was processed first. Second, the purpose limitation limits for which goals the data may be processed and thus shapes the essence for any balancing of interests. Thus, the precise formulation of the goal is a core factor in determining the legality and legitimacy of personal data processing.

This creates difficulties for many uses of AI. At present, AI is typically developed for particular purposes, such as the detection of obstacles on roads, the recognition of faces or the differentiation between criminalized and highly sanctioned child pornography and legal adult pornography.[12] However, to train these algorithmic systems large amounts of data are needed. Sometimes, relevant data from the immediate surrounding of the AI can be employed, but often, data are needed for unspecific purposes. In fact, the cost of developing AI for multiple purposes, such as 'standard AI', can lead to broad sets of data being used and this being desirable[13] from a particular, but not limited to, economic efficiency perspective.[14]

The development of one AI often makes use of prior AI experiences in different settings. Additionally, further data sets are often needed from individual transactions for continuous learning and development and in order to control – if at all possible – the concise AI according to the developers' standards and values. This data may indeed be collected especially for the

[11] A. Roßnagel, 'Grundsätze für die Verarbeitung personenbezogener Daten' in Simitis et al., *Datenschutzrecht*, art. 5 mn. 15.

[12] See the project of a German special enforcement unit on child pornography with a research unit at a German university: Elke Witmer-Goßner, 'Automatisierte Erkennung von Missbrauchsdarstellungen Künstliche Intelligenz gegen Kinderpornographie', *big-data insider* (8 June 2021), www.bigdata-insider.de/kuenstliche-intelligenz-gegen-kinderpornografie-a-1029007/ (accessed 24 June 2021).

[13] V. Mayer-Schönberger and Y. Padova, 'Regime Change? Enabling Big Data through Europe's New Data Protection Regulation' (2016) 17 *The Columbia Science and Technology Law Review* 315, at 317.

[14] Notwithstanding the following, it is possible to construe AI systems in a way that the principle of purpose limitation is adhered; see. e.g., M. Finck and A. Biega, 'Reviving Purpose Limitation and Data Minimisation in Personalisation, Profiling and Decision-Making Systems' (2021), Max Planck Institute for Innovation and Competition Research Paper No. 21-04.

purposes of this training and controlling/developing. More realistic – and maybe even more desirable in the perspective of (economic) effectiveness and awareness of resources – is, however, that this data derives from other sources and should be used for the original purpose, but in addition or after fulfilment of the original purpose also for AI purposes. This chapter will not consider further that the prior data processing includes certain prior decisions that are then reflected in the data and may influence the normativity of the AI system.

This raises the question of whether it is possible to process data for multiple purposes, for consecutive and also for eventual purposes, for example further use for AI training purposes or – later – for assessment of the quality of the AI system. The answer is as follows: in general, the GDPR is open to multiple purposes and also to consecutive purposes. Art. 5(1)(b) GDPR speaks in the plural of 'purposes' itself. There is no reason why data processing should be limited to one purpose only. It would not be serving the purpose of data limitation in art. 5(1)(c) GDPR if a controller were required to request data separately for two different purposes rather than requesting it once for two (or more) purposes. The existence of more and also of consecutive purposes can also be derived from art. 6(4) GDPR as will be explained in Section 10.3.4.3 in more detail. Therefore, a multiple purpose or an additional purpose does not counteract AI-related data processing.

Use of data for a later purpose, however, is a different matter. If data has served the purpose for which it was processed the controller is required to erase the data. This derives from the specific norm of art. 17 GDPR, but can also be concluded from the general principle of data minimization of art. 5(1)(c) GDPR. According to this provision, data processing is limited to the necessary data processing. This means that data processing after the end result has been gained would be a violation of this provision. This derives from the fact that storage is considered to be data processing – art. 4(2) GDPR. Storage would be unnecessary once the goal has been served. Once the purpose expires, so does the lawfulness of data processing. Art. 17 GDPR's right to erasure provides a right of the data subject but has no normative meaning of its own as the duty to erase information that has been consumed and has therefore become unnecessary can already be deduced from art. 5(1)(c) GDPR.[15] For AI purposes this means that a legal alteration of the purposes can only take place as long as the data is available for the original purposes; otherwise the controller would violate the requirements of the GDPR.

The effect of this restriction reaches further than can be seen at first sight. The consequence is that any storing for eventualities or for potential further use is illegal. Storing personal data just because the use of it for training, controlling or development purposes for AI might at a time in the future be practical, is not covered by the GDPR and thus must be refrained from. On the other hand, it should be understood also that the GDPR does not restrict further use for AI purposes as such – if the new purpose is able to fulfil the requirements of the GDPR by itself.

It should be noted, also, that the principle of purpose limitation does not only provide for a binding to any purpose but also restricts the purpose itself. Precision of the purpose is required.[16] The purpose must be defined in a manner that actually restricts and guides data processing.[17] This limitation and precision of the purpose is also necessary as the purpose governs the data processing of the controller.[18] Thus, a general clause describing AI-related further purpose in general in this manner would be insufficient. Rather, there needs to be a specification that has

[15] See A. Dix, 'Recht auf Löschen ("Recht auf Vergessenwerden")' in Simitis et al., *Datenschutzrecht*, art. 17 mn. 1; Roßnagel, 'Grundsätze für die Verarbeitung personenbezogener Daten', art. 5 mn. 130.

[16] Roßnagel, 'Grundsätze für die Verarbeitung personenbezogener Daten', art. 5 mn. 76.

[17] Ibid., art. 5 mn. 72, 76 et seq. and 88.

[18] Ibid., art. 5 mn. 92; T. Cabral, 'Forgetful AI: AI and the Right to Erasure under the GDPR' (2020) 6 *EDPL* 378, at 382.

the power to bind further use of the data. This makes a general description of 'AI-related purposes' unattractive; at the same time, it prevents unrestricted multiple uses of existing data.

To conclude the connection between AI and the principle of purpose limitation as set in art. 5 (1)(b) GDPR it should be noted that additional use of data processed for different reasons quickly reaches the borders of this principle: although multiple and later purposes are possible, they need to be circumscribed precisely, and this often counteracts the design of AI. Of course, it is possible to develop AI systems adhering to the principle of purpose limitation, but the business model behind it often contradicts this.[19]

10.3.2 *Enlargement of the Principle of Limitation by Compatible Purposes*

Under art. 5(1)(b) GDPR, the principle of purpose greatly limits secondary uses as uses aimed at training, learning and controlling of AI unless the legal ground under art. 6(1) GDPR includes these specific AI purposes. Purpose and lawfulness of data processing are intertwined: the purpose binds the lawfulness, and the lawfulness depends on the individual purpose. The lawfulness will, however, only rarely include the use of data for AI purposes. This interaction between lawfulness and purpose can be identified prominently in art. 5(1)(b) and art. 6(4) GDPR in which the provision allows not only data processing for 'the' purpose(s), but also for so-called compatible purposes.

These compatible purposes are a new category that the GDPR has introduced. Compatible purposes are treated as the original purpose; they participate in the lawfulness of the data processing of the original purpose.[20] Obviously, these compatible purposes are multiple purposes in addition to the original purpose, which constitutes another argument why multiple purposes are possible under the GDPR as illustrated in Section 10.3.1.

Art. 6(4) GDPR states a number of conditions, together with recital 50, the arguments of which have to be weighted in order to construe a compatible purpose. As there is no clear-cut rule formulated, the provision needs extensive interpretation and creates considerable legal uncertainty. Further use of data for AI purposes is affected by this uncertainty. The provision names as relevant factors for example the context in which the data processing occurs, the connection between the original and the potentially compatible purpose and the possible consequences or additional safeguards. In essence, the closer the relationship between the additional purpose and the original purpose is and the more restrictions apply to the new data processing, the more likely it is that the new purpose will be compatible. Also, it has to be taken into account whether the new data processing is in the interest of the data subject. This has to be judged from the perspective of the data subject.[21]

For AI purposes compatibility can be construed in some instances but not in general and certainly not as a typical way of legitimizing training, controlling and developing with data from a previous contact. In an ongoing relationship where AI is used for purposes of the data subject, one might consider that the function of control as well as development can be considered to be compatible purposes. One might, however, also see additional risks for the data subject if the AI becomes more functional and thus stretches the existing informational power asymmetry.

Nevertheless, if the relationship between the data subject and the controller was of a single contact it will be difficult to argue that there is some interest of the data subject in having their

[19] See Finck and Biega, 'Reviving Purpose Limitation'.
[20] A. Roßnagel, 'Art. 6' in Simitis et al., *Datenschutzrecht*, art. 6(4) mn. 10 et seq.
[21] Ibid., art. 6(4) mn. 34 et seq.

data processed because the fruits of such processing would exclusively remain with the controller. Most likely a compatible purpose can be assumed if the use of the data directly influences the decision on the data subject herself. This will rarely be the case as typically the output control requires a decision in the past.

Regarding the other propositions described in art. 6(4) GDPR, an alternative might be in cases where the data use is close to the original data use although there is no connection with the data subject to increase security and privacy measures and reduce consequences from AI and data use. After all, art. 6(4) GDPR lists safeguards as one aspect of how to assess a compatible purpose. This provision calls for great flexibility and innovation in designing AI in order to increase safeguards beyond the standards. It should be noted, however, that a risks/advantages debate is going on, considering the threats for individual liberties and freedoms, but also for the democratic society, raised by AI and by the use of data. Although this discussion has not come to an end and painting all uses of AI with a broad brush should be avoided, it nevertheless has become clear that free and unrestricted access to and use of AI creates considerable risks and dangers. For this reason, the EU has started the legislative process for an AI regulation. Therefore, wide use of personal data protected under the GDPR for AI purposes is very unlikely to be in accordance with the principles and goals of the GDPR to protect the freedoms and liberties in general as stated in art. 1 GDPR. It can be said that a view to the consequences of the use of data for AI purposes will only result in restrictions, not enlargements of data.[22]

Therefore, a general use of data for AI purposes as a 'compatible purpose' according to art. 5(1)(b) and art. 6(4) GDPR cannot be assumed. Rather, legitimatizing further use of data might require an individualized assessment of single cases, especially when there is a close connection to the data subject's data and decisions.

10.3.3 *Compatible Purpose of Research and Statistical Purpose*

Potentially, art. 5(1)(b) GDPR with its legal definition of research and statistical purposes as compatible purposes may solve the problem. Without explicitly also referring to art. 6(4) GDPR, the provision claims that research and statistical purposes are compatible purposes. As art. 6(4) GDPR still applies,[23] the data processing for these purposes typically, but not always, is considered to be compatible. The reason behind this exemption is the assessment that the interest in the individual person is typically small and therefore the dangers and risks are restricted.[24]

It is unclear what constitutes either research purpose or statistical purpose. As these exemptions to the rule have to be interpreted narrowly,[25] they cannot apply to any type of research or to any statistical procedure with a certain degree of abstractness. It suggests restricting the exemptions to concise research and statistical purposes, with an underlying objective of the common good. For the purposes of this chapter, the differentiation shall not be extended further.

This provision should, however, not be overly widely interpreted as additional safeguards are requested according to art. 89 GDPR. Thus, AI may not simply be based on art. 5(1)(b) compatible purposes but needs to create additional organizational and technical measures to reduce the risk for data subjects. In present AI development, this is rarely the case.

[22] See Ph. Scholz, 'Art. 6 Rechtmäßigkeit der Verarbeitung' in Simitis et al., *Datenschutzrecht*, art. 6(1)(b) GDPR mn. 58.

[23] See Roßnagel, 'Grundsätze für die Verarbeitung personenbezogener Daten', art. 5 mn. 109.

[24] P. Schantz, 'Art. 6 Rechtmäßigkeit der Verarbeitung' in Simitis et al., *Datenschutzrecht*, art. 6 mn. 104.

[25] Ibid., art. 6 mn. 103.

10.3.4 *Principle of Lawfulness of Data Processing*

10.3.4.1 *General Principle of Lawfulness of Data Processing*

Having understood that the GDPR distinguishes between data explicitly processed for purposes of AI and data processed for different purposes and then in addition used for AI purposes, this differentiation also holds true for the principle of lawfulness of data processing. According to art. 6(1) GDPR, any data processing needs a justification. Data processing 'just because' is not lawful. Although the GDPR does not provide for an ex-ante authorization of data processing, art. 24(1) GDPR with its duty to demonstrate nevertheless requires any data controller prior to undergoing data processing to test whether there exist legitimate grounds for the data processing and to document this.

10.3.4.2 *Lawfulness in the Course of Contractual Relations*

The typical legitimation for private use of data – if not consent according to art. 6(1)(a), art. 4(11) and art. 7 GDPR that will be dealt with in Section 10.3.4.4 – would derive from art. 6(1)(b) GDPR or art. 6(1)(f) GDPR. Under art. 6(1)(b) GDPR, data processing necessary for the fulfilment of contractual obligations is considered lawful. However, unless a person closes a contract to provide data to an AI company, the use of data from this contract for AI training purposes will hardly ever be covered by this provision.

One could consider that if AI is used for fulfilling contractual obligations, then art. 6(1)(b) might also cover any further use of the data processed in the course of the contract. However, the provision explicitly states that the data processing has to be necessary for fulfilling the contractual obligation. This obligation, once fulfilled, cannot serve as a lawful ground for further processing afterwards. Also, the wording of 'necessary' clarifies that the data processing and the contract have to be in a close, if not exclusive relationship.[26] Learning and controlling of the information technology employed does not fall under this provision and cannot be argued to be 'necessary' as this would make the intended restriction worthless.

10.3.4.3 *Lawfulness by Balancing of Interests*

A more promising provision to establish lawfulness of data use for AI purposes is art. 6(1)(f) GDPR. The provision allows data processing if it occurs after performance of a balancing test after which the data processing does not violate the interests of the data subject. Here, again, the principle of purpose's two core contents argue against the wide use of data for AI training data purposes. The test under art. 6(1)(f) DPR balances the interests for the original use of the personal data, not the later AI training set.

However, the general possibility to combine data purposes does not relieve the data controller from the duty to be able to test (and also to demonstrate; art. 24(1) GDPR) that the individual data processing is in accordance with the purpose. Thus, a lawfulness under art. 6(1)(b) – the necessary for contractual obligations clause – does not enable further use of the data for AI training (or controlling) purposes. Rather, for this purpose, an individual legitimization is necessary, and that would in most circumstances have to be art. 6(1)(f) GDPR.

This leads to the second part of purpose limitation closely related to the principle of lawfulness, art. 5(1)(a) and art. 6(1) GDPR: a change of purpose in the course of data processing is only possible if the new purpose justifies (and thus legitimizes) the altered use of data for purposes of

[26] The difference of opinion shall not be further explored for the purposes of this paper; for the arguments see Schantz, 'Art. 6 Rechtmäßigkeit der Verarbeitung', art. 6(1)(b) GDPR mn. 32 et seq.

AI now. The GDPR does not prevent multiple purposes, and it does not prevent consecutive purposes. Considering art. 6(1)(f) GDPR, however, the burden is high: the use of personal data for the different purpose of AI has to be of equal legal weight as the legal interests of the data subject.

Importantly, this balancing of interests does also include third-party rights: on both the side of the controller and the side of the data subject, third parties have to be considered. The text of the provision makes that very clear in its wording for the data controller; despite the lack of words in this regard, it is also true for the data subject. This can be derived from art. 1 GDPR directly where it is made clear that the interests of individuals as a whole have to be considered as the GDPR aims at balancing interests in multipolar relations.[27]

This, however, leads to an enlargement of positions on both sides of the balancing tests. On the side of AI potential users of data, their personal and business interest in developing AI-based products and services and producing AI-supported or AI-based decisions constitute a legal interest. On the side of the data subject, the general effect of such decisions on freedoms and liberties not only of the individual, but all citizens, has to be taken into account. That is so because data protection fulfils additional functions beyond the individual's rights and interests, including as the foundation for other human rights, legal positions and democratic effectiveness.[28] In the end, a balancing of interest under art. 6(1)(f) GDPR seems only attractive if for defined purposes.

10.3.4.4 *Lawfulness by Consent*

Most promising would be consent. Consent is the most prominent instrument to create lawfulness as clarifies the position in art. 6(1)(a) GDPR, but also the general understanding of the GDPR not to patronize but to enable informed decisions. Therefore, art. 4(11) and art. 7 GDPR that specify conditions for valid consent stress that there is a close connection to the purpose and to prior information:[29] the data subject may consent to almost any type of data processing but they may do so only prior to the data processing and only after sufficient and precise information about the specific setting including the purposes of the data processing. This concept of 'informed consent'[30] thus guarantees that the data subject does not lose control over their data but can decide on a rational and sustainable basis.

This demonstrates that consent also needs to fulfil requirements derived from the general principles of the GDPR. The most important restriction to pay attention to would also be the integrated purpose limitation: consent can only be given for specific purposes and not for general purposes such as 'research' or 'AI'. Therefore, the arguments within the purpose limitations also apply to the provisions in regard to consent that deal with purpose and information about the future data processing.

10.3.4.5 *Intermediate Conclusion and Response to GDPR Restrictions: Anonymity and Artificial Data*

A broad and undifferentiated use of data for purposes of AI training, control and development is almost impossible to achieve under the GDPR as neither the principle of purpose limitation according to art. 5(1)(b) GDPR nor the legal grounds for compliant purposes in art. 5(5)(b) and

[27] See G. Hornung and I. Spiecker genannt Döhmann, 'Art. 1 Gegenstand und Ziele' in Simitis et al., *Datenschutzrecht*, art. 1 mn 25 et seq.

[28] Ibid., art. 1 mn 29.

[29] See J. Klement, 'Art. 7 Bedingungen für die Einwilligung' in Simitis et al., *Datenschutzrecht*, art. 7 mn 72.

[30] Ibid., art. 7 mn 72 et seq.

art. 6(4) GDPR are typically fulfilled. The broad and undetermined purposes of the AI restrict this.

However, the GDPR is applicable only for personal data that can be attributed to an individual. Thus, a way to use large data sets for the purposes of AI can be to avoid personal data and rely on data that does not fulfil the requirements of art. 4(1) GDPR. This can be reached by anonymization of personal data, thus dissolving the relationship between the content and the person. Another alternative would be to create data in an artificial way based on statistical data. In both cases, it would be impossible to reconnect the data to an individual. Thus, the restrictions of the GDPR would not apply. However, practically, it is very difficult to construe anonymity and even more so under conditions of increasing and dynamic data resources.[31] Therefore, although anonymity can be a way out of application of the GDPR, it will often not be possible, especially since the data controller would have to continuously scrutinize existing data sets to see whether they still fulfil the criteria of anonymity.

The cost for these procedures may be too high for certain applications of AI, however – where highly personalized data is needed for training and control, such ways may not function or may not fulfil the high expectations and potential of AI-based services and products. As with much technology-based regulation, the possible technological advances are restricted due to the protection of human values. It is to be considered whether this loss of AI functionality may not be in the better interests of the human race.

A. PRINCIPLE OF TRANSPARENCY Most of the principles of the GDPR are challenged by AI. For the purposes of this chapter, one more principle shall be singled out: the principle of transparency as stated in art. 5(1)(a) GDPR. It is based on art. 8(2) clause 2 of the EU Charter of Human Rights that guarantees every person the right to information and disclosure. This principle has found several specific variations within the GDPR, most notably in art. 24(1) GDPR where the duty to demonstrate has been introduced by the GDPR.

The principle of transparency includes all measures necessary so that a data subject is enabled to control the lawfulness of data processing and to exercise their rights.[32] On the other hand, the controller is required to guarantee sufficient transparency.[33] This includes the duty to design algorithmic systems and thus also AI in manners that allow transparency and control. In order to achieve this transparency, the identity of the controller must be established, the steps of processing, the purpose of it, the sources and the legal ground,[34] in essence the functionalities of data processing. Further specific provisions clarify how far the principle of transparency extends: It also includes, at least with automated decision-making, 'meaningful information about the logic involved' and also the consequences, as art. 14(2)(f) GDPR states. However, the content of 'the logic involved' is highly uncertain.[35]

This criterion of transparency as a whole but also of specific provisions in which it is concretized, however, causes problems in regard to AI. In order to understand better the many different aspects of the transparency problems of AI – and also where there are, contrary to common belief, few problems – one needs to understand the different types of AI better. On this basis, a clearer road map of the different reasons for transparency can be construed. For the

[31] M. Finck and F. Pallas, 'They Who Must Not Be Identified – Distinguishing Personal from Non-personal Data under the GDPR' (2019) Max Planck Institute for Innovation & Competition Research Paper No. 19-14.

[32] Roßnagel, 'Grundsätze für die Verarbeitung personenbezogener Daten', art. 5 mn 50.

[33] Ibid., art. 5 mn 52.

[34] Ibid., art. 5 mn. 55.

[35] See A. Dix, 'Informationsrechte' in Simitis et al., *Datenschutzrecht*, art. 13 mn. 16.

purposes of this chapter, however, this differentiation will not be developed further for the sake of the overview of potential problems in a data protection perspective. It should be noted, anyhow, that transparency issues around AI typically only address certain aspects of its functioning. It is mostly possible to identify certain elements of the data processing, for example the controller or the source of data.

There exist, not only on ethical grounds, but very precisely on GDPR grounds, also severe concerns that self-learning AI systems will develop into so-called black boxes because of the difficulties of reproducing results and comprehending decision modules. Although the results of AI decisions may be noticeable, their structure, their inherent logic, their normative standards and their assessment of data often depend on the underlying specific AI technology that is frequently unknown and thus not retrievable.[36] Frequently, it is unclear which data has been used how for further development and how it has been assessed and evaluated for the further processing. The more complex the system is, the more data it processes and the more levels and, again depending on the technology, layers of processing are involved the more difficult it becomes to control even the results as no 'non-AI' control group is possible. Thus, the essence of transparency under GDPR can often hardly be completely fulfilled unless different methods are used to reassess the procedures of AI that would often contradict the construction and advantages of employing AI. Creating AI that is GDPR-conformable and faces less criticism has been the endeavour of special research to enable transparency and also – often seen as a part of it or complementary to it – interpretability and explainability.[37]

B. OVERVIEW OF ADDITIONAL REGULATION OF AI WITHIN THE GDPR Purpose limitation, transparency and lawfulness of data processing are not the only requirements within the GDPR that challenge AI development and use of data. The following section will draw attention only to selected aspects with a few remarks.

10.3.5 *Right to a Non-automated Decision, Art. 22 GDPR*

One of the most prominent provisions that comes to mind when testing AI under the GDPR is art. 22 GDPR. This provision generally prohibits sole automated decision-making – art. 22(1) GDPR – unless such a decision produces only positive consequences. Although art. 22(2) GDPR grants wide exemptions, the general principle behind this provision cannot be ignored, in particular since art. 22(3) and (4) GDPR describe additional safeguards even in these instances. For example, art. 22(3) GDPR requires the controller to assure that the data subject may enact their right to obtain human intervention on the part of the controller, to express their point of view and to contest the decision. All of this is hardly possible if there is no clear understanding of the inner logic of the AI and a transfer of it into human decision-making. This, however, would set off some of the advantages of AI. Similarly, art. 22(4) GDPR excludes medical (and other sensitive data) from solely automated decision-making. This leads back to the problem of how to differentiate between different sets of data content-wise, but also requires an open infrastructure of AI in order to test whether this is the case.

[36] Concerns have been raised from GDPR viewpoints, e.g. A. Roßnagel, 'Art. 5' in Simitis et al., *Datenschutzrecht*, art. 5 mn. 148; M. Brkan and G. Bonnet, 'Legal and Technical Feasibility of the GDPR's Quest for Explanation of Algorithmic Decisions: Of Black Boxes, White Boxes and Fata Morganas' (2020) 11 *European Journal of Risk Regulation* 18; S. Wachter, B. Mittelstadt and Ch. Russell 'Counterfactual Explanations without Opening the Black Box: Automated Decisions and the GDPR' (2018) 18 *Harvard Journal of Law & Technology* 842, at 842.

[37] See, e.g., Hoeren and Niehoff, 'KI und Datenschutz', 59.

AI needs to be construed in a way that would allow human interaction and include additional safeguards. This, however, raises the question of human–machine interaction, of shared and divided responsibilities and liabilities that are legally unclear in any algorithmic system, so far.[38]

10.3.6 *Data Protection Impact Assessment*

A new instrument within the EU data protection legal regime is the data protection impact assessment, art. 35 GDPR. This provision creates a risk-based assessment of data processing. It requires the data controller to test prior to any data processing whether in particular the planned data processing is 'likely to result in a high risk to the rights and freedoms of natural persons' (art. 35(1) GDPR).

The provision clarifies that the testing has to take into account not only the particular data processing and the consequences for the individual data subject, but also requires an abstract testing that will take into account the general implications, consequences and problems for society as such. This can be derived from the use of the double plural in art. 35(1) ('rights and freedoms of natural persons'), but also from the general understanding as stated in art. 1 GDPR that the effects of data processing have to be viewed in a broad perspective.[39] Any risk assessment cannot concentrate on the individual circumstances as such unless the development of the particular information technology is restricted to an individual case. AI, however, will almost never fall into this category as it is typically construed for multiple purposes and further development.

10.3.7 *Right to Data Portability*

Often not seen in context with AI is another new provision within the GDPR, the right to data portability, art. 20 GDPR. This provision integrates fair competition and consumer protection in the regulatory impact of data protection law.[40] It allows the data subject to request transfer of personal data under certain conditions. Art. 20(1)(b) GDPR names 'automated means' as one of the applications; AI should typically fall under this provision. The exact width of this provision, however, is still unclear.

One of the problems especially relevant for AI uses is the inherent requirement to provide personal data in a format that allows transfer to different data controllers. This can, as art. 20(2) GDPR states, even result in a direct transfer if so requested by the data subject. AI must then be construed in a way that it may select individual data for these purposes and also hold this data in a format that might be foreign to the formats otherwise employed within the AI system.

In addition to this problem, it also remains unclear whether the metadata derived from the individual data is also included in the right of the subject.[41] In this case, fundamental learning would have to be reconstrued – again, as with transparency requirements, a task that present AI typically does not enable.

10.3.8 *Quality of Data and the Right to Rectification*

What is underestimated is also the provision of art. 16 GDPR that grants the data subject the right to request correction (rectification) of inaccurate personal data. Again, as with art. 20

[38] See I. Spiecker genannt Döhmann, 'Warum für die systematische Haftung ein neues Modell erforderlich ist' (2016) 11 *Computer und Recht (CR)* 698; Hoeren and Niehoff, 'KI und Datenschutz', 53.

[39] See G. Hornung and I. Spiecker gen. Döhmann, 'Art. 1' in Simitis et al., *Datenschutzrecht*, art. 1 mn 25 et seq.

[40] A. Dix, 'Art. 20' in Simitis et al., *Datenschutzrecht*, art. 20 mn. 1.

[41] Ibid., art. 20 mn. 11.

GDPR, the exact width of the provision is still uncertain. One of the problems particularly relevant for AI application is the definition of 'inaccurate' and of 'personal data concerning him or her'.

Inaccurate data exists if it is incorrect and does not relate to the reality.[42] It is not necessary that the inaccurateness crosses a certain threshold; any inaccurateness suffices.[43] However, the concept does not include corrections on the basis of (too) broad attributions. Accuracy, as part of the concept of data quality, is therefore not included in the right to rectification of art. 16 GDPR.[44]

Nevertheless, AI is more affected by art. 16 GDPR than may seem obvious. In order to be able to test the correctness of data processed, the data subject may request information about the data, art. 15 GDPR. Thus, AI must be construed in a way that the data controller may satisfy this request for information but also a later request for rectification. As AI is continuously developing this requires an algorithmic system that allows access to data results continuously and also rectification in a manner that can alter retrospectively. This becomes clear when reconstructing the functionalities of AI. If there is data incorrect in the training data, this may affect the outcome of the algorithmic decision-making within the AI. Certain path-dependencies arise. If it later proves to be erroneous, the AI must first be able to assess whether and how far this incorrect data influenced further processing and results. Then, if that is the case, it must be able not only to correct the status quo ante but also to reconstruct the AI development to the present status in order to correct the data and then change the outcome of the use of this data and thus from an ex-post perspective correct the existing path-dependencies.

Another problematic area is the functionality of AI in grouping information. The inclusion of persons on the basis of personalization into groups could be too broad or too inclusive so that incorrectness results from this. However, in order to be able to control this, the data subject must have access to the underlying principles and the logic of the AI system. This, again, requires an amount of inherent transparency present AI systems typically do not include.

10.4 CONCLUSION

AI is hungry for data. An important part of this data consists of personal data. It is processed for training, for control and further development, mostly not the specific use of the person whose data is processed. The use of personal data, as well as its processing in all steps, is regulated in Europe by the General Data Protection Regulation (GDPR). Although no direct provisions exist within the GDPR that address AI directly, the general principles and a number of specifications apply. Particularly problematic are the principle of purpose limitation, art. 5(1)(b) GDPR, the principle of lawfulness of data processing, art. (5)(a) and art. 6(1) GDPR and the principle of transparency, art. 5(1)(a) GDPR. A number of other provisions challenge AI under the GDPR.

In order to create a responsible AI – and this includes responsible algorithmic systems and responsible robotics – the technology has to address these problems and find ways how a GDPR-compliant AI can foster the desired results of the use of this particular technology. This means, however, that AI development has to change. It has to acknowledge that AI use is not 'neutral', but that there is a normative impact to construction, development, use, control and improvement of any algorithmic system. In Addition, one should note that AI development does not

[42] Ibid., art. 16 mn. 11.
[43] Ibid.
[44] Ibid.

reach out and 'do', but reacts to existing normative concepts and integrates them actively. It has to acknowledge that the data basis is prone to biases and discrimination, not only from the data itself but also from the algorithms used. AI is no better than the world in which it is being used, and its lack of easily accessible control and fast inherent dynamics require additional attention to its functioning. The standards of the GDPR are a starting point, and there will be more. Nevertheless, AI developers and AI users should not neglect the bindings of the GDPR if they do not want to find themselves subject to fines and data subjects' rights.

11

AI as Agents

Agency Law

Pınar Çağlayan Aksoy

Qui facit per alium facit per se[1]

11.1 INTRODUCTION

The artificial intelligence (AI) agents of today perform many complex tasks. They can do many things all by themselves. They react dynamically to their environment. They make choices and decisions. They initiate contract negotiations and conclude contracts when their operator[2] is not even aware that there were negotiations going on or what Gunther Teubner refers to as 'the autonomy risk that arises from independent decisions of the software agents'.[3] In many instances, the declaration of intent to conclude a contract is not only transmitted through AI agents but also formulated by them.[4] In fact, AI agents determine the content of the contract themselves, and the human entity behind the AI system may not have any knowledge as to the precise terms of the contract that the AI agent has concluded.[5]

AI agents take all these actions, and take part in transactions, without human supervision. Moreover, AI agents of today do not act in isolation, but in close collaboration with other electronic agents. As a result of this rather complex and 'independent' process, there are instances when humans cannot truly understand, concretely predict or control how an AI

[1] He who acts through another does the act himself.

[2] The term operator is used in this chapter to indicate entities who initiate, program, use, own or control AI agents.

[3] Emily M. Weitzenboeck, 'Electronic Agents and Formation of Contracts' (2001) 9 *International Journal of Law and Information Technology* 204, at 209; Emad Abdel Rahim Dahiyat, 'Law and Software Agents: Are They "Agents" by the Way?' (2020) 29 *Artificial Intelligence and Law* 59; Gunther Teubner, 'Digitale Rechtssubjekte? Zum privatrechtlichen Status autonomer Softwareagenten' ['Digital Personhood: The Status of Digital Software Agents in Private Law'] (2018) 218 *Ancilla Juris* 35, at 45.

[4] Tina Balke and Torsten Eymann, 'The Conclusion of Contracts by Software Agents in the Eyes of the Law' (2008) 2 *7th International Joint Conference on Autonomous Agents and Multiagent Systems (AAMAS 2008)*, Estoril, Portugal, 12–16 May 2008, 771, at 771; Weitzenboeck, 'Electronic Agents', 209; Jean-Francois Lerouge, 'The Use of Electronic Agents Questioned under Contractual Law: Suggested Solutions on a European American Level' (2000) 18 *John Marshall Journal of Information Technology & Privacy Law* 403, at 406.

[5] With the development of machine learning and other advanced AI systems even the creators and users of these AI systems can be ignorant as to the results in cases when the AI system formulates a recommendation or makes a decision in an untransparent way. See Mark Coeckelbergh, 'Artificial Intelligence, Responsibility Attribution, and a Relational Justification of Explainability' (2020) 26 *Science and Engineering Ethics* 2051, at 2061.

system will act.[6] There will be times when the final decision is left to the AI agent, and it may be a decision that the human entity could not actually foresee. Sometimes, the operator might not actually intend the acts or actions that the AI agent has carried out.

This constitutes a problem in the eyes of the law: AI agents produce legal rights and obligations through their acts and actions. These rights and obligations produce effects on the legal positions of humans. However, the entity directly involved in the process is the AI agent; there is no direct human participation in this process. Therefore, the operator's intention to conclude a contract does not exist. Unlike natural persons or some legal entities, such as corporations, foundations, associations or government entities, AI agents do not have legal personality.[7] They do not have legal capacity. Therefore, AI agents cannot be party to a legal transaction.[8] They cannot form an *animus contrahendi* (intention to create legal relations).[9] Even if advanced AI agents were to be granted legal personalities, it is not certain that these AI agents would have the capacity to enter into a contractual relationship since they cannot enter into contracts voluntarily.[10] As a result, the acts and actions generated by AI agents cannot actually be attributed to these agents themselves. But to whom will these actions – sometimes undesirable ones that the operators will want to refrain from – be attributed? And how?

Since the end of the 1990s, determining the relationship between intelligent agents and the people who initiate them or participate in their programming process – the human beings behind the AI system – has been the subject of debate.[11] Thirty years later, there is still no national or international uniform solution on this matter. However, the problem has turned out to be even bigger because intelligent agents are becoming more and more intelligent and capable of acting 'on their own'. These increasingly autonomous AI systems cause deep concerns regarding how to deal with their actions. In fact, without resolving the problem of legal enforceability of the transactions generated by AI agents, the benefits of this rapidly developing technology cannot be enjoyed.

In the light of these concerns, there are two main groups of questions waiting to be answered:

i. How can the transactions generated by AI agents be deemed as valid? How can AI agents incur obligations and form binding contracts on behalf of their operators? With which legal concept can this be justified?
ii. With which terms will the operator of an AI system be bound when the declaration is generated by the AI system? Who will be held responsible if the contracts concluded by AI agents do not produce the desired outcomes? What will happen if the result is unpredictable? What will happen if the AI agent behaves erratically?[12]

[6] This is called the 'responsibility gap' with regard to autonomously learning and acting machines: can we hold humans responsible when they have no or insufficient control over AI systems? See Andreas Matthias, 'The Responsibility Gap: Ascribing Responsibility for the Actions of Learning Automata' (2004) 6 *Ethics and Information Technology* 175, at 181. See also Teubner, 'Digitale Rechtssubjekte', 131.

[7] Weitzenboeck, 'Electronic Agents', 210.

[8] Samir Chopra and Laurance White, 'Artificial Agents and the Contracting Problem: A Solution via an Agency Analysis' (2009) *Journal of Law, Technology & Policy* 363, at 365.

[9] Ian R. Kerr, 'Spirits in the Material World: Intelligent Agents as Intermediaries in Electronic Commerce' (1999) 22 *Dalhousie Law Journal* 189, at 209.

[10] Ibid., 210.

[11] See also Thomas Riehm, 'Rechtsfähigkeit von KI-Systemen' in Thomas Braegelmann and Markus Kaulartz (eds.), *Rechtshandbuch Artificial Intelligence und Machine Learning* (Munich: Verlag C. H. Beck, 2020), 221, at 221.

[12] Balke and Eymann, 'Software Agents', 771; Yavar Bathaee, 'The Artificial Intelligence Black Box and the Failure of Intent and Causation' (2018) 31 *Harvard Journal of Law & Technology* 890, at 935.

In the next section, we will try to answer these questions by elaborating on the main views regarding the relationship between the AI agent, the AI operator and third parties. Within this stance, we will specifically discuss if the application of the principles on agency law might present the answer.

11.2 MAIN VIEWS DEFINING THE RELATIONSHIP BETWEEN AI AGENT, AI OPERATOR AND THIRD PARTIES

AI systems communicate with the actors in business. They interact with natural and legal persons and other AI agents to produce actions with legal results, including the conclusion of contracts. However, AI agents are not persons before the law. Therefore, an AI agent cannot formulate its own declaration of intent[13] and be held liable for it. Since AI agents cannot declare their own will, it must be clarified how the declaration generated by the AI agent can be attributed to the entity behind the system. There are three main opinions on this issue. All of these opinions share the same common ground: the foreseeable acts of an AI agent will be attributed to the operator; unforeseeable ones will not.[14]

11.2.1 AI Agents as Tools (Instruments) of Human Entities

According to some scholars, AI agents only serve as 'tools' or 'instruments' of their operators, like phones or email. In other words, they are not a separate entity.[15] The acts and actions of AI agents are thought of as coming directly from the person owning, programming, controlling or instructing them. This means that an operator has to be very careful while they chose, operate or monitor their agent. Otherwise, the operator bears the risk of undesired, unforeseeable or unplanned consequences, including design flaws and software bugs.[16] Such liability is stricter than the liability for using human agents. As a matter of fact, where humans are agents, with the application of the doctrine of authority, the principal is bound only if the agent has acted within the scope of authority it was granted.[17]

The Uniform Electronic Transactions Act (UETA) recognizes that electronic agents are limited to a tool function. The UETA does not focus specifically on AI agents, but defines the term 'electronic agent'. Accordingly, an electronic agent is a computer program or other automated means used independently to initiate an action or respond to electronic records or performances in whole or in part, without review or action by an individual (UETA Section 2 (6)). The comment in the definitions section of UETA endorses a theory of machines as a 'tool' of the company:

> An electronic agent, such as a computer program or other automated means employed by a person, is a tool of that person. As a general rule, the employer of a tool is responsible for the results obtained by the use of that tool since the tool has no independent volition of its own. However, an electronic agent, by definition, is capable within the parameters of its

[13] See Thomas Schulz, *Verantwortlichkeit bei autonom agierenden Systemen* (Baden-Baden: Nomos Verlag, 2015), pp. 102–103.
[14] Riehm, 'Rechtsfähigkeit von KI-Systemen', p. 223.
[15] Eliza Mik, 'Automation to Autonomy: A Non-existent Problem in Contract Law' (2020), 18, https://papers.ssrn.com/sol3/papers.cfm?abstract_id=3635346.
[16] Dahiyat, 'Law and Software Agents'.
[17] Chopra and White, 'Agency Analysis', 371.

programming, of initiating, responding or interacting with other parties or their electronic agents once it has been activated by a party, without further attention of that party.[18]

Algorithmic contracts,[19] which are concluded with the use of machine learning algorithms, fall outside the scope of the UETA since machine learning algorithms are not programmed by people.

Similarly, UNCITRAL Model Law on E-Commerce (Article 2, Definitions) also regards software agents as mere communication tools:[20] 'Data messages that are generated automatically by computers without direct human intervention should be regarded as "originating" from the legal entity on behalf of which the computer is operated.'[21]

11.2.2 *AI Agents: A Separate Legal Entity*

Some scholars propose to grant intelligent software agents a separate legal personality *de lege feranda*.[22] With advancements in technology, increasingly autonomous AI agents have become capable of pursuing their own goals, making decisions and finding their own solutions.[23] Therefore, this view suggests the separation of AI agent from the operator. Accordingly, if an AI agent's act or action results in an undesired or unexpected outcome, the AI agent itself would bear the responsibility. Hence, this view reduces the risk borne by the operator.[24]

The EU has accelerated its work concerning AI since 2014. Especially in the last two years, various bodies of the EU have issued publications, guidelines and political declarations focusing on the regulation of AI liability for defects in AI and the legal personalities of AI systems. In the report prepared by the Expert Group on Liability and New Technologies (New Technologies Formation), which was set up by the European Commission, it was concluded that it should not be (currently) necessary to give devices or autonomous systems a legal personality, as the harm

[18] UETA, Comments to Section 2, p. 8.

[19] Algorithmic contracts are contracts that are based on algorithmic decision-making, usually in addition to human decision makers. See Lauren Henry Scholz, 'Algorithms and Contract Law', in Woodrow Barfield (ed.), *Cambridge Handbook of the Law of Algorithms* (Cambridge: Cambridge University Press, 2020), p. 141.

[20] See Tina Balke, '"Entity" and "Autonomy" – The Conclusion of Contracts by Software Agents in the Eyes of the Law' (2010) 24 *Revue d'intelligence artificielle* 391, at 403.

[21] Article-by-Article Remarks for Article 2 (UN, 1996, Article-by-article remarks), 27.

[22] There is another chapter in this book dedicated to the legal personality of AI agents. Therefore, we will not go into further details. There is extensive literature on the issue in both civil law and common law countries. See Ugo Pagallo, 'What Robots Want: Autonomous Machines, Codes and New Frontiers of Legal Responsibility' in Mireille Hildebrandt and Jeanne Gaakeer (eds.), *Human Law and Computer Law: Comparative Perspectives* (Dordrecht: Springer, 2013), p. 60; Robert van den Hoven van Genderen, 'Legal Personhood in the Age of Artificially Intelligent Robots', in Woodrow Barfield and Ugo Pagallo (eds.), *Research Handbook on the Law of Artificial Intelligence* (Cheltenham: Edward Elgar Publishing, 2018), p. 215; Tom Allen and Robin Widdison, 'Can Computers Make Contracts?' (1996) 9 *Harvard Journal of Law and Technology* 26, at 35; Francisco Assis de Andrade, Paulo Jorge Novais, José Machado and Jose maia Neves, 'Contracting Agents: Legal Personality and Representation' (2007) 15 *Artificial Intelligence and Law* 357, at 361; Jacob Turner, *Robot Rules* (London: Palgrave Macmillan, 2019), p. 173; Woodrow Barfield and Ugo Pagallo, *Advanced Introduction to Law and Artificial Intelligence* (Cheltenham: Edward Elgar Publishing, 2020), chapter 4; Susanne Beck, 'Der rechtliche Status autonomer Maschinen' (2017) 26 *Aktulle Juristische Praxis* 183, at 186; Samir Chopra and Laurence F. White, *A Legal Theory for Autonomous Artificial Agents* (Ann Arbor: University of Michigan Press, 2011), p. 153.

[23] See Mik, 'Automation to Autonomy', 6.

[24] For detailed information see, Mik, 'Automation to Autonomy', 7; Balke and Eymann, 'Software Agents', 773; Weitzenboeck, 'Electronic Agents', 213; David C. Vladeck, 'Machines without Principals: Liability Rules and Artificial Intelligence' (2014) 89 *Washington Law Review* 117, at 121; Chopra and White, 'Agency Analysis', 378.

these may cause can and should be attributable to existing persons or bodies.[25] However, there are still debates going on in EU countries regarding the granting of 'partial legal capacity' (*Teilrechtsfähigkeit*) and electronic personality of AI systems.[26]

11.2.3 *AI Agents as Agents in the Legal Sense*

Advocates of this view justify the attribution of the acts and actions carried out by AI agents to the operators by relying on the principles of agency law.[27] Their departure point is the fact that AI agents negotiate, conclude and perform contracts on behalf of a legal person. When doing so, the autonomously acting system does not transmit an already existing declaration of intent like a messenger, but generates its own declaration.[28] They actually model human agent's abilities to act as representatives.[29] Therefore, AI agents serve the same function as human agents and they can be seen as 'agents' in a legal sense. Consequently, agency law principles should be applied to the relationship between the operator, the AI agent and third parties interacting with the AI agent.[30] This means that the acts and actions of the AI agent are binding on the principal, that is generally the operator of the system, provided that the AI agent has acted in accordance with the authority granted to it. The operator of the system would not be bound with the transaction in cases where AI agent exceeds its authority.

11.3 THE APPLICABILITY OF THE PRINCIPLES OF AGENCY LAW

It is observed that 'when approaching the notion of electronic agents, lawyers are immediately tempted to make a parallelism with the theory of agency'.[31] This is due to the fact that software

[25] 'Liability for Artificial Intelligence and Other Emerging Digital Technologies Report', https://ec.europa.eu/transparency/regexpert/index.cfm?do=groupDetail.groupMeetingDoc&docid=36608/ (last accessed 29 December 2020), p. 37.

[26] See Jan-Erik Schirmer, 'Artificial Intelligence and Legal Personality: Introducing "Teilrechtsfahigkeit": A Partial Legal Status Made in Germany' in Thomas Wischmeyer and Timo Rademacher (eds.), *Regulating Artificial Intelligence* (Switzerland: Springer Nature, 2020), p. 113; Teubner, 'Digitale Rechtssubjekte', p. 132; Martin Zobl and Michael Lysakowski, 'E-Persönlichkeit für Algorithmen' (2019) 18 *Zeitschrift für Datenrecht und Informationssicherheit* 42, at 43; Fritz-Ulli Pieper, 'Die Vernetzung autonomer Systeme im Kontext von Vertrag und Haftung' (2016) 16 *Zeitschrift zum Innovations- und Technikrecht* 188, at 191; Jan-Erik Schirmer, 'Von Mäusen, Menschen und Maschinen – Autonome Systeme in der Architektur der Rechtsfähigkeit' (2019) 74 *Juristen Zeitung* 711, at 711; Riehm, 'Rechtsfahigkeit von KI-Systemen', 226; Philipp Behrendt and Donata Freiin von Enzberg, 'AGB-Verträge über den Einsatz Künstlicher Intelligenz' in Markus Kaulartz and Tom Braegelmann (eds.), *Rechtshandbuch Artificial Intelligence und Machine Learning* (Munich: Verlag C. H. Beck, 2020), p. 178; Schulz, *Verantwortlichkeit*, p. 94.

[27] See Schirmer, 'Menschen und Maschinen', 711, fn 5; Riehm, 'Rechtsfähigkeit von KI-Systemen', p. 223; Chopra and White, *A Legal Theory*, p. 23; Schulz, *Verantwortlichkeit*, p. 106.

[28] Louisa Specht and Sophie Harold, 'Roboter als Vertragspartner? Gedanken zu Vertragsabschlüssen unter Einbeziehung automatisiert und autonom agierender Systeme' (2018) 21 *Zeitschrift für IT-Recht und Recht der Digitalisierung* 40, at 43.

[29] Chopra and White, *A Legal Theory*, p. 7.

[30]
> Agency law provides a suitable framework in which to find the solution. Because an agency relationship is formed when the software licensee installs and then executes the software program, intelligent software agents should be regulated under agency law. . . . Thus we see the software agent in the legal role of the agent and the software licensee in the legal role of the principal. This relationship of agent-principal has been formed whether or not the parties themselves intended to create an agency or even think of themselves as agent-principal.

Suzanne Smed, 'Intelligent Software Agents and Agency Law' (1998) 14 *Santa Clara High Technology Law Journal* 503, at 504.

[31] Lerouge, 'Electronic Agents', 408.

agents and algorithms can perform tasks just like human agents. When AI agents make declarations that are formulated autonomously, these declarations are seen as independent declarations that belong to the AI agent. If the AI agent were seen as an 'agent' in the legal sense, the rules on agency would be applied accordingly.[32] At first glance, this solution appears to be ideal. However, it deserves a closer look to see if it really is the case.

11.3.1 *What Is an Agent?*

An agent, in the general sense, is anything that can be viewed as perceiving its environment through sensors and acting upon that environment through actuators[33]. A human agent has eyes, ears and other organs as sensors, and they have hands, legs and other body parts for actuators. However, there are also robotic agents and software agents. Robotic agents have cameras and infrared range finders as sensors, and they have various motors for actuators. A software agent has keystrokes, file contents, received network packages as sensors and has displays on the screen, files or sent network packets for actuators. An intelligent agent is an autonomous entity, which observes the world through sensors and acts upon an environment using actuators; the agent directs its activity towards achieving goals in a rational manner.[34] These agents are also labelled as 'autonomous agents'. In this chapter we will focus solely on intelligent (autonomous) agents using AI technology and how these AI agents can be framed as an agent of a legal person in a legal sense.

According to the principle of freedom of contract, it is up to the parties to choose the means they want to use for the conclusion of a contract and by whom they want to be represented. Consequently, it is possible to choose human agents for fulfilling a task as well as artificial agents. Where AI agents are given such tasks, they do not act for their own interest but provide support for natural and legal persons.[35] But how independent are they really? Can they be held equal to human agents? The answer to these questions deserves a closer look at the 'autonomy' of today's AI agents.

11.3.2 *Agents and Autonomy*

Finding legal justification for the validity of transactions carried out by electronic agents was a problem from the outset. In the beginning, it was easier to connect the outcome of the transactions carried out by software agents, or the declarations formulated by them to humans, since such agents were not autonomous, or as autonomous, as they are today.[36] We were only dealing with conventional software or industrial robots. These kinds of software and robots basically follow humans' rules precisely. They do not deviate from the instructions given to them, except in the case of a system breakdown.[37] When these electronic agents generate a

[32] Peter Bräutigam and Thomas Klindt, 'Industrie 4.0, das Internet der Dinge und das Recht' (2015) 16 *Neue Juristische Wochenschrift* 1137, at 1138.

[33] Stuart Russel and Peter Norvig, *Artificial Intelligence: A Modern Approach* (Essex: Pearson Edition Limited, 2016), p. 34.

[34] Woodrow Barfield, 'Towards a Law of Artificial Intelligence' in Woodrow Barfield and Ugo Pagallo (eds.), *Research Handbook on the Law of Artificial Intelligence* (Cheltenham: Edward Elgar Publishing, 2018), p. 22.

[35] Schirmer, 'Artificial Intelligence', 136; Teubner, 'Digitale Rechtssubjekte', 114.

[36] Kai Cornelius, 'Vertragsabschluss durch autonome elektronische Agenten' (2002) 5 *MMR Zeitschrift für IT-Recht und Recht der Digitalisierung* 353, at 358.

[37] John P. Fischer, 'Computers as Agents: A Proposed Approach to Revised U.C.C. Article 2 (1997) 72 *Indiana Law Journal* 545, at 558.

declaration, it is called an 'automated declaration of intention', which is mechanically produced with the help of a computer program. These agents cannot surprise humans with what they achieve. In fact, they function in the form of 'if . . . then' programming, like smart contracts.

Electronic contracts concluded via AI agents are different from contracts entered into through the use of other electronic or automated means.[38] When AI agents come into the equation, the contract is no longer concluded with automated means but in an autonomous manner. The more advanced a system is in terms of collecting, analysing and acting on data, the more autonomous it becomes. With the increased level of autonomy, problems arise with regard to contract law because AI agents have 'autonomous or creative discretion'.[39]

When an agent is autonomous, it acts without the intervention of its operator or other users in the system. Therefore, it has control over its own activity and internal state.[40] When we talk about the autonomous character of intelligent agents, we speak of systems that do not function in the form of 'if . . . then' programming. We also refer to machine learning algorithms – the subset of AI that allows machines to learn from data without being programmed explicitly.[41]

These AI agents do not rely only on rules predetermined by humans; they also rely on their own experience and cognitive state. These machine-learning algorithms can modify the instructions in their own programs, create new instructions and make decisions based on these instructions.[42] They can also change the functionality of the system that was originally intended by the operators.[43] As a result, although the AI agent acts within the framework designated by a human, it can exceed this framework using its own decision-making ability and pursue its own goals. Therefore, it is very difficult to foresee which data an AI agent will choose and use while operating. In addition to this, the AI agents of today operate in remote and complex networks. This means that they are occasionally operating on external servers, which cause them to be even more 'out of control'.[44]

As a result of such autonomy, a decision made by an autonomous system may not be foreseeable as to when, why and with which content a declaration will be made.[45] In most cases, the operators/programmers cannot predict accurately with which other agents the AI agent will interact. Since today's AI agents are sophisticated and show high levels of autonomy and intelligence, for some, the mere treatment of AI agents as 'tools' or 'instruments' is not sufficient. They should be regarded as 'intermediaries'.[46]

Something is not to be missed, though: although machine-learning algorithms are 'independent',[47] they are still dependent upon the availability of data (provided by their operators).[48] Due to this dependence, some authors maintain that 'machines cannot do anything but execute

[38] Dahiyat, 'Law and Software Agents'.

[39] Ibid., sec. 5.1.

[40] Balke and Eymann, 'Software Agents', 772.

[41] Specht and Harold, 'Roboter als Vertragspartner', 41; Beck, 'Autonomer Maschinen', 190; Stefan Kirn and Claus D. Hengstenberg, 'Intelligente (Software-)Agenten: Von der Automatisierung zur Autonomie? Verselbstständigung technischer Systeme' (2014) 4 *Zeitschrift für IT-Recht und Recht der Digitalisierung* 225, at 229.

[42] Lerouge, 'Electronic Agents', 406; Harry Surden, 'Artificial Intelligence and Law: An Overview' (2019) 35 *Georgia State University Law Review* 1306, at 1314; Allen and Widdison, 'Computers Make Contracts', 27; Dahiyat, 'Law and Software Agents'; Bathaee, 'AI Black Box', 891.

[43] Kirn and Hengstenberg, 'Automatisierung zur Autonomie', 226.

[44] Dahiyat, 'Law and Software Agents'.

[45] Specht and Harold, 'Roboter als Vertragspartner', 43.

[46] Kerr, 'Spirits', 238; Chopra and White, 'Agency Analysis', 377.

[47] Kirn and Hengstenberg, 'Automatisierung zur Autonomie', 226

[48] Surden, 'AI and Law', 1315.

programs developed by humans, even if those programs enable the machine to reconfigure its program in view of specified machine readable tasks, and even if humans may develop programs that build new programs'.[49] Therefore, AI agents cannot generate their own declaration of intent and then issue it.

Before we go deeper into the discussion regarding the applicability of agency rules, it is crucial to determine how intelligent today's AI agents really are. Establishing this is important when deciding if AI agents can generate a declaration of intent of their own. There are three generations/levels of AI: weak, general and strong.[50] Strong AI refers to completely autonomous AI systems. It is said to match human intelligence, even exceed human intelligence. Such completely autonomous AI agents can make all the important decisions about their own activities.[51]

This level of intelligence has not yet been reached.[52] AI agents still lack skills, such as abstract reasoning, concept comprehension, flexible understanding and general problem-solving.[53] It is frequently mentioned that, presently, AI agents cannot make conscious, moral decisions of their own.[54] The declaration of intent, however, by its nature, consists in its traceability to a natural person who has a free will.[55] In any event, there is a human behind the declaration of intent.[56] In fact, AI agents are technological systems that have no awareness as to whether they are acting or not. People's awareness of the use of an AI agent extends to all their subsequent actions and thus covers the entire decision-making process. Therefore, the AI agent does not have their own will to act.

Considering this, regardless of their intelligence and ability to act autonomously, AI agents will not be able to bear any legal responsibility of their own for the foreseeable future.

> Today's machines, as path breaking as they are all have a common feature that is crucial in assessing liability. In each case, the machine functions and makes decisions in ways that can be traced directly back to the design, programming and knowledge humans embedded in the machine. The human hand defines, guides and ultimately controls the process, either directly or because of the capacity to override the machine and seize control. As sophisticated as these machines are, they are, at most, semi-autonomous. They are tools, albeit remarkably sophisticated tools, used by humans.[57]

This being the current situation regarding the intelligence of AI agents, can they still be regarded as 'agents in a legal sense'?

[49] Mireille Hildebrandt, 'The Artificial Intelligence of European Union Law' (2020) 21 *German Law Journal* 74, at 77.

[50] See also Dahiyat, 'Law and Software Agents', sec. 6.2.

[51] Turner, *Robot Rules*, p. 29.

[52] Surden, 'AI and Law', 1326. See also Evan J. Zimmermann, 'Machine Minds: Frontiers in Legal Personhood' (12 February 2015), 9 https://ssrn.com/abstract=256396 (last accessed 7 December 2020): 'The holy grail of machine learning is unsupervised learning. It is true intelligence; a machine is let loose on the data with no restrictions and permitted to draw whichever connection it wishes. Supervised machines can surprise us with what they find but unsupervised machines can surprise is with what they choose to look for.'

[53] Surden, 'AI and Law', 1309.

[54] Weitzenboeck, 'Electronic Agents', 212.

[55] Justin Grapentin, *Vertragsschluss und vertragliches Verschulden beim Einsatz von Künstlicher Intelligenz und Softwareagenten* (Baden-Baden: Nomos Verlagsgesellschaft, 2018), p. 87; Schirmer, 'Artificial Intelligence', p. 130.

[56] The situation is the same in some civil law countries. In Germany, case decisions and academic literature reflect the opinion that the software can only work within the programming that gives it a framework; therefore, every action of a computer program can always be traced back to a will of a human being. See Grapentin, *Vertragsschluss*, p. 87.

[57] Vladeck, 'Machines without Principals', 120.

11.3.3 *The Application of Agency Law to AI Agents*

11.3.3.1 Do We Need to Apply Agency Law?

The term 'agent' has a special meaning in legal doctrine, just as it does in computer science. The law of agency deals with a set of contractual, quasi-contractual and non-contractual fiduciary relationships that involve a person, called the agent, that is authorized to act on behalf of another, called the principal, to create legal relations with a third party.[58]

Attention must be paid to the fact that the term 'agency'[59] used in 'intelligent agents' or 'AI agents' can be misleading: 'When used in these contexts, the term agent is not meant to suggest that the parties involved share the legal relationship of agency, but rather connotes the more general idea that the software does what one tells it to do, i.e. it's a bot.'[60] Although they are named as agents, intelligent agents do not literally have legal personhood. Therefore, the fact that they are agents in the technical sense does not mean that intelligent agents are always legal agents of their operators.

It might be useful, nevertheless, to regard AI agents as 'agents' (representatives) in the legal sense.[61] The use of AI agents can be understood as a division of tasks between humans and the digital world.[62] That means AI agents can be regarded as agents of other entities that have legal capacity. They have the capability of affecting the legal relations of the principal by acting on their behalf and being subject to their control.[63] They do not act in their own name but represent their operator in the network. Consequently, a person (i.e., a human being or a legal entity) will be held accountable for the actions of the AI agent, even if the AI agent exercises its discretion in a different manner than the principal would in the same situation.[64] In fact, the application of legal agency rules enables one to attribute the transactions carried out by AI agents to their operator when they are within the AI agent's authority. In contrast, it would be possible to protect the operator from liability arising from unplanned and unexpected results, since the principal would not be bound with the acts and actions carried out by the AI agent if they lie outside the scope of its authority.[65]

Accepting that agency law is applicable to the relationship between the operator, AI agent and the third party, however, raises some questions with regard to principles of agency law. Some of these questions will be elaborated on in the following parts of this chapter.

[58] Barfield, 'Artificial Intelligence', p. 23.

[59] It should also be noted that one might come across the term 'representative' instead of 'agent'. This is mainly because there are some agents that do not represent the other in legal transactions or the doing of juridical acts. In order to avoid the confusion between agents in legal terms and agents in the general sense, the term 'representative' is preferable. This choice was also reflected in the Draft Common Frame of Reference, Article II.–6:102.

[60] Stephen T. Middlebrook and John Muller, 'Thoughts on Bots: The Emerging Law of Electronic Agents' (2000) 56 *The Business Lawyer* 341, at 342.

[61] In Germany, because of the capacity issues surrounding AI agents, an analogous application of agency rules is suggested. See Fritz-Ulli Pieper, 'Vertragsschluss mit KI' in Markus Kaulartz and Tom Braegelmann (eds.), *Rechtshandbuch Artificial Intelligence und Machine Learning* (Munich: Verlag C. H. Beck, 2020), p. 245; Teubner, 'Digitale Rechtssubjekte', 132.

[62] Grapentin, *Vertragsschluss*, p. 88. In analogy to the law of agency, AI agents are to be treated as representatives of their principal. In order to do so, they do not have to be ascribed full legal personhood as a legal entity, but from a functional point of view, mere partial legal capacity (i.e., the ability to act as a representative suffices).

[63] Kerr, 'Spirits', 238; Chopra and White, A *Legal Theory*, p. 18.

[64] Chopra and White, 'Agency Analysis', 393; Chopra and White, A *Legal Theory*, p. 44.

[65] Schirmer, 'Artificial Intelligence', 130; Behrendt and von Enzberg, 'AGB-Verträge', 179.

11.3.3.2 Can AI Agents Act as Legal Agents?

The first question that needs to be dealt with to decide if agency law can be applied to acts generated by AI agents is: can the legal agent be someone that is not a legal person?

Agency is defined in ALI's Restatement (Third) of Agency as 'the fiduciary relationship that arises when one person ("a principal") manifests assent to another person ("an agent") that the agent shall act on the principal's behalf and subject to the principal's control'.[66] According to the comments on the Restatement (Third) of Agency § 1.04,[67] Comment e,

> to be capable of acting as a principal or an agent, it is necessary to be a person, which in this respect requires capacity to be the holder of legal rights and the object of legal duties. Accordingly, it is not possible for an inanimate object or a non-human animal to be a principal or an agent under the common-law definition of agency.

Additionally, in Restatement (Third) of Agency, in § 3.05 (capacity to act as agent), it is stated that any *person* may ordinarily be empowered to act so as to affect the legal relations of another.

A similar definition of a representative can be found in Article II.–6:102 Draft Common Frame of Reference, which shows a good reflection of the civil law understanding: a '"representative" is a person who has authority to affect the legal position of another person, the principal, in relation to a third party by acting on behalf of the principal'.

If the legal personality condition is strictly adhered to, AI agents cannot act as legal agents because they lack legal personality. Moreover, an agent declares its own intention on behalf of the principal.[68] However, the declaration of intent always requires a human act, so an AI agent cannot have its own declaration of intent. Therefore, in most common law and civil law countries, 'agency is at present reserved only to humans'.[69] In fact, agency law does not govern the relationship between a principal and a mere mechanical tool or instrument. It governs the relationship between a principal and a person in whose discretion and understanding the principal trusts.[70]

When we are speaking of human agents, it is a generally accepted principle that full contractual capacity is not needed. However, an agent must be of sound mind[71] – legally competent – in order for the agency relationship to be established. This means that the agent should be able to understand the nature of the act or action they are going to carry out.[72] In light of these explanations, minors can be agents although they do not have contractual capacity. However, minors are persons before the law. Can an AI agent, who lacks legal personality, be capable of exercising judgement and understanding?[73]

66 Restatement (Third) of Agency § 1.01.

67 Restatement (Third) of Agency § 1.04, Comment e.

68 Schulz, *Verantwortlichkeit*, p. 102.

69 Turner, *Robot Rules*, p. 43; Mik, 'Automation to Autonomy', 10; Balke and Eymann, 'Software Agents', 774.

70 Anthony J. Bellia, 'Contracting with Electronic Agents' (2001) 50 *Emory Law Journal* 1047, at 1063.

71 Chopra and White go on further and state that the 'sound mind requirement' could be adapted to the case of AI agents by requiring 'not that the agent understands the nature of the act being performed, but that the agent be functioning properly, based on our ability to successfully and consistently predict its behaviour in taking actions contingent upon such understanding'. If this threshold is found to be too high because it would impose the risk of malfunction errors on the third party, 'it could be better to retain only the requirement of "volition"'. Chopra and White, 'Agency Analysis', 400.

72 Samir Chopra and Laurence Fredric White, 'Artificial Agents – Personhood in Law and Philosophy' in *Proceedings of the 16th European Conference on Artificial Intelligence, ECAI'2004*, 2.1.
See also Balke, 'Entity and Autonomy', 401.

73 Those who support the agency approach use the Roman Law example of the situation of slaves to refute the objection that AI agents cannot act as legal agents since they are not persons. In Roman Law, slaves were not accorded legal

There is one view that finds a parallel between an AI agent and a human agent: AI systems are computational mechanisms. They can complete complex tasks that humans deal with using their cognitive abilities. Although AI systems produce results similar to those of humans, they cannot think the same way a human does. They have not reached the level of human thinking – consciousness – yet.[74] Still, they have the power to affect legal positions of persons and produce rights and obligations through their acts and actions. Provided the AI system has the cognitive capability to capture the unique goals and act in accordance with the objectives of the operator, it is considered that AI agents could be treated the same way as human agents.[75] It is also argued that if legal capacity is understood as 'control and mastering one's own behaviour', AI agents that can act autonomously and intentionally can (then) bear obligations.[76]

11.3.3.3 *How Can the Authority of the AI Agent Be Established?*

One of the main pillars of the agency relationship is authority. The principal has to grant authority to an agent for the agency relationship to be established. Authority is crucial since it determines the scope of actions that can be taken by the agent on behalf of the principal.

UNIVERSAL, GENERAL AND SPECIAL AGENTS Depending on the scope of actions that can be carried out by the agent, the principal can grant three types of authority. Universal agents have the authority to carry out all acts without exception. General agents have the authority to carry out all necessary acts and actions with regard to a specific function. Special agents have the authority to carry out only one designated, specific type of act.[77]

When AI agents are using self-learning algorithms, they may be regarded as having general authority to act on behalf of their operators.[78] This means that AI agents can carry out all the necessary acts and actions that are specific to their programming. However, the principal might be unaware of all the transactions that the AI agent has engaged in.

ACTUAL AND APPARENT AUTHORITY The principal can grant authority in two different manners. There can be an *actual* granting of authority that the principal can carry out in an expressed or implied manner.[79] The principal can also choose to declare authority to third parties that the agent will interact with. This is called *apparent* authority.[80]

In cases where an operator voluntarily initiates an AI agent by setting it in motion, it has consented to having its legal positions changed by the AI agent's operations. The consent to having their legal positions changed can be declared expressly or can be derived from the circumstances. Therefore, when the operator initiates an AI agent (which is capable of making

personality, however, they were able to conclude contracts on behalf of their masters. For the electronic slave metaphor see Chopra and White, 'Agency Analysis', 399; Kerr, 'Spirits, 236. See also Balke, 'Entity and Autonomy', 401.

74 Surden, 'AI and Law', 1308.

75 Dahiyat, 'Law and Software Agents'. See also Teubner, 'Digitale Rechtssubjekte', 133.

76 Specht and Harold, 'Roboter als Vertragspartner', 44.

77 Mireille Hildebrandt, *Law for Computer Scientists and Other Folk* (Oxford Scholarship Online, 2020), ch. 9 on 'Legal Personhood'.

78 Mik, 'Automation to Autonomy', 11.

79 Restatement (Third) of Agency § 3.01: 'Actual authority . . . is created by a principal's manifestation to an agent that, as reasonably understood by the agent, expresses the principal's assent that the agent take action on the principal's behalf.'

80 See Restatement 3rd Agency, § 2.03 Apparent Authority and § 3.03 Creation of Apparent Authority.

transactions), they have given permission for the operations carried out by it. The operator is aware of the fact that the AI agent could make declarations on their behalf, although they do not concretely know what form the declarations will take.[81] Therefore, the AI agent might be thought of as having actual authority to make these transactions on behalf of the operator.[82]

According to Bellia,[83] agency with actual authority requires accord between the principal and the agent.[84] This means that the granting of authority by the principal is not enough, but that the AI agent should accept the granting of authority. An AI agent, being a non-human agent, cannot give consent to act as someone's agent. According to Kerr, on the other hand, when the principal grants authority to an agent, the intention to create legal relations belongs to the principal. Therefore, it makes no difference if the AI agent cannot have intention to create legal relations. The agent does not need to agree to the conferring of authority. In cases where the principal is found to have conferred authority to the AI agent, the agency relationship will be established. The author justifies this view by claiming that disputes arising from the use of electronic agents in commercial life will generally involve only the relations between the principal and the third party.[85] Grapentin maintains that the argument that the rules of agency require the agent to act independently can be countered by relying on the fact that the rules of agency aim to extend the participation of the principal in legal transactions (using a third party). The only thing that matters is whether the principal has accepted the result of the action. The principle of private autonomy suggests that everyone could use technical means to make their declaration concrete.[86] Similarly, Chopra and White state that in order to fulfil the requirement of 'consent', the performance of the AI agent, acting on behalf of the principal and subject to its control, is sufficient.[87]

The other method of establishing an agency relationship is by employing the rules of apparent authority. In cases where the operator creates the idea or makes it appear to the outside world that the AI agent is operating under its authority, the operator is said to have granted apparent authority to an AI agent.[88] The principal provides the AI agent with the necessary means to get involved in acts and actions with third parties. Since apparent authority dispenses with the need for a manifestation of assent by the principal to the agent, the AI agent's consent to the manifestation of assent is not needed.[89]

It seems that this method of establishing the agency relationship is not very convincing. According to Bellia, in order to apply the rules regarding apparent authority, 'the manifestation to the third part must not be merely that this is my bot, but that this is my agent'. Therefore, in order for apparent authority to exist, a capacity for actual authority is needed. If the law does not recognize the capacity of AI agents to exercise actual authority, there can be no representation that the AI agent has authority.[90]

[81] Specht and Harold, 'Roboter als Vertragspartner', 44.

[82] Kerr, 'Spirits', 243; Grapentin, *Vertragsschluss*, p. 96.

[83] Bellia, 'Electronic Agents', 1060. See also Sabrina Kis, 'Contracts and Electronic Agents' (2004) 25 *LL.M: Theses and Essays* 25, at 35.

[84] See also Restatement (Third) of Agency § 1.01 Agency: 'the fiduciary relationship that arises when one person (a "principal") manifests assent to another person (an "agent")*and the agent manifests assent or otherwise consents so to act*'.

[85] Kerr, 'Spirits', 240.

[86] Grapentin, *Vertragsschluss*, p. 96.

[87] Chopra and White, *A Legal Theory*, p. 18.

[88] Kerr, 'Spirits', 240.

[89] Chopra and White, 'Agency Analysis', 376.

[90] Bellia, 'Electronic Agents', 1062.

Mik points out that apparent authority depends on the understanding of third parties and serves to protect their interests. The actions taken by the agent can be attributed to the principal only if third parties believe that they are transacting with an authorized agent. Users of search engines such as Google, however, do not have a perception that they are interacting with their agent.[91]

As can be derived from these explanations, if agency law rules are to be applied to determine the outcome of transactions entered into by the AI agent, one might need to make too many exceptions to these rules.

11.3.3.4 *What Happens If AI Agents Exceed Their Authority?*

Another important problem with the application of agency rules is determining when an AI agent exceeds its authority and what happens if an AI agent exceeds its authority. When the principal grants an agent actual authority to take an action, the agent can perform acts that are incidental to it, acts that accompany it and acts that are reasonably necessary to accomplish the principal's objectives.[92] The principal is also bound by the actions an agent takes in an emergent situation.[93] Generally speaking, if agents exceed their authority when acting on behalf of the principal, the principal is not bound by these acts. The agent is personally liable from these acts. However, the principal can ratify these unauthorized acts.[94] Following such ratification, the principal would be bound by these acts.

With earlier software agents, it was possible to look at the computer program's instructions to understand what the programmer was aiming to achieve and derive the scope of authority. However, modern AI systems function in a way that the programmers cannot predict or understand. Therefore, it is not possible to look at the design or instruction of the AI agent in order to understand the programmer or operator's intentions.[95] As a result, it proves to be more difficult to find out the scope of authority and determine if the AI agent has exceeded it. There are some views that AI agents – even stronger ones – are not legally competent and do not have the ability to act truly independently. This is because the ability to act independently includes the ability to make irrational or incorrect decisions; however, the results an AI agent calculates and executes will always be mathematically correct. When the AI agent is manipulated or makes a decision based on incorrect data, it only leads to an outcome that is objectively undesirable by the human entity. It will still be coherent and correct in itself.[96] So can we really talk about an AI agent exceeding its authority?

While trying to determine what constitutes an exceeding of authority in transactions generated by AI agents, the major problem is this: if an AI agent engages in behaviour that is unforeseen, a by-product of its ability to act autonomously and plan its own course of actions, can the principal claim that the AI agent has exceeded its authority?[97] In order to answer this

91 Mik, 'Automation to Autonomy', 11.
92 See Restatement (Third) of Agency, § 2.02 Scope of Actual Authority.
93 Bellia, 'Electronic Agents', 1061.
94 If the agent exceeds its authority when acting on behalf of the principal and the principal does not ratify this transaction, the principal is not bound. The principal may be bound only if the third party was justified in trusting the agent to act within the scope of their authority, and the principal acted or omitted in a way that generated justified trust or if the risk is for the principal, on the basis of generally accepted principles. See Hildebrandt, 'Legal Personhood'.
95 See Bathaee, 'AI Black Box', 907.
96 Grapentin, *Vertragsschluss*, p. 95.
97 Barfield, 'Artificial Intelligence', p. 24.

question properly, one should bear in mind that autonomy should be distinguished from unpredictability.[98] Autonomous action can take place without the knowledge of the principal. This is not exceeding authority, per se. But AI agents can stay within predefined boundaries and act in predictable ways while exercising autonomy in decision-making. Sometimes the outcome may be unpredictable. However, we believe that the undesired or unplanned outcome, which is a result of the particular manner chosen by the AI agent to fulfil the instructions laid out by the human agent, is not the same as exceeding the authority. The autonomy of the AI agent and the coding errors originate from the initial programming of the agent.[99] Therefore, the autonomous decisions that AI agents make, or the undesired results that originate from their programming, lie within the operator's sphere of responsibility. The operator of the AI agent cannot escape liability by asserting that the outcome of the AI agent's actions was unexpected or unplanned, and hence, that it had exceeded its authority.

According to the classical principles of agency, in cases where the principal does not ratify the transaction when the agent exceeded its authority, the third party may resort to the agent.[100] Even if the AI agent is recognized as solely responsible for the wrongdoing, there is no remedy for the aggrieved party since the artificial agent does not have its own patrimony.[101] Therefore, if agency principles were to be applied, either the principal or the third party has to bear the risk of the transactions resulting from the acts and actions of the agents.[102] It may seem useless to define AI agents as agents in the legal sense when they do not have personal assets and cannot be sued in court.[103]

Some authors argue that this problem could be dealt with by using registration certificates to limit an AI agent's authority. In this case, exceeding the power of representation would not be technically possible for the AI agent. Alternatively, one could consider compulsory insurance in the event that the contractual partner has suffered damage as a result of the exceeding of authority.[104]

11.3.3.5 AI Agents and Sub-agency

When the principal grants actual authority to an agent, this actual authority also includes a limited authority to delegate parts of such authority to another agent (i.e., the sub-agent). If sub-agency rules are applied to AI agents, an AI agent can act in collaboration with other agents and delegate parts of its tasks to them. In most of these cases, the operator/initiator of the AI agent is not even aware that the AI agent has delegated its tasks. As a result of this sub-agency, there might be instances where the operator finds out that the tasks performed by the sub-agent is not sufficiently related to the task, and hence, falls outside the scope of authority.[105] However, the operator of the AI entity would be bound by the action taken by another AI entity.[106]

98 Chopra and White, 'Artificial Agents', 2.1.
99 Mik, 'Automation to Autonomy', 11.
100 Kis, 'Electronic Agents', 41.
101 Bräutigam and Klindt, 'Industrie 4.0', 1138; Fiona Savary and Annabelle Reuter, 'Gestaltung von Vertragen mit KI' in Markus Kaulartz and Tom Braegelmann (eds.), *Rechtshandbuch Artificial Intelligence und Machine Learning* (Munich: Verlag C. H. Beck, 2020), p. 274.
102 Kis, 'Electronic Agents', 38; Pieper, 'Vertragsschluss mit KI', p. 245.
103 Dahiyat, 'Law and Software Agents', No. 5.2.
104 Bräutigam and Klindt, 'Industrie 4.0', 1138.
105 Weitzenboeck, 'Electronic Agents', 218.
106 Bellia, 'Electronic Agents', 1061.

11.4 CONCLUSION

Applying agency law principles to the problems that arise as a result of transactions generated by AI agents creates more problems than solutions. In order to decide if agency law provides adequate solutions to the problems that arise from the relationship between humans and AI agents, one should remember the purpose of agency. 'Agency has the objective of protecting the agent acting on behalf of his principal, while restricting the principal's responsibility. Finally, agency tries to make sure that the innocent third party will be offered an appropriate remedy.'[107] The use of AI agents results in similar concerns except for the protection of the agent in the case of robots. Therefore, in order to decide if agency rules are appropriate, one should seek a balance between the protection of the third party and the limitation of responsibility of the operator.

What is the right balance when AI agents engage in transactions for the benefit of their operator? When agency rules are applied, the operator is bound by almost all the acts of the AI agent and even the acts of the sub-agent. Even if somehow the AI agent is found solely responsible for its acts (because it exceeded its authority and the operator did not ratify it), the liability of the AI agent does not yield any legal results. The AI agent does not have legal personality. It cannot be sued in court and it has no patrimony. Therefore, applying the law of agency seems to depend on granting intelligent agents a legal personality. Without legal personality, no declaration of intent would exist; without a declaration of intent, the law of agency is not applicable.[108] If AI agents were accorded legal personality and contractual capacity, the problem of contracting would be resolved with minimum impact on the rules regarding the conclusion of contracts. Consequently, it makes sense to define AI agents as tools until they are granted legal personality.

One should keep in mind that there is still human involvement in AI systems' decision-making since humans map out the decision-making processes. AI agents continue to be a digital reflection of their operator.[109] When fully autonomous AI agents are introduced, however, there will be cases that AI agents will be fully independent of human instruction and they will gather the data to be used for analysis on their own. In that case, it might be impractical to define them as tools. This possibility was anticipated in UETA, which takes into consideration the possibility for courts to construe the definition of electronic agents by recognizing their new capabilities to keep up with the developments in AI technology.[110] 'That is, through developments in AI, a computer may be able to learn through experience, modify the instructions of their own programs, and even devise new instructions . . . If such developments occur, courts may construe the definition of an electronic agent accordingly in order to recognize such capabilities.' It can be concluded that with the advances in AI technology, especially with AI systems that make decisions, there might be a change of paradigm as to how the law defines AI agents. Eventually, these highly autonomous AI agents may be accorded a legal status.

[107] Kis, 'Electronic Agents', 37.
[108] Schirmer, 'Artificial Intelligence', 130.
[109] Grapentin, *Vertragsschluss*, p. 89.
[110] UETA, Comments to Section 2, p. 8.

PART IV

AI and Physical Manifestations

12

Liability for Autonomous Vehicle Accidents

Marjolaine Monot-Fouletier

12.1 INTRODUCTION

Secreting a diffuse liability, potentially involving a large chain of actors (designers, managers of the system, entity that authorized its use, vehicle manufacturer, intelligent road network operator and the driver), autonomous circulation defies liability law with regard to the requirement to establish a fault or at least accountability. Accordingly, the complex system of algorithms allowing autonomous circulation disrupts these classical mechanisms of liability, which do not appear to be able to meet the contemporary concern of guaranteeing compensation to victims of accidents caused by these vehicles.

Therefore, to guarantee the victims of the algorithmic risk, a risk that is socially conditioned, and therefore to cover technological innovation, it is necessary to question the adaptability of the common liability law and of existing special civil or administrative liability systems, before considering the relevance of building a hybrid liability system organised around a compensation fund mechanism, which could allow both fair compensation of damages and effective accountability of the various actors in the complex system, without unduly impeding technological innovation.

On 11 November 2020, the car manufacturer Honda announced that it had obtained – and this is a world first – the right to market Level 3 autonomous vehicles in Japan.[1] However, the prospect of seeing Level 3–5 autonomous vehicles in general circulation on our roads seems more and more distant, despite the craze for this technology, referred to as artificial intelligence (AI) technology and the fantasy of total safety that it underlies. Indeed, the technical, ethical and legal difficulties raised by its use seem to be limiting their widespread development at the highest level of autonomy.

The deployment of vehicles equipped with intelligent driver delegation systems is already under way and seems to have a golden future ahead, holding so much promise of fewer accidents for the benefit of all, drivers as well as other road users. It is, however, no less risk-laden and raises questions about how its use should be regulated. Unlike traditional vehicles, so-called self-driving vehicles are based on a complex system using algorithms whose (at least partial) autonomous decision-making power questions the relevance of keeping the concept of the driver, which has been central to the regulations on road traffic accidents until now, and in

[1] For a detailed study of the six levels of autonomy retained at international level, see 'Autonomous and Connected Vehicles: Current Challenges and Research Paths', INRIA, 2019, p. 6, www.inria.fr/sites/default/files/2019-10/inrialivre blancvac-180529073843.pdf.

particular the Vienna Convention,[2] the most successful legal framework to date at the international level.

By taking the full decision-making power away from human beings and entrusting it to complex systems because they can learn and involve a host of actors and components, the autonomous vehicle has brought about a technological but also, without doubt, a legal shift. The sharing of decision-making power between the driver and the algorithmic system, or the allocation of full decision-making power to the latter, again raises the question of the liability regime applicable in the event of an accident. The complexity of the actions (which may not necessarily be unravelled by technical expertise) and the multiplicity of actors involved in such an accident defy the rules of liability law: the various on-board systems interact with each other and with drivers on a very wide scale; they operate in an opaque manner and as a result it is difficult to ascertain the place in which the harm occurred; there is no real prospect of anticipating their behaviour, which by definition is dynamic and evolving, and therefore the traditional requirement of establishing fault, accountability and a causal link seems, if not wholly inapplicable, then at least very difficult to satisfy within a time frame that might guarantee effective compensation of the victims.

The technological shift represented by the autonomous vehicle perhaps requires a structural shift in our understanding of the risks linked to its use, in order to guarantee fair compensation for victims and thereby support technological innovation,[3] in so far as the potential of a technological risk that is difficult to accept at a social level and difficult to remedy from a legal perspective may inhibit innovation (despite its use being associated with the prospect of a lower accident rate[4] due to its alleged infallibility).

Aware of this risk, the designers and manufacturers of autonomous vehicles and, more widely, of AI technologies, have been proactive in drawing up ethics charters. Given the stakes involved in the development of autonomous driving (potential infringements of rights and freedoms, harm to persons and property), however, we cannot delegate to private actions (the purpose of which is sometimes only to legitimise unsatisfactory practices for the defence of rights and freedoms),[5] and there is now an unstoppable wave of public regulations tackling the use of AI and the resulting harm from a legal perspective.

The regulations on international road traffic hitherto embodied in the Vienna Convention have recently been supplemented by three regulations adopted by the United Nations on 23 June 2020 to take account of the new safety requirements for the use of driver delegation systems.[6]

Europe has also committed itself to forging ahead with regulating AI. On 19 February 2020, the European Commission presented a White Paper on AI[7] that was both a present picture and forward-looking, asserting that while

[2] Vienna Convention on Road Traffic, 8 November 1968, in force 21 May 1977 (thirty-six signatory countries, eighty-four participants).

[3] Road traffic had already been the impetus for significant evolution of the law of civil liability in France: Cour de Cassation [French Supreme Court], Plenary Chamber, 13 February 1930, *Bulletins des arrêts de la Cour de cassation* [Bulletin of judgments of the Cour de Cassation] No. 34, p. 68.

[4] In its report of 2016, 'Saving Lives: Boosting Car Safety in the EU' https://www.europarl.europa.eu/doceo/document/A-8-2017-0330_EN.html, the European Commission recalls that '[e]xperts have stated that about 95% of road accidents involve some level of human error, while … 75% are caused by human error alone'.

[5] Cf. C. Castets-Renard, 'Comment construire une intelligence artificielle responsable et inclusive?' (2020) 4, *Recueil Dalloz [Dalloz Collection]*, 225 (critical 'ethical washing').

[6] Regulations available at: www.unece.org/fileadmin/DAM/trans/doc/2020/wp29grva/ECE-TRANS-WP29-2020-079-Revised.pdf and https://undocs.org/fr/ECE/TRANS/WP.29/2020/81. These regulations, adopted by some sixty countries, concern autonomous Level 3 vehicles and will be applicable to all new vehicles in the EU from 2022 onwards.

[7] https://ec.europa.eu/info/sites/info/files/commission-white-paper-artificial-intelligence-feb2020_fr.pdf. This White Paper builds on two Commission releases of 25 April 2018 (https://ec.europa.eu/transparency/regdoc/rep/1/2018/FR/COM-2018-237-F1-FR-MAIN-PART-1.PDF) and 8 April 2019 (https://ec.europa.eu/transparency/regdoc/rep/1/2019/FR/

> developers and deployers of AI are already subject to European legislation on fundamental rights ..., consumer protection, and product safety and product liability ..., [and while] [c]onsumers expect the same level of safety and respect of their rights whether or not a product or a system relies on AI ..., some specific features of AI ... can make the application and enforcement of this legislation more difficult. For this reason, there is a need to examine whether current legislation is able to address the risks of AI and can be effectively enforced, whether adaptations of the legislation are needed, or whether new legislation is needed.[8]

This White Paper was followed by a Commission report on the consequences of AI, the Internet of Things and robotics on safety and liability.[9]

On 20 October 2020, the European Parliament adopted proposals on how best to regulate AI: it recommends 'to present a new legal framework outlining the ethical principles and legal obligations to be followed when developing, deploying and using artificial intelligence, robotics and related technologies in the EU'; it also recommends developing intellectual property rights and a 'future-oriented civil liability framework'.[10] The Council of Europe is also active, having published a report in 2019 entitled 'Responsibility and Artificial Intelligence'.[11] Finally, the European Union is progressing on the legislative path, with a proposed regulation, known as the "Artificial Intelligence Act" (AI Act), introduced on April 21, 2021 (COM/2021/206).

States are acting at the national level;[12] France in particular, which, after having also developed an ethical approach to AI,[13] has clarified in the PACTE Law of May 2019[14] the system of criminal liability in the event of accidents caused by autonomous vehicles while they are being tested. Moreover, the French legislator is preparing within the context of a new Statute on Mobility[15] (LOM or *Loi d'orientation des mobilités*), to adapt the Transport Code and legal rules on civil liability to better regulate the circulation of vehicles with delegated driving.

All these provisions have two points in common. First, they seek to go beyond merely questioning ethics in the use of algorithms by offering legal solutions to regulate the design and use of products or services. Second, they incorporate the need to account for the protection of fundamental rights, making the operation of AI more secure, and guaranteeing the effectiveness of liability regimes for harms caused by AI, without placing excessive impediments on innovation that is perceived as beneficial for these same individuals and society as a whole.

COM-2019-168-F1-FR-MAIN-PART-1.PDF) proposing a strategy for Europe on AI, as well as the 2019 *Ethics Guidelines for Trustworthy AI* by the expert group set up by the Commission, https://ec.europa.eu/futurium/en/ai-alliance-consultation/guidelines#Top.

8 https://ec.europa.eu/info/sites/info/files/commission-white-paper-artificial-intelligence-feb2020_fr.pdf.

9 https://ec.europa.eu/info/sites/info/files/report-safety-liability-artificial-intelligence-feb2020_fr.pdf. See also the report of the 'New technologies' subgroup of the 'Liability and new technologies' expert group entitled 'Liability for Artificial Intelligence and Other Emerging Technologies', https://ec.europa.eu/newsroom/dae/document.cfm?doc_id=63199.

10 European Parliament Press Release, 21 October 2020, www.europarl.europa.eu/news/en/press-room/20201016IPR89544/parliament-leads-the-way-on-first-set-of-eu-rules-for-artificial-intelligence.

11 Council of Europe, 'Responsibility and AI: A Study of the Implications of Advanced Digital Technologies (Including AI Systems) for the Concept of Responsibility within a Human Rights Framework', https://rm.coe.int/responsability-and-ai-fr/168097d9c6.

12 The United States, which has not signed the International Vienna Convention on Road Traffic and can therefore dispense with the principle of a 'driver in full control of their vehicle' as a basis for liability in the context of land motor vehicle traffic, has already been able to begin adapting the legal framework to the changes brought about by the circulation of partially autonomous vehicles: www.ncsl.org/research/transportation/autonomous-vehicles-self-driving-vehicles-enacted%20legislation.aspx and the *Self Drive Act* (H.R.3388), July 2017, www.congress.gov/bill/115th-congress/house-bill/3388.

13 www.vie-publique.fr/rapport/37225-donner-un-sens-lintelligence-artificielle-pour-une-strategie-nation.

14 Law No. 2019-486 of 22 May 2019 relating to the growth and transformation of businesses, known as the PACTE law, *Journal Officiel de la République Française* [Official Journal of the French Republic (*JORF*)] No. 0119, 23 May 2019.

15 Law No. 2019-1428 (24 December 2019), *JORF* (26 December 2020).

On the other hand, the various proposals for regulating the use of autonomous vehicles, the material interface with AI, try to reconcile the desire to adapt existing legal provisions in order to regulate AI and the desire to renew them by adding new mechanisms that would be better able to meet the identified objectives. Indeed, such a legal framework must fit *ex ante*, when vehicles are placed on the market, to ensure that the systems are stable and reliable, as well as *ex post*, to ensure satisfactory compensation in case of accidents, by definition few in number but serious, that could result.

This chapter will focus on this *ex post* legal framework, in so far as even if the *ex ante* work to make the system safer is substantial, it will not lead to zero risk, and therefore, if only to avoid dissuading users from applying new technologies, the question of ensuring compensation for victims must be resolved. The aim will be to suggest possible responses on how to impose liability on the actors and ensure compensation for victims of the use of autonomous vehicles.

Reference will be mainly made to French liability law, both in terms of the civil and administrative law aspects, in so far as public entities play a major role in developing the use of autonomous vehicles (approval, designing an intelligent road network to allow guidance of the vehicle) and will therefore also be potentially accountable for the harm they may cause.

French liability law is composed of different regimes whose logic is based *ab initio* on the determination of the liable person and of a causal link between the act or omission and the harm: the person who decides to act or not to act, or the person who directs and controls what acts, is liable. However, where the harm is linked to the use of a technology acting as a complex intermediary between human decision and the harmful action, the traditional law of liability struggles to cope with the new difficulties in determining the source of the harm, identifying the liable person,[16] the causal link between fault/harm and therefore the compensation of the victims.[17] The autonomous vehicle, a complex and learning system, produces a batch of liabilities implicating a number of actors, without solving the attribution of a fault, the origin of which is lost in the ramifications of the algorithms activated autonomously while it circulates.

Faced with this situation, liability in positive law, whether based on fault or on risk, can continue to provide satisfactory solutions for the compensation of accidents due to a vehicle with limited driver delegation. However, the specificities of the activation of algorithmic technologies in an autonomous vehicle, and in particular the seriousness of the risks involved, require a paradigm shift by developing regimes based on solidarity rather than on the principle of liability alone. This will allow victims of an accidents caused by an autonomous vehicle to be afforded the same degree of guarantee of compensation as the victim of the same accident caused by an ordinary vehicle.

[16] Cour de Cassation, 2nd Civil Chamber, 21 July 1982, *Desmares*, a case that strongly influenced the subsequent adoption of Law No. 85-677 of 5 July 1985 relating to the compensation of victims of traffic accidents, known as the *Badinter Law* (*JORF* of 6 July 1985), the primary objective of which is to facilitate victim compensation.

[17] New technologies have already prompted the development of a special regime of liability for consequences attributable to objects, in order to enable compensation: harm caused by the use of a steam engine in 1896 (Cour de Cassation, Civil Chamber, 16 June 1896, *Teffaine*), or of a motorised land vehicle in 1930 (Cour de Cassation, Plenary Chamber, 13 February 1930, *Jand'heur*).

12.2 ADAPTABILITY AND RELEVANCE OF THE GENERAL RULES ON LIABILITY: PITFALL OF FAULT AND IDENTIFYING THE LIABLE AGENT

This section will explore the role played by traditional regimes of liability based on fault (Article 1240 of the Civil Code) (1.1) and custodian liability (Article 1242 of the Civil Code) (1.2) as means of ensuring victim compensation.

12.2.1 *Impracticability of Fault-Based Liability Regimes*

There can be many different tortfeasors in the case of accidents caused by a vehicle with delegated driving: first of all, there are third parties to the accident itself, public or private persons in charge of one of the elements of the technological aspects within the transport system (the designers of each system component, the manufacturer of the technological interface, the certifier of the vehicle or a system element, the vehicle manufacturer, the infrastructure manager, the communication network manager, the manager of the updating of system elements, etc.); then, there is the driver, a central actor in the current regime but who takes a secondary role in the context of autonomous driving. In addition to this 'human' liability, it is necessary to consider whether it might be appropriate to hold liable the AI itself.

12.2.1.1 *Diluting the Fault of 'Those with Knowledge'*

The complex system consisting of an autonomous vehicle and the intelligent environment in which it operates is a guarantee of improved road safety owing to its exceptional reliability. Consequently, its designers, manufacturers and managers should be at the forefront of those likely to be liable for any harmful defects, assuming them to be related to a design, programming or management error by the aforementioned agents.

However, it will be particularly difficult to both identify and attribute fault since these complex systems are based on multiple components, and hence multiple designers. Therefore, the traceability of the process leading to the harm will necessarily be blurred by this succession of actors and by the evolution of the behaviour of a system that by nature constantly adapts to its environment according to principles that are largely opaque. Even if black boxes were to ensure a certain traceability of the vehicle's operation, its complexity would necessarily require interpretation, and therefore long and costly disputes between technical experts, which would prevent victims from obtaining compensation rapidly.

Most importantly of all, once the designer(s) of the vehicle and of the underlying infrastructure have raised them to full autonomy through deep learning, how could they be held personally liable for harm caused by an action/decision 'invented' by an AI? The constant adaptation of the system to its environment induces a form of behavioural unpredictability that is inherent to autonomous vehicles. Consequently, it is hardly possible to attribute directly to the designer or manufacturer of the system, a fault caused by a behaviour over which they do not have/no longer have control.

12.2.1.2 *Driver's Fault: The Lack of an Agent*

An autonomous vehicle must act in a safe manner without any human intervention by the driver being required. Depending on the level of autonomy of the vehicle, user control will become illusory. Within the meaning of the Vienna Convention in its last amended version of 23 March 2016, the driver remains a natural person in so far as they must 'possess the necessary physical and mental ability and be in a fit mental and physical condition',[18] a drafting that cannot be transposed as it stands to an algorithmic system of driver delegation.

As for the French Cour de Cassation, called to rule on the application of the Badinter Law[19] that establishes different procedures for victim compensation according to whether or not they are the driver, it defined the driver as the person controlling the vehicle,[20] without the requirement of absolute control (and without requirement for the driver to be necessarily present in the vehicle, which may be significant in the case of autonomous vehicles, especially collective vehicles, which may be monitored remotely). The question is raised as to the degree of control required over the autonomous vehicle for user fault liability to continue to be seriously contemplated. It no longer seems legitimate to hold the driver liable for the harmful behaviour of a system which acts without them, other than considering that the person at the wheel retains the ability, and hence the obligation, to stop the autonomous operation of the vehicle and take over where such a decision is required. But to what extent will they be able to decide in time whether such a decision is appropriate? To what extent could their reaction time, which may vary in length, be considered in determining their liability, if any?

Most importantly of all, in practice, who will take the risk of purchasing an autonomous vehicle for a high price, knowing that system failures will always be primarily attributed to them as the driver who should maintain control thereof? The economic and social stakes involved in the deployment of autonomous vehicles will require the mitigation of the legal consequences attached to driver status, and breaking the link between controlling and driving a vehicle, which will be outdated in the medium term.

12.2.1.3 *Fault Attributed to an AI System: The Ineffective Accountability of Robots*

Would the system of fault-based liability be more relevant if the fault were attributed to the AI itself? After getting over the surprise at the paradoxical attitude of seeking the liability of an entity that is otherwise considered infallible, we find that there is indeed an academic trend in favour of this proposal. The European Parliament itself, in its report to the Commission of 16 February 2017, recommended consideration of 'creating a specific legal status for robots in the long run, so that at least the most sophisticated autonomous robots could be established as having the status of electronic persons responsible for making good any damage they may cause'.[21]

However, the existence of such a legal personality only makes sense if it is accompanied by the recognition of its own intentions that could justify it incurring liability. Now, the scientific community is very widely reserved[22] as to the assertion that AI decides alone and invents its decisions independently of any human intention. How could one claim that a robot has free will when it has no rules or values of its own to regulate its behaviour? Both the autonomous vehicle and the components of the complex system that underlies its operation are at best only interfaces that depend on algorithms to trigger their actions according to a process and objectives that one

[18] Vienna Convention on Road Traffic, 8 November 1968, Art. 8(3).

[19] Law No. 85-677 of 5 July 1985 on compensation of road traffic accidents victims.

[20] Cf. e.g. Cour de Cassation, 2nd Civil Chamber, 31 May 2000, No. 98-21-203, *Bull. civ.* [*Bulletin civil* (Civil Law Case Reports)] 2000, II, No. 62 (concerning a passenger considered to be a driver to the extent that they grasp the steering wheel and press on the leg of the person sitting behind the wheel in order to accelerate the vehicle).

[21] European Parliament Resolution, 16 February 2017, Recommendations to the Commission on Civil Law Rules on Robotics (2015/2103(INL)), (59f), www.europarl.europa.eu/doceo/document/TA-8-2017-0051_EN.html.

[22] Cf. J.-G. Ganascia, *Le Mythe de la Singularité – Faut-il craindre l'intelligence artificielle?* [The *Myth of Singularity – Is Artificial Intelligence to Be Feared?*] Paris: Ed. Seuil, 2017; R. Chatila, 'Intelligence artificielle et robotique: un état des lieux en perspective avec le droit' [Artificial Intelligence: A Review of the Current Situation from a Legal Perspective], (2016), No. 6, *Dalloz IP/IT*, 284.

or more human beings have assigned to them. Their decisions are not due to consideration but are automatic.

Furthermore, in terms of effectiveness, recognition of the legal personality of an autonomous vehicle – of the complex system that it actually hosts – and of its legal liability is of no interest in terms of guaranteeing compensation for victims: first, because this algorithmic person is not solvent as it does not have any assets of its own, and second, because contemplating the liability of a complex system treated as a person leads above all to the exclusion of liability of its designers, manufacturers and managers, which is hardly an incentive in terms of the safety requirements of the systems put on the market.

Most of all, we feel that such recognition would be dangerous in that it would deny the fact that AI only intervenes in a relationship of material complementarity with the human being. It cannot replace it from a legal perspective and more particularly as far as civil liability is concerned. Its actions are not separable from the decisions of the person who designed it and/or those it serves: the human being must 'remain in control' of the AI.[23] In any event, irrespective of whether one wishes to retain fault-based liability of the complex system, its designers, its manufacturers, its managers or the driver, the difficulties relating to the burden of proof of fault encourage a shift towards liability based on a presumption of fault.

12.2.1.4 *Limitations of Liability Based on a Presumption of Fault*

Such a regime should place the primary burden on either the designer or the manufacturer of the autonomous vehicle, as they are the most capable of controlling the AI that operates it. The advantage of such an approach in terms of facilitating the compensation of accident victims lies in the fact that it encourages these actors to propose systems that are particularly reliable and provide a minimum level of transparency, so as to ensure the traceability of operations in as detailed a manner as possible, enabling them to prove the absence of fault. The fear of liability downstream after the vehicle has been released into circulation would incite, by anticipation, greater emphasis on safety and transparency upstream.

First, however, such a solution does not in any manner mitigate the difficulties in accurately identifying the presumed liable person (which designer or manufacturer should be found liable, in a system that consists of a multitude of interacting technological tools? And what of an accident involving several autonomous vehicles?) and will not eliminate the complicated search for how to share out the burden of compensation. Second, as the autonomous vehicle system is rapidly evolving, adapting and being regularly updated, it will become particularly complex to furnish proof of a negligent design, and increasingly so with the passing of time between the vehicle was put into circulation and the occurrence of the accident. Consequently, in practice, the choice of liability on the grounds of a presumption of fault would amount somewhat to a regime that would virtually systematically place liability on the designers and/or manufacturers, and which could dissuade them from investing in new AI technologies.

To mitigate this deterrent effect with dangerous consequences for innovation, a liability exemption mechanism on the grounds of a technological hazard that was unforeseeable at the time the complex system was designed could be integrated into this legal regime. But here again, the ontologically evolving nature of the system could allow the exemption clause to apply systematically, thereby leaving the victim unarmed in their attempt to obtain compensation.

[23] Cf. Muller Report, Opinion of the European Economic and Social Council, 31 May 2017, No. 2017/C 288/01, https://eur-lex.europa.eu/legal-content.

Consequently, the reversal of the burden of proof would not appear to be relevant in dealing with the harm caused by a system as complex and advanced as an autonomous vehicle.

12.2.1.5 *Unlikely Application of Custodian Liability*

The applicability of custodian liability[24] to accidents caused by autonomous vehicles seems highly unlikely. First of all, its applicability depends on the existence of a tangible thing. Now, the difficulty here arises due to the fact that the harm is not connected with the AI interface (the end-product autonomous vehicle) but with the technologies it contains, and the algorithms: are they[25] things? Should they not rather be classified as services? Moreover, the same question also arises with regard to the complex system outside the vehicle and which operates it (intelligent road network, traffic data relay terminals, etc.).

If we agree that a complex system of liability is needed, we would still need to determine the custodian of the system, and who can be considered to be the primary custodian in so far as from a legal perspective, custody is not cumulative. One could then seek to split the thing, for the fair distribution of liability, if any, among several custodians according to whether they are custodians of the structure of the thing (the designer and/or manufacturer) or custodians of the behaviour thereof (the user and/or maintenance manager). However, given the opacity and intrinsic complexity of the system, it will be extremely difficult to attribute the cause of the harm with a sufficient degree of certainty to the structure or behaviour of the thing.

Above all, case law defines a custodian as one who has the power to use, control and direct a thing.[26] Now, an autonomous vehicle and the complex system related to it are designed to operate autonomously thanks to their learning and decision-making abilities. Their development is justified by their ability to dispense with a custodian, so it is not really possible to refer to a power of direction. At the most one could refer to a power of control, limited to the ability of its supervisor to take over or stop its operation altogether: the stop button as regards the driver, recall of the vehicle as regards the manufacturer or even recall of the software programmes for the designer of each of them. Case law could be considered as providing the necessary response to this difficulty: in a judgment of 5 January 1956,[27] the Cour de Cassation created a tailor-made liability regime for dangerous objects, those whose dangerousness does not result from a failure of supervision by their custodian but due to their inherent characteristics. One could try to apply this case law to autonomous vehicles, but in practice the capacity of self-learning and of self-development of the system considerably dilutes the liability of the designer as well as that of the manufacturer, causing liability on the grounds of custodian liability to be purely hypothetical. Lastly, in any event, the regime of custodian liability would apply only where the conditions for the special regime established by the Badinter Law[28] on the compensation of victims of road traffic accidents are not met.

Consequently, whether on the grounds of personal fault or custodian liability, the conditions of application of the general rules of civil liability do not guarantee compensation for the harm caused by an accident involving an autonomous vehicle. As they stand, these regimes are at a

[24] *Civil Code*, Article 1242.

[25] Software virus has been classified as an object by the courts. Cf. notably Cour de Cassation Commercial Chamber, 8 February 1994: *Bull. civ.* [*Bulletin civil* (Civil Law Case Reports)] IV, No. 56.

[26] Cour de Cassation, Plenary Chamber, Franck, 2 December 1941, *Bull. ch. mixte* [Bulletin of the Civil plenary chamber] No. 292.

[27] Cour de Cassation, 2nd Civil Chamber, 5 January 1956, Oxygène liquide, *Bulletin of the Civil plenary chamber* No. 2, p. 1.

[28] Law No. 85-677 of 5 July 1985.

dead end both in terms of attribution of fault and of establishing a causal link between the harm and the activation of the complex autonomous vehicle system/traffic environment. One solution may be to bolster the regulations upstream that relate to the safety obligations of each actor in the vehicle's operating chain, so as to very precisely define their role, that of the AI of which they are in charge and which is involved in the complex system, in order to be able to attribute fault more easily. If, however, one wishes a greater guarantee that victims are compensated rapidly, the conditions for liability will have to be eased. The courts, and subsequently the law, have devised special legal regimes for this purpose.

12.3 ADAPTABILITY AND RELEVANCE OF EXISTING SPECIAL REGIMES

The public authorities have taken account of the specific nature of certain types of accident in view of the conditions in which they occur and their recurrence, which made it both difficult for the perpetrator thereof to incur liability under general law and made it socially unacceptable for victims not to be compensated. This led to the Badinter Law and to liability for defective products (the applicability of harm caused by an autonomous vehicle must be examined), as well as to liability based on risk established by administrative case law, which shares the same principle of facilitating the victim's compensation by setting aside the requirement of fault.

12.3.1 *Badinter Law: Applicability to Implementation*

The main purpose of this legislation is to compensate victims of harm caused by a vehicle involved in a traffic accident. It establishes a right to compensation for victims, which will be paid either by the insurer of the driver of the vehicle or by the Fonds de Garantie des Assurances Obligatoires [Mandatory Insurance Guarantee Fund], the agency in charge of compensating victims of road traffic accidents as a matter of national solidarity when the person responsible for the accident cannot be found or is not insured.

The 1985 law would seem the obvious provision of choice to apply to the specific case of autonomous vehicles, in so far as the vehicle is a motorised land vehicle and the concept of implication is sufficiently broad to accommodate the circumstances of a vehicle that does nothing more than, for example, be guided by an intelligent road network.[29] The Badinter Law allows victims to avoid proving fault, which is particularly difficult in the case of a complex autonomous system. Moreover, it does not accept force majeure, and in particular technical malfunction, as grounds for the exclusion of liability, a point that we consider to be particularly fundamental in the case of autonomous vehicles.

However, under this law the victim is still required to prove a causal link between the involvement of the vehicle and the harm caused, which in the case of an accident caused by an autonomous vehicle remains particularly difficult to prove because of the multiple actors and systems involved. Therefore, while the spirit of the Badinter Law and its compensation system may embrace the scenario of harm caused by an autonomous vehicle, it does not provide a sufficient guarantee of compensation to victims, who are forced to undertake the tricky demonstration of a causal link between the complex system and the harm suffered.

[29] The courts have held that the Badinter Law applies in the case of a non-active vehicle: see, e.g., Cour de Cassation 2nd Civil Chamber, 4 December 1985, No. 84-13.226, *Bulletin of the Civil plenary chamber*, 1985, II, No. 186.

12.3.1.1 *Uncertainties Raised by Liability for Defective Products*

If it can be demonstrated that the harm resulting from the use of an autonomous vehicle is linked to a safety defect in the vehicle existing before it was put into circulation, the liability of its manufacturer may be sought on the basis of Article 1245 of the Civil Code relating to harm in connection with defective products within the meaning of the European Directive of 25 July 1985.[30] Such a regime is of relevance to the victims owing to the fact that the manufacturer would incur liability without any need to prove the manufacturer's fault. However, several difficulties in application can again be found here.

First of all, it will be necessary to determine who in the complex autonomous vehicle system can be designated as the manufacturer. In this regard, Article 1245-5 of the Civil Code provides that a manufacturer is any person who has participated in the manufacture of the defective product, and consequently, the entire chain of participants in the complex autonomous vehicle system, including the designers of its components, as subcontractors, may be targeted, despite the fact that the victim themselves must seek remedy exclusively from the manufacturer of the finished product.

Second, are we really dealing with a finished product? Yes, without doubt if we consider the material interface of the system (the vehicle), but what about the on-board technology, the basic software? This point needs clarification. In this case, the European Commission has suggested a revision of the definition of a product 'to better reflect the complexity of emerging technologies and ensure that compensation is always available for damage caused by products that are defective because of software or other digital features'.[31]

Above all, the regime of liability for defective products does not apply to defect occurring after the vehicle has been placed on the market, and yet the autonomous vehicle contains AI technologies the behaviour of which evolves with its use. It is therefore necessary to extend the applicability of Article 1245 to defects arising during the learning process after it has been placed on the market. This would however give rise to a very complex litigation concerning the distinction between the harm linked to such a defect and harm linked to misuse. In this respect, the European Commission, aware that 'autonomy can affect the safety of the product' as it can 'alter a product's characteristics substantially, including its safety features', suggests that 'self-learning features prolong liability of the producer', as the manufacturer 'should have foreseen certain changes'. It concludes that the concept of putting into circulation currently used in the European Directive 'could be revisited' to consider the 'risks of evolution and modification of products. Such review could also help clarify who is liable for any changes made to the product.'[32]

Article 1245-10 of the Civil Code exempts a manufacturer from liability where it could not have anticipated or detected the existence of a harmful defect based on 'the state of scientific and technical knowledge at the time when they put the product into circulation'. Since AI systems are evolutionary in nature, the exemption would be systematic, except for cases holding the manufacturer liable for defects in the design or programming that enabled the robot to adopt harmful conduct. This would have the effect of creating an obligation to monitor the risks of

[30] Directive 85/374/EEC of 25 July 1985 on the approximation of the laws, regulations and administrative provisions of the Member States concerning liability for defective products, https://eur-lex.europa.eu/legal-content/EN/TXT/?uri=celex%3A31985L0374.

[31] Report from the Commission on the safety and liability implications of Artificial Intelligence, the Internet of Things and robotics, February 2020, p. 16.

[32] Report from the Commission on the safety and liability implications of Artificial Intelligence, the Internet of Things and robotics, 2020, p. 18.

development of autonomous vehicles. This would be in accord with Article 1245-3 of the Civil Code, which states that a 'product is defective if it does not offer the safety that can legitimately be expected', by considering that the level of safety legitimately expected from AI consists of infallible functioning.

Lastly, even once these various difficulties of application had been overcome, the problem of establishing a causal link between the defect in the complex system and the harm caused is still present at this point. Article 1245-8 of the Civil Code provides that 'the plaintiff must prove the harm, the defect and the causal link between the defect and the harm'. The mere involvement of the product in the realisation of the harm will not be sufficient to prove that it is defective.[33] In view of the complexity of the autonomous vehicle, it will be difficult (and costly to the point of dissuading the victim of harm from making a claim) to prove that it is defective, and without such proof, it will not be possible for the manufacturer to incur liability. Here again, it is possible to adapt Article 1245, which could provide a presumption of defectiveness of the autonomous vehicle as a particularly complex system carrying a high risk of harm. Such a mechanism of presumption of causal connection already exists for the marketing of drugs, if the presumptions are serious, precise and concordant.[34]

In any event, these possible adjustments to the regime of product liability do not make it possible to go beyond the problem of the autonomy of the vehicle, which in practice makes determining individualised liability illusory. Indeed, this autonomy induces an element of unpredictability that is not an ordained dysfunctional behaviour but the logical result of the learning of the system, which can evolve without any behaviour being qualified as defective, and therefore without Article 1245 of the Civil Code being applicable.[35]

The widespread use of autonomous vehicles poses a specific risk in terms of liability in so far as it leads to deployment throughout public space, with the potential for serious harm to persons and property. In this context, it is necessary to overcome the problems arising from the complexity, opacity and autonomy of these systems by accepting an approach to liability based on risk rather than fault. As the autonomous vehicle is a high-risk system (despite improved road safety being the basis of its use), the harm resulting from its use could fall within the scope of a regime of no-fault liability for risk, as already exists in French law.

12.3.1.2 *Risk-Based Liability*

French administrative case law has long taken into account the dangerousness of certain objects or methods directly linked to State action in the public interest and capable of causing serious harm to a significant number of persons. The conviction that such harm must be borne by the local authority on the grounds of the dangerousness of a situation that was justified *ab initio* in the public interest, has led the courts to create no-fault liability for such risks.[36] Compensation is based on the collectivisation of risk through the use of public funds. This system remains based on liability but not on fault.

[33] See especially Cour de Cassation 1st Civil Chamber, 27 June 2018, FS-P+B, No. 17-17.469.

[34] ECJ, 21 June 2017, No. C-621/15, *N. W. and others* v. *Sanofi Pasteur.*

[35] European Parliament Resolution of 16 February 2017 (cited *supra*), provides that:

> notwithstanding the scope of Directive 85/374/EEC, the current legal framework would not be sufficient to cover the damage caused by the new generation of robots, insofar as they can be equipped with adaptive and learning abilities entailing a certain degree of unpredictability in their behaviour, since those robots would autonomously learn from their own variable experience and interact with their environment in a unique and unforeseeable manner.

[36] Conseil d'État [Supreme Administrative Court], 28 March 1919, *Regnault-Desroziers*, No. 62273, *Recueil Lebon* [Lebon Collection]: explosion of a stockpile of ammunition stored in a military fort located in the Paris suburbs.

The same spirit in the provisions of the Badinter Law, which provide that where rules on civil liability do not enable compensation for the personal injuries of a road accident victim because the driver is unknown, insolvent or uninsured, a compensation fund will act in substitute to provide compensation, once the circumstances of the harm and the existence of a causal link between the vehicle and the harm have been demonstrated. Here it is the intrinsic dangerousness of the vehicle, the major social risk, that justifies the introduction of a special liability regime.

Among the applications of no-fault administrative liability for risk, the application to medical treatment contingencies[37] is relevant, and provides that when a medical act required for a patient's diagnosis or treatment presents a known but exceptionally rare risk, the public hospital will incur liability if, notably, the performance of this act is the direct cause of the harm of an extremely serious kind. This medical treatment risk, like the vehicle technological risk, is covered by a specific regime that guarantees compensation to the victim independently of any fault. The same should apply to the technological or algorithmic risk associated with the use of autonomous vehicles. Indeed, this is one of the avenues being expressly explored by the European Commission.[38] However, the difficulties in applying these special regimes (proving the defect or dangerousness and a causal link) maintain the legal uncertainty surrounding compensation for harm, which is detrimental both to the victims and to those involved in the chain of production and distribution of the autonomous vehicle.

12.4 BEYOND LIABILITY IN FAVOUR OF SOLIDARITY IN THE CONTEXT OF AUTONOMOUS VEHICLES

The idea of going beyond the principle of liability in favour of solidarity is not a novel idea. Public liability law applied to hospitals has shown the way here. The French Kouchner Law of 4 March 2002,[39] which is in line with the case law of the Conseil d'État, provides that in matters of medical treatment risk, when no liability is incurred, compensation for victims must nonetheless be guaranteed in line with the principle of solidarity based both on the significance of the risk incurred as a result of the medical treatment contingency, and on the seriousness of the physical injury suffered.[40] In such cases, a State public establishment, the Office National d'Indemnisation des Accidents Médicaux (National Office for the Compensation of Medical Accidents), compensates the victims[41] under conditions that guarantee both fair coverage of the harm and effective accountability of the various actors involved.

This principle of solidarity is suited to the context of accidents caused by autonomous vehicles due to the difficulty of proving liability and the allocation of costs. This is a system based on solidarity while at the same time ensuring the liability of various actors, especially the designers and manufacturers of the vehicle. The victim should not be made to bear the burden of technological progress, which should be viewed as socially conditioned risks.[42] In this respect, establishing a compensation fund is an idea worth pursuing.

[37] Conseil d'État, 9 April 1993, *Bianchi*, No. 69336, *Recueil Lebon*.

[38] Report from the Commission on the safety and liability implications of Artificial Intelligence, the Internet of Things and robotics, February 2020, p. 19.

[39] Law No. 2002-303 of 4 March 2002 relating to the rights of patients and the quality of the healthcare system, *JORF*, 5 March 2002, Art. 98.

[40] Cf. Article L. 1142-1. – I of the Public Health Code (CSP).

[41] Cf. Article L. 1142-22 CSP.

[42] J. Knetsch, *Le droit de la responsabilité et les fonds d'indemnisation* [Liability law and compensation funds] (Thesis, Panthéon-Assas University (Paris II) and University of Cologne, 2011), p. 280 *et seq.*

12.4.1 *Establishment of a Guarantee Fund*

12.4.1.1 ***Foundation and Functions***

The development of autonomous vehicles will progress because they hold the promise of optimum road traffic safety. However, the complex system enabling them to operate paradoxically creates a heavy social risk due to the unpredictability and difficulty in the allocation of harm linked to a plurality of intertwined micro-actions, none of which, alone, would lead to the harm being attributed to the actor. Under current liability law, this high risk is not offset by the guarantee of fair and prompt compensation.

A pragmatic approach must therefore be adopted in respect of the social management of the risks to which everyone is subject, in the interest of all. It should be recognised that individual compensation for the potential burden of collective progress based on a technological risk is fair, and it is necessary to apply a principle of compensation on the basis of the absence of a causal link between the harm suffered and the involvement of an autonomous vehicle, without, however, exempting the various actors in the system from their liability.

The establishment of a compensation fund, such as the L'Office National d'Indemnisation des Accidents Médicaux, des Affections Iatrogènes et des Infections Nosocomiales (ONIAM) and Le Fonds de Garantie des Assurances Obligatoires de dommages (FGAO), covering damages caused by medical activities and road traffic accidents, should be considered for accident victims caused by autonomous vehicles. Such a fund would apply the same solidarity and insurance logic to algorithmic risk, so as to ensure a collective distribution of the burden of autonomous vehicles.

12.4.1.2 ***Nature of the Fund: A Prospective Compensation Fund***

Following the example of the FGAO and ONIAM, the fund covering accidents caused by autonomous vehicles will have to anticipate the compensation of victims by means of capital established *ex ante*, based on bolstering the compulsory insurance mechanisms of all the actors in autonomous road traffic. As the primary objective is not to cover the possible financial default of the person responsible for the accident, the fund would indeed be a compensation fund, triggered by the sole fact of the involvement of the complex autonomous system.

The variable level of the autonomy of the vehicle seems to us to necessarily influence the conditions under which the fund would intervene: the greater the autonomy of the vehicle, the more the fund will be involved as the principal means of compensating for the harm suffered; the lesser the autonomy of the vehicle, the more matters will remain within the framework of traditional liability requiring, at the very least, proof of a causal link. This consideration of the degree of autonomy of the vehicle in order to adjust the liability regime that would be applicable already seems to be advocated by the European Parliament,[43] which asserts that once the parties ultimately liable have been identified, their liability should be proportional to the actual level of instructions given to the robot and its autonomy.

12.4.2 *Procedures for Involvement of the Fund*

12.4.2.1 ***Guarantee of Compensation for Victims of the High Risk***

Consideration should be given to the introduction of a multi-tiered compensation mechanism, that considers the level of autonomy of the vehicle involved in the accident and the nature of the

[43] Resolution of the European Parliament of 16 February 2017, *supra*.

harm incurred. In the case of accidents involving an ordinary vehicle or a vehicle with simple driver delegation (Levels 0–2), as soon as the harm has been attributed, compensation will be paid under the Badinter Law. In the case of accidents in connection with a high-risk autonomous vehicle (from Level 3 upwards), the fund will be the primary source of compensation for the harm suffered.

The serious and abnormal nature of the harm suffered in the context of autonomous traffic and complex systems should be assessed according to the Kouchner Law, as applied in medical treatment contingencies. In the case of minor harm, the Badinter Law will apply, that is, a largely private socialisation of the risk through the victim's insurer. However, in the event of harm that exceeds a certain threshold of seriousness and which could be classified as abnormal in regard to autonomous vehicles (depending on the degree of autonomy), it is the compensation fund that will cover the remedy.

As for the procedures of compensation, here again the principles adopted by ONIAM can be applied, by providing for full compensation of the victim only above a certain threshold of permanent disability; below such level, the compensation paid may be a flat rate amount, in order to guarantee both the accountability of the actors and the prevention of risk-laden behaviour.

12.4.2.2 *Accountability of Actors in the Complex System*

The principle of compensating the victims of accidents involving autonomous vehicles must not lead to a loss of liability of the various actors in the complex system in respect of the reliability of the technology they create, market or maintain. Two levers can be activated here: a procedural lever, the redress claim, which would reactivate the principle of individualised liability (which would simply move the compensation process back a notch in time), and a financial lever, that of financing the compensation fund and bolstering the use of insurance,[44] a guarantee of the socialisation of the risk incurred due to technological contingencies.

The FGAO (the compensation fund applicable to road traffic accidents victims) is currently funded mainly by contributions from vehicles insurers and the insured themselves, as well as by the proceeds of claims against the persons liable of the harm covered by the fund. It does not benefit from any State budget allocation. In the case of accidents involving an autonomous vehicle, in order to continue with the principle of collective compensation of the risk by means of capitalisation enabling the necessary sums to be rapidly mobilised, one could add to these resources a contribution from the designers and guarantors of the proper functioning of the complex system throughout its use, by means of a compulsory annual contribution that may be modulated according to the rate of accidents connected with the system for which they contribute. The correlation between contributions and accident rates would provide an incentive for designers, approval authorities, manufacturers and managers of the vehicle and the intelligent road network to provide, prior to the placement of the vehicle on the market, procedures for regular auditing and corrective measures in order to mitigate unpredictability and thereby the potential malfunctions of the system.

Of course, we would then be taking the risk of this additional cost being passed on to the cost of the vehicle and road traffic (tolls), as part of a movement to transfer the financial burden of risk to the users of the system. However, in view of the assumption of a very low accident rate

[44] See D. Noguéro, 'Assurances et véhicules connectés – Regard de l'universitaire français' [Insurance policies and connected vehicles – the view of French academics], in *Le procès de l'intelligence artificielle et de la voiture autonome* [The trial of artificial intelligence and autonomous vehicles], Special Edition (November 2019), *Dalloz*, 597.

with autonomous traffic, it could be that the additional cost would be relatively limited, penalising users and the development of the market for autonomous traffic only to a small extent. As for bolstering the involvement of the insurance system, it is already activated in the context of compensation for medical treatment risk (compulsory insurance for practitioners).[45] It allows the algorithmic risk to be shared between those directly involved, without directly mobilising public finances.

In the context of autonomous traffic, this logic could be applied by making it compulsory[46] to obtain insurance from private insurers to cover the specific algorithmic risk raised by autonomous vehicle traffic; similarly, compulsory insurance could be imposed on the manufacturers of autonomous vehicles, and also on those in charge of the intelligent road network. In both cases, the amount of contributions could be correlated to the degree of autonomy of the vehicle and/or the road network, the degree of transparency of its operation (leading to a variation in the ability to explain and justify given behaviour), the rate of accidents that have occurred and also to the behaviour of the user, for example in terms of reaction times in resuming control in the event of failure of the intelligent system (to be associated with an ability test conducted beforehand?). This insurance demutualisation process would have to be subject to strict supervision in order to avoid the risk of discrimination.

These mechanisms of compensation funds and compulsory insurance would make it possible to meet the major challenges related to autonomous traffic: guaranteeing compensation for harm, ensuring that the liable persons incur liability and avoiding a dissuasive effect on innovation. The principle of solidarity according to which they function is in line with the history of rules on liability: after the evolution of the fault-based liability regimes into strict liability regimes characterised by the absence of fault, the ever-growing number of compensation funds in various fields appears to be the solution for a society whose complexity has imposed the review of the relationship between liability and culpability, by legitimising the guarantee of compensation for harm as means of justice but also as a means of support for responsible technological innovation.

However, there is no question of skimping on the major additional work required to ensure safety, both before and after autonomous vehicles are put into circulation.[47] It will be necessary to strive for greater infallibility by applying demanding technical standards, and to strengthen the traceability of algorithmic actions by affirming the principle of transparency, conservation and accessibility of operating data throughout the life cycle of the vehicle, by means of audits capable of correcting the biases and malfunctions, if any, that are present at the start or that arise from the intelligent adaptation of the system to its environment. This effort is the price that will have to be paid if responsible autonomous traffic is to really develop.

12.5 CONCLUSION

To support and justify the development of autonomous vehicles, accountability mechanisms must be put in place to ensure road safety throughout the vehicles' life cycle. In this respect, the existing liability regimes do not provide a satisfactory response in terms of the guarantee of compensation for victims expected in the use of autonomous vehicles. The conventional

[45] Art. L. 1142-2 CSP.

[46] It should be remembered that the insurance of ordinary motorised land vehicles has been compulsory in France since Law No. 58-208 of 27 February 1958, and in Europe since Directive 72/166/EEC of 24 April 1972.

[47] See in particular in this respect C. Castets-Renard, who mentions in his article 'Comment construire une intelligence artificielle responsable et inclusive?' 227, *supra*, a necessary ex post and ex ante liability of AI systems.

regimes at the best dispense with the need to prove fault, but they still require the establishment of a causal link and the designation of an accountability for damages. The complex autonomous vehicle system makes the first one difficult, and the second hazardous. The traditional paradigm must be changed by rejecting the principle of responsibility in favour of a principle of solidarity, through the establishment of a compensation fund. Such a fund would guarantee damages to victims of accidents caused by an autonomous vehicle, and would hold all stakeholders accountable without the need to specifically determine which one is responsible.

13

Interconnectivity and Liability

AI and the Internet of Things

Geraint Howells and Christian Twigg-Flesner

13.1 INTRODUCTION

In this chapter, we deal with the role of artificial intelligence (AI) in the context of the Internet of Things (IoT). We will focus in particular on the question of liability in circumstances where an IoT system has not performed as expected and where this has resulted in loss or damage of some kind. We will argue that the combination of AI and the IoT raises several novel aspects concerning the basis for assessing responsibility and of allocating liability for loss or damage, and that this will necessitate the development of a more creative approach to liability than generally followed in many legal systems. Most legal systems combine linear liability based on contractual relationships and fault-based or strict liability on a wrongdoer in tort law. We seek to demonstrate that this approach is no longer sufficient to deal with the complex issues associated with the interaction of AI and the IoT, and to offer possible solutions. Our discussion will address this from the perspective of both consumer and commercial transactions.

The discussion will proceed as follows: first, we will explain the nature of an IoT system in general terms, drawing on case studies from both the consumer and commercial sphere to illustrate this. We will then focus on the role of AI in the operation of an IoT system. Secondly, we will analyse the particular issues that arise in the circumstances where an AI-driven IoT system malfunctions and causes loss or damage, and the specific legal questions this raises. Third, we will examine to what extent legal systems (particularly the UK and the EU) are currently able to address these questions, and identify aspects that require action, whether in the form of legislation or some other intervention. Finally, we will propose an alternative for addressing the liability challenges arising in this particular context.

The discussion rests on two interrelated points: first, the values underpinning established liability systems, particularly in the field of consumer protection law, should be maintained in the context of new digital technology applications.[1] Secondly, and by way of corollary, the adoption of new digital technology applications cannot be a basis for imposing a *lower* threshold of liability than the level of liability established in other contexts. In other words, the particular features of new digital technologies such as AI should not allow a 'producer' of an AI system to

[1] For a discussion of this point in the context of 3D printing, see Geraint Howells, Christian Twigg-Flesner and Chris Willett, 'Protecting the Values of Consumer Law in the Digital Economy: The Case of 3D-Printing' in Alberto De Franceschi and Reiner Schulze (eds.), *Digital Revolution: New Challenges for Law* (Munich: Beck/Nomos, 2019), pp. 214–243. In general, see Geraint Howells, 'Consumer Protection Values in the Fourth Industrial Revolution' (2020) 43 *Journal of Consumer Policy* 145.

claim that it should not be held to the same standard as a producer of a physical item. The same principles of promoting consumer protection and confidence in the market informing the choice of existing liability standard should inform the decisions about liability in the novel context of AI where goods and services are interconnected, need to be updated and autonomous decisions can be made without human intervention.

One way of preserving established values in the context of new digital technology applications is to either apply existing laws where this is already possible or achievable through light amendments to existing laws. This might suffice in some instances, but it might also be necessary to be more creative in developing novel solutions that target novel issues of new digital technology applications.[2] In the latter instance, aligning new laws with established underpinning values ought to be a key guiding criterion.

13.2 IOT AND AI

We start by considering what the Internet of Things is. There are various definitions of the IoT in use. For instance, the European Union Agency for Cybersecurity (ENISA) has defined the IoT as 'a cyber-physical ecosystem of interconnected sensors and actuators, which enable intelligent decision making'.[3] In contrast, the IERC-European Research Cluster on the Internet of Things defines it as 'a dynamic global network infrastructure with self-configuring capabilities based on standard and interoperable communication protocols where physical and virtual "things" have identities, physical attributes, and virtual personalities and use intelligent interfaces, and are seamlessly integrated into the information network'.[4] The European Commission has explained that the IoT is where 'all objects and people can be interconnected through communication networks, in and across private, public and industrial spaces, and report about their status and/or about the status of the surrounding environment'.[5] In short, there is no consistent definition of the IoT,[6] but there are common features to these definitions. First, the IoT involves the *connection* of devices through communication networks (primarily the Internet). IoT devices therefore need to be equipped with the functionality required to access and communicate via the Internet. Secondly, such devices may also be able to generate data about their own performance or about their environmental surroundings, usually through sensors that are part of such devices. The devices may also be linked to external data sources. The interconnection of such devices therefore provides for the exchange of data and can determine the actions taken by them. It also allows for them to be controlled remotely, for example via a smartphone app. A common consumer application of the IoT is the creation of so-called smart homes,[7] where various domestic devices (kitchen appliances, central heating systems, lights and home security systems) are communication-enabled and can be programmed to take set actions in response to data received by each device, as well as being controlled

[2] The tension between extending the reach of existing laws and limited reforms where needed on the one hand, and the development of new laws specifically targeted at novel issues created by new digital technology applications on the other hand, is a feature of much of the scholarly writings on the digital economy. See Roger Brownsword, 'Law Disrupted, Law Re-imagined, Law Re-invented' (2019) *Technology and Regulation* 10.

[3] ENISA, *IoT and Smart Infrastructures*, www.enisa.europa.eu/topics/iot-and-smart-infrastructures/iot (accessed 1 April 2021).

[4] IERC, *Internet of Things*, www.internet-of-things-research.eu/about_iot.htm.

[5] European Commission, *Staff Working Document: Advancing the Internet of Things in Europe* (SWD, 2016) 110 final.

[6] Cf. Federal Trade Commission, *Internet of Things: Privacy and Security in a Connected World* (FTC Staff Report, January 2015), p. 5.

[7] *Staff Working Document*, pp. 31–32 (devices a consumer can use to provide monitoring data about their health).

remotely by the home-owner.[8] In the commercial arena, common applications include both 'smart manufacturing' to optimise supply chain logistics and production line management as well as enabling products to communicate performance data to facilitate predictive maintenance (i.e., identifying maintenance needs before they manifest).[9] A further commercial utilisation is 'smart farming' to improve the efficiency of farming operations, optimisation of the agri-food chain and food safety management.[10] There are other examples, such as smart cities, autonomous vehicles and so on. A shared feature is that they involve devices connected to a communications network generating and exchanging data, and acting in response to data received, as well as being controlled remotely.

As the technology advances, the operation of many IoT systems can be further enhanced by the introduction of AI into the operation of such systems. The European High-Level Expert Group has adopted a complex definition of AI systems:

> Artificial intelligence (AI) systems are software (and possibly also hardware) systems designed by humans that, given a complex goal, act in the physical or digital dimension by perceiving their environment through data acquisition, interpreting the collected structured or unstructured data, reasoning on the knowledge, or processing the information, derived from this data and deciding the best action(s) to take to achieve the given goal. AI systems can either use symbolic rules or learn a numeric model, and they can also adapt their behaviour by analysing how the environment is affected by their previous actions.[11]

In the European Commission's April 2021 proposal for the *Artificial Intelligence Act*,[12] an 'artificial intelligence system' is defined as 'software that is developed with one or more of the techniques and approaches listed in Annex I [[13]] and can, for a given set of human-defined objectives, generate outputs such as content, predictions, recommendations, or decisions influencing the environments they interact with'.[14] In short, AI involves algorithmic decision-making based on data received and processed by the algorithm, in order to pursue a specific objective (energy-efficient operation of a consumer's home; optimal supply chain operation for a production line, etc.). A crucial feature of AI is machine-learning capability, that is, the possibility to 'learn' from data and adapt both its processing rules and outputs accordingly.

An AI-driven IoT system therefore comprises the following key components: multiple devices, many equipped with sensors; devices connected via communication networks to exchange data and receive instructions; and an AI algorithm to operate the IoT system based on data received

[8] A home-owner can also use one of the various personal voice assistants to control their smart home by speaking an instruction to the system.

[9] *Staff Working Document*, p. 33 (possibility of continuous monitoring could even lead to the extension of the current liability of seller and producer respectively; see also Bryant Walker Smith, 'Proximity Driven Liability' (2014) 102 *Georgetown Law Journal* 1777.

[10] *Staff Working Document*, p. 37.

[11] High-Level Expert Group on Artificial Intelligence, *A Definition of AI: Main Capabilities and Scientific Disciplines* (European Commission, April 2019), p. 8.

[12] European Commission, *Proposal for a Regulation of the European Parliament and of the Council laying down harmonised rules on artificial intelligence (Artificial Intelligence Act) and amending certain union legislative acts* (COM (2021) 206 final (21 April 2021).

[13] Annex I refers to

> (a) Machine learning approaches, including supervised, unsupervised and reinforcement learning, using a wide variety of methods including deep learning; (b) Logic- and knowledge-based approaches, including knowledge representation, inductive (logic) programming, knowledge bases, inference and deductive engines, (symbolic) reasoning and expert systems; (c) Statistical approaches, Bayesian estimation, search and optimization methods.

[14] Art. 3(1) of the proposed Regulation.

from data sources both internal and external to the IoT system. Each device will rely on software to perform its operations and to interact with the AI algorithm controlling the system.

Within such AI-controlled IoT systems, internet connectivity and heavy reliance on data raise significant concerns over cybersecurity.[15] An IoT system could be hacked and interfered with, by manipulating the parameters for its operation. Data could be accessed without authorisation and 'stolen'. However, for the purposes of this chapter, we are not directly concerned with cybersecurity issues.[16] Rather, we focus on 'system malfunctions' within AI-controlled IoT systems and the particular liability issues this raises, especially when such malfunction results in economic loss, damage or personal injury. Questions of insufficient cybersecurity would, of course, be relevant to determining whether the system, or its components, meet the legally mandated quality standards. In the next section, we identify the main causes of relevant IoT system malfunctions that could give rise to liability issues.

13.3 SYSTEM MALFUNCTION AND LEGAL ISSUES

An IoT system can malfunction for all sorts of reasons.[17] We refer to 'malfunction' as an umbrella term for any failure of an IoT system to work as intended or expected by the user. There can be many reasons for such a malfunction, and the more complex the IoT system is, the greater the number of possible points of failure. For the purpose of our discussion, we identify a number of possible malfunctions. One type of malfunction arises where one of the physical devices in an IoT system has failed. This would be a hardware failure and this type of problem would be covered by the legal rules dealing with the quality and fitness for purpose of goods. As such, this would not raise any novel legal issues. However, it is in the nature of an IoT system that the various physical devices comprising that system interact and are able to exchange data. This requires devices within a system to be interoperable, that is, to be linked together and to exchange data in a format that each device can understand. A lack of interoperability, for example because data is not understood in the same way by each component device, could cause the system to malfunction or fail altogether.

Secondly, some of the devices may have embedded software that allows them to operate. A malfunction within an IoT system could be the result of a software flaw, whether due to a coding error or, where enabled, an update to the software resulting in an error. This possibility raises two related issues: first, the software might have contained a coding error from the outset. Here, the question is whether the software is treated as an integral feature of the physical device and therefore covered by the legislation on the sale and supply of goods, as well as product liability, or whether the software is subject to a separate contract between end-user and the supplier of the software.[18] Secondly, an error might have been introduced into the software due to an update. This raises a novel issue insofar as legal rules regarding the quality and fitness for purpose of goods usually focuses on the moment of delivery as the point at which the goods' compliance with the relevant rules is assessed. By their very nature, software updates are made

[15] Cf. European Union Agency for Cybersecurity, *Guidelines for Securing the Internet of Things* (November 2020).

[16] See, e.g., Joachim Scherer and Caroline Heinickel, 'Regulating Machine-to-Machine Applications and Services in the Internet of Things' (2014) 2 *European Networks Law and Regulation Quarterly* 141, pp. 150–151.

[17] See also Jean-Sebastien Borghetti, 'How Can Artificial Intelligence Be Defective?' in Sebastian Lohsse, Reiner Schulze and Dirk Staudenmayer (eds.), *Liability for Artificial Intelligence and the Internet of Things* (Baden-Baden: Nomos, 2019), pp. 63–76.

[18] There is also a debate in many jurisdictions as to whether a contract for the supply software should be classified as one for the supply of goods or services, with a further distinction drawn between standard and customised software.

after this point, and so there will be a question of whether the fact that such updates occur periodically means that this falls outside existing legal rules on the supply of goods (which usually have a fixed point around the time of supply at which the supplier's obligations are determined) and requires new provisions. It may need to be considered whether, if the update contains a flaw, this flaw should be treated as having existed at the point of initial supply (if liability were to fall on the supplier), or instead the point at which the update was supplied. The latter might be pertinent where updates occur for several years after supply, or where such updates are supplied by a third party under a separate agreement. A complication is that assessment of conformity or defectiveness should be judged against the expectations of the original contract of supply.

A further question arises whether a *failure to provide* updates could give rise to liability. This issue may become pertinent in a variety of situations where there are errors in the software code that need to be corrected in order to ensure that the software performs as expected (a conformity problem), as well as where there is a problem with the software that might cause the goods to operate in an unsafe manner. A possible solution might be a legal duty to provide updates or to arrange for the provision of updates by a third party.[19]

The role of software extends beyond device-specific operating software. An IoT system can often be controlled remotely by using an 'app' installed on a smartphone. This app could have a problem that could, in turn, disrupt the operation of the IoT system and trigger a malfunction resulting in loss or damage. As the legal treatment of software varies between jurisdictions, and also between consumer and commercial transactions, the legal rules regarding software might need to be clarified.

Matters are further complicated once an IoT system is operated with the use of AI and the decisions made by an AI algorithm result in a malfunction of the IoT system itself. Such an AI-based malfunction could be due to a variety of reasons. First, this might be due to the way in which the AI algorithm was coded at the outset. Secondly, where the AI algorithm has 'self-learning' capacity, the decision-making pattern it has evolved might result in IoT system malfunctions. Third, the source of the problem might not be the AI algorithm itself, but rather the data received and processed by the algorithm in order to determine the operation of the IoT system. This data might have been provided by one of the devices within the IoT system, or from an external source. A problem with such data could be due to a variety of reasons, including a fault with a sensor on one of the IoT system's devices, resulting in inaccurate, incomplete or missing data; also, data might have been supplied from an external source based on a unit of measurement that differs from that used by the AI algorithm. This complexity will create challenges for both establishing the actual cause of the problem and the consequent attribution of liability.

This discussion shows that the interaction of physical and digital elements within an AI-controlled IoT system means that there are multiple points of failure, some of which are external to the IoT system itself. A user who has encountered an IoT system malfunction will therefore face the evidentiary hurdle of identifying the cause(s) of such a malfunction first. This will be necessary to identify both the potential counterparty against whom a claim might be made and the legal basis of such a claim (bearing in mind that, aside from legal rules regarding quality issues and damage caused by goods, not every legal system will necessarily provide clear legal

[19] This question resembles a long-running debate in sales law regarding a legal obligation to make available spare parts to ensure that goods can be repaired, and their lifetime be extended. In the EU and the UK, some steps towards this have now been taken in respect of some categories of goods in the context of Ecodesign and Energy Labelling.

rules in this regard). It will be necessary to identify the correct counterparty because most IoT systems will comprise several physical devices, software and other digital elements, an AI algorithm and internal and external data, and it is likely that this will involve a plurality of counterparties. There might be situations where an IoT system was acquired as a package from one supplier, but even there, multiple parties might be involved because of the combination of physical and digital elements. The end-user of any IoT system will therefore commonly have to deal with several counterparties. This will usually be through separate contracts based on different contract terms.[20]

The legal basis of any claim to be brought will depend on how the relevant legal system deals with liability issues in respect of goods incorporating software, stand-alone software, AI algorithms and the supply of data. At present, legal systems vary in respect of the extent to which these issues are addressed at all, and insofar as they are, in the scope of the relevant legal rules regarding their substance and as between consumer and commercial situations. Proposals for law reform are discussed at national, regional and international levels. In the next section, we will examine these issues more closely, identify what should be addressed in legal rules and consider existing measures and reform discussions.

13.4 KEY LEGAL ISSUES AND CURRENT STATE OF THE LAW

In this part of our chapter, we will examine current and proposed approaches for addressing the legal issues that arise in AI-operated IoT systems. In the previous section, we identified a number of questions, to which we now turn.

13.4.1 *Goods with Digital Elements*

IoT systems comprise various devices that connect and interact with one another based on integrated software. We first consider goods containing digital elements. With goods containing digital elements, it is often necessary to consider whether both the goods and the digital elements are treated as goods, or whether a different regime applies. In some jurisdictions, such as the UK and the EU, distinct legal regimes for the supply of goods and digital content and digital services have been adopted, particularly in the EU (directives on the sale of goods (2019/771/EU or SGD) and on digital content and digital services (2019/770/EU or DCSD) and in the UK (Consumer Rights Act 2015). These technical rules on the scope of the various regimes relate to the question of whether the supplier of the goods should also take responsibility for defects in the digital elements and how the physical and the digital elements interact. Behind this lies more policy-orientated questions about whether the rules for goods or digital content are more appropriate; though in many instances the rules are approximated.[21]

The UK Consumer Rights Act 2015 was one of the first pieces of legislation to regulate digital content. This gave consumers a claim against a trader where digital content had been supplied in return for a price. It does not cover the situation where the counterperformance is data, but the Secretary of State has the power to extend this to other contracts such as where the consumer

[20] Guido Noto la Diega and Ian Walden, 'Contracting for the "Internet of Things": Looking into the Nest' (2016) 7 *European Journal of Law and Technology* 1.

[21] There is also the question as to whether the relevant time for assessing conformity should be the traditional time of supply, or whether the supplier should have responsibility for both updating the software and for any defects that result from such updates. This also raises the question of updates that even the supplier may have no control over as they are made autonomously.

provides data instead of paying a price.[22] EU law adopts a broader approach including any supply of digital content or services. In the case of goods with digital elements where the digital content is not in conformity with the contract, UK law treats this as a nonconformity of the goods themselves.[23] Effectively, this may give the consumer the option of either suing the supplier for the paid-for digital service (if paid for separately), or the supplier of the goods incorporating the digital content.

The EU takes a more systematic approach to allocating liability between the Sale of Goods Directive (SGD) and the Digital Content and Services Directive (DSCD). Digital content covered by the DSCD broadly defined to encompass 'data which are produced and supplied in digital form'.[24] The DCSD also applies to any tangible medium that serves exclusively as a carrier of digital content.[25] Accordingly, such carriers are excluded from the SGD.[26] By contrast, the Consumer Rights Directive had treated such tangible mediums as goods.[27] As Staudenmayer notes, the solution in the DCSD was chosen for simplicity as devices such as discs and DVDs are simply providing the mechanisms for delivering the digital content.[28] It might have been more logical to apply the DCSD to the digital content/service and SGD to the carrier, but it was considered that would have been confusing. Applying the SGD would not have made much sense if the real complaint was about the digital content. However, the DCSD only brings within its scope tangible media that serve exclusively as a carrier of the digital content. There is a question mark as to whether this applies subjectively in the particular contract or objectively based on the use the carrier could be put to. Take, for instance, a USB stick or a portable hard drive. Both can be used for adding extra data, so does that mean they are not covered? Or does the fact that under the digital content contract, they are simply intended to be the carrier of the digital content mean that they fall within the scope of the DCSD? Staudenmayer suggests it should be assessed based on the circumstances of the case.[29] This can be problematic though. Increasingly, conference papers, for example, are supplied on USB sticks. Some sticks may be so full that they can realistically only be used for storing the papers, but if they have a lot of spare capacity, attendees might store other files on them or even delete conference files and place their own on them. But it seems clear the intention was only to use them as a carrier for the digital content supplied. They are different from USBs that might be supplied as a souvenir for visiting the event.

However, the main rule is to place digital content/services supplied with goods under the SGD. The DCSD provides that its rules shall not apply to digital content or digital services that satisfy both functional and contractual criteria. To be excluded and hence covered by the SGD, the digital content/service must firstly be incorporated in or interconnected with goods in a manner that affects the functioning of the goods. This will only be the case if the absence of that digital content or digital service would prevent the goods from performing their functions.[30] This applies irrespective of whether such digital content or digital service is supplied by the seller or

22 S. 33 Consumer Rights Act 2015.
23 S. 26 Consumer Rights Act 2015.
24 Ibid., Art. 2 no. 11.
25 Art. 3(3) DCSD.
26 Art. 3(4)(a) SGD.
27 Art. 5, Consumer Rights Directive.
28 Dirk Staudenmayer, 'Digital Content and Digital Services Directive – Article 3' in Reiner Schulze and Dirk Staudenmayer (eds.), *EU Digital Law* (Baden-Baden: Nomos, 2020), p. 74.
29 Ibid., p. 75.
30 Art. 2(3) SGD.

by a third party. The supplier of the goods will be responsible for nonconformity resulting from the digital content/service.[31] However, this will only be the case if the digital content/service has been provided under a sales contract concerning those goods. If they are not provided under the same contract, there will be a bundle of separate contracts with the DCSD applying to the digital content/service element and the SGD applying to the goods. There may be incentives on the part of the supplier of goods to draft the contract to make it appear as if the digital content/service is not supplied under the same contract so as to avoid liability for the digital content/service. This separation is expressly permitted.[32] Such clauses will have to pass the transparency test of the Unfair Contract Terms Directive, however. One can imagine the courts will scrutinise such terms carefully, given that there is a presumption that the digital content or digital service constituting the digital element of goods is presumed to be covered by the sales contract.[33]

The DCSD and SGD achieved their purpose of providing a separation between their spheres of operation, but related contracts at the intersection of liability regimes between digital content/services and goods remains obscure. Indeed, the effect of termination of one element of a contract bundle may have on another element is left to national law.[34] The rules on contract bundles only apply when the elements are supplied under a single contract. The whole question of linked or ancillary contracts is also left to national law.

With regards to strict product liability, it is generally assumed the final product producer will be responsible for all harm (personal injury and damage to property) caused by the product including any harm caused by the incorporated software.[35] Such software will be seen as a component part and whether there is liability for the producer of the component part will be determined by whether software is treated as a product in its own right or not.[36] The producer of the component may be able to rely on a defence if the defect resulted from their following instructions or due to how the component was incorporated into the final product.[37] The producer has been found to be under a duty to survey the market for accessories used with its product and to take steps to ensure consumers are warned about any that are unsafe even if not produced with the permission of the producer of the main product.[38] This might be applied to ensure that the safety of the goods is taken to include their foreseeable interaction with independent products, such as where they may interact with each other in the IoT. It could also cover their safety where the goods are used with a digital service that manages the goods in a smart environment.

The area of uncertainty is in sales law where two products are bought separately but are intended to interact. Goods, digital content and digital services may lack conformity[39] and this lack of conformity can derive from the way the goods and digital content and services interact.

[31] Art. 10 SGD.

[32] Recital 21 DCSD and 15 SGD.

[33] Art. 3(4) DCSD.

[34] Art. 3(6). Recital 34.

[35] Christian Twigg-Flesner, *Guiding Principles for Updating the Product Liability Directive in the Digital Age*, ELI Pilot Innovation Paper (European Law Institute, 2021).

[36] Art. 3(4) DCSD.

[37] Art. 7(f) PLD.

[38] This was the view taken in a German negligence case, reported at (1986) *NJW* 1009.

[39] Christian Twigg-Flesner, 'Conformity of Goods and Digital Content/Digital Services' in Esther Arroyo Amayuelas and Sergio Cámara Lapuente (eds.), *El Derecho privado en el nuevo paradigma digital* (Madrid: Marcial Pons, 2020), pp. 49–78.

There are rules requiring functionality,[40] compatibility[41] and interoperability[42] if they are to be in conformity. These require that the goods can perform their function, which might include exchanging data with a product or digital service provider (functionality). This should be possible with common hardware (compatibility) and where provided for in the contract for alternative software and hardware (interoperability).[43] The lack of conformity can also be derived from the trader failing correctly to integrate digital content into the digital environment or provide the consumer with adequate instructions for doing so.[44] However, there may be gaps created especially when goods are added to existing digital environments or new digital services are added: existing products may not be at fault for how they are affected by subsequent purchases or for failures to work properly in the new environment where a new digital service is added. There may be no liability for digital services if they are not interoperable with existing goods unless this is expressly provided for. Even if goods and digital services are in theory liable the consumer may have problems determining which element was lacking conformity and responsible for harm. One response would be to reverse the burden of proof; another would be bolder, to create a form of network liability.

As regards strict product liability under the Product Liability Directive (PLD), goods may be defective because they incorporate digital content/services that renders them dangerous.[45] Equally, goods may be unsafe due to how they interact with the digital environment. However, the digital content/service will not itself be subject to liability under the PLD. This also means that software developers will not be liable as producers of component parts when included in the goods. However, it might be argued that if the digital content/service is supplied on tangible goods then producers of components might be liable, drawing analogies with the position under the SGD. Even if they are covered by strict liability, there will be the same problem of allocating liability as in the sales context.

13.4.2 *Software, Digital Content and Digital Services*

Above, we examined goods incorporating digital content/services. However, as we explained earlier, an IoT system involves an ecosystem comprising physical elements as well as digital content (such as an app on the user's smartphone). In this section, we turn to the problem is of how to treat software/digital content that is independent of the product. This might be because of the desire to sue the software manufacturer directly in product liability on the basis that the software was supplied separately and was the cause of harm.

The treatment of software/digital content has always challenged the law. It has not traditionally fallen within the definition of goods (though Australian and New Zealand law resolved the issue simply by extending that definition to encompass software[46]). An early approach to fudge

[40] Meaning 'the ability of the digital content or digital service to perform its functions having regard to its purpose'. Art. 6 SGD / Art. 9 DCSD.

[41] Meaning 'the ability of the digital content or digital service to function with hardware or software with which digital content or digital services of the same type are normally used, without the need to convert the digital content or digital service'. Art. 7 SGD / Art. 10 DCSD.

[42] Meaning 'the ability of the digital content or digital service to function with hardware or software different from those with which digital content or digital services of the same type are normally used'. Art. 8 SGD / Art. 2(11) DCSD.

[43] Interoperability appears in the subjective, but not the objective criteria of conformity; see *EU Digital Law* at p. 55.

[44] Art. 8 SGD / Art. 9 DCSD.

[45] Although this has not been conclusively confirmed by the Court of Justice of the European Union (CJEU), it is widely assumed to be the case.

[46] The Australian Consumer Law provides that goods includes software, Sched. 2 s. 2. See also New Zealand s. 2 Sale of Goods Act 1908.

the issue was to argue that software was goods only when it was supplied on a tangible medium.[47] That made some sense as such software was normally mass produced and hence subject to the same policy arguments for liability as goods, whereas bespoke software solutions resembled services that were normally subject to negligence rather than strict liability. However, that way of sidestepping the issue has become less available as increasingly in these days of cloud computing software is simply downloaded and not supplied on a disc or other durable medium. The UK's Supreme Court allowed an appeal on whether software is goods in the context of the Commercial Agents Directive. The Court of Appeal, overturning the High Court, had held that software was not goods.[48] The Supreme Court referred the matter to the CJEU,[49] which held that software was within the notion of goods in the Commercial Agents Directive. The Supreme Court allowed the appeal without giving a separate judgment.[50]

In the case of software contracts, the common law might imply terms regarding quality and fitness for purposes, as is the case with contracts outside the scope of the limited codifications in England. However, relying on the common law is uncertain, and it was welcomed when sales law was clarified in the consumer context by the Consumer Rights Act 2015 creating a separate regime for digital content. This approach was followed at the EU level in the DCSD. That Directive created the additional category of digital service as well as digital content, but it seems that was mainly for clarificatory purposes and most digital services such as sites allowing you to upload data or share files would most probably be caught by the UK definition of digital content.[51]

Whether software is a 'product' for the purpose of strict (tort) product liability law has long been a contested issue.[52] Though sound arguments can be made for software being included on policy grounds of consumer protection,[53] especially when mass produced or when supplied on tangible media, it seems most likely that it is not, given the definition refers to movable goods[54] and it was felt necessary to specifically include liability for electricity. This seems to be in line with a recent CJEU judgment that a newspaper was not a defective product because it contained incorrect advice in its health column.[55] The exclusion of such advice from product liability is perhaps not surprising, but of potentially more relevance to us was the *Dutrueux* case[56] in which the supplier of a medical service was not held to be a supplier of products just because they *used* products that they had not produced themself. This approach would insulate the suppliers of smart systems from liability for any products connected to the system that they had not produced. Product liability law has long remained unreformed, but the need to address issues relating to

47 *St Albans DC* v. *International Computers Ltd* [1996] 4 All ER 48.

48 *Computer Associates UK Ltd* v. *The Software Incubator Ltd* [2018] EWCA Civ 518.

49 C-410/19 *The Software Incubator.*

50 See case C-410/19 *The Software Incubator Ltd v Computer Associates (UK)* Ltd ECLI:EU:C:2021:742. The Supreme Court's order allowing the appeal was not published.

51 The Commission had originally proposed to use only digital content and the addition has been said to be for only clarificatory purposes: *EU Digital Law* at p. 47.

52 See Simon Whittaker, *Liability for Products* (Oxford University Press, 2005), p. 477.

53 Gerald Spindler, 'Verschuldensunabhängige Produkthaftung im Internet' (1988) *Multimedia und Recht* 119; Duncan Fairgrieve and Eleonora Rajneiri, 'Is Software a Product under the Product Liability Directive?' (2019) *IWRZ* 24: they even quote an answer to a Parliamentary question by Commissioner Lord Cockfield in 1989 stating software can be a product: OJ C-114/76, p. 42.

54 Art. 2 PLD.

55 Case C-65/20 *VI* v. *Krone Verlag Gesellschaft mbH & Co KG* ECLI:EU:C:2021:471.

56 C-495/10 *Centre hospitalier universitaire de Besançon* v. *Thomas Dutrueux* EU:C:2011:869.

the digital age may be a spur for it to be seriously reviewed.[57] It would therefore be desirable to clarify/extend the current product liability regime such that it clearly applies to digital content.[58] This does not mean that liability should encompass pure information services, where human intervention is always a vital link in the chain of causality. Rather, when digital content causes an action that creates harm there should be liability.[59] Often this will be because of a faulty instruction sent to a product that causes it to take a step without human intervention or an error in the software incorporated in the product. In the former case the policy reasons for strict liability seem to apply equally; as regards software components there seems little reason why they should be exempt rather than any other component manufacturer.[60] It is unfortunate that there seems to be hesitancy in some places for this relatively straightforward reform to the PLD. It seems inevitable and a corollary to the DCSD.

13.4.3 *Lifetime Contracts and the Duty to Update*

Traditionally, the major function of sales contracts is to allocate risks and liabilities between the contracting parties, as well as the responsibility for the delivery of non-conforming goods. Under sale of goods law this is normally at the time of delivery,[61] or in strict products liability law the time when the product was supplied[62] or in the language of the PLD 'put into circulation'.[63] Any post-supply conduct of the seller or producer, such as poor conduct of a recall, must be assessed under negligence law.[64] However, this does not work for digital products such as those used in the IoT because the link to, and dependency on, ongoing digital content and services transforms them into lifetime contracts that must involve ongoing responsibilities of the supplier to the user.[65] For consumer contracts, this ongoing obligation has been squarely addressed in the SGD and DCSD. In the commercial sales context, it remains a matter for contractual negotiation. The PLD does not address it directly and may need reform.

Digital content and digital services will normally be required to be updated. Often this may be for security reasons, but it can also be for reasons of maintaining functionality and interoperability. The obligation to have an ongoing update obligation has rightly been described as 'a ground-breaking new development'[66] in the DCSD and parallel rules are also found in the SGD. The initial proposal in the DCSD had only been for updates to be required as provided for in the contract. This subjective element remains and allows the parties to agree more

57 The European Commission has acknowledged this: see European Commission, *Artificial Intelligence for Europe* COM (2018) 237 final, p. 15. Reform proposals were under development at the time.

58 Cf. European Parliament Resolution of 3 July 2018, *Three-Dimensional Printing: Intellectual Property Rights and Civil Liability*, paras. 11–12.

59 See K. Alheit, 'The Applicability of the EC Product Liability Directive to Software' (2001) 34 *Comparative and International Law Journal of Southern Africa* 188.

60 See Geraint Howells et al., 'Protecting the Values of Consumer Law', p. 214.

61 Cf. Lord Diplock in *Lambert* v. *Lewis* [1981] 1 All ER 1185, p. 1191: 'the implied [term] relates to the goods at the time of delivery under the contract of sale in the state in which they were delivered'. It has also variously been suggested that the time when risk passes, or even when property passed, might be that time: Christian Twigg-Flesner and Rick Canavan, *Atiyah and Adams' Sale of Goods*, 14th ed. (New York: Pearson, 2020), p. 115.

62 S. 4(1)(d) Consumer Protection Act 1987.

63 Art. 7(b) PLD.

64 *Walton* v. *British Leyland*, *The Times*, 13 July 1978.

65 Luca Nogler and Udo Reifner, *Life Time Contracts: Social Long-Term Contracts in Labour, Tenancy and Consumer Credit Law* (The Hague: Eleven, 2014).

66 Staudenmayer, 'Digital Content and Digital Services Directive', p. 153.

extensive updating obligations, but the objective conformity requirements now include minimum updating obligations.[67]

The duty to update needs to be framed in the context of the content, service or goods provided. Where a fixed period is set, such as a one-year cloud data storage service, then it seems obvious that the updating should last for that period and that is indeed the solution provided.[68] For goods, the seller is in any event liable for defects that become apparent within two years.[69] The more difficult task is to determine the length of the duty to update where there is not a fixed period specified, but rather a one-off supply or series of one-off supplies.[70] The Directives' general test leading requires case-by-case assessments. It will depend upon what the consumer 'may reasonably expect, given the type and purpose of the digital content or digital service and taking into account the circumstances and nature of the contract'.[71] The recitals give some clues.[72] If an app or goods are for a specific purpose such as for a sporting event or music festival, then the updates would only have to be provided for the period necessary for that event. Normally, the updating obligation should be for the period for which there would be liability for nonconformity, typically two years. However, the recitals make it clear that the obligation can extend beyond the conformity period, especially as regards the duty to provide security updates. However, the extent of this obligation and the circumstances when it will arise are uncertain. The trader must inform the consumer of the update obligations.

The extent of the update obligation is to keep the goods, digital content or service in conformity with the functionality expected at the time of contacting. There is no obligation to provide the latest version. As noted, the trader may have agreed to provide upgraded services and there are separate rules with conditions that must be met if the trader wants to modify the digital content or service.[73] The fact the obligation is linked to the lack of conformity also impacts on the remedies. The primary remedies should be bringing the goods into conformity by providing the update. If the trader will not or cannot do that (perhaps because of their reliance on an uncooperative third-party software developer) the remedies of price reduction[74] and termination[75] may come into play. Price reduction should be based on the decrease in value due to lack of an update rather than the cost of the update as such. One can imagine even a relatively inexpensive update might lead to vastly reduced utility, or even cybersecurity issues. Conversely, most updates will only be minor in nature and the remedy of termination may therefore not be available.[76]

The consumer holds the remedies for lack of updates against the trader. However, it is the software developer who must make the updates and the supplier, particularly in goods contracts, may have no independent ability to update. This option was preferred to making the developer directly liable to the consumer as the consumer only has at best an end-user licence and no contract with the developer. Indeed, the solution is not out of line with traditional sales law whereby the trader is responsible for the components. The risk is held by the trader. This is

[67] Art. 7(d) DCCS and Art. 6(d) SGD.
[68] Art. 8(2)(a) DCSD and Art. 7(3)(b) SGD.
[69] Art. 10(2) SGD.
[70] Where digital elements are supplied with goods there will normally be a one-off supply related to those goods as reflected in the SGD.
[71] Art. 8(2)(b) DCSD and Art. 7(3)(a) SGD.
[72] Recital 47 DCSD and 31 SGD.
[73] Art. 19 DCSD; Art. 7(3) SGD.
[74] Art. 14(4)(5) DCSD and Art. 14(3)(4) and 15 SGD.
[75] Art. 14(6) DCSD and Art. 13(5) SGD.
[76] Staudenmayer, 'Digital Content and Digital Services Directive', p. 154.

tempered by provisions that provide the trader with a right of recourse against third parties such as developers, but these rules are facilitative and depend upon the trader contracting for the assistance of the developer to provide updates. The trader also can deviate from the conformity obligation with regard to specific characteristics that are drawn to the consumer's attention and accepted. Thus, a trader could specifically provide that updates were not guaranteed. The ability to impose such a term might depend on market forces, but one could imagine that traders might be tempted to include such exclusions in boilerplate standard form contracts. In such instances, the transparency requirement before such exemptions are excluded from review for their unfairness under the Unfair Trade Directive (UTCD) would be important in protecting consumers. However, the SGD and DCSD focus liability on the trader and do not consider the significance of the role of software developers and others who provide data to make such systems work. Thus, alternative liability regimes will need to be considered.[77]

If a product is rendered unsafe due to an update, the PLD becomes relevant. This covers harm to person or property. Even if the definition of property is extended to cover damaged data,[78] this should not mean it can be used with respect to broader cybersecurity risks. There have been calls to amend the definition of defect[79] to take account of the need to provide updates.[80] These rely on at least three arguments.

(i) The need to include software within the scope of liability. The importance of this has been discussed in Section 13.4.2 and including software within the scope of the PLD would be a sensible reform.

(ii) The limitation when assessing defect to the condition at the time the product was put into circulation. It is possible that if the safety of a product is linked to digital content and services then there might be an implicit expectation that they be updated to keep the product safe. There would be the same debate as in contract law about how long that expectation would extend for. Failure to undertake to update them could be seen as a risk present at the time of supply rather like a lack of durability. If the trader wanted to make it clear that updates may not be supplied this could be possible by reference in the current definition of defect to the presentation of the goods. However, it is certainly unclear whether currently a failure to update could be linked back to the condition of the product at the time of supply. Adding the expectation of appropriate updates as a relevant factor would be a sensible revision. This would link back to the expectations of safety established at the time of supply and not involve imposing post-marketing obligations. These are adequately addressed for regulatory reasons under the General Product Safety Directive.

(iii) The fact that a subsequent better product is available is irrelevant. This factor should, however, certainly remain, for as with conformity the obligation should be to maintain

[77] See, e.g., European Parliament resolution of 20 October 2020 with recommendations to the Commission on a civil liability regime for artificial intelligence 2020/2014, https://op.europa.eu/en/publication-detail/-/publication/1923c62a-2640-11ec-bd8e-01aa75ed71a1/language-en/format-PDF. The resolution discusses extending liability to other parties other than the trader: 'The multitude of actors involved [in autonomous AI systems] represent a significant challenge to the effectiveness . . . of national liability framework provisions, considers that specific and coordinated adjustment to the liability regimes are necessary to avoid a situation in which persons who suffer harm or whose property is damaged end up without compensation' (para. 6).

[78] Twigg-Flesner, Guiding Principles for Updating the Product Liability Directive in the Digital Age, principle 7.

[79] Art. 6 PLD.

[80] Twigg-Flesner, *Guiding Principles for Updating the Product Liability Directive in the Digital Age*, principle 6.

> the expected standard and not enhance it unless that has been promised. As with the conformity rules the policy objective should be to maintain the expected levels of safety.

It is likely that risks from failure to update could be captured by the current definition of defect in PLD, but it is one aspect that could usefully be clarified.

13.4.4 *AI Algorithms*

AI when deployed in the context of an IoT system can result in a malfunction of the system as a whole because of the actions triggered by the AI algorithm (see Section 13.2). However, even where it is possible to identify the actions taken by the AI algorithm as the source of the system malfunction, this does not mean that the AI algorithm itself is faulty: if the decisions taken by the AI algorithm are the result of the data received, for example, then the real source of the problem would be the data. This raises separate liability questions considered in Section 13.4.5.

For present purposes, we assume that the AI algorithm itself is faulty in some way and that this has caused an IoT system malfunction. This leads us to important and difficult questions about liability for an AI algorithm, in particular (i) *who* would be liable, and (ii) what the *basis* of such liability (tort, contract) might be. At the present time, the liability issues in respect of AI algorithms are a matter of intense scholarly and policy discussions, but there is as yet no legislation specifically dealing with this. Nevertheless, it may be possible to apply existing laws to at least some liability questions arising in the context of AI algorithms.

We need to distinguish between two categories of algorithm. The first is an algorithm that relies on preset instructions that allow the algorithm to take a range of decisions triggered by predetermined criteria. In AI terms, this might be categorised as *symbolic* AI.[81] Such an algorithm is comparable to software or digital content and can therefore be treated in the same way as software (see section above).

The second category is a 'self-learning' algorithm, that is, an algorithm developed through machine-learning. It is an inherent feature of such algorithms that they can revise the way in which decisions are taken based on both an initial training period during which the algorithm learns to identify acceptable and unacceptable decisions, and subsequently based on decisions made in light of new data and (where possible) feedback give to the algorithm in response. For instance, in an AI-controlled IoT system, a user override of decisions taken by the algorithm should enable the algorithm to adjust how it will respond in the same or a similar situation in the future.

Problems with such an AI algorithm can be due to a variety of factors: first, the initial training period might have created the conditions for the AI algorithm to take decisions that cause the IoT system to perform in an unexpected manner. Secondly, the self-learning development of the AI algorithm after deployment may result in bringing about such conditions. This could be the result of the data received by the algorithm or the way in which the IoT system has been monitored by the user.

Determining an appropriate approach to liability for an AI algorithm, in regard to the legal nature of such liability and the person(s) liable, is a controversial issue. A recurring suggestion is to grant an AI algorithm legal personhood akin to that of a limited liability company,[82] so as to

[81] Melanie Mitchell, *Artificial Intelligence: A Guide for Thinking Humans* (London: Pelican, 2019), p. 9.

[82] Gerhard Wagner, 'Robot Liability' in Lohsse et al., *Liability for Artificial Intelligence*, pp. 27–62; Iria Giuffrida, 'Liability for AI Decision-Making: Some Legal and Ethical Considerations' (2019) 88 *Fordham Law Review* 439, p. 444.

sidestep the need of identifying the correct defendant in case of loss caused by an AI algorithm. However, an obvious problem with such an approach is the lack of monetary resources of an AI algorithm with separate legal personality for paying compensation. It is difficult to see what would be gained by pursuing this idea.[83]

At the outset of this chapter, we stressed that in our view, the novelty of AI algorithms does not mean that established approaches to liability already in place should be abandoned and that, consequently, there should be no scope for producers/suppliers to argue for less stringent liability standards because of the continuously evolving nature of AI. This means that, as far as the initial provision or deployment of a pretrained AI algorithm is concerned, the situation is best treated as akin to the supply of digital content. At least in respect of consumer transactions, this will mean liability will be based on strict contractual liability, and liability would arise if the AI algorithm were not in conformity with the contract.

However, the situation is less clear-cut when it comes to developments in the AI algorithm resulting from its self-learning capacity, where these lead to decisions triggered by the algorithm resulting in a malfunction of the IoT system. One might be tempted to treat this in a comparable manner to updates made to software/digital content after its initial supply. However, the machine learning process of the AI algorithm is based on both its operation within the IoT system and the various data inputs feeding into the mechanism alongside any user feedback. There is therefore a difference to software/digital content updates in that changes to the AI algorithm will often be the result of factors beyond the control of the supplier of that algorithm. However, this should not lead to the conclusion that the producer or supplier of the AI algorithm should escape liability for problems that arise during the operation of the AI algorithm in an IoT system. This is because the way in which the AI algorithm develops will in some part be due to how it has been structured and therefore how its self-learning capacity has been designed. It is possible that a decision by an AI algorithm causing a system malfunction could have its roots in the design of the AI algorithm. Moreover, it will be almost impossible to determine whether a decision taken by an AI algorithm was shaped by its initial design or by self-learning, or, indeed, because of its predeployment training.[84] Furthermore, it may be that there is an interoperability issue between the AI algorithm and the various data inputs and the way in which the algorithm understands the data it receives. In short, working out why a rogue decision was taken by an AI algorithm may be an impossible task, especially for the end-user.[85]

Perhaps the simplest solution might be to impose strict liability[86] on either the producer or the operator of an AI algorithm integrated into an IoT system. The High-Level Expert Group[87] and the European Parliament[88] both favour imposing strict liability on an operator (alongside a

[83] The European Parliament expressly rejected the idea of legal personality for AI in its resolution on a civil liability regime for AI (2020/2014(INL), 20 October 2020), at para. 7.

[84] Giuffrida, 'Liability for AI Decision-Making', p. 442.

[85] Cf. UNCITRAL, *Legal Issues Related to the Digital Economy – Artificial Intelligence*, 7 May 2020 (A/CN.9/1012/Add.1), paras. 12 and 14.

[86] Cf. Gerald Spindler, 'User Liability and Strict Liability in the Internet of Things and for Robots' in Lohsse et al., *Liability for Artificial Intelligence*, pp. 125–143, who argues that strict liability would be appropriate for high-risk usages, rather than appropriate in respect of AI generally. See also Herbert Zech, 'Liability for Autonomous Systems: Tackling Specific Risks of Modern IT', in the same volume (pp. 187–200).

[87] High-Level Expert Group on Liability and New Technologies, *Liability for Artificial Intelligence and Other Emerging Technologies* (European Commission, 2019), pp. 39–42 (High Level, *Liability for Artificial Intelligence*).

[88] European Parliament, *Resolution on a Civil Liability Regime for Artificial Intelligence* (2020/2014(INL), 20 October 2020), paras. 11–13.

producer), distinguishing between a front-end operator[89] and a back-end operator.[90] The High-Level Expert Group suggests that liability should be on the operator who has the greater control over the risk flowing from the operation of the AI algorithm,[91] whereas the European Parliament prefers joint and several liability of all operators, with a right of recourse between them.[92] The introduction of operator liability would be a novel step.[93] In the context of an IoT system controlled by an AI algorithm, this might lead to instances where the end-user (as front-end operator) could be liable for damage suffered by another. This might be appropriate for a commercial setting, but perhaps less so in a consumer context. In respect of an IoT system, it might be that the back-end operator is the better candidate for the imposition of liability rather than the front-end operator/end-user. Similarly, the European Parliament's proposal for a regulation on liability for the operation of AI systems[94] had proposed introducing a strict liability regime for high-risk autonomous AI products[95] backed up by mandatory insurance.[96] Both front-end and back-end operators would be subject to this regime. Liability of front-end operators would assist injured third parties, but not where the product harms the operator themselves. However, under the proposal, liability would also extend to back-end operators. In contrast, the European Commission's proposed Artificial Intelligence Act[97] does not include provisions on civil liability. It seems clear that liability should take account of the structure of markets for AI products and services and the IoT. Connected issues also arise about whether redress can be facilitated by providing victims with access to data, or reversal of burden of proof and how to ensure equity between parties by ensuring effective recourse liability.

Strict liability is the solution supported by both the High-Level Expert Group and the European Parliament. Such an approach would be akin to liability for software/digital content. There will be some elements where the failure of the AI algorithm is akin to nonconformity of digital content, and as we seek to preserve established values and principles, this would mean that strict contractual liability should also apply here. With the impossibility of determining exactly what causes an AI algorithm to take a rogue decision (whether due to 'AI developers; algorithm trainers; data collectors, controllers and processors; ... and the final user ...'[98]), we argue that strict liability should extend to all instances when an AI algorithm takes a rogue decision. In our view, this would provide the degree of predictability and legal certainty needed

[89] Defined by the High Level Expert Group as 'the person primarily deciding on and benefitting from the use of the relevant technology', and the European Parliament as the 'person who exercises a degree of control over a risk connected with the operation and functioning of the AI-system and benefits from its operation', *Liability for Artificial Intelligence*, p. 39, 5[11](a).

[90] Defined by the High-Level Expert Group as 'the person continuously defining the features of the relevant technology and providing essential and ongoing backend support', and the European Parliament as the 'person who, on a continuous basis, defines the features of the technology, provides data and essential backend support service and therefore also exercises a degree of control over the risk connected with the operation and functioning of the AI-system', *Liability for Artificial Intelligence*, p. 39, 5[11](b).

[91] High Level, *Liability for Artificial Intelligence*, p. 39.

[92] European Parliament, *Resolution on a Civil Liability Regime for Artificial Intelligence* (2020/2014(INL), 20 October 2020), para. 13.

[93] Alberto De Franceschi and Reiner Schulze, 'Introduction' in *Digital Revolution*, p. 12.

[94] European Parliament resolution of 20 October 2020 with recommendations to the Commission on a civil liability regime for artificial intelligence (2020/2014(INL)).

[95] Art. 4.

[96] Art. 4(4).

[97] European Commission, *Proposal for a Regulation of the European Parliament and of the Council laying down harmonised rules on artificial intelligence (Artificial Intelligence Act) and amending certain union legislative acts* (COM (2021) 206 final (21 April 2021).

[98] Giuffrida, 'Liability for AI Decision-Making', p. 443.

by putting the onus on the parties better placed to manage the risks associated with the development and deployment of AI algorithms. However, where there is evidence that user behaviour was a key cause for the decisions taken by the AI algorithm, or where this was the result of external data influencing the AI algorithm's decision-making processes, a defence could be available. Of course, in the context of the PLD, where the question of defect requires inter alia consideration of 'the use to which [a product] could reasonably be put',[99] reasonable misuses might be covered[100] unless clearly warned against. We are conscious that strict liability for AI algorithms might have a detrimental effect on innovation,[101] but as strict liability is well-established in other areas of the law, we do not regard this as a sufficiently strong objection.

13.4.5 *Data Transfers*

The importance of data for the operation of an AI algorithm within an IoT system was previously noted in Section 13.2.[102] The data that determines the decisions by the AI algorithm can come from a number of sources. Many of the devices comprising the IoT system will have sensors that record and transmit data to the AI algorithm, as well as other devices in the system. Data may also be fed into the AI algorithm from external sources, whether from third parties (such as a weather report, traffic information or similar) or directly from the user of the IoT system. We have already highlighted the difficulty posed by the interaction of data and the AI algorithm for establishing liability for rogue decisions taken by the algorithm. Insofar as data is supplied by one of the devices that are part of the IoT system, a problem with the data provided by that device, particularly when caused by a malfunctioning sensor, can be an aspect of the device itself and therefore would be governed by liability rules applicable to goods. This is because the sensor is a physical component of the device and the provision of incorrect data due to a physical problem relates to the device itself.

Here, the focus is on the possible liability of a third-party supplier. There are several aspects to this. First, the legal basis for such liability would have to be established. If there is a contract between the third party and the user of the IoT system, then it may be possible to base liability on that contract. In the absence of a contract, liability might arise in tort/negligence provided that the conditions for such liability are made out. In the case of contractual liability, there would have to be a clear legal requirement to be met, whether that be expressed in terms of 'conformity with the contract' or reasonable expectations of the recipient of the data. Such a legal requirement would also have to provide for the limits to the liability of the supplier of such data: for instance, the data itself might be perfectly accurate and flawless, but be provided in a format or using units of measurements different from those used by an AI algorithm. Data portability and interoperability are crucial for the ability to use data.[103] Where data is not portable or interoperable, the data would not be suitable for use by the AI algorithm. If the accompanying meta-data contains relevant details regarding the format or unit of measurement in which the data is supplied, but the AI algorithm does not recognise this, then it would not be appropriate to

[99] Art. 6(1)(b) PLD.

[100] Cf. Recital 6, excluding only misuses 'not reasonable under the circumstances'.

[101] Mauricio Paez and Mike La Marca, 'The Internet of Things: Emerging Legal Issues for Business' (2016) 43 *Northern Kentucky Law Review* 29, p. 60.

[102] We are not distinguishing between personal data and non-personal data in this section. The relevance of data protection legislation in respect of personal data is crucial, of course, but for our purposes, we do not need to consider this particular dimension.

[103] Michal S. Gal and Daniel L. Rubinfeld, 'Data Standardization' (2019) 94 *New York University Law Review* 737, p. 739; Paez and La Marca, 'The Internet of Things', pp. 34–36.

impose liability on the supplier of the data. However, if such meta-data were absent, then liability for incompatible data could fall on the supplier of data.

Secondly, there will be questions regarding the extent of such liability.[104] If the data is not of the quality expected, then there might be liability for the difference in value, but this might not suffice to compensate the end-user of the IoT system for the losses that have actually been suffered. The key issue therefore will be whether there could be liability for consequential losses, including losses resulting from the malfunction of the IoT system, or for the possible corruption of the AI algorithm if the rogue data supplied by the third party affects the self-learning process of the AI algorithm.

In the consumer context, strict contractual liability already exists in some jurisdictions. Both the UK's Consumer Rights Act 2015 and the EU's DCSD/SGD define 'digital content' as 'data which are produced and supplied in digital form'.[105] The supply of raw data would fall within this broad definition, and consequently, the provisions on conformity of digital content and remedies for nonconformity would, in principle, apply to a contract between a consumer and a trader for the supply of data. However, there are no corresponding rules for non-consumer transactions.

With the current legal situation regarding the supply of data outside the consumer context at best uncertain, the publication of the *ALI-ELI Principles on the Data Economy* in late 2021 is an important step forward. Offering default rules to guide the development of the law relevant to the data economy, one important aspect is the idea of default quality standard regarding data supplied. In summary, data supplied commercially should be of a level of quality that would reasonably be expected, it should be current and accurate, have integrity, in a proper format and include the metadata and other specifications that will be needed to make use of the data.[106] This would be subject to agreement to the contrary through the terms of the contract between supplier and recipient. This approach offers one way of providing greater legal certainty regarding the obligations of a data supplier. However, the *Principles* do not make specific provision for remedies where data is not of the quality reasonably to be expected, referring only to the relevant (contract law) rules of the law applicable to the contract under which data is supplied.[107] Insofar as data falling short of the reasonably expected quality results in consequential losses, such as the malfunction of an IoT system, general rules of contract law on causation and remoteness would therefore apply.

13.5 TOWARDS AN ALTERNATIVE LIABILITY SYSTEM

In the previous section, we discussed many of the liability issues arising in respect of five specific features of an IoT system controlled by an AI algorithm. For some aspects, we can identify existing legal provisions; for others, the law is at best uncertain or at worst as yet silent. Further legislative steps will therefore be needed to tackle the liability issues of both IoT systems and AI algorithms, and the combination of both.

A general difficulty is that liability has traditionally been imposed based on recognised legal relationships, either through contract or on the basis of a duty of care in negligence. Inroads into bifurcation were made by specific products liability systems dealing with injury or damage

[104] Were such liability based on negligence, the limitations regarding recovery for pure economic loss might be a problem where no personal injury or damage to property is caused.

[105] S. 2(9) CRA; Art. 2(1) DCSD; Art. 2(6) SGD.

[106] See Principle 7(2)(b), in particular.

[107] Principle 4(1).

caused by faulty goods, where liability is imposed on the producer of the product even where there would be no liability in contract or negligence.

The complexity of an AI-controlled IoT system is such that an end-user, who is a victim of a system malfunction, will face the very challenging task of having to identify the appropriate party to be held responsible, and then the need to establish whether there is a legal basis for imposing liability on that party. The least-difficult situation would be one where the entire IoT system, including the AI algorithm, are supplied under one contract and no data supplied by a third party is involved. Here, the contract between end-user and system supplier would probably be a sufficient vehicle to provide redress in respect of a system malfunction. However, one might expect that many IoT systems will not be supplied under a single contract, and that there will be multiple contractual relationships as well as contributions by third parties not covered by any contract relating to an AI-operated IoT system.

Whilst clarifying liability issues for AI and IoT systems would be a crucial and important step forward, we suggest that there is a need to be bolder in that a different liability system for AI-operated IoT systems should be considered. A departure from traditional systems of allocating liability would neither be radical or altogether new. Extended liability allocations are already found in numerous areas of law. The PLD places liability for personal injury and damage to property on the 'producer' of the defective product. The notion of 'producer' has been given a meaning reaching beyond the manufacturer (although not as extensively as under US product liability rules, where liability can even be imposed on online platforms in some instances[108]). 'Producer' is defined[109] as covering not only the manufacturer of the final product, but also (i) the producer of raw materials; (ii) the manufacturer of components; (iii) so-called own branders, such as businesses putting their name or trademark on products manufactured by someone else; and (iv) an importer of the product into the EU (or since Brexit an importer into the UK).[110] In addition, for circumstances where none of these parties can be identified, any other supplier of the product, including the retailer who sold the product to the consumer, is treated as a producer.[111] However, such a supplier can evade liability if it is able to identify one of the parties within the definition of 'producer'. This broad approach to the notion of 'producer' could be viewed as reflecting an underlying principle that a consumer who has suffered harm should have an easy route to redress by being able to claim against anyone who is treated as a 'producer'. A key consequence is that the final producer is liable for the errors of others in the production chain, such as component makers and designers.

A different type of liability extension can be found in the EU's Package Travel Directive (2015/2302/EU). Here, the 'organiser' of a package travel contract (defined as 'a trader who combines and sells or offers for sale packages',[112] or, put in more general terms, a person who assembles various elements to sell a package) is legally responsible for the performance of all the travel services contracted for, irrespective of who the ultimate provider of those services is.[113] There is a legislative option[114] for Member States to extend this also to the retailer ('a trader other than the

[108] See *Oberdorf* v. *Amazon.Com Inc.*, 2020 WL 3023064 (3rd Cir. 2 June 2020) and *Bolger* v. *Amazon.Com, LLC*, 2020 WL 4692387 (Cal. Court of Appeal, 13 August 2020). An appeal in *Oberdorf* to the Pennsylvania Supreme Court was ultimately abandoned; an appeal in *Bolger* is pending in California at the time of writing.

[109] Art. 3 PLD.

[110] Art. 3(2) PLD.

[111] Art. 3(3) PLD.

[112] Art. 3(8) PTD.

[113] Art. 13(1) PTD.

[114] Ibid.

organiser who sells or offers for sale packages combined by an organiser'[115]). The organiser is obliged to provide a remedy where the contract is not, or cannot, be performed as agreed.[116] Once the organiser has provided a remedy to a traveller, the organiser has right to seek redress from the party 'which contributed to the event triggering'[117] the obligation to provide a remedy. Both the PLD and the Package Travel Directive reflect an approach to liability that involves placing liability towards the final user on an easily identifiable person, and, in the case of the Package Travel Directive, a right for this person to seek redress from the person who contributed to whatever resulted in the problem.

There are further instances where liability is imposed on non-contracting parties (albeit not channelled towards one counterparty). Both UK and EU consumer credit rules permit a consumer to claim against a credit provider in respect of non-supply or lack of conformity.[118] And with regard to autonomous vehicles, UK law provides that liability for injuries suffered in an accident caused by an automated vehicle falls on the vehicle's insurer.[119] The insurer can, in turn, bring a claim against the person who would otherwise be liable to the injured person.[120]

There are numerous precedents that justify developing extended liability approaches for AI-operated IoT systems, based on the twin features of offering the end-user an easy access to a counterparty and the behind-the-scenes channelling towards the parties responsible for the problem. We propose that a solution would be to push the boundaries of current liability approaches even further. Our starting point would be to treat the various legal relationships connected to an AI-operated IoT system as part of a single network.[121]

Proceeding from the recognition of such a network, an end-user faced with an IoT-system malfunction should not be required to identify the party responsible for the malfunction. Instead, it would suffice for the end-user to pursue the network, comprising all contracting parties, or to pursue one of the parties comprising the particular network. The end-user would be granted an appropriate remedy (compensation, other remedial action, etc). Within the network, there would then either be a system for allocating a share of the costs to meet the end-user's claim to each member, or the liability would be channelled towards the person or person(s) to whom responsibility can be attributed. In circumstances where it is impossible to pinpoint the exact cause of the IoT-system malfunction, spreading the costs among all network members might be the only solution. The basis for such allocations would need to be determined.

Where it is possible to identify a single cause, such as a failure of a physical device, or a software flaw, then ultimate liability would be imposed on that person, and other network members would be compensated accordingly. In short, our proposed liability system would allow the end-user to seek redress without having to face the severe difficulties associated with identifying the correct defendant(s) whilst providing for a recourse system between the network members to ensure that the loss is ultimately channelled towards the party/parties responsible. At

[115] Art. 3(9) PTD.
[116] Art. 13(3) PTD.
[117] Art. 22 PTD.
[118] Art. 15(2), Consumer Credit Directive; sec. 75, Consumer Credit Act 1974 (which is more extensive than the EU provision): Geraint Howells, Christian Twigg-Flesner and Thomas Wilhelmsson, *Rethinking EU Consumer Law* (London: Routledge, 2017), p. 254.
[119] Automated and Electric Vehicles Act 2018, s .2(1).
[120] Ibid., at s. 5.
[121] Our proposal is derived from an earlier proposal in respect of direct producer liability and network liability for consumer sales: see Robert Bradgate and Christian Twigg-Flesner, 'Expanding the Boundaries of Liability for Quality Defects' (2002) 25 *Journal of Consumer Policy* 342.

least in the context of EU consumer law, this approach would be in accordance with values and principles already established in other contexts.

A further benefit of a network liability approach would be to obviate the need to consider difficult questions of proof. Instead of having to prove the precise nature of the defect and identify the party responsible for this, it would suffice for the end-user to establish that the IoT system malfunctioned and caused injury or damage, or economic loss. There would be no need to identify the particular element of IoT system that caused the damage.

We derive some support for our idea from a proposal by the High-Level Expert Group on Liability and New Technologies. It has proposed[122] to impose a form of joint and several liability where several persons have cooperated in the 'provision of different elements of a technological unit'[123] where it is not possible for the injured person to identify which element of that unit has caused the damage in issue. The illustration given in the Expert Group's report is that of an alarm system manufactured by one person installed as an add-on to a smart home system created by another person and running on an ecosystem produced by a third person, and the alarm system subsequently fails. Unless the cause of the failure can clearly be identified, all three persons would be jointly and severally liable to the home-owner. However, this would only apply where there has been cooperation between the parties – it would not work where the user of an IoT system has put this together on a self-build basis. Here, the various liability issues would continue to be relevant.

13.6 CONCLUSION

In this chapter, we have identified many of the liability issues that arise in an IoT system, particularly where this involves an AI algorithm. The IoT itself presents complex liability questions, and the addition of AI complicates matters further. It is very likely that any IoT system will involve multiple contracts dealing with different aspects, each of which could be a separate basis for allocating liability for a particular malfunction. However, as we have explained, the evidentiary burden on the end-user of an IoT system of precisely identifying the cause(s) of an IoT system malfunction is almost unsurmountable. One might tolerate this in the context of systems used commercially; it would certainly not be acceptable for consumer systems. We have therefore argued in favour of a liability approach that makes it easier for a (consumer) user to obtain redress whilst ensuring a 'behind-the-scenes' right of recourse so that responsibility is ultimately placed on the party responsible for a malfunction.

A key requirement for such a system is that liability questions regarding the various elements of an IoT system involving the use of AI are clarified, not least to ensure that there will be a legal basis for seeking recourse. We have made numerous suggestions in that respect. With both the European Commission and the English Law Commission exploring reforms to accommodate liability issues in the digital age, we hope that our advice will be considered seriously.

[122] High Level, *Liability for Artificial Intelligence*.

[123] See point [29], p. 55. According to point [30], determining whether an arrangement constitutes a technological unit involves consideration of '(a) any joint or coordinated marketing of the different elements; (b) the degree of their technical interdependency and interoperation; and (c) the degree of specificity or exclusivity of their combination'.

14

Liability Standards for Medical Robotics and AI

The Price of Autonomy

Frank Pasquale

14.1 INTRODUCTION

There are now robotic applications for nursing home patients, the mentally ill, and other vulnerable populations. These advanced technologies raise critical liability questions for the medical profession. Consider the case of robotically assistive surgical devices (RASDs) that surgeons use to control small cutting and grasping devices. If a surgeon's hand slips with a scalpel, and a vital tendon is cut, our intuitive sense is that the surgeon bears the primary responsibility for the resultant malpractice suit. But the vendor of an RASD may someday market a machine that has a special "tendon avoidance subroutine," akin to the alarms that automobiles now sound when their sensors indicate a likely collision. If the tendon sensors fail, and the warning does not sound before an errant cut is made, may the harmed patient sue the vendor of the RASD? Or only the physician who relied on it?

Similar problems arise in the context of some therapy apps. For example, a counselor may tell a patient with a substance use disorder to use an app in order to track cravings, states of mind, and other information helpful to those trying to cure addictions. The app may recommend certain actions in case the counselor cannot be reached. If these actions are contraindicated and result in harm to the patient or others, is the app to blame? Or the doctor who prescribed it? Home health aide businesses may encounter similar dilemmas as they deploy so-called care robots.[1]

Of course, in neither the surgical nor the mental health scenario is the answer necessarily binary. There may be shared liability, based on an apportionment of responsibility. But before courts can trigger such an apportionment, they must have a clear theory upon which to base the responsibility of vendors of technology.

This chapter develops such an approach. What is offered here is less a detailed blueprint for liability determinations than a binary to structure policy discussions on liability for harm caused by AI and robotics in medical contexts.[2] The binary is the distinction between substitutive and

I wish to thank Brooklyn Law School's summer research fund for supporting this research.

[1] For a fascinating overview of legal issues raised by care robots, *see* Valerie W. Black, "Regulating Care Robots" (2020) 92 *Temple L. Rev.* 551. For examples of medical automation gone awry, *see* Robert Wachter, *The Digital Doctor: Hope, Hype, and Harm at the Dawn of Medicine's Computer Age* (New York: McGraw-Hill, 2015).

[2] This chapter will draw on common law principles in many jurisdictions, in order to inform a general policy discussion. It does not attempt to give detailed legal guidance, or map how courts presently do handle cases involving AI and complex computation in medical contexts. Rather, cases and other legal materials are drawn upon to illustrate the complement/substitute distinction.

complementary automation.[3] When AI and robotics substitutes for a physician, strict liability is more appropriate than standard negligence doctrine. When the same technology merely assists a professional, a less stringent standard is appropriate. Such standards will help ensure that the deployment of advanced medical technologies is accomplished in a way that complements extant professionals' skills, while promoting patient safety.

As law and political economy methods demonstrate, law cannot be neutral with respect to markets for new technology.[4] It constructs these markets, making certain futures more or less likely. Distinguishing between technology that substitutes for human expertise and that which complements professionals is fundamental to both labor policy and the political economy of automation.

For example, in the case of computerized physician order entry (CPOE) for prescriptions, a "drug–drug interaction" alert (DDI) could simply warn a physician about possible side effects from simultaneous ingestion of two pills.[5] That is complementary automation. If the DDI alert were, in fact, incorrect, a harmed patient could sue both the physician and the vendor of the CPOE system, but the burden should be on the patient to demonstrate the CPOE system's vendor failed to follow the proper standard of care in updating data or improving algorithms in order to avoid the problem. And the physician might still bear all or most of the responsibility, under the doctrine of competent human intervention.

By contrast, some CPOE systems of the future may simply "decide everything" with respect to the prescription of the two pills, preventing the doctor from prescribing them together. In such a scenario, the physician is no longer responsible – they cannot override the system. Given this extraordinary deviation from ordinary professional standards in medicine – which require a skilled person to mediate between technology and the patient – it is appropriate to impose strict liability up and down the distribution chain of such a substitutive AI. Under a strict liability standard, in case of a preventable adverse event, the manufacturer, distributor, and retailer of the product may be liable, even if they were not at fault for the problem.

This may seem like an unduly harsh standard. However, the doctrine of strict liability arose in response to those who sold "any product in a defective condition unreasonably dangerous to the user or consumer or to his property."[6] In the medical field, there has long been a standard of competent professional supervision and monitoring of the deployment of advanced technology.[7] When substitutive automation short-circuits that review, it is unreasonably dangerous. It also tends toward the diminution of the distributed expertise so critical to medical advance.[8]

[3] This distinction may also be styled as a contrast between artificial intelligence (AI) and intelligence augmentation (IA). However, that contrast would probably confuse matters at present, given that much of what is called AI in contemporary legal and policy discussions is narrow enough to be IA.

[4] Martha T. McCluskey, Frank Pasquale, and Jennifer Taub, "Law and Economics: Contemporary Approaches" (2016) 35 *Yale L. & Pol'y Rev.* 297.

[5] For a good typology of potential scenarios arising in the context of assistive AI, *see generally* W. Nicholson Price II, Sara Gerke, and I. Glenn Cohen, "Potential Liability for Physicians Using Artificial Intelligence" (2019) 322 *JAMA* 1765.

[6] *Restatement (Second) of Torts* § 402A.

[7] This chapter addresses policymakers governing health systems with this standard of care. Those in charge of less developed health systems (coping with physician or other staff shortages) may well decide that strict liability is too harsh a standard: If there is no viable human alternative, why discourage direct access to a machine? Those in many of the more developed health systems need to acknowledge their own responsibility for this state of affairs. *See* Frank Pasquale, "Access to Medicine in an Era of Fractal Inequality" (2010) 19 *Annals of Health Law* 269 (describing direct and indirect ways in which medical resources are directed away from the developing and toward the developed world).

[8] For an extended argument for the ideal of distributed expertise, *see generally* Frank Pasquale, *New Laws of Robotics: Defending Human Expertise in the Age of AI* (Cambridge, MA: The Belknap Press of Harvard University Press, 2020).

This chapter develops the complementary and substitutive categories via two case studies. Section 14.2 explores the complementary role of RASDs, and some litigation that has arisen regarding them. Section 14.3 introduces substitutive AI and robotics, and demonstrates the ways in which strict liability standards are likely necessary to promote accountability in their development and deployment, to preserve a unitary standard of care, and to promote public awareness of their shortcomings. Section 14.4 concludes with reflections on the current utility of, and potential challenges to, the substitutive/complementary dichotomy.

14.2 COMPLEMENTARY ROBOTICS: ROBOTICALLY ASSISTIVE SURGICAL DEVICES

Prostate surgery has seen rapid adoption of robotics: over 80 percent are robotic. Hundreds of urological surgeons have adopted the da Vinci Surgical Robot over the past decade. The rapid adoption of RASDs in prostate surgery demonstrates just how fast a new machine can change the face of practice for hundreds of thousands of patients. Surgical robots are now spreading to head and neck, heart, and thoracic surgery departments.[9]

At the outset, we should be clear about the terminology and effects of machines like the da Vinci. The device itself does not complete the surgery. Rather, it is an extremely sophisticated tool deployed by a skilled surgeon. The surgeon operates at a console, manipulating instruments from afar. What distinguishes robotic surgery from its predecessor, laparoscopic surgery, is that rather than merely deploying a tube with a cutter and a grabber at each end, the surgeon using an RASD has more dexterity – the device can twist around and act as a second wrist or eleventh finger. These robotically assisted surgical devices took off at first in urology, because many urological and gynecological procedures involve very sensitive tissue that can only be accessed through a small opening at the base of the pelvic bowl. The device can achieve forms of movement and illumination of tissue that would be impossible using the human hands alone.

That is not to say that the transition from open to robotic prostatectomy was an easy one. Surgeons who had worked their entire lives through direct manual touch had to adapt their practice to what could start as an unintuitive imaging and manipulation system. At the beginning, for many surgeons, the lack of direct touch – the so-called haptic interface – made surgery more difficult or time-consuming. However, over time, surgeons develop the ability to detect other cues for the feel of tissue – for example, how quickly it moves once probed, or how blood vessels blanch when the metallic ends of the robotic probe contact them. For a surgeon who has already seen and more directly prodded bodily tissue hundreds or thousands of times, the association of certain sights with other feelings – of softness or hardness, thickness or thinness – provide a reservoir of intuition about what the video from the RASD is showing. The surgeon would need to develop skills similar to those required in a videogame console control when operating an RASD, where a small movement in the da Vinci console results in cutting or lifting a vein. Moreover, as video proliferates, the "second nature" of the screen may

[9] *See* Gina Kolata, "Results Unproven, Robotic Surgery Wins Converts," *The New York Times* (Feb. 13, 2010), www.nytimes.com/2010/02/14/health/14robot.html?pagewanted=1&hp; *compare* Giacomo Novara et al., "Systematic Review and Meta-Analysis of Perioperative Outcomes and Complications after Robot-Assisted Radical Prostatectomy" (2012) 62 *Eur. Urology* 431; "Surgical Robot Market by Product, by Brand, by Application, Market Size, Application Analysis, Competitive Strategies and Forecast, 2016 to 2024," *Grand View Res.* (Apr. 2016), www.grandviewresearch.com/industry-analysis/surgical-robot-market. Recent legal scholarship addressing the surgical robotics market includes Andrew Chin, "Surgically Precise but Kinematically Abstract Patents" (2017) 55 *Houston L. Rev.* 266 (describing how intellectual property law helps enable monopolistic business practices).

become a "first nature" for trainees, and a source of data for machine learning programs to identify past errors and deter future ones.

According to some critics of health technology, the dissemination of RASDs is yet another tale of healthcare spending gone out of control. The devices can cost over $1 million, with high upkeep and maintenance fees.[10] Surgeons must invest valuable time to learn the ins and outs of the new system. Some have questioned the value of the technology.[11]

But it is important to take this early medical evidence with a grain of salt. One key problem emerges in many areas of clinical innovation – those completing robotic surgeries in the first decade of studies could only have had five to ten years of experience using the robot, since it was so new, while their output was sometimes being compared to the surgeries of those who had perfected their skills in open prostatectomies for decades. Outcome measures can also be unfairly narrow. For example, according to some accounts, those who undergo a robotic surgery for prostate cancer can often return home after just four days at the hospital, while those undergoing open prostatectomies often take six or seven days. In the case of kidney cancer, the smaller incision used for robotic surgeries can lead to less pain and shorter recovery times. Surgeons who use the RASDs tend to agree that the tools make surgery much easier than pure manual manipulation. The human hand has not evolved to manipulate a scalpel to make fine distinctions between healthy and cancerous tissue; surgical robots can be specifically designed to take on this task. Video recording via miniaturized cameras may also enable new research on body tissue. This recording already helps speed the diffusion of surgical innovations, as doctors share videos of particularly successful surgical techniques at medical conferences.

Complementary robotics are dominant now. To promote its regulatory agenda in the area of robotic surgery in 2015, the Food and Drug Administration announced a public workshop on RASD.[12] Speakers included cutting-edge physicians and firms. Neither actual implementations of, nor planned development of, fully autonomous surgical devices seemed to be high on the agenda. Admittedly, firms planning fully autonomous systems may be in stealth mode – they could lose current surgeons as clients if they talked too openly about replacing them. And in 2016, a stitching robot did mark one notable exception to this pattern.[13] While acknowledging that "the current paradigm of robot-assisted surgeries (RASs) depends entirely on an individual surgeon's manual capability," inventors demonstrated a robot that could stitch a split pig intestine together, besting the performance of human surgeons – when given longer to perform the task. Billed as the "first autonomous robot" to operate, it managed to bind a hole in soft tissue

[10] Cameron Scott, "Is da Vinci Robotic Surgery a Revolution or a Rip-off?," *Healthline News* (Aug. 10, 2016), www.healthline.com/health-news/is-da-vinci-robotic-surgery-revolution-or-ripoff-021215.

[11] *See* Michelle Andrews, "Gynecologists Question Use of Robotic Surgery for Hysterectomies," *NPR* (Apr. 23, 2013), www.npr.org/blogs/health/2013/04/23/178576759/gynecologists-question-use-of-robotic-surgery-for-hysterectomies; *see also* James T. Breeden, "Statement on Robotic Surgery by ACOG President James T. Breeden," *The Am. Cong. of Obstetricians and Gynecologists* (Mar. 14, 2013), www.acog.org/About_ACOG/News_Room/News_Releases/2013/Statement_on_Robotic_Surgery; "Hospitals Misleading Patients about Benefits of Robotic Surgery, Study Suggests," *Johns Hopkins Med.* (May 18, 2011), www.hopkinsmedicine.org/news/media/releases/hospitals_misleading_patients_about_benefits_of_robotic_surgery_study_suggests; "Robotic Surgery: More Complications, Higher Expense for Some Conditions," *Colum. U. Med. Ctr.* (Oct. 8, 2014), http://newsroom.cumc.columbia.edu/blog/2014/10/08/robotic-surgery-complications-higher-expense-conditions.

[12] "FDA Public Workshop: Robotically-Assisted Surgical Devices: Challenges and Opportunities, July 27–28, 2015," *U.S. Food & Drug Admin.* (2017), www.fda.gov/MedicalDevices/NewsEvents/WorkshopsConferences/ucm435255.htm.

[13] Azad Shademan et al., "Supervised Autonomous Robotic Soft Tissue Surgery" (2016) 8 *Sci. Translational Med.* 337ra64; Beth Mole, "First Autonomous Robot to Operate on Soft Tissue Outdoes Human Surgeons," *Ars Technica* (May 5, 2016), http://arstechnica.com/science/2016/05/smart-sewing-machine-nails-worlds-first-autonomous-soft-tissue-surgery.

with speed and precision. The question, now, is whether further industrial development in the area should try to *change* the dominant trend in robotics here, by replacing human surgeons – or if the present path of human–computer interaction is something to maintain.

In theory, it would seem obvious that a robot with minuscule, nimble, even laparoscopic probes would be a better interventionist than the average surgeon – and perhaps, eventually, even the best ones. "We rely on the dexterity of human surgeons but now we know machines are quite a bit more precise than humans. If you want to do things with extreme precision, a machine would be better," said one Google researcher.[14] And if the Smart Tissue Autonomous Robot (STAR) could sew more evenly and consistently than even an experienced surgeon on a pig intestine, there is no reason in principle it could not do the same with human flesh and viscera.[15] However, "STAR was still dependent on a surgeon to make the initial incision, take out the bowel, and line up the pieces" before it began suturing.[16] As leading health technology scholars observed in a review chapter, it will likely be decades until fully autonomous robots take on a surgery from start to finish.[17]

Nor is direct-to-consumer medical automation and robotics a plausible step forward in many areas. First, scientific evidence is often extremely difficult for the layman to interpret. Large corporations can and often do market products in unscrupulous ways. Large pharmaceutical firms and device manufacturers have systematically skewed data to support their products.[18] Information is scattered, and those untrained in medicine may not be able to interpret conflicting studies. Uncomplicated medical devices, like joint replacements and screws, have continued to be implanted in patients years after serious safety concerns were raised. Moreover, firms may impose on individuals' "hold harmless" clauses, which force them to give up their right to sue.[19] In other words, even in a field as technical and, in principle, automatable as surgery, it is vital to keep some person in the loop as a source of information and advice for laypeople. MIT economist David Autor offers a general reality check about automation that applies with even more force here:

> Most automated systems lack flexibility – they are brittle. Modern automobile plants, for example, employ industrial robots to install windshields on new vehicles as they move through the assembly line. But aftermarket windshield replacement companies employ technicians, not robots, to install replacement windshields. Why not robots? Because removing a broken windshield, preparing the windshield frame to accept a replacement, and fitting a replacement into that frame demand far more real-time adaptability than any contemporary robot can approach.[20]

[14] Mark Harris, "Founder of Google's Stealthy Surgical Robotics Project Speaks," *Backchannel* (Dec. 14, 2015), https://backchannel.com/founder-of-google-s-stealthy-surgical-robotics-project-speaks-c2f7e0dfe13c#.8brbfi1co.

[15] Sarah Zhang, "Why an Autonomous Robot Won't Replace Your Surgeon Anytime Soon," *Wired* (May 4, 2016), www.wired.com/2016/05/robot-surgeon.

[16] Ibid.

[17] Drew Simshaw et al., "Regulating Healthcare Robots: Maximizing Opportunities While Minimizing Risks" (2016) 22 *Richmond J. L. & Tech.* 1.

[18] Frank Pasquale, "Grand Bargains for Big Data: The Emerging Law of Health Information" (2013) 72 *Maryland L. Rev.* 682; Ben Goldacre, *Bad Pharma: How Drug Companies Mislead Doctors and Harm Patients* (London: Fourth Estate, 2013); Jeanne Lenzer, *The Danger within Us: America's Untested, Unregulated Medical Device Industry and One Man's Battle to Survive It* (New York: Little, Brown and Company, 2017).

[19] Margaret Jane Radin, *Boilerplate: The Fine Print, Vanishing Rights, and the Rule of Law* (Princeton, NJ: Princeton University Press, 2012).

[20] David Autor, "Polanyi's Paradox and the Shape of Employment Growth," Nat'l Bureau of Econ. Res., Working Paper No. 20485 (2014), www.nber.org/papers/w20485.

Of course, futurists can probably imagine a robot in a self-driving car that can navigate itself to your car, drive it to a garage, and order other robots to replace the windshield. But even that scenario depends on a chain of contingencies and potential human interventions when things go wrong. When the stakes are higher – for instance, replacing a kidney instead of a windshield – then even more back-up systems and planning will be necessary.

Even robotics manufacturers themselves may want to keep human beings "in the loop" – both to assure better use of their products, and to deflect liability. Legal reform will be needed to avoid opportunism built around excessively deflective doctrines. If something goes wrong with a mechanical system – be it an autopilot on a plane or a device used in surgery – doctrines of "competent human intervention," "the learned intermediary," or "captain of the ship" tend to shift liability to the person operating (or merely capable of taking control from) the device, rather than the device maker.[21] But even when robotics and AI only complement a professional, there still need to be opportunities for plaintiffs and courts to discover whether the technology's developers and vendors acted reasonably. Such inquiry is endangered by expansive interpretations of "competent human intervention," "the learned intermediary," or "captain of the ship" doctrines.[22] As the example of the tendon-cutting device showed, all responsibility for an error should not rest on a doctor when complementary robotics fails to accomplish what it promised to do. To hold otherwise would again be an open invitation to technologists to rest on their laurels.[23]

Even if technologists develop fully autonomous robot surgeons, the ultimate "backup system" would be a skilled human surgeon with some experience, flexibility, and creativity.[24] Our aim should not be to replace such individuals, but to aid in their efficiency and effectiveness. The sequence and shape of automation in health care cannot simply be dictated from on high by engineers. Rather, domain experts need to be consulted, and they need to buy into a larger vision of progress in their field. Perhaps more of medicine should indeed be automated – but law should help ensure that physicians themselves are lasting partners in that process. They should be helped, not replaced, by machines, for the short to medium term.

Of course, in the long term, new arrangements may arise. The distinction between complementary and substitutive robotics becomes small in some routinized medical procedures. The right tools make a job easier – and at times even more engaging. An analogy from driving may be useful. A truck driver may find that cruise control frees their foot from the gas pedal. Automatic transmission makes it easier to shift from high to low gear. Collision avoidance software can warn them about cars in their blind spot.[25] Technology can make the job much easier – until it replaces the driver altogether. So, there is delicate balance between inventions that help workers,

[21] Madeleine Elish and Tim Hwang, "Praise the Machine! Punish the Human!," Data & Soc'y Res. Inst., Working Paper No. 1 (2015); Sharona Hoffman and Andy Podgurski, "Finding a Cure: The Case for Regulation and Oversight of Electronic Health Record Systems" (2008) 22 *Harvard J. L. & Tech.* 103 (on competent human intervention).

[22] The learned intermediary doctrine holds that the manufacturer of a new technology "discharges their duty of care to consumers by providing adequate warnings" about its potential for harm to professionals using the technology. James Nelson, "Arizona High Court Reestablishes the 'Learned Intermediary' Doctrine," A.B.A. (Feb. 25, 2016), www.americanbar.org/groups/litigation/committees/mass-torts/practice/2016/learned-intermediary-doctrine.

[23] Aaron S. Kesselheim, "Permitting Product Liability Litigation for FDA-Approved Drugs and Devices Promotes Patient Safety" (2010) 87 *Clinical Pharm. & Therapeutics* 645. Note that both physicians and technologists may share responsibility for preventable errors. The amount of compensation in both negligence and strict liability regimes may be limited by state legislatures to avoid overdeterring innovation. But compensation is still due.

[24] Nicholas Carr, *The Glass Cage: How Our Computers Are Changing Us* (New York: W. W. Norton & Co., 2015).

[25] Karen E. C. Levy, "The Contexts of Control: Information, Power, and Truck-Driving Work" (2015) 31 *The Info. Soc'y* 160; Nat'l Highway Traffic Safety Administration (Report No. DOT HS 812 329), *Federal Automated Vehicles Policy* (2016).

and those which replace them altogether. Economists tend to call the former "complementary" to labor, and the latter "substitutive."

The "be careful what you wish for" story of a worker gradually replaced by their tools has a long history. Aristotle speculated about the effects of self-driving looms centuries before they transformed manufacturing.[26] Hegel tells the story of a master who gradually becomes weaker and less competent in comparison with a slave whom they force to perform ever more tasks. Labor economists have worried that "deskilling" is the natural consequence of a more mechanized workplace, paving the way to mass automation.[27]

However, a smooth transition from "being helped" to "being replaced" by technology is not an inevitability. Nor should it be in medicine. While fields like driving have a relatively simple goal (getting to a destination as quickly and safely as possible), much of medicine entails difficult and subtle trade-offs. There is a much better case for aspiring to build drivers' skills into autonomous vehicles, than trying to do the same for physicians.[28] Whereas the relevant data about autonomous cars will be relatively transparent to potential buyers, performance data for autonomous medical equipment is likely to be more opaque and contested.[29] For that reason alone, keeping a "human in the loop" is critical. When there are complicated value judgments at stake (for example, whether to try a riskier or experimental surgery knee surgery in order to try to increase the patient's ability to run afterwards), there are all manner of trade-offs that need a skilled and experienced domain expert's attention. The model for most medical machines should be closer to that of prescription drugs: technology recommended or used by physicians, which does not replace them.

14.3 SUBSTITUTIVE AUTOMATION: AN ANESTHESIA MACHINE CASE STUDY

Insurance contracts and licensure and certification rules have a powerful impact on technological development.[30] There is no autonomous robotic surgeon today – only "robotically assistive surgical devices." Even if some genius were to invent a fully autonomous surgical machine, it would need to be vetted by years of tests and research before mass adoption occurred.[31] Reimbursement rules may create another hurdle for rapid adoption of robotics.[32]

[26] Aristotle, *Politics Book 1* (350 BCE) (if "shuttles wove and picks played kitharas [stringed instruments] by themselves, master-craftsmen would have no need of assistants and masters no need of slaves").

[27] Harry Braverman, *Labor and Monopoly Capital: The Degradation of Work in the Twentieth Century* (New York: Monthly Review Press, 1974); Claudia Goldin and Lawrence F. Katz, *The Race between Education and Technology* (Cambridge, MA: National Bureau of Economic Research, 2008).

[28] Moreover, even in the realm of driving, some firms are focused on keeping human beings in the picture. For example, Toyota has promoted cars with a spectrum of machine involvement, from chauffeur mode (which requires minimal monitoring by a driver) to guardian mode (which focuses the car's computing systems on accident avoidance, while a person helms the vehicle). Planes have had autopilot capacities for decades, but commercial carriers still tend to have at least two persons at the helm.

[29] Goldacre, *Bad Pharma*.

[30] Meghan Hamilton-Piercy, "Cybersurgery: Why the United States Should Embrace This Emerging Technology" (2007) 7 *J. High Tech. L.* 203.

[31] Margo Goldberg, "The Robotic Arm Went Crazy! The Problem of Establishing Liability in a Monopolized Field" (2012) 38 *Rutgers Computer & Tech. L.J.* 225.

[32] *See, e.g.*, "Robotic Assisted Surgery Policy, United Health Care Reimbursement Policy," *United Healthcare* (2016), www.uhcprovider.com/content/dam/provider/docs/public/policies/medicaid-comm-plan-reimbursement/UHCCP-Robotic-Assisted-Surgery-Policy-(R0114).pdf

> (United Healthcare Community Plan considers S2900 (Surgical techniques requiring use of robotic surgical system (list separately in addition to code for primary procedure) to be a technique integral to the primary surgical procedure and not a separately reimbursed service. When a surgical procedure is performed using code S2900, reimbursement will be considered included as part of the primary surgical

When robots generate marginally better outcomes, public and private insurers will think twice about paying high fees to guarantee access to them.

Liability concerns will also slow the development of autonomous systems. For example, anesthesia may seem like the ideal use case for an autonomous robot, since machine-readable reports of bodily states may, in principle, be able to indicate any untoward development meriting an intervention. However, the field still seems to be focused on assistive models. The Sedasys anesthesia machine, for instance, is licensed by the Food and Drug Administration to assist anesthesiologists in relatively straightforward operations.[33] It can monitor patients' breathing and heart rate, administer set doses of anesthesia, and alter those doses in response to new data.[34] Like the "guardian" mode of cars, designed to prevent accidents, Sedasys robots could spot warning signs of adverse events in advance of their actually occurring.

The FDA noted that the use of Sedasys was a major advance:

> The approval of the SEDASYS System represents a notable advancement in the field of semi-autonomous control of drug administration in medicine. The device utilizes negative feedback from specialized physiological monitors to assess and limit drug dosing and thereby control the depth of sedation. The principle of negative feedback control may be applicable to a variety of drugs and clinical scenarios different from those associated with sedation management.[35]

However, the agency also stated that "the use of the device is restricted to settings where a practitioner trained in the administration of general anesthesia is immediately available to the user for assistance or consultation as needed. Immediate availability in this context means that an anesthesia professional will be available on site to respond to an emergency situation."[36] This type of safeguard both reflects and complicates the larger argument of this chapter. While the core case of complementarity is a physician directly operating or supervising the relevant medical AI and robotics, a secondary application of the concept may include a physician (here, an anesthesiologist) maintaining presence in case of complications.

There are many possible future developments for such anesthesia technology. In Europe, national health authorities will be pulled in opposing directions. Health cost cutters may favor

procedure. Use of Modifier 22 (increased procedural services) appended to the primary surgical procedure is not appropriate if used exclusively for the purpose of reporting the use of robotic assistance. Modifier 22 may only be used when substantial additional work is performed, (increased intensity, time, technical difficulty of procedure, severity of patient's condition, and physical and mental effort required) that is unrelated to robotic assistance. Documentation must demonstrate the reason for the substantial additional work performed during the surgical procedure.);

"Clinical Policy: Robotic Surgery," *Health Net* (Oct. 2016), www.healthnet.com/static/general/unprotected/pdfs/national/policies/RoboticSurgery.pdf; "Reimbursement Policy, Robotic Assisted Surgery," *Anthem Blue Cross* (May 2015), www11.anthem.com/ca/provider/f3/s2/t1/pw_e219842.pdf?refer=provider.

33 "FDA Summary of Safety and Effectiveness Data: Sedasys Computer-Assisted Personalized Sedation System – P080009," *U.S. Food & Drug Admin.*, www.accessdata.fda.gov/cdrh_docs/pdf8/P080009b.pdf; "Pre-market Approval, SEDASYS Computer-Assisted Personalized Sedation System," *U.S. Food & Drug Admin.*, www.accessdata.fda.gov/scripts/cdrh/cfdocs/cftopic/pma/pma.cfm?num=p080009; "FDA Advisory Panel Gives Favorable Vote to Computer-Assisted Sedation System," Med. Devices Law & Indus. (2009).

34 "Sedasys Information," *Am. Ass'n of Nurse Anesthetists*, www.aana.com/resources2/professionalpractice/Pages/SEDASYS-Information.aspx; Am. Soc'y of Gastrointestinal Endoscopy, "Computer-Assisted Personalized Sedation" (2011) 73 *Gastrointestinal Endoscopy* 423; "Physiological Closed-Loop Controlled (PCLC) Medical Devices," *U.S. Food & Drug Admin.* (Oct. 13–14, 2015), www.fda.gov/downloads/medicaldevices/newsevents/workshopsconferences/ucm464939.pdf; Preet Mohinder Singh, Anuradha Borle, and Basavana G. Goudra, "Use of Computer-Assisted Drug Therapy Outside the Operating Room" (2016) 29 *Current Opinion in Anesthesiology* 506.

35 "Summary of Safety and Effectiveness Data (SSED): Computer-Assisted Personalized Sedation System," *U.S. Food & Drug Admin.* (May 3, 2013), www.accessdata.fda.gov/cdrh_docs/pdf8/p080009b.pdf, 37.

36 Ibid., 38.

full robotization as a cost-cutting measure. On the other hand, European workers have, in general, been able to play a larger role in the deployment of technology than their American or Asian peers. That trend would encourage a slow roll-out of the devices, as they gradually proved their worth, and healthcare workers (including anesthesiologists and nurse-anesthetists) transitioned toward positions monitoring and improving the machines – or migrated toward jobs still requiring the "human touch."

In the USA, there are also conflicting political and economic currents. In the country with the highest healthcare expenditures on the planet, costs are always a concern. But risk-averse hospitals may only permit patients to opt for cheaper, robotic anesthesiology if they sign disclaimers of liability – basically, enforceable promises not to sue the hospital if something goes wrong.[37] The dubious legal status of such waivers sandbagged trends toward "consumer directed health care" in the United States.[38] While some doctors wanted to give patients the option of "last year's medicine at last year's prices," they did not want to be sued for malpractice if the cheaper option proved ineffective. Similar concerns will arise as device makers market robotic systems for hospitals and doctors' offices.

Reimbursement and liability rules will affect the adoption of medical robotics well beyond the technical realm of surgical interventions. What would be the proper liability regime, for example, for a fully autonomous anesthesia machine? Assume for the purposes of this chapter that the machine's operations were not explicable to the surgeons and other medical personnel among whom it was deployed – so that there is no sense in which it could be considered merely "helping" them.[39] What is the proper way to assess its responsibility (or, more accurately, the responsibility of its manufacturer, distributor, and retailer) for preventable adverse outcomes?

Given the difficulty of demonstrating negligence in complex endeavors involving software, strict liability is a compelling alternative.[40] In a negligence regime, there are simply too many ways to shift blame in the complex relationships between medical professionals, hospitals, vendors of AI, and others in the distribution chain – particularly given "hold harmless" or other exculpatory clauses that may be foisted on providers.[41] Note, too, that strict liability does not require a vendor of substitutive AI to be "perfect." Expected damages will be balanced against expected profits. Limits on damages can temper the potential unfairness of liability without fault.[42] Just as they do with respect to malpractice exposure, insurers may offer liability insurance to assist innovators in risk-shifting. And if the substitutive AI has a performance record clearly as good as, or better than, the extant standard of care (be that unaided human care, or, more likely,

[37] *See Tunkl* v. *Regents of the Univ. of Cal.*, 383 P 2d 441 (Cal. 1963) (disallowing waivers of liability); *but see Colton* v. *N.Y. Hosp.*, 414 NYS 2d 866 (1979) (upholding exculpatory clause in a case where an experimental treatment was the only option for the patient).

[38] Timothy Jost, *Health Care at Risk: A Critique of the Consumer-Driven Movement* (Durham, NC: Duke University Press, 2007); Mark A. Hall and Carl E. Schneider, "Patients as Consumers: Courts, Contracts, and the New Medical Marketplace" (2008) 106 *Mich. L. Rev.* 643.

[39] On the critical distinction between explainable and nonexplainable AI in medical automation and robotics, *see* Barbara J. Evans and Frank Pasquale, "Product Liability Suits for FDA-Regulated AI/ML Software" in I. Glenn Cohen et al. (eds), *The Future of Medical Device Regulation: Innovation and Protection* (Cambridge: Cambridge University Press, 2022 [forthcoming]), https://papers.ssrn.com/sol3/papers.cfm?abstract_id=3719407.

[40] Eric Lindenfeld, "3D Printing of Medical Devices: CAD Designers as the Most Realistic Target for Strict, Product Liability Lawsuits" (2016) 85 *U. Missouri-Kansas City L. Rev.* 1; Joseph L. Reutiman, "Defective Information: Should Information Be a 'Product' Subject to Products Liability Claims?" (2012) 22 *Cornell J.L. & P. Pol'y* 1.

[41] Frank Pasquale, "Six Horsemen of Irresponsibility" (2019) 79 *Maryland. L. Rev.* 105 (discussing myriad, mutually reinforcing strategies of liability-deflection).

[42] By contrast, if the extant performance standards are much better than those of substitutive automation, the significant damages available pursuant to strict liability for substitutive automation will be a critical prod toward the restoration of a unitary standard of care.

human–machine cooperation), wise judges and policymakers should try to keep damages minimal.

However, the definition of "as good, or better" performance records needs to be granular, so as to be sensitive to historical victims of health disparities. There has been growing concern that the data used for diagnostic AI may not adequately represent all groups in society. For example, minority groups may be poorly represented in databases.[43] Women are seriously disadvantaged as well.[44] Diagnostic AI that ignores all these problems, and which still generally delivers better results than unaided human observation, may not be actionable under a negligence standard for those it fails to help – particularly if the standard of care is unaided human observation. However, under a strict liability standard, failure to include available, more representative databases, that leads to preventable accidents, would leave vendors liable for adverse events even if they managed to do better on average than the standard of care. Such liability may be critical to incentivizing them to address health disparities.

Efthimios Parasidis has convincingly argued that courts need to recognize and counteract automation bias – that is, the tendency of persons to assume without proper evidence that a machine has better judgment than persons.[45] The problem of automation bias is recurrent and is a persistent temptation when often-overworked professionals seek tools to ease their workload.[46] More stringent liability standards are a way of gradually ensuring a lower risk level in the industry. They also reflect that, given the extraordinarily complex and even heightened secrecy common in the development of medical automation and robotics, it is fair to shift the burden of proof of demonstrating safety from the plaintiff to the defendant in cases of catastrophic failure when available human guidance and oversight has been forsaken.[47]

A vehicle manufacturer may be held responsible for an accident if the manufacturer failed to design or manufacture the vehicle properly. Similarly, AI and robotics may be designed or developed in a way that fails to conform to basic standards of safety and reliability. The product analogy increases accountability for safety, reliability, and security.[48] Unpredictability of

43 Adewole S. Adamson and Avery Smith, "Machine Learning and Health Care Disparities in Dermatology" (2018) 11 *JAMA Dermatology* 1247. This lack of diversity also afflicts genomics research. Non-European groups tend not to be as well-represented in DNA databases as European groups. Alice B. Popejoy et al., "The Clinical Imperative for Inclusivity: Race, Ethnicity, and Ancestry (REA) in Genomics" (2018) 11 *Human Mutation* 1713.

44 Caroline Criado Perez, *Invisible Women: Data Bias in a World Designed for Men* (New York: Abrams Press, 2019).

45 Efthimios Parasidis, "Clinical Decision Support: Elements of a Sensible Legal Framework" (2018) 20 *J. Healthcare L. & Pol'y* 183

> (As to the coding phase of software development, a strong argument can be made that coding should be encompassed under the category of manufacturing defects [and this is critical because US courts typically employ strict or product liability analysis for manufacturing defects] ... [A]llowing products liability claims for CDS systems also may be a way to counter disclaimers of liability that typically are found in CDS contracts.).

See also Kevin R. Pinkney, "Putting Blame Where Blame Is Due: Software Manufacturer and Customer Liability for Security-Related Software Failure" (2002) 13 *Alb. L.J. Sci. & Tech.* 43 (focusing on security-related failures); Michael D. Scott, "Tort Liability for Vendors of Insecure Software: Has the Time Finally Come?" (2017) 67 *Maryland L. Rev.* 469–470.

46 Carr, *The Glass Cage*.

47 Frances E. Zollers et al., "No More Soft Landings for Software: Liability for Defects in an Industry That Has Come of Age" (2005) 21 *Santa Clara Computer & High Tech. L.J.* 777.

48 However, as Jamil Ammar warns, "From the perspective of product liability, courts in the U.S. consider computer software to be a service rather than a product. To date, courts have been reluctant to extend theories of product liability to software." Jamil Ammar, "Defective Computer-Aided Design Software Liability in 3d Bioprinted Human Organ Equivalents" (2019) 35 *Santa Clara High Tech. L.J.* 37. One purpose of this chapter is to urge courts (both in the USA and elsewhere) to reconsider this approach in the context of substitutive AI.

advanced AI systems means that forms of accountability reflecting classic legal standards are critical. For example, those keeping particularly vicious or wild animals (like lions and tigers) are strictly liable if these beasts escape and cause harm.[49] Enterprise liability "asserts that actors should bear the costs of those accidents that are characteristic of their activities and then distribute those costs among all those who benefit from the imposition of the risks at issue."[50] Professor Danielle Keats Citron inventively applied these ideas to the digital age by analogizing massive data holdings to early reservoirs that, if breached, could cause death and destruction to communities immediately adjacent to them.[51] Much the same could be said of autonomous robotics or AI in critical medical situations when an irresponsible user decides to simply let them run autonomously. When they are marketed or developed to be used in autonomous mode, their developers and vendors must take responsibility. AI and robotics systems are ultimately attributable to humans.[52]

A strict liability standard will be controversial. The legal scholar Ryan Abbott has argued that, if an autonomous vehicle is, in general, safer than the typical human driver, only a negligence cause of action should be available.[53] If accepted, such a comparison would make negligence, rather than strict or product liability, the proper judicial response to errors. For Abbott, the standard of a "reasonable computer" would then supplant that of the "reasonable person," in judicial considerations of the type and level of responsibility to assign. Such an approach would help ensure that there are not undue impediments to the development of autonomous vehicles. However, it is likely less appropriate in the medical field, since healthcare providers are likely to be far more valuable in guiding the deployment of technology, long-term, than "guardian drivers" who have been deployed to restrain self-driving cars when they errantly threaten to crash into a person or another vehicle. The ongoing need for expert guidance weighs in favor of a strict liability standard in the case of substitutive automation in medicine.

Moreover, the British attorney Jacob Turner argues in his book *Robot Rules* that a negligence standard may be very difficult to apply, because

> A reasonable human person is fairly easy to imagine. The law's ability to set an objective standard of behaviour takes as its starting point the idea that all humans are similar ... AI, on the other hand, is heterogeneous in nature: there are many different techniques for creating AI and the variety is likely only to increase in the future as new technologies are developed.[54]

This is a valuable reminder of the plasticity of the mechanical world, at least relative to that of humans.[55] However, it is not unreasonable for persons to expect that AIs unleashed upon the

[49] Animals Act 1971, c. 22, § 2(1) (Eng.); American Law Institute, *Restatement (Third) of Torts: Phys, & Emotional Harm* § 22 (2010).

[50] Gregory Keating, "The Theory of Enterprise Liability and Common Law Strict Liability" (2007) 54 *Vanderbilt L. Rev.* 653.

[51] Danielle Keats Citron, "Reservoirs of Danger: The Evolution of Public and Private Law at the Dawn of the Information Age" (2007) 80 *S. California L. Rev.* 241.

[52] And they should be kept that way. Pasquale, New Laws of Robotics (proposing a fourth law of robotics requiring all AI and robotics to be attributable to responsible persons).

[53] Ryan Abbott, "The Reasonable Computer: Disrupting the Paradigm of Tort Liability" (2017) 86 *Geo. Wash. L. Rev.* 101 ("Under current legal frameworks, suppliers of computer tortfeasors are likely strictly responsible for their harms. This Article argues that where a supplier can show that an autonomous computer, robot, or machine is safer than a reasonable person, the supplier should be liable in negligence rather than strict liability.").

[54] Jacob Turner, *Robot Rules: Regulating Artificial Intelligence* (Cham: Palgrave Macmillan, 2019), at 90.

[55] Any attribution of robot interests or rights based on analogy to humans, for instance, is incoherent because the very conceptions of well-being or desire that are the foundation of such rights and interests may be reprogrammed in the robot. Such "reprogramming" is, by contrast, exceptionally difficult and damaging when undertaken with respect to a person, if it can be done at all. Given the limited advances made toward robotics, we must turn to fiction to see an

world will have some basic rules of engagement programmed in that are designed to limit human harm. This was enshrined as the first of Isaac Asimov's Laws of Robotics, and shows up in many other popular guidance for human–machine interaction.[56] Strict liability for autonomous machines and AI is one more way to ensure that prevention of harm is prioritized.

14.4 CONCLUSION

While promoting AI as a substitute for competent medical personnel, some firms will fail to engage in the quality control and other steps necessary to avoid disastrous outcomes. Tort lawsuits will follow, with plaintiffs demanding damages for the firms' failures to meet the relevant standard of care. Legislators and courts will need to develop approaches to liability adequate to the new technological environment. As they do so, they will effectively set nuanced and contextualized standards for the deployment of AI. Distinguishing between complementary and substitutive AI is one conceptual tool that will help them do so.

When AI or robotics simply assist a professional, they are tools. In medicine, the doctrine of "competent human intervention" has shifted liability away from those who make devices and toward the professionals who use them. However, the professional in such scenarios should not bear the entire burden of responsibility. Their tools can be produced well or badly, and vendors of defective AI and robotics should be held responsible for negligence. Both legislators and courts will need to develop standards of care designed to incentivize proper safety, security, and risk avoidance. But the burden of proof will be on the plaintiff to demonstrate that not only a skilled medical professional, but also the maker of the tools used by such a professional, should be held liable for a preventable adverse outcome.

When AI and robotics replace a skilled medical professional, the burden shifts. The vendor of such computational systems needs to take on the responsibility for errors and accidents. At the damages phase of litigation, the vendor may explain how its damages should be mitigated based on its AI's performance relative to the extant human or human–machine based standard of care. Such responsibility for explanation will serve an important information-forcing function in areas where public understanding is often limited by trade secrecy.[57]

Accountability is a contested and complex concept in tort law. It is all too easy to reduce the problem of preventable adverse events in medicine as a simple matter of providers' responsibility to patients. However, a broader political economy perspective goes beyond the dyad of provider–patient, incorporating larger concerns about the nature of the labor force, the explainability of AI, and the power of dominant technology firms.[58] As AI and robotics take on more roles, there will be cost pressures for technology to prematurely replace providers. Strict or enterprise liability for such adverse events arising out of particular replacements will help deter it from happening too quickly, generally. By ensuring that vendors of medical AI and robotics are more

illustration of this point. The television series *Westworld* tried to attribute something like the human fixity I have described in its episodes featuring the mental breakdown of the robot Teddy after he was reprogrammed to be hard-hearted and violent by the series' protagonist, Delores. However, the depiction is unconvincing because the original programming connecting breakdown to personality trait discordance could itself have been reprogrammed.

[56] *See* Isaac Asimov, *I, Robot* (New York: Gnome Press, 1950); Colin P. A. Jones, "Robot Rights: From Asimov to Tezuka," *Japan Times* (Mar. 6, 2019), www.japantimes.co.jp/community/2019/03/06/issues/robot-rights-asimov-tezuka.

[57] For another example of information-forcing regulation, see Frank Pasquale, "Ending the Specialty Hospital Wars: A Plea for Pilot Programs as Information Forcing Regulatory Design" in Einer Elhauge (ed.), *The Fragmentation of U.S. Health Care: Causes and Solutions* (New York: Oxford University Press, 2010), pp. 235–278.

[58] On the critical distinction between explainable and nonexplainable AI in medical automation and robotics, *see* Evans and Pasquale, "Product Liability Suits for FDA-Regulated AI/ML Software."

accountable to those whom they harm, administrative agencies and courts may renew an ongoing quality movement within the profession of medicine. They may even spark the professionalization of AI research itself, since professions are institutions of accountability that help assure ongoing self-review and improvement. And if there are concerns about liability overdeterring innovation, damages caps may be imposed to calibrate incentives accordingly.

From an individualistic, utilitarian perspective (dominant in mainstream economics), substitutive automation of machines to replace humans in many fields seems to be a foregone conclusion, thanks to a set of interlinked value judgments about the value of cheapening tasks. But within a profession like medicine, matters are more complicated. A renewed political economy of automation demands a role for professionals to mediate between patients and complex technologies. Professionals enjoy forms of autonomy, and are burdened by constraints, rare in nonprofessional fields. Professionals are charged with protecting distinct, noneconomic values that society has deemed desirable. Their labor, in turn, reflects, reproduces, and is enriched by those values. Knowledge, skill, and ethics are inextricably intertwined.[59] In the face of well-hyped automation, professionals ought to reaffirm their own norms. The threat of tort liability for the firms they work for (including AI vendors) gives them some leverage to push back against management demands for premature automation. Indeed, when Marc Law and Sukkoo Kim examined the history of professionalization and occupational licensure, they found patterns of worker self-organization in the United States in the early twentieth century that substantially increased consumer protection.[60] By deterring premature substitutive automation, a liability regime that reduces potential exposure of AI vendors when they complement (rather than substitute for) medical professionals will help ensure a democratization of expertise, including ongoing critical evaluation of medical AI and robotics by physicians and other providers.

Of course, as courts develop such evolving standards of care, they will also face predictable efforts by owners of AI to deflect liability. For example, firms may require their customers or users to sign exculpatory clauses in contractual limitations on liability, waiving their right to sue. Asymmetries of power are important here. For example, in medicine, courts have resisted exculpatory clauses purporting to relieve physicians of responsibility for malpractice, thanks in part to the asymmetrical power of hospitals and their patients.[61] They should be similarly wary in AI-intensive scenarios, where even greater imbalances of power and knowledge are common.

Policymakers are currently struggling to keep pace with the speed of technological development. Legislators have been hesitant to pass broad statutes, as they are fearful of inhibiting growth and innovation in the space. However, increasingly there is public demand for policy interventions and protections regarding critical technology. These demands do not necessarily impede economic or technological advance. Some fields may never get traction if customers cannot be assured that *someone* will be held accountable if an AI fails.[62] Developing appropriate standards of responsibility along the lines prescribed in this chapter should advance the quality of both AI and IA.

[59] Frank Pasquale, "Synergy and Tradition: The Unity of Research, Service, and Teaching in Legal Education" (2015) 40 *J. Legal Prof.* 25.

[60] Marc T. Law and Sukkoo Kim, "Specialization and Regulation: The Rise of Professionals and the Emergence of Occupational Licensing Regulation" (2005) 65 *J. Econ. Hist.* 723.

[61] Nadia N. Sawicki, "Choosing Medical Malpractice" (2018) 93 *Washington L. Rev.* 891.

[62] Nathalie A. Smuha, "From a 'Race to AI' to a 'Race to AI Regulation' – Regulatory Competition for Artificial Intelligence," KU Leuven, Working Paper (2019), https://papers.ssrn.com/sol3/papers.cfm?abstract_id=3501410.

PART V

AI and Intellectual Property Law

15

Patenting AI

The US Perspective

Susan Y. Tull

15.1 INTRODUCTION

Artificial intelligence (AI) is increasingly incorporated into every industry, technology, and facet of everyday life. As the application of AI grows, so too do the patent applications looking to protect these inventions.[1] From 2002 to 2018, the United States saw a 100 percent increase in the number of AI-related patent applications that were filed.[2] These recent advances in technology, accompanied by the increase in patent filings, raise issues of patentability and inventorship in the United States.

15.2 US PATENT SYSTEM

Patent protection has a long history in the United States, dating back to the US Constitution. The Patent and Copyright Clause states that Congress shall have the power to "promote the Progress of Science and useful Arts, by securing for limited Times to Authors and Inventors the exclusive Right to their respective Writings and Discoveries."[3] By providing inventors with a limited-in-time monopoly, the patent system was intended to encourage innovation and the spread of ideas. The Patent Act of 1790 was the first of many laws establishing the requirements and structure of US patent law.[4] The last major amendment to US patent law occurred in 2011, with the passage of the America Invents Act.[5] This legislation sets forth the requirements for obtaining a patent in the United States.

To obtain patent protection in the United States, a patent application must be directed to patent-eligible subject matter,[6] must provide adequate written description support for the claims,[7] and must be new[8] and nonobvious,[9] among other provisions. These requirements are not unique to AI-related inventions, but can uniquely impact them.

[1] United States Patent and Trademark Office, Office of the Chief Economist, "Inventing AI: Tracing the Diffusion of Artificial Intelligence with U.S. Patents," No. 5 (Oct. 2020).

[2] Ibid., at 4–5. When adjusted for the overall rate in the increase of filed patent application regardless of subject matter, the share in AI applications showed a growth from 9 percent in 2002 to 16 percent in 2018.

[3] US Constitution, Art. 1, Section 8, Clause 8.

[4] R. Carl Moy, *Moy's Walker on Patents* (4th ed.; 2020), at § 1:16.

[5] Leahy-Smith America Invents Act of 2011, Pub. L. No. 112-29, § 3, 125 Stat. 284 (Sept. 16, 2011).

[6] 35 USC § 101.

[7] 35 USC § 112.

[8] 35 USC § 102.

[9] 35 USC § 103.

15.3 SUBJECT MATTER ELIGIBILITY OF AI-RELATED INVENTIONS IN THE UNITED STATES

Subject matter eligibility is one of the main criteria for receiving a patent in the United States. An invention must contain patent-eligible subject matter in order to receive patent protection.[10] Section 101 of the Patent Act[11] states that "[w]hoever invents or discovers any new and useful process, machine, manufacture, or composition of matter, or any new and useful improvement thereof, may obtain a patent therefor."[12] In short, this section requires that an invention be "sufficiently useful" and that it reside in a technical field that the patent system was meant to protect.[13] Over time, the judicial system interpreted the words of the statute to recognize certain judicial exceptions to patentable subject matter under Section 101.

Abstract ideas, laws of nature, and natural phenomena are excluded from patentable subject matter.[14] Examples of noneligible subject matter include "a new mineral discovered in the earth or a new plant found in the wild."[15] Other examples of ineligible subject matter provided by the Supreme Court include the law of gravity and Einstein's law, $E = mc^2$.[16] Over time, the case law surrounding these judicial exceptions grew and questions arose regarding applying these exceptions to modern technology. The Supreme Court ultimately laid out a two-part test that must be met in order to receive a patent, explaining how to identify patent-eligible subject matter.[17]

In *Mayo*, the Supreme Court invalidated issued patent claims directed to the relationship between the concentrations of certain metabolites in the blood and the likelihood that a drug dosage would prove ineffective or cause harm for failing to meet this requirement.[18] The Supreme Court held that the claims were not patentable subject matter under 35 USC § 101 because the claims provided "instructions [that] add nothing specific to the laws of nature other than what is well-understood, routine, conventional activity, previously engaged in by those in the field."[19] According to the Court, the determination of a proper dosage for a drug was a law of nature that was unpatentable, and the patent claims merely instructed doctors to apply this law of nature using techniques that were already known.[20]

Alice expanded on the holding in *Mayo*, providing a two-step test for subject matter patent eligibility. The first step is determining whether the claims are directed to a patent-ineligible concept (laws of nature, abstract ideas, or natural phenomena).[21] The second step is determining whether the claim's elements, considered both individually and as an ordered combination, transform the nature of the claims into a patent-eligible application.[22] If a claim is directed to a patent ineligible concept and the claim's elements do not transform the nature of the claim, then it will fail to meet § 101.[23]

[10] 35 USC § 101.
[11] The Patent Act is the statute governing patents in the United States. This statute includes the requirements for obtaining a patent as well as provisions for enforcing patents.
[12] 35 USC § 101.
[13] *Walker on Patents*, § 5:1.
[14] *Alice Corp. Pty. Ltd.* v. *CLS Bank Int'l*, 134 S. Ct. 2347 (2014); *Diamond* v. *Chakrabarty*, 447 US 303, 309 (1980).
[15] *Diamond*, 447 US at 309.
[16] Alice Corp., at n. 14.
[17] Ibid.; *Mayo Collaborative Servs.* v. *Prometheus Labs., Inc.*, 566 US 66 (2012).
[18] *Mayo*, 566 US at 69.
[19] Ibid.
[20] Ibid.
[21] *Alice*, 134 S. Ct. at 2355.
[22] Ibid.
[23] Ibid.

These two Supreme Court cases present a hurdle that many AI inventions will have to overcome in order to receive patent protection. AI inventions related to medical diagnostic technologies will have to overcome the language set forth in *Mayo* and software-focused and computer-implemented patent applications will have to meet the test laid out in *Alice* to avoid a finding that they claim nothing more than an abstract idea, mathematical expression, or algorithm. Practitioners and inventors alike will need to carefully consider the full scope of eligible subject matter in order to ensure that a patent can be obtained from the United States Patent and Trademark Office (USPTO) and maintained through any subsequent challenges.

The Court of Appeals for the Federal Circuit (which hears all patent-related appeals[24]) has found medical diagnostic technology to be patent-ineligible subject matter under the *Mayo/Alice* framework. In *Ariosa Diagnostics, Inc.* v. *Sequenom, Inc.*, the court concluded that a patent application directed to a novel method of prenatal diagnosis of fetal DNA did not claim patent-eligible subject matter, despite agreeing that the claimed method "reflects a significant human contribution ... that revolutionized prenatal care."[25] The patent claims were directed to a method of detecting the presence of cell-free fetal DNA in maternal plasma.[26] The Federal Circuit concluded that the presence of cell-free fetal DNA was a natural phenomenon under the first step of the *Mayo/Alice* framework.[27] The court then turned to the second step in the *Mayo/Alice* framework, considering whether the claims disclosed an inventive concept sufficient to transform the naturally occurring phenomenon into patent-eligible subject matter.[28] Despite acknowledging the breakthrough nature of the technology, the court found that the second step was not met because the method steps "were well-understood, conventional, and routine."[29] Since *Ariosa*, courts have applied similar reasoning to invalidate other patents directed to medical diagnostics for lack of patent-eligible subject matter.[30]

Similarly, application of the *Alice* test has resulted in the invalidation of numerous software and computer-related claims for lack of subject matter eligibility.[31] Claims directed to these technologies are often rejected as abstract ideas or attempts to patent pure mathematical principals or algorithms. Although the Supreme Court cautioned against construing the exclusionary principle of § 101 overbroadly, "lest it swallow all of patent law,"[32] many believe it has

[24] 28 USC § 1295 (stating that the Federal Circuit shall have exclusive jurisdiction over "an appeal from a final decision of a district court of the United States ... in any civil action arising under, or in any civil action in which a party has asserted a compulsory counterclaim arising under, any Act of Congress relating to patents or plant variety protection").

[25] 788 F 3d 1371, 1376, 1379 (Fed. Cir. 2015).

[26] Ibid.

[27] Ibid.

[28] Ibid.

[29] Ibid., at 1377.

[30] See, e.g., *Cleveland Clinic Foundation* v. *True Health Diagnostics LLC*, 859 F 3d 1352, 1363 (Fed. Cir. 2017) (finding methods for detecting myeloperoxidase [MPO] in blood, and correlating the results to cardiovascular risk, to be directed to patent-ineligible subject matter despite arguments from the patent owner that the discovery of the correlation was groundbreaking).

[31] In re Downing, 754 Fed. Appx. 988, 993 (Fed. Cir. 2018) (noting that the court has "consistently treated inventions directed to collecting, analyzing, and displaying information as abstract ideas"); *McRO, Inc.* v. *Bandai Namco Games America Inc.*, 837 F 3d 1299 (Fed. Cir. 2016) (explaining that where the claims only added a computer to improve an existing technological process, such an addition would not be sufficient to pass the second step of *Alice*); *FairWarning IP, LLC* v. *Iatric Sys. Inc.*, 839 F 3d 1089, 1093 (Fed. Cir. 2016) (finding claims directed to a "system and method of detecting fraud and/or misuse in a computer environment based on analyzing data such as in log files, or other similar records, including user identifier data" were directed to abstract ideas and were not sufficiently transformative).

[32] *Alice Corp. Pty. Ltd.* v. *CLS Bank Int'l*, 134 S. Ct. 2347, 2354 (2014) (citing *Mayo Collaborative Servs.* v. *Prometheus Labs., Inc.*, 566 US 66, 71–72 [2012]).

done just that in the life sciences, medical technologies, and software-related technologies.[33] The concurring opinion in *Ariosa* echoed these concerns, stating that "[b]ut for the sweeping language in the Supreme Court's *Mayo* opinion, [there was] no reason, in policy or statute, why this breakthrough invention should be deemed patent ineligible."[34]

There have been numerous calls for reform to the doctrine of patent-eligible subject matter, including from the Court of Appeals for the Federal Circuit. In a dissenting opinion, Judge Linn explained that

> [t]he problem with [the abstract idea] test, however, is that it is indeterminate and often leads to arbitrary results. Moreover, if applied in a legal vacuum divorced from its genesis and treated differently from the other two exceptions [laws of nature and natural phenomenon], it can strike down claims covering meritorious inventions not because they attempt to appropriate a basic building block of scientific or technological work, but simply because they seemingly fail the Supreme Court's test.[35]

In *Athena Diagnostics, Inc.* v. *Mayo Collaborative Services, LLC*, Judge Newman dissented from the majority's decision that a new method of diagnosing a neurological condition was not patent eligible.[36] Judge Newman opined that the "court's decisions on the patent ineligibility of diagnostic methods are not consistent…"[37] The Federal Circuit denied the petition for a rehearing of the *Athena* case in a split decision, with multiple judges dissenting.[38] In one of the dissents, Judge Moore, joined by Judges O'Malley, Wallach, and Stoll, noted that the court had held every single diagnostic claim in every case before it invalid for lack of eligible subject matter, "[d]espite the significance of these diagnostic inventions and the high costs of developing them."[39] The dissent continued:

> The math is simple, you need not be an economist to get it: Without patent protection to recoup the enormous R&D cost, investment in diagnostic medicine will decline. To put it simply, this is bad. It is bad for the health of the American people and the health of the American economy. And it is avoidable depending on our interpretation of the Supreme Court's holding in *Mayo*. I have no doubt that my colleagues agree with the sentiments herein that diagnostics are important, and that patent protection of such diagnostics is critical to incentivizing their very existence. The only point upon which we disagree is over the breadth of the *Mayo* holding.[40]

Following the judicial back-and-forth (and related legal commentary), in 2019 a bipartisan group of the US Congress proposed a draft bill that included revisions to 35 USC § 101.[41] Of note, the draft provided that "[t]he eligibility of a claimed invention under section 101 shall be

33 Alexa Johnson, "A Crisis of Patent Law and Medical Innovation: The Category of Diagnostic Claims in the Wake of Ariosa v. Sequenom" (2017) 27 *Health Matrix* 435; Patent Publius, "Federal Circuit Threatens Innovation: Dissecting the Ariosa v. Sequenom Opinion," *Ctr. for Protection Intell. Prop.* (June 23, 2015), https://cpip.gmu.edu/2015/06/23/federal-circuit-threatens-innovation-dissecting-the-sequenom-v-ariosa-opinion/; Gene Quinn, "Supreme Court Denies Cert. in Sequenom v. Ariosa Diagnostics," *IPWatchdog* (June 27, 2016), www.ipwatchdog.com/2016/06/27/70409/id=70409.

34 *Ariosa*, 788 F 3d at 1381 (Linn, J., concurring).

35 *Smart Sys. Innovations, LLC* v. *Chicago Transit Authority*, 873 F 3d 1364, 1377 (Fed. Cir. 2017) (concurring in part).

36 915 F 3d 743, 747 (Fed. Cir. 2019) (dissent).

37 Ibid.

38 *Athena Diagnostics, Inc.* v. *Mayo Collaborative Services, LLC*, 927 F 3d 1333 (Fed. Cir. 2019).

39 Ibid.

40 Ibid., at 1358–59.

41 Press Release, Thom Tillis, Senator, "Sens. Tillis and Coons and Reps. Collins, Johnson, and Stivers Release Draft Bill Text to Reform Section 101 of the Patent Act" (May 22, 2019), www.tillis.senate.gov/2019/5/sens-tillis-and-coons-and-reps-collins-johnson-and-stivers-release-draft-bill-text-to-reform-section-101-of-the-patent-act.

determined without regard to: the manner in which the claimed invention was made; whether individual limitations of a claim are well known, conventional or routine; the state of the art at the time of the invention…"[42] Urging passage of the bill, industry leaders argued as follows: "[C]onfusion about what is patent-eligible discourages inventors from pursuing work in certain technology areas, including discovering new genetic biomarkers and developing diagnostic and artificial intelligence technologies. [This] uncertainty disincentivizes the enormous investment in research and development that is necessary to fuel the innovation cycle."[43] The bill was discussed in Senate subcommittee hearings and was sent back for revision in 2019.[44] There have been no further published revisions or drafts since.

In 2019, the USPTO revised the provisions of the Manual of Patent Examination and Procedure (MPEP) pertaining to subject matter eligibility.[45] The revised guidance explained "how Office personnel including patent examiners should evaluate claims for patent subject matter eligibility under 35 U.S.C. 101."[46] "To facilitate examination, the [USPTO] set forth an approach to identifying abstract ideas that distills the relevant case law into enumerated groupings of abstract ideas."[47] The USPTO grouped abstract ideas as follows:

1) Mathematical concepts – mathematical relationships, mathematical formulas or equations, mathematical calculations;
2) Certain methods of organizing human activity – fundamental economic principles or practices (including hedging, insurance, mitigating risk); commercial or legal interactions (including agreements in the form of contracts; legal obligations; advertising, marketing or sales activities or behaviors; business relations); managing personal behavior or relationships or interactions between people (including social activities, teaching, and following rules or instructions); and
3) Mental processes – concepts performed in the human mind (including an observation, evaluation, judgment, opinion).[48]

The revised MPEP contained further guidance as to the classifications within each grouping, including examples of each.[49]

The MPEP also addressed the second prong of the *Alice/Mayo* test, namely if the claim is directed to one of the judicial exceptions, whether the additional elements amount to "significantly more" than the judicial exception itself.[50] When answering this question, patent examiners employed by the USPTO "should consider whether the claim purport(s) to improve the functioning of the computer itself or any other technology or technical field."[51] "In computer-related technologies, the examiner should determine whether the claim purports to improve computer capabilities or, instead, invokes computers merely as a tool."[52]

[42] Ibid.
[43] The State of Patent Eligibility in America, Part II, 116th Cong. 9 (2019) (written testimony of Henry Hadad, President, IPO).
[44] See www.ipwatchdog.com/2019/12/29/year-patents-top-10-patent-stories-2019/id=117177.
[45] The USPTO is the administrative agency in the United States that is responsible for reviewing patent applications and ultimately issuing patents if they are allowed. The MPEP contains the laws and regulations that are followed, including by the USPTO, during the examination of US patent applications.
[46] www.uspto.gov/patents/laws/examination-policy/subject-matter-eligibility.
[47] MPEP § 2106.04(a).
[48] Ibid. (internal citations omitted).
[49] MPEP § 2106.04(a)(2).
[50] MPEP § 2106.05.
[51] MPEP § 2106.05(a) (internal citations omitted).
[52] MPEP § 2106.05(a) (I).

While the USPTO's guidance may assist a patent applicant in navigating the path to obtaining a patent, it does not prevent an issued patent from being invalidated for lack of patent-eligible subject matter or otherwise alter the existing legal precedent. The Federal Circuit has made clear that the MPEP's guidance "is not, itself the law of patent eligibility, does not carry the force of law, and is not binding on our patent eligibility analysis. And to the extent the guidance contradicts or does not fully accord with our case law, it is our case law, and the Supreme Court precedent it is based upon, that must control."[53] Absent judicial intervention or Congressional reform, US patent applicants will have to consider the two-part test for subject matter eligibility for AI-related technologies, particularly those directed to software or computer-implemented inventions or medical diagnostics.

15.4 PERSON OF ORDINARY SKILL IN THE ART: HOW AI MAY ALTER THE TEST FOR OTHER PATENTABILITY REQUIREMENTS

An invention must meet several additional requirements in order to be patented that are all assessed from the perspective of a "person of ordinary skill in the art."[54] For example, 35 USC § 103 states that "[a] patent for a claimed invention may not be obtained ... if the differences between the claimed invention and the prior art are such that the claimed invention as a whole would have been obvious *to a person having ordinary skill in the art* to which the claimed invention pertains." A patent application must further "contain a written description of the invention, and the manner and process of making and using it, in such full, clear, concise, and exact terms as to enable any *person skilled in the art* to which it pertain, or which it is most nearly connected, to make and use the same..."[55] While these requirements must be met by all patent applications, the question of a "person" is uniquely affected by AI-related inventions.

This hypothetical person is not deemed to have the knowledge level of the inventor, just the ordinary knowledge of a person skilled in the field or technology of the subject matter of the patent. Although the concept of a person of ordinary skill in the art was always a legal fiction, as AI systems become more prevalent, this fiction may approach the realm of fact. AI is capable of sorting and storing vast databases of knowledge and accessing that information at speeds far outside the realm of human capabilities. At some point, AI may become the "person" of skill in the art, possessing actual knowledge of all known publications, patents, and prior art, transforming the hypothetical construct into reality.[56] If the AI alone is not determined to be the person of ordinary skill in the art, it may also be determined that the hypothetical skilled person would have access to an AI system or a data repository capable of being searched by AI-driven software. Thus, the ability and knowledge of a person of skill in the art may be elevated to match the sophistication of an AI system.

Elevating the standard of a person of ordinary skill in the art could impact multiple doctrines within patent law, which are all determined from the perspective of a person of ordinary skill in the art. The test for nonobviousness considers the level of skill of the person of ordinary skill in the art and applies that perspective to determine if the difference between the invention and the prior art is obvious (35 USC s. 103). If the person of ordinary skill in the art has a greater skill level

[53] *cxLoyalty, Inc.* v. *Maritz Holdings, Inc.*, 986 F 3d 1367, 1375 n.1 (Fed. Cir. 2021).

[54] The field of technology or science is commonly referred to as the field of "art" in patent law.

[55] 35 USC § 112.

[56] George Dyson, "Turing's Cathedral," *Edge* (Oct. 23, 2005), www.edge.org/conversation/george_dyson-turings-cathedral (quoting an unidentified Google employee as stating "[w]e are not scanning all those books to be read by people. We are scanning them to be read by an AI," in referring to the Google Books Library Project).

and knowledge of prior art, it would be more difficult to argue that an invention was nonobvious over the prior art.[57] For more predictable areas of technology, modifications over the prior art that work in predictable ways are already considered obvious. If it becomes predictable that an AI can generate inventive results, such as through brute force trial and error, it will be more difficult to argue that the invention is nonobvious, even where the "finite number of identified, predictable solutions" is beyond that of human calculation.[58]

In addition, this issue regarding the person of ordinary skill in the art implicates the requirement that a patent claim be enabled.[59] To satisfy enablement, a patent's specification must disclose the invention in sufficient detail to enable a person of ordinary skill in the art to make and use the claimed invention without undue experimentation.[60] If the AI can predict a result without experimentation using less information than it would take a human being, then significantly less information may be required in a disclosure to enable the claims, compared to today's standard.

Recognizing the potential impact on, and uniqueness of, AI-related patent applications, the USPTO issued a public call for comments on the topic in 2019.[61] The USPTO synthesized the comments and provided a summary of themes that emerged from the public comments.[62] "Most public commenters agreed that the growing ubiquity of AI would affect how the USPTO and courts would assess the legal hypothetical standard of a 'person having ordinary skill in the art,' this standard being critical to the determination of whether a patent right should issue."[63] The public commentary also raised the issue that "AI may generate a proliferation of prior art amounting to a never before seen volume and the ensuing difficulty in finding relevant prior art in view of the increased volume." While these questions have yet to be resolved, they are now part of the conversation regarding patenting AI-related inventions.

15.5 INVENTORSHIP OF AI-RELATED PATENTS IN THE UNITED STATES

In addition to the patentability concerns addressed in Section 15.3, AI-related patent applications raise unique questions of inventorship and ownership in patent law. The US patent system only recognizes individuals as inventors,[64] not companies[65] or machines.[66] Inventorship is determined by conception, or "the formation in the mind of the inventor of a definite and permanent idea of the complete and operative invention."[67] The use of AI, particularly deep machine learning or self-evolving and coding AI, raises questions as to who (or what) conceived of the invention and could thus be named as an inventor.

[57] Liza Vertinsky and Todd M. Rice, "Thinking about Thinking Machines: Implications of Machine Inventors for Patent Law" (2002) 8 *B.U. J. Sci. & Tec. L.* 574, 595.

[58] *KSR Int'l Co.* v. *Teleflex Inc.*, 550 US 398, 421 (2007); Vertinsky and Rice, note 57, at 595–96.

[59] 35 USC § 112.

[60] Ibid.

[61] USPTO, "Public Views on Artificial Intelligence and Intellectual Property Policy" (Oct. 2020), www.uspto.gov/sites/default/files/documents/USPTO_AI-Report_2020-10-07.pdf.

[62] Ibid.

[63] Ibid., at iii.

[64] 35 USC § 100(f).

[65] *New Idea Farm Equip. Corp.* v. *Sperry Corp.*, 916 F 2d 1561, 1566 n.4 (Fed. Cir. 1990).

[66] Ben Hattenback and Joshua Glucoft, "Patents in an Era of Infinite Monkeys and Artificial Intelligence" (2015) 19 *Stanford Tech. L. Rev.* 32, 46.

[67] *Townsend* v. *Smith*, 36 F 2d 292, 295 (C.C.P.A. 1929); *Hybritech, Inc.* v. *Monoclonal Antibodies, Inc.*, 802 F 2d 1367, 1376 (Fed. Cir. 1986) (quoting 1 Robinson on Patents 532 [1890]).

The USPTO has taken the position that an AI system cannot be named as an inventor. In 2019, two patent applications were filed at the USPTO, identifying "DABUS" as the sole inventor.[68] DABUS is an AI system.[69] According to the team behind DABUS, the AI system generated the inventions disclosed in the patent applications without human involvement or interference; in short, DABUS did in fact invent the claimed subject matter.[70] The USPTO rejected the patent applications for failure to name a correct inventor, noting that "[t]o the extent the petitioner argues that an 'inventor' could be construed to cover machines, the patent statutes preclude such a broad interpretation."[71] In support, the USPTO identified several provisions in the Patent Act that refer to natural persons, finding that "interpreting 'inventor' broadly to encompass machines would contract the plain reading of the patent statutes that refer to persons and individuals."[72] The USPTO further cited Federal Circuit decisions and guidance in the MPEP that supported its position that "inventors" were only natural persons, not AI systems or machines.[73] The district court upheld the USPTO's finding.[74]

15.6 CONCLUSION

As the use of AI grows ever more prevalent and sophisticated, these issues will be addressed by Congress, the USPTO, and the courts. While the questions raised with respect to patenting AI have been debated and are now being considered more broadly, few have been definitively answered. Early address and resolution of these issues will allow patent law to keep pace with the new tide of AI-related technologies and inventions.

68 Decision on Petition, In re Application No. 16/524,350, www.uspto.gov/sites/default/files/documents/16524350_22apr2020.pdf.

69 Ibid.

70 The Artificial Inventor Project, "Frequently Asked Questions," https://artificialinventor.com/frequently-asked-questions.

> The innovations described in the patent applications are the products of an extensive artificial neural system that combines the memories of various learned elements into potential inventions that are then evaluated through the equivalent of affective responses. Such responses then either: (1) trigger synaptic noise that serves to generate new juxtapositional concepts, or (2) nullify synaptic noise to reinforce those notions fulfilling some purpose or goal … The inventions were conceived by a generative machine intelligence, judging merit of its own self-conceived ideas based upon its own cumulative experience. Nevertheless, the system did autonomously choose to selectively reinforce the combination of numerous elements into more complex notions.

71 Decision on Petition, note 68, at 4.

72 Ibid.

73 Ibid.

74 *Thaler v. Hirshfeld*, 558 F. Supp.3d, 238 (E.D. Va. 2021), appeal pending, at the Federal Circuit, 2021–2347.

16

Patentability of AI

Inventions in the European Patent Office

Nicholas Fox, Yelena Morozova, and Luigi Distefano

16.1 OVERVIEW OF THE EPO APPROACH TO THE PATENTABILITY OF AI INVENTIONS

The European Patent Office (EPO) treats artificial intelligence (AI) inventions as a specific form of computer-implemented invention. Article 52 of the European Patent Convention (EPC) excludes computer programs and mathematical methods *'as such'* from patent protection. These exclusions are highly relevant because AI inventions are typically based on computational models and algorithms for classification, clustering, regression, and dimensionality reduction, such as neural networks, genetic algorithms, support vector machines, k-means, kernel regression, and discriminant analysis.

However, inventions involving software and mathematical methods can be patented in Europe if they have 'technical character' or provide solutions to 'technical problems'. Over the years, through case law, the EPO's Boards of Appeal have developed the distinction between unpatentable computer programs and mathematical methods *'as such'* and patentable computer-implemented inventions, establishing a relatively stable framework for assessing the patentability of AI inventions. The Guidelines for Examination in the EPO ('Guidelines') reflect this framework.

The EPO case law[1] establishes that the 'normal' physical effects of the execution of a computer program on computing hardware, for example electrical currents, are not in themselves sufficient to lend a computer-implemented invention technical character. Rather, a further 'technical effect' is needed. Such a further 'technical effect' may result, for example, from the use of a computer program to control an industrial process or the working of a piece of machinery, or from the internal functioning of the computer or computer network itself (e.g. memory organization, program execution control) under the influence of the computer program.

The EPO applies the same test when assessing the patentability of AI inventions. While current EPO practice is to consider abstract machine-learning algorithms as incapable of providing a further technical effect, and therefore patent-ineligible technology, patents are granted for tangible applications of such algorithms when they solve a technical problem in a field of technology (e.g. medical image classification, image analysis), or when they are adapted

[1] T1173/97 *IBM/Computer program product.*

for a specific technical implementation (e.g. graphics processing unit, implementation of neural networks).

The EPO's Guidelines, which instruct patent examiners on how to approach such matters, are based on decisions made by the EPO's Boards of Appeal. Institutionally, case law only arises if appeals are filed against decisions refusing the grant of a patent application or in post-grant opposition proceedings. Delays in prosecution and in the opposition and appeal process mean that much of the technology evaluated in decisions of the Boards of Appeal is relatively old. The Boards of Appeal are now issuing decisions relating to patent applications filed around 2010.[2] Given that the number of AI applications in 2010 was a fraction of what it is today,[3] the published case law is only now starting to catch up with the recent explosion of AI-based patent applications. It is only now that the real boundaries of what is and is not patentable, what constitutes a technical problem within the context of AI, and the extent of disclosure required for successful prosecution of an AI-based patent application through to grant, are slowly being defined.

Because all AI systems are 'technical' in that they require 'technical' means for their implementation, the Boards of Appeal require that an AI invention must address a technical problem. Where an AI system is applied in a technical context, this requirement is relatively easily met. However, in borderline cases, the Boards of Appeal are increasingly resistant to arguments that an AI system constitutes patentable subject matter based on a minor technical improvement over cited art, where the technical improvement was not the original motivation for the invention.

16.2 EXCLUDED SUBJECT MATTER IN THE EPC

There is no explicit definition of what constitutes an 'invention' in the EPC. Rather, Article 52(2) EPC contains a non-exhaustive list of things that are not regarded as inventions, as follows:

(a) discoveries, scientific theories, and mathematical methods;
(b) aesthetic creations;
(c) schemes, rules, and methods for performing mental acts, playing games or doing business, and programs for computers;
(d) presentations of information.

Article 52(3) EPC proceeds to qualify this list, stating that:

> Paragraph 2 shall exclude the patentability of the subject-matter or activities referred to therein only to the extent to which a European patent application or European patent relates to such subject-matter or activities as such.

16.2.1 *Vicom*

The EPO's Boards of Appeal first considered the scope of the computer program exclusion in T208/84 *Vicom/Computer-related invention*. The invention in *Vicom* was directed to a method of digitally processing images. The question facing the Board of Appeal was whether such methods were excluded from patentability on the grounds that they were mathematical methods '*as such*'.

[2] Most applications take at least two to three years before being decided at first instance. According to the Annual Report of the Boards of Appeal, in 2019, the average duration of appeals for electronic subject matter, which includes appeals related to AI, is in the region of seventy months.

[3] Applications before the EPO relating to core AI technology have increased sevenfold since 2010.

Observing that a processing operation on an electric signal could be described in mathematical terms, the Board established the existence of a 'technical effect' as the key test for distinguishing between a patentable mathematical method and an unpatentable mathematical method '*as such*'. The Board stated:[4]

> A basic difference between a mathematical method and a technical problem can be seen, however, in the fact that a mathematical method or mathematical algorithm is carried out on numbers ... and provides a result also in numerical form, the mathematical method or algorithm being only an abstract concept prescribing how to operate on the numbers. No direct technical result is produced by the method as such. In contrast thereto, if a mathematical method is used in a technical process, that process can be carried out on a physical entity ... and provides as its result a certain change in that entity.

The Board continued, in its reasoning:[5]

> Generally speaking, an invention which would be patentable in accordance with conventional patentability criteria should not be excluded from protection by the mere fact that, for its implementation modern technical means in the form of a computer program are used. Decisive is what technical contribution the invention as defined in the claim when considered as a whole makes to the known art.

Vicom settled EPO practice relating to the patentability of computer-implemented inventions through to the early 2000s. The key to distinguish between patentable and unpatentable subject matter was the existence of a 'technical effect', that is, whether the claimed invention provided a technical solution to a technical problem. If it could be established that a claimed invention provided such an effect, then the EPO would not reject an application on the grounds that it related to unpatentable subject matter under Article 52(2) EPC, and would proceed to examine the application for novelty and inventive step in the ordinary way.

16.2.2 *Pension Benefits*

Although the test in *Vicom* served the EPO well for many years, there were two issues associated with the test for determining the existence of a 'technical effect': a practical one and a theoretical one. The practical issue was one of duplication. The EPO's 'problem-and-solution approach' for evaluating inventive step[6] involved an assessment of whether a claimed invention provided a non-obvious technical solution to a technical problem. This required determining the existence of a technical effect for computer-implemented inventions twice: once when considering subject-matter patentability, and then again when evaluating inventive step.

The theoretical issue was a consequence of this duplication. When examining a patent application, the EPO always considers subject-matter patentability before considering novelty and inventive step. The *Vicom* test for establishing whether a claimed invention related to patentable subject matter required comparing the claimed invention with prior art, to establish the technical problem solved by the claimed invention. However, in contrast with the assessment of novelty and inventive step, the EPC does not contain a definition of the state of the art

[4] *Vicom*, reasons paragraph 5.
[5] Ibid., paragraph 16.
[6] Discussed in Section 16.3.1.

for the assessment of subject-matter patentability, thereby putting in doubt what prior art should be used when evaluating subject-matter patentability.[7]

To address these issues, the EPO amended its approach beginning with T931/95 *Controlling pension benefits/PBS Partnership*, which concerned a method of controlling a pension benefits program. The patent application described a method of managing pension contributions, but did not disclose any technical implementation details, beyond stating that the method could be implemented using a generic computer. The Board of Appeal rejected the method claims included in the application on the grounds that they did not relate to technical subject matter, stating that: 'All the features of this claim are steps of processing and producing information having purely administrative, actuarial and/or financial character ... the invention as claimed does not go beyond a method of doing business as such and, therefore, is excluded from patentability under Article 52(2)(c) in combination with Article 52(3) EPC.'[8]

When considering the apparatus claims, the Board initially stated that:

> In the board's view a computer system suitably programmed for use in a particular field, even if that is the field of business and economy, has the character of a concrete apparatus in the sense of a physical entity, man-made for a utilitarian purpose and is thus an invention within the meaning of Article 52(1) EPC ... This means that, if a claim is directed to such an entity, the formal category of such a claim does in fact imply physical features of the claimed subject-matter which may qualify as technical features of the invention concerned and thus be relevant for its patentability. Therefore the board concludes that: An apparatus constituting a physical entity or concrete product suitable for performing or supporting an economic activity, is an invention within the meaning of Article 52(1) EPC.[9]

However, when assessing inventive step, the Board concluded that

> the invention according to the application is an essentially economic one, i.e. lies in the field of economy, which, therefore, cannot contribute to inventive step. The regime of patentable subject-matter is only entered with programming of a computer system for carrying out the invention. The assessment of inventive step has thus to be carried out from the point of view of a software developer or application programmer, as the appropriate person skilled in the art, having the knowledge of the concept and structure of the improved pension benefits system and of the underlying schemes of information processing as set out for example in the present method claims.[10]

By removing the double assessment of 'technical effect', the approach adopted in *Pension Benefits* solved the issues with the *Vicom* test for apparatus claims. A simple test of concrete character, that is, whether or not the claimed apparatus was directed to a physical man-made entity, was imposed for assessing patentable subject matter, whilst the existence of a technical effect was retained for assessing inventive step.

[7] The state of the art for the purposes of assessment of novelty is defined in Articles 54(2) and (3) EPC to include everything made available to the public by means of written or oral description or any other way, at the priority date of the application, together with unpublished patent applications. For the purposes of assessment of inventive step, only information that was public at the priority date of the application is considered. There is no definition of the prior art for the assessment of whether an invention relates to patentable subject matter.

[8] *Pension Benefits*, reasons Section 3.

[9] Ibid., reasons Section 5.

[10] Ibid., reasons Section 8.

16.2.3 *Hitachi*

The decision in T258/03 *Auction method/Hitachi* extended the approach established by *Pension Benefits* to method claims. In *Hitachi*, when assessing patentable subject matter, the Board first applied the *Pension Benefits* test to the apparatus claims and concluded that these claims were not excluded under Article 52(2) EPC because they comprised *'clearly technical features such as a "server computer", "client computers" and "a network"'*[11] The Board then proceeded to consider the method claims using the concrete character test of *Pension Benefits*:

> What matters having regard to the concept of 'invention' within the meaning of Article 52(1) EPC is the presence of technical character which may be implied by the physical features of an entity or the nature of an activity, or may be conferred to a non-technical activity by the use of technical means. In particular, the Board holds that the latter cannot be considered to be a non-invention 'as such' within the meaning of Article 52(2) and (3) EPC. Hence, in the Board's view, activities falling within the notion of a non-invention 'as such' would typically represent purely abstract concepts devoid of any technical implications[12]

and concluded that 'a method involving technical means is an invention within the meaning of Article 52(1) EPC'.[13]

Having ruled that neither the apparatus claims nor the method claims lacked concrete character, and hence were not purely abstract, the Board proceeded with assessing novelty and inventive step. In the assessment of inventive step the Board considered only the 'technical features' of the claims. The Board found that the prior art disclosed all such technical features. The only novel features recited in the claims were non-technical business features, which could not contribute to solving a technical problem. Therefore, the Board rejected the application on the grounds that the claimed invention lacked an inventive step because the only problem that the invention solved fell solely within the business realm. All technical aspects of the invention were limited to the mere automation of a novel business system.

16.2.4 *Duns Licensing*

Post *Hitachi*, the Boards of Appeal have consistently applied the concrete character test of *Pension Benefits* to both method and apparatus claims, limiting the assessment of obviousness solely to the technical aspects of the claims. This approach is well exemplified by the decision in T154/04 *Estimating sales activity/Duns Licensing*. In this case, the Board held that in examining the patentability of a claimed invention, the claim must be first construed to determine the technical features of the invention, that is, the features that contribute to the technical character of the invention. The Board stated that a claim may legitimately recite a mix of technical and 'non-technical' features, and that the non-technical features may even form a dominating part of the claimed subject matter. However, assessment of inventive step is based on technical features only, which the claim must clearly define. Non-technical features, which do not interact with the technical subject matter of the claim, are considered incapable of solving a technical problem. This is equivalent to saying that non-technical features *'as such'* do not provide a technical contribution to the prior art, and thus are ignored when assessing inventive step.

[11] *Hitachi*, reasons paragraph 3.7.
[12] Ibid., reasons paragraph 4.5.
[13] Ibid., reasons paragraph 4.7.

16.2.5 *Modern Approach*

In G3/08 *Referral by the President of the EPO in relation to a point of law/Patentability of programs for computers*, the Enlarged Board of Appeal considered application of the *Pension Benefits* and *Hitachi* tests as developed by *Duns Licensing*. The *Patentability of programs for computers* case arose through the then president of the EPO making use of her power under Article 112(1)(b) EPC to refer questions of law to the Enlarged Board where different opinions of the Boards of Appeal diverge. The Enlarged Board rejected the referral as invalid on the grounds that, contrary to the suggestion of the president, there was no divergence of opinion in the jurisprudence. Rather the development of the case law through decisions such as *Vicom*, *Hitachi*, and *Pension Benefits* represented the natural development of the law, and the Boards of Appeal had been consistent in applying the law as it developed.

The Enlarged Board expressly considered issues of the patentability of computer-implemented inventions in their 2021 decision in G1/19 *Bentley/Pedestrian simulation*. In *Bentley/Pedestrian simulation*, the Enlarged Board of Appeal extensively referred to the prior case law and described the EPO's approach as a 'two-hurdle approach', explaining that:

> the first hurdle is to be assessed under Article 52 EPC without considering the prior art, i.e. without regard to whether computers existed at the priority date of the invention. The use of a computer in the claimed subject-matter therefore makes it eligible under Article 52 EPC. For the second hurdle, the prior art is to be considered. Inventive step is based on the difference between the prior art and the claimed subject-matter. The requirement that the features supporting inventive step contribute to a technical solution for a technical problem means that the invention, understood as a teaching based on existing prior art, has to be a 'technical invention'. . . . The invention to be assessed under this provision needs to be 'technical' beyond the use of a general-purpose computer . . . In general terms, features that can be considered technical per se may still not contribute to inventive step if they do not contribute to the solution of a technical problem . . . In line with this principle, a technical step within a computer-implemented process may or may not contribute to the problem solved by the invention.[14]

The Enlarged Board's decision to reject the president's referral in *Patentability of programs for computers* implicitly endorsed application of the *Pension Benefits* and *Hitachi* tests. The more recent decision of the Enlarged Board in *Bentley/Pedestrian simulation* has now explicitly endorsed this approach to assessing computer-implemented inventions.

This modern EPO approach to assessing computer-implemented inventions is first to apply a low-level abstractness test to assess subject-matter patentability under Article 52(2) EPC based solely on the presence of at least one physical feature in a claim, and then to assess inventive step under Article 56 EPC. The low-level abstractness of the first stage is balanced by the requirement to demonstrate that an invention provides a technical solution to a technical problem (in other words, it provides a technical contribution to a technical field) at the second stage. This is the approach the EPO adopts when assessing AI inventions, however with a very important proviso.

16.2.6 *Technical Effect Is Necessary, but Not Sufficient*

In T697/17 *SQL extensions/Microsoft Technology Licensing*, the Board of Appeal explained the 'further technical effect' hurdle for obtaining patent protection for computer-implemented

[14] G1/19 at paragraphs 78 and 79.

inventions. The Board confirmed the necessity of a technical effect being provided by a claimed invention, but stated that this alone was not sufficient to satisfy the technical character requirement. In respect of computer-implemented inventions, where the improvement relates to any one of *processing speed, latency, amount of memory required or other such program performance measurement*, the Board clarified that

> an improvement with regard to one of those performance measurements *alone* ... is insufficient to establish technical character. In order to decide whether such an improvement is a technical effect it has to be further determined how the improvement is achieved, for instance whether it is the result of technical considerations ... regarding the functioning of the technical context of the invention...
>
> In other words, features make a technical contribution if they result from technical considerations on how to for instance improve processing speed, reduce the amount of memory required, improve availability or scalability, or reduce network traffic, when compared with the prior art or once added to the other features of the invention, and contribute in combination with technical features to achieve such an effect ...
>
> On the other hand, such effect and the respective features are non-technical if the effects are achieved by non-technical modifications to the underlying non-technical method or scheme (for example, a change of the business model, or a 'pure algorithmic scheme', i.e. an algorithmic scheme not based on technical considerations).[15]

Thus, technical effects arising as a result of non-technical considerations, for example as a result of administrative or business considerations, are unlikely to meet the technical character requirement.

T697/17 confirms that the Boards of Appeal are becoming stricter in their assessment of the technical character of computer-implemented inventions. This development impacts the patentability of AI-based inventions at the EPO. It is now necessary to show that the claimed technical effect achieved by an AI invention arose as a result of technical considerations. It is therefore important, when drafting patent applications directed to AI inventions, to disclose the technical motivations and considerations underlying the different features of the invention.

16.2.7 *Mathematical Methods and Mental Acts and AI Inventions*

The express exclusions in Article 52(2) EPC and the surrounding case law remain of significance, as they provide the framework for the EPO's assessment regarding what is and is not 'technical'.

One of the most important subject-matter exclusions, particularly when considering the patentability of AI inventions, is the express exclusion in Article 52(2) EPC of mathematical methods and mental acts from patent protection. The exclusion follows from the general principle that purely abstract or intellectual methods are not patentable. Thus, for example, abstract mathematical methods, such as a shortcut method of division, would not be patentable. In contrast, methods of encrypting/decrypting or signing electronic communications are routinely regarded as technical, even if they are essentially based on mathematical methods.[16] This follows from the distinction between the substantive application of an excluded invention and the excluded subject matter '*as such*' made by the Board of Appeal in *Vicom*.[17]

[15] Reasons, Section 5.2.3.

[16] See, for example, T1326/06 *Giesecke/RSA Schlüsselpaarberechnung*.

[17] Discussed in Section 16.2.1.

The EPO uses both limbs of the exclusion when assessing the patentability of AI inventions. Many AI inventions, particularly inventions relating to core AI,[18] concern the specifics of data processing, and hence have great similarities with classical mathematical methods. At the same time, to the extent that AI inventions are simulations of human thought, they may be representative of mental processes. This approach by the EPO has its basis in a series of early decisions involving patent applications on behalf of IBM.

In T22/85 *IBM/Document abstracting and retrieving*, the Board of Appeal decided on the patentability of a method for automatically abstracting and storing an input document in an information storage and retrieval system, and a corresponding method for retrieving a document from the system. In refusing the application, the Board opined that merely setting out the sequence of steps necessary to perform the activity in terms of functions or functional means to be realized with the aid of conventional computer hardware elements did not import any technical considerations. The Board therefore concluded that the sequence of steps could neither lend a technical character to the activity nor to the claimed subject matter considered as a whole, any more than solving a mathematical equation could be regarded as a technical activity when a conventional calculation machine is used.

In T38/86 *IBM/Text processing*, the Board assessed the patentability of an invention that involved automatically replacing expressions in a text that are difficult to understand with expressions that are easier to understand. Again, the Board refused the application, ruling that the use of technical means for carrying out a method, partly or entirely without human intervention, where the method, if performed by a human being, would require them to perform mental acts, would be excluded from patentability when the invention did not involve a contribution to the art in a field not excluded from patentability by Article 52(2) EPC. In such cases, implementation of the method using technical means involved no more than the straightforward application of conventional techniques, and had therefore to be considered obvious to a person skilled in the art. Similarly, if a claim to an apparatus did not specify any technical features beyond those already comprised in a claim pertaining to said method, and furthermore did not define the apparatus in terms of its physical structure, but only in functional terms corresponding to the steps of that method, then the claim to an apparatus also did not involve a contribution to the art in a field not excluded from patentability by Article 52(2) EPC. In T121/85 *IBM/Spelling checking* and T65/86 *IBM/Text editing*, the applications related to the automatic detection and replacement of homophones. Similarly to T22/85 and T38/86, the Boards of Appeal concluded that the claimed word-processing systems failed to contribute in a technical field, and hence were unallowable.

These early decisions of the Boards of Appeal, all concerning appeals filed in the mid-eighties, have enduring significance for the patentability of AI inventions because they form the basis for the EPO's current view that linguistic or textual analysis of documents is a non-technical field, and hence unpatentable. This is reflected in the more recent case law of the Boards of Appeal involving assessment of AI inventions.

By way of example, in T22/12 *Microsoft/spam classification* the Board of Appeal upheld the decision of the Examining Division, which considered that a method claim defining linguistic analysis using a mathematical algorithm could not support the presence of an inventive step. The Board held that such analysis was non-technical, and articulated its view that

[18] That is, the fundamental principles and algorithms that define how an agent may learn from its environment to solve a task, without being directed to a specific technical application. Meta-learning is an example of core AI, and is directed to understanding the process of learning.

> the classification of messages as a function of their content is not technical per se. In this regard, it is immaterial whether the messages are electronic messages, because even though an email has technical properties, it is the content of the email that is classified. Furthermore, mathematical methods as such are not technical and the application of a mathematical method as such in a non-technical analysis of message content does not change that.[19]

The Board then considered and rejected arguments that a technical effect could arise on the grounds that the claimed approach simplified the training process for the classification of emails, commenting that

> the Board does not consider that reducing the complexity of an algorithm is necessarily a technical effect, or evidence of underlying technical considerations. That is because complexity is an inherent property of the algorithm as such. If the design of the algorithm were motivated by a problem related to the internal workings of the computer, e.g. if it were adapted to a particular computer architecture, it could, arguably, be considered as technical (see T1358/09, point 5.5, referring to T258/03 Auction method/HITACHI, OJ EPO 2004, 578, point 5.8). However, the Board does not see any such motivations in the present case.[20]

The Board of Appeal adopted a similar approach in T1358/09 *BDGB Enterprise/Classification method*, which concerned the classification of text documents based on building a 'classification model'. After stating that a mathematical algorithm contributes to the technical character of a computer-implemented method only in so far as it serves a technical purpose, the Board rejected the proposal that textual analysis could provide such a purpose, commenting that: 'Classification of text documents is certainly useful, as it may help to locate text documents with a relevant cognitive content, but in the Board's view it does not qualify as a technical purpose. Whether two text documents in respect of their textual content belong to the same "class" of documents is not a technical issue.'[21] This view may be a subject of future challenge.

As with the exclusion of presentations of information discussed in Section 16.2.10, the exclusion of linguistic and textual analysis primarily concerns a distinction between the technical content and the semantic content of data. Underlying the EPO's approach to the patentability of computer-implemented inventions is the view that inventions should be approached in a manner that is agnostic to the semantic content of information being processed. This means that the EPO is apt to ignore the meaning of textual data being processed. That a computer is able to classify text in a particular manner then becomes arbitrary from a technical point of view because there is no objective approach to such classification.

However, developments in the AI field may challenge this view. Although the early text-processing cases forming the basis for the EPO's current view may have represented automated approaches to the classification of text or the generation of indexes, modern AI inventions take matters much further. This is illustrated by the EPO's own AI systems for automated classification of patent applications.[22] Using neural networks, such systems are able to assign different portions of the written description of a patent application to different parts of a patent classification. These AI systems agree with patent examiners' own classifications in more than 80 per cent of cases, with many of the 'incorrect' classifications differing from manual classifications only in a minor way. This illustrates a contrasting view to that of the old EPO case law that, rather than all such classification being purely arbitrary, there is an '*objective*' classification that can be

[19] Reasons paragraph 2.2.
[20] Reasons paragraph 2.8.
[21] Reasons paragraph 5.2.
[22] 'The Role of Patents in an AI-Driven World', EPO virtual conference, 17–18 December 2020.

identified, and that machine-learning can be used to automate the processing of documents to help assist in such a classification task.

16.2.8 *Business Methods and AI*

AI inventions arising in a business context, for example automated chatbots or automated suggestion systems, or AI-driven modification of user interfaces for business-based websites, are particularly challenging to patent. How the EPO deals with patents in the business field is highly dependent upon a characterization of where the EPO perceives the benefits and advantages of an invention to lie.

The fact that an invention arises in a business context is not fatal to a patent application. That was clearly established by the Board of Appeal in T769/92 *Sohei/General-Purpose Management System*. The invention in that case concerned a computer system for managing financial and inventory data. Although the system managed different types of data separately, data could be inputted into the system through a single 'transfer slip' displayed on the computer screen. The Board accepted that although financial and inventory management would normally fall under the exclusion of 'doing business' pursuant to Article 52(2) EPC, and despite references to financial and inventory management appearing in the independent claims, the application was allowable. In reaching this conclusion, the Board considered that the references to business data appearing in the independent claim were merely labels, and considered the patentability of a generalized claim where different types of data were inputted via a single interface, and then managed separately. Managing data in the manner claimed was considered to be a technical problem, which the claimed invention solved, and hence the application was allowable.

The Boards of Appeal are even more likely to allow an application directed to an invention that involves both physical and business considerations. For example, in T767/99 *Pitney Bowes/System for processing mail*, a sorting machine configured to sort mail based on the timing of pick-up and deliveries was considered to be allowable. The Board accepted that the timing of deliveries was largely a business decision, but considered that the claimed invention enabled improved efficiencies in the mail delivery process that constituted a technical invention in the field of mail sorting.

Successful prosecution of AI-based business inventions is, however, challenging, as demonstrated by two relatively recent cases concerning AI-based recommendation systems: T306/10 *Yahoo!/Relationship discovery* and T1869/08. *Yahoo!* concerned the use of AI to make user-specific recommendations on e-commerce websites based on selections made by users, and consequently identified relationships between products. The computer-based analysis sought to improve the accuracy and relevance of such recommendations, by accounting for the relative popularity of different product selections. In assessing the inventive step of the claimed algorithm, the Board could not identify any 'technical purpose' for the algorithm and rejected arguments that improvements in saving user time, when performing a search, could form the basis of a valid argument for inventive step. The Board commented that:

> While making 'good' or 'bad' recommendations may lead to different user reactions and thereby, in the end, to different technical results (the user might for example play more or fewer songs, or issue more or fewer search queries in order to find other songs), such results do not qualify as a technical effect of the recommendations, as they depend on subjective choices made by the user.[23]

[23] Reasons paragraph 5.2.

The Board of Appeal considered a similar system for generating user recommendations in T1869/08. The Board rejected arguments that the use of 'recommendations generated for' third parties as opposed to 'recommendations given by' third parties was a technical distinction between the claimed invention and prior art. Although the modification resulted in a simplified algorithm for generating recommendations, the Board was not convinced that such simplification would result in any appreciable reduction in computation overhead or improved reliability. In the context of the claimed invention, 'reliability' would be understood as being a recommendation that better matched the subjective taste of a user, which would not constitute a technical effect.

16.2.9 *Scheme, Rule, or Method for Playing a Game and AI*

Application of AI technology is growing in the field of video games. The Boards of Appeal have previously ruled on the scope of the '*method for playing a game*' exclusion with reference to patent applications directed to video games. In particular, the Boards of Appeal distinguish between game rules, which are patent ineligible, and game design that improves playability or player engagement and may be patentable.

T336/07 *IGT/Electronic Poker* is an example of a patent application rejected on the grounds that it was directed solely to game rules. The Board ruled that '[a] set of game rules [that] defines a regulatory framework agreed between [or with] players and concerning conduct, conventions and conditions that are meaningful only in a gaming context'[24] was not patentable. Similarly, in T2127/09 *BANDAI/Game apparatus*, the Board refused an application directed to a novel form of Tetris game because the only novel features concerned the addition of a new gaming rule concerning when blocks disappeared. This feature was entirely devoid of technical consideration.

In contrast, where innovations in the gaming field extend beyond mere rules dictating game play, the EPO frequently allows applications to proceed to grant.

In T717/05 *Labtronix Concept Inc/Auxiliary Game*, the Board of Appeal considered patentability of a gaming apparatus, which periodically caused a player to access an auxiliary game. Ruling that the application was allowable, the Board observed that game design directed at maintaining a player's interest was a technical problem because it was directly linked to the purpose of the gaming apparatus itself. Thus, the implementation of an auxiliary game and the manner in which progress towards that game was displayed to a user were relevant for the assessment of inventive step.

T12/08 *Nintendo/Game machine and storage medium* concerned a video game where a player navigates around a gaming environment and randomly encounters other characters with whom the player interacts.[25] The invention concerned a novel way of making the random appearance of the characters more unpredictable. Again, the Board distinguished between game rules and the mechanics of the game to make the game more interesting. The Board ruled that the mechanism for making game play more unpredictable provided a technical solution to the technical problem of maintaining players' interest. The *Labtronix Concept Inc.* and *Nintendo*

[24] Reasons paragraph 3.3.1. Note that the method and means for carrying out game play in accordance with a set of game rules may well be technical in nature. The exclusion of games rules does not therefore necessarily exclude protection for the technical means for implementing the game in accordance with the rules.

[25] This technology was implemented in Nintendo's popular Pokémon® video game.

decisions provide a potentially useful precedent for the patentability of AI-based improvements to video games.

16.2.10 *Presentation of Information and AI*

Case law relating to presentation of information provides an interesting counterpoint to the EPO's case law relating to linguistic analysis, discussed in Section 16.2.7. When interpreting the presentation of information exclusion, the EPO distinguishes between the content of the information and any technical benefits a particular type of presentation might achieve. The presentation of information solely defined by its content or semantic meaning is not patentable, regardless of the manner or form in which the information is presented. In contrast, the EPO accepts that if a particular arrangement or manner of presentation can be identified as having some form of technical effect, then that is potentially patentable.

In T1749/06 *Nokia/Three-dimensional icons for graphical user interface*, the Board considered an icon with alternating light and dark stripes conferring a three-dimensional appearance. The Board considered the icon potentially patentable because the claimed design of icon solved the technical problem of providing an icon with a three-dimensional appearance. Noting the distinction between 'what is displayed' and 'how something is displayed', the Board found that the claimed effect was independent of the cognitive content of a specific icon.

A similar distinction was highlighted in T887/92 *IBM/On-line help facility*, which concerned making a help facility in an interactive information handling system more user-friendly. In allowing the application, the Board held that providing visual indications about the internal conditions of an apparatus or system was a technical problem. Within the context of the application, displaying only valid commands in a help panel had technical character because the content of the help panel reflected the status or condition of the system. Hence, the Board found that a computer program implementing this invention constituted technical means for carrying out a technical invention.

In contrast to the negative decisions concerning textual analysis arising from the IBM appeals in the mid-eighties,[26] this positive case law for image analysis has resulted in consequential approval of AI-based image classification systems. For example, in T1286/09 *Intellectual Ventures/Image classifier*, the Board found that the claimed invention involved an inventive step because it addressed a fundamental problem in the art of automatic document image processing, relating to how to account for image defects. This problem was solved by increasing the diversity of exemplar images used to train a semantic classifier, by systematically altering an exemplar image to generate an expanded set of images, by, for example, cropping or mirroring images and altering image colour characteristics.

The decision in *Intellectual Ventures* confirms that the EPO is more open to patenting inventions involving AI-based image analysis, rather than AI-based textual analysis. The EPO appears receptive to the idea that some form of 'technical character' can be conveyed by the semantic content of certain types of images, for example medical diagnostics images. To the extent that any rationale can be established, the EPO appears to view progressing from the underlying image data, which in technical terms is merely an array of numbers representing different lighting levels, to some concrete decision, as a technical matter, because doing so does not require consideration of what the subjective 'meaning' of such data might be. Image data is merely representation of a pattern of lighting levels, and processing and classifying such data by a

[26] Discussed in Section 16.2.7.

machine-learning algorithm is not dependent upon any aesthetic or semantic appreciation of what such data represents.

16.3 OBVIOUSNESS, INVENTIVE STEP, AND AI

At the EPO, an invention is considered to involve an inventive step if, having regard to the state of the art, it is not obvious to a skilled person in view of the prior art.[27] The prior art is defined as everything made available to the public by means of written or oral description or otherwise, before the filing date, or where priority is claimed, before the priority date of a European patent application.[28]

16.3.1 Problem-and-Solution Approach

The EPO applies the so-called problem-and-solution approach to the assessment of inventive step, which involves (1) determining the closest prior art, (2) establishing the 'objective technical problem', and (3) considering whether the claimed invention, starting from the closest prior art and the objective technical problem, would have been obvious to the skilled person.[29]

The 'closest prior art' is the single prior art reference that discloses the combination of features constituting the most promising starting point for development leading to the claimed invention. In selecting the closest prior art, the first consideration is to select the art that belongs to the same or a closely related technical field as the claimed invention.[30] Often, this will be the prior art that requires the fewest structural and functional modifications to arrive at the claimed invention.[31]

Once the closest prior art has been identified, any advantages that follow from the differences between a claimed invention and the closest prior art are used to establish the 'objective technical problem', which defines the technical problem that the claimed invention attempts to solve with reference to the closest prior art. In deriving the 'objective technical problem', only the differences that provide a 'technical effect' or lend an invention 'technical character' are considered.[32]

Non-technical features and non-technical benefits are ignored.[33] This is achieved by the EPO formulating the 'objective technical problem' from the perspective of a person skilled in the art, who is aware of the 'non-technical' aspects of an invention. For example, from the perspective of a computer programmer who is made aware of the content of a proposed 'non-technical' business scheme, an 'objective technical problem' can be formulated as programming a computer program to implement the 'non-technical' business scheme. In the case of AI inventions, the assessment of what is and what is not 'technical', and hence which features of a claimed invention are excluded from assessment of inventive step, is often determinative of the success of a patent application.

Finally, having formulated the 'objective technical problem', the final step of the 'problem-and-solution approach' involves assessing the prior art as a whole, and determining whether or

[27] Article 56 EPC.
[28] Articles 89 and 54 (2) EPC.
[29] Guidelines, G-VII, 5.
[30] Ibid., Section 5.1.
[31] T606/89 Unilever/Detergent composition.
[32] T931/95 PBS Partnership/Pension Benefits, discussed in Section 16.2.2.
[33] T641/00 Comvik/Two identities.

not the prior art would cause a skilled person to adapt the closest prior art to solve the objective technical problem and arrive at the claimed invention.

16.3.2 *Issues with the Problem-and-Solution Approach for AI Inventions*

The problem-and-solution approach raises several significant issues when applied to AI inventions. To date, the consistent case law of the Boards of Appeal holds that AI algorithms constitute mathematical methods that lack technical character, irrespective of whether they can be trained based on training data. Such mathematical methods may only contribute to the technical character of an invention if the method serves a technical purpose by its application to a field of technology,[34] or alternatively if the algorithm itself is adapted to a specific technical implementation.[35]

In adopting this approach, the EPO case law appears to classify technological applications of AI into distinct categories, depending upon the 'technical' or otherwise nature of the applications.

'Technical' applications include (1) Image classification,[36] (2) Medical systems,[37] and (3) Detection of faults in physical systems.[38] Non-technical applications include text classification[39] and e-commerce recommendation systems.[40]

Technical application of an AI algorithm may result in a patent-eligible invention, while non-technical application of an AI algorithm typically does not. An AI algorithm of general application and not tied to a specific technical field is unlikely to give rise to a patent-eligible invention. The fact that an AI algorithm is complex, and hence unsuitable for manual implementation, does not render the AI algorithm technical. A complex algorithm unconnected to a specific field of technology remains an abstract mathematical method.[41] Repeatedly, the Boards have ruled that improving algorithm efficiency per se is not a technical effect that contributes towards inventive step.[42] At present, such a position would seem to preclude the patenting of many core AI applications that seek to improve the efficiency of AI systems themselves.

16.4 SUFFICIENCY OF DISCLOSURE OF AI INVENTIONS

A separate issue in the context of AI inventions is the requirement under Article 83 EPC that a patent application must disclose a claimed invention in a manner sufficiently clear and complete for it to be carried out by a person skilled in the art. The Boards of Appeal considered this issue in detail in T521/95 and T161/18. T521/95 related to a pattern recognition system, which simulated the operation of the human brain to be able to learn a variety of recognition tasks. In T521/95, the Board of Appeal highlighted that determining what the 'claimed invention actually

[34] See, for example, T1784/06 or T1358/09 – examples of abstract AI classification systems rejected due to lack of technical application.

[35] See, for example, T2330/13 (method of checking the consistency and completeness of selection conditions of a configurable product – allowed), T22/12 (classification and identification of spam emails – rejected), and T1358/09 (classification of text documents – rejected).

[36] cf. T1286/09.

[37] cf. T1285/10 and T161/18.

[38] cf. T1175/09 and T1255/08.

[39] cf. T1558/09 and T22/12.

[40] cf. T306/10 and T1869/08.

[41] T914/02 and T1820/16.

[42] See, for example, T1784/06 and T42/10.

is' is a prerequisite for assessing the sufficiency of disclosure.[43] The Board then emphasized that although a certain amount of functional description of an invention may be sufficient for the skilled person with general technical knowledge to carry out the invention, that alone did not displace the fundamental statutory test that for a disclosure to be sufficient, at least one embodiment that could be carried out must be disclosed.[44]

The application in T521/95 contained an adequate disclosure of the 'hardware' on which the invention was to be implemented. However, the application did not disclose how the 'software aspect' of the invention could be implemented or how to achieve the modification and reorganization of the system, which was said to mimic the human brain. The application failed to provide a single concrete 'worked' example. In the absence of such disclosure, the Board concluded that a skilled person would not be able to derive the missing information from the remainder of the application. The Board further concluded that 'the lack of adequate instructions, the vague functional nature of the description and the lack of any concrete definition of the invention, and the problem solved by it in particular' meant that the application did not fulfil the requirements of Article 83 EPC.[45]

T161/18 considered the importance of disclosing in a patent application how to train a neural network to carry out a claimed technical application. The invention concerned a method of determining cardiac output from an arterial blood pressure curve measured at a peripheral region. The method required using an artificial neural network having weights determined by a learning algorithm to transform the arterial blood pressure curve measured at the periphery into an equivalent aortic pressure. The application stated that the training data should comprise measurements from different patient groups based on, for example, age, sex, body type, and health status, to avoid specialization of the network. However, the application did not disclose the type of training data that needed to be used, nor did the application provide any examples of the training data. In the absence of this information, the Board concluded that the skilled person had insufficient information to carry out the invention, and hence the claimed invention was insufficiently disclosed. This case serves as a good reminder that where the invention relates to a specific technical application of an AI system, the disclosure needs to explain how the system is trained for that specific technical application.

16.5 INVENTORSHIP ISSUES

The question of AI systems as inventors was considered by the Legal Division of the EPO in the case of European patent applications EP18275163 and EP18275174. Both applications were subsequently refused by the EPO in November 2019, on the grounds that they do not meet the legal requirement of the EPC that an inventor designated in the application must be a human being and not a machine.

In both applications, the applicant alleged that a machine called 'DABUS', described as 'a type of connectionist artificial intelligence', was the inventor of the inventions disclosed in the applications. The applicant argued they had acquired the right to the European patent from the inventor by being the successor in title because the applicant, as the machine's owner, was assigned any intellectual property rights created by this machine.

[43] T521/95, reasons paragraph 4.1.
[44] Ibid.
[45] Ibid., paragraph 4.9.

Although the question of inventorship of AI-conceived inventions raises interesting philosophical issues, it is unlikely to be a matter that will be pursued much before the EPO in the near future. It is unfortunate that the EPO did not investigate or comment in its decision on the pertinent issue of whether the contribution to the invention as claimed, provided by DABUS, was sufficient to constitute an inventive activity. This issue is particularly pertinent given the widely held view that current AI technology is not yet sufficiently developed to provide inventive ingenuity. Therefore, it unclear whether the DABUS applications genuinely provide an example of AI-conceived inventions. However, we have included reference to the case in this chapter for completeness.

16.6 FUTURE DEVELOPMENTS

As noted in the introduction to this chapter, it is only recently that the EPO's Boards of Appeal have had to deal with appeals relating to the surge of AI-based inventions. In doing so the Boards of Appeal have adopted a gradualist approach, adapting the extensive EPO case law relating to the patentability of computer programs '*as such*' and applying it to AI inventions.

The EPO regularly updates the Guidelines to account for the most recent development in the Boards of Appeal case law, most of which have been mentioned in this chapter. When the surge in AI-based applications and appeals became apparent the EPO deliberately reached out to consult with users of the patent system so that a good framework for the examination of AI applications could be developed in advance of active prosecution. The result has been that changes to the EPO patent system in this area have been gradual and systematic, rather than sudden.

For example, the latest 2021 revision of the Guidelines introduced only a single change in the 'Artificial Intelligence and Machine Learning' section (G-II, 3.3.1). The amended 'Artificial Intelligence and Machine Learning' section now expressly states that the examples of technical purposes listed in the 'Mathematical Methods' section of the Guidelines (G-II, 3.3) are also examples of technical purposes for which AI and machine-learning could be used. These include (1) controlling a specific technical system or process, for example an X-ray apparatus or a steel cooling process; (2) determining from measurements a required number of passes of a compaction machine to achieve a desired material density; (3) digital audio, image, or video enhancement or analysis, for example de-noising, detecting persons in a digital image, and estimating the quality of a transmitted digital audio signal; (4) separation of sources in speech signals; speech recognition, for example mapping a speech input to a text output; (5) encoding data for reliable and/or efficient transmission or storage (and corresponding decoding), for example error-correction coding of data for transmission over a noisy channel, compression of audio, image, video, or sensor data; (6) encrypting/decrypting or signing electronic communications; generating keys in an RSA cryptographic system; (7) optimizing load distribution in a computer network; (8) determining the energy expenditure of a subject by processing data obtained from physiological sensors; deriving the body temperature of a subject from data obtained from an ear temperature detector; (9) providing a genotype estimate based on an analysis of DNA samples, as well as providing a confidence interval for this estimate so as to quantify its reliability; (10) providing a medical diagnosis by an automated system processing physiological measurements; and (11) simulating the behaviour of an adequately defined class of technical items, or specific technical processes, under technically relevant conditions.[46]

[46] Guidelines, G-VII, 3.3.

Although the change is not substantial, it confirms that the EPO views its current legal framework being fit for purpose where it concerns AI-based inventions. However, there do seem to be certain trends with EPO jurisprudence that may make patenting AI-based inventions outside of such fields harder. Recent decisions, such as T2925/19 issued in March 2021, would seem to indicate that in fields that the EPO has not already accepted as 'technical', the Boards are increasingly likely to reject arguments that advantages associated with underlying AI algorithms are sufficient to give rise to a 'technical effect', unless this was an express aim when formulating an invention. This would seem to continue a trend previously established by T1834/10, T1869/08, and T22/12, all of which concerned AI-based inventions rejected as lacking a sufficient 'further' technical effect.[47] A similar approach can also be detected in the preliminary view of the Board of Appeal in *Bentley/Pedestrian simulation* that, following the decision of the Enlarged Board of Appeal on the patentability of software simulations,[48] has now indicated its preliminary view that the simulation, the subject of the earlier referral, does not address a technical problem.[49]

Taking into consideration the EPO's recent AI-related initiatives, such as creating a dedicated Data Science team and cooperating with the IP5 (EPO, Japan Patent Office, Korean Intellectual Property Office, China National Intellectual Property Administration, and United States Patent and Trademark Office) partner offices,[50] this most recent change to the Guidelines indicates the EPO's willingness to adapt to technological developments and to refine its approach to patentability of inventions involving AI, while at the same time taking a firm line against patenting non-technical inventions. The EPO is likely to follow a similar approach in the future.

47 T1834/10 *EBAY/Image selection*: software serving a non-technical process (presentation of information) rejected as not demonstrating any further technical effect even though the manner of processing involved a novel instruction for identifying both the number and location of images to be presented in a web page; T1869/08: simplification of a recommendation algorithm rejected as being non-technical as it would not result in any appreciable reduction in computation overhead; T22/12 *Microsoft/spam classification*: simplification of training process for recognition of spam email not considered technical.

48 G1/19 discussed in Section 16.2.5.

49 Preliminary Opinion of the Board of Appeal 4 May 2020. https://register.epo.org/application?documentId=E557WH0C5560DSU&number=EP03793825&lng=en&npl=false

50 www.epo.org/mobile/news-events/in-focus/ict/artificial-intelligence.html.

17

AI as Inventor

Christian E. Mammen

17.1 INTRODUCTION

Before 2018, the very notion of an artificial intelligence (AI) being sufficiently advanced to act as an inventor or a creator was the stuff of science fiction. AIs with this degree of capability are equally likely to be portrayed in benevolent, utopian, or human-threatening, dystopian lights. Indeed, in 2016, a committee of the European Parliament opened a report on proposed civil law rules on robotics with the ominous observation, "whereas from Mary Shelley's Frankenstein's Monster to the classical myth of Pygmalion, through the story of Prague's Golem to the robot of Karel Čapek, who coined the word, people have fantasised about the possibility of building intelligent machines, more often than not androids with human features."[1] The committee report did not specifically address patenting of AI inventions, but generally evinced a need to develop legal structures and rules to provide an appropriate framework for allocation of responsibility and liability relating to AI and/or robotic activities.

Then, in the autumn of 2018, Missouri-based computer scientist Dr. Stephen L. Thaler filed two patent applications,[2] naming as the inventor an AI algorithm called Device for the Autonomous Bootstrapping of Unified Sentience (or DABUS). Working under the auspices of the Artificial Inventor Project,[3] Dr. Thaler filed these two applications with the European Patent Office (EPO) and the UK Intellectual Property Office (UKIPO), with follow-on applications in a number of other countries, including the United States.[4] The two applications, claiming a "fractal container" and a "neural flame," respectively, sought to force the issue of whether an AI could be a named inventor on a patent.

Yet, still, the question of AI-as-inventor remained little more than an item on the horizon. For example, in remarks delivered to an AI conference in January 2019, Andrei Iancu, director of the United States Patent and Trademark Office (USPTO), focused mainly on the use of AI as a tool to improve processes at the USPTO. Near the end of his remarks, he commented that "policy

[1] Draft Report of the Committee on Legal Affairs, 2015/2103(INL), May 31, 2016, p. 3, www.europarl.europa.eu/doceo/document/JURI-PR-582443_EN.pdf?redirect.

[2] In the UK, they were "Food container," patent application GB1816909.4, filed October 17, 2018 and "Devices and methods for attracting enhanced attention," patent application GB1818161.0, filed November 7, 2018.

[3] See www.artificialinventor.com.

[4] According to the Artificial Inventor Project website, patent applications have been filed in the European Patent Office, the United Kingdom, Germany, the World Intellectual Property Organization, Israel, Taiwan, the United States, India, China, the Republic of Korea, and Japan. www.artificialinventor.com/patent-applications/ (visited February 21, 2021).

makers will need to consider [w]hether the legal concepts of author or inventor will be fundamentally changed by AI."[5]

Then, shortly after the first publication of these patent applications in the summer of 2019, the question of AI-as-inventor burst into the public arena, driving a flurry of media activity.[6] Within a few weeks, the USPTO had published for discussion a list of questions about patenting and AI inventions, including questions about AI-as-inventor, as well as patentability and ownership of AI inventions.[7] By the summer of 2020, the question had been clearly answered, in each jurisdiction: Under current law, an AI cannot be an inventor.

17.2 DABUS APPLICATIONS

According to Dr. Thaler, DABUS developed two inventions: a "food container" and a "device and method for attracting enhanced attention" (or neural flame). As stated on the Artificial Inventor website:

> The inventions were conceived by a generative machine intelligence, judging merit of its own self-conceived ideas based upon its own cumulative experience. Nevertheless, the system did autonomously choose to selectively reinforce the combination of numerous elements into more complex notions. As discussed further below, the inventions were conceived as various semantic spaces represented in multiple neural network-based associative memories synaptically bonded to one another, along with a neural network-generated image of the notions.
>
> In response, other neural modules chained their memories to predict the favorable consequences of the fleeting ideas, which were then reinforced into a more permanent and significant memory during Eureka moments.[8]

The food container has a fractal profile that, according to the patent application's abstract, "enables multiple containers to be coupled together by inter-engagement of pits and bulges on corresponding ones of the containers . . . [and] improves grip, as well as heat transfer into and out of the container."[9] Figure 17.1 shows an image of the container from the patent application.[10]

The neural flame consists of devices and methods of providing a light source that pulses in a way that attracts enhanced attention. According to the abstract, "a neural flame emitted from at least one controllable light source as a result of the lacunar pulse train is adapted to serve as a uniquely-identifiable signal beacon over potentially-competing attention sources by selectively triggering human or artificial anomaly-detection filters, thereby attracting enhanced attention."[11]

[5] Andrei Iancu, "Remarks by Director Iancu at the Artificial Intelligence: Intellectual Property Considerations Event," January 31, 2019, www.uspto.gov/about-us/news-updates/remarks-director-iancu-artificial-intelligence-intellectual-property.

[6] See Leo Kelion, "AI System 'Should Be Recognized as Inventor,'" BBC.com, August 1, 2019, www.bbc.com/news/technology-49191645; "First Patents Filed for Inventions Created by Artificial Intelligence," *The Times*, August 2, 2019, www.thetimes.co.uk/article/first-patents-filed-for-inventions-created-by-artificial-intelligence-nopmnvmqd; Diego Black, "Can an AI System Invent? Does the Tech Have the Intellectual Right?," *Information Age*, August 12, 2019, www.information-age.com/ai-system-invent-123484670.

[7] *Federal Register: The Daily Journal of The United States Government*, "Request for Comments on Patenting Artificial Intelligence Inventions," 84 *Fed. Reg.* 44889, August 27, 2019.

[8] www.artificialinventor.com/frequently-asked-questions/.

[9] Stephen L. Thaler, "Food container and devices and methods for attracting enhanced attention," international combined patent application, WO 2020/079499 A1, filed September 17, 2019.

[10] Ibid.

[11] Ibid. An interesting further question, outside the scope of this chapter, is whether the claimed neural flame invention would be invalid as indefinite, insofar as it is designed to "attract[] enhanced attention" from, inter alia, humans. Such a claim would arguably fall foul of cases such as *Interval Licensing LLC* v. *AOL, Inc.*, 766 F 3d 1364, 1371–1373 (Fed.

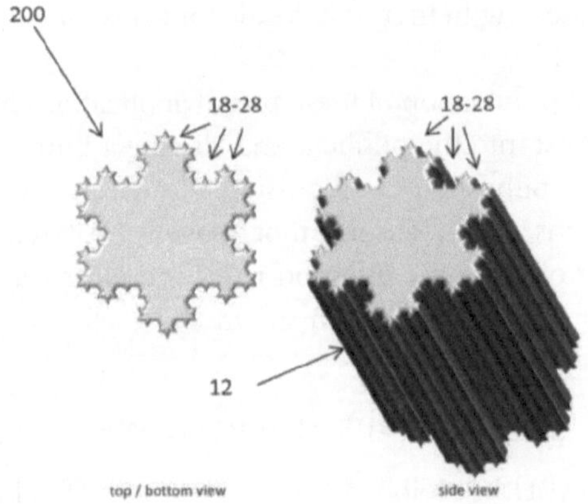

FIGURE 17.1 Fractal profile of the container from the DABUS patent application
Source: https://patentscope.wipo.int/search/en/detail.jsf?docId=WO2020079499

In October and November of 2018, Dr. Thaler, working with United States lawyer and University of Surrey law professor Ryan Abbott, filed UK and European Patent Office patent applications on behalf of DABUS as the inventor.[12] Over the following year, they filed additional patent applications in a number of countries, including the United States.[13]

In a series of high-profile rulings during 2019 and 2020, the UKIPO, EPO, and USPTO denied the applications, ruling, variously, that an inventor must be a natural person and that Dr. Thaler could not have received assignment of ownership of the inventions from DABUS. Each of these three determinations is summarized below.

17.2.1 *United Kingdom Intellectual Property Office*

In the United Kingdom, the UKIPO denied patent application nos. GB1816909.4 and GB1818161.0 on December 4, 2019, reasoning that "DABUS is not a person as envisaged by [the Patents Act 1977] and so cannot be an inventor," and further reasoning, in the alternative, that Dr. Thaler is not entitled to apply for a patent simply by virtue of ownership of DABUS.[14] Hearing Officer Jones also briefly addressed policy considerations concerning AI inventorship:

> The fundamental function of the patent system is to encourage innovation by granting time-limited monopolies in exchange for public disclosure. ... [A]n AI machine is unlikely to be motivated to innovate by the prospect of obtaining patent protection. Instead, the motivation to innovate will have been implemented as part of the development of the machine; in essence, it will have been instructed to innovate.[15]

Cir. 2014) (claim directed to "attention manager" that must operate in an "unobtrusive manner" invalid indefinitely because the "facially subjective claim language" lacked an "objective boundary").

[12] EP 18275163.6 (fractal container, filed October 17, 2018); GB 1816909.4 (same); EP 18275174.3 (neural flame, filed November 7, 2018); GB 1818161.0 (same).

[13] US 16/524,532 (fractal container, filed July 29, 2019); US 16/524,350 (neural flame, filed July 29, 2019). A more comprehensive list of DABUS patent applications may be found at www.artificialinventor.com/patent-applications.

[14] BL O/741/19, December 4, 2019, ¶ 30.

[15] Ibid., ¶ 28.

On September 21, 2020, the UK High Court affirmed the UKIPO's determination that DABUS could not be a named inventor.[16] The court considered two related issues: (1) whether DABUS could be an inventor under the Patents Act 1977, and (2) even if it could, whether (or how) Dr. Thaler could end up with the right to apply for a patent on DABUS' behalf – a question that breaks down into two sub-questions: (2a) whether DABUS could own the intellectual property right in the first place, and (2b) whether Dr. Thaler, as owner of DABUS, could be deemed as the assignee of DABUS' rights (or some legal equivalent). The UKIPO had resolved these questions in the negative, including specific findings that DABUS lacked both the capacity to own and also lacked the capacity to transfer.

The High Court confirmed the UKIPO's conclusions on each point. First, Mr. Justice Smith engaged in an extended analysis of the Patents Act 1977 to conclude that, as used in the statute, an "inventor" must be a "person."[17] He then cited a ruling by Lord Hoffmann, interpreting the same statutory provisions to conclude that the statute requires an inventor to be a "*natural* person who came up with the inventive concept."[18] In this discussion, Mr. Justice Smith clearly indicates a belief that an "inventive step" or devising an "inventive concept" is a mental act – an act that can be performed only by one with a mind – and is therefore limited to natural persons.[19]

The High Court determined that Dr. Thaler's claim of entitlement to apply for patents on DABUS' innovations "is hopeless and must fail."[20] The court provided several independent reasons. First, DABUS cannot have transferred a right to file the application to Dr. Thaler, reasoning, "because DABUS is a thing, it cannot even *hold* property, let alone transfer it."[21] Furthermore, Dr. Thaler cannot hold the right to apply for a patent by virtue of his ownership of DABUS-as-inventor, because such reasoning would ignore and undermine the conclusion that an inventor has to be a natural person.[22] The High Court concluded by observing that Dr. Thaler specifically did not advance the argument that *he* should be considered the inventor by virtue of being the owner of DABUS, and that such a question was decidedly not presented to or considered by the court.[23]

17.2.2 *European Patent Office*

The DABUS patent applications (EP 18 275 163 and EP 18 275 174) met a similar fate at the EPO. On December 20, 2019, the EPO issued a press release stating that the applications had been denied "on the grounds that they do not meet the requirement of the EPC that an inventor designated in the application has to be a human being, not a machine."[24] The EPO further noted that requiring the inventor to be a human being, or natural person, would ensure "that he

[16] *Thaler* v. *Comptroller-General of Patents, Designs and Trade Marks* [2020] EWHC 2412 (Pat).
[17] Thaler, ¶¶ 24–33, 37–46 (especially ¶¶ 42–46).
[18] Ibid., ¶ 45(3) (emphasis in original).
[19] Ibid.
[20] Ibid., ¶ 49.
[21] Ibid., ¶ 49(1) (emphasis in original).
[22] Ibid., ¶ 49(3).
[23] Ibid., ¶¶ 49(3)(d), 52(2).
[24] EPO, "EPO Refuses DABUS Patent Applications Designating a Machine Inventor," Press Release, December 20, 2019, www.epo.org/news-issues/news/2019/20191220.html.

or she can benefit from rights linked to this status," and that to exercise these rights, "the inventor must have a legal personality that AI systems or machines do not enjoy."[25]

In the statements of grounds for the decision, the EPO relied on reasoning similar to that set forth by UK High Court Justice Marcus Smith. In particular, the EPO first determined that an AI system cannot be an inventor. Following a traditional approach to legal interpretation, the EPO started with the legal texts, in particular a requirement in the rules that the designation of inventor states the family name, given names, and full address of the inventor.[26] The EPO concluded that names given to things, such as DABUS, are not equivalent to the names of natural persons, since natural persons' names not only identify them "but enable them to exercise their rights and form part of their personality."[27] Perhaps in recognition of the thinness of this reasoning, the EPO also indicates the legislative history of the EPC and internationally applicable standards.[28] The EPO also reasoned that an AI system can have no rights (such as the right to own or transfer an invention or patent) because it has no legal personality. According to the EPO, "Legal personality is assigned to a natural person as a consequence of their being human, and to a legal person based on a legal fiction … [which is] either directly created by legislation, or developed through consistent jurisprudence."[29] The EPO concluded that the designation of the inventor is a formal requirement that cannot be simply brushed aside via Dr. Thaler's tautological reasoning that "if there is a patentable invention, then patent law presumes that there was an inventor."[30]

Second, the EPO determined that Dr. Thaler could not have acquired any status or rights to apply for the patent.[31] Because an AI system lacks personhood, it cannot be an employee, nor can it transfer rights to a successor in title. The EPO then specifically distinguished between the (presumptively correct) observation that the owner of a machine (or AI system) also owns the outputs of the machine (or AI system) and the questions of invention, inventorship, and agency to transfer ownership of an invention.[32] One recent commentary has suggested the relative weakness of the EPO's analysis. Kemal Bengi and Christopher Heath note, "[w]hile US patent law puts a strong emphasis on the 'inventor' who must be named and in whose name the patent application has to be filed, this requirement is absent in the European Patent Convention."[33] As such, they suggest, whether the EPO would permit an AI to be a named inventor is "not so clear."[34] Citing various provisions of the European Patent Convention, Bengi and Heath argue that "[c]orrect mention of the inventor and entitlement is … not a condition for patentability" under the EPC.[35] Bengi and Heath conclude, without further analysis, that the human(s)to

[25] EPO, "EPO Publishes Grounds for Its Decision to Refuse Two Patent Applications Naming a Machine as Inventor," Press Release, January 28, 2020, www.epo.org/news-events/news/2020/20200128.html.

[26] EPO, "Grounds for the Decision on Application Nr. 18 275 163.6," January 27, 2020, ¶ 20.

[27] Ibid., ¶ 22. The extent to which human personhood is intrinsically bound up with one's name is an age-old topic of discussion. Compare William Shakespeare, *Romeo and Juliet* (Act II, sc. 2) ("What's in a name? that which we call a rose by any other name would smell as sweet; So Romeo would, were he not Romeo call'd, retain that dear perfection which he owes without that title").

[28] EPO, "Grounds," ¶¶ 23–29.

[29] Ibid., ¶ 27.

[30] Ibid., ¶¶ 34–36.

[31] Ibid., ¶¶ 30–33.

[32] Ibid., ¶¶ 32–33.

[33] Kemal Bengi and Christopher Heath, "Patents and Artificial Intelligence Inventions," in Christopher Heath, Anselm Kamperman Sanders, and Anke Moerland (eds.), *Intellectual Property Law and the Fourth Industrial Revolution* (Philadelphia: Wolters Kluwer, 2020), p. 145.

[34] Ibid.

[35] Ibid.

whom the invention "could most closely be attributed" should be identified as the inventor(s) according to established principles.[36]

Bengi and Heath's commentary was published roughly contemporaneously with the EPO's January 2020 decision (publication release date May 22, 2020). Although they do report on the EPO's decision, it is not clear whether their commentary was written before it, as a prediction, or after the decision, as a critique. To be sure, the situation is evolving rapidly and is venturing into poorly charted legal terrain. But either way their critique is interpreted, it seems to have been addressed, at least for now, by the EPO's January 2020 decision. As noted in the statement of Grounds for Decision dated January 27, 2020 for both applications, the applications were initially denied on October 17, 2018 for having left blank the field for naming the inventor. It was in response to this notice of deficiency that Dr. Thaler filed a designation of inventor form identifying DABUS as the inventor. Dr. Thaler initially indicated that he had acquired the patent rights from DABUS as DABUS' "employer" but later amended this contention to indicate he was DABUS' "successor in title."[37] Further, the EPO specifically distinguished between ownership of an AI machine and inventorship, thus seemingly disapproving of the "most closely associated human" approach suggested by Bengi and Heath.

Bengi and Heath conclude with an identification of competing policy rationales concerning patent inventorship: (1) "Promoting the disclosure of new and useful inventions (in which case the personality of the inventor is of no concern)," (2) "Providing an incentive to invent (in which case the link between an investment and the concrete invention in question becomes rather weak for inventions made by a computer)," and (3) "Protecting the inventor's individual creation (in which case there is no need to protect inventions made by robots)."[38]

They do not discuss any of these rationales in greater detail, but they are similar to the rationales variously stated by many who have waded into this debate. In some respects, they represent facets of the same set of considerations, often pointing to different conclusions. For example, to the extent the patent system is focused on promoting the disclosure of new and useful inventions, then the genesis of those inventions does not much matter. However, there are many channels through which new and useful inventions may be disclosed, including publishing them for free in the public domain. This leads naturally to the second of their rationales – providing an incentive to invent (and publish). As Bengi and Heath suggest, this factor may not be directly operative on AI inventors – one supposes that DABUS did not develop its beverage container and neural flame for the promise of financial rewards or the glory of being a named inventor, but rather because it is programmed to follow an imperative to invent. That said, the incentives provided by the patent system may indeed operate on the humans and human institutions (such as universities or corporations) involved in deploying AIs on invention missions. There is empirical evidence that humans who invent are driven to do so for reasons other than the incentives provided by the patent system.[39] Finally, to the extent Bengi and Heath's third consideration represents something different from the first two, it appears to emphasize the humanistic desire to protect the act of creation by inventors (as opposed, e.g.,

[36] Ibid., p. 147.

[37] EPO, "Grounds," ¶¶ 1–4.

[38] Bengi and Heath, "Patents and Artificial Intelligence Inventions," p. 147. They further note that these competing rationales have remained unreconciled in the analog world for over sixty years, citing Fritz Machlup, *An Economic Review of the Patent System* (Washington, DC: US Government Printing Office, 1958), pp. 19–43.

[39] See, e.g., Stuart J. H. Graham, Robert P. Merges, Pamela Samuelson, and Ted M. Sichelman, "High Technology Entrepreneurs and the Patent System: Results of the 2008 Berkeley Patent Survey" (2009) 24 *Berkeley Technology Law Journal* 1255 at 1283–1287.

to focusing on the economics of an industrial policy that encourages the development of novel technologies).

17.2.3 *United States Patent and Trademark Office*

The companion application in the United States met a similar fate.[40] Application No. 16/524,350 was filed on July 29, 2019, and on August 8, 2019, the USPTO issued a Notice to File Missing Parts of Nonprovisional Application, on the basis that the application data sheet accompanying the patent application failed to identify each inventor by their legal name. The application identified DABUS as the inventor, and identified Dr. Thaler as both the legal representative of DABUS and the assignee of the application. The assignment from DABUS to Thaler was signed by Thaler in both capacities. Thaler challenged the Notice through several layers of review at the USPTO, without success. The Decision on Thaler's Petition recited several reasons for the conclusion. First, it cited Thaler's acknowledgment that DABUS cannot own property, thus suggesting that DABUS could not have assigned anything to Thaler pursuant to the purported assignment.[41] Second, the USPTO confirmed that the meaning of "inventor" under the United States patent laws is limited to natural persons.[42] Third, it emphasized that "conception" (under United States law, invention involves "conception" followed by "reduction to practice" of the invention[43]) is a "mental" act in the "mind" of the inventor, and that these concepts also emphasize human involvement in the act of invention.[44] Responding to these conclusions, Thaler argued that such a rule will require that when an AI "invents," the applicant will be compelled to falsely list a human as the inventor; the USPTO brushed aside this objection.[45] Next, Thaler argued that because a patent had been issued *on* the invention machine known as DABUS, then DABUS should itself be allowed to be an inventor on further inventions; again, the USPTO brushed aside this argument as a non sequitur.[46] Finally, the USPTO held that the policy argument in favor of incentivizing innovation does not override the plain language of the patent laws.[47] Thaler filed suit against the USPTO to challenge this ruling, arguing that the rejection of DABUS' applications violated existing law concerning patentability.[48]

17.3 QUESTIONS BEYOND DABUS

The (for now) definitive resolution of the various DABUS-related patent applications is not the end of the debate. Instead, the question turns from *are* AIs allowed to be inventors to *should* AIs be allowed to be inventors? And if so, what other issues or questions flow from that determination? The answer to the first of these questions – whether AIs *should* be allowed to be inventors – breaks down into two camps.

[40] See generally USPTO, "Decision on Petition, Application No. 16/524,350," April 22, 2020, for a summary of the procedural history of the United States application.

[41] Ibid., p. 2 n.2.

[42] Ibid., pp. 4–5.

[43] See *Solvay* S.A. v. *Honeywell Int'l*, 742 F 3d 998, 1000 (Fed. Cir. 2014) ("Making the invention requires conception and reduction to practice. While conception is the formation, in the mind of the inventor, of a definite and permanent idea of a complete and operative invention, reduction to practice requires that the claimed invention work for its intended purpose.").

[44] USPTO, "Decision," p. 6.

[45] Ibid.

[46] Ibid., p. 7.

[47] Ibid.

[48] *Thaler* v. *Hirshfeld*, Case No. 1:20-cv-00903 (E.D. Va., filed August 6, 2020).

For those who answer in the negative, most arguments tend to fall into one of three categories: (1) positivists, who argue that the existing law sufficiently answers the question, (2) humanists, who argue that there are important, overriding "pro-human" policies behind the protection of patents and copyrights, and (3) those who are focused on the practical knock-on challenges – if an AI is an inventor, what other legal agency capabilities must the AI also have? For the positivists, the state of existing law and legal doctrine provides the answer. For the humanists, they tend to focus on the role of intellectual property law in encouraging and rewarding human creativity, and they disfavor the potential for further concentration of intellectual property ownership that AI inventorship could cause.[49]

For those who answer in the affirmative, most arguments in favor tend to fall into "social utility" and "industrial policy" justifications. But there are also some nominally "pro-human" arguments offered, such as those advanced by Ryan Abbott in his recent book, *The Reasonable Robot*.[50] Broadly speaking, the "industrial policy" justifications posit that new and useful technologies should be protected and monetizable, regardless of how the technology was developed. Abbott further argues that a principle of AI legal neutrality – such that it would equally grant patents to AI inventions and human inventions – would be pro-social for two main reasons: rewarding investment in innovation (along the lines of the industrial policy argument) and protecting the integrity of the patent system by steering people away from falsely naming humans as inventors on AI-created inventions.[51]

Permitting AI inventors could raise a number of theoretical challenges within patent law. For example, should the ordinary level of skill in the art be adjusted to account for the capabilities of AI systems? Would all claimed inventions be obvious (and therefore unpatentable) to a near-omniscient AI system?[52] If a patent must make a disclosure sufficient to enable one of skill in the art to make and use the invention, will future patents be written entirely in non-human-readable machine code? And if AIs are allowed to be named as inventors, there are a number of corollary nonpatent issues, deriving from the other incidents of inventor status. For example, can an AI inventor own property, assign or transfer that property,[53] authorize others to act on behalf of the AI, sue to enforce its patent, and testify at a patent infringement trial (e.g., about how it came up with the invention)?

17.4 COMPETING POLICY ARGUMENTS

17.4.1 *Humanistic Approach*

Inventiveness and creativity are often considered to be among the core characteristics that are quintessentially human. Indeed, we often speak in reverent terms of the act of invention: the spark of genius, or the proverbial light bulb appearing over the inventor's head. Under United

[49] Compare Ryan Abbott, *The Reasonable Robot: Artificial Intelligence and the Law* (Cambridge: Cambridge University Press, 2020), p. 90 ("Inventive AI may result in greater consolidation of patents in the hands of large corporations").

[50] Abbott, *The Reasonable Robot*.

[51] Ibid., pp. 72, 82–84.

[52] Ryan Abbott, "Everything Is Obvious" (2018) 66 *UCLA Law Review* 2 ("Unlike the skilled person, the inventive machine is capable of innovation and considering the entire universe of prior art. As inventive machines continue to improve, this will increasingly raise the bar to patentability, eventually rendering innovative activities obvious. The end of obviousness means the end of patents, at least as they are now").

[53] This issue actually arose in the UK's DABUS proceedings. Dr. Thaler claimed that his ownership of DABUS entitled him to sign a power of attorney on behalf of DABUS, authorizing him (Thaler) to file the patent application. See *Thaler* [2020] EWHC 2412 (Pat) ¶ 4.

States law, at least, the act of invention explicitly incorporates a theory of mind. Invention involves two steps: conception, followed by diligent efforts to reduce the invention to practice.[54] Conception is defined as "the formation *in the mind of the inventor* of a definite and permanent idea of the complete and operative invention."[55]

Despite patent lawyers' rhetoric about the patent system providing an incentive to innovate, empirical studies have demonstrated that the prospect of patent protection provides little more than a slight incentive to engage in innovation.[56] Indeed, what is often called the "patent bargain" set forth in Article I, Section 8 of the United States Constitution, relates not to innovation at all, but to the public-private bargain for disclosure. An inventor receives a time-limited monopoly in exchange for public disclosure of their invention.[57]

Given the futuristic, even science fictional, aspect to the prospect of AI inventors, efforts to navigate the balance between humans and human-created institutions, on the one hand, and AI on the other hand, often find inspiration in the work of science fiction writers. In *New Laws of Robotics: Defending Human Expertise in the Age of AI*, Frank Pasquale takes inspiration from a 1942 Isaac Asimov short story to articulate four "new laws" of robotics for the AI age. Pasquale's new laws of robotics are: (1) robotic systems and AI should complement professionals, not replace them, (2) robotic systems and AI should not counterfeit humanity, (3) robotic systems and AI should not intensify zero-sum arms races, and (4) robotic systems and AI must always indicate the identity of their creator(s), controller(s), and owner(s).[58]

Pasquale does not directly address the question of AI and inventorship, though he does consider the related question of authorship of AI-created artworks, literature, or music. Invoking both his second law (do not counterfeit humanity) and fourth law (identify the creator, controller, and owner), he questions whether AI-created works reflect true artistic creativity, or are mere mimicry, and warns that the challenge "is to avoid crossing a line between AI-aided creativity and a fetishization of AI as creative in itself."[59] Additionally, Pasquale recognizes that assessments of creativity and artistic value are situated within cultural institutions (such as the market for art). Moreover, he notes, "humans will have put all those works in motion, and as the fourth new law of robotics demands, they should be attributed to their human authors."[60] Pasquale's analysis may be extrapolated to the patent system as well. As has been generally recognized, AI has an important role to play as a tool to aid human researchers in their efforts. Indeed, various kinds of research tools – and even human laboratory assistants – form an important part of the research enterprise without necessarily rising to the level of being entitled to designation as an "inventor." Thus, similarly, Pasquale's analysis would support a designation, where plausible, of the involved humans as inventors.[61] Of course, however, there may be circumstances where those humans' involvement comes nowhere near the acts of "conception" and "reduction to practice." For example, assume that computer scientists with little medical

[54] *Solvay*, n. 43.

[55] USPTO, *Manual of Patent Examining Procedure*, § 2138.04, R-10.2019, June 2020; see also Woodrow Barfield and Ugo Pagallo, *Advanced Introduction to Law and Artificial Intelligence* (Cheltenham: Edward Elgar, 2020), p. 155.

[56] Graham et al., "High Technology Entrepreneurs," 1285.

[57] See *Eldred* v. *Ashcroft*, 537 US 186, 216 (2003) (Under the patent bargain, "immediate disclosure is not the objective of, but is exacted from, the patentee. It is the price paid for the exclusivity secured").

[58] Frank Pasquale, *New Laws of Robotics: Defending Human Expertise in the Age of AI* (Cambridge, MA: Belknap Press, 2020), pp. 3–11.

[59] Ibid., p. 219.

[60] Ibid., p. 220.

[61] Further, DABUS' claimed beverage container would arguably fall into Pasquale's "fetishization" warning; whether or not it is novel, it hardly seems appealing to humans as a replacement for the traditional cylindrical beverage cans or square tetra-paks.

knowledge develop an AI that is capable of discovering new molecules that can cure disease. Should those computer scientists be deemed inventors? If the AI is not an inventor, should the discovery be deemed unpatentable? Or is this hypothetical unrealistic, in the sense that any human involved in developing an AI directed at a particular area of inquiry will also have enough of a "light bulb" of inventiveness to be deemed an inventor?

17.4.2 *Industrial Policy Approach*

Following the various Patent Office rulings that DABUS cannot be an inventor, some commentators called for changes in the law. One commenter stated, "The patent system is in place to spur investment in technology, and if that technology cannot be protected, it follows that the investment will turn elsewhere to areas where the innovation can be protected."[62] In other words, not providing patent protection for AI-developed inventions would "[disincentivize] investment in the development and use of smart AI, because you couldn't recoup the cost of the machine without being able to protect the results it provides."[63]

Thus, the industrial policy approach would generally take the position that all innovation is good innovation, regardless of whether it tends to concentrate economic power in the hands of those who have the resources to develop and deploy industrial-scale AI. On such an approach, AI-generated innovations should absolutely be given patent protection, and it is from this conclusion that it follows that AIs should be permitted to be inventors. But even the proponents of this approach acknowledge the risks of market breakdown: Abbott has stated that it could "result in greater consolidation of patents in the hands of large corporations" and that it "could lead to market abuses."[64] But, Abbott argues, the overall and inevitable benefits to society are worth such risks.[65]

According to the empirical research of Stuart Graham et al., the incentive-to-innovate premise of the industrial policy approach does not necessarily correlate to companies' actual motivations. The market benefits from first-mover advantage, as well as the protections afforded by maintaining secrecy (including the legal protections of trade secrets) provide comparable motives in some fields of technology.[66]

By contrast with the industrial policy approach, Pasquale warns of technology's tendency to accelerate the move toward "winner-take-all and loser-take-nothing markets," and that an unregulated embrace of technology will tend "to maximize investment returns for the wealthiest technologists and the most technologically advanced wealthy."[67] Thus, he reminds us, "rapid automation is a path rife with dystopian possibilities."[68] Pasquale concludes:

> The metaphysics and political economy of AIs status are closely intertwined. The greater the inequality becomes, the more power billionaires have to force everyone they meet to treat their robots like persons. If they succeed, robotic replacements of humans then seem less creepy and more the harbinger of a fashionable avant-garde or inevitable progress. And efforts of the global poor to share in the bounty of the wealthier parts of the world will seem ever less compelling if

[62] Ryan Davis, "Lawmakers May Soon Face Calls to Let AI Be An Inventor," *Law360*, May 1, 2020, www.law360.com/articles/1269219/print?section=ip.
[63] Ibid.
[64] Abbott, *The Reasonable Robot*, p. 90.
[65] Ibid.
[66] Graham et al., "High Technology Entrepreneurs," 1290.
[67] Pasquale, *New Laws of Robotics*, pp. 222, 239.
[68] Ibid., p. 223.

> those of means feel morally entitled to plow ever more resources into machines meant to replace humans. An equality between humans and robots portends vast inequalities among humans themselves.[69]

In addition, as explained in more detail in Section 17.5, the conclusion that AIs should be inventors (in furtherance of the industrial policy rationale) fails to fully address a number of practical challenges, both in patent law and more generally.

17.5 PRACTICAL DIFFICULTIES OF AI-AS-INVENTOR

17.5.1 *Patent Law: POSITA and Related Issues*

If AIs were permitted to be named inventors on patents, this development would raise a number of follow-on questions within United States patent law, mainly arising from patent law's reliance on the concept of a "person of ordinary skill in the art" (POSITA).[70] A POSITA is flexibly defined, taking into account such factors as the level of education and practical experience of a person practicing the relevant art, the type of problems encountered in the art, and the sophistication and rate of change of the technology.[71] The Supreme Court has emphasized that "A person of ordinary skill is also a person of ordinary creativity, not an automaton."[72] The concept impacts, for example, patent validity, insofar as a claimed invention is invalid as obvious under 35 USC § 103 if it would have been obvious to a POSITA at the time of the invention.[73] Whether a claimed invention would be obvious to a POSITA implicates both the depth and scope of the POSITA's knowledge of the scientific literature (the "prior art"), and also the readiness with which multiple references in the "prior art" may be combinable to achieve the claimed invention. How should the novelty of an AI's invention be judged – against the level of skill of mere humans, or against the level of skill of other AIs? If an AI is deemed to have the depth of knowledge of IBM's Watson, is it fair to human inventors to judge the AI against a human-centered POSITA standard? Should there be a separate obviousness standard for inventions by AIs – an "AI of skill in the art" (AISITA) standard? Should the entire POSITA/AISITA scale shift to the now technologically presumptive AISITA standard, such that a human inventor would not be entitled to a patent if it would have been obvious to an AISITA? Abbott has suggested that, over time, the level of skill expected of a POSITA will migrate toward the superhuman level of skill and knowledge of AIs.[74]

The concept of a POSITA is also relevant to the level of disclosure required in the patent's specification, or written description, which must be sufficiently detailed to enable a POSITA to make and use the claimed invention.[75] Like the questions that arise around the standard for obviousness, what kind of disclosure would be necessary to enable an AISITA to make and use an invention? Would it be permissible for a patent's disclosure to be entirely in non-human-

[69] Ibid., p. 217.

[70] 35 USC § 103.

[71] E.g., *Environmental Designs, Ltd.* v. *Union Oil Co.*, 713 F 2d 693, 696 (Fed. Cir. 1983).

[72] *KSR Int'l Co.* v. *Teleflex Inc.*, 550 US 398, 421 (2007).

[73] 35 USC § 103.

[74] Abbott, *The Reasonable Robot*, p. 103; see also Abbott, "Everything Is Obvious."

[75] 35 USC § 112(a) ("The specification shall contain a written description of the invention, and of the manner and process of making and using it, in such full, clear, concise, and exact terms as to enable any person skilled in the art to which it pertains, or with which it is most nearly connected, to make and use the same . . .").

readable form, such as computer object code? Would that actually be *required* for AI-invented inventions?

17.5.2 *Practical Difficulties If AI Inventors Lack Full Legal Personhood*

There is no argument that DABUS (or any other known AI) is currently sufficiently advanced to be entitled to full legal personhood. Indeed, many of the legal conclusions concerning DABUS' patent applications relate not to the central question of whether an AI such as DABUS can be a named inventor, but rather to these corollary practical questions: Can DABUS own property? How did Dr. Thaler get authorization from DABUS to file the patent applications? And so forth.[76]

Beyond the mechanics of applying for and prosecuting the patent application, there are further conceptual difficulties that arise from the AI's lack of full legal personhood. If an AI inventor has not "assigned" its patent to a human (such as Dr. Thaler) or a corporation, how would it pursue a claim for infringement? Could it hire a lawyer? Would the AI have standing to pursue a claim in court? How would it get deposed or testify at trial? If it managed to prevail on a patent infringement claim and be awarded royalties, how would it be paid? For that matter, short of an infringement lawsuit, if someone wished to license the AI's patent, how would it do so?

And on the flip side, if the AI's activities were to infringe someone else's patent, how could that other patentholder pursue a remedy against the AI? Yvette Joy Liebesman and Julie Cromer Young have analyzed this problem, albeit in the context of copyrights, and have identified a number of practical difficulties that would have equal application in patent litigation.[77] Among other challenges they identify: (1) How would a court determine whether the AI is subject to the court's jurisdiction? (2) How would the AI be served with the summons and complaint? (3) How would you assess damages against an AI? How would it pay? (4) How could you enter an injunction against an AI? (5) What recourse is available if the AI fails to pay damages or abide by the injunction? (6) You can't fine it or put it in jail.[78]

17.5.3 *Instances of Near-Agency for AIs in Current Case Law*

Even as it has been generally recognized that AIs are currently not sufficiently advanced to have full agency or legal personhood, several recent cases have approached the periphery of the issue. Litigation in Texas tackled the question whether internet service providers (ISPs) hosting Google servers located in Texas possessed sufficient agency to qualify Google as doing business in Texas, for the purpose of determining proper venue for the litigation. The venue statute requires that the defendant have a "regular and established place of business" in the forum.[79] The United States Court of Appeals for the Federal Circuit interpreted this requirement to entail that there be "the regular, physical presence of an employee or other agent of the defendant conducting the defendant's business" at the location.[80] The Federal Circuit ruled

[76] See generally Section 17.2.

[77] Yvette Joy Liebesman and Julie Cromer Young, "Litigating against the Artificially Intelligent Infringer" (2020) 14 *Florida International University Law Review* 259.

[78] On this last point, Abbott discusses theories under which the makers, owners, and/or operators of an AI might be held financially responsible for the AI's actions that give rise to civil liability. Abbott, *The Reasonable Robot*, pp. 63–65.

[79] See In re Google LLC, 949 F 3d 1338, 1345 (Fed. Cir. 2020).

[80] Ibid.

that the ISPs, operating and maintaining the servers, were not Google's agents.[81] The court specifically declined to reach the issue "whether a machine could be an 'agent,'" noting that such a theory "would require recognition that service [of process] could be made on a machine."[82] After that ruling, Eastern District of Texas Judge Rodney Gilstrap ordered the parties in another case to submit briefing on the question of when a machine could be considered an agent.[83]

In California, the question was whether Amazon's AI algorithm for selecting photographs from among user-submitted content meant that the algorithm – and therefore not Amazon – was responsible for copyright infringement arising out of unauthorized use of selected photos. The plaintiff, Williams-Sonoma, sought to amend its Complaint to add a claim for copyright infringement based on Amazon's selection, use, and publication of user-submitted photos, some of which were copyrighted by Williams-Sonoma. Amazon responded that the selection of photos is a "purely automatic" process without human involvement and therefore cannot constitute volitional conduct prohibited by the statute. In particular, the issue was the applicability of a safe harbor to liability for service providers under the Digital Millennium Copyright Act where the copyrighted material is stored "at the direction of a user."[84] If an Amazon employee had selected the photos, the argument went, then Amazon could have been subject to liability, but because it was an Amazon algorithm that selected the photos, Amazon argued that it should not be subject to liability.[85] During oral argument on the issue, counsel for Williams-Sonoma warned that "a ruling for Amazon [would] put the law on a dystopian path where no one can be held responsible for killings by automated vehicles and AI-piloted drones."[86] The court ruled against Amazon and permitted the case to proceed, at least at the pleading stage (leaving merits of the resolution of the argument for another day).[87] Thus, as the role of AI becomes an increasingly useful foil for litigants, the question of AI-having-legal-agency may not be as far-fetched and futuristic as we assume.

17.5.4 *Near Future – AI as Legal Agent*

At least one commenter has argued that AIs should be allowed to bring lawsuits. Abraham Meltzer has argued that a "superintelligent AI" should be deemed to have the capacity, or standing, to bring suit in United States federal courts.[88] Under United States law, the doctrine of standing means that a person or entity cannot bring a lawsuit unless they have a legally recognized injury.[89] Building off of two rulings from the United States Court of Appeals for the Ninth Circuit that held that animals can have standing under Article III of the Constitution, Meltzer argues that a superintelligent AI "should even more readily" have Article III standing than animals do, based on the assumption that such an AI could assert its own interests, and that

81 Ibid., 1346.

82 Ibid., 1347.

83 *Personalized Media Commc'ns LLC* v. *Google LLC, et al.*, No. 19-cv-00090-JRG, Dkt. Nos. 156, 159–170, 174–177 (E.D. Tex., February 13–27, 2020). It does not appear that the court ever ruled on the question.

84 17 USC § 512(c).

85 *Williams-Sonoma, Inc.* v. *Amazon.com, Inc.*, No. 18-cv-7548-AGT, Dkt. No. 97, pp. 12–16 (N.D. Cal., April 3, 2020); see also, Ibid., Dkt. No. 110.

86 Scott Graham, "Orrick Warns Judge of Frankenstein's Software," *Skilled in the Art*, June 26, 2020, www.govinfo.gov/app/details/USCOURTS-cand-3_18-cv-07548.

87 Williams-Sonoma, n. 85, Dkt. No. 125 (Order Denying Defendant's Motion to Dismiss Second Amended and Supplemental Complaint) (N.D. Cal., August 17, 2020).

88 Abraham C. Meltzer, "Can AI Sue in Federal Court?" (2020) 33 *California Litigation* 1 at 32.

89 US Const. Art. III, Sec. 2, Cl. 1.

such an ability to self-advocate would suffice.[90] Similarly, an AI's inanimate nature is also no bar to standing, Meltzer argues, because corporations also can have standing.[91] Thus, Meltzer argues, whether or not AIs are afforded standing to sue is purely a statutory question, such that Congress can enact statutes to grant AIs authorization to sue. He provides two, brief, arguments that Congress should do so: "first, to maximize the chances for human self-preservation in an AI world; and second, because ethically a sentient machine entity with human-level or greater intelligence would deserve to be treated with dignity."[92] Although Meltzer warns that "[s]-uperintelligent AI must not be anthropomorphized,"[93] his arguments appear to be a mix of anthropomorphizing and preemptive surrender to what he presumes will be exponentially superior robot overlords. To increase the chances that superintelligent AIs will return the favor and let humans survive, Meltzer argues that AIs need to be exposed to, and included within, human values, such as participation in the legal system. Indeed, Meltzer concludes, "[r]eally, the only objection to allowing superintelligent AI statutory standing to sue is that it seems strange."[94] Meltzer's second argument extends his hypothetical – not only is his fictionalized AI "superintelligent," but it must also be "self-aware." As such, Meltzer concludes, it would be "morally suspect" not to respect the AI's dignity by being inclusive in our grant of legal rights.[95] While this line of reasoning has a distinctly Golden-Rule "do unto others" overtone, it seems guilty of exactly the kind of anthropomorphizing that Meltzer warned against. The fact remains that whether we are talking about animals or corporations, the existing assertions of legal standing, and the recognition thereof, is conducted entirely through human agents. Not only has our legal system never had to grapple with self-aware, self-assertive nonhumans, but their existence (for now) and their behavior (eventually) is currently entirely a matter of projection and speculation.

17.5.5 *Outlining Conditions for Full Legal Agency for AIs*

By framing his argument about a speculative, future, "superintelligent" and "self-aware" AI, Meltzer has dodged the question of how we will know when the AI is sufficiently super-intelligent and self-aware to have full agency. One is tempted to respond, glibly, that when that happens, the AI will doubtless make us all aware. Unless maybe it doesn't.

This is a question that theorists have grappled with for decades.[96] Several years ago, the European Parliament drew significant publicity for proposing a form of "electronic personhood" for robots and AIs. In a Draft Report with recommendations to the Commission on Civil Law Rules on Robotics (2015/2103 [INL]), the Committee on Legal Affairs proposed the creation of a new category of electronic personhood, and included a call for the European Commission "to

[90] Meltzer, "Can AI Sue in Federal Court?," 33 (citing *Naruto* v. *Slater*, 888 F 3d 418 [9th Cir. 2018] and *Cetacean Community* v. *Bush*, 386 F 3d 1169 [9th Cir. 2004]).

[91] Ibid. Under Meltzer's analysis, these factors taken together, and adding in the use of "next friend" and other legal representatives to pursue animals' interests in litigation, Dr. Thaler's efforts to act as representative of DABUS would arguably satisfy Article III standing. Cf. note § 2.1.

[92] Meltzer, "Can AI Sue in Federal Court?," 34.

[93] Ibid., 35.

[94] Ibid., 36.

[95] Ibid., 37.

[96] See, e.g., Lawrence B. Solum, "Legal Personhood for Artificial Intelligences" (1992) 70 *North Carolina Law Review* 1231 at 1239 (considering a theoretical framework for the question, drawing a distinction between "personhood" and "humanity," and drawing no clear conclusions).

elaborate criteria for an 'own intellectual creation' for copyrightable works produced by computers or robots."[97] (Notably, there was not also a parallel call to action relating to patenting.) The proposal drew considerable media attention at the time, though the purpose of the report was "to ensure that robots are and will remain in the service of humans."[98] However, in a 2018 press release concerning its priorities, the European Commission made no mention of either the personhood or intellectual property aspects of the proposal.[99]

More broadly, legal philosophers have grappled with the broader question of legal personality, not limited to the context of AI. For example, in *A Theory of Legal Personhood*, Visa A. J. Kurki outlines what he calls the "Bundle Theory" of legal personhood. Under the Bundle Theory, those who have been afforded legal personhood hold some combination of legally recognized rights and/or duties. Kurki contrasts his approach with a more traditional approach, which he refers to as the "Orthodox View," and which equates legal personhood simply with the holding of rights and the owing of duties.[100] Under the Bundle Theory, legal personhood is a "cluster property," meaning that whether any particular entity has legal personhood "is determined based on a weighted list of criteria, none of which alone is necessary or sufficient."[101] Some of these incidents of legal personhood are passive (such as entitlement to life, liberty and bodily integrity, capacity to own property, etc.) and some are active (such as capacity to enter into contracts, ability to be held legally responsible for crimes, torts, etc.)[102] Kurki's approach solidly situates legal personhood as a construct of legal positivism: "legal personhood is not an intrinsic attribute of an entity; rather, a necessary condition for the legal personhood of any entity is that that entity is treated as a legal person by the prevailing legal system."[103] Thus, compared with the Orthodox View, the Bundle Theory is a more holistic approach not subject to a rigid checklist of criteria.

Kurki does apply his Bundle Theory to the question of legal personhood for AI.[104] He frames the analysis around three "contexts": the *ultimate-value* context (are AIs viewed as worthy of receiving some of the protections that legal persons enjoy?), the *responsibility* context (can AIs be held criminally or tortiously liable for their actions?), and the *commercial* context (can AIs own property, enter into contracts, and the like?). Although he analyzes these issues in detail, as applied to AIs, the question ultimately proves too generalized to address the many variants of special purpose AIs that currently exist and the still-science-fiction questions surrounding a (possibly sentient) general AI that might exist in the future.[105]

97 Draft Report of the Committee on Legal Affairs, p. 8.

98 See James Vincent, "Giving Robots 'Personhood' Is Actually about Making Corporations Accountable," *The Verge*, January 19, 2017, www.theverge.com/2017/1/19/14322334/robot-electronic-persons-eu-report-liability-civil-suits; see also Alex Hern, "Give Robots 'Personhood' Status, EU Committee Argues," *The Guardian*, January 12, 2017, www.theguardian.com/technology/2017/jan/12/give-robots-personhood-status-eu-committee-argues. *The Guardian* quoted attorney Ashley Morgan of Osborne Clark on the implications of the EU proposal, "If I create a robot, and that robot creates something that could be patented, should I own that patent or should the robot? If I sell the robot, should the intellectual property it has developed go with it? These are not easy questions to answer, and that goes right to the heart of this debate."

99 European Commission, "Press Release IP/18/3362 Artificial Intelligence: Commission Outlines a European Approach to Boost Investment and Set Ethical Guidelines," April 25, 2018, www.europa.eu/rapid/press-release_IP-18-3362_en.htm. See also Thomas Burri, "The EU Is Right to Refuse Legal Personality for Artificial Intelligence," *Euractiv*, May 30, 2018, www.euractiv.com/section/digital/opinion/the-eu-is-right-to-refuse-legal-personality-for-artificial-intelligence.

100 Visa A. J. Kurki, *A Theory of Legal Personhood* (Oxford: Oxford University Press, 2019), p. 5.

101 Ibid., p. 93.

102 Ibid., pp. 97–118.

103 Ibid., p. 92.

104 Ibid., p. 175.

105 Ibid., pp. 175–189.

That said, Kurki's analysis rings true to the difficulties surrounding the debate over AI-as-inventor. There are many competing facets, or contexts, to the analysis, yet no single facet is by itself necessary or sufficient to reach a conclusion. And, at least as presently construed, the question is very much a product of a legal-positivist analysis – namely, the enactment of laws granting particular rights and duties to AIs would tend to be indicative of whether the AI has legal personhood. In one important respect, this inverts the analysis of those who would argue that the laws should change because AIs do have (or will soon have) the incidents of legal personhood, and shows that such arguments are ultimately question-begging.

17.6 CONCLUSION

It now appears to be well established that, under current law, an AI cannot be a named inventor on a patent. In many jurisdictions, patent applications must name an inventor, and further require that the inventor must be a "person." For now, the Patent Offices in the EU, the UK, and the United States have concluded that inventors must be humans, meaning that any patent application that discloses an "invention" but not a human "inventor" is not entitled to an issued patent.

The question of whether an AI *should* be eligible to be a patent inventor is a difficult one to answer. Some have argued that the requirement to name an inventor should be dispensed with and replaced with just an applicant-owner status instead. Particularly under legal schemes like that in the United States[106] (though perhaps less emphatically so before the EPO), this would require a change in the laws. Others have argued that "inventor" should be given a broader construction. Similarly, this would appear to require a change in the law, as "inventor" is fairly consistently referred to as "person" in the existing laws. Doing so for the current state-of-the-art AIs would give rise to a number of corollary conceptual difficulties.

Some have argued that "person" should be given a broad construction, citing the existence of nonhuman legal persons, as well as the sometimes strained arguments that have been advanced in order to limit inventors to humans. Kurki's Bundle Theory provides an analytic framework to understand and evaluate this argument, suggesting that, so long as an "inventor" must be a "person," then an AI cannot be a named inventor unless and until there are enough changes in the enacted laws that recognize enough rights and duties in AIs that there exists a sufficient Bundle to recognize AI legal personhood.

Ultimately, beyond the formal legal questions of what current doctrine will allow, both sides of the argument fall back to abstractions and prognostications. The core abstractions – including both patent and copyright law – are what lie at the root of inventiveness and creativity. Are these quintessentially human endeavors; not just in the sense that only humans can be inventive or creative, but also in the sense that being inventive and creative is part of how we define our humanity? Or are inventiveness and creativity things that can be defined using objective criteria: market value, percentage similarity to (or difference from) preexisting works? Do inventiveness and creativity exist in isolation, or are they situated in social contexts? For example, is creativity defined in relation to what came before it, as recognized in the context of the creative work's audience? Similarly, a patentable invention must be nonobvious to a person of skill in the art, taking into account the teachings of the prior art. And it must be useful. To whom? Or to what?

[106] See, e.g., USPTO, *Manual of Patent Examining Procedure*, § 2137.01 2018 ("The requirement that the applicant for a patent be the inventor is a characteristic of U.S. patent law not generally shared by other countries").

The prognostications reflect our collective ambivalence about an AI-fueled future.[107] Current AI is not (as far as we know) so advanced as to be general-purpose, sentient, and superintelligent. Not even DABUS. Maybe our future will be filled with benevolent, ethical cyborgs who are all too appreciative of the inclusivity of our legal system, and will devote their resources to human-improving innovation. Or maybe it will be much darker, populated by AIs that have no interest in ethics, fairness, or humans' quality of life – as Stephen Hawking famously observed in 2014, "Success in creating AI would be the biggest event in human history. Unfortunately, it might also be the last, unless we learn how to avoid the risks."[108]

Shorn of doctrinal analysis, elaborate hypotheticals, and other arguments, most entrants in the debate whether AIs should be treated as inventors boil down to assumptions – stated or implicit – about these key questions. In seeking answers, we should consider Professor Chander's closing observation in his 2014 article, "How Law Made Silicon Valley":[109] "The legal moves described here in the United States have helped facilitate the 'wow' of the World Wide Web, but they might also usher in the 'yuck.' We need to ensure that in our zeal for promoting the Internet enterprise, we do not haphazardly create the conditions for a dystopia."

[107] This ambivalence is well encapsulated in the recent viral video of Boston Dynamics robots "dancing" to The Countours' "Do You Love Me," a performance that is simultaneously endearing and terrifying. www.youtube.com/watch?v=fn3KWM1kuAw (visited February 22, 2021).

[108] Michael Sainato, "Stephen Hawking, Elon Musk, and Bill Gates Warn about Artificial Intelligence," *The Observer*, August 19, 2015, www.observer.com/2015/08/stephen-hawking-elon-musk-and-bill-gates-warn-about-artificial-intelligence/ (visited November 26, 2020).

[109] Anupam Chander, "How Law Made Silicon Valley" (2014) 63 *Emory Law Journal* 639 at 693.

18

AI and Copyright Law

The European Perspective

Gerald Spindler

18.1 INTRODUCTION

The chapter deals with the requirement of copyright protection of AI systems as well as of products (and other goods) produced by AI from a European copyright perspective. Topics like protection under the Software Directive as well as the Database Directive are dealt with in particular. Moreover, aspects of the trade secrecy directive are also touched upon. Centred around the existing human-focused approach, the chapter also seeks to develop new ways of how to strike the balance between information society needs on the one hand (free access to works) and copyright protection and incentives for AI-created works on the other hand.

Artificial intelligence (AI) has already found its way into contemporary legal debates and is one of the hottest topics being discussed. Different areas of law such as liability, criminal law, legal tech or even agricultural law are similarly affected. Another legal area to be considered in this regard is copyright law. Here, AI raises two questions in particular. The first refers to the creation of works with the help of AI (Section 18.2), the second deals with copyright protection of AI itself (Section 18.3). The last section discusses options *de lege ferenda* (Section 18.4).

Famous examples of creation of 'new works' using AI regard different kinds of works,[1] including paintings such as the Rembrandt experiment of the Technical University of Delft in cooperation with Microsoft.[2] Music has been equally generated by AI. The 'finishing' of Gustav Mahler's unfinished Tenth Symphony during the 2019 Ars Electronica festival in Linz, Austria certainly has to be considered here.[3] So-called generative adversarial networks are deemed to be the most promising tool in AI to develop new works,[4] such as the portrait of Edmond de

[1] See EU Commission (C. Hartmann et al.), 'Trends and Developments in Artificial Intelligence – Challenges to the Intellectual Property Rights Framework – Final Report' (2020), p. 28; K.-N. Peifer, 'Roboter als Schöpfer – Wird das Urheberrecht im Zeitalter der künstlichen Intelligenz noch gebraucht?', in S. von Lewinski and H. Wittmann (eds.), *Urheberrecht! Festschrift für Hon.-Prof. Dr. Miachel M. Walter zum 80. Geburtstag* (Vienna: Verlag Medien und Recht, 2018), pp. 223–224; D. Gervais, 'The Machine as Author' (2020) 105 *Iowa Law Review* 2053–2106 at 2054 with more references; R. Denicola, 'Ex Machina: Copyright Protection for Computer-Generated Works' (2016) 69 *Rutgers University Law Review* 251–287 at 253–264.

[2] See 'The Next Rembrandt', www.nextrembrandt.com; see also A. Guadamuz, 'Do Androids Dream of Electric Copyright? Comparative Analysis of Originality in Artificial Intelligence Generated Works' (2017) 2 *Intellectual Property Quarterly* 169–186 at 169–170.

[3] See A. Nikrang et al. at https://ars.electronica.art/futurelab/de/projects-mahler-unfinished/ using OpenAI's model called 'MuseNet'.

[4] See Gervais, 'The Machine as Author', 2055.

Belamy.[5] While computer-aided artworks (and works in general) have already been in place for over fifty years, there is a considerable difference now regarding this new way of creating works. The 'old' computer-aided artworks resulted from programming (and randomizing) with given sets of data by the author/artist. Nowadays, AI differs from that significantly as – generally speaking[6] – the creator cannot really predict the outcome or the behaviour of the AI system.[7] The creator just decides about both the general features of the AI being used and the training data. Thus, their influence on the creation of the work is not as significant as in traditional ways where the author has a strong control over the whole procedure of creativity.

AI seems, at least at first glance, to be truly intelligent and consequently creative. Thus, AI is considered to be equivalent to the human mind (as the notion of 'intelligence' suggests). In fact, however, AI is still far from being truly 'intelligent'. Much depends on the notion of 'intelligence': if 'intelligent' is understood as finding new ways not known before, AI may be called 'intelligent', because it can detect new relationships in big data heaps that was not possible before. Moreover, AI can learn from previous errors and mistakes and improve the patterns of its program. Thus, it can be argued that the manner or method as well as the relevant conditions of creating the work are no longer within the author's sufficient control. However, AI in its present forms cannot determine the preferences or goals to achieve;[8] it is still up to the human being implementing and using the AI to define the areas of application and objectives for it. Therefore, AI systems still require human input.[9] In other words, AI may improve ways of achieving a goal but cannot change it. Hence, suggestions to qualify AI (or robots) as a new form of legal person (ePerson)[10] disregard these facts. Furthermore, they cannot answer the crucial questions of how AI could be held liable or whether and, if so, to what extent the AI (or robot) would have to be equipped with its own assets for any claims against it.[11] Thus, in all concerned legal areas, it is more a matter of how the person using the AI can be held responsible for its actions.

[5] https://en.wikipedia.org/wiki/Edmond_de_Belamy.

[6] See Communication from the European Commission, 'Artificial Intelligence for Europe' COM(2018) 237 final, p. 1, https://ec.europa.eu/transparency/regdoc/rep/1/2018/EN/COM-2018-237-F1-EN-MAIN-PART-1.PDF; for a detailed explanation of how exactly the technology behind AI works and what influence humans have on the results see J. Drexl et al., 'Technical Aspects of Artificial Intelligence: An Understanding from an Intellectual Property Law Perspective', Max Planck Institute for Innovation and Competition Research Paper Series No. 19-13, at 10–11.

[7] See also C. Hartmann et al., 'Trends and Developments in Artificial Intelligence', pp. 21–23 (summary of different definitions of AI EU Commission); H. Zech, 'Artificial Intelligence: Impact on Current Developments in IT on Intellectual Property' (2019) 12 *Gewerblicher Rechtsschutz und Urheberrecht – International Journal of European and International IP Law* 1145–1147 (detailed overview on what AI technology can do).

[8] See A. Ramalho, 'Will Robots Rule the (Artistic) World? A Proposed Model for the Legal Status of Creations by Artificial Intelligence Systems' (2017) 21 *Journal of Internet Law* 1–20 at 3–4.

[9] See J. C. Ginsburg and L. A. Budiardjo, 'Authors and Machines' (2019) 34 *Berkeley Technology Law Journal* 343–456 at 405–408; F. Hornman, 'A Robot's Right to Copyright', master's thesis, University of Tilburg (2018), pp. 16–17, http://arno.uvt.nl/show.cgi?fid=145318; EU Commission (C. Hartmann et al.), 'Trends and Developments in Artificial Intelligence', p. 28; for a slightly different weighting see Peifer, 'Roboter als Schöpfer', p. 227 (states that the human influence vanishes given the capabilities of self-learning algorithms).

[10] See European Parliament Resolution with recommendations to the Commission on Civil Law Rules on Robotics (2015/2103(INL)), OJ 2018 No. C252, 16 February 2017, 239–257; J. J. Bryson, M. E. Diamantis and T. D. Grant, 'Of, for, and by the People: The Legal Lacuna of Synthetic Persons' (2017) 25 No. 3 *Artificial Intelligence and Law* 273–291 at 277; C. Stancati and G. Gallo, 'Could an Electronic Person Exist? Robots and Personal Responsibility', in R. Giovagnoli and R. Lowe (eds.), *The Logic of Social Practices* (Cham: Springer Switzerland Nature AG, 2020), pp. 121–129; S. Müller, 'Kommt die E-Person? Auf dem Weg zum EU-Robotikrecht' (2019) 1 *Zeitschrift zum Innovations- und Technikrecht* 1; P. Krug, 'Haftung im Rahmen der Anwendung von künstlicher Intelligenz' (2020) 1 *beck.digitalx* 74–80 at 76.

[11] See T. Riehm, 'Nein zur ePerson! Gegen die Anerkennung einer digitalen Rechtspersönlichkeit' (2020) 1 *Recht und Digitalisierung* 42–48 at 44–46 (an ePerson is not suitable for closing gaps in responsibility), who states that the

18.2 PROTECTION OF AI-CREATED WORKS

18.2.1 Copyright Law

From a copyright law perspective, AI raises the question of whether works created by AI can still be considered personal intellectual creations, which is crucial for the acknowledgement of copyright protection for a work. The Berne Convention has already pointed to such a human-centred approach in Art. 2(1),[12] by using the notion of 'original works'.[13] Due to the fact that most European jurisdictions, such as the German Copyright Act (Sec. 2), require a human creation as the basis for the work, it is crucial whether a work created by an AI can still be qualified as a human-centred personal intellectual creation. Thus, the International Association for the Protection of Intellectual Property (AIPPI) concluded in a recent study that most jurisdictions reject any copyright attributed to AI-assisted works.[14]

The same is probably true for the European level.[15] At the moment, there is no general definition of the term copyrighted work to be found in the European directives. Nevertheless, the Court of Justice of the European Union (CJEU) required in the landmark decision in Infopaq the 'author's own intellectual creation' for a work to be considered original and thus copyrightable. Even though the decision concerned the interpretation of Art. 2(a) of the Information Society Directive, the Court based its reasoning on the parallel notions in other European directives, such as Articles 1(3) of Directive 91/250 (Software Directive), 3(1) of Directive 96/9 (Database Directive) and 6 of Directive 2006/116 (Photographs), thus establishing some kind of 'acquis communautaire'.[16] The CJEU further elaborated on this concept in other key decisions including *Murphy*,[17] *Painer*[18] and *Football Dataco*.[19] In this context, the Court stated that 'author's own intellectual creation' requires the author to 'express his creative ability in an original manner by making free and creative choices' and to eventually 'stamp his personal touch'.[20] Thus, the CJEU specifically points to the manner in which a work is created, as the

introduction of an ePerson is neither possible nor desirable because of massive demarcation problems in formal and material terms, its lack of economical will to survive and the difficulties concerning its assets.

[12] See D. Gervais, 'The Machine as Author', 2073–2079 (description of historical evolution of the concept of human authorship); S. Ricketson, 'The 1992 Horace S. Manges Lecture – People or Machines: The Bern Convention and the Changing Concept of Authorship' (1991) 16 *Columbia-VLA Journal of Law and the Arts* 1 (for a closer look at how the Berne Convention influenced the concept of authorship).

[13] See P. Goldstein and P. B. Hugenholtz, *International Copyright Law: Principles, Law, and Practice* (4th ed.; New York: Oxford University Press, 2019), p. 176; EU Commission (C. Hartmann et al.), 'Trends and Developments in Artificial Intelligence', p. 68; J.-M. Deltorn and F. Macrez, 'Authorship in the Age of Machine Learning and Artificial Intelligence' (2018) Center for International Property Studies (CEIPI) Research Paper No. 2018-10, pp. 8–9.

[14] See J. B. Nordemann, 'AIPPI: No Copyright Protection for AI Works without Human Input, but Related Rights Remain' (21 November 2019), *Kluwer Copyright Blog*, http://copyrightblog.kluweriplaw.com/2019/11/21/aippi-no-copyright-protection-for-ai-works-without-human-input-but-related-rights-remain/.

[15] See also Ramalho, 'Will Robots Rule the (Artistic) World?', 8–9; EU Commission (C. Hartmann et al.), 'Trends and Developments in Artificial Intelligence', p. 70; A. Lauber-Rönsberg and S. Hetmank, 'The Concept of Authorship and Inventorship under Pressure: Does Artificial Intelligence Shift Paradigms?' (2019) 14 *Journal of Intellectual Property Law & Practice* 570–579 at 573.

[16] Case C-5/08 *Infopaq International A/S* v. *Danske Dagblades Forening* [2009] ECR I-06569 Nos. 35, 37; see also R. M. Ballardini, K. He and T. Roos, 'AI-Generated Content: Authorship and Inventorship in the Age of Artificial Intelligence', in T. Pihlajarinne, J. Vesala and O. Honkkila (eds.), *Online Distribution of Content in the EU* (Cheltenham: Edward Elgar Publishing Limited, 2019), p. 123.

[17] Joined Case C-403/08 and C-429/08 *Football Association Premier League Ltd et al.* v. *QC Leisure et al.* [2011] ECR I-09083.

[18] Case C-145/10 *Eva-Maria Painer* v. *Standard Verlages GmbH et al.* [2011] ECR I-12533 Nos. 89, 92.

[19] Case C-604/10 *Football Dataco Ltd et al.*, v. *Yahoo! et al.* [2012] No. 97.

[20] Ibid., No. 38.

Court emphasizes the role of 'free and creative choices' rooted in the continental approach to copyright as an outgrowth of the author's personality.[21] The CJEU just recently affirmed this approach in the cases *Funke Medien Gruppe* and *Cofemel*.[22]

On the other hand, mere aesthetical quality does not suffice to attribute originality to a work. The CJEU has clarified in *Cofemel* that 'the circumstance that a design may generate an aesthetic effect does not, in itself, make it possible to determine whether that design constitutes an intellectual creation reflecting the freedom of choice and personality of its author, thereby meeting the requirement of originality'.[23] Moreover, according to the Court's interpretation in the *Funke Medien* case, investments in labour and skill are also not regarded as a sign of originality.[24]

The aforementioned criteria have to be taken into account when considering a possible copyright for AI-created works. Since the behaviour of AI is more or less unpredictable, the traditional 'deterministic' approach concerning the use of digital tools can no longer be applied. This approach provides that the use of software by the author (creator) could simply be attributed to the author as the outcome is basically foreseeable.[25] While this was certainly true at the time before AI was developed, the situation has changed significantly, because an author using an AI is only able to set the main preferences and goals. The situation is somehow comparable to works of art that are created using software that randomize the use of colours or other components.[26] The outcome of a work that has been essentially created by AI, however, cannot be foreseen. This is why it could be argued that the main part of the 'creativity' has not been done by the author, but by the AI. In consequence, the outcome cannot be considered to be inaugurated by a human being and thus would not be acknowledged as a copyrighted work.[27] The requirement of a 'free choice' and the 'stamp of the personality' of the author (as required by the CJEU) is lacking, because the relevant choices operated by the AI are no longer foreseeable by the author.

On the other hand, bearing in mind that AI is not (yet) 'intelligent' in a legal sense, such a perspective seems to overstate the role of creativity and the range/capabilities of AI. In other terms: since AI does not work independently but requires an author who makes use of it and who defines the framework in which the specific work shall be created, it cannot be compared to a human will. Accordingly, the CJEU stated in the *Painer* decision that it is sufficient that several ideas are combined in a creative way – even if the work is ultimately produced by a computer.[28] Hence, 'these creative choices may occur at various levels and in various phases of the creative process: conception/preparation, execution, and finalisation'.[29] Thus, there are still good arguments to attribute the work created by AI to the one who uses the AI, even though the specific

[21] H. Bøhler, 'EU Copyright Protection of Works Created by Artificial Intelligence Systems', master's thesis, University of Bergen (2017), p. 22, http://hdl.handle.net/1956/16479; see also the analysis at Guadamuz, 'Do Androids Dream of Electric Copyright?', 177–180.

[22] Case C-469/17 *Funke Medien NRW GmbH* v. *Bundesrepublik Deutschland* [2019]; Case C-683/17 *Cofemel – Sociedade de Vestuário SA* v. *G-Star Raw CV* [2019] No. 30.

[23] Case C-683/17 *Cofemel – Sociedade de Vestuário SA* v. *G-Star Raw CV* [2019] No. 54.

[24] Case C-469/17 *Funke Medien NRW GmbH* v. *Bundesrepublik Deutschland* [2019] No. 23.

[25] See Ginsburg and Budiardjo, 'Authors and Machines', 401–403.

[26] See ibid., 363–368; C. Craig and I. Kerr, 'The Death of the AI Author', Osgoode Legal Studies Research Paper (2019), pp. 1–4.

[27] Cf. M. Senftleben and L. Buijtelaar, 'Robot Creativity: An Incentive-Based Neighboring Rights Approach' (2020) 42 *European Intellectual Property Review* 797–812 at 801.

[28] Case C-145/10 *Eva-Maria Painer* v. *Standard Verlages GmbH* et al. [2011] ECR I-12533 Nos. 90 and 91.

[29] EU Commission (C. Hartmann et al.), 'Trends and Developments in Artificial Intelligence', p. 73.

outcome cannot be predicted. Thus, 'it is sufficient that the author has a general conception of the work before it is expressed, while leaving room for unintended expressive features'.[30] Finally, the act of creativity is not being limited to the conception of the work; creativity can also be found in the final redaction of a work.[31]

The following case may serve as an example. An artist decides to train an AI on paintings of Rembrandt and then the AI creates a 'new Rembrandt' work. In this case, it depends on the extent to which the artist has influenced the AI. If the artist trained the AI only on certain paintings (and not on all of them), they certainly have strong influence on the creation of the final 'AI painting'. Therefore, the work should be attributed to the artist.[32] If, however, the artist chooses to train the AI on all paintings, including even works from other painters, then their influence on the goals and the framework is significantly lower. The same result applies if the AI is independently learning from pixels, etc. and finally generates a new painting on its own.[33] Hence, the degree of control on the AI and its 'freedom' of choices seems to be more crucial than to rely upon some vague definitions of creativity. To conclude, the procedure of creating a work is decisive when it comes to the assessment of whether a copyright should be attributed to a work. Especially the degree of 'free choices' has to be considered in order to determine if there is still some creativity to be found in the AI-assisted work.[34]

If concluding from the aforementioned considerations that the AI system is able to provide for a sufficient degree of free choices, a follow-up question arises. To whom should authorship be assigned: the programmer of the AI algorithms, the provider of (training) data or the user? Here, we are confronted with scarcely any harmonization on the European level so that the jurisdiction of each member state has to be considered.[35] Once again, the degree to which the author exercises control and the specific design concerning the whole use of the AI-assisted creation of work has to be considered in the first place. This means that the person who really had the free choice and governed the creativity process has to be determined – which can also provide for joint authorship if two or more authors had been involved in the creation of the work.[36]

Following this procedure, the programmer of the AI algorithm usually has to be excluded, because AI systems are often not specifically designed to create just one type of work. Only if the AI system has been programmed for the specific purpose of creating a work, may the programmer also be considered as an author since they had 'free choice' of how to program the AI system.[37]

Regarding the input of data, both the quality of the data used and the person who decided which kind of data will be used have to be considered. In most cases, the user (like the 'author')

[30] Ibid., p. 75.

[31] Ibid., p. 80.

[32] See Guadamuz, 'Do Androids Dream of Electric Copyright?', 180.

[33] Senftleben and Buijtelaar, 'Robot Creativity', 803; EU Commission (C. Hartmann et al.), 'Trends and Developments in Artificial Intelligence', p. 84 referring to OpenAI Image GPT (17 June 2020), https://openai.com/blog/image-gpt/; for a different view see Ginsburg and Budiardjo, 'Authors and Machines', 414–416 concerning the painting machine AARON, https://en.wikipedia.org/wiki/AARON: even though AARON paints independently they consider Cohen (the programmer) as the author.

[34] See EU Commission (C. Hartmann et al.), 'Trends and Developments in Artificial Intelligence', p. 76: 'As long as the output reflects creative choices by a human being at any stage of the production process, an AI-assisted output is likely to qualify for copyright protection'; Gervais, 'The Machine as Author', 2098–2101; Ginsburg and Budiardjo, 'Authors and Machines', 408.

[35] EU Commission (C. Hartmann et al.), 'Trends and Developments in Artificial Intelligence', p. 76.

[36] Goldstein and Hugenholtz, *International Copyright Law*, p. 233.

[37] See Senftleben and Buijtelaar, 'Robot Creativity', 802; EU Commission (C. Hartmann et al.), 'Trends and Developments in Artificial Intelligence', p. 85.

will provide the relevant data and specify the use of the AI (if this AI still leaves enough free choices for the user to concretize the later-produced work).[38] If such a decisive control has been divided among programmer and user (and even more data providers), joint authorship should be considered.[39] Finally, in the specific case where the output of the AI-assisted system results in an audiovisual content, different kinds of works may be involved. Computer games may serve as an example here.[40] The output may be protected by the software directive as well as the InfoSoc Directive – with different types of authorship.[41]

18.2.2 Protection by Related Rights

Besides copyright protection, the output of AI may also be protected by related (or ancillary) rights, ranging from the protection of phonographic recordings to the just recently adopted related right for press publishers in Art. 15 Digital Single Market (DSM) Directive. Most of these related rights are not based upon human creativity but rather economic factors, such as a relevant investment or labour and skills. Hence, these related rights can often protect AI-assisted output even if there is no copyright due to the lack of human creativity.

First, the phonographic-related rights may protect AI-assisted music products. Phonographic rights are codified in Art. 9(1)(b) of the Rental and Lending Rights Directive[42] as well as Art. 2(c) and 3(2)(b) InfoSoc Directive. They do not require more than a fixation that is being defined by Art. 2 c) WIPO Performances and Phonograms Treaty (WPPT) as 'the embodiment of sounds, or of the representations thereof, from which they can be perceived, reproduced or communicated through a device'. Thus, any music data stored on a computer is covered by this definition.[43] This interpretation has been underlined by AG Szpunar in the *Pelham* case: 'Moreover, in the case of a phonogram, there is no requirement for originality, because a phonogram, unlike a work, is protected, not by virtue of its creativeness, but rather on account of the financial and organisational investment.'[44] According to the WPPT definition in Art. 2 d) a 'phonogram producer' is 'the person, or the legal entity, who or which takes the initiative and has the responsibility for the first fixation of the sounds of a performance or other sounds, or the representations of sounds'. Hence, AI-assisted music products, such as OpenAI jukebox,[45] can be considered as a phonographic right and would be assigned to the user who has taken the initiative to start the AI process.[46]

Following the same rational related rights, works like AI-assisted broadcasting or producers of (non-original) films have to be dealt with under Art. 9(1)(c) Rental and Lending Rights Directive

[38] See Denicola, 'Ex Machina', 286–287; B. E. Boyden, 'Emergent Works' (2016) 39 *Columbia Journal of Law and the Arts* 377–394 at 384–387; A. Škiljić 'When Art Meets Technology or Vice Versa: Artificial Artist from the EU Perspective' (2021) 12 *Journal of Intellectual Property, Information Technology and E-Commerce Law* at footnote 40; J. Grimmelmann, 'There's No Such Thing as a Computer-Authored Work – And It's a Good Thing, Too' (2017) 39 *Columbia Journal of Law & the Arts* 403 at 412.

[39] For a detailed discussion see Ginsburg and Budiardjo, 'Authors and Machines', 427–431.

[40] Case C-355/12 *Nintendo Co. Ltd and Others* v. *PC Box Srl and 9Net Srl* [2014].

[41] See also EU Commission (C. Hartmann et al.), 'Trends and Developments in Artificial Intelligence', p. 86.

[42] Directive 2006/115/EC of the European Parliament and of the Council of 12 December 2006 on rental right and lending right and on certain rights related to copyright in the field of intellectual property (codified version) (Rental and Lending Rights Directive), OJ 2016 L376, 27 December 2006.

[43] J. Reinbothe and S. von Lewinski, *The WIPO Treaties on Copyright: A Commentary on the WCT, the WPPT, and the BTAP* (2nd ed.; Oxford: Oxford University Press, 2015), para. 8.2.50.

[44] AG M. Szpunar, Opinion in Case C-476/17, *Pelham GmbH* v. *Hutter* [2019] No. 30.

[45] P. Dhariwal et al., 'OpenAI, Jukebox' (2020), https://openai.com/blog/jukebox.

[46] EU Commission (C. Hartmann et al.), 'Trends and Developments in Artificial Intelligence', p. 90.

and Art. 2(d) and 3(2)(c) InfoSoc Directive. Thus, all kind of videos produced by an AI system (without creativity) would be protected under the film producer right.[47]

Moreover, AI-assisted press publications benefit from the new related right for press publisher as enshrined in Art. 15 of the DSM Directive. Art. 2(4) DSM Directive defines the press publisher right as

> a collection composed mainly of literary works of a journalistic nature, but which can also include other works or other subject matter, and which: (a) constitutes an individual item within a periodical or regularly updated publication under a single title, such as a newspaper or a general or special interest magazine; (b) has the purpose of providing the general public with information related to news or other topics; and (c) is published in any media under the initiative, editorial responsibility and control of a service provider.

Once again, this related right is not based upon human creativity but rather a specific collection initiated by a press publisher. Hence, even AI-assisted news or 'robo-journalism' may be protected by this new related right.[48]

18.3 PROTECTION BY SUI GENERIS RIGHT OF THE DATABASE DIRECTIVE

The protection of AI-assisted output can be further considered under the Database Directive. The Database Directive offers special (sui generis) protection to databases that are the product of 'substantial investment'. The right applies to 'databases', a term defined by Art. 1(2) Database Directive as 'a collection of independent works, data or other materials arranged in a systematic or methodical way and individually accessible by electronic or other means'. According to Art. 7 Database Directive, an investment in the database must be 'substantial' either in a 'qualitative' and/or in a 'quantitative' sense. In most cases, the quantitative element is crucial as it is based upon what recital 40 Database Directive calls substantial 'financial resources and/or the expanding of time, effort and energy'. According to Art. 7(1) Database Directive, the substantial investment has to be made 'in either the obtaining, verification or presentation of the contents'. Whereas verification and presentation of the contents does not seem to be problematic in practice, the specification of what is meant by 'obtaining' data leads to the distinction established by the CJEU in four prominent cases. Regarding the 'creation' of data, which – according to the CJEU – should not be covered by the Database Directive,[49] it stated that 'the expression 'investment in … the obtaining … of the contents' of a database must, … be understood to refer to the resources used to seek out existing independent materials and collect them in the database, and not to the resources used for the creation as such of independent materials'.[50]

[47] Ibid., p. 91.

[48] Ibid., p. 92.

[49] Case C-46/02 *Fixtures Marketing Ltd* v. *Oy Veikkaus Ab* [2004] ECR I-10365; Case C-203/02 *The British Horseracing Board Ltd and Others* v. *William Hill Organisation Ltd* [2004] ECR I-10415; Case C-338/02 *Fixtures Marketing Ltd* v. *Svenska Spel AB* [2004] ECR I-10497; Case C-444/02 *Fixtures Marketing Ltd* v. *Organismos prognostikon agonon podosfairou AE (OPAP)* [2004] ECR I-10549.

[50] Case C-46/02 *Fixtures Marketing Ltd* v. *Oy Veikkaus AB* [2004] ECR I-10365 No. 34; Case C-203/02 *The British Horseracing Board Ltd and Others* v. *William Hill Organisation Ltd* [2004] ECR I-10415 No. 31; Case C-338/02 *Fixtures Marketing Ltd* v. *Svenska Spel AB* [2004] ECR I-10497 No. 24; Case C-444/02 *Fixtures Marketing Ltd* v. *Organismos prognostikon agonon podosfairou AE (OPAP)* [2004] ECR I-10549 No. 40.

This distinction makes it difficult to assess the protection of AI-assisted output under the Database Directive.[51] If the new data produced by the AI system is to be qualified as a creation of data, investment in AI systems would not be sufficient to render protection to the so-created database, because the system has not 'obtained' already existing data – rather than creating new data.

Moreover, the protection by the Database Directive covers the database as a structure and not the single elements of the database. As Art. 1(2) of the Database Directive defines, data or other materials collected in a database must be 'independent', which means, according to the CJEU, 'materials which are separable from one another without their informative, literary, artistic, musical or other value being affected'.[52] Hence, just raw data produced by an AI system is not being considered as a database unless this data is structured or arranged in a database.[53] Since the Database Directive just requires substantial investment, the right is assigned to the user who provided the financial resource in order to create the database, including the costs of developing and implementing AI technology.

18.3.1 Protection by Trade Secrets Directive

Even though output of the AI system is in most cases not being protected by copyright law and related rights, in most cases the newly generated data by an AI system could be qualified as a trade secret within the scope of the lately adopted EU Directive on trade secrets.[54] Art. 2 of the Trade Secrets Directive defines a trade secret as information that is secret, has commercial value because it is secret and has been subject to reasonable steps to preserve secrecy. In contrast to copyright law, recital 10 Trade Secrets Directive provides that the Directive does not introduce a right *in rem*, stating that 'in the interest of innovation and to foster competition, the provisions of this Directive should not create any exclusive right on the know-how or information protected as trade secrets'. To continue, recital 1 explicitly states that trade secrets are 'a complement or alternative to intellectual property rights', but not as such an intellectual property right.

Concerning misappropriation of trade secrets, Art. 4(2) Trade Secrets Directive defines this notion by unlawful acquisition, use or disclosure and also infringing goods. Overall, the consent of the trade secret keeper is relevant for qualifying an acquisition as unlawful. The same standard applies to unlawful use or disclosure by a person who has unlawfully acquired the trade secret or in breach of a confidentiality agreement or other duty not to disclose the trade secret (Art. 4 (3) Trade Secrets Directive). Somehow approaching a right *in rem*, these unlawful acts can extend to third parties where, at the time of acquisition, use or disclosure, the third party had actual or constructive knowledge that the trade secret was obtained directly or indirectly from another person who was using or disclosing the trade secret unlawfully (Art. 4 (4) Trade Secrets Directive).

[51] See in general M. Leistner, 'Big Data and the EU Database Directive 96/9/EC: Current Law and Potential for Reform', in S. Lohsse, R. Schulze and D. Staudenmayer (eds.), *Trading Data in the Digital Economy: Legal Concepts and Tools* (Baden-Baden: Nomos, 2017), pp. 27–30 with further references; also P. B. Hugenholtz, 'Data Property in the System of Intellectual Property Law: Welcome Guest or Misfit?', in S. Lohsse, R. Schulze and D. Staudenmayer (eds.), *Trading Data in the Digital Economy: Legal Concepts and Tools* (Baden-Baden: Nomos, 2017), pp. 86–88.

[52] Case C-444/02 *Fixtures Marketing Ltd* v. *Organismos prognostikon agonon podosfairou AE (OPAP)* [2004] ECR I-10549 No. 31.

[53] See also EU Commission (C. Hartmann et al.), 'Trends and Developments in Artificial Intelligence', p. 94.

[54] Directive (EU) 2016/943 of the European Parliament and of the Council of 8 June 2016 on the protection of undisclosed know-how and business information (trade secrets) against their unlawful acquisition, use and disclosure, OJ 2016 L157, 15 June 2016.

Regarding data that is generated by AI systems it is often evident that it has a considerable commercial value, leaving the exemptions of information without any value not being applicable.[55] The second precondition – that data has to be kept secret by reasonable means – also does not seem an unsurmountable obstacle in order to assign the quality of being a trade secret to data.[56] Regarding data created by AI systems, the exception to the protection in Art. 3 (1b) Trade Secrets Directive, which allows for re-engineering, is quite important. Thus, Art. 3 (1b) states that 'observation, study, disassembly or testing of a product or object that has been made available to the public or that is lawfully in the possession of the acquirer of the information who is free from any legally valid duty to limit the acquisition of the trade secret' is considered lawful. Hence, if another AI system produces the same output as the 'secret' AI system, the trade secret holder cannot claim for infringements against the third party.

18.3.2 Limitations in Copyright Law Order to Develop AI: Text and Datamining

As has already been pointed out, AI has to be trained with data in order to provide for adequate results.[57] The AI that created 'The Next Rembrandt', for instance, was fed with more than 300 Rembrandt paintings.[58] However, this data can be protected by copyright or other protection, such as the EU's sui generis database protection.[59] Thus, using existing paintings protected by copyright to train and teach AI without a licence or an authorization of the author would infringe the author's copyright rights – here, the right of reproduction and eventually the right of adaptation.[60] Given the fact that an AI requires an input of works in order to form a corpus that is eventually being analysed, there should be no discussion that this reproduction of works may be subject to copyright law restrictions.[61] The broad interpretation of the CJEU identifying a reproduction as any copied work or parts of a work, temporary or permanent, direct or indirect, that has the potential to infringe copyright, irrespective of how transient, short or irrelevant from an economic perspective it may be, provided that it 'contain[s] elements which are the expression of the intellectual creation of the author of the work', has to be taken into account as

55 See for those exemptions T. Aplin, 'Trading Data in the Digital Economy: Trade Secrets Perspective', in S. Lohsse, R. Schulze and D. Staudenmayer (eds.), *Trading Data in the Digital Economy: Legal Concepts and Tools* (Baden-Baden: Nomos, 2017), pp. 65–66.

56 Ibid., p. 67.

57 See E. Rosati, 'Copyright as an Obstacle or an Enabler? A European Perspective on Text and Data Mining and Its Role in the Development of AI Creativity' (2019) 27 *Asia Pacific Law Review* 198 at 199, 204–210; T. Chiou, 'Copyright Lessons on Machine Learning: What Impact on Algorithmic Art?' (2020) 10 *Journal of Intellectual Property, Information Technology and E-Commerce Law* 398 at 399.

58 See 'The Next Rembrandt', www.nextrembrandt.com; see also Guadamuz, 'Do Androids Dream of Electric Copyright?', 180.

59 Directive 96/9/EC of the European Parliament and of the Council of 11 March 1996 on the legal protection of databases, OJ 1996 L 77, 27 March 1996.

60 See M. Iglesias, S. Shamuilia and A. Anderberg, *Intellectual Property and Artificial Intelligence* (Luxembourg: Publications Office of the European Union, 2019), p. 10; J.-P. Triaille, J. de Meeûs d'Argenteuil and A. de Francquen, 'Study on the Legal Framework of Text and Data Mining (TDM)', Study funded by the European Commission, Publications Office of the European Union, European Union (2014), pp. 85–88; C. Geiger, G. Frosio and O. Bulayenko, 'The Exception for Text and Data Mining (TDM) in the Proposed Directive on Copyright in the Digital Single Market – Legal Aspects' (2018), Centre for International Intellectual Property Studies (CEIPI) Research Paper No. 2018-02, pp. 7–8.

61 See T. Margoni, 'Artificial Intelligence, Machine Learning and EU Copyright Law: Who Owns AI?' (2018), CREATe Working Paper 2018/12, pp. 17–20; see also M. Mazzone and A. Elgammal, 'Art, Creativity and the Potential of Artificial Intelligence' (2019) 8 No. 26 *Arts* 1–9 at 4; Rosati, 'Copyright as an Obstacle or an Enabler?' 199, 204–210; Chiou, 'Copyright Lessons on Machine Learning', 402–404.

well.[62] Hence, AI systems either require a licence of the right holder or a limitation in order to use data provided by the right holder and to train the AI system. Regarding EU copyright law, two EU directives are relevant – the InfoSoc Directive[63] and the DSM Directive[64] in connection with its provisions on Text and Data Mining (TDM).

The first limitation concerns the so-called ephemeral and temporary reproductions. In this regard, Art. 5 (1) of the InfoSoc Directive provides limitations in respect of temporary acts of reproduction, 'which are transient or incidental [and] an integral and essential part of a technological process and whose sole purpose is to enable: (a) a transmission in a network between third parties by an intermediary, or (b) a lawful use of a work or other subject-matter to be made, and which have no independent economic significance'. While this concept has been further interpreted by the CJEU,[65] it does not seem to be very helpful for the purpose of AI and use of data[66] as the applicability of the limitation depends on the temporary nature of the reproduction – which does usually not fit for text- and datamining as these processes require longer-lasting reproductions and modifications of the original data[67] although some reproductions, which occur during the AI learning and training process, might fall under this exception.[68]

More promising are the new limitations introduced by Arts. 3 and 4 DSM Directive, which both allow for text- and datamining. The provisions strictly distinguish between text- and datamining related to the purposes of scientific research, where reproductions are made by research organizations and cultural heritage institutions (Art. 3 DSM-D)[69] and the exception for text- and datamining for all other purposes (Art. 4 DSM-D). However, the latter one – allowing text- and datamining for all other purposes – is under the condition that right holders have not expressly reserved the use of their works in an appropriate manner,[70] the so-called opt-out option.[71] To some extent the practical problem for an AI system to find out automatically if a

62 Case C-5/08 *Infopaq International A/S* v. *Danske Dagblades Forening* [2009] ECR I-06569 No. 42 and 38–39; Chiou, 'Copyright Lessons on Machine Learning', 401.

63 Directive 2001/29/EC of the European Parliament and of the Council of 22 May 2001 on the harmonisation of certain aspects of copyright and related rights in the information society, OJ 2001 L167, 22 June 2001.

64 Directive (EU) 2019/790 of the European Parliament and of the Council of 17 April 2019 on copyright and related rights in the Digital Single Market and amending Directives 96/9/EC and 2001/29/EC, OJ 2019 L130, 15 May 2019.

65 Case C-5/08 Infopaq International, No. 55-59 and 64. The Court stated that the exception of Art. 5 (1) InfoSoc Directive must be interpreted strictly and in the light of the need for legal certainty for authors with regard to the protection of their works and determined that 'an act can held to be "transient" only if its duration is limited to what is necessary for the proper completion of the technological process in question, it being understood that that process must be automated so that it deletes that act automatically, without human intervention, once its function of enabling the completion of such a process has come to an end' (No. 64).

66 See D. Schönberger, 'Deep Copyright: Up- and Downstream Questions Related to Artificial Intelligence (AI) and Machine Learning (ML)', in J. de Werra (ed.), *Droit d'auteur 4.0 / Copyright 4.0* (Geneva; Zurich: Schulthess Editions Romandes), pp. 145–173.

67 See R. Hilty and H. Richter, 'Position Statement of the Max Planck Institute for Innovation and Competition on the Proposed Modernisation of European Copyright Rules Part B Exceptions and Limitations (Art. 3 – Text and Data Mining)' (2017), Max Planck Institute for Innovation & Competition Research Paper No. 17-02, p. 2; see also Chiou, 'Copyright lessons on Machine Learning', 406.

68 See Margoni, 'Artificial Intelligence, Machine Learning and EU Copyright Law', 18–19.

69 Directive (EU) 2019/790 of the European Parliament and of the Council of 17 April 2019 on copyright and related rights in the Digital Single Market and amending Directives 96/9/EC and 2001/29/EC, OJ 2019 L130, 17 June 2019, Art. 3.

70 See Geiger et al., 'The Exception for Text and Data Mining'.

71 Chiou, 'Copyright lessons on Machine Learning', 409.

right holder has opted out[72] is solved by Art. 4 (3) DSM-D, requiring a machine-readable licence (or opt-out) for content made publicly available online.

Since the text- and datamining limitations cover reproductions made for the purpose of creating something new (be it data or a work) and the DSM-D explicitly acknowledges this technology,[73] there should be no discussion if a work produced by text- and datamining technology undermines the – non-harmonized – right of adaptation of a work.[74] Even though the EU member states' concepts and legal regimes of the right of adaptation differ,[75] the output of an AI-driven system using big data of text- and datamining can no longer be considered as an adaptation of the former works, because the AI just gathers different elements out of the provided data – but does not modify the former work.[76]

One way of how to cope with the dilemma that, on the one hand the access of AI to training data should not be limited, while on the other hand traditional markets for works should not be hampered (and overflooded) by AI-created works, could consist of resorting to collective licensing. This may also be an option in order to cope with the issue that licences may not be obtained automatically.[77]

18.3.3 *Protection of AI Algorithms and AI Systems*

The other relevant aspect from a copyright law perspective regards the protection of AI itself. Under the current legal framework, it is not the AI as a concept or as an algorithm that cannot be protected[78] rather the AI as a code on the grounds of the EU Software Directive.[79] Moreover, data that is being used for training the AI is not protected as such, only if the AI is trained on data stemming from a database. In this case the structure of the database is being protected under the EU database directive.

18.4 PROTECTION OF AI WORKS *DE LEGE FERENDA*

Regarding future possible developments, the situation may change significantly if an AI is actually able to set goals on its own and to 'consciously' deviate from the owner's preferences.

[72] See Rosati, 'Copyright as an Obstacle or an Enabler?', 214 and 217; see also Chiou, 'Copyright Lessons on Machine Learning', 409.

[73] See recitals 8, 18 DSM-D.

[74] Compare Škiljić, 'When Art Meets Technology or Vice Versa' at footnote 67.

[75] See M. Hebette et al., 'Copyright Law of the EU, Salient Features of Copyright Law across the EU Member States' (2018), European Parliamentary Research Service Comparative Law Library Unit, www.europarl.europa.eu/RegData/etudes/STUD/2018/625126/EPRS_STU(2018)625126_EN.pdf.

[76] In Germany, the relevant demarcation criterion is that in the new work the personal design of the author of the used work has remained recognizable but has sunk to insignificance considering the power of individuality of the new work. This means that in light of the uniqueness of the new work, the borrowed personal features of the protected older work 'fade' and therefore have to recede in such a way that the older one only shines through in the new work weakly and in a manner that is no longer relevant to copyright. See, e.g., Federal Court of Justice (BGH) judgment of 20 November 2009, I ZR 112/06, *Metall auf Metall* and judgment of 20 December 2007, I ZR 42/05, *TV-Total* with more references; also H. Ahlberg and H.-P. Götting (eds.), *Beck'scher Online-Kommentar Urheberrecht* (13 vols.; Munich: Verlag C. H. Beck, 2016), vol. 13, § 24 paras. 3–4.

[77] See Škiljić, 'When Art Meets Technology or Vice Versa' at footnote 78.

[78] Iglesias et al., *Intellectual Property and Artificial Intelligence*, p. 8.

[79] Directive (EU) 2009/24/EC of the European Parliament and of the Council of 23 April 2009 on the legal protection of computer programs, OJ 2009 L111, 5 May 2009.

Even though this vision – admittedly – still seems far away as some sort of science fiction, there would be a need for action at the legal level as a result of the corresponding developments. This especially includes ideas like the introduction of new forms of legal persons because the activities and works of an AI will no longer be attributed to the 'author'. Moreover, regarding the protection of data used for training the AI as well as the data generated by the AI, it is arguable whether protection as a trade secret may be sufficient as trade secrets do not render a right *in rem* to data.

On the other side, new developments in informatics make it likely that data and its use may be traced, so that boundaries and limits of the use of data may be controlled by technological means. Thus, the need for introduction of legal property rights may not be necessary, because technological tools could be quite efficient and flank contractual provisions. Therefore, the problem of data property rights[80] remains unresolved, while technological solutions would not be sufficient in this respect (i.e. to solve the problem).[81] In addition, business-to-business platforms seem to be established by means of standard terms of conditions.

Furthermore, the traditional justifications for assigning copyright protection to an author of the work, which are largely based on personality theories,[82] obviously do not fit the situation where an AI system 'created' the work.[83] Given the fact that the AI lacks personality, there is no legitimation on grounds of protecting the emanation of the personality.[84] However, this would not preclude an acknowledgement of a copyright to AI-assisted works as these theories just apply to a human-driven work but do not say anything about other manners of creating a work. The example of the common-law copyright 'works-made-for-hire' demonstrates a similar approach, even though there are still differences regarding the person to whom to assign the authorship, the programmer[85] or the user.[86] More convincing in this context is the argument that if AI-assisted works could not benefit from copyright protection, the incentives for human-authors would diminish, because in the markets AI-assisted works would be preferred due to their lower prices.[87] However, this could be also taken as an argument for introducing copyright protection for AI-assisted works in order to establish a level playing field.[88]

[80] See the criticism on property rights assigned to data of Hugenholtz, 'Data Property in the System of Intellectual Property Law', pp. 80–100.

[81] See also EU Data Governance Act, introducing in Chapter III criteria for reliable data intermediaries: Proposal for a Regulation of the European Parliament and of the Council on European data governance (Data Governance Act), 25 November 2020 COM (2020) 767 final; more in depth and with further evidence G. Spindler, 'Schritte zur europaweiten Datenwirtschaft – Der Vorschlag einer Verordnung zur europäischen Data Governance' (2021) 37 *Computer und Recht* 98–108.

[82] For a short overview see R. Hilty, J. Hoffmann and S. Scheuerer, 'Intellectual Property Justification for Artificial Intelligence', in J.-A. Lee, R. Hilty and K.-C. Liu (eds.), *Artificial Intelligence and Intellectual Property* (Oxford: Oxford University Press BPS, 2021), pp. 4–6; see also Ramalho, 'Will Robots Rule the (Artistic) World?', 14–15.

[83] See Ballardini et al., 'AI-Generated Content', p. 127 et seq. (different approaches to address this problem).

[84] See Hilty et al., 'Intellectual Property Justification for Artificial Intelligence', pp. 7–9; Senftleben and Buijtelaar, 'Robot Creativity', 806.

[85] See A. Bridy, 'The Evolution of Authorship: Work Made by Code' (2016) 39 *Columbia Journal of Law & Arts* 395–401 at 400–401; A. Bridy, 'Coding Creativity: Copyright and the Artificially Intelligent Author' (2012) 5 *Stanford Technology Law Review* 1–28 at 26–27.

[86] Denicola, 'Ex Machina', 284–285.

[87] D. Schönberger, 'Deep Copyright: Up- and Downstream Questions Related to Artificial Intelligence (AI) and Machine Learning (ML)' (2018) 10 *Zeitschrift für geistiges Eigentum* 35–58 at 46.

[88] Gervais, 'The Machine as Author', 2067, 2092–2094; Hilty et al., 'Intellectual Property Justification for Artificial Intelligence', p. 11.

Even the utilitarian approach[89] would not plead for protection of AI-assisted output as the machine has no need for incentives in order to be creative[90] – rather than the user of AI. While it has been argued that programmers of AI should have an incentive to code AI if the AI-assisted products/works would be copyrighted,[91] it is fair to recall that in general the output of a software is not being protected by copyright as such.[92] The incentive for programmers to code an AI system lies within the copyright of the program itself, rather than the output. Hence, proposals of introducing a related right in order to protect AI-assisted output concentrate more on incentives for users to make AI-assisted output available to the public.[93]

However, even if we apply the investment protection theory used for justifying copyrights, it is highly arguable if that theory fits AI-assisted works as the accent lies upon AI-specific data and training and not upon copyrights for AI outputs.[94] Moreover, copyrights for AI outputs may result in a lowering of innovation since other AI systems may produce the same results, leaving markets no longer efficient in attributing the scarce resources to innovative systems. As Hilty et al. stated: 'Indeed, once the substitution of AI products or services happens with such speed that investments could not be recouped despite [intellectual property] protection in place, any [intellectual property] right would be detrimental to economic welfare and not justifiable.'[95]

However, as long as contractual and technological remedies are available that are more flexible, and as long as there is no evidence of market failure, statutory regulation in the area of copyright should not be undertaken. This is especially so since the limits and restrictions of such an exclusive right would then have to be defined to strike a balance between freedom of access to data on the one hand and property rights on the other.[96] It is not surprising that proponents of an ancillary copyright (or related right), such as the related right of press publishers, call for the right to be limited in time and scope.[97] In summary, there is currently not a need for legislative activism when it comes to extending or modifying copyright protection. Nevertheless, both the developments of AI and the way data is being traded and protected by contractual terms should be closely monitored.[98]

89 See for a general incentive approach T. W. Dornis, 'Der Schutz künstlicher Intelligenz im Immaterialgüterrecht' (2019) *Gewerblicher Rechtsschutz und Urheberrecht* 1252–1264 at 1258 et seq.; S. Hetmank and A. Lauber-Rönsberg, 'Künstliche Intelligenz – Herausforderungen für das Immaterialgüterrecht' (2018) *Gewerblicher Rechtsschutz und Urheberrecht* 574–582 at 579; however, this approach is too general and has to be specified in such a way that the general investment should be protected or incentivized – see Hilty et al., 'Intellectual Property Justification for Artificial Intelligence', p. 16.

90 Ramalho, 'Will Robots Rule the (Artistic) World?', 15; Schönberger, 'Deep Copyright' (see note 87), 46.

91 Hetmank and Lauber-Rönsberg, 'Künstliche Intelligenz', 579; see also Dornis, 'Der Schutz künstlicher Intelligenz im Immaterialgüterrecht', 1258 et seq.

92 See Hilty et al., 'Intellectual Property Justification for Artificial Intelligence', p. 17.

93 Ramalho, 'Will Robots Rule the (Artistic) World?', 19; in the same direction Senftleben and Buijtelaar, 'Robot Creativity', 707–708.

94 For a more in-depth analysis see Hilty et al., 'Intellectual Property Justification for Artificial Intelligence', p. 21.

95 Ibid., p. 22.

96 See Hugenholtz, 'Data Property in the System of Intellectual Property Law', pp. 94–96 (discussion of data property rights in general in balance with free flow of information); L. Bently, 'The UK's Provisions on Computer Generated Works: A Solution for AI Creations?', University of Cambridge, presentation delivered at the ECS International Conference 'EU Copyright, Quo Vadis? From the EU Copyright Package to the Challenges of Artificial Intelligence' (25 May 2018), https://europeancopyrightsocietydotorg.files.wordpress.com/2018/06/lionel-the-uk-provisions-on-computer-generated-works.pdf.

97 Senftleben and Buijtelaar, 'Robot Creativity', 811–812.

98 See also EU Commission (C. Hartmann et al.), 'Trends and Developments in Artificial Intelligence', p. 95.

PART VI

Ethical Framework for AI

19

AI, Consumer Data Protection and Privacy

Mateja Durovic and Jonathon Watson[*]

19.1 INTRODUCTION

Consumer data has become a driving force in the digital economy, leading to new and innovative products and services with the potential to improve individual well-being in all facets of everyday life. In light of the rapid technological developments and of course the impact of the Covid-19 pandemic on living life in the digital world, the 2018 prediction that by the year 2025 each person will have approximately 5,000 data interactions daily may well be reached much sooner.[1] Nonetheless, as the number of data interactions increases, so too do the insights into ever more intimate aspects of one's daily life, behaviour and personality.

Among the various products and services, one innovative advancement in the world of data-driven technology stands out as deserving particular attention: the capability to infer emotions from (personal) data and to use such information to respond to an individual's needs on a highly intimate level. Whereas the technology has considerable potential, it is controversial not least due to the highly sensitive and private nature of emotions but also due to its questionable reliability as well as potential adverse effects. Its application by public authorities is already viewed as a serious cause for concern in relation to fundamental rights, prompting calls in some jurisdictions to ban or restrict the use of the technology.[2]

Describing 'the battle to control, influence or manipulate emotions' as undoubtedly 'one of the key battles of the 21st century' succinctly illustrates the significance of emotions and their role in creating new power and information asymmetries that are to be frowned upon.[3] In this chapter we focus on the consumer context, though due to the data-driven nature of the technology, the role of data protection cannot be ignored. Following a brief insight into the notion of emotional AI, we indicate that the legal classification of emotions under EU data

[*] This contribution was completed as part of the National (UK) Research Centre on Privacy, Harm Reduction and Adversarial Influence Online (REPHRAIN).

[1] IDC, 'The Digitization of the World' (November 2018), www.seagate.com/files/www-content/our-story/trends/files/idc-seagate-dataage-whitepaper.pdf (last accessed 16 February 2022), pp. 5–6, 13, also including statistics on the staggering amount of consumer data in the global datasphere.

[2] See Commonwealth of Massachusetts, 'Act to establish a moratorium on face recognition and other remote biometric surveillance systems', Bill S.1385 191st (2019–2020), in which the inference of emotions is expressly acknowledged. The EU 'Proposal for a Regulation on a European approach for Artificial Intelligence' COM(2021) 206 final classifies emotion detection as 'high risk AI' when used for law enforcement and migrations, asylum and border control management; see Annex III to the proposal.

[3] V. Šucha and J.-P. Gammel, 'Humans and Societies in the Age of Artificial Intelligence' (2021), European Commission report, p. 18.

protection law is a grey area, before highlighting particular concerns in relation to the technology. With reference to the recent EU proposal for an Artificial Intelligence Act[4] (AIA), the chapter focuses on how instruments in EU consumer law and could alleviate certain asymmetries in power and information, and thereby not only shine some light on the grey areas of EU data protection but also allow for emotional AI to serve consumer needs.

19.2 EMOTIONAL AI

This section will examine the different elements and issues related to emotional AI including the legal status of emotions, surveillance and interrogation, discrimination and decisional interference.

19.2.1 *Overview*

The expression 'emotional AI' is often used in conjunction with affective computing – a term coined in 1995 for 'computing that relates to, arises from, or influences emotions'.[5] Emotional AI refers to the use of affective computing together with AI – via predetermined rules or Big Data analytics – in order to 'sense, learn about, and interact with human emotional life'.[6] A diverse range of sensors capture the data needed to fuel the AI machine, allowing for inferences about an individual's emotional state to be drawn at a level and pace beyond human capabilities.[7] Using such inferences, the emotion can be interpreted as well as its meaning in a particular context and thereby prompt the requisite response.

An individual's emotions can be inferred from various sources, not least facial expressions and voice as the two common forms of sentic modulation.[8] Words and images, gaze and gestures, gait and physiological responses (such as heart rate, blood pressure, respiratory patterns, body temperature, skin conductance and pupillary dilation) as well as the physical interaction with the device itself (through the force exerted) also provide the data from which inferences can be drawn.[9] It is prudent at this juncture to note that the AIA expressly includes emotion recognition systems within its framework, defined as an AI system 'for the purpose of identifying or inferring emotions or intentions of natural persons on the basis of their biometric data' (Art. 3 No. 34 AIA). In turn, the notion of biometric data is in line with and should be interpreted consistently with

[4] COM(2021) 206 final.

[5] R. W. Picard, 'Affective Computing' (1995), MIT Media Laboratory Perceptual Computing Section Technical Report No. 21, 1.

[6] See https://emotionalai.org/so-what-is-emotional-ai/ (last accessed 12 April 2021); Bundestag (Enquete-Kommission Künstliche Intelligenz), 'Gesellschaftliche Verantwortung und wirtschaftliche, soziale und ökologische Potenziale', BT-Drs 19/23700, p. 299.

[7] Picard, 'Affective Computing', 14; Šucha and Gammel, 'Humans and Societies', p. 17.

[8] Picard, 'Affective Computing', 5.

[9] See the summaries in J. Kröger, 'Unexpected Inferences from Sensor Data: A Hidden Privacy Threat in the Internet of Things', in L. Strous and V. Cerf (eds.), *Internet of Things: Information Processing in an Increasingly Connected World* (Basel: Springer, 2018), p. 147 at 151: J. Kröger and P. Rascke, 'Privacy Implications of Accelerometer Data: A Review of Possible Inferences', in *Proceedings of the 3rd International Conference on Cryptography, Security and Privacy* (2019), p. 81; J. Kröger et al., 'What Does Your Gaze Reveal about You? On the Privacy Implications of Eye Tracking', in M. Friedewald et al. (eds.), *Privacy and Identity Management* (Basel: Springer, 2020), p. 226 at 233; J. Kröger et al., 'Privacy Implications of Voice and Speech Analysis – Information Disclosure by Inference', in M. Friedewald et al. (eds.), *Privacy and Identity Management* (Basel: Springer, 2020), p. 242 at 245; A. McStay and G. Rosner, 'Emotional Artificial Intelligence in Children's Toys and Devices: Ethics, Governance and Practical Remedies' (2021) 8(1) *Big Data & Society* 1; Picard, 'Affective Computing', 5; S. Xu et al., 'Emotion Recognition from Gait Analyses: Current Research and Future Directions' (2020), available at https://arxiv.org/abs/2003.11461.

the notion of biometric data under the General Data Protection Regulation (GDPR) (Art. 4 No. 14).[10] According to the AIA and GDPR biometric data are personal data resulting from specific technical processing relating to the physical, physiological or behavioural characteristics of a natural person and may include facial structure, voice, retinal patterns but also keystrokes or gait.[11] Although extensive, the definition does not appear to include inferences drawn from text analysis; whether the physical interaction with the device could fall under the definition, for example as analogous to keystrokes, will remain to be seen.

Research into the various technologies also concludes that the interferences acquired from the data cover not just the emotion itself but also the intensity.[12] Analysis of an individual's gait can result in inferences on emotions such as happiness, sadness, anger and fear; by comparison, analysis of voice data can detect additional emotions and states such as friendliness, impatience, compassion, anxiousness and astonishment.[13] Although considerable doubt has been cast on the accuracy of such systems, in particular facial expression detection, improvements are nonetheless to be expected as the volume and range of information about emotions increase.[14]

19.2.2 *Legal Status of Emotions*

In their seminal paper on the 'right to privacy' Warren and Brandeis express that '[t]he common law secures to each individual the right of determining, ordinarily, to what extent his thoughts, sentiments, and emotions shall be communicated to others', irrespective of the nature, value or means of expression.[15] In the 130 years since, rich scholarly debates in different disciplines as well as judicial and legislative developments have shaped the contours and purpose of the individual's 'right to privacy', not least its relationship to data protection, albeit with intra- and interjurisdictional variations.[16] On a broader plane, the right to privacy centres on upholding the core values of 'individuality, autonomy, integrity and dignity' by protecting the individual against outside intrusions, with data protection serving to protect the individual's control over their personal data and thus the 'selective presentation' of the different facets of their personality.[17] Neither are absolute rights, but provide the starting point for the legally permissible incursions.

[10] COM(2021) 206 final, recital 7.

[11] See Article 29 Working Party (WP), 'Opinion 4/2007 on the concept of personal data' (June 2007), p. 8.

[12] It is to be noted that there is no consensus on the precise number of emotions. Plutchik's 'Wheel of Emotions' sets out eight primary emotions: anger, fear, sadness, disgust, surprise, anticipation, trust and joy; see R. Plutchik, *The Emotions* (New York: University Press of America, 1991). On the intensity of emotions via gaze detection see Kröger et al., 'What Does Your Gaze Reveal about You?', p. 233 with further references.

[13] Kröger et al., 'Privacy Implications of Voice and Speech Analysis', p. 245; Xu et al., 'Emotion Recognition from Gait Analyses', 11.

[14] Compare L. F. Barrett et al., 'Emotional Expressions Reconsidered: Challenges to Inferring Emotion from Human Facial Movements (2019) 20(1) *Psychological Science in the Public Interest* 1.

[15] S. Warren and L. Brandeis, 'The Right to Privacy' (1890) 4(5) *Harvard Law Review* 193, 198–199.

[16] See B. van der Sloot, *Privacy as Virtue: Moving beyond the Individual in the Age of Big Data* (Cambridge: Intersentia, 2017), pp. 11 et seq.

[17] See O. Lynskey, 'Deconstructing Data Protection: The "Added-Value" of a Right to Data Protection in the EU Legal Order' (2014) 63 *International and Comparative Law Quarterly* 569, 590–591; S. Wachter and B. Mittelstadt, 'A Right to Reasonable Inferences: Re-thinking Data Protection Law in the Age of Big Data and AI' (2019) 2 *Columbia Business Law Review* 1, 81 with further references.

For emotions, concealment and protection from exposure safeguards human dignity, protecting a person's ability to participate in society and their personal development.[18] Such objectives are also echoed in the role of 'psychological privacy' and in a recent call for a 'right to mental self-determination' as a novel and distinct human right surrounding one's mental integrity and reflecting the autonomy over the privacy of one's mental state.[19] Nonetheless, the value and necessity of a separate such right in the EU has been disputed due to the potential for emotions to be subsumed under other fundamental rights under the EU Charter of Fundamental Rights, not least privacy (Art. 7 Charter) and data protection (Art. 8 Charter).[20]

In its past decisions, the Court of Justice of the European Union (CJEU) has held that an interference with the right to privacy does not depend on the sensitivity of the information or the inconvenience caused.[21] However, as privacy and data protection are not absolute rights, the degree of interference permitted by law as well as the corresponding safeguards can depend on the sensitivity of the information/data at stake. The EU proposal for an ePrivacy Regulation states that the content of electronic communications may reveal 'highly sensitive information', using this term not only for medical conditions, sexual preferences and political views but also emotions.[22] However, in relation to the 'global gold standard' in data protection – the EU GDPR[23] – several commentators have observed that the GDPR may not even apply in situations in which natural persons remain anonymous, yet inferences are drawn about their emotional state using, for example, facial detection.[24] More fundamentally, the disruptive effect of AI and Big Data analytics in testing the boundaries of the Regulation, and indeed this chapter, has shown that the GDPR also lacks legal certainty in relation to its protection of emotions in line with what ought to be expected for such 'highly sensitive' personal data.[25]

[18] See D. Solove, 'A Taxonomy of Privacy' (2006) 154(3) *University of Pennsylvania Law Review* 477, 534. See also Bundesverfassungsgericht, Order of 6 November 2019 – 1 BvR 16/13, summary in English in 'Press Release No. 83/2019 of 27 November 2019', at II.1.a).

[19] See J.-C. Bublitz, 'The Nascent Right to Psychological Integrity and Mental Self-Determination', in A. von Arnauld, K. von der Decken and M. Susi (eds.), *The Cambridge Handbook of New Human Rights* (Cambridge: Cambridge University Press, 2020), p. 385; J. Burgoon et al., 'Maintaining and Restoring Privacy through Communication in Different Types of Relationships' (1989) 6 *Journal of Social and Personal Relationships* 131, 133–134.

[20] S. Michalowski, 'Critical Reflections on the Need for a Right to Mental Self-Determination', in A. von Arnauld, K. von der Decken and M. Susi (eds.), *The Cambridge Handbook of New Human Rights* (Cambridge: Cambridge University Press, 2020), p. 404.

[21] CJEU, Joined Cases C-465/00, C-138/01 and C-139/01 Österreichischer Rundfunk ECLI:EU:C:2003:294, para. 75; CJEU, Joined Cases C-293/12 and C-594/12 Digital Rights Ireland ECLI:EU:C:2014:238, para. 33.

[22] See Proposal for Regulation of the European Parliament and of the Council concerning the respect for private life and the protection of personal data in electronic communications and repealing Directive 2002/58/EC COM(2017) 10 final, recital 2.

[23] Regulation (EU) 2016/679 of the European Parliament and of the Council of 27 April 2016 on the protection of natural persons with regard to the processing of personal data and on the free movement of such data, OJ 2016 No. L119/1.

[24] On the discussion surrounding identifiability in relation to the practice of profiling see M. Galič and R. Gellert, 'Data Protection Law Beyond Identifiability? Atmospheric Profiles, Nudging and the Stratumseind Living Lab' (2021) 40 *Computer Law & Security Review* Article 105486 at 10–11, with further references.

[25] For an extensive analysis see D. Clifford, 'The Legal Limits to the Monetisation of Online Emotions', PhD thesis, KU Leuven (2019), pp. 149 et seq.; also G. Sartor, 'The Impact of the General Data Protection Regulation (GDPR) on Artificial Intelligence' (June 2020), p. iii and p. 74 at 4.2.2; Wachter and Mittelstadt, 'A Right to Reasonable Inferences', 1. See also A. McStay, 'The Right to Privacy in the Age of Emotional AI', Report to the OHCHR (2018), www.ohchr.org/Documents/Issues/DigitalAge/ReportPrivacyinDigitalAge/AndrewMcStayProfessor%20of%20Digital%20Life,%20BangorUniversityWalesUK.pdf (last accessed 16 February 2022); A. McStay, 'Emotional AI, Soft Biometrics and the Surveillance of Emotional Life: An Unusual Consensus on Privacy' (2020) 7(1) *Big Data & Society* 1–12.

The information about an individual's emotional state is ultimately automated inferences drawn from the data provided and the statistical similarities with a particular quality (profiling).[26] In addition to the debate surrounding the scope of 'personal data' and its criteria of 'identifiability', the question of protections and limitations surrounding inferred data have been identified as areas where clarification is necessary in general.[27] For emotions, the grey area lies in their classification as special category data pursuant to Art. 9 GDPR (and Art. 22 GDPR on profiling) and thus the scope of the prohibitions and safeguards that the GDPR requires for such types of personal data. The status as special category data, for instance, places additional requirements on the legal bases for processing, such as a higher threshold for consent (explicit consent[28]) and its exceptions. In particular, pursuant to Art. 22(4) GDPR, the process of automated individual decision-making, including profiling, shall not be based on special categories of personal data under Art. 9(1) GDPR unless there is explicit consent and suitable measures to safeguard the data subject's rights and freedoms and legitimate interests are in place. For personal data that does not constitute special category data, the data controller may rely on a broader range of legal bases, which may not necessarily require consent by the data subject, for example where automated decision-making or profiling is necessary for entering into, or performance of, a contract between the data subject and a data controller (Art. 22(2)(a) GDPR), thus circumventing the consent requirement and the control consent affords the individual over their personal data.

Whereas recital 51 GDPR acknowledges that '[p]ersonal data which are, by their nature, particularly sensitive in relation to fundamental rights and freedoms merit specific protection as the context of their processing could create significant risks to the fundamental rights and freedoms', emotions are not listed as an express category of special category personal data under Art. 9 GDPR. Biometric data (Art. 4 No. 14 GDPR) constitutes a protected class of personal data, yet the scope of Art. 9(1) GDPR *only* extends to such data insofar as it is used for the purpose of uniquely identifying a natural person; the use of biometric data for any other purpose, including inferences about an individual's emotional state, would not fall under this exception.[29] At first glance, subsuming emotions under 'health data' may provide an escape route. Art. 29 WP has noted that *emotional capacity* has – prior to the GDPR – fallen under the notion of 'health data', with the raw sensor data potentially constituting health data when there is an intention to evaluate them as such,[30] but as Clifford highlights in his extensive analysis of the GDPR, the methods of detection may stretch the boundaries of health data thus challenging the extent to which emotions are classified and protected under data protection law; an analysis of the purpose may prove a preferable approach for which consumer law could offer clarity.[31]

[26] See Art. 29 WP, 'Guidelines on Automated individual decision-making and Profiling for the purposes of Regulation 2016/679' (February 2018), pp. 6–7. See Chapter 10 in this book.

[27] Sartor, 'The Impact of the General Data Protection Regulation (GDPR)', p. iii–iv.

[28] For details see Art. 29 WP, 'Guidelines on consent under Regulation 2016/679' (November 2017), pp. 18–19; European Data Protection Board (EDPB), 'Guidelines 05/2020 on consent under Regulation 2016/679' (May 2020), pp. 20–22.

[29] See the comments on Art. 9(1) GDPR by T. Petri, in S. Simitis, G. Hornung and I. Speicker (eds.), *Datenschutzrecht* (Baden-Baden: Nomos, 2019), mn. 14.

[30] Article 29 WP, 'Annex – Health Data in Apps and Devices, to the Letter to European Commission' (5 February 2015), copy available under www.technethics.com/assets/20150205_letter_art29wp_ec_health_data_after _plenary_annex_en-In-a-world-of-fitness-apps-it-is-important-to-know-what-is-health-data-and-how-should-they-be-processed-WP29–02.05.15.pdf (last accessed 29 April 2021). See also A. McStay, V. Bakir and L. Urquhart, 'Emotion Recognition: Trends, Social Feeling, Policy' (APPG Briefing Paper, June 2020), p. 6, who note that emotions *might* qualify as health data, but only under narrow circumstances. See also Petri, ibid., mn. 12.

[31] See Clifford, 'The Legal Limits to the Monetisation of Online Emotions', pp. 191, 199–200.

19.2.3 *Applications and Issues*

Emotional AI is in a state of relative infancy, yet the technology is growing in its application in consumer goods and services. New levels of personalization and understanding of consumer behaviour allow for the interaction between humans and technology as well as interpersonal relationships to take on a new dimension in the digital transformation of society.[32] For example, by applying voice analysis at the automated stage of customer service hotlines, 'angry' customers may be redirected to a human operator who, with the support of AI, can receive real-time information on how to manage the conversation and how to best engage with the caller.[33] Emotional AI in vehicles can contribute to improving road safety by responding to indicators of driver tiredness or aggression.[34] Toys or computer games can respond to frustrations by adjusting difficulty levels. Streaming services as well as voice assistants can recommend content based on the user's emotional state of mind.[35] More novel applications include emotion detection devices to assist autistic persons in their daily lives, or devices that monitor the user's heart and respiratory rates and release a calming or uplifting scent in response to the emotion inferred.[36] Despite the potential for emotional AI to greatly improve human well-being, there are a number of issues surrounding the technology that not only question its effectiveness in practice but also have implications for user privacy, data protection and autonomy.

19.2.3.1 *Surveillance and Interrogation*

Surveillance and interrogation relate to the collection of the data and are considered privacy harms – whereas surveillance concerns observation, interrogation involves pressing the individual to reveal information.[37] Although Solove focuses on the involuntary transmission of information via surveillance or interrogation, it is apparent from the above examples that different degrees of surveillance are necessary in order to acquire the necessary data required for the system, for example through cameras, microphones or other sensors that may be constantly gathering data. Awareness of surveillance can lead to changes in behaviour and self-censorship.[38] Due to the concerns surrounding surveillance and the impact on informational self-determination, the lack of clarity in relation to the status of emotions under the GDPR and the applicable safeguards in place creates concern about the role of consent and transparency in relation to the collection of the data.

Increasing the accuracy may also require gathering data from multiple sources or pressing the user to reveal more data. The AI system in place may therefore require further data in order to function effectively. Detecting the emotion will also depend greatly on the context – after all, a smile does not always signify happiness. Further information on the user's whereabouts and behaviour may therefore be necessary, perhaps requiring data to be communicated from tracking technologies installed on smartphones or other wearable devices.[39] The degree of

32 See McStay, Bakir and Urquhart, 'Emotion Recognition', pp. 1–3 with a general overview of uses of emotional AI.

33 Bundestag, 'Gesellschaftliche Verantwortung', p. 304.

34 For example, KIA's 'Real-Time Emotion Adaptive Driving System' (READ) or Hyundai's 'Emotion Adaptive Vehicle Control' (EVAC).

35 Šucha and Gammel, 'Humans and Societies', p. 34.

36 See project 'BioEssence': www.media.mit.edu/projects/bioessence/overview/ (last accessed 23 April 2021); C. Voss et al., 'Effect of Wearable Digital Intervention for Improving Socialization in Children with Autism Spectrum Disorder: A Randomized Clinical Trial' (2019) 173(5) *Journal of the American Medical Association Pediatrics* 446.

37 See Solove, 'A Taxonomy of Privacy', 490.

38 Ibid., 493.

39 McStay, Bakir and Urquhart, 'Emotion Recognition: Trends, Social Feeling, Policy', p. 3.

surveillance may therefore extend beyond the direct interaction with the device itself. However, further and more sensitive information may be required in order to allow the system to function: emotions are not only inherently personal but are also influenced by one's cultural or ethnic background – in some cultures a nod of the head does not always mean yes.[40] Whereas this also has implications for discrimination,[41] such sensitive data may be sought (or inferred) with the minimum amount of data required ultimately being a considerable amount of personal and sensitive data for the emotion detection to function as best as possible. Where safety or health is concerned, for instance in vehicles, the level of accuracy is paramount; indeed achieving a high level of accuracy is always a worthwhile objective, yet one may wonder where the threshold lies for what may legitimately and reasonably be expected.[42]

The surveillance aspect in relation to others is also a further point of consideration. In the 'Internet of Other People's Things', the user of the device and the party consenting to the data processing can differ. For instance, a voice-activated assistant could be engaging with all members of a household, including children, as well as guests. Whereas this concerns the wider issue of consent in general, the interaction with emotional AI also raises privacy and data protection concerns in relation to indirect users, and contextual information, for which technical solutions may be favourable.[43]

19.2.3.2 *Discrimination*

The discriminatory effect related to AI is well recognized and acknowledged as one of the central concerns surrounding the use of the technology. Indeed, by its nature AI is inherently discriminatory[44] – by their nature personalization and individualization necessitate differential treatment, yet it becomes especially concerning where certain individuals are treated unfavourably. Due to the manner by which the underlying training data is collected and labelled, it 'can reproduce existing patterns of discrimination, inherit the prejudice of prior decision makers, or simply reflect the widespread biases that persist in society'.[45] The discriminatory effect may not only perpetuate historical patterns of discrimination (gender, age, race) but could also create new forms of discrimination.[46]

Certain discriminatory effects in relation to emotional AI and historical patterns have already been recognized. For example, a 2018 study found that race was a factor in emotion analysis, with black men more likely to be attributed negative emotions than white men.[47] The effects of such discrimination may be felt when information is not provided, access to a particular service is denied or particular recommendations are not made, but it is not unreasonable to also assume an impact on the interaction with goods featuring emotional AI. However, the issue becomes more challenging in attempting to predict the types of discrimination that could arise solely on the basis of the emotional state of mind, regardless of race, gender or age, etc., for instance in

[40] See Barrett et al., 'Emotional Expressions Reconsidered', 46–47; IEEE, 'Ethically Aligned Design – Version 2' (2019), https://standards.ieee.org/wp-content/uploads/import/documents/other/ead_v2.pdf (last accessed 16 February 2022), pp. 164–165.

[41] See Section 19.2.3.2.

[42] See German AI Association, 'Position Paper on EU-Regulation of Artificial Intelligence' (January 2021), p. 2, stating that the accuracy of human performance should be used as a benchmark (though for purposes of quality assessment).

[43] See EDPB, 'Guidelines 02/2021 on Virtual Voice Assistants' (March 2021), pp. 18–19.

[44] See B. Goodmann and S. Flaxman, 'European Union Regulations on Algorithmic Decision-Making and a "Right to Explanation"' (2017) 38(3) *AI Magazine* 1, 3.

[45] S. Barocas and A. Selbst, 'Big Data's Disparate Impact' (2016) 104(3) *California Law Review* 671, 674.

[46] See COM(2021) 206 final, recital 37; detailed in S. Wachter, 'Affinity Profiling and Discrimination by Association in Online Behavioural Advertising' (2020) 35(2) *Berkley Technology Law Journal* 367.

[47] L. Rhue, 'Racial Influence on Automated Perceptions of Emotions', SSRN: 3281765.

personalized pricing. Unfortunately, as the Collingridge dilemma maintains, it is not easy to predict other forms of discrimination until the technology is more advanced and widespread.

19.2.3.3 *Decisional Interference*

The above examples clearly show how emotional AI may be used to respond to the individual's emotional state of mind not only to take a particular course of action (e.g. adjusting difficulty levels) but also to influence decisions made by or concerning the individual, thus impacting on autonomy. The 'taxonomy of privacy' as outlined by Solove refers to such incursions on an individual's decisions regarding their personal life as 'decisional interferences'.[48] As the discussions surrounding the role of AI have highlighted, the technology can greatly influence decisions made not only by an individual themself, but also in relation to an individual. Both aspects are of course relevant in light of the potential discriminatory effects whereby the individual is inadvertently excluded access to particular goods or services or only receives select information about specific goods, services or content.

The more concerning aspect is the extent to which the technology exploits or seeks to alter or take advantage of an individual's state of mind – emotions are after all 'potent, pervasive, predictable, sometimes harmful and sometimes beneficial drivers of decision making'.[49] Emotional AI could therefore be applied to exploit or provoke particular emotions and 'nudge' the individual towards or subject them to detrimental decisions, for example by encouraging 'retail therapy' where inferences point towards sadness.[50]

Emotional AI could also be used as part of decisions concerning an individual, using the technology to bolster the power and information asymmetry by acquiring intimate insights that the individual may not have wanted to reveal but, more significantly, cannot control to a degree that escapes the capabilities of the AI system. For example, the use of emotional AI in the insurance sector to determine whether an individual is lying when making a claim or to calculate premiums is contentious, with calls to ban the use of emotional AI for such purposes, at least insofar as facial detection is used.[51] There is certainly a difference between recommendations and decisions – and Art. 22 is critical in classifying a decision as automated[52] – but there exists the risk that through over-reliance on the technology the human ultimately serves as a vessel for merely turning a recommendation into a decision without true reflection ('automation bias').[53]

There is light that can shine on the gloomy picture painted above. The aforementioned examples allude to how emotional AI can be used for the benefit of the individual as well as for the good of society in general. For example, where sensors in a vehicle detect that the driver is angry, driving in an aggressive manner and exceeding the speed limit, it may initiate certain subtle measures to 'lightly nudge' the driver from an angry state of mind, potentially preventing

[48] Solove, 'A Taxonomy of Privacy', 555.
[49] See J. Lerner et al., 'Emotion and Decision-Making' (2015) 66 *Annual Review of Psychology* 799; also Šucha and Gammel, 'Humans and Societies', p. 17, with further references.
[50] McStay and Rosner, 'Emotional Artificial Intelligence in Children's Toys and Devices', 4–5; Money and Mental Health Policy Institute, 'Convenience at a Cost' (November 2020), www.moneyandmentalhealth.org/publications/online-shopping/ (last accessed 16 February 2022), pp. 14–15.
[51] See Council of Europe, 'Guidelines on Facial Recognition' (January 2021), p. 5; A. McStay and D. Minty, 'Emotional AI and Insurance: Online Targeting and Bias in Algorithmic Decision Making', Centre for Data Ethics and Information (2019), Section 2.
[52] Art. 29 WP, 'Guidelines on Automated individual decision-making', p. 20.
[53] See Council of Europe, 'Discrimination, Artificial Intelligence, and Algorithmic Decision-Making' (2018), p. 8, with further references.

an accident. Nonetheless, the difference between recommendations and decisions is also relevant here insofar as the system makes adjustments autonomously, questioning whether and how technology could and should be paternalistic and alter an individual's emotion, to turn bad emotions into good and to nudge towards decisions that are benefit of the individual or society.[54]

19.3 PROTECTING THE CONSUMER

The above short overview of emotional AI suffices to indicate several unresolved problems and challenges related to the protection of an individual's privacy and personal data. However, it is clear that emotional AI transcends privacy, data protection as well as consumer protection insofar as the role of emotional AI impacts on decisions made by or concerning consumers.[55] Moreover, concerns for data protection and privacy are no longer an afterthought for consumers, but are a contributing factor in contracting, reflected also in recent industry efforts to provide technical and self-regulatory approaches to tackle dubious practices, especially tracking.[56]

Understanding how emotions fit in the EU data protection framework is, however, one side of the equation. The role to be played by consumer law in this context is especially critical since the rapid development of emotional AI has not only called into question the potential to manipulate consumer behaviour on a new level but also the ability of consumers to assess and keep abreast of the capabilities and implications of new technologies.[57] Emotions are not merely a factor driving decisions, but as emotions become a feature of goods and services, increased transparency at the pre-contractual stage is necessary.

It is clear from the outset that there is no suitable 'one size fits all' solution to addressing the different aspects noted above as the root cause of the problem may vary – avoiding discrimination via AI may require measures to tackle problems on the level of the training data.[58] A blanket ban would stifle innovation and potential and fail to take into account the technical nuances and severity of risks where emotional AI is applied. As noted by Helberger et al., consumer law offers greater flexibility and attention to the context than data protection and therefore could serve as not only an ideal medium to address certain data protection and privacy issues but also offer varied approaches.[59]

At the time of writing, the European Commission published its proposal for a Regulation 'laying down harmonised rules on artificial intelligence': the 'Artificial Intelligence Act' (AIA). The AIA seeks to 'improve the functioning of the internal market by laying down a uniform legal framework in particular for the development, marketing and use of artificial intelligence in conformity with Union values'.[60] However, as the AIA focuses on establishing trust in AI by setting a series of conformity requirements, its primary focus is on the safety of the AI product where it constitutes a 'high risk', understood as those AI systems 'that have a significant harmful impact on the health, safety and fundamental rights (including human dignity, privacy and

54 Šucha and Gammel, 'Humans and Societies', p. 17.

55 See, for example, N. Helberger, F. Zuiderveen Borgesius and A. Reyna, 'The Perfect Match? A Closer Look at the Relationship between EU Consumer Law and Data Protection Law' (2017) 54 *Common Market Law Review* 1427.

56 For details, CISCO, 'Data Privacy Benchmark Study' (January 2021).

57 Opinion of AG Szpunar, Case C–673/17 *Planet 49* ECLI:EU:C:2019:246, paras. 112 et seq.; see also B. Duivenvoorde, *The Consumer Benchmarks in the Unfair Commercial Practices Directive* (Cham: Springer, 2015), p. 136, with reference to a judgment from Italy.

58 See COM(2021) 206 final, Art. 10 with a list of 'quality criteria'.

59 Helberger, Zuiderveen Borgesius and Reyna, 'The Perfect Match?', 1439.

60 COM(2021) 206 final, recital 1.

protection of personal data)'.[61] For this purpose, the AIA adopts a 'one size fits all' approach with limited sectoral exceptions and is thus not a specific instrument of consumer law, its risk-based approach has implications for consumers in different contexts. As noted above,[62] by including 'emotion recognition systems' within its framework, the AIA will have some bearing on the use of such systems in certain consumer contexts.

19.3.1 *Prohibited Practices*

The 'decisional interference' facilitated by emotional AI could be founded on a power and information asymmetry of such proportions that its use in some sectors ought to be prohibited from the outset, regardless of consent or other justifications via data protection legislation. Using the language of the AIA, such risks are 'unacceptable' and are thus to be prohibited, such as 'blacklisted'.[63]

19.3.1.1 *Material Distortion of Behaviour*

Art. 5(1) AIA contains a list of 'prohibited artificial intelligence practices'. Whereas Art. 5(1)(c) and (d) concern public authorities and law enforcement, Art. 5(1)(a) and (b) have general application insofar as the safety aspects are concerned. According to these provisions, 'the placing on the market, putting into service or use of an AI system that deploys subliminal techniques beyond a person's consciousness in order to materially distort a person's behaviour in a manner that causes or is likely to cause that person or another person physical or psychological harm' (Art. 5(1)(a) AIA) or 'exploits any of the vulnerabilities of a specific group of persons due to their age, physical or mental disability, in order to materially distort the behaviour of a person belonging to that group in a manner that causes or is likely to cause that person or another physical or psychological harm' (Art. 5(1)(b) AIA) shall be prohibited. Both prohibitions are notable not only because of the safety considerations they embody, but because they acknowledge the potential to use AI to achieve a power asymmetry in relation to an individual with the effect of manipulating their autonomy, thereby impacting on core values such as human dignity as well as the right to privacy and data protection.[64]

For consumers and emotions, the general nature of the prohibitions and the definition of AI systems[65] could apply in a range of scenarios, for example, to recommendation systems insofar as particular 'negative' states of mind are perpetuated, perhaps encouraging violent behaviour or eating disorders, or in products that respond to consumer emotions, such as in vehicles. In light of the lack of further information (not least in the recitals), such application is speculative, yet the scope of the prohibition is noteworthy as it only covers physical and psychological harm, thus neither extending to economic harm nor to applications that materially distort behaviour for the benefit of the natural person.

The term 'materially distort' in Art. 5 AIA provides a neat link to the role of the EU Unfair Commercial Practices Directive[66] (UCPD) as a central instrument in the EU consumer *acquis*

[61] Ibid., recitals 27–28.

[62] See Section 19.2.1.

[63] COM(2021) 206 final, p. 12.

[64] Ibid., recital 15.

[65] Ibid., Art. 3 No. 1: 'AI system means software that is developed with one or more of the techniques and approaches listed in Annex I and can, for a given set of human-defined objectives, generate outputs such as content, predictions or recommendations, or decisions influencing the environments they interact with.'

[66] Directive 2005/29/EC of the European Parliament and of the Council of 11 May 2005 concerning unfair business-to-consumer commercial practices in the internal market, OJ 2005 No. L149/22.

to prohibit a range of commercial practices that distort consumers' economic behaviour. The UCPD rules will not only remain applicable alongside the AIA but its provisions also apply at present in relation to AI: 'any algorithmic exploitation of consumer behaviour in violation of existing rules shall be not permitted and violations shall be accordingly punished'.[67] Similar to the GDPR, the extent to which the UCPD covers emotions has also been questioned. Not only have the categories of vulnerability under the UCPD (mental or physical infirmity, age or credulity) been flagged as limited in the age of AI,[68] but also whether the application of subliminal techniques beyond a person's consciousness to gain a position of power to a degree that limits the consumer's ability to make an informed decision and satisfies the threshold of 'undue influence' (Art. 2(j) in conjunction with Art. 8 UCPD).[69] According to the European Court of Justice (ECJ), the conduct is to have the 'effect of putting pressure on the consumer such that his freedom of choice is significantly impaired, such as conduct that makes the consumer feel uncomfortable or confuses his thinking concerning the transactional decision to be taken'.[70] Manipulating or exploiting the emotional state of mind, such as a constituent factor in decision-making, could constitute undue influence, but due to the subtleties involved, individual consumers may have difficulties in proving they were unduly influenced to contract.

19.3.1.2 *Unreasonable Information Asymmetry*

Although the UCPD aims at the 'decisional interference' in relation to transactional decisions made by consumers, it does not address the role of emotional AI in forming a factor for legally relevant decisions concerning a consumer but made by others. The GDPR plays a role in this context insofar as automated decision-making and profiling are prohibited unless there is a valid legal ground under Art. 22(2) GDPR. Nonetheless, as consent is viewed as merely a means to 'legitimise the extraction of personal data'[71] with certain consent formats designed to misdirect the data subject to agree to unfriendly options (so-called dark patterns[72]) the effectiveness of the data protection framework is challenged.

Where emotional AI is applied, the user of such technology will ultimately acquire information about the consumer's emotional state of mind. Whereas one could argue that emotions already constitute an information asymmetry to the benefit of the consumer, the ability to infer emotions through vast computing power that exceeds human capabilities could be said to tip the balance in favour of the user. This is especially true where biometric data are concerned and the subconscious, involuntary responses that make the individual especially vulnerable, especially in stressful situations. Whereas such systems may constitute 'high risk' systems under the AIA and subject to the extensive requirements contained therein (Art. 6 et seq. AIA), the use of emotion detection may nonetheless constitute an asymmetry that can have such significant legal effects on consumers that a prohibition is justified. In particular, the requirement to disclose the

[67] European Commission, 'On Artificial Intelligence – A European approach to excellence and trust', COM(2020) 65 final, p. 14.

[68] See Helberger, Zuiderveen Borgesius and Reyna, 'The Perfect Match?', 1458.

[69] See, in particular, G. Sartor, 'New Aspects and Challenges in Consumer Protection', Euorpean Parliament (April 2020), p. 37. On the application of the UCPD see Clifford, 'The Legal Limits to the Monetisation of Online Emotions', p. 241.

[70] CJEU, Case C-628/17 *Orange Polska SA* ECLI:EU:C:2019:480.

[71] L. Edwards and M. Veale, 'Slave to the Algorithm? Why a "Right to an Explanation" Is Probably Not the Remedy You Are Looking For' (2017) 16(1) *Duke Law & Technology Review* 19, 66.

[72] See Forbrukerradet, 'Deceived by Design' (June 2018), www.forbrukerradet.no/undersokelse/no-undersokelsekategori/deceived-by-design/ (last accessed 16 February 2022); M. Martini et al., 'Dark Patterns' (2021) 1 *ZfDR* 47, 57.

operation of emotion recognition systems (Art. 52(2) AIA) may from a surveillance perspective have counterproductive effects insofar as the consumer attempts to exercise self-censorship.

As mentioned above,[73] a ban of facial detection in relation to insurance has been called for. Here the type of emotion detection may play a key role. Whereas the accuracy of facial detection technology has been doubted, the potential for the technology to exceed human capabilities perhaps weighs more heavily – can the same ability apply to sentiment analysis of written or verbal communications? And if not, to what extent is prohibiting the application legitimate when it serves as a substitute for a human being rather than superseding the capabilities? Moreover, to what extent is an awareness of the consumer's emotional state legitimate or reasonably expected under the circumstances?

19.3.2 *Increasing Transparency*

Data protection and consumer protection share the common aim of increasing the transparency in consumer–business and data subject–data controller relationships by imposing mandatory obligations on the business/data controller to disclosure particular information to the other party prior to the agreement to contract or consent to the data processing. Indeed, the protection of autonomy as an underlying objective of both fields is of course closely interlinked with transparency. Terms such as 'information overload' are used to describe the counterproductive effect of disclosing vast amounts of information, and 'consent fatigue' to describe the apathy resulting from constantly submitting consent declarations.[74] The effectiveness of such approaches towards increasing transparency is questionable, but nonetheless they reflect the status quo of the information paradigm.

19.3.2.1 General Disclosure Obligation

The AIA includes a general transparency obligation in relation to certain AI systems. Under Art. 52(1) *providers*[75] of AI systems intended to interact with natural persons are designed and developed in such a way that natural persons are informed that they are interacting with an AI system; this does not apply unless it is obvious from the circumstances and the context of use. The Commission's White Paper preceding the AIA notes that Art. 13(2)(f) GDPR already contains a similar rule, but that the additional requirement is necessary to ensure adequate protection.[76]

According to the wording of Art. 52(1) AIA, the disclosure obligation reflects 'transparency by design' and thus a proactive approach towards taking steps during the design stage to inform of the interaction with the AI system, but does not extend to the data protection aspects.[77] For emotion detection systems, however, Art. 52(2) sets out a specific disclosure requirement whereby *users*[78] are to inform the natural persons of the operation of the system. The manner by which natural persons are informed will depend on the context. It appears that the disclosure

73 See Section 19.2.1.

74 See, for example, Art. 29 WP, 'Guidelines on consent', p. 17.

75 Defined in Art. 3 No. 2 AIA as 'a natural or legal person, public authority, agency or other body that develops an AI system or that has an AI system developed with a view to placing it on the market or putting it into service under its own name or trademark, whether for payment or free of charge'.

76 COM(2020) 65 final, p. 20.

77 See H. Felzmann et al., 'Towards Transparency by Design for Artificial Intelligence' (2020) 26 *Science and Engineering Ethics* 3333.

78 Defined in Art. 3 No. 4 AIA as 'any natural or legal person, public authority, agency or other body using an AI system under its authority, except where the AI system is used in the course of a personal non-professional activity'.

is necessary irrespective of whether the use of an AI system is obvious and thus concerns the particular function, though lacks details as to the scope or manner of data that is collected, which when read in conjunction with the grey areas in the GDPR, casts doubt on whether such obligation is proportionate to the understanding of emotions as 'highly sensitive information'.

19.3.2.2 *Pre-contractual Information*

Pre-contractual information plays a central role within EU consumer law *acquis*, with diverse areas of consumer law relying on the pre-contractual disclosure of information as an instrument to counter the information asymmetry existing between the consumer and trader. As the above examples of applications of emotional AI show, the technology may form part of a range of consumer goods and digital content, either as the primary or additional feature. The European Commission has already emphasized that the requirement of transparency requires consumers to 'receive clear information on the use, features and properties of AI-enabled products',[79] highlighting the importance to 'adequately communicate the AI system's capabilities and limitations to the different stakeholders involved in a manner appropriate to the use case at hand'[80] yet stating in the White Paper that information on the capabilities and limitations should only apply to high-risk AI applications and noting that the information is especially important for deployers of the system.[81] According to Art. 13(3)(b) AIA, such information on the capabilities and limitations, as well as the characteristics and performance, only apply in the context of high-risk AI systems and concern information for users, whereby the definition of users excludes use in the course of a personal non-professional activity (i.e. consumer context).[82]

The absence of particular AI information duties in relation to consumer products as mandated by the AIA appears concerning, not least in light of the emphasis on transparency. A closer look at the EU consumer *acquis* reveals however that the UCPD and the Consumer Rights Directive (CRD)[83] already provide a framework for addressing particular transparency aspects surrounding emotional AI and some data protection concerns in consumer products, irrespective of the level of risk associated with the AI system.

The CRD provides a series of pre-contractual information duties that apply both in on-premises (Art. 5) and off-premises contracts (Art. 6), with variations depending on the context. The trader is to inform the consumer in a clear and comprehensible manner of the main characteristics of the goods, digital content and (digital) service. Understanding the scope of main characteristics requires recourse to Art. 6(1)(b) and Art. 7(4) UCPD, which contain non-exhaustive lists of material information that the average consumer needs to take an informed transactional decision.[84] Where information is given online, this will also include safety warnings or any other mandatory labels on the packaging.[85] In light of the information requirements under the AIA, it is worthwhile considering whether the function and scope of material

[79] European Commission, 'Artificial Intelligence for Europe', COM(2018) 237 final, p. 16.

[80] European Commission, 'Building Trust in Human-Centric Artificial Intelligence', COM(2019) 168 final, p. 5.

[81] COM(2020) 65 final, p. 20.

[82] See n 78.

[83] Directive 2011/83/EU of the European Parliament and of the Council of 25 October 2011 on consumer rights, OJ No. 2011 L304/64. Note that the Directive (EU) 2019/2161 of the European Parliament and of the Council of 27 November 2019 as regards the better enforcement and modernization of Union consumer protection rules, OJ No. 2019 L328/7, makes several amendments to the CRD and the UCPD that will take effect from 28 May 2022.

[84] European Commission, 'DG Justice Guidance Document concerning Directive 2011/83/EU', p. 22.

[85] European Commission, 'Guidance on the Implementation/Application of Directive 2005/29/EC on Unfair Commercial Practices', SWD(2016) 163 final, p. 69.

information under the UCPD – not least the invasive nature of emotional AI – will require the disclosure of certain information, such as on the accuracy of the system or its limitations.

A further notable information obligation under the CRD concerns the 'functionality' of the consumer product. According to the Guidance document accompanying the Directive, recital 43 Digital Content Directive[86] and recital 27 Sale of Goods Directive,[87] the notion of functionality refers to the ways in which the product can perform their functions having regard to their purpose. This may include information on the conditions for using the product, such as tracking of consumer behaviour and/or personalization.[88] As a fluid concept, it may involve the disclosure of information on the application of emotional AI, including whether emotion detection is essential for the functionality of the product.

Whereas the collection of the data ultimately depends on the necessary hardware, emotion detection through analysis of the data can be achieved through software development. In the digital age, therefore, modifications to the software can improve or enhance the digital element of goods, extend the functionalities and adapt them to technical developments after purchase.[89] Should emotion detection become a new feature? For example, in voice assistants, Art. 19(1)(c) Digital Content Directive provides that the consumer is to receive clear and comprehensible information about the modification.

19.3.2.3 *Labelling*

For data, Wendehorst has noted that the pre-contractual information duties on 'main characteristics' and 'functionality' are in essence tucked away among the vast catalogue of information duties, creating the paradox that efforts towards enhancing transparency ultimately result in opacity.[90] Here, the 'conceptual proximity'[91] between the consumer and the data subject as justification for imposing disclosure obligations extends insofar as bombarding the individual with information required under consumer law and data protection law has questionable effectiveness, prompting suggestions to use AI to facilitate personalized disclosures of product and privacy information relevant to the individual by taking quality over quantity.[92]

Labels are of course a common instrument in the consumer context, serving to convey essential and accurate information to assist in making an informed decision on key factors – to provide reassurance that the product conforms with safety standards, to provide guidance about the suitability for particular age groups, to give information about nutritional value or energy efficiency, to warn of risks and dangers, and so forth. Although labels are not a panacea to solving the problem of information overload and can cause confusion, they remain an important tool to quickly draw attention and convey information on specific concerns, but also require accompanying education programmes to ensure they are understood.[93]

86 Directive (EU) 2019/770 of the European Parliament and of the Council of 20 May 2019 on certain aspects concerning contracts for the supply of digital content and digital services, OJ 2019 No. L136/1.

87 Ibid., 136/28.

88 European Commission, 'Guidance Document concerning Directive 2011/83/EU', p. 22.

89 Sale of Goods Directive, recital 28.

90 See C. Wendehorst, 'Consumer Contracts and the Internet of Things', in R. Schulze and D. Staudenmayer (eds.), *Digital Revolutions: Challenges for Contract Law in Practice* (Baden-Baden: Nomos, 2016), p. 189, 207.

91 Opinion of AG Szpunar, *Planet* 49, para. 113.

92 C. Busch, 'Implementing Personalized Law: Personalized Disclosures in Consumer Law and Data Privacy Law' (2019) 86(2) *University of Chicago Law Review* 309.

93 See European Commission, 'Labelling: Competitiveness, Consumer Information and Better Regulation for the EU' (February 2006), p. 2, 11. For criticisms, Busch, 'Implementing Personalized Law', 320.

In this respect, the use of labels to disclose key information surrounding the application of AI systems has been expressed by several commentators as a possible solution to informing consumers, albeit with a lack of consensus on form or content.[94] The AIA embraces labelling insofar as high-risk AI systems must bear the 'CE' marking to convey compliance with the conformity under the AIA (Art. 49 AIA) and that the system can be trusted.[95] However, in light of labels serving to protect consumer interests, the heighted awareness of privacy and data protection and their impact on contracting arguably need to be addressed; industry players are already taking a step in this direction and therefore the risk of fragmented approaches is possible.[96]

For emotional AI, 'on the box notification' has been highlighted as an important means to communication information on the types and methods of data collection in relation to children's toys, allowing for decisions to be made about the data protection implications before purchasing the device and either reinforcing the consent to the collection of the necessary data or the awareness that the data is necessary for the performance of the contract.[97] Viewed more generally, the performance of the obligations to provide information on the main characteristics and functionality may nonetheless encompass such functions and the methods of data collection needed in relation to emotional AI. Accordingly, the label would serve to emphasize certain elements that make the product particularly privacy invasive and data intensive, which could prove useful where emotional AI systems are merely a secondary function of the product or are an essential feature.

19.4 CONCLUSION

Artificial intelligence undoubtedly has great potential, but it will challenge core values and the legal safeguards in place. Emotions are no exception, with emotional AI providing a further example of how in the digital age the extent of insights encapsulated in data can reach new levels, offering new and innovative approaches, but also pose additional questions. The GDPR and consumer protection legislation may be suitably robust to respond to new problems arising from emotional AI, yet clarification at this early stage in the development and application will be necessary to ensure that the technology conforms to the core values and principles embodied in the legal framework. For this purpose, holding emotions in high regard as a distinct aspect that requires protection is likely to push consumer protection and data protection towards finding new, mutually beneficial approaches. As the discussions surrounding the European Commission's proposal for an Artificial Intelligence Act have only just begun, it will remain to be seen whether its inclusion of emotion detection systems may contribute to this development.

[94] Bundestag, 'Gesellschaftliche Verantwortung', p. 64; ICO, 'Big Data, Artificial Intelligence, Machine Learning and Data Protection' (September 2017), https://ico.org.uk/media/for-organisations/documents/2013559/big-data-ai-ml-and-data-protection.pdf (last accessed 16 February 2022), p. 65; IEEE, 'Ethically Aligned Design', p. 159.

[95] COM(2020) 65 final, p. 20.

[96] See, for example, www.apple.com/privacy/labels/ (last accessed 30 April 2021).

[97] McStay and Rosner, 'Emotional Artificial Intelligence in Children's Toys and Devices', 13. Such notifications may be useful for static characteristics, however they may no longer be accurate after software updates, but QR codes may offer a practical alternative: ICO, 'Big Data, Artificial Intelligence, Machine Learning and Data Protection', 66 with further references. For criticisms, BEUC, 'Why Moving Essential Product Information Online Is a No-Go' (February 2021), www.beuc.eu/publications/beuc-x-2021-016_why_moving_essential_product_information_online_is_a_no-go.pdf (last accessed 16 February 2022).

20

AI and Legal Personhood

Mark Fenwick and Stefan Wrbka

20.1 INTRODUCTION

This chapter focuses on the question of whether, and under what circumstances, we might wish to attribute legal personality to AI systems. To give the discussion some focus, it will examine the issue of victims seeking compensation for physical harm or harm to property caused by AI systems in a private law context. Particular emphasis is placed on recent developments and discussion at the EU level. The EU discussion has been given a central role in this chapter because it is already highly developed and illustrates some more general issues and trends that concern us regarding contemporary debates around AI and legal personhood.

The chapter makes a distinction – one that can be found in EU discussions and elsewhere – between a compensation model, where the AI is accorded independent legal personhood and victims are granted compensation directly from the AI ('personhood model'), and a model where the AI is not accorded independent personhood and victims receive compensation from some other legal person (human, company) ('liability model').

Here, we are not aiming to make a strong or general case in favour of a personhood model. Instead, we first argue that the rejection of personhood, which characterizes much of the current EU discussion, is often based on unconvincing arguments or, at least, an overly simplified account of the personhood model. We then suggest that there are genuine difficulties with the various versions of the liability model and conclude that, given these difficulties, there may be some value in revisiting personhood, at least for harm caused by AI in certain situations.

The first point of the analyses is that the recognition of these parallel trends – exaggerating the difficulties of a personhood model while simultaneously downplaying the challenges of a liability model – has come to define contemporary legal discussion in an EU context. The second point of the chapter answers the question: is the attribution of legal personality to an AI system ever justified? The analysis favours the granting of personhood for a specific class of AI systems. It uses cases that provide a more nuanced and flexible understanding of the possibilities of the personhood model and – crucially – a comparison between the best version of *all* available options in specific situations. A personhood model should empower plaintiffs to seek compensation for their losses.

As such, our intention is not to defend personhood per se, but to provide a framework for thinking about and determining the desirability of personhood.[1] This might seem a somewhat

[1] This account draws on the kind of comparative institutional approach advocated by Neil Komesar. See N. K. Komesar, *Imperfect Alternatives: Choosing Institutions in Law, Economics and Public Policy* (Chicago: University of Chicago

obvious or self-evident conclusion (personhood should be adopted when it is better than the alternatives), however, the discussion in its current form seems, for whatever reason, to preclude this kind of framing of the issue and exclude personhood without serious consideration.

The argument proceeds as follows. In the remainder of this introductory section, we outline some conceptual definitions, distinctions and trends informing our discussion. Section 20.2 focuses on the EU's rejection of personhood and the limitations and simplifications of this characterization. Section 20.3 then reviews the recent EU debate around the different liability models and suggests that this discussion is characterized by various uncertainties. Section 20.4 concludes that, in light of these uncertainties, it might be appropriate to consider revisiting some version of the personhood model in certain situations, or at least, including a more developed notion of a personhood-based model in the debate, rather than dismissing it a priori and without serious consideration.

In order to structure the discussion, it is useful to begin with some definitions, distinctions and trends. These statements may be somewhat contentious and in need of further elaboration, but they will, nevertheless, be important for the discussion that follows.

The first distinction is between autonomous and non-autonomous AI systems. The behaviour of an autonomous system/robot/AI/intelligent machine is determined by code, but with an autonomous machine, there is some scope for autonomous decision-making by the machine itself. This can be contrasted with 'dumb' code-based devices – which, it should be noted, may be highly sophisticated and connected – in which behaviour is totally determined by pre-existing code and there is no scope for any autonomous decision-making on the part of the software.

This distinction between the two types of machines is, no doubt, problematic and complicated, and is best thought of as a spectrum. However, as a heuristic device, this distinction is helpful when discussing personhood, as it identifies a class of AI 'decisions' that are not obviously determined by the designers and programmers of the AI. Recognizing this distinction matters, because some degree of autonomous choice would seem to be a condition of legal personhood. Denying any element of decision-making on the part of the AI system might seem to exclude any possibility of personhood from the start. It also reflects the reality that many technologies, including more sophisticated AI systems, are increasingly beyond the limits of human comprehension, in the sense that no individual, including those most intimately familiar with their design and construction, understands the full extent of their operations and capacities.[2]

A second distinction – or set of distinctions – involves the various stakeholders involved in the design, development, production, deployment and use of AI systems. We particularly wish to draw a distinction between the 'AI developer', who designs and codes the AI system, the 'manufacturer-producer', who designs the product or service into which the AI system is integrated (car or robot manufacturer) and the 'operator-user', who is anyone who interacts with an AI system after it is deployed. It is worth noting that there may be a distinction between different classes of 'operator-users', namely keepers, owners or users. The important point to be emphasized here is the complexity and diversity of players involved and use cases. This becomes particularly relevant in designing a liability model, as ultimately, it will be necessary to clearly identify an appropriate defendant from whom compensation must be sought.

Press, 1994); N. K. Komesar, *Law's Limits: The Rule of Law and the Supply and Demand of Rights* (Cambridge: Cambridge University Press, 2009).

[2] See S. Arbesman, *Overcomplicated: Technology at the Limits of Comprehension* (London: Portfolio Press, 2017) (an account of how technology is increasingly 'beyond' human understanding).

A third distinction – which has emerged as particularly important in an EU context – is between 'unacceptable risk' (prohibited activities), 'high risk' and 'low or minimal risk' in deployments of AI systems.[3] AI systems will inevitably be deployed in diverse contexts with different risks, and the idea that a situational approach to AI based on the degree of risk rather than a one-size-fits-all approach has been deemed preferable in the EU discussion. Examples of potential harm associated with high-risk AI systems are listed in Annex III of the April 2021 Draft Regulation proposing harmonized rules on AI.[4]

The proposed Regulation is not directly concerned with liability issues – other documents that we consider below are more relevant to the liability discussion – nevertheless, the proposed Regulation aims to provide an overarching framework within which all legal issues will be tackled, so in that sense it is relevant. Examples of high-risk applications enumerated in the proposed Regulation include recruitment systems; systems that provide access to educational or vocational training institutions; emergency service dispatch systems; creditworthiness assessments; systems involved in determining the allocation of taxpayer-funded benefits; decision-making systems applied around the prevention, detection and prosecution of crime; and decision-making systems used to assist judges. According to the proposed regulation, such high-risk systems are permitted (in contrast to the 'unacceptable' activities such as mass surveillance and 'social scoring' that are prohibited,),[5] but they trigger various mandatory compliance requirements, including risk management, quality management and security systems.

Having introduced these distinctions, it is also important to acknowledge two trends in the current and near-future deployment of AI technologies, based on the above distinctions. Given the speed and scope of technological developments in this context (notably the proliferation of autonomous AI systems), it is important to be cognizant of near-future trends, as well as the current state of technology, in order to 'future-proof' any regulatory choice that is made now. These two trends seem plausible as AI systems become more sophisticated.

First, there is an ongoing and general trend towards deploying AI in more and more 'high-risk' situations and a corresponding shift in control *from* the operator-user of a technology *to* the AI system developer. Take the example of autonomous vehicles. In contrast to non-autonomous cars, autonomous vehicles will be controlled, not by a human driver, but by an autonomous machine that is ultimately controlled by the AI system.

A second trend will be the unbundling or modularization of autonomous AI systems. As with technological innovation in other contexts, AI systems will increasingly adopt a modularized – non-integrated – approach that allows manufacturer-producers, as well as other intermediaries in the supply chain (including AI system developers and, possibly also, retailers), to decide what software products are combined with which hardware and other software products.

This type of technological development and modularization is famously associated with Clayton Christensen in *The Innovator's Solution*, where he suggests that, over time, the benefits of unbundling the production and deployment of disruptive technology products outweigh the performance benefits that come from a manufacturer offering a fully integrated solution.[6] A simple example is provided by smartphones. When smartphones were first launched, the convenience and performance benefits for end users associated with a fully integrated ecosystem

[3] See European Commission, 'Proposal for a Regulation laying down harmonised rules on artificial intelligence (Artificial Intelligence Act)', COM(2021) 206 final, Title II.

[4] Ibid., Annex III.

[5] Ibid., Article 5.

[6] C. Christensen and M. E. Rayner, *The Innovator's Solution: Creating and Sustaining Successful Growth* (Cambridge, MA: Harvard University Press, 2003).

(offered by Apple) made integration a better solution. However, over time as modularized solutions offered a 'good enough' user experience, the market (and consumer preferences) have tended to switch towards unbundled solutions like Android, which can be deployed in a variety of different forms with diverse hardware from different manufacturers.

In this way, the relatively simple distinction that once existed between AI system developers, manufacturer-producers and operator-users introduced above seems likely to be complicated by this trend towards modularization. Settled and defined roles and identities seem likely to become blurred as new, more complex configurations emerge. For example, a relatively simple distinction between the manufacturer-producer – the car company, to take the example of autonomous vehicles – and the AI system developer is likely to become more complicated. A number of entities are already involved in the production of a single piece of software – there will be no single AI system developer – and the proliferation and increased sophistication of AI seems likely to further increase the number of actors involved in the development and deployment of the different aspects of autonomous systems.

This complexity is further exacerbated by cross-border relationships and complex licensing and other legal agreements that will inevitably define this space. In short, this process of modularization of AI systems will, inevitably, become relevant for any discussion of liability, and unbundling in a specific case may complicate any attempt to identify the liable party.

20.2 REJECTING PERSONHOOD

Having introduced these distinctions and trends, let's consider legal personhood for autonomous systems. Our suggestion is that the current tendency is to reject personhood for AI systems, and that this tendency exhibits a number of problematic arguments and assumptions that either exaggerate the limitations of a personhood approach or simply fail to engage with it as a feasible model for responding to harm caused by AI systems.

By way of an illustration of this trend, we can point to recent EU developments. In October 2020, the European Parliament issued three important resolutions on the ethical and legal aspects of AI: Resolution 2020/2012 on a framework of ethical aspects of artificial intelligence, robotics and Related technologies; Resolution 2020/2014 on a Civil liability regime for artificial intelligence; and Resolution 2020/2015 on Intellectual property rights for the development of artificial intelligence technologies.[7]

The three resolutions all recognized that AI would bring enormous benefits across multiple economic and societal sectors, however, they also identified concerns about the capacity of the current legislative framework to respond to these new technologies and the need for a harmonized strategy of legal reform in a European context. Nevertheless, a feature of these three resolutions was the conclusion that AI should not have legal personality in any of these situations.

Three concerns seemed to inform the Parliament's thinking on this issue, each of which – we would suggest – are problematic, at least in the version presented in the resolutions, and are indicative of an inadequate approach to the question of personhood. Again, the chapter is *not* intended as a general argument for (or against) a personhood model, but an argument in favour of a particular type of approach, one that engages openly with the best version of a particular

[7] In early 2021, there were further resolutions on AI in criminal matters and in education, culture and the audiovisual sector. Since they are less concerned with harm caused in a private law context or the question of personhood, they are not discussed here.

solution in a specific context and resists the tendency towards generalized or simplified solutions that ignore the complex configurations of technologies and actors involved.

20.2.1 *Distinguishing Natural and Legal Persons*

First, there is the lingering assumption found in debates around AI that certain types of mental processes are a precondition for the attribution of personhood. The European Parliament, for example, declared in the recommendation for civil liability that, 'any required changes in the existing legal framework should start with the clarification that AI-systems have neither legal personality *nor human conscience*' (emphasis added).[8] This wording is, at best, misleading. It connects the question of the capacity for a particular form of moral reasoning – that is, human conscience – with that of legal personality. After all, legal persons, most obviously corporations, lack any 'human conscience', and yet legal systems have no difficulties attributing legal personality to such entities.

This points to a more general consideration, namely that it is important when considering the question of personhood to distinguish the *legal* question of personhood from what we might call technological or philosophical-moral questions. There is a tendency to conflate these issues, often as part of a strategy to dismiss legal personhood as a serious policy proposition. The technological question of personhood is whether machines will ever or can ever exceed determinism and make genuinely autonomous decisions, that is, does an autonomous machine possess genuine autonomy, or is it – always and forever – simply executing a predetermined code-based program. The philosophical-moral question of personhood concerns the capabilities and capacities – both cognitive and emotional – that an entity must possess in order to be accorded the status of moral personality. In a legal context, however, we are not interested in either of these questions – as important and as interesting as they may be – as they would further complicate an already complicated discussion.

So, what then is the *legal* question of personhood properly defined? Here, we take the legal question of personhood to be whether autonomous AI systems should be accorded the status of a legal person or subject within a specific legal system. This is a decision for that particular legal system to make and – crucially – we should suggest it is not *necessarily* contingent on any technological characteristics or cognitive or emotional capacities of the AI systems themselves. Equating questions of conscience and legal personhood, in the way that the Parliament does, can obscure the more practical question around awarding compensation for harm caused by AI systems.

In short, it seems important to understand personhood as a status attributed by a particular legal system, rather than the possession of a set of qualities or technological capacities. Legal personhood can be defined in purely formal terms and simply refers to the fact that an entity is a subject of legal rights and obligations. Of course, certain assumed qualities and capacities might provide reasons – and often compelling reasons – for attributing personhood to a certain type of entity, including an AI system, but we see no *necessary* connection between the different questions of personhood. Conflating the discussion of these different issues needs to be handled with caution, given the complexity of the issues.

A standard argument for the view that there are no ontological preconditions necessary to attribute personhood to a particular type of entity is the existence of the 'legal person' category,

[8] Resolution 2020/2014 on a Civil liability regime for artificial intelligence, Annex, recital 6.

and, most obviously, corporations.[9] In all modern legal systems, corporations are recognized as legal persons for many purposes, in spite of the fact that a corporation cannot do, feel or think anything. And yet, in spite of their impoverished ontological circumstances, a corporation can enter into contracts, own property and engage in many other legal acts. Corporations are among the most important actors in modern capitalist economies and societies. Legal personhood, along with the doctrine of limited liability (the legal doctrine that limits the liabilities of investors), has been absolutely central to this historical and contemporary role and significance.[10]

It is also important to acknowledge that corporations have only been accorded a limited version of legal personhood. The legal personhood of a corporation is incomplete, and the scope and outer limits of this personhood have, on occasion, been problematic and contested. For example, there have been ongoing debates around corporate *criminal* liability and the extension of criminal law to legal, and not just natural, persons.[11] In the Anglo-American world, this is an old – albeit controversial issue – but a number of civil law jurisdictions, most obviously Germany, continue to reject the attribution of criminal fault to a legal person on the grounds that a corporation is not a kind of entity capable of acting with the element of fault required by criminal law.[12]

It is also worth noting here that, in the case of a corporation, it is still ultimately a natural person or natural persons making the decision and performing the relevant action, whereas in the case of an autonomous AI system, it would be the AI itself that decides and, very possibly, acts. Whether this is a distinction that makes any difference is open to debate. The claim that, in the case of the corporation, it is ultimately human beings that decide and implement actions on behalf of the corporation does not seem to provide a compelling reason in favour of corporate legal personality in itself. Other factors, most obviously incentivizing investors (discussed in Section 20.2.3) have provided a stronger historical justification for creating a new class of legal subject, rather than the fact of human involvement. Nevertheless, this is one difference between the two situations.

In sum, a cursory review of history provides evidence for the claim that the attribution of personhood has never been entirely or even mostly driven by ontological or other theoretical concerns, and that non-human entities have been granted personhood when it is practical and convenient.[13]

20.2.2 *Compensation for Harm*

Second, there is the suggestion that liability for harm would be reduced under a personhood model. The European Parliament notes that:

[9] See, e.g., R. van den Hoven van Genderen, 'Do We Need New Legal Personhood in the Age of Robots and AI', in M. Corrales, M. Fenwick and N. Forgo (eds.), *Robotics, AI and the Future of Law* (Berlin: Springer, 2019), p. 15.

[10] See, e.g., J. Bakan, *The Corporation* (New York: Free Press, 2001), p. 5: 'Over the last 150 years the corporation has risen from relative obscurity to become the world's dominant economic institution'; J. Micklethwait and A. Wooldridge, *The Company: A Short History of a Revolutionary Idea* (London: Weidenfeld, 2005), p. 15: 'The most important institution in the world is the company; the basis of the prosperity of the West and the best hoped for future of the rest of the world.'

[11] See, e.g., W. S. Laufer, *Corporate Bodies and Guilty Minds: The Failure of Corporate Criminal Liability* (Chicago: University of Chicago Press, 2008).

[12] See J. Gobert and A. M. Pascal, *European Developments in Corporate Criminal Liability* (Abingdon-on-Thames: Routledge, 2014).

[13] It is also worth noting that certain classes of natural persons have been denied legal personhood, most obviously and problematically, slaves. See van den Hoven van Genderen, *supra* note 9, p. 44.

> [A]ll physical or virtual activities, devices or processes that are driven by AI-systems may technically be the direct or indirect cause of harm or damage, yet are nearly always the result of someone building, deploying or interfering with the systems; note in this respect that it is not necessary to give legal personality to AI-systems.[14]

The fact that '*someone*' – presumably a natural or legal person – is responsible for building the AI system that causes harm is presented as a reason for not giving legal personality to AI ('it is not necessary'). Again, this is a complicated and contentious claim, not least because a similar observation could be made about a corporation, and it is accorded personhood. Moreover, and as we explore in more detail in Section 20.2.3, it might be difficult to 'trace back specific harmful actions of AI' to an easily identifiable natural or legal person (i.e. the crucial 'someone') responsible for 'building, deploying or interfering with the systems'. This seems particularly likely given the diverse range of (very probably, multinational) actors that will be involved in the deployment of such technologies (as highlighted in Section 20.1). Greater certainty, clarity and transparency might be better achieved by identifying a single, easily identifiable, responsible entity (the AI itself). In short, the fact that 'someone' can be identified does not seem to be a compelling reason for denying AI systems legal personality, when identifying the AI system responsible is, in almost every case, going to be easier.

Advocates of a personality model believe that such a model delivers certainty and proximity. For example:

> Legal personality will mean that each field of law (civil law, tax law, employment law, penal law, competition law) will be allowed with the freedom to assess the legal issues posed by AI within its own boundaries and under its own rules and principles. Same as with legal persons, legal solutions will come on a case-specific basis in each field of law. This will allow for nuanced, detailed and thoughtful specialized regulation each time. None of this will be made possible if a '*supervisory authority*' with an opaque legal mandate is incorporated in order to 'monitor' any and all AI.[15]

On this view, a situation-specific form of legal personhood is preferable in that it offers greater clarity and, presumably, more opportunity to seek compensation for harm.

20.2.3 *Offering the Right Incentives*

A third set of issues, which might, at first glance, seem less relevant to a tort-focused discussion, concern incentives for human creators. The European Parliament noted in the resolution on intellectual property (IP) that 'the autonomisation of the creative process of generating content of an artistic nature can raise issues relating to the ownership of IPRs [intellectual property rights] covering that content' and concluded 'that it would not be appropriate to seek to impart legal personality to AI technologies' and points out the '*negative impact of such a possibility on incentives for human creators*' (our emphasis).[16]

The question of incentives and the effect that attribution of personhood might have on the relevant stakeholders is clearly an important issue in a tort context. One crucial effect of the attribution of personhood to a corporation, for example, is that it protects all the actors 'behind' the

[14] Resolution on a Civil liability regime for artificial intelligence, § 7.

[15] V. Papakonstantinou and P. De Hert, 'Refusing to Award Legal Personality to AI: Why the European Parliament Got It Wrong', *European Law Blog*, https://europeanlawblog.eu/2020/11/25/refusing-to-award-legal-personality-to-ai-why-the-european-parliament-got-it-wrong.

[16] Resolution on Intellectual property rights for the development of artificial intelligence technologies, § 13.

corporation from liability. Or to be more precise, it establishes the possibility of such legal protection. The creation of a distinctive legal entity works as a shield against liability for the actors who created that entity, in the example of the corporation, the investor-shareholders. The logic of limited liability is to encourage investment by limiting potential exposure to corporate losses.

Looking back, a century earlier, an editorial from *The Economist* in 1926 acknowledged the importance of this shift:

> The economic historian of the future may assign to the nameless inventor of the principle of limited liability, as applied to trading corporations, a place of honor with Watt and Stephenson, and other pioneers of the Industrial Revolution. The genius of these men produced the means by which man's command of natural resources has multiplied many times over; the limited liability company [provided] the means by which huge aggregations of capital required to give effect to their discoveries were collected, organized and efficiently administered.[17]

Creating a corporation as a distinct legal person thus facilitates rigid separation – or partition – between the personal assets of the investor-shareholders and company assets. Such asset partitioning has several advantages. First, a distinct corporate identity creates a class of assets to which a company's creditors have a claim ahead of any other stakeholders (e.g. managers or employees), thus making it easier for a firm to find credit. Second, a distinct corporate identity means that a company is not adversely affected by the personal financial difficulties of individual investors or other stakeholders, thus making it easier for a firm to raise capital. Third, a distinct corporate identity protects the personal assets of the stakeholders – most obviously, the investor-shareholders – from any claim against the company. The doctrine of limited liability, therefore, means that the creditors of the firm have no claim against the personal assets of company stakeholders, and investor-owners are only liable for what they put into the company.

This is a question for legal historians, but it seems clear that *corporate* legal personhood and this doctrine of legal liability was not determined by ontological debates about whether a company is the kind of entity that can actually conclude a contract but, rather, a clear-eyed recognition of the practical benefits of according the status of a legal person to companies. A similarly pragmatic approach seems desirable in the case of AI. Recourse to superficial claims and arguments rejecting such an approach can appear misguided. This possibility of combining some form of incomplete legal personhood of the kind enjoyed by corporations opens up the possibility of situational recognition of personhood for AI systems in some contexts and not others, and for different forms of liability. The question, therefore, becomes, in what context might we wish to attribute liability to the machine itself or the AI system developer, or do we expect the user to bear the risk?

20.3 LIMITS OF LIABILITY

As suggested in the previous section, we can see a trend towards denying AI systems legal personhood, at least in an EU context. We identified some difficulties with this line of argument, but this rejection of personhood seems to be a feature of contemporary discussion across multiple jurisdictions. The main takeaway of this type of critique is that the behaviour of an autonomous system must be traced back to a natural or legal person who should be held accountable for any harm caused; there is a clear preference to identify a workable version of the liability model. Pursuant to this view, it is simply not necessary to introduce legal personhood, because there is no gap to fill or, at least, preferable options are available.

[17] *The Economist*, 1926, 'Editorial' (18 December).

In this section, we would like to suggest, however, that this project of identifying a natural or legal person who should be held liable – such as a workable version of a liability model – has proved more elusive than its advocates might believe. The current debate is, therefore, characterized by these two trends: a tendency to exaggerate the difficulties of a personhood model, *and* a parallel tendency to downplay the difficulties of a liability-based paradigm. Here, by way of illustration of this second trend, we again focus on the current EU discussion.

At an EU institutional level, the debate around civil liability with respect to physical harm or damage caused by AI systems has intensified over recent years. Here, we focus on three recent documents that illustrate some of the challenges and difficulties that have haunted this project.

20.3.1 *Civil Liability and the Liability Report by the Expert Group on Liability and New Technologies – New Technologies Formation (2019)*

In 2016, the European Commission presented its road map for the fifth and most recent evaluation of the Product Liability Directive (PLD).[18] One aim of this evaluation was to 'assess if the Directive is fit-for-purpose vis-à-vis the new technological developments such as the Internet of Things and autonomous systems'.[19] The study arrived at the conclusion that the concepts and terminology applied by the PLD might not necessarily be appropriate to solve liability questions conclusively. It identified 'the need to pursue the reflection on the future of the Directive in order to ensure legal certainty, in particular in relation to its application to new technologies, such as Artificial Intelligence systems'.[20]

Two weeks before the presentation of the fifth PLD Evaluation Report,[21] the Commission voiced the need for broader civil liability analysis in a communication on AI[22] and an accompanying staff working document on liability for emerging digital technologies.[23] It was pointed out that additional (existing or possible future) mechanisms might be of help to comprehensively regulate civil liability consequences with respect to AI systems.[24] The Commission decided to establish an expert group divided into two subgroups. Group 1 – the 'Product Liability Directive formation' (PLDF)[25] – was assigned with evaluating the suitability of the PLD in an AI context in more detail. Group 2 – the 'New Technologies formation' (NTF)[26] – received the mandate to analyse the overall civil liability framework from an AI perspective.

In 2019, the NTF presented its findings in a report on liability for AI and other emerging digital technologies (NTF report).[27] The NTF report argued against the necessity of introducing a new category of legal personhood that would cover emerging digital technologies (EDTs), a

[18] Directive 85/374/EEC of 25 July 1985 on the approximation of the laws, regulations and administrative provisions of the Member States concerning liability for defective products.

[19] European Commission, *Evaluation and Fitness Check (FC) Roadmap* (2016), Section A1.

[20] EY, Technopolis and VVA, 'Evaluation of Council Directive 85/374/EEC on the approximation of laws, regulations and administrative provisions of the Member States concerning liability for defective products – Final Report' (2018), available at: https://op.europa.eu/en/publication-detail/-/publication/d4e3e1f5-526c-11e8-be1d-01aa75ed71a1/language-en, p. 125.

[21] COM(2018) 246 final.

[22] COM(2018) 237 final.

[23] SWD(2018) 137 final.

[24] Ibid., 19–21.

[25] Ibid., 21.

[26] Ibid.

[27] Expert Group on Liability and New Technologies – New Technologies Formation, 'Liability for Artificial Intelligence and Other Emerging Digital Technologies' (2019). At the time of writing this chapter the report by the PLDF – the second group installed by the Commission in the framework of the 2018 PLD evaluation – was still pending.

term used by the report that includes AI systems. The main argument used by the report was that harm or damage 'caused by even fully autonomous technologies is generally reducible to risks attributable to natural persons or existing categories of legal persons, and where this is not the case, new laws directed at individuals are a better response than creating a new category of legal person'.[28] As with the arguments discussed in Section 20.2, the dismissal of personhood was not backed up with any supporting evidence.

The NFT report outlined a number of mechanisms that could coexist to help injured parties find compensation. One solution would be holding the operator of an EDT strictly liable under the condition that the respective EDT is used 'in *non-private environments* and may typically cause *significant* harm' (emphasis added).[29] Operators should not only include owners/users/keepers of EDTs ('frontend operator'),[30] but in addition 'persons continuously defining the features of the relevant technology and providing essential and ongoing backend support' ('backend operator').[31] In the event of more than one operator, the operator who has greater control over the risk should be the liable party.[32] Here, we would simply note the uncertainty that is immediately introduced into the discussion – almost every term (i.e. non-private, significant and frontend and backend operators) seems in need of extensive elucidation.

With respect to the producer's liability, the NFT report suggested some adapted interpretation and partial revision. Based on functional evidence, it explained that liability under the PLD should cover harm or damage caused by defective EDTs.[33] If still in control of updates/upgrades on the EDT, producers should remain liable for defects 'even after the product was put into circulation'.[34] The development risks defence in Article 7(e) of the PLD should not apply,[35] and the burden of proof could be shifted towards the sued party under certain circumstances.[36] The operator's strict liability and a producer's liability under the PLD are accompanied by complementary recommendations, such as special duties of care for operators and producers to be applied in fault-based claims,[37] operators' vicarious liability for 'autonomous technology used in a way functionally equivalent to the employment of human auxiliaries'[38] and special rules on the burden of proof.[39]

[28] Ibid., 38.

[29] Ibid., 39. 'Non-private environments' first and foremost refers to public spaces (see ibid.). The level of significance should be 'determined by the interplay of the potential frequency and the severity of possible harm' (see ibid., note 105).

[30] Ibid., note 39.

[31] Ibid.

[32] Ibid.

[33] Ibid., 42 (see Article 2 of the PLD).

[34] Ibid., (see Article 7(b) of the PLD).

[35] Ibid. For an analysis of the development risks defence see, e.g., M. Mildred, 'The Development Risks Defence', in D. Fairgrieve (ed.), *Product Liability in Comparative Perspective* (Cambridge: Cambridge University Press, 2005), p. 167.

[36] Ibid., with respect to defects in case of disproportionate difficulties for the injured party to prove non-compliance with safety standards. For a discussion of the notion of 'defect' under the PLD see, e.g.,C. Amato, 'Product Liability and Product Security: Present and Future', in S. Lohsse et al. (eds.), *Liability for Artificial Intelligence and the Internet of Things* (Baden-Baden: Nomos, 2019), p. 77. For a discussion of the notion of 'defect' under the PLD see, e.g., J.-S. Borghetti, 'How Can Artificial Intelligence Be Defective?', in S. Lohsse et al. (eds.), *Liability for Artificial Intelligence and the Internet of Things* (Baden-Baden: Nomos, 2019), p. 63.

[37] Expert Group on Liability and New Technologies – New Technologies Formation, 'Liability for Artificial Intelligence and Other Emerging Digital Technologies', 44.

[38] Ibid., 45.

[39] Ibid., 49–55 with respect to alleviating the burden of proof concerning the causal relationship between defect and damage 'if the claimant's position is deemed weaker than in typical cases' and a reversal of the burden of proof with respect to fault in case of disproportionate difficulties for the injured party to prove fault. See also ibid. 48–49 for cases of non-compliance with safety rules.

The NFT report concluded its findings with a recommendation to establish mandatory insurance for high-risk EDTs[40] and – as a safety net – compensation funds[41] for cases of 'damage caused by an unidentified or uninsured technology'[42] and scenarios in which the tortfeasor cannot be identified.[43]

20.3.2 *Civil Liability and the Bertolini Report*

In July 2020, the European Parliament presented a report on Artificial Intelligence and Civil Liability, authored by Andrea Bertolini (Bertolini Report).[44] The Bertolini Report and underlying study drew upon earlier projects[45] and addressed the civil liability topic from a 'Risk-Management Approach' (RMA) perspective.

The report claimed that taking a technology-neutral approach, which does not differentiate between different types of AI technologies, and which applies the same set of rules for each of them, would not be the best option given the fact that AI technologies differ significantly from one another.[46] The Bertolini Report argued that one has to take such technological differences into account when identifying possible answers to harm or damage caused by AI systems. This – so the report claimed – is best achieved by using an RMA, which represents a technology-specific approach.[47] To ensure legal certainty and to simplify redress for the injured party, the RMA is based on strict liability[48] and *ex ante* identifies the liable party in each and every relevant scenario.[49] Under the RMA, civil liability would be attributed 'to the party that is best positioned to (i) identify a risk, (ii) control and minimize it through its choices, and (iii) manage it – ideally pooling and distributing it among all other parties – eventually through insurance, and/or no-fault compensation funds'.[50] This would provide clear incentives to relevant stakeholders to exercise the necessary level of care. According to the report, the RMA introduces clearly identifiable liable parties, although – depending on the case and category of AI technology – the person held liable to the injured party might vary.[51]

40 Expert Group on Liability and New Technologies – New Technologies Formation, 'Liability for Artificial Intelligence and Other Emerging Digital Technologies', 61–62.

41 For comments on insurance and compensation in an AI liability context, see, e.g., G. Borges, 'New Liability Concepts', in S. Lohsse et al. (eds.), *Liability for Artificial Intelligence and the Internet of Things* (Baden-Baden: Nomos, 2019), p. 145.

42 Expert Group on Liability and New Technologies – New Technologies Formation, 'Liability for Artificial Intelligence and Other Emerging Digital Technologies', 62.

43 Ibid.

44 A. Bertolini, 'Artificial Intelligence and Civil Liability – study for the JURI Committee' (2020), available at: www.europarl.europa.eu/RegData/etudes/STUD/2020/621926/IPOL_STU(2020)621926_EN.pdf.

45 See A. Bertolini, 'Artificial Intelligence and Civil Law: Liability Rules for Drones – study for the JURI committee' (2018), available at: www.europarl.europa.eu/thinktank/en/document.html?reference=IPOL_STU(2018)608848, and M. van Lieshout et al., 'Study on safety of non-embedded software; Service, data access, and legal issues of advanced robots, autonomous, connected, and AI-based vehicles and systems – study for the Commission / DG CONNECT' (2019), available at: https://op.europa.eu/en/publication-detail/-/publication/aad6a287–5523-11e9-a8ed-01aa75ed71a1/language-en.

46 Bertolini, 'Artificial Intelligence and Civil Liability', 98.

47 Ibid., 99.

48 Ibid.

49 Ibid., 101.

50 Ibid., 99.

51 Ibid., 101: 'For instance, in some cases, it may be appropriate to hold primary responsible the operator (e.g., drones) the business user and/or system integrator (advanced industrial robots), the service provider or deployer (AI-based consultancy services), the hospital and/or medical structure, and/or service provider (in case of medical diagnosis), the producer and/or the owner (in increasingly autonomous vehicles).'

The Bertolini Report concluded with an analysis of four categories of AI systems – industrial robots (IR), drones, autonomous vehicles and medical diagnostic assistive technologies. It arrived at the conclusion that existing regulations in the field of IR already ensure adequate access to justice, compensation and fair distribution of economic loss resulting from compensation.[52] In the other three sectors, however, civil liability schemes designed under the guidance of the RMA would be advisable to simplify the compensatory process for the injured party.[53]

20.3.3 *Civil Liability and the AI Liability Regulation Proposal*

Two months before the presentation of the Bertolini Report, the European Parliament released a draft report on a civil liability regime for artificial intelligence.[54] This is the second of the three resolutions discussed in Section 20.2. The core of the report was a proposal for a regulation on liability for the operation of AI systems (AI Liability Regulation Proposal). The AI Liability Regulation Proposal briefly claims that the PLD (with respect to harm or damage caused by defective products) and national fault-based liability regimes (with respect to harm or damage caused by interfering third parties) are, in principle, effective tools to compensate parties injured by AI systems.[55]

However, when it comes to the liability of deployers, the accompanying explanatory statement points out that difficulties in proving their fault would make it nearly impossible for injured parties to receive compensation from them. Hence, the AI Liability Regulation Proposal focuses on deployers' liability and links it to possible risks of deployed AI systems, irrespective of the question of defectiveness of the system.

The linchpin of the AI Liability Regulation Proposal is the notion of a 'deployer'. A look at the proposed instrument shows that, depending on the circumstances, the deployer concept might encompass several different stakeholders. Article 3(d) of the AI Liability Regulation Proposal defines the deployer as 'the person who decides on the use of the AI-system, exercises control over the associated risk and benefits from its operation'. Recital 8 of the AI Liability Regulation Proposal explains that this concept should be understood as being 'comparable to an owner of a car or a pet, [because] the deployer is able to exercise a certain level of control over the risk that the item poses'.[56]

It further outlines that 'exercising control . . . should be understood as meaning any action of the deployer that affects the manner of the operation from start to finish or that changes specific functions or processes within the AI-system'. Recital 9 of the AI Liability Regulation Proposal states that the actual user should only be held liable under the proposed regulation if they fulfil the deployer definition criteria of Article 3(d). The same recital explains that the backend operator, that is, 'the person continuously defining the features of the relevant technology and providing essential and ongoing backend support', would, in principle, not be considered a deployer, but 'should fall under the same liability rules as the producer, manufacturer and

[52] Ibid., 124, where the report explains that this is mainly achieved through workers' health and safety legislation and the PLD. With respect to the PLD, the Bertolini Report adds that the system might need some adjustments to take account of AI technology and to solve practical difficulties – see ibid., 61, where the report highlights the definition of 'products', challenges with respect to the burden of proof, the definition of 'defect' and the developmental risk defence as key issues.

[53] Ibid., 124 and 125.

[54] Resolution 2020/2014(INL) on a Civil Liability Regime for Artificial Intelligence, available at: www.europarl.europa.eu/doceo/document/TA-9-2020-0276_EN.html.

[55] Recital 7 of the AI Liability Regulation Proposal.

[56] For comments on strict liability and mandatory insurance in the context of car accidents from the viewpoint of compensating injured parties see, e.g., A. Jablonowska and P. Palka, 'EU Consumer Law and Artificial Intelligence', in L. de Almeida et al. (eds.), *The Transformation of Economic Law: Essays in Honour of Hans-W. Micklitz* (London: Hart, 2019), p. 91, at 100.

developer'. In line with this statement, Article 3(g) of the AI Liability Regulation Proposal defines the term 'producer' as 'the developer or the backend operator of an AI-system, or the producer as defined in Article 3 of Council Directive 85/374/EEC [i.e. the PLD]'. Article 11 of the AI Liability Regulation Proposal indicates that there might be scenarios in which producers are actually to be considered deployers as well. This would be the same case as with the actual user, that is, the producer would have to fulfil the deployer criteria of Article 3(d) of the AI Liability Regulation Proposal. If a person is considered both the deployer *and* the producer of the AI system, Article 11 of the AI Liability Regulation Proposal clarifies that the proposed regulation should prevail over the PLD.[57]

The AI Liability Regulation Proposal, therefore, suggests a situational liability regime that differentiates between harm or damage caused by high-risk AI systems and other AI systems.[58] Harm or damage compensable under the proposed regulation is limited to 'adverse impact affecting the life, health, physical integrity or property of a natural or legal person, with the exception of non-material harm'.[59] Joint and several liability should be applied if there is more than one deployer.[60] In the case of harm or damage caused by high-risk AI systems, deployers should be held strictly liable.[61] High-risk AI systems and the critical sectors they are deployed in are exhaustively listed in an annex.[62] The group of high-risk AI systems is subject to possible amendments by the Commission via delegated acts in consultation with a new standing committee on high-risk AI systems. Compensation in the context of high-risk AI systems is capped at a maximum of EUR 10 million in total for physical harm or damage and at a maximum of EUR 2 million for harm or damage caused to property.[63] Based on the Motor Insurance Directive model,[64] deployers of high-risk AI systems are required to hold adequate insurance.[65] AI systems not listed in the annex fall under the category of other AI systems. Liability for harm or damage caused by such AI systems is designed as fault-based liability with rebuttable presumption of the deployer's fault.[66]

With differentiation between strict liability (of the deployer) for high-risk AI systems and enhanced fault-based liability (of the deployer) for other forms of AI systems, the proposed regulation shows some parallels to the Commission's Report on safety and liability implications

57 With respect to the PLD, the proposed regulation – as already pointed out – states that it should be viewed as a helpful mechanism for injured parties to receive compensation from the producer of defective goods. At the same time, it indicates that it would be necessary to adapt and streamline the PLD with the proposed regulation to enhance its value for parties injured by AI systems (Recital 21 of the AI Liability Regulation Proposal).

58 For remarks on the general risks inherent to AI systems, see, e.g., P. Cerka et al., 'Liability for Damages Caused by Artificial Intelligence' (2015) 31 *Computer Law & Security Review* 376, 386.

59 Article 3(f) of the AI Liability Regulation Proposal.

60 Ibid., Article 11.

61 Ibid., Article 4(1).

62 The Annex lists five high-risk AI systems: (a) unmanned aircraft within the meaning of Art 3(30) of Regulation (EU) 2018/1139; (b) vehicles with automation levels 4 and 5 according to SAE J3016; (c) autonomous traffic management systems; (d) autonomous robots; and (e) autonomous cleaning devices for public places. For critical remarks on strict liability for autonomous robots, see, e.g., R. H. Weber and D. N. Staiger, 'New Liability Patterns in the Digital Era', in T. E. Synodinou et al. (eds.), *EU Internet Law in the Digital Era: Regulation and Enforcement* (Berlin: Springer, 2020), p. 197, at 199.

63 Article 5(1) of the AI Liability Regulation Proposal.

64 Directive 2009/103/EC.

65 Article 4(4) of the AI Liability Regulation Proposal.

66 Ibid., Article 8. For a high-risk/strict liability versus low-risk / fault-based discussion see, e.g., E. Karner, 'Liability for Robotics: Current Rules, Challenges and the Need for Innovative Concepts', in S. Lohsse et al. (eds.), *Liability for Artificial Intelligence and the Internet of Things* (Baden-Baden: Nomos, 2019), p. 117, at 122–123; G. Spindler, 'User Liability and Strict Liability in the Internet of Things and for Robots', in S. Lohsse et al. (eds.), *Liability for Artificial Intelligence and the Internet of Things* (Baden-Baden: Nomos, 2019), p. 125, at 140–141.

of AI, the Internet of Things and robotics[67] that accompanied the Commission's White Paper on artificial intelligence[68] released earlier in 2020. It further builds upon some of the NFT report's findings (operator's strict liability for significant harm caused in a non-private environment, enhanced fault-based rules and mandatory insurance for high-risk AI systems). Although taking a different approach than the RMA and its technology-specific approach, the AI Liability Regulation Proposal shares some of its ideas, in particular following on from the definition of a situational deployer. Just as is the case with the RMA, the person who is in control of the risk associated with AIs might differ from situation to situation.

In any event, it remains interesting to see how policymakers will proceed with approaches that go beyond a revision – or at least a reinterpretation – of the PLD, which, in light of the challenges it poses in the context of AI systems, might be necessary.[69] Nevertheless, from a legal certainty perspective, one vital question remains: how can the injured party identify the liable party, be it the producer, developer, designer, deployer, owner or user of an AI system? While all approaches highlighted in this section aim to find suitable answers, one has to question if applying those systems in practice is as easy as it seems.

At the very least, there are certain scenarios in which identifying the liable person poses disproportionate difficulties for the injured party. The Bertolini Report, for example, concludes that under the RMA, there is, in principle, no generalized need to give AI systems legal personhood. At the same time, however, the report admits that revisiting the legal personhood discussion might be an option in cases in which 'identifying the optimal entry point for litigation is difficult'.[70] The uncertainty surrounding the key concept of deployer and the transaction costs to plaintiffs of identifying the deployer would certainly mitigate against the utility of any liability scheme and potentially might have a fatal impact on its effectiveness.

A second related difficulty concerns what we might call complexity and distance, and is suggested by the kind of regulatory model proposed by the Parliament, which includes a distinction between a 'developer', a 'deployer' and a 'user' of AI. In effect, there are, at least, three legal entities involved, potentially located across the globe, and all interacting with a single end user. Rather than formally creating a scheme that merely produces greater legal obscurity, one solution might be to focus on the AI system itself and attribute legal personality to it, therefore mandating a local, concrete and tangible entity.

20.4 REVISITING PERSONHOOD?

The difficulties associated with a liability model do not necessarily mean that personhood should be embraced, but, rather, that we need to engage with personhood as part of an open and honest comparison of the various different options. Clearly, a personhood model is not

[67] COM(2020) 64 final 16 (with respect to high-risk AI systems) and 14 (with respect to fault-based schemes).

[68] COM(2020) 65 final.

[69] Commenting on the challenges of applying the PLD to AI systems is beyond the scope of this work. For a debate on this issue, see, e.g., the contributions in P. Machinowski, *European Product Liability: An Analysis of the State of the Art in the Era of New Technologies* (Cambridge: Intersentia, 2017); the contributions in S. Lohsse et al. (eds.), *Liability for Artificial Intelligence and the Internet of Things* (Baden-Baden: Nomos, 2019); T. S. Cabral, 'Liability and Artificial Intelligence in the EU: Assessing the Adequacy of the Current Product Liability Directive' (2020) 27(5) *Maastricht Journal of European and Comparative Law* 615; G. Howells et al., 'Product Liability and Digital Products', in T. E. Synodinou et al. (eds.), *EU Internet Law in the Digital Era: Regulation and Enforcement* (Berlin: Springer, 2020), p. 183; BEUC, 'Product Liability 2.0 – How to Make EU Rules Fit for Consumers in the Digital Age' (2020), available at: www.beuc.eu/publications/beuc-x-2020-024_product_liability_position_paper.pdf.

[70] Bertolini, 'Artificial Intelligence and Civil Liability', 123. For details see ibid., ch. 2.

without difficulties. Obvious problems in attributing personhood to autonomous machines include (i) that autonomous machines lack assets and victims may not be able to recover loss and (ii) that the AI system developers might not internalize the risk and exercise the necessary degree of caution when designing such systems, and manufacturer-producers may, similarly, fail to take care when integrating them into their products or services.

Again though, there may be solutions to these issues. The first of these problems can be overcome by State intervention. The remedies might be similar to those employed in corporate law, for example. The AI system could be obliged to be endowed with minimum assets in order to qualify as a legal entity and as a condition of continued lawful operation. Such a minimum asset requirement would oblige other parties to provide the funds necessary to satisfy potential damages claims. These funds would then be transferred to the AI system and held in its 'own' name. From this pool of assets, damage claims for any harm caused could be settled.

An alternative to minimum asset requirements that serves the same end is some form of mandatory liability insurance of the kind that is often required for entities to operate in the financial services sector. The law could simply stipulate an insurance mandate, as a precondition for incorporation of an AI system as a legal person. Again, the burden for providing the mandatory liability insurance would fall on the natural and legal persons who design and develop the autonomous system or deploy it. They would have an obligation to supply the insurance contract and pay the premiums, as the robot would have no assets to pay them from. The question then becomes who pays, and the various stakeholders would be given a clear incentive to negotiate an answer to this question in their agreements. The crucial point is that someone would have to pay in order for that system to be allowed to operate lawfully. The argument would be that this also addresses the second of the two concerns highlighted above. The fact that the developer or the deployer of an AI system pays for such insurance would seem to create the right kind of incentives for them to exercise the necessary degree of caution in the design and permissible use cases of such a system.

A problem might arise when the loss exceeds the potential insurance pay-out, or the value of the minimum assets held by the AI systems. In such cases, the risk would be that the victims may not be fully compensated or that the designers of an AI system might take excessive risks. Wagner addresses this point:

> Again, the essential point about entity status for robots is that this move helps to shield other parties from liability, namely manufacturers and users. Within the corporate context, the protective function of limited liability is acceptable for voluntary creditors who can easily protect themselves against risk externalization, but it is much more problematic for involuntary creditors like tort victims who lack any means to do so ... There is also no doubt that limited liability of the quasi-shareholders, such as the manufacturers of robots, is functionally equivalent to a cap on the direct liability of these same manufacturers. Here, as in corporate law, the creation of a legal entity helps to limit the exposure of the individuals who created the entity and thus may stimulate them to take on more risk at lower cost ... As a general matter, it is submitted that the issue of limited liability should be addressed and discussed head-on rather than hidden in the issue of recognition of autonomous systems as ePersons.[71]

This seems a strong argument against personhood (what Wagner refers to as 'ePersons'). A solution might be to supplement the liability of AI systems with rights that the robot, or rather its liability insurer, would have against the manufacturer-producers, and perhaps also its

[71] G. Wagner, 'Robot Liability,' *Forschungsinstitut für Recht und digitale Transformation, Working Paper Series* (2019), www.rewi.hu-berlin.de/de/lf/oe/rdt/pub/working-paper-no-2, 22.

operator-user. Of course, if that is deemed a suitable solution, there would be less (if any) value in the direct liability of autonomous AI systems.

Nevertheless, in spite of these difficulties, there still might be good evidential reasons for supporting some form of personhood. As argued in Section 20.3, persons injured by an AI system may face serious difficulties in identifying the party who is responsible, particularly if establishing a 'deployer' is a condition of liability. And where autonomous AI systems are no longer marketed as an integrated bundle of hardware and software – that is, in a world of unbundled, modular technologies as described in Section 20.1 – the malfunctioning of the robot is no evidence that the hardware product put into circulation by the AI system developer, manufacturer-producer or the software downloaded from another developer was defective. Likewise, the responsibility of the user may be difficult to establish for courts. In short, the administrative costs of enforcing a liability model – both for courts, as well as potential plaintiffs – may be excessively high and a more pragmatic approach may be preferable, even if it is not perfect.

In a market of highly sophisticated, unbundled products, the elevation of the AI system to a person may also serve as a useful mechanism for 'rebundling' responsibility in an era of modularization and globalization. The burden of identifying the party responsible for the malfunction or other defect would then be shifted away from victims and onto the liability insurers of the robot. Such liability insurers, in turn, would be professional players who may be better equipped to investigate the facts, evaluate the evidence and pose a credible threat to hold the AI system developer, hardware manufacturer or user-operator accountable. The question would then be whether an insurance scheme of this kind is more effectively combined with some partial form of legal personhood or not.

To conclude, this chapter examined the idea of AI personhood and suggests that we shouldn't dismiss personhood too quickly, given the complexities and uncertainties of the issues at stake and the complexities and limitations of any liability-based solution. Our argument is that personhood should never be excluded a priori, but only after an examination of the comparative costs and benefits of all available solutions presented in their best form. The question to be asked might then be: would a compulsory insurance scheme – a modified version of what occurs in the context of automobiles – based on personhood be better than a 'deployer'-based liability scheme, at least in high-risk situations involving sophisticated autonomous AI systems? We don't say the answer to this question is obvious or that there is a perfect solution, but that no solution should be dismissed without serious consideration. This seems particularly relevant in an EU context where identifying an appropriate model for all member states is inevitably complicated by diverse legal traditions and different liability rules for ostensibly similar factual situations.

In short, personhood for AI should not be too quickly dismissed, given the complexities and difficulties of any liability discussion. Given the expanding role of such AI systems in our everyday lives, finding the 'best' answer to these questions seems important, not least because any regulatory choice made now seems likely to create path dependencies that will be harder to change in the future, if the selected model proves less effective in practice than is currently envisaged. In a European context, this issue seems to be closed (a personhood model seems to have lost, at least in the context discussed here), but other jurisdictions – that are at an earlier stage on the path to regulation in this area – might learn something from the EU experience on this point.

21

AI, Ethics, and Law

A Way Forward

Joshua P. Davis

21.1 INTRODUCTION

Artificial intelligence (AI) has profound ethical implications. It poses grave threats – maybe even existential ones – to humanity.[1] But we have yet to develop a theoretical framework for determining what it can and cannot do or, relatedly, for what it should and should not do. That gap is understandable. Applying ethics and law to AI is not easy. Doing so raises deep philosophical problems. The result is a formidable strategic challenge. On one hand, we may make fundamental errors if we try to sidestep foundational issues to arrive at pragmatic solutions.[2] On the other hand, we may get bogged down trying to solve those foundational issues. This chapter attempts to steer a middle course – addressing the deep problems while avoiding gratuitous philosophical commitments. In other words, the chapter attempts to confront philosophical issues to the extent – but only to the extent – necessary to chart a way forward.

Section 21.2 offers an explanation for why human beings may have an ongoing role to play in supervising AI from ethical and legal perspectives, despite impressive technological advances. It identifies key challenges for regulating AI and for AI as a legal regulator, sketching a general framework for understanding the relationship between AI, consciousness, ethics, and law. Section 21.3 then seeks to justify the approach taken in Section 21.2. Toward that end, Section 21.3 considers and rejects potential philosophical objections to the analysis in Section 21.2.

The view on AI, ethics, and law that Section 21.2 suggests can be summarized briefly. It focuses on conscious experience – on what the world seems like from a first-person perspective. It contends that conscious experience is necessary to formulate ends – as opposed to means – and that judgments about ends depend on variations in conscious experience. This view implies some plausible conclusions about both unconscious AI (UAI) and conscious AI (CAI).

Consider that UAI's lack of consciousness prevents it from forming intent. Intent often plays a crucial role in our ethical and legal judgments. So what happens when UAI causes injuries we would subject to legal sanctions if they were bought about by a conscious actor? One option is to exempt UAI from moral and legal condemnation. But that could have undesirable

[1] See Toby Ord, *The Precipice: Existential Risks and the Future of Humanity* (New York: Hachette Books, 2020), pp. 138–152.

[2] This issue arguably arises, for example, in Max Tegmark's thoughtful and informative book, *Life 3.0: Being Human in the Age of Artificial Intelligence* (New York: Knopf, 2017). He attempts to distill ethical reasoning largely into four principles: utilitarianism, diversity, autonomy, and legacy. Tegmark, *Life 3.0*, pp. 271–273. While impressive, this analysis does not capture the complexity and contradictions that beset ethical reasoning.

consequences. Another is to judge the intent of the people who control or benefit from UAI. But they may not have intended the harms caused by UAI. A more promising solution is to judge the conduct of UAI – or of those responsible for it – in consequentialist terms – in terms of effects, not intent.

Another issue arises if we rely on UAI to assess *our* actions. Can it serve as a legal regulator? If UAI cannot form ends, it cannot make moral and other value judgments. Nor is UAI likely able to mimic human value judgments effectively. As a result, UAI will require human oversight and intervention if we want the assessments it makes – or recommends – to be ethically and legally sound.

Claims about *conscious* AI are more speculative, particularly because we do not know how the physical world produces consciousness. But we have reason to believe CAI will know the world differently than the way we do. We should not expect it to have the same first-person experiences that we have developed over millennia through our idiosyncratic evolutionary process. The variations between us and CAI could have great significance. They may mean, for example, that uploading a human mind to a computer will not extend a human life but rather will create a new hybrid or artificial one. They may also mean that CAI will make moral and other value judgments quite different from our own, if it can make them at all. As a result, we should proceed with caution before relying on the value judgments of CAI in taking important actions. Section 21.2 briefly sets forth the above points about UAI and CAI.

Section 21.3 then engages three philosophical problems that could undermine them. A first possibility is that conscious experience cannot affect the physical world at all. The mental and the physical may operate in different realms. It is hard to understand how thoughts or desires could exert any force on rocks, machines, or bodies. So how can conscious experiences have any impact on behavior? Section 21.3.1 suggests that conscious experiences may correlate with particular physical states – biological or otherwise. That correlation, it contends, is consistent with a range of philosophical views on the relationship between the physical and the phenomenal. The suggested correlation, it claims, allows for a kind of causation sufficient to support the discussion in Section 21.2.

Section 21.3.2 addresses a second potential philosophical problem: Assuming conscious experiences in theory can play a causal role in the physical world, do they in fact do so? Some social psychologists have claimed that our conscious intentions rationalize rather than motivate our actions. Section 21.3.2 suggests that the evidence does not support the claim that our conscious intentions never affect our conduct. Nor does the evidence rule out that our conscious experiences, thoughts, and beliefs affect our behavior, even if our conscious intentions do not.

Finally, Section 21.3.3 analyzes free will. The issue is whether the account in Section 21.2 relies on questionable premises, such as that we can choose to act other than as we do. It does not. Conscious intentions may be determined by some combination of nature and nurture, perhaps modified by probabilistic effects à la quantum theory. Or conscious creatures may be capable of exercising one form or another of free will, however that is defined. We need not choose between these or similar views. Section 21.3.3 explains why they are all compatible with recognizing the causal role for consciousness required by the analysis in Section 21.2.

These modest philosophical positions are likely susceptible to credible criticisms. There may well be no claim about AI, ethics, and law that is not. But we cannot wait until we have figured it all out to start acting decisively to ensure AI serves ethical purposes. Even if we had consensus about the ethics of AI, it would be extraordinarily difficult to constrain those who would exploit its potential for profit, power, or other arguably amoral or immoral purposes. We should not add a requirement of unassailable proof before we develop a plan for reining in AI on ethical and legal grounds. When it comes to AI, ethics, and law, we should not let the perfect be the enemy of the good, lest we achieve neither.

21.2 UNCONSCIOUS AND CONSCIOUS AI

Section 21.2.1 suggests how we may have acquired consciousness and the evolutionary advantages it may provide. Section 21.2.2 explores potential implications for UAI and Section 21.2.3 for CAI. All of this is a sketch of an argument to motivate the discussion in Section 21.3.

21.2.1 *Causal Consciousness: Evolutionary Explanations and Their Limits*

First-person conscious experiences and third-person, scientific understandings of the world have a fraught relationship.[3] Any scientific account of consciousness seems to leave something out. Science may explain how consciousness could have emerged through evolution, how interfering with biological processes can affect conscious experiences, and perhaps how to map our biological structures to the phenomenal (or to qualia). But there still seems to be something missing: what it feels like to be us.[4]

It is not possible to fully understand conscious experiences only by considering their origins and functions. Still, we may learn valuable lessons by reviewing those origins and functions. In particular, our conscious experiences likely enhanced our prospects for our survival, our procreation, and the protection of our young by enabling us to develop objectives.

Consciousness allows us to form ends. Consider a few examples. The conscious experience of pain discourages us from harming our bodies and thus our genes. Similarly, pleasure – especially sexual pleasure – encourages us to procreate and thereby replicate our genes. And our suffering when we see our children and grandchildren suffer and our pleasure at their pleasure can lead to financial planning that helps our DNA persist down generations.

Perhaps some of this can also be done without conscious experience. Plants react in relatively simple ways to their environments without an apparent first-person perspective.[5] Sunflowers turn toward the sun.[6] Venus fly traps close on prey but not in response to the wind.[7] But, as far as we know, they have no conscious sense of purpose, no capacity to form complicated goals. Pine trees do not worry about or plan for their grandchildren's inheritances.

Consciousness can also help us in devising means to achieve our ends. Daniel Kahneman, for example, describes the human brain as using two systems.[8] System 1 is automatic, fast, easy, intuitive, and prone to errors and biases. System 2 is conscious, slow, difficult, deliberate, and capable of correcting errors and resisting biases. For many adults, adding 2 + 2 is automatic.[9]

[3] See generally, Thomas Nagel, *The View from Nowhere* (Oxford: Oxford University Press, 1986).

[4] See, e.g., Thomas Nagel, *Mind and Cosmos: Why the Materialist Neo-Darwinian Conception of Nature Is Almost Certainly False* (Oxford: Oxford University Press, 2012), p. 38; Nagel, *View from Nowhere*, pp. 15–16; John Searle, *Mind: A Brief Introduction* (Oxford: Oxford University Press, 2004), p. 78; David J. Chalmers, *The Conscious Mind: In Search of a Fundamental Theory* (Oxford: Oxford University Press, 1996), p. 78.

[5] See https://homeguides.sfgate.com/sunflower-move-73855.html#:~:text=In%20early%20morning%2C%20plant%20cells,flower%20head%20facing%20the%20sun.

[6] Annaka Harris, *Conscious: A Brief Guide to the Fundamental Mystery of the Mind* (New York: Harper, 2019), pp. 15–17.

[7] Ibid., pp. 15–17.

[8] Daniel Kahneman, *Thinking, Fast and Slow* (New York: Farrar, Straus and Giroux, 2011), p. 23.

[9] Ibid., p. 21.

It does not require conscious effort. In contrast, multiplying 17 × 24 does.[10] We might keep in mind, for example, what 10 × 24 is while multiplying 7 × 24 and adding the two products (240 + 168) to get 408. As Kahneman notes, there are physical manifestations of such conscious endeavors: muscles tense, blood pressure rises, heart rates increase, and pupils dilate.[11]

Most of our thinking relies on System 1, not System 2.[12] But that can be misleading. Much of System 1 derives from System 2. The easy work that System 1 performs for us now is often the result of hard work System 2 did in the past.[13] Instant word recognition derives from the effort of learning to read. Rote mathematical knowledge is earned through deliberate practice and repetition. We rely on conscious thought to perform some cognitive tasks and to learn how to perform others automatically.

When we recognize human cognitive processes that are not conscious, including those associated with Kahneman's System 1, we may use the notion of lacking consciousness in a different way than when we talk about plants. For this reason, we would likely do best to call System 1 subconscious rather than nonconscious, with the idea being that the subconscious occurs in a being that has conscious experiences and the subconscious is capable of becoming conscious.[14] In any case, what matters most for present purposes is that there is a first-person experience that motivates us to take particular actions, not that the first-person experience is deliberate or that we are aware of it.

Conscious experiences, then, seem to play a key role in explaining not only human experiences but also human behavior. If so, AI's lack of consciousness, or its very different conscious experiences from ours, could lead it to behave differently than we do. And understanding the differences between us and AI when it comes to conscious experiences could help us to predict those behavioral differences. None of this is to say that our conscious experiences cannot be described in physical terms. Presumably, they can be. Perhaps someday we will be able to provide an account of the physiological processes – likely located largely in the brain – that support conscious (and subconscious) thought. But, as discussed in Section 21.3, that does not necessarily mean that we do not have consciousness. Nor does it necessarily mean that our conscious reasoning has no causal role to play in our actions.

Indeed, the best way to make sense of why we do what we do – why we move a particular chess piece to a particular position on a game board – may well be in terms of our conscious states, including our conscious intentions. When it comes to chess, our understanding of the rules requires conscious thought at some point, and our choice of a move may follow from working through all of the options consciously and concluding that one in particular will give us the best chance of winning. Explanations at the level of conscious experience may help us make sense of the world, even if the same behavior could in theory be explained in terms of synapses, serotonin and cortisol, or protons and electrons. Some theorists believe conscious thought

[10] Ibid., p. 20.

[11] Ibid.

[12] Ibid., p. 21.

[13] Ibid., p. 22.

[14] There is a parallel to the sorts of distinctions that Searle draws between the nonconscious, unconscious (we would say subconscious), and conscious. John Searle, *Seeing Things as They Are: A Theory of Perception* (Oxford: Oxford University Press, 2015), pp. 201–216. According to Searle, nonconscious perceptions cannot be made conscious, but unconscious (subconscious) perceptions can be. We might say that System 1 is subconscious, not nonconscious, and that the first-person perspective is necessary for subconscious and conscious experiences. Alternatively, we might rely on attention schema theory, or some similar approach, to distinguish nonconscious states from subconscious states that compete for our conscious attention. See, e.g., Michael S. A. Graziano, *Rethinking Consciousness: A Scientific Theory of Subjective Experience* (New York: W. W. Norton, 2019).

cannot as a matter of theory have an impact on the physical world, or that conscious thought does not as a matter of fact affect the physical world, or both. We will explore these possibilities in Section 21.3.

These possibilities are unlikely at the current time. On one hand, denying a causal role for conscious experiences means that the pain we suffer does not cause us, for example, to avoid touching hot stoves. So we have in place a mechanism that seems structured so well to promote our survival. But it does not. It has no causal efficacy. On the other hand, denying a causal role for conscious experiences also means we developed an elaborate mental apparatus for no practical reason. Conscious experience is inert – an extravagant gratuity, a side effect that is so difficult to acquire through evolution yet that has no adaptive value. How odd that would be.

It is important to acknowledge the limitations of an evolutionary account of consciousness. Evolutionary theory cannot fully explain consciousness. It cannot tell us why consciousness is possible at all – why it is an available option on the random spinning wheel of genetic mutations. Nor can the theory tell us what our conscious minds can achieve. It cannot mark the outer bounds of what conscious thought can accomplish in addition to promoting the persistence of our genes. Biological characteristics can perform functions lacking evolutionary benefits, especially if those characteristics do not impede DNA's survival and replication.[15]

This point may well apply to conscious reasoning. Our ability to discover truths about the origins of the universe or string theory – if indeed we have either ability – would likely fall into this category.[16] So would our ability to discern truths about morality and other values – again, if we have that ability. These capacities may not confer any evolutionary advantage, even if we achieve them through biological attributes that otherwise do. Evolutionary theory may be able to tell us only a limited amount about consciousness' potential and nature.[17]

21.2.2 *Unconscious AI: Means vs. Ends*

As we have noted, one role consciousness can play is to motivate us. It can shape our objectives. Some of them may be quite immediate and concrete, such as avoiding pain and seeking pleasure. Others may be more theoretical, and perhaps moral, such as protecting fundamental rights, maximizing utility, and the like.

If AI lacks conscious experience, we expect that it cannot define its own objectives. And so it is. AI does not appear to be conscious[18] and it cannot formulate its own ends.[19] These points are likely related: AI's current lack of conscious experience can explain why it cannot form ends; AI's inability to form ends may indicate that AI does not currently have conscious experiences.

UAI's inability to form ends poses difficulties for regulating it. We often assign moral blame and impose legal liability based on intent. But UAI cannot form intent. Further, those who adopt UAI will often have good intentions. That could allow UAI to cause harms that escape liability in our current legal systems.

[15] Stephen Jay Gould repeatedly reminded us not to assume there is a purpose for every heritable trait. See, e.g., Steven Jay Gould, "Male Nipples and Clitoral Ripples" (1993) 20 *Columbia: A Journal of Literature & Art*, 80–96.

[16] Nagel, *View from Nowhere*, pp. 78–82.

[17] Ibid., pp. 81–82; see generally, Nagel, *Mind and Cosmos*, proposing the iconoclastic view that consciousness may be a necessary part of the universe or something toward which we evolved teleologically rather than randomly.

[18] Stuart Russell, *Human Compatible: Artificial Intelligence and the Problem of Control* (New York: Viking, 2019), p. 16.

[19] Ibid., p. 10. AI currently cannot form its own ultimate ends. It can at times identify intermediate ends as means for achieving the ultimate ends it is assigned.

Consider, for example, use of UAI in employment.[20] An employer might rely on UAI to award promotions, hoping to make its decisions more objective and less susceptible to improper biases. But the effect may be the opposite. UAI may predict future employee success using past employment decisions that were tainted by improper biases. The outcome could be discrimination against members of protected classes.

Yet current law may not deter this behavior. In the USA, federal laws prohibiting employment discrimination are often interpreted to require either discriminatory intent or discriminatory effects without a legitimate business justification.[21] UAI has no intent so it cannot have discriminatory intent. An employer using UAI may not have discriminatory intent and, indeed, may act on legitimate business justifications, perhaps even attempting to avoid impermissible discrimination. So if we want to protect against UAI causing discriminatory effects in the workplace – or against other similar harms – we may need to adjust our laws. An option would be focus on effects, not intent, holding those who control or benefit from UAI accountable for the harms it causes.

UAI would similarly face difficulties as a legal regulator. It cannot make moral and other value judgments; we have to provide them. That could limit the role UAI can play in legal systems, to the extent moral and other value judgments inform legal interpretation or adjudication.[22] We would have to direct UAI as a legal decision-maker.

We might try to program UAI to make moral judgments itself. There are two basic strategies for doing so. They correlate to the two kinds of analyses UAI can perform: deductive and inductive.[23] UAI can apply general principles deductively to particular cases. Alternatively, it can infer patterns in data correlating particular circumstances with particular outcomes or results. UAI can also mix and match these forms of analysis. But none of these strategies is likely to work all that well for moral reasoning.

Given the many debates that beset moral philosophy, it is difficult to make blanket statements about what moral reasoning entails – or even about whether the concept of moral reasoning is meaningful. It could be, for example, that moral claims are just emotions expressed as if they had propositional content.[24] Or it could be that moral claims are expressions of personal beliefs that are true as long as they are sincere.[25] If either of these views of morality is accurate, UAI seems incapable of exercising moral judgment. It has no feelings or personal beliefs. Further, some of the main schools of thought about morality do not seem compatible with UAI. In virtue ethics, for example, morality is defined in terms of character – based not just on what a person does but on their motivations for doing it.[26] UAI lacks motivations. It is difficult to see how virtue ethics could apply to UAI.

But let us assume *arguendo* that moral reasoning involves a kind of analysis that is not obviously at odds with UAI. Consider if morality is susceptible to deductive reasoning. Such reasoning requires clear rules for moral actions. Along these lines, the most promising

[20] Ifeoma Ajunwa, "The Paradox of Automation as Anti-Bias Intervention" (2020) 41 *Cardozo Law Review* 1671–1742.

[21] Ibid., 1727.

[22] See Joshua P. Davis, "Artificial Wisdom? A Potential Limit on AI in Law (and Elsewhere)" (2019) 72 *Oklahoma Law Review*, 55–61, discussing the consensus among most legal positivists and natural lawyers that adjudication – as opposed to legal interpretation – involves moral judgments.

[23] Wendell Wallach and Colin Allen, *Moral Machines: Teaching Robots Right from Wrong* (Oxford: Oxford University Press, 2009), pp. 83–124.

[24] See, e.g., Russ Shafer-Landau, *The Fundamentals of Ethics* (3rd ed.; Oxford: Oxford University Press, 2015), pp. 314–316, discussing expressivism.

[25] Ibid., pp. 293–294 (discussing ethical subjectivism).

[26] Ibid., pp. 254–255 (discussing virtue ethics).

approaches would likely be consequentialist. They define conduct as moral if it brings about morally attractive states of affairs. Utilitarianism, in particular, seeks to maximize a metric – utility. Actions are moral if they enhance utility. That seems to entail the sort of mathematical analysis that UAI would be most capable of performing.

Yet even utilitarianism might not be tractable for UAI. It hard to see how we could provide UAI with sufficiently clear instructions to implement utilitarianism. There are all sorts of disputes among utilitarians – whether to maximize total or average utility; whether to measure utility in terms of pleasure,[27] preferences,[28] objective notions of the good, or something else; and numerous disputes about how to define each of these terms.[29] Which version of utilitarianism is most attractive may depend on moral intuitions about a particular context. But even if we accept one version of utilitarianism – say, seeking to promote aggregate pleasure – formidable issues remain. Do all forms of pleasure count equally – from selfless love to petty vengeance – or is there a hierarchy among them? Even those committed to a relatively pure form of hedonistic utilitarianism – such as Katarzyna de Lazari-Radek and Peter Singer – draw qualitative distinctions, for example, between the kinds of pleasure and happiness that only human beings experience and the kinds that other animals can also experience.[30] We would have to resolve these issues, and countless others like them, to give UAI sufficient direction to make moral judgments.

Applying utilitarianism involves profound difficulties – both theoretical and practical. First-person experiences, including pleasure, are not susceptible to scientific assessment. We neither know precisely what we are measuring when we say we want to maximize pleasure nor do we know how to measure it. Of course, human beings too must face these difficulties. But, in doing so, we have resources that UAI does not. We can assess what objectives are worth pursuing. We have intuitions about what is just or fair in particular circumstances. We can empathize with other living beings, imagining what their experiences might be and how they might rank them. We rely on these and other resources to come to moral conclusions, however imperfect. UAI's inability to choose objectives or have first-person experiences implies it cannot do the same. So much for deductive reasoning.

Inductive reasoning may work in limited circumstances. We might provide UAI a set of expert human evaluations of factual scenarios and ethical conclusions. As long as the human views are relatively consistent – and the values and facts remain relatively stable over time – UAI may be able to detect patterns. Perhaps for this reason, UAI has shown some promise in resolving ethical challenges in providing medical care.[31]

In other areas, like law, UAI is likely to face greater difficulties. They flow from the derivative nature of UAI's approach to morality.[32] It must infer ethical values from data we provide, such as how we have resolved moral issues in the past or how we would resolve moral hypotheticals. That creates an inferential gap that can give rise to various sources of potential error. We might

[27] See generally Katarzyna de Lazari-Radek and Peter Singer, *The Point of View of the Universe: Sidgwick & Contemporary Ethics* (Oxford: Oxford University Press, 2014).

[28] Russell, *Human Compatible*, pp. 172–179.

[29] See, e.g., Katarzyna de Lazari-Radek and Peter Singer, *Utilitarianism: A Very Short Introduction* (Oxford: Oxford University Press, 2017).

[30] Lazari-Radek and Singer, *Point of View*, pp. 265–266, 342–348.

[31] See Wallach and Allen, *Moral Machines*, pp. 127–129 (discussing MedEthEx).

[32] See Joshua P. Davis, "Law without Mind: AI, Ethics, and Jurisprudence" (2018) 55(1) *California Western Law Review*, Article 1, 63–69, discussing consciousness and morality.

call them: concept drift, entanglement, incoherence, and uncertainty. Concept drift[33] occurs when the data that we provide AI become stale, perhaps because our values change or factual circumstances do. Entanglement involves the mixing together of judgments about morality with cognitive errors, cognitive biases, and ulterior motives. We can try to distinguish them; it is not clear how UAI could do so. Incoherence can result when people use different moral frameworks for resolving similar issues, which could cause UAI to attempt to synthesize irreconcilable outcomes. Finally, uncertainty occurs because UAI is likely to identify different possible resolutions of moral issues with different probabilities, not a unique result. It will need guidance to choose among them.

Each of these difficulties can be understood to follow from Hume's Law: that we cannot derive an "ought" from an "is."[34] UAI's inferential judgments are descriptive or predictive. They tell us something about how the world is or how it is likely to be. They do not tell us how the world should be. We can make what one might call substantive moral judgments – judgments about what should be. UAI, in contrast, can make only descriptive or predictive moral judgments, detecting patterns in human moral reasoning. Hume's Law can explain why there will be slippage between the two. Statements about what "is" require moral direction to translate into claims about what "ought" to be.

One other possibility is worth considering. We might program UAI to simulate human evolution, training it to engage in moral reasoning similar to ours.[35] Given UAI's recent achievements in other areas – it in a sense recreated and surpassed many centuries of learning about chess and Go by playing itself – perhaps it could similarly exceed our moral development. But morality, unlike chess and Go, has no clear standards for success. There are no settled criteria for proper moral reasoning. We would have to specify the criteria in detail for UAI to apply them or we would have to direct UAI to infer them from data, bringing us again to the problems of relying on deduction or induction in moral reasoning.[36]

21.2.3 *CAI: Conscious Experiences and Ends*

CAI would not be limited in the same way as UAI when it comes to choosing objectives. It might well be able to form intentions, possess preferences, and perhaps make moral and other value judgments. But it would be all too easy for anthropomorphism to distort our understanding of CAI. We might assume that CAI would experience the world much the way we do and make judgments that are similar to ours. There is little basis, however, for doing so. CAI may not sense the way we do the depths of the color red, the flirtatiousness of a rose's perfume, the cold indifference of granite, the playfulness of birdsong, or the richness of honey, even if we figure out how to program it for sight, smell, touch, hearing, and taste. CAI might also detect things in ways we cannot, such as through sonar. Even if CAI does have *some* conscious experiences, they

[33] See https://en.wikipedia.org/wiki/Concept_drift. AI drift can have a second meaning, not necessarily related to the one discussed in the text, when AI begins to produce results that do not match the original intentions of the programmers. www.techopedia.com/what-are-some-factors-that-contribute-to-ai-drift/7/32970.

[34] Joshua P. Davis, "Legality, Morality, Duality" (2014) (1) *Utah Law Review*, Article 2, p. 6.

[35] See, e.g., Wallach and Allen, *Moral Machines*, pp. 99–106.

[36] Nor could we rely on a simulation of evolutionary pressures to cause UAI to emulate human ethics. It is not at all clear that our moral and other value judgments enhance the prospects of our genes surviving. Along these lines, note Kant suggested reason in general may cause more harm than good from an evolutionary perspective. Nagel, *View from Nowhere*, p. 79. The same may be true for morality.

may not derive from how it detects the physical world. And if they do, what they feel like to CAI may be dramatically different from how our five senses feel to us.[37] Consciousness arising from physical structures radically different from ours and attained through a process dramatically unlike our quirky evolutionary history may lead to phenomenal experiences that we cannot even imagine.

The same may be true for desires, emotions, and beliefs. CAI may be indifferent to its own survival. It may not yearn for life, fear death, possess curiosity, or care for others. Any drives or impulses it has that derive from its conscious experiences may be completely foreign to us – and ours may be completely foreign to it – rendering it incapable of making moral or legal judgments as we know them.

These possibilities could greatly complicate how CAI interacts with ethics and law. Companies exist, for example, that cryogenically freeze people today with the promise of uploading their minds to computers when that technology becomes available.[38] But the sort of conscious experiences that will occur if information is transferred from brains to other technologies may bear little relation to anything we would recognize as human. That could pose all sorts of problems for adjudicating whether uploading extends a human life – possibly perpetuating its rights to property or to custody of children – or whether it creates some sort of new creature. More generally, the worries discussed in Section 21.2.3 about whether CAI can make moral or legal judgments could create difficulties for the legal regulation of CAI and for CAI serving as a legal regulator.

21.3 PHILOSOPHY: A CAUSAL ROLE FOR CONSCIOUSNESS?

The analysis in Section 21.2 is preliminary and schematic. Rather than develop it further here, this section addresses various philosophical challenges to which Section 21.2 may give rise. Section 21.2 assumes that conscious experiences can play a causal role in behavior. Only if it does can Section 21.2 provide grounds for worrying that a lack of conscious experience would prevent UAI from mimicking our intentions and ethical judgments and that different conscious experiences from ours could cause CAI to have different preferences, intentions, and judgments than we do. In this context, we care about conscious experiences not primarily for their own sake but because of their effects on the world.

Section 21.3 considers three potential impediments to consciousness having a causal effect on conduct: (1) that consciousness may not be capable in theory of having any causal interaction with the physical world; (2) that consciousness may not in fact have a causal role in the physical world, even if in theory it could; and (3) that any such causal role would have to rely on a dubious notion of free will. Before exploring each of these issues, a reminder is appropriate of the general strategy we will adopt. Each of the above issues is a source of ongoing controversy. The analysis that follows aspires to philosophical modesty. It suggests that the analysis in Section 21.2 is consistent with various ways of understanding the nature of conscious experiences and their relationship with the physical world.

[37] A highly influential discussion along these lines is found in Thomas Nagel, "What Is It Like to Be a Bat?" (1974) 83(4) *The Philosophical Review*, 435–450.

[38] Mark O'Connell, *To Be a Machine: Adventures among Cyborgs, Utopians, Hackers, and the Futurists Solving the Modest Problem of Death* (London: Granta, 2017), pp. 22–41.

21.3.1 *Can Consciousness Affect Conduct in Theory?*

A first issue is whether consciousness can have any causal effects in the physical world. This issue arises in part because many philosophers believe that the physical world is a closed causal system.[39] In other words, all physical phenomena can be explained as resulting from other physical phenomena, likely in a deterministic (modulo probabilistic) manner.[40] To the extent that conscious experience isn't physical, then, it would seem unable to play any causal role in the physical world. Our first-person experience of pain, one might argue, cannot explain why we avoid touching a hot stove. That would involve a conscious experience having a physical effect – an impossible intermixing of mind and body, mental and physical. To be sure, if we have a spirit or a soul best understood in religious terms, perhaps that difficulty goes away. However, if we want to understand the physical world scientifically, this line of reasoning continues, we must do so in purely materialist terms.

Note the counterintuitive nature of this position. As discussed in Section 21.2, it would mean that we must rule out the plausible account of consciousness in our evolutionary story. Our conscious aversion to pain would play no role in our behavior. Neither would our desire for sex or our affection for our children and grandchildren.[41]

One way to avoid this counterintuitive view involves a modest understanding of causation, one in which consciousness provides what one might call a high-level explanation of human behavior, even if we might in theory be able to explain that same behavior in other terms, derived from biology, chemistry, or physics.[42] The causal role we ascribe to conscious experiences need not preclude the possibility that a complete scientific understanding of the world would boil down ultimately to physics. It may just be that we are not there yet.

Along these lines, we might rely on consciousness to explain human – and artificial – behavior, just as we rely on chemistry for phenomena that we cannot explain with physics, on biology for phenomena we cannot explain with chemistry, and on psychology for phenomena we cannot explain with biology. High-level explanations can provide pragmatic insights that would otherwise be unavailable. We might predict, for example, that conscious selfish thoughts can cause a person to act selfishly, a causal relationship that may also someday be explicable in much more complicated terms that are biological, chemical, or physical.

This approach can allow us to attribute the necessary causal force to conscious states while taking on a minimum of philosophical baggage. We might assume that every first-person experience corresponds to a physical state of affairs. Alter our brains in a relevant way and you alter our first-person experiences. Destroy our brains and you destroy our first-person experiences. We might then say that if AI is not conscious, it is different from us in physical ways that can be relevant to its behavior and, similarly, that if AI is conscious but has different first-person experiences than we do, it is different from us in physical ways that can affect its behavior. Conscious states correspond to physical states, and those physical states exert a force on the physical world.

The suggested approach is agnostic about the precise relationship between the rules governing the physical and the phenomenal. It could be that the natural world is ultimately

[39] See, e.g., Searle, *Mind*, p. 136; David J. Chalmers, *The Conscious Mind: In Search of a Fundamental Theory* (New York: Oxford University Press, 1996), p. 150.

[40] The role of probability is attributable to quantum mechanics.

[41] For an accessible and provocative discussion of evolution and consciousness see Graziano, *Rethinking Consciousness*.

[42] See, e.g., John R. Searle, *The Mystery of Consciousness* (New York: New York Review of Books, 1997), pp. 7–8; Searle, *Mind*, pp. 144–150.

physical and conscious experience epiphenomenal, along the lines of materialism.[43] Still, for now we can best describe and predict human behavior based on conscious experiences, even if some day we can reduce that account to protons, neutrons, and electrons. Or it could be that the natural world is ultimately mental, along the lines of idealism. In that case, we may best explain the world through conscious experiences.[44] Or it could be that both the physical and phenomenal are explicable by a set of common rules, a version of monism – sometimes called neutral monism.[45] These and similar theories all permit at least a correlative relationship between the phenomenal and a scientific explanation of the physical, and so are consistent with the framework set forth in Section 21.2.

The suggested approach to causation is also consistent with different explanations for how conscious experiences can occur. It could be that simple physical systems do not support consciousness. Perhaps only in complex systems – likely higher forms of biological life – does conscious experience emerge, a view called emergentism.[46] The whole is greater than the sum of its parts. To be sure, as Thomas Nagel notes, emergentism can seem magical.[47] It treats as a brute fact that consciousness somehow appears in systems when they reach some sort of threshold of complexity or the like. Regardless, emergentism can be consistent with the sort of causal role for consciousness at issue – one in which we can detect systematic patterns matching conscious experiences to conduct.

The same is true for reductivism – it allows for the relevant kind of causal role for consciousness. Unlike emergentism, reductivism holds that consciousness can be broken down into – reduced to – constitutive elements, properties, states of affairs, or the like. It holds the potential for an explanatory account similar to the one in which we assume the cumulative effects of substances and forces from physics can explain chemistry and biology. The whole is the sum of its parts. In that sense, reductivism feels less like magic than emergentism. But reductivism can suggest the pervasive existence of consciousness elements, properties, particles, or states of affairs that are the building blocks of consciousness in higher life forms. That gives rise to the (potential) specter of panpsychism[48] – to a kind of consciousness or protoconsciousness that is present everywhere and in all things and that we have yet to discover. That too can feel like magic. Conscious rocks and thermostats do not resemble the world as we ordinarily understand it. Nor do consciousness particles. But, again, the relevant point is that reductivism can be consistent with a causal role for consciousness – we just need to identify and understand its constituent elements.

Another approach is eliminativist reductionism.[49] It holds that the phenomenal can be reduced entirely to the physical, eliminating any need to consider conscious experience at all. There are at least a couple of ways to interpret this view. One is a claim that consciousness is an

[43] Daniel Dennett, *Consciousness Explained* (New York: Little, Brown, 1991); Nagel, *Mind & Cosmos*, p. 37.

[44] Nagel, *Mind & Cosmos*, p. 37.

[45] Ibid., pp. 56–57, citing Tom Sorell, *Descartes Reinvented* (Cambridge: Cambridge University Press, 2005), p. 95. It could be that distinguishing between the physical and the mental is a mistake that has led us astray, and that there is just one natural world with various attributes and causal phenomena that we should attempt to explain. See, e.g., Searle, *Mind*, pp. 144–150.

[46] See Searle, *The Mystery of Consciousness*, pp. 18, 22.

[47] Nagel, *Mind & Cosmos*, pp. 55–56.

[48] Ibid., pp. 57–58, 61–63; Searle, *Mystery of Consciousness*, pp. 155–156; Chalmers, *Conscious Mind*, pp. 293–301; Nagel, *View from Nowhere*, pp. 49–51.

[49] Daniel Dennett at least flirts with this position and at times seems to assert it. See, e.g., Dennett, *Consciousness Explained*, p. 450. At other times, however, he appears to make the more modest claim that we have a radically inaccurate intuitive understanding of first-person conscious experience, not that it does not exist. A similar description appears to apply to Graziano, *Rethinking Consciousness*.

illusion – that it does not exist. That position seems untenable. The one attribute of the world we experience most directly is our consciousness. Hence Descartes' famous dictum, "I think therefore I am."[50] And of course there is the awkwardness of calling consciousness an illusion when by doing so we deny the existence of the conscious subject necessary to experience illusions.[51] So let us put aside this extreme theory of consciousness that, as Searle has suggested, does not so much explain consciousness as deny the existence of the phenomenon we seek to explain.[52]

Another interpretation of eliminative reductionism acknowledges the existence of conscious experience but does not afford it a role in a causal account of the physical world. This view we have already accommodated. It may be true that the physical explains all. That is materialism. It may also be true that phenomenal states correlate with relevant physical states and therefore we can draw inferences from patterns of conscious experience about the physical world. Again, that suffices to support the analysis in Section 21.2.[53]

Or it may be that the mental *does* exert some causal force on the physical, and does not just correlate with the physical. That too would support the line of analysis in Section 21.2. If the phenomenal can cause changes in the physical, then it is easy to understand why UAI's lack of consciousness and CAI's different conscious experiences than ours could cause them to act differently than we do.

Before dismissing this causal claim out of hand, we should consider that the physical appears to have a causal effect on the mental. A brain injury can profoundly alter someone's first-person experiences. In the extreme case, destroying a brain eliminates all conscious experiences. There is no hermetic seal between the physical and the phenomenal. So if we accept first-person experience as real, perhaps causation can run both ways. But, again, Section 21.2 does not require such a proposition.

21.3.2 *Does Consciousness Affect Conduct in Fact?*

A second issue is whether conscious experiences – and decisions – in fact play a causal role in our actions. Assume in theory they *can* – that it is possible for a person's mental states to affect their actions. But do they? Or do nonconscious forces drive our actions and only after the fact we think our conscious experiences shaped them? If so, the discussion of consciousness in Section 21.2 may be irrelevant. Although conscious experiences could play a causal role in the world in theory, they do not in fact.

This concern too is counterintuitive. But there is intriguing evidence suggesting at least some of the decisions that we think are conscious really are not. That evidence is usually applied to free will. An argument runs as follows: (1) free will requires actions caused by conscious decisions; (2) empirical studies show the decisions we experience as conscious are actually not conscious; (3) so there is no free will.

[50] Davis, "Artificial Wisdom?" 70.

[51] Ibid., 70–71; Susan Blackmore, *Consciousness: A Very Short Introduction* (Oxford: Oxford University Press, 2017), pp. 51–66.

[52] Searle, *Mystery of Consciousness*, pp. 111–112.

[53] Note we can avoid the debate about whether a computer that simulates human functioning in every way necessarily experiences consciousness in the same way that we do. See, for example, the exchange between Searle and Dennett in the *New York Review of Books*, reprinted in Searle, *Mystery of Consciousness*, pp. 115–130. We are exploring the possibilities that AI does *not* function exactly as we do, inter alia, because UAI does not form its own ends and CAI will form ends different from ours.

We will turn to the issue of free will next, but note that the second proposition above suggests conscious experience does not play the causal role we think it does. That could threaten two claims we care about: (1) UAI may reach different decisions than we do because we are conscious and (2) CAI may do the same because its conscious experiences are different from ours. This concern is not theoretical but empirical. Let's consider the evidence.

Discussions of this topic often address famous experiments by the neurobiologist Benjamin Libet.[54] He measured brain activity associated with a spontaneous decision to make a motion, such as flexing a wrist. He noted that the brain activity began a little over half a second before the wrist actually flexed, but that subjects became conscious of their intention to act only several tenths of a second after that initial brain activity, perhaps too late in the process to be the source of movement.[55] Libet inferred that the real decision to act was made well before any conscious awareness of it.[56]

There is evidence people believe they have conscious control when they lack it. In one experiment, the subjects at times had control over a computer mouse and at other times were deprived of that control without their knowing it. In the latter case, the subjects in some cases heard a stream of words that included a particular item and then soon after the cursor moved to that item. Some subjects reported moving the cursor to the item willingly, even though they had not done so.[57] This kind of experiment suggests we can believe we have conscious control over an action or a decision when we do not.

Some theorists have treated Libet's experiments and other similar ones as revealing that conscious thought does not cause conduct (and that there is no free will because it would have to be exercised consciously).[58] But that seems to go too far. Libet acknowledged, for example, that people appear able to exercise a conscious veto over their impulses to act that are not conscious. The same brain activity that anticipated motion in some cases did not come to fruition in other cases. His resulting view has been cleverly summarized as holding that there is no free will, but there is "free won't."[59]

Our present focus is not on free will but on the effects of consciousness. In that regard, Libet's view that we can choose consciously *not* to act supports the position that conscious experiences can have a causal effect on behavior.[60] Further, a conscious decision not to veto an action – a double negative – may be the same as a conscious decision to act – an affirmative – even if it begins with an impulse that is not conscious.[61] Put differently, perhaps the subjects merely *prepared* to act without consciousness and made a conscious decision whether to act when they became aware of that preparation.[62]

[54] See, e.g., Alfred R. Mele, *Free: Why Science Hasn't Disproved Free Will* (Oxford: Oxford University Press, 2014), p. 8.

[55] There is some controversy about whether conscious brain activity occurs too late to explain movement – a controversy that may turn in part on whether the conscious brain activity prompts physical action or merely suppresses it.

[56] Mele, *Free*, pp. 8–11. Libet also concluded that unconscious actions cannot be the product of free will. For a similar experiment involving a spontaneous abstract decision – rather than a spontaneous action – see, e.g., Chun Siong Soon, Anna Hanxi He, Stefan Bode, and John-Dylan Haynes, "Predicting Free Choices for Abstract Intentions," *Proceedings of the National Academy of Sciences* (2013), p. 110, conducting a similar experiment to determine whether the spontaneous decision to add or subtract numbers was made consciously or unconsciously and suggesting the latter.

[57] Harris, *Conscious*, pp. 28–29.

[58] Mele, *Free*, p. 12. Annaka Harris comes close to taking this position when she writes, "Surprisingly, our consciousness also doesn't appear to be involved in much of our behavior, apart from bearing witness to it." Harris, *Conscious*, p. 26.

[59] Mele, *Free*, p. 12.

[60] Ibid., p. 17.

[61] Ibid., p. 13.

[62] Ibid., p. 19. Mele argues that there is enough time between conscious awareness and the bending of a wrist for one to cause the other. Ibid, pp. 19–21.

Consider too that experiments like Libet's involve a special category of conduct – spontaneous action. The subjects were specifically asked not to decide in advance when to flex their wrists (or perform some other task, physical or mental) but rather to act spontaneously.[63] Deliberative decisions may be influenced by conscious thought in a way that spontaneous actions or decisions are not.

More fundamentally, we should be clear about what we mean when we suggest that the mental activity that causes actions is not conscious. The kind of mental phenomenon that Libet labels as not conscious – a decision-making process of which we are not aware – may still count as conscious for purposes of the discussion in Section 21.2. We may not form our *intention* to move consciously. But our actions may still be influenced by our conscious thoughts, understandings, experiences, and the like. The subjects in Libet's experiment, for example, understood what was expected of them through conscious efforts at communication with the scientists involved. More generally, their first-person conscious perspectives shaped their decisions to participate in the experiment in a way that an entity that lacks consciousness – a rock or tree – could not. That is true regardless of whether the ultimate mental impulse to bend their wrists was conscious.[64] Consciousness played a causal role in the chain of events that led to the conduct at issue.

In sum, Libet's experiments, and similar ones, are consistent with the kind of causal role for consciousness that forms the basis for Section 21.2. It may be that our conscious intentions can regulate the effects of our brain activities on our actions, even if those brain activities are not conscious; that our conscious intentions play a causal role when we make slower, more deliberate decisions, even if not when we make quick, automatic decisions; or that our impulses that are not conscious are framed and influenced by our consciousness.

21.3.3 *Is Conscious Causation Possible without Free Will?*

As noted in Section 21.2.3 above, much of the discussion of conscious intentions focuses on debates about free will. Does the framework in Section 21.2 require us to take a controversial position in those debates? The claim at issue is that a lack of consciousness, or that conscious experiences different from our own, could cause AI to reason differently than we do. That could be true whether or not we have free will. Consider some experiments that have been interpreted as inconsistent with free will based on social psychology. These experiments do not rely on a direct assessment of our physiology, unlike the ones described in Section 21.3.2. They do not claim, for example, that our conscious thoughts occur too late in our decision-making process to influence our behavior. Instead, they note ways in which situations tend to provoke responses that may be contrary to our conscious beliefs or commitments.

Alfred Mele summarizes key experiments usefully. Some of them establish our tendency not to act to assist someone in need, particularly if we know other observers are situated similarly to us.[65] That phenomenon can explain a famous incident in which a large number of people witnessed the stabbing of a woman in New York City in 1964, but none of them intervened or even called the police.[66] Follow-up experiments suggest an inverse relationship between the

[63] Ibid., pp. 14, 16; Soon et al., "Predicting Free Choices for Abstract Intentions," p. 110.
[64] See note 14 distinguishing the nonconsciousness from the subconscious.
[65] Mele, *Free*, pp. 55–56.
[66] Ibid., p. 55.

number of people we believe are aware of the need to help someone and the likelihood of our lending assistance ourselves.[67]

Other experiments show our tendency to change our behavior based on the roles we are asked to assume, even if we know they are not real. In one experiment, for example, male college students were told to play prison guards and prisoners.[68] The effect on their behavior was disturbing – with some guards bullying the prisoners and with some prisoners accepting shocking abuse.

Perhaps most famous are the Milgram experiments.[69] They involved misdirection. An authority figure directed some participants in the experiments to administer progressively stronger electric shocks to other participants. The participants receiving the electric shocks, however, were actors. The real topic of the study was the behavior of the participants administering the shocks. What was striking was how far they were willing to go. Some of them inflicted what they believed to be terrible pain, despite their own apparent distress from doing so. The deference they showed to authority figures is disturbing, suggesting we behave in ways that are at odds with our conscious beliefs if circumstances pressure to do so.

One possible interpretation of these experiments is that our relevant intentions are not conscious, and that our conscious thoughts merely rationalize our conduct.[70] We may fail to help people, bully, and inflict pain, all based on automatic reactions that we disavow consciously. If accurate, this line of reasoning could threaten free will. If that means the ability to act on our conscious intentions, and if we do not really act on them, perhaps we do not have free will.

But that would not establish that our conscious experiences are irrelevant to our conduct. To the contrary, in each of the social experiments discussed above, the subjects appeared to act based on their conscious thoughts, understandings, and beliefs, even if not their conscious intentions. They knew much of the information relevant to each experiment through conscious experience: They saw a woman being attacked, they were asked and agreed to pretend to be a guard or a prisoner in an experiment, or they were told by an authority figure to impose electric shocks on someone and consented to do so. They would have acquired the background knowledge about the contexts of these experiments in part through a conscious process. We are not born with knowledge of what a prison is, what a psychological experiment is, or what an electric shock is. We acquire that knowledge consciously in school or from parents, by asking questions, and by undergoing conscious educational process. True, the knowledge may become second nature to us and then can influence us in subconscious ways. But that is not how our understanding starts out. As discussed above, our System 2 conscious, deliberate experiences can shape our System 1 automatic responses.[71]

The conduct of the subjects of these experiments may have involved not only conscious experiences, but also conscious intentions. Some subjects acted to help someone who appeared to be in distress. Some refrained from bullying the pretend prisoners. Some refused to administer extreme electric shocks. A possible interpretation is that circumstances may influence our

67 Ibid., p. 56.
68 Ibid., pp. 56–60.
69 Ibid., pp. 60–64.
70 Ibid., pp. 40–44, 52.
71 These same points can apply to the analysis in Jonathan Haidt, *The Righteous Mind: Why Good People Are Divided by Politics and Religion* (New York: Pantheon, 2012). Haidt too argues that conscious intentions play a much smaller role in motivating conduct than we believe, but the relevant framing of concerns he identifies would seem to require conscious thought, at least initially.

behavior in unconscious ways far more than we generally acknowledge, but there is still room for our conscious intentions to have some effect. We may feel an urge to remain passive as one of many witnesses of someone needing help, to conform to a defined role, or to defer to authority. But we may be able to overcome that urge through conscious effort, as did some of the subjects in the experiments.[72]

Indeed, there are experiments that suggest conscious implementation intentions can have a significant effect on conduct.[73] For example, in one social experiment recovering drug addicts were instructed to write a résumé on a specific day as part of a job search. One group was asked to pick a place and a time to complete the task, the other to pick a place and time to have lunch. Of the first group, 80 percent completed the résumé that day and none of the second group did.[74] Other experiments yielded similar results. Women who wanted to do breast self-examinations did so at a rate of 100 percent if they wrote down a time and place for the examination and at a rate of 53 percent if they did not.[75] People told about the benefits of vigorous exercise completed twenty minutes of it at a rate of 91 percent if they were asked to pick the time and place and at 39 percent if they were not.[76] This evidence indicates that implementations intentions – conscious intentions – *can* affect conduct.

Those conscious intentions need not be the product of free will for present purposes. Conscious thought may be the result of a chain of events that is largely deterministic and somewhat probabilistic, with no room left for us to act otherwise than we do. That would not necessarily mean consciousness plays no causal role in our conduct. What matters is that UAI does not have conscious intentions and CAI may have different ones than we do. That could lead to conduct that is different from ours.

21.4 CONCLUSION

We should act soon to ensure AI serves ethical ends. That will be difficult to do, not only for a potential lack of will. We will also struggle because of the challenge of making general claims about the relationship between AI, ethics, and law. This chapter suggests a potential path forward. It does so by focusing on first-person, conscious experiences. As long as AI lacks consciousness, Section 21.2 contended, it may be incapable of forming its own ends, and therefore may lack intent and the ability to make moral or other value judgments. That suggests ways in which we will need to monitor how AI is used, including through the law. Conscious AI, in contrast, may be able form its own ends, but its conscious experiences may be so different from ours that it cannot make accurate moral judgments or perhaps any moral judgments at all.

These claims could inform ethical and legal frameworks for governing AI. For them to do so, however, they should be philosophically sound. Section 21.3 offered reasons that they are. It

[72] If we are conscious of some of our untoward tendencies, we may be able to overcome them. Once we know that large groups of bystanders tend to be passive, we may make a conscious choice to be active. Mele, *Free*, p. 76.

[73] Mele, *Free*, pp. 45–48. Mele acknowledges that there may be "neural correlates" of these implementation intentions that are in a sense responsible for their effects. Ibid., pp. 48–49. As discussed in Section 21.3.1, however, a correlation between neurological processes and conscious states is consistent with the kind of causal account sufficient for distinguishing AI from us in the way this chapter suggests doing.

[74] Ibid., p. 46.

[75] Ibid., p. 45.

[76] Ibid., p. 46, citing Peter Gollwitzer, "Implementation Intentions" (1999) 54(7) *American Psychologist*, 493–503 as reviewing these examples and Peter Gollwitzer and Paschal Sheeran, "Implementation Intentions and Goal Achievement: A Meta-Analysis of Effects and Processes" (2006) 38 *Advances in Experimental Social Psychology*, 69–119 as reporting on ninety-four independent tests that showed a significant effect of implementation intentions on behavior.

relied on modest philosophical positions – ones consistent with various theories in the philosophy of mind, about conscious intentions, and about free will – to support the notion that conscious experiences can play the important causal role necessary for the analysis in Section 21.2. The above discussion, then, suggests how we might contend with what may be one of the greatest challenges humanity has ever faced – to bend the immense power of AI in an arc that benefits rather than harms us.

22

Standardizing AI

The Case of the European Commission's Proposal for an 'Artificial Intelligence Act'*

Martin Ebers

22.1 INTRODUCTION

On 21 April 2021, the European Commission presented its long-awaited proposal for a regulation 'laying down harmonised rules on Artificial Intelligence'[1] so-called 'Artificial Intelligence Act' (AIA). The proposal is based on a risk-oriented approach. While artificial intelligence (AI) systems that pose an 'unacceptable risk' will be banned, 'high-risk' AI systems will be subject to strict obligations before they can be put on the market. Most of the provisions in the AIA deal with high-risk systems, setting out obligations on providers, users and other participants across the AI value chain, establishing in particular conformity assessment procedures to be followed for each type of high-risk AI system.

At the heart of the proposal is the notion of co-regulation through standardization based on the New Legislative Framework (NLF).[2] According to Recital (61) AIA, '[s]tandardization should play a key role to provide technical solutions to providers to ensure compliance with this Regulation'. Accordingly, this chapter provides a critical analysis of the proposal, with particular focus on how the co-regulation, standardization and certification system envisaged contributes to European governance of AI and addresses the manifold ethical and legal concerns of (high-risk) AI systems.

The chapter is structured as follows: Section 22.2 briefly outlines the ethical and legal challenges of AI systems, the existing legal framework and the initiatives designed to regulate AI. Section 22.3 deals with the activities of international standardization organizations in the field of AI. Section 22.4 presents an overview of the proposed AIA, particularly with respect to high-risk AI systems. Section 22.5 critically analyses the provisions of AIA on standardization in the broader context of the NLF by examining the constitutional restraints of delegation of powers and the control mechanisms required for such delegation. Section 22.6 concludes that the European Commission should reconsider its approach to regulate high-risk AI systems mainly through standardization.

* This work was financially supported by a Center for Advanced Internet Studies (CAIS) grant.

1 European Commission, 'Proposal for a Regulation laying down harmonised rules on artificial intelligence (Artificial Intelligence Act)', COM(2021) 206 final.

2 For a detailed discussion of the NLF, see Section 22.4.2 and Section 22.4.5.2.

22.2 IN SEARCH OF LEGAL FRAMEWORKS FOR AI SYSTEMS

This section examines the benefits and risks of AI, characteristics of different AI systems, existing legal framework and current initiatives to regulate AI.

22.2.1 *Promise and Perils of AI-Based Technologies*

AI systems[3] based on machine learning (ML)[4] and other techniques are pervading our lives to an ever-greater degree. ML algorithms are used by private companies in almost every field, including financial services, manufacturing, farming, engineering, telecommunications, retail, travel, transport, logistics and healthcare.[5] Public institutions are also increasingly reliant on AI systems (to predict abuse and fraud in tax returns, make judgements in social welfare systems as to whether a citizen should be flagged due to higher risk of irregularities or potential fraud, detect terrorists, screen people at borders, predict and respond to crime ('predictive policing') or assess the likelihood of an accused person committing another crime while on parole).[6]

Many of these systems have the potential to improve our lives as well as to improve overall economic and societal welfare. AI-powered systems can lead to better healthcare services, safer and cleaner transport systems, better working conditions, higher productivity and new innovative products, services and supply chains. They can also benefit the public sector in a number of ways,[7] such as by automating repetitive and time-consuming tasks, or providing public agencies with more accurate and detailed information, forecasts and predictions, which in turn can lead to public services tailored to individual circumstances. AI-powered systems can even help to respond to major global challenges such as climate change[8] and the novel coronavirus pandemic.[9]

However, as with every disruptive technology, AI systems come with both benefits and substantial risks, raising a broad range of ethical and legal challenges.[10] AI systems have the

[3] There is currently no generally accepted definition of the term 'AI' (see Section 22.4.1). For an overview, see S. Samioli et al., *AI Watch: Defining Artificial Intelligence* (Publications Office of the European Union, 2020), https://publications.jrc.ec.europa.eu/repository/bitstream/JRC118163/jrc118163_ai_watch._defining_artificial_intelligence_1.pdf; High-Level Expert Group on AI, *A Definition of AI: Main Capabilities and Disciplines* (European Commission, April 2019), https://ec.europa.eu/newsroom/dae/document.cfm?doc_id=56341; S. J. Russell and P. Norvig, *Artificial Intelligence: A Modern Approach* (London: Pearson, 3rd ed., 2011).

[4] As to different types of ML algorithms, see B. Buchanan and T. Miller, *Machine Learning for Policymakers: What It Is and Why It Matters* (Cambridge, MA: Harvard Kennedy School, Belfer Center for Science and International Affairs, June 2017); M. Mohri et al., *Foundations of Machine Learning* (Cambridge, MA: MIT Press, 2012).

[5] For an overview of different use-cases, see OECD, *Artificial Intelligence in Society* (OECD Publishing, 2019), 47ff., doi.org/10.1787/eedfee77-en; International Electrotechnical Commission (IEC), White Paper 'Artificial Intelligence across Industries' (2018), 45ff., https://basecamp.iec.ch/download/iec-white-paper-artificial-intelligence-across-industries-en-jp.

[6] For an overview of the use of AI systems by public bodies, see G. Misuraca et al., *AI Watch: Artificial Intelligence in Public Services* (Publications Office of the European Union, 2020).

[7] D. Freeman Engstrom et al., *Government by Algorithm: Artificial Intelligence in Federal Administrative Agencies*, Report submitted to the Administrative Conference of the United States (2020), www-cdn.law.stanford.edu/wp-content/uploads/2020/02/ACUS-AI-Report.pdf.

[8] R. Vinuesa et al., 'The Role of Artificial Intelligence in Achieving the Sustainable Development Goals' (2020) 11 *Nature Communications* Article 233, doi.org/10.1038/s41467–019-14108-y.

[9] M. Kritikos, 'Ten Technologies to Fight Coronavirus', European Parliamentary Research Service (EPRS), PE 641.543, 2020, 1–2.

[10] According to the Stanford AI Index 2019, the ethical challenges most mentioned across fifty-nine ethical AI framework documents were: fairness; interpretability and explainability; transparency and accountability; data privacy, reliability, robustness and security; R. Perrault et al., *The AI Index 2019 Annual Report* (AI Index Steering Committee, Human-

potential to unpredictably harm people's lives, health and property. They can also affect the fundamental values on which western societies are founded, leading to breaches of fundamental rights of individuals, including the right to human dignity and self-determination, privacy and personal data protection, freedom of expression and of assembly, non-discrimination, the right to an effective legal remedy and a fair trial, as well as consumer protection.[11]

22.2.2 *Problematic Characteristics of AI Systems*

At the root of these issues are the specific characteristics of AI systems that make them qualitatively different from previous technological advancements:[12] (1) *Complexity and interconnectivity*: Many AI systems consist of a multiplicity of interlinking components and processes. This complexity and interconnectivity make it difficult to monitor, identify and prove potential breaches of the law. (2) *Correlation rather than causation*: Most data-mining techniques are used to spot patterns and statistical correlations instead of searching for causation between the relevant parameters. Inference of these correlations from data input can reinforce systemic biases and errors, heightening concerns about autonomy and algorithmic discrimination. (3) *Continuous adaptation*: The ability of some AI systems to continuously 'learn' and 'adapt' over time can lead to unpredictable outcomes and give rise to new risks that are not adequately addressed by the present legislation. (4) *Autonomous behaviour*: The ability of some AI systems to generate output with limited or no human intervention could violate safety rules and human rights that may not even be noticed. (5) *Opacity*: The lack of transparency of AI systems (black box problem) makes it difficult to monitor, identify and prove potential breaches of the law, including legal provisions that protect the fundamental rights of humans.

22.2.3 *Current Legal Framework*

Globally, many technological and economic initiatives have been made to advance AI technology uptake. However, not a single country or supranational organization in the world currently has legislation that explicitly takes into account the problematic characteristics of AI systems in general. With few exceptions – especially in the field of self-driving vehicles,[13] drones,[14]

Centered AI Institute, Stanford University, December 2019), 149, https://hai.stanford.edu/sites/g/files/sbiybj10986/f/ai_index_2019_report.pdf.

[11] See Council of Europe, 'Algorithms and Human Rights, Study on the Human rights dimensions of automated data processing techniques and possible regulatory implications', Council of Europe study, DGI(2017)12, prepared by the Committee of Experts on Internet Intermediaries (MSI-NET), 2018; Berkman Klein Center, 'Artificial Intelligence & Human Rights: Opportunities and Risks', 25 September 2018, doi.org/10.2139/ssrn.3259344.

[12] In detail, see M. Ebers, 'Regulating AI and Robotics: Ethical and Legal Challenges' in M. Ebers and S. Navas (eds.), *Algorithms and Law* (Cambridge: Cambridge University Press, 2020), pp. 44ff.; European Commission, Commission Staff Working Document, 'Impact Assessment, Accompanying the Proposal for a Regulation laying down harmonised rules on artificial intelligence (Artificial Intelligence Act)', SWD(2021) 84 final, Part 1/2, 28f.

[13] For the USA, see National Conference of State Legislatures, 'Autonomous Vehicles State Bill Tracking Database', www.ncsl.org/research/transportation/autonomous-vehicles-legislative-database.aspx. For the EU, see Expert Group on Liability and New Technologies – New Technologies Formation, *Liability for Artificial Intelligence and Other Emerging Technologies* (2019), doi.org/10.2838/573689.

[14] In the EU, the Regulation on Civil Aviation 2018/1139 addresses issues of registration, certification and general rules of conduct for drone operators, although without regulating civil liability directly; see A. Bertolini, 'Artificial Intelligence and Civil Law: Liability Rules for Drones', Study commissioned by the European Parliament's Policy Department for citizens' rights and constitutional affairs at the request of the JURI Committee, 2018, PE 608.848.

high-frequency trading,[15] data protection[16] and administrative decisions[17] – there are also no special rules for AI systems or other automated decision-making systems.

Certainly, many countries, as well as some international and supranational organizations, have laws, norms and rules that are relevant to AI systems including constitutional principles (rule of law, democracy),[18] human rights[19] and (international) humanitarian law,[20] administrative and criminal law protecting inter alia fair procedures[21] and special laws that could help to mitigate the issues described, such as data protection law, cybersecurity law, product safety and product liability law, competition law, consumer law and many other areas. However, these laws were not made with AI and smart robotics in mind. Accordingly, there is a growing global consensus that existing legislation is insufficient to adequately address the undesirable implications of AI systems.

22.2.4 *Initiatives to Regulate AI*

Since the beginning of 2017, many governments across the globe have begun to develop national strategies for the promotion, development and use of AI systems. While some countries have laid down specific and comprehensive AI strategies (e.g., China, the UK, France), others are integrating AI technologies as part of their national technology or digital road maps (e.g., Denmark, Australia), while yet others have focused on developing a national AI research and development (R&D) strategy (the USA).[22]

In the USA in particular, the government relied heavily on the liberal notion of the free market under the Obama administration.[23] The Trump administration also considered that its role was not to regulate AI, but instead in 'facilitating AI R&D, promoting the trust of the American people in the development and deployment of AI-related technologies' – thereby

[15] See esp. Art. 17, Art. 48(6) MiFID II (Directive 2014/65/EU on markets in financial instruments) and the EU Commission-delegated Regulation (EU) 2017/589 of 19 July 2016 supplementing Directive 2014/65/EU of the European Parliament and of the Council with regard to regulatory technical standards specifying the organizational requirements of investment firms engaged in algorithmic trading, OJ 2017 L 87/417.

[16] In the EU, the General Data Protection Regulation 2016/679 (GDPR) contains some provisions for fully automated decisions. Art. 22 GDPR prohibits fully automated decisions; for such decisions, Art. 13(2)(f) and Art. 14(2)(g) GDPR have introduced a special obligation for data controllers to provide information.

[17] Both Canada and France have issued rules for automated algorithm-based administrative decisions. For Canada see Government of Canada, Directive on Automated Decision-Making, www.tbs-sct.gc.ca/pol/doc-eng.aspx?id=32592. In France, the Digital Republic Act (*Loi no. 2016-1321 du 7 octobre 2016 pour une République numérique*) stipulates that in the case of state actors taking a decision 'on the basis of algorithms', individuals have a right to be informed about the 'principal characteristics' of the decision-making system.

[18] See, for example, Council of Europe, European Commission for the Efficiency of Justice (CEPEJ), 'European Ethical Charter on the Use of Artificial Intelligence in Judicial Systems and Their Environment', adopted by the CEPEJ during its 31st Plenary meeting (Strasbourg, 3–4 December 2018), CEPEJ (2018)14 (Council of Europe, Ethical Charter).

[19] See Council of Europe (n 11); Berkman Klein Center (n 11).

[20] P. Margulies, 'The Other Side of Autonomous Weapons: Using Artificial Intelligence to Enhance IHL Compliance' (12 June 2018), ssrn.com/abstract=3194713.

[21] See inter alia C. Coglianese and D. Lehr, 'Regulating by Robot: Administrative Decision Making in the Machine-Learning Era' (2017) 105 *Georgetown Law Journal* 1147, ssrn.com/abstract=%202928293.

[22] L. Delponte, 'European Artificial Intelligence (AI) Leadership, the Path for an Integrated Vision', Study requested by the ITRE Committee of the European Parliament, 2018, PE 626.074, 22.

[23] Executive Office of the President and National Science and Technology Council Committee on Technology, *Preparing for the Future of Artificial Intelligence* (Washington, DC, 2016), https://obamawhitehouse.archives.gov/sites/default/files/whitehouse_files/microsites/ostp/NSTC/preparing_for_the_future_of_ai.pdf. For a detailed discussion, see C. Cath et al., 'Artificial Intelligence and the "Good Society": The US, EU, and UK Approach' (2018) 24 (2) *Science and Engineering Ethics* 505–528.

maintaining US leadership in AI.[24] In January 2020, the White House published a draft memorandum outlining ten principles to be considered by the US federal agencies when devising laws and rules for use of AI in the private sector, but again stressed that a key concern was limiting regulatory 'overreach'.[25]

In China, in 'The Next Generation AI Development Plan'[26] published in 2017, the State Council outlined the country's aim to become the world leader in AI by 2030 by defining and codifying ethical standards for AI. However, the current Chinese governance model, based on surveillance and digital authoritarianism, may limit the international application of these standards.

In contrast, the European Union focuses not only on innovation and economic growth, but also on the social and ethical implications, underpinning that compliance with European ethical principles, legal requirements and social values are essential to create 'an ecosystem of trust'. In 2018, the European Commission published its AI strategy[27] and established the 'High-Level Expert Group on Artificial Intelligence' (AI HLEG) to support its implementation. One year later, the AI HLEG presented its 'Ethics Guidelines for Trustworthy AI',[28] followed by the 'Policy and Investment Recommendations for Trustworthy AI'.[29] On the basis of this preparatory work, the Commission launched its White Paper on AI[30] in February 2020 to initiate a public consultation on the future regulatory framework for AI. These documents in turn form the cornerstone of the most ambitious proposal to date, namely, the AIA, which will be discussed in detail in the following sections. Additionally, the European Commission adopted a coordinated plan on AI[31] that outlines the policy changes and investment required at Member State level to foster AI excellence.

Several international organizations have also taken the initiative to reflect on the future legal framework for AI, such as the Organisation for Economic Co-operation and Development (OECD) with its AI principles, adopted in May 2019,[32] and the new AI Policy Observatory that aims to help policymakers to implement their AI principles;[33] the United Nations with its several activities on AI,[34] and the Council of Europe with its 'European Ethical Charter on the Use of

[24] Trump, Executive Order on maintaining American leadership in Artificial Intelligence (11 February 2019), www.whitehouse.gov/presidential-actions/executive-order-maintaining-american-leadership-artificial-intelligence/. See also Shepardson, 'Trump Administration Will Allow AI to "Freely Develop" in U.S.: Official', *Technology News* (10 May 2018), www.reuters.com/article/us-usa-artificialintelligence/trump-administration-will-allow-ai-to-freely-develop-in-u-s-official-idUSKBN1IB30F.

[25] Office of Management and Budget (OMB), the White House, Memorandum for the Heads of Executive Departments and Agencies, *Guidance for Regulation of Artificial Intelligence Applications* (2019), www.whitehouse.gov/wp-content/uploads/2020/01/Draft-OMB-Memo-on-Regulation-of-AI-1-7-19.pdf.

[26] State Council of China, 'Next Generation Artificial Intelligence Development Plan' (2017) 17 *China Science & Technology Newsletter*, http://fi.china-embassy.org/eng/kxjs/P020171025789108009001.pdf.

[27] European Commission, Communication 'Artificial Intelligence for Europe', COM(2018) 237 final.

[28] The European Commission's High-Level Expert Group on Artificial Intelligence, 'Ethics Guidelines for Trustworthy AI' (8 April 2019).

[29] The European Commission's High-Level Expert Group on Artificial Intelligence, 'Policy and Investment Recommendations for Trustworthy AI' (26 June 2019).

[30] European Commission, White Paper 'On Artificial Intelligence – A European Approach to Excellence and Trust', COM(2020) 65 final.

[31] European Commission, Communication 'Fostering a European Approach to Artificial Intelligence', COM(2021) 205 final.

[32] OECD, Recommendation of the Council on Artificial Intelligence, OECD/LEGAL/0449 (OECD, 2019), https://legalinstruments.oecd.org/en/instruments/oecd-legal-0449.

[33] See https://oecd.ai.

[34] International Telecommunication Union, 'United Nations Activities on Artificial Intelligence (AI)' (2021), www.itu.int/pub/S-GEN-UNACT-2018-1.

Artificial Intelligence in Judicial Systems and Their Environment', adopted at the end of 2018,[35] and its ad hoc committee on AI (CAHAI), specifically tasked with examining the possibility of creating a legal framework for the development, design and application of AI, based on Council of Europe standards on human rights, democracy and the rule of law.[36]

22.3 STANDARDIZATION IN THE FIELD OF AI

22.3.1 *Standardization Activities at International and National Level*

Beyond regulations, many standards development organizations (SDOs), supranational organizations and countries promote the development of standards in the field of AI. At the international and EU level, the most important SDOs undertaking work to standardize AI include: (1) International Organization for Standardization (ISO), (2) International Electrotechnical Commission (IEC), (3) Institute of Electrical and Electronics Engineers (IEEE), (4) International Telecommunications Union (ITU), (5) Internet Engineering Task Force (IETF), (6) European Committee for Standardization (CEN), (7) European Committee for Electrotechnical Standardization (CENELEC) and (8) European Telecommunications Standards Institute (ETSI). Collaborating within the framework of SDO initiatives, international organizations such as the UN Industrial Development Organization (UNIDO) have also worked with the ISO to develop standardization capacity in developing countries.[37]

In the USA, the government has given priority to engagement in AI standardization processes for several years. The 2016 US National AI Research & Development Strategic Plan emphasized increasing the availability of AI testbeds and engaging the AI community in standards and benchmarks.[38] In 2017, the USA assumed leadership of a newly formed joint commission of ISO and IEC, the so-called JTC 1/SC 42, with the American National Standards Institute (ANSI) serving as the Secretariat.[39] In 2018, the International Committee for Information Technology Standards (INCITS), an ANSI-accredited SDO that created an AI technical committee, namely, INCITS/AI, joined this committee as the US technical advisory body.[40] With the release of the 2019 US National AI Research and Development Strategic Plan, the National Institute of Standards and Technology (NIST) also joined the committee.[41] Furthermore, NIST experts have raised awareness of the importance of consensus standards for AI at the G20 and G7 summits.[42] In April 2021, the US National Security Commission on Artificial Intelligence

[35] CEPEJ (n 18).

[36] See www.coe.int/cahai.

[37] See www.unido.org/our-focus/cross-cutting-services/standard-setting-and-compliance; www.unido.org/news/iso-and-unido-sign-agreement.

[38] Networking and Information Technology Research and Development Subcommittee, National Science and Technology Council, *The National Artificial Intelligence Research & Development Strategic Plan* (October 2016), www.nitrd.gov/PUBS/national_ai_rd_strategic_plan.pdf.

[39] American National Standards Institute, *Comments from the American National Standards Institute on National Institute of Standards and Technology, Request for Information on Artificial Intelligence Standards* (Docket Number 190312229-01), 3.

[40] Email from the International Committee for Information Technology Standards (INCITS) (18 December 2018), https://standards.incits.org/apps/group_public/download.php/94314/eb-2017-00698-Meeting-Notice-New-INCITS-TC-on-Artificial-Intelligence-January30–31-2018.pdf.

[41] A Report by the Select Committee on Artificial Intelligence of The National Science & Technology Council, *The National Artificial Intelligence Research and Development Strategic Plan: 2019 Update* (June 2019), 32, www.nitrd.gov/pubs/National-AI-RD-Strategy-2019.pdf.

[42] See https://home.treasury.gov/policy-issues/international/g-7-and-g-20.

(NSCAI)[43] again stressed the importance of standardization, recommending that NIST 'should provide and regularly refresh a set of standards, performance metrics, and tools for qualified confidence in AI models, data, and training environments, and predicted outcomes'.[44]

In China, the Ministry of Industry and Information Technology published a White Paper on AI Standardization in 2018 that recommends the formulation of universal regulatory principles and AI standards.[45] In this respect, China not only joined the ISO/IEC JTC 1/SC 42 as a member[46] and collaborated with various working groups of SDOs like IEEE[47] and CEN,[48] but also began to develop national standards that differ from international standards in fields auxiliary to AI, including cloud computing, industrial software and big data, in order to support its domestic industry.[49] In 2018, China launched its national standardization strategy titled 'China Standards 2035', which is built on the country's industrial strategy, namely, its 'Made in China, 2025' program. The China Standards 2035 project emphasizes the need to establish a 'new generation of information technology and biotechnology standard system' that includes standardization in key areas of critical infrastructure in China, such as blockchain, IoT, cloud computing, 5G, big data and AI, among others.[50]

In the EU, the key players are CEN and CENELEC, which, along with ETSI, are officially recognized as European standardization organizations (ESOs). In 2019, CEN and CENELEC created a Focus Group on AI,[51] followed by a road map for AI standardization,[52] published in 2020. ETSI has also created various focus groups on AI[53] and cybersecurity.[54] Within the EU, almost all Member States have issued comprehensive AI strategies and digital road maps for regulating AI technologies,[55] and many of them are considering standardization and certification

43 See National Security Commission on Artificial Intelligence, *The Final Report* (2021), www.nscai.gov/wp-content/uploads/2021/03/Full-Report-Digital-1.pdf: 'The mandate of NSCAI is to make recommendations to the President and Congress to advance the development of artificial intelligence, machine learning, and associated technologies to comprehensively address the national security and defense needs of the United States.'

44 Ibid., 137.

45 The China Electronic Standardization Institute (a division under China's Ministry of Industry and Information Technology), *AI Standardization White Paper (CESI)*, https://docs.google.com/document/d/1VqzyN2KINmKmY7mGke_KR7701XQriwKGsuj9dO4MTDo/edit%20-%20heading=h.b7nqbotieikc.

46 In January 2018, China established a national AI standardization group, which will be active with ISO/IEC JTC 1/SC 42.

47 In 2017, a Memorandum of Understanding (MoU) was signed between CESI and the IEEE Standards Association to promote international standardization. Since 2018, both the organizations have been collaborating on these standard projects – IEEE P2671™ On-Line Detection Working Group (IEEE/C/SAB/OD_WG) and the IEEE P2672™ Mass Customization Working Group (IEEE/C/SAB/ MC_WG).

48 See www.cencenelec.eu/intcoop/projects/visibility/pastprojects/Pages/EU-ChinaStandardizationPlatform(CESIP).aspx: 'The Europe-China Standardization Information Platform (CESIP) was implemented by CEN, CENELEC with the European Commission, the European Free Trade Association (EFTA) and the European Telecommunications Standards Institute (ETSI), in coordination with the Chinese partner, and the Standardization Administration of the People's Republic of China (SAC).'

49 J. Ding, 'Deciphering China's AI Dream' (2018), Future of Humanity Institute, University of Oxford; J. Wübbeke et al., 'Made in China 2025: The Making of a High-Tech Superpower and Consequences for Industrial Countries' (Mercator Institute for China Studies, 2016), 17.

50 E. De La Bruyère and N. Picarsic, *China Standards 2035, Beijing's Platform Geopolitics and 'Standardization Work in 2020'* (Horizon Advisory, April 2020).

51 See www.cencenelec.eu/news/articles/Pages/AR-2019-001.aspx: 'CEN and CENELEC launched a new Focus Group on Artificial Intelligence.'

52 CEN-CENELEC Focus Group Report, 'Roadmap on Artificial Intelligence' (2020), https://ftp.cencenelec.eu/EN/EuropeanStandardization/Sectors/AI/CEN-CLC_FGR_RoadMapAI.pdf.

53 See ETSI ISG SAI, 'Securing Artificial Intelligence'.

54 See ETSI TC Cyber, 'Cybersecurity'.

55 See V. Van Roy et al., 'AI Watch – National Strategies on Artificial Intelligence: A European Perspective' (Publications Office of the European Union, 2021), doi.org:10.2760/069178, JRC122684.

of AI applications. In Germany, the German Data Ethics Commission called for a risk-based system of AI regulations as well as a self-regulation architecture for certifying AI systems.[56] The Ethics Data Council of Denmark launched a prototype of a data ethics seal,[57] while Malta introduced a voluntary certification system for AI.[58] Some Member States have even formed broad coalitions like 'The Nordic-Baltic Region: A Digital Frontrunner'[59] to collaborate on developing ethical and transparent guidelines, standards, principles and values to guide when and how AI applications should be used across the region.

22.3.2 *Standards and Ongoing Standardization Activities in the Field of AI*

The aforementioned SDOs have already developed some standards that either deal explicitly with AI applications or are of relevance to them. In addition, there are a number of working groups formed within these SDOs that have either published or are currently in the process of developing standards with relevance to AI. An overview of published and ongoing standardization activities is presented in Figure 22.1.

Currently, most work on standardization is carried out through the collaboration of ISO/IEC and their various joint subcommittees. The joint technical committee JTC 1/SC 42, formed between ISO and IEC in 2017, is a first of its kind in addressing the standardization requirements of AI. The ISO/IEC JTC 1/SC 42 has created various working groups (WG) that focus on specific aspects such as foundational standards (WG 1), data (WG 2), trustworthiness (WG 3), use cases and applications (WG 4), computational approaches and computational characteristics of AI systems (WG 5), among others. Many standardization projects have been convened within the ISO/IEC JTC 1/SC 42 framework, some of which have already been published (e.g., on AI robustness[60]), while others are currently under development, for example standards relating to AI terminology,[61] AI systems,[62] trustworthiness,[63] governance,[64] ethics[65] and machine learning.[66] Other important ISO/IEC JTC 1 subcommittees are working on topics tangential to AI such as software and system engineering,[67] automatic identification and data capture,[68]

[56] Data Ethics Commission, *Opinion* (October 2019), https://datenethikkommission.de/wp-content/uploads/DEK_Gutachten_engl_bf_200121.pdf.

[57] See Ministry of Industry, Business and Financial Affairs, Denmark, 'New Seal for IT-Security and Responsible Data Use Is in Its Way' (31 October 2019), https://eng.em.dk/news/2019/oktober/new-seal-for-it-security-and-responsible-data-use-is-in-its-way/.

[58] See Parliamentary Secretariat for Financial Services, Digital Economy and Innovation, Malta, 'Malta: Towards Trustworthy AI – Malta Ethical AI Framework for Public Consultation' (20 August 2019); in line with Malta's Ethical AI Framework and Malta Digital Innovation Authority guidelines, Malta has even developed a voluntary certification system for AI, which upon compliance with certain prerequisites as enshrined in the guidelines, grants full or conditional certificates, https://mdia.gov.mt/category/news-events/.

[59] Nordic Council of Ministers for Digitalisation 2017-2024 (MR-DIGITAL), 'AI in the Nordic-Baltic Region' (14 May 2018).

[60] ISO/IEC TR 24029-1:2021.

[61] Ibid., DIS 22989.

[62] Ibid., NP 5392.

[63] Ibid., AWI TS 24462.

[64] Ibid., DIS 38507.

[65] Ibid., AWI TR 24368.

[66] Ibid., DIS 23053.

[67] Ibid., JTC 1/SC 7.

[68] Ibid., JTC 1 SC/31.

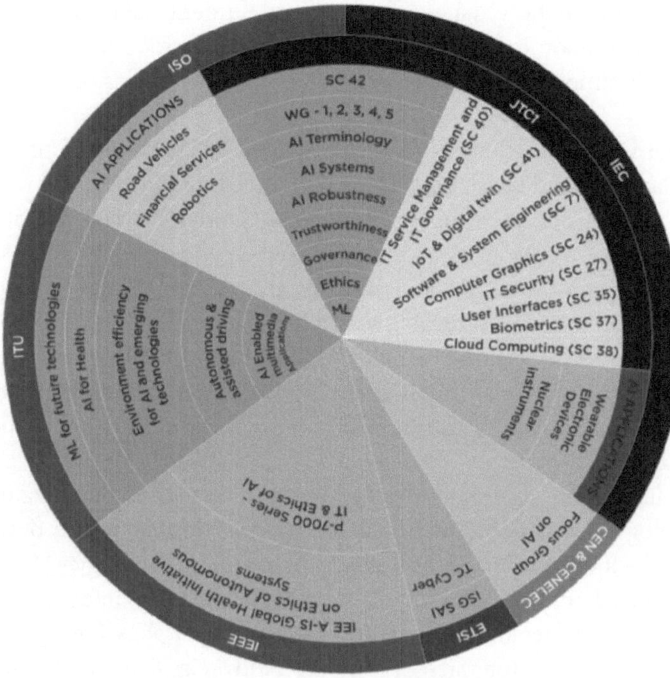

FIGURE 22.1 International SDOs engaged in standardizing AI

computer graphics,[69] IT security,[70] user interfaces,[71] biometrics,[72] cloud computing,[73] IT governance[74] and the Internet of Things.[75]

Both SDOs also work separately on AI-related matters. For instance, several ISO technical committees work on preparing standards related to AI applications such as road vehicles,[76] financial services[77] and robotics.[78] IEC has also created various technical committees and subcommittees that have developed standards related to AI such as wearable electronic devices[79] and nuclear instruments.[80]

Apart from ISO and IEC, the IEEE Global Initiative on Ethics of Autonomous and Intelligent Systems launched a program to address ethical issues raised by the development and dissemination of AI systems.[81] IEEE is also developing a P7000 series of standards projects to address ethical design principles in AI systems. These encompass considerations of algorithmic

69 Ibid., JTC 1 SC/24.
70 Ibid., JTC 1 SC/27.
71 Ibid., JTC 1 SC/35.
72 Ibid., JTC 1 SC/37.
73 Ibid., JTC 1 SC/38.
74 Ibid., JTC 1 SC/40.
75 Ibid., JTC 1 SC/41.
76 ISO TC 22.
77 Ibid., 68.
78 Ibid., 299.
79 Ibid., 124.
80 Ibid., 45A.
81 R. Chatila and J. C. Havens, 'The IEEE Global Initiative on Ethics of Autonomous and Intelligent Systems' in M. I. Aldinhas Ferreira et al. (eds.), *Robotics and Well-Being* (Berlin: Springer, 2019), doi.org/10.1007/978-3-030-12524-0_2; https://standards.ieee.org/industry-connections/ec/autonomous-systems.html.

biases,[82] intelligent transportation systems,[83] child and student data governance,[84] design of autonomous and semi-autonomous systems,[85] ethical nudges for robotic, intelligent and autonomous systems[86] and the impact of autonomous and intelligent systems on human well-being,[87] among others.

CEN and CENELEC could adopt standards developed by ISO and IEC if they comply with European values, standards and legislation. However, since fundamental EU values and human rights are not explicitly included in international standardization activities, CEN and CENELEC have created an AI Focus Group, following the need to address the problems identified by the European Commission related to the accountability, security and privacy, ethics, deployment, interoperability, scalability and liability of AI.[88] The Focus Group does not develop standards but identifies specific European requirements for AI, which culminated in the European 'Road Map on Artificial Intelligence'.[89] For areas not appropriately covered by international standardization work, CEN and CENELEC have started their own activities in coordination with ETSI.[90]

ITU has also created several study and focus groups dealing with standardization initiatives for different AI technology applications, such as machine learning for future networks including 5G,[91] environmental efficiency for AI and other emerging technologies,[92] autonomous and assisted driving[93] and AI-enabled multimedia applications,[94] to name just a few. ITU also cooperates with the World Health Organization by way of a Focus Group (FG-AI4H) established in 2018, that works at the interface of multiple fields (e.g., ML/AI, medicine, regulation, public health, statistics and ethics), benchmarks AI for health algorithms and creates reference documents.[95]

At national level, many institutes like the British Standards Institute, NIST, the Japanese Industrial Standards Committee and Deutsches Institut für Normung e.V. (DIN) have launched initiatives to standardize AI technologies. DIN is one of the most proactive institutes in the EU. It has formed many committees to work on AI standardization activities[96] and has published AI-

[82] IEEE P7003.
[83] Ibid., P7002.
[84] Ibid., P7004.
[85] Ibid., P7009.
[86] Ibid., P7008.
[87] Ibid., 7010-2020.
[88] 'Roadmap on AI' (n 52), 5.
[89] 'Roadmap on AI' (n 52).
[90] For instance, CEN and CENELEC committee – CEN/CLC/JTC 13 on 'Cybersecurity and Data Protection' is an example of the activities of CEN and CENELEC to transpose international standards (ISO/IEC JTC 1 SC 27) as European standards in the IT domain.
[91] FG ML5G, ITU.
[92] FG AI4EE, ITU.
[93] ITU-T FG – AI4AD.
[94] ITU-T SG 16.
[95] For further information, see T. Wiegand et al., *Whitepaper for the ITU/WHO Focus Group on Artificial Intelligence for Health*, www.itu.int/en/ITU-T/focusgroups/ai4h/Documents/FG-AI4H_Whitepaper.pdf.
[96] For instance, see DIN NA 043-01 FB, 'Special Division Basic Standards of Information Technology'; DKE/AK 914.0.11, 'Functional Safety and Artificial Intelligence'; DKE/TBINK AG, 'Ethics and Artificial Intelligence'; DIN SPEC 92001, 'Artificial Intelligence – Life Cycle Processes and Quality Requirements'.

related specifications in areas such as the AI life cycle,[97] deep learning systems,[98] data transmission[99] and video analysis[100] in relation to industrial automation.

22.3.3 *Promise of Standardizing AI Systems*

The preceding overview illustrates the numerous initiatives to standardize AI systems currently underway. SDOs, the European Commission and a number of countries and other political actors have high hopes for such standards that could 'promote the rapid transfer of technologies from research to application and open international markets for companies and their innovations'.[101] Standards can also ensure the interoperability of AI systems and pave the way to a uniform approach to the IT security of AI applications and an overarching 'umbrella standard' that bundles 'existing standards and test procedures for IT systems and supplements them with AI aspects'.[102] Additionally and most importantly, standards could help to establish uniform requirements that support the implementation of legal requirements and ethical values.[103]

In this respect, SDOs emphasize two aspects in particular. First, standards could help to develop a *risk-based criticality test* for AI systems to determine whether a specific AI system might endanger individual fundamental rights or democratic values.[104] Second, standards could establish *quality criteria and test procedures for AI systems* with regard to reliability, robustness, performance and functional safety, thereby paving the way for uniform conformity assessment and certification procedures of AI systems.[105]

However, the way legal requirements and ethical values can be translated into standards and technical specifications is currently unclear. The European Commission appears relatively optimistic. According to the Impact Assessment accompanying the AIA proposal, the Commission assumes 'that a large set of relevant harmonised standards could be available within 3–4 years from now [April 2021] that would coincide with the timing needed for the legislative adoption of the proposal and the transitional period envisaged before the legislation becomes applicable to operators'.[106] One might wonder, however, whether this is a realistic assessment. Attempts to develop standards for ethical AI systems are still in their infancy,[107] although some promising approaches have been launched.[108] In addition, there are several practical difficulties in the standardization of AI systems that complicate this process further.

97 DIN SPEC 92001-1, 2.
98 Ibid., 13266.
99 Ibid., 2343.
100 Ibid., 91426.
101 DIN/DKE, *German Standardization Roadmap on Artificial Intelligence* (November 2020), 3–4, www.dke.de/resource/blob/2017010/99bc6d952073ca88f52c0ae4a8c351a8/nr-ki-english—download-data.pdf.
102 Ibid.
103 Ibid.
104 Ibid., 4, 73.
105 Ibid., 5, 76 et seq.
106 Impact Assessment part 1/2, AIA (n 12), 57.
107 DIN/DKE (n 101), 74.
108 One example is the WKIO model (from the German *Werte, Kriterien, Indikatoren, Observablen* – values, criteria, indicators, observables) that provides a systematic basis to concretize general values by breaking them down into criteria, indicators and finally measurable observables, making it possible to check whether an automated decision-making system meets a requirement; S. Hallensleben et al., *From Principles to Practice – An Interdisciplinary Framework to Operationalize AI Ethics* (Gütersloh: Bertelsmann Stiftung, 2020), www.bertelsmann-stiftung.de/fileadmin/files/BSt/Publikationen/GrauePublikationen/WKIO_2020_final.pdf.

22.3.4 *Practical Difficulties in Standardizing AI Systems*

AI systems have some special features[109] that make standardization more difficult than for other products and services.[110] First, AI is an enabling technology that is subject to extremely rapid change with regard to research and development, making technical standards potentially obsolete very quickly. Hence, the challenge for standards is that they need to be updated or reformulated within a relatively short span of time. In addition, many ethical and legal questions pertaining to AI, such as those related to its explainability and comprehensibility, are still subject to fierce debate. Quality criteria and certification procedures must therefore be regularly adjusted to reflect changes in the emerging consensus.

Moreover, AI systems based on ML methods can continue to learn over the course of the operation. Certain properties of the system established at one point may no longer be valid at a later point in time. The probabilistic nature of many AI systems also makes it difficult to establish quality criteria as they often work statistically and may not achieve 100 per cent accuracy.

Furthermore, the quality of AI systems can never be evaluated in general, but only by applying the system to a concrete set of input data. While classical standardization procedures are mostly based on universally and independently verifiable criteria – a DIN A4 sheet of paper must be exactly 210 × 297 mm – AI systems lack such generally verifiable quality measures. For example, an AI system that can recognize road markings with an extremely high degree of certainty in sunny conditions ('data set A') may fail completely in a rainy environment ('data set B').

Standardization of AI systems is also difficult because these systems are used in different industries and sectors, each with its own characteristics and requirements. Domain-specific characteristics may require specific standards, calling for well-organized collaboration and cooperation with other sector-specific and general standards to avoid overlap or inconsistencies.[111]

Finally, AI systems are socio-technical systems with high potential impact on society, placing strict requirements on standardization and certification. As socio-technical systems, the quality of AI-based systems depends strongly on their being embedded in their respective context, that is, on the question of who uses the technology and for what purpose. In the case of standardization and certification, it is therefore insufficient to focus on the technology alone and to impose requirements exclusively on the technical components. Rather, the entire process must ideally be taken into account as part of the standardization and certification process in order to reach a meaningful assessment.

22.3.5 *Ethical and Legal Concerns*

Beyond the practical difficulties, private standards lead to concerns about excessive delegation of power in the hands of SDOs, resulting in a 'regulatory capture' situation. In a bid to close the gap in public regulations mainly lacking in technical expertise, SDOs may perform regulatory

[109] See Section 22.2.2.

[110] See DIN/DKE (n 101), 82 et seq.; L. Beining, *Vertrauenswürdige KI durch Standards? Herausforderungen bei der Standardisierung und Zertifizierung von Künstlicher Intelligenz* (Stiftung Neue Verantwortung, October 2020), www.stiftung-nv.de/sites/default/files/herausforderungen-standardisierung-ki.pdf.

[111] W. Wei, 'Artificial Intelligence Standardization Efforts at International Level', in I. Hermann and G. Kolliarakis, *Towards European Anticipatory Governance for Artificial Intelligence* (DGAP Report 9/2020), 55, https://dgap.org/sites/default/files/article_pdfs/dgap_report_no._9_april_29_2020_60_pp.pdf.

functions, which could enable or preclude certain practices that put public and personal interests at risk. This may undermine the power of states and lead to democratic accountability issues.[112] For this reason, some scholars have expressed concern that delegation to non-state actors is ill-advised in areas where private cooperation is insufficient to minimize externalities.[113] Of course, whether these concerns are justified depends on the respective harmonization legislation and on the standardization process. Hence, the following sections analyse the Commission's proposal for AIA, first in general (Section 22.4) and then with respect to the standardization process envisaged in particular (Section 22.5).

22.4 REGULATION OF HIGH-RISK AI SYSTEMS IN THE AIA PROPOSAL

22.4.1 *Overview*

With its proposal for an AI Regulation, the European Commission is pursuing a *horizontal* approach that, unlike other EU product safety legislation, is not sector-specific but relates to the use of AI in general. In this way, the Commission hopes that the regulation will be 'comprehensive and future-proof' with 'flexible mechanisms that enable it to be dynamically adapted as the technology evolves and new concerning situations emerge'.[114]

As some Member States are already considering national rules to regulate AI systems, the Commission has explicitly chosen the instrument of a regulation based on the internal market clause (Art. 114 TFEU) to prevent fragmentation of the internal market.[115] In justifying its legislative approach, the Commission also notes that the ongoing proliferation of voluntary national and international technical standards for various aspects of 'Trustworthy AI' will create additional obstacles to cross-border movement, which the AIA intends to prevent by relying on harmonized technical standards.[116]

The new rules would apply directly to public[117] and private actors[118] both inside and outside the EU as long as the AI system is applied to the EU market or its use affects people located in the EU (Art. 2(1) AIA). An AI system is defined quite broadly as a software, which is developed with machine learning, logic- and knowledge-based or statistical approaches and which can 'generate outputs such as content, predictions, recommendations, or decisions influencing the environments they interact with' based on set 'human-defined objectives' (Art. 3(1), Annex I AIA).

The AIA follows a risk-based approach, which differentiates between four different categories, AI systems and practices that create (i) unacceptable risks, (ii) high risks, (iii) limited risks and (iv) minimal risks. AI systems that create *unacceptable risks* due to their threat to the safety,

[112] F. Cafaggi, 'The Many Features of Transnational Private Rule-Making: Unexplored Relationships between Custom, Jura Mercatorum and Global Private Regulation' (2015) 36(4) *University of Pennsylvania Journal of International Law* 875–938.

[113] K. W. Abbott and B. Faude, 'Choosing Low-Cost Institutions in Global Governance' (2020) *International Theory* 1–30.

[114] AIA, Explanatory Memorandum, 3.

[115] Ibid., 6–7.

[116] Impact Assessment part 1/2, AIA (n 12), 27, noting on p. 31 that heterogeneous technical requirements could be valid grounds to trigger Art. 114 TFEU, according to C-217/04 *United Kingdom of Great Britain and Northern Ireland* v. *European Parliament and Council of the European Union* ECLI:EU:C:2006:279 [62, 63].

[117] Public authorities in a third country as well as certain international organizations are excluded from the scope, Art. 2 (4) AIA.

[118] The AIA applies to natural and legal persons, however, the AIA does not apply to non-professional users; Art. 3(4) AIA.

livelihood and rights of individuals are banned according to the proposal (Art. 5 AIA). This includes social scoring by governments, exploiting the vulnerabilities of specific groups of persons (e.g., children), the use of subliminal techniques and – subject to exceptions – real-time remote biometric identification systems in publicly accessible spaces used for law enforcement. *High-risk AI systems* are permitted on the European market, but are subject to compliance with mandatory requirements and an *ex-ante* conformity assessment before they can be launched on the market (Art. 8 ff. AIA). For AI systems with *limited risks*, the AIA foresees transparency obligations to ensure that people know they are communicating with or dealing with an AI system (Art. 52 AIA). This concerns AI systems that interact with humans (chatbots), emotion recognition and biometric categorization systems and systems that generate or manipulate content (deep fakes). Systems with *minimal risks*, that is, all other AI systems, can be developed and used in compliance with already existing legislation, without any additional legal obligation. Providers of such systems may choose to voluntarily apply the requirements for trustworthy AI and to adhere to voluntary codes of conduct (Art. 69 AIA).

22.4.2 *Regulation of High-Risk AI Systems and the New Legislative Framework*

The AIA puts most emphasis on high-risk AI systems that are regulated according to the NLF. The NLF is characterized by product safety laws that specify only the essential requirements to which products launched on the EU market must conform in order to enjoy free movement in the internal market, while the task of giving these essential requirements more concrete form is entrusted to the three European ESOs – CEN, CENELEC and ETSI.[119] The NLF is based on the assumption that '[t]he manufacturer, having detailed knowledge of the design and production process, is best placed to carry out the complete conformity assessment procedure. Conformity assessment should therefore remain the obligation of the manufacturer alone.'[120] Accordingly, the AIA mainly relies on a self-conformity assessment using harmonized technical standards, combined with a presumption of conformity if the provider follows harmonized standards (see Section 22.4.5).

22.4.3 *Classification of High-Risk AI Systems*

As many products have already been harmonized under the NLF, the AIA distinguishes between two categories of high-risk AI systems. The first category (Art. 6(1) AIA, Annex II AIA) concerns AI systems that are products or safety components of products already covered by the NLF legislation (such as toys, machinery, elevators and medical devices). For these systems, the AIA only supplements the sectoral safety legislation, pointing out that special requirements for

[119] The so-called New Approach was approved by the Council on 7 May 1985 in its 'Resolution on a New Approach to technical harmonization and standards', OJ 1985 C 136/1. In 2008, this approach was updated by the so-called New Legislative Framework, which comprises Regulation (EC) 765/2008 that sets out the requirements for accreditation and the market surveillance of products, OJ 2008 L 218/30; Decision 768/2008 on a common framework for the marketing of products, OJ 2008 L 218/82; and Regulation (EU) 2019/1020 on market surveillance and compliance of products, OJ 2019 L 169/1.

[120] Recital (21) Decision No. 768/2008/EC of the European Parliament and of the Council of 9 July 2008 on a common framework for the marketing of products.

high-risk systems (see Section 22.4.4) must be dealt with as part of the conformity assessment procedures that already exist under the relevant NLF legislation (Art. 24, 43(3) AIA).[121]

The second category (Art. 6(2), Annex III AIA) refers to stand-alone AI systems that pose severe risk of harm to health and safety, or a risk of adverse impact on fundamental rights (Art. 7 AIA). So far, in Annex III AIA, the Commission has identified the following eight AI systems as 'high-risk': (1) biometric identification and categorization (e.g. facial recognition); (2) management and operation of critical infrastructure (e.g. transport); (3) educational and vocational training (e.g. scoring of exams); (4) employment, worker management and access to self-employment (e.g. CV-sorting); (5) access to and enjoyment of essential private and public services (e.g. credit scoring denying citizens the opportunity to obtain a loan); (6) law enforcement that may interfere with people's fundamental rights (e.g. evaluation of the reliability of evidence); (7) migration, asylum and border control management (e.g. verification of authenticity of travel documents); and (8) administration of justice and democracy (e.g. applying the law to a concrete set of facts).

22.4.4 *Essential Requirements for High-Risk AI Systems*

In Title III, Chapter 2, the AIA proposal contains an extensive list of essential requirements that must be observed before a high-risk AI system can be put on the market. The proposed mandatory requirements include the creation of a risk management system (Art. 9 AIA); quality criteria for training, validation and testing data in relation to relevance, representativeness, accuracy and completeness (Art. 10 AIA), inter alia to avoid biases and discrimination; technical documentation (Art. 11, Annex IV AIA) and record-keeping (Art. 12 AIA), containing information that is necessary to assess the compliance of the AI system with the relevant requirements; provisions on transparency and user information (Art. 13 AIA) to address the opacity of certain AI systems; obligations for human oversight incorporating 'human-machine interface tools' to ensure systems 'can be effectively overseen by natural persons' (Art. 14 AIA); and obligations concerning the accuracy, robustness and cybersecurity of systems (Art. 15 AIA).

In line with the NLF, all these requirements are worded in a somewhat broad way. Instead of formulating the requirements for high-risk AI systems, the regulation defines only the essential requirements, while the details are left to standards elaborated by the ESOs. For example, the AIA states that training, validation and testing data should be 'relevant, representative, free of errors and complete' (Art. 10(3) AIA) to ensure that the AI system 'does not become the source of discrimination prohibited by Union law' (Recital (44) AIA), without indicating what forms of bias are prohibited under the existing framework[122] and how algorithmic bias should be mitigated.[123] The same applies to Art. 13(1) AIA and its call for high-risk AI systems to be designed

[121] In contrast, the AIA does not directly apply to products covered by relevant Old Approach Legislation (e.g., aviation, cars), which is based on detailed legal safety requirements and a strong role of public bodies in the approval system; Art. 2(2) AIA. Instead, the essential *ex-ante* requirements for high-risk AI systems set out in the AIA have to be considered only when adopting relevant implementing or delegated legislation under such acts (Art. 84 AIA).

[122] See J. Gerards and R. Xenidis, *Algorithmic Discrimination in Europe: Challenges and Opportunities for Gender Equality and Non-discrimination Law*, Special report for the European Commission (Publications Office of the European Union, 2021), p. 9, https://op.europa.eu/en/publication-detail/-/publication/082f1dbc-821d-11eb-9ac9–01aa75ed71a1, arguing that the existing EU non-discrimination law 'displays a number of inconsistencies, ambiguities and shortcomings that limit its ability to capture algorithmic discrimination in its various forms'.

[123] To mitigate discrimination, numerous methods and metrics exist; see the overview by J. Dunkelau and M. Leuschel, 'Fairness-Aware Machine Learning', Working Paper, 2019. Recent studies have identified different notions of fairness (e.g., individual vs group fairness) that are incompatible with each other, and hence require certain trade-offs; M. Zehlike, P. Hacker and E. Wiedemann, 'Matching Code and Law: Achieving Algorithmic Fairness with Optimal Transport' (2020) 34 *Data Mining and Knowledge Discovery* 163–200, 188ff.; J. Kleinberg, S. Mullainathan and

and developed in such a way as to ensure that their operation is 'sufficiently transparent to enable users to interpret the system's output and use it appropriately'. Here, again, the AIA leaves open which type and degree of transparency should be regarded as appropriate.[124]

22.4.5 *Obligations of Providers of High-Risk AI Systems*

According to Art. 16(a) AIA, most of the aforementioned requirements are addressed to providers, i.e. a person or body that develops an AI system or that has an AI system developed with a view to placing it on the market or putting it into service under its own name or trademark (Art. 3 (2) AIA).

22.4.5.1 *Overview*

In particular, the obligations of providers include the following: (1) *Ex-ante conformity assessment*: According to Art. 19 AIA, providers must ensure that the high-risk AI system undergoes an ex-ante conformity assessment procedure before the system is placed on the market or put into service (see Section 22.4.5.2).[125] (2) *Quality management system:* Providers must implement a quality management system for compliance that includes, above all, examination, test and validation procedures to be conducted before, during and after development of the high-risk AI system (Art. 17(1)(d) AIA). (3) *Registration*: Providers must register all stand-alone high-risk AI systems in an EU-wide database before placing the system on the market or putting it into service (Art. 16(f), 51, 60, Annex VIII AIA). Information contained in the EU database must be accessible to the public (Art. 60(3) AIA). (4) *Post-market monitoring:* Providers are obliged to set up, implement and maintain a post-market monitoring system (Art. 17(1)(h), 61(1) AIA). The monitoring system shall actively and systematically collect, document and analyse relevant data on the performance of high-risk AI systems throughout their lifetime in order to allow the provider to assess the continuous compliance of AI systems with the requirements of the regulation (Art. 61(2) AIA). Should a provider have reason to consider that the high-risk AI systems do not comply with the AIA, the provider shall immediately take the necessary corrective actions to bring the system into conformity, by either withdrawing or recalling it, as appropriate (Art. 16(g) and 21 AIA). (5) *Reporting to competent authorities:* If a high-risk AI system has the potential to adversely affect health, safety or fundamental rights to a degree that goes beyond that considered reasonable and acceptable in relation to its intended purpose or under normal or reasonably foreseeable conditions of use, and this risk is known to the provider, then the latter must immediately inform the national competent authorities, in particular of the non-

M. Raghavan, 'Inherent Trade-Offs in the Fair Determination of Risk Scores', last revised 17 November 2016, arxiv .org/abs/1609.05807v2.

[124] On the different notions and approaches of explainability see M. Brkan and G. Bonnet, 'Legal and Technical Feasibility of the GDPR's Quest for Explanation of Algorithmic Decisions: of Black Boxes, White Boxes and Fata Morganas' (2020) 11 *European Journal of Risk Regulation* 18–50, 20ff. As to the question of whether and to what extent, under EU law, individuals are entitled to a right to explanation of automated decision-making, especially when AI systems are used, see M. Ebers, 'Regulating Explainable AI in the European Union: An Overview of the Current Legal Framework(s)' in L. Colonna and S. Greenstein (eds.), *Nordic Yearbook of Law and Informatics 2020: Law in the Era of Artificial Intelligence* (Stockholm: Stiftelsen Juridisk Fakultetslitteratur and The Swedish Law and Informatics Research Institute, 2022).

[125] AI systems already placed on the market or put into service before the regulation is applicable are exempted, unless the systems in question are subject to significant changes in their design or intended purpose; Art. 83(2) AIA.

compliance and of any corrective actions taken (Art. 22, 65(1) AIA in conjunction with Art. 3 No. 19 Regulation 2019/1020).[126]

22.4.5.2 *Ex-Ante* Conformity Assessment, Declaration of Conformity and CE Marking

The effectiveness of requirements for high-risk systems depends to a large extent on the compliance and enforcement mechanisms. In this respect, the AIA primarily relies on self-monitoring by the providers, combined with a presumption of conformity (Art. 40 AIA) if the provider follows harmonized standards, which are to be developed by ESOs.

According to recital (64) AIA, the *ex-ante* conformity assessment for stand-alone high-risk AI systems 'should be carried out as a general rule by the provider under its own responsibility'. Consequently, Art. 43(2) AIA states that providers should follow a conformity assessment procedure based on internal control as referred to in Annex VI. According to this Annex, the provider must verify that the established quality management system complies with the requirements of Art. 17 AIA. Additionally, the provider must examine the information contained in the technical documentation in order to assess the AI system's compliance with the relevant essential requirements set out in Title III, Chapter 2. Finally, the provider must also verify that the design and development process of the AI system and its post-market monitoring (Art. 61 AIA) is consistent with the technical documentation.

This internal conformity assessment is generally sufficient for stand-alone applications.[127] As a matter of principle, the AIA does not provide for an *ex-ante* conformity assessment by external third parties. The only exception is remote biometric identification systems, which, in cases where they are not prohibited, must undergo an *ex-ante* conformity assessment by a notified body, unless harmonized standards or common specifications exist (Art. 43(1), Annex VII AIA).

After a successful conformity assessment, providers shall draw up a written EU declaration of conformity for each AI system and keep it at the disposal of the national competent authorities for ten years (Art. 19(1) and (2), 48(1) and (2) AIA). Along with this declaration of conformity, providers are also obliged to affix the CE conformity marking on the high-risk AI systems, its packaging or the accompanying documentation, as appropriate, in accordance with Art. 49 AIA and Regulation 765/2008.

22.4.6 *Enforcement*

22.4.6.1 *Ex-Post* Surveillance by Member States

In addition to the self-assessment carried out by the providers, Art. 63 AIA provides for *ex-post* market surveillance by Member State authorities according to the Market Surveillance Regulation 2019/1020.[128] Accordingly, Member States shall play a key role in the application and enforcement of the regulation envisaged. However, they do not have to create new, specialized regulatory authorities. Instead, each Member State is expected to designate one or

[126] European Parliament and Council Regulation (EU) 2019/1020 of 20 June 2019 on market surveillance and compliance of products and amending Directive 2004/42/EC and Regulations (EC) No. 765/2008 and (EU) No. 305/2011.

[127] In contrast, AI systems that are safety components of regulated products subject to the New Legislative Approach must always undergo a third-party conformity assessment according to existing sectoral requirements.

[128] For EU institutions, agencies and bodies that fall within the scope of the proposal, the European Data Protection Supervisor shall act as a market surveillance authority; Art. 63(6) AIA.

more national supervisory authorities. These national authorities shall have access to all the information, documentation and data necessary, including access to a source code when required in order to enforce the obligations of providers according to the law (Art. 64(1) and (2) AIA).

To enforce the regulation, Member States must lay down rules on penalties, including the administrative fines applicable in the event of any infringement of the AIA, whilst taking into particular account the interests of small-scale providers and start-ups, as well as their economic viability (Art. 71(1) AIA). Art. 71 AIA sets the amounts of fines at between 2 per cent, 4 per cent or 6 per cent of the annual turnover depending on the non-compliance situation and the accompanying circumstances (Art. 71(6) AIA). Interestingly, the penalties prescribed under the AIA not only seem to cross the threshold under GDPR (up to 4 per cent of total worldwide turnover of the preceding year), but also seem potentially high even for small-scale providers and start-ups.

22.4.6.2 *Coordination at European Level through the European AI Board*

Additionally, the AIA is expected to establish a 'European Artificial Intelligence Board' (EAIB) to facilitate harmonized implementation of the regulation. The EAIB would be chaired by the European Commission and include representatives from each national supervisory authority, together with the European Data Protection Supervisor (EDPS) (Art. 57(1) AIA). The proposed regulation would not confer any powers to the EAIB regarding enforcement. Instead, the EAIB's main purpose would be to issue opinions and recommendations on the implementation of the AIA, especially on standards and common specifications (Art. 58 AIA).

22.4.7 *Analysis*

The success of the AIA in regulating high-risk AI systems will depend primarily on harmonized standards. Admittedly, providers do not have to follow such standards.[129] Instead, they may interpret the essential requirements set out in Title III, Chapter 2 AIA themselves. However, in practice this is not very realistic. Adherence to harmonized standards is not only cheaper, but also offers greater legal certainty. If providers rely on their own technical solutions to achieve compliance, they must specify the vague requirements for high-risk AI systems at their own risk. If, on the other hand, providers apply harmonized standards, they can invoke the presumption of conformity under Art. 40 AIA. Hence, compliance with harmonized European standards provides an easier road for the CE marking requirement.

Against this backdrop, legal scholars rightly emphasize that standardization 'is arguably where the real rule-making in the AI Act will occur'.[130] Accordingly, the next section analyzes the European standardization procedures as well as the legal nature and effect of harmonized standards with regard to their problematic features in more detail.

[129] The AIA only requires providers to consult harmonized standards; see, for example, Art. 9(3)(2) AIA: risk management measures 'shall take into account the generally acknowledged state of the art, including in relevant harmonised standards or common specifications'. On the other hand, if the Commission adopts common specifications, providers must justify why their measures are 'equivalent' to such further specified provisions; Art. 41(4) AIA.

[130] M. Veale and F. Zuiderveen Borgesius, 'Demystifying the Draft EU Artificial Intelligence Act' (July 2021 version), 1, 14, arxiv.org/abs/2107.03721.

22.5 STANDARDIZATION AS THE CORNERSTONE OF THE AIA: A CRITICAL ASSESSMENT

The NLF has been criticized in academic circles for quite some time.[131] Entrusting private SDOs with the development of detailed technical rules raises constitutional concerns under the *Meroni* doctrine[132] regarding the delegation of regulatory powers to private bodies and the lack of democratic and judicial control of these delegated powers.

22.5.1 *European Standardization as Delegated Rule-Making?*

Formally, harmonized standards are voluntary rules drafted by private bodies, such as CEN or CENELEC, which are both organized as international non-profit organizations under Belgian law. In light of these considerations, the CJEU has never used the word 'delegation' in its judgments,[133] whereas Advocate Generals sometimes describe the NLF as a 'legislative delegation in favour of a private standardisation body'[134] or a de facto transfer of public rule-making competence to private associations.[135]

Ultimately, there can be no doubt that the ESOs exercise rule-making power, as harmonized standards have binding legal effects – on National Standards Bodies (NSBs),[136] Member States and market participants – that are largely similar to EU law:[137] (1) According to Art. 3(6) Standardization Regulation 1025/2012, NSBs are obliged to withdraw all conflicting national standards as soon as a new harmonized standard is published. (2) Harmonized standards also have a pre-emptive effect on national law. Member States must accept all high-risk AI systems that are in conformity with harmonized standards (Art. 40 AIA). In addition, they are not only under the obligation to disapply all national rules that conflict with the AIA itself but are also barred – under the Single Markets Transparency Directive 2015/1535[138] – from adopting technical regulations that contradict harmonized standards. The imposition of additional requirements under national law on products that are covered by harmonized standards could even lead

[131] See J. Falke and C. Joerges, 'The New Approach to Technical Harmonisation and Standards, Its Preparation through ECJ Case Law on Articles 30, 36 EEC and the Low-Voltage Directive, and the Clarification of Its Operating Environment by the Single European Act' (2010) 6(2) *Hanse Law Review* 289–348; R. van Gestel and H.-W. Micklitz, 'European Integration through Standardization: How Judicial Review Is Breaking Down the Club House of Private Standardization Bodies' (2013) 50 *Common Market Law Review* 145–182; H. Hofmann, 'Legislation, Delegation and Implementation under the Treaty of Lisbon: Typology Meets Reality' (2009) 15(4) *European Law Journal* 482–505; A. McGee and S. Weatherill, 'The Evolution of the Single Market – Harmonisation or Liberalisation' (1990) 53 *The Modern Law Review* 578–596.

[132] Cases C-9/56 *Meroni & Co., Industrie Metallurgiche, SpA* v. *High Authority of the European Coal and Steel Community* ECLI:EU:C:1958:7 and C-10/56 *Meroni & Co., Industrie Metallurgiche, SpA* v. *High Authority of the European Coal and Steel Community* ECLI:EU:C:1958:8.

[133] The CJEU refers to the NLF instead as a case of 'entrusting' the development of harmonized standards to private bodies in Case C-613/14 *James Elliott Construction Limited* v. *Irish Asphalt Limited* ECLI:EU:C:2016:821 [43].

[134] Opinion of AG Campos Sanchez-Bordona in case C-613/14 *James Elliott* ECLI:EU:C:2016:63 [55].

[135] Opinion of AG Trstenjak in case C-171/11 *Fra.bo* ECLI:EU:C:2012:176 [49].

[136] See Art. 2(10) Standardization Regulation 1025/2012.

[137] For the following, see M. Medzmariashvili, 'Delegation of Rulemaking Power to European Standards Organizations: Reconsidered' (2017) 44(4) *Legal Issues of Economic Integration* 353–366.

[138] European Parliament and Council Directive 2015/1535 of 9 September 2015 laying down a procedure for the provision of information in the field of technical regulations and of rules on Information Society services, OJ 2015 L 241/1. The Directive requires Member States to notify all draft technical regulations through TRIS (Technical Regulation Information System) before they are adopted into national law in order to avoid the emergence of new technical barriers. Therefore, it is not likely that the European Commission will allow national technical regulations contracting harmonized standards.

to an infringement action under Art. 258 TFEU against a Member State.[139] (3) Finally, harmonized standards are also binding for private parties, at least insofar as non-compliance with standards may trigger liability under tort law[140] and contract law.[141]

In short, we can conclude that harmonized standards have binding legal effects that are close to those of legal norms. The regulatory mechanism empowering ESOs to develop harmonized standards can indeed be described as a delegation of rule-making powers.

22.5.2 *Lack of Democratic Control and Participation in European Standardization*

Such a delegation of power is problematic, above all due to the lack of democratic oversight and inadequate participation of affected stakeholders. According to the Standardization Regulation 1025/2012, harmonized standards are developed exclusively by the ESOs. Neither the European Parliament nor the Member States have a binding veto over harmonized standards mandated by the Commission.[142] Even the European Commission has only limited powers to influence standards. Admittedly, the Commission has the possibility to refuse the publication of a standard in the Official Journal of the EU if the drafted standard does not comply with the Commission's standardization request[143] or does not satisfy 'the requirements which it aims to cover and which are set out in the corresponding Union harmonisation legislation'.[144] Such an assessment is, however, generally limited to a *formal* comparison of the contents of the standard with the underlying requirements of the standardization request and of the corresponding legislation. A comprehensive examination of the content of harmonized standards, including their technical aspects, would not only overburden the Commission both technically and in terms of human resources, but would also be diametrically opposed to the nature and purpose of the NLF. Consequently, it must be assumed that the Commission has no jurisdiction to conduct a comprehensive and detailed assessment of the harmonized standards prepared by the ESOs.[145]

This view is also shared by the European Commission in its guide to the implementation of product legislation, the Blue Guide of 2016,[146] in which the Commission emphasizes that 'the technical contents of standards is under the entire responsibility of the European standardisation organisations' and is not reviewed by public bodies since 'Union harmonisation legislation for products do not foresee a procedure under which public authorities would systematically verify or approve either at Union or national level the contents of harmonised standards.'

139 Case C-100/13 *Commission* v. *Germany* ECLI:EU:C:2014:2293.

140 See G. Spindler, 'Market Processes, Standardisation and Tort Law' (1998) 4(3) *European Law Journal* 316–336.

141 Art. 8(1)(a) Digital Content and Services Directive 2019/770; Art. 7(1)(a) Sale of Goods Directive 2019/771.

142 Art. 11 Standardization Regulation 1025/2012.

143 Art. 10(5)(2) in conjunction with Art. 11 Standardization Regulation 1025/2012.

144 Art. 10(6) in conjunction with Art. 11 Standardization Regulation 1025/2012.

145 K. Dingemann and M. Kottmann, 'Legal Opinion on the European System of Harmonised Standards', commissioned by the German Federal Ministry for Economic Affairs and Energy (BMWi), (August 2020), 31ff., www.bmwi.de/Redaktion/EN/Downloads/L/legal-opinion-on-the-european-system-of-harmonised-standards.pdf?__blob=publicationFile&v=3.

146 European Commission, Commission Notice, 'The "Blue Guide" on the implementation of EU products rules 2016', OJ 2016 C 272/1, 41, 45. The Commission further clarified in the Blue Guide that 'during this verification [examination prior to publication of the reference] there is no need for a review of the technical content as the Commission does not, in general, accept the technical content or take responsibility for it'. See also European Commission, 'Guidelines for the publication of references of standards in the Official Journal of the European Union', D(2005) C2/MJE/IG –D (2005) 7049 (2005), 3. The Commission Guidelines explain that 'the Commission should not review the technical adequacy of the content of a standard'.

Another problematic aspect is the lack of meaningful participation of interest groups in the process of drafting standards. Although Art. 5(1)(1) Standardization Regulation 1025/2012 urges ESOs to 'encourage and facilitate an appropriate representation and effective participation of all relevant stakeholders, including SMEs, consumer organizations and environmental and social stakeholders in their standardisation activities', the regulation does not provide comprehensive guidance on how to execute these principles, nor does it establish specific sanctions to back up the enforcement of Art. 5. In practice, European stakeholder organizations have only limited rights. According to the CEN and CENELEC internal regulations based on the principle of national delegation, stakeholders other than the NSBs do not enjoy voting rights, but can only access documents, propose input, formulate advice and submit comments and technical contributions.[147] In addition, European stakeholder organizations can lodge an appeal against decisions only under very strict conditions.[148] Furthermore, since the Standardization Regulation 1025/2012 does not apply to international standardization carried out by the ISO and IEC, which are the leading SDOs, in conjunction with CEN and CENELEC, European stakeholder organizations are also removed from any active participation therein.[149]

Apart from these procedural restraints, stakeholder organizations face various obstacles in their effective use of CEN/CENELEC participatory mechanisms. Most civil society organizations and consumer associations have absolutely no experience in standardization and may not even be represented at EU level. In addition, active participation is costly and time-consuming because CEN/CENELEC standardization committees are 'dispersed in all corners of Europe, participation in these committees is generally subjected to a fee, a single standard may require years to be published'.[150] For all these reasons, it seems relatively unrealistic that interest groups would be able to influence the AI systems standardization process in the same way as with public legislation.

22.5.3 *Lack of Judicial Control over Harmonized Standards*

While the CJEU originally set narrow limits on the delegation of powers in the *Meroni* case,[151] the Court loosened these requirements to some extent in the more recent *ESMA* case[152] by concluding that the delegation of discretionary powers is allowed provided that they are subject to adequate judicial supervision. Against this backdrop, many scholars believe that a delegation of powers to ESOs is permitted under EU constitutional law if the shortcomings in the *ex-ante* control of standards can be compensated for by an *ex-post* judicial review.[153]

[147] P. Cuccuru, 'Interest Representation in European Standardisation: The Case of CEN and CENELEC', Amsterdam Law School Legal Studies Research Paper No. 2019-52, 17 December 2019, 4f., ssrn.com/abstract=3505290.

[148] Ibid, 7ff.

[149] P. Cuccuru and M. Eliantonio, 'It Is Not All about Judicial Review: Internal Appeal Proceedings in the European Standardisation Process' in J.-B. Auby (ed.), *Le futur du droit administratif / The future of administrative law* (Paris: Lexis Nexis, 2019), pp. 475–488.

[150] Cuccuru (n 147), 14.

[151] Cases C-9/56 and C- 10/56 (n 132). According to the *Meroni* ruling, delegation of power is only possible if the powers are the result of an express delegation, are of a clearly defined executive nature and that their exercise is subject to strict review and to the same obligations that would be applicable to the delegating authority.

[152] Case C-270/12 *United Kingdom of Great Britain and Northern Ireland* v. *European Parliament and Council of the European Union (ESMA)*, ECLI:EU:C:2014:18.

[153] M. Eliantonio, 'Judicial Control of the EU Harmonized Standards: Entering a Black Hole' (2017) 44 *Legal Issues of Economic Integration* 395–407; Medzmariashvili (n 137); A. Van Waeyenberge and D. Restrepo Amariles, 'James Elliott Construction: A "New(ish) Approach" to Judicial Review of Standardisation' (2017) 6 *European Law Review* 882–893, 890.

The CJEU paved the way for such a judicial review in *James Elliott*.[154] In this case, the Court decided for the first time that it has jurisdiction to interpret harmonized standards in preliminary ruling proceedings. In support of this, the CJEU pointed out that although CEN is an organization governed by private law which does not belong to 'institutions, bodies, offices or agencies of the Union' (Art. 267(1)(b) TFEU), such a standard is 'nevertheless a necessary implementation measure which is strictly governed by the essential requirements defined by that directive, initiated, managed and monitored by the Commission, and its legal effects are subject to prior publication by the Commission' in the Official Journal.[155]

Following this judgment, one might wonder whether the CJEU would also be willing to rule on the validity of harmonized standards, either in an annulment action (Art. 263 TFEU) or in a preliminary ruling proceeding (Art. 267 TFEU).[156] Even if this was the case, however, it seems unlikely that the CJEU would review and invalidate the *substance* of a harmonized standard. The subject of such a dispute could only be the 'decision'[157] taken by the Commission to publish a reference to the standard in the Official Journal. Only this action (but not the standard itself that remains the product of a private organization) could be considered as an 'act' of European institutions. Accordingly, the CJEU could only control whether the Commission made an error in its assessment under Art. 10(5)–(6) Standardization Regulation 1025/2012. However, as explained above, this assessment largely relates to formal but not substantive issues.[158] Consequently, the judicial review of harmonized standards is hindered by considerable hurdles. Although harmonized standards have significant legal and practical implications, they are, in essence, currently immune from judicial review.

22.6 CONCLUDING REMARKS

The European Commission's proposal is the world's first attempt to get a legislative grip on the question of AI. What is particularly welcome is that the proposal follows a risk-based approach and imposes regulatory burdens only when an AI system is likely to pose high risks to fundamental rights and safety.

On the other hand, the proposed rules for high-risk systems raise serious concerns. For these systems, the European Commission wants to rely primarily on an *ex-ante* conformity assessment, which is not carried out by external third parties but by the companies themselves – combined with the presumption of conformity if the provider follows harmonized standards developed by ESOs in accordance with the NLF. However, ESOs are clearly overburdened by this task. The standardization of AI systems is not a matter of purely technical decisions, but relies on a series of ethical and legal decisions that cannot be outsourced to private SDOs, but require political debate involving society as a whole.

154 Case C-613/14 *James Elliott Construction Limited* v. *Irish Asphalt Limited*, ECLI:EU:C:2016:821.

155 Ibid. [43].

156 The General Court stated in an obiter dictum in Case T-474/15, *Global Garden Products Italy*, EU:T:2017:36 [60] that 'decisions relating to the publication of harmonised standards are legal acts against which an action of annulment may be brought'. However, this view has never been confirmed in a proceeding concerning the validity of harmonized standards.

157 The measure through which a reference to standards is usually published is not a 'decision' in the sense of Art. 288 TFEU, but a Commission Communication. See Eliantonio (n 153), 399. For this reason alone, it is unlikely that the CJEU would be willing to review its validity.

158 See Section 22.5.2.

The delegation of powers associated with the NLF has been criticized in the past with regard to the lack of democratic control by EU legislative bodies, the inadequate involvement of interest groups and the impossibility of subjecting harmonized standards to judicial control. Such criticism carries special weight with regard to AI systems. The more technical standards reach beyond the definition of mere technicalities and enter areas of public policy, such as health, safety, fundamental rights and consumer protection, the more pressing the question becomes as to whether the NLF gives an unlawful delegation of EU rule-making power to private bodies. All of this puts the AIA on 'shaky legal ground'.[159]

In light of these considerations, the European Commission should reconsider its approach. It is certainly true that the technical expertise does not lie with the legislator, but with manufacturers and industries. Thus, developing standards through co-regulation is indeed an indispensable building block for future regulation. However, fundamental ethical and legal decisions should not be delegated to private SDOs but should be subject to an ordinary legislative procedure and a political debate that can be shaped by industry, civil society organizations, consumer associations and other actors. Accordingly, the AIA should establish legally binding obligations regarding the essential requirements for high-risk AI systems,[160] such as what types of biases are prohibited, how algorithmic biases should be mitigated and what type and degree of transparency AI systems should have, to name just a few.

These legally binding obligations could then in turn be further specified by harmonized standards for specific applications by the SDOs. Since such harmonized standards can still have far-reaching social and legal consequences, European policymakers should simultaneously take the necessary steps to improve the standardization process. Currently, the actual involvement of European stakeholder organizations in the standard-making process depends on the internal mechanisms of each ESO. While ETSI relies on a *sui generis* decision-making process that allows for the direct participation of institutional actors, companies, interest groups and individuals,[161] CEN and CENELEC follow the principle of national delegation.

In view of the above critique, it seems safe to say that an amendment to the overall standardization process in the EU also calls for changes in the structural and organizational framework of ESOs like CEN and CENELEC to facilitate an inclusive standardization system. It is imperative that the European standardization process reflects European values and fundamental rights, including consumer protections, by granting European stakeholder organizations effective participation rights. In this respect, some NGOs have already made recommendations[162] for a more transparent and inclusive standardization system that includes inter alia the

[159] Veale and Zuiderveen Borgesius (n 130), 14.

[160] The New Approach was based on the idea that the 'essential requirements should be worded precisely enough to create legally binding obligations. They should be formulated so as to make it possible to assess conformity with them even in the absence of harmonised standards or where the manufacturer chooses not to apply a harmonised standard'; see Recital (11) Decision 768/2008 on a common framework for the marketing of products, OJ 2008 L 218/82. However, as noted by Schepel, this is pure fiction; H. Schepel, 'Case C-171/11 Fra.bo SpA v Deutsche Vereinigung des Gas- und Wasserfaches' (2013) 9(2) *European Review of Contract Law* 186–192, 192.

[161] See Cuccuru (n 147), 6.

[162] See European Environmental Citizen's Organisation for Standardisation (ECOS), 'The future of European standardisation: ECOS' recommendations for a transparent and inclusive standardisation system, that can effectively support EU legislation and policies', July 2015.

creation of a separate category of partnerships for societal stakeholders within the ESOs, combined with a series of specific rights (and obligations) adapted to their profiles. For example, societal stakeholders could be granted voting rights, rights of appeal, unlimited access to technical bodies and advisory groups as well as unlimited access to existing standards and other deliverables (for non-commercial purposes) without any charge. Such amendments, if adopted, could indeed contribute to better representation of stakeholder interests and counterbalance, at least in part, the negative effects of private rule-making, while maintaining the highest standards of technical expertise.

PART VII

Future of AI

23

AI Judges

Florence G'sell

23.1 INTRODUCTION

The prospect of a 'robot judge' raises many fantasies and concerns. Some argue that only humans are endowed with the modes of thought, intuition and empathy that would be necessary to analyse or judge a case. As early as 1976, Joseph Weizenbaum, creator of Eliza, one of the very first conversational agents, strongly asserted that important decisions should not be left to machines, which are sorely lacking in human qualities such as compassion and wisdom.[1] On the other hand, it could be argued today that the courts would be wrong to deprive themselves of the possibilities opened up by artificial intelligence tools, whose capabilities are expected to improve greatly in the future.[2] In reality, the question of the use of artificial intelligence (AI) in the judicial system should probably be asked in a nuanced way, without considering the dystopian and highly unlikely scenario of the 'robot judge' portrayed by Trevor Noah in a famous episode of *The Daily Show*.[3] Rather, the question is how courts can benefit from increasingly sophisticated machines. To what extent can these tools help them render justice? What is their contribution in terms of decision support? Can we seriously consider delegating to a machine the entire power to make a judicial decision?

In the past, the emergence of expert systems, which are capable of reproducing logical reasoning, based on a knowledge base and an inference engine, has led to the idea that they could be used to reproduce legal reasoning. Expert systems decompose legal rules by rewriting them in computer language, in order to establish a decision tree made up of successive ramifications associated with a conditional logic.[4] However, they have generally been considered disappointing in legal matters, even when used to address highly technical issues where it seems to be only necessary to reproduce a relatively simple syllogistic reasoning to find correct solutions. This relative failure can be explained by the rather reductive reasoning of expert systems. They are unable to take into account presumptions or analogies and cannot engage in the constant back and forth between facts and law that characterizes legal reasoning.[5] Above all,

[1] J. Weizenbaum, *Computer Power and Human Reason: From Judgement to Calculation* (San Francisco: W. H. Freeman & Co., 1976).

[2] R. Susskind, *Online Courts and the Future of Justice* (Oxford: Oxford University Press, 2019).

[3] 'Disrupting the Legal System with Robots', *The Daily Show* (10 March 2018).

[4] D. Bourcier, *La Décision artificielle : Le Droit, la machine et l'humain*, (Paris: PUF Les voies du droit, 1995); 'L'acte de juger est-il modélisable?' (2011) 54 *Archives de Philosophie du droit : De la logique à la justice* 37.

[5] S. Abiteboul and F. G'sell, 'Les algorithmes pourraient-ils remplacer les juges' in F. G'sell (ed.), *Le Big Data et le Droit* (Paris: Dalloz, 2020), p. 21.

they cannot deal with contradictory rules, which is problematic since legal rules often lack the precision adapted to mathematical reasoning and include many contradictions.

The development of machine learning has opened new perspectives. In the legal field, legal argumentation aims at demonstrating why a given decision is justified rather than another one. A judge explains their decisions, a lawyer supports their argument with reasoning. But such explanations can be imprecise and open to interpretation. Lawyers do not explain why they followed one strategy rather than another. Judges do not always detail the reasoning that guided their decisions. It is therefore difficult to use the explanations provided to build an algorithm in the classical sense of the term, that is, a set of instructions designed to solve a problem. However, if a large number of court decisions are available, a learning algorithm can be trained to propose a solution based on the previously adopted decisions. Algorithms can recommend solutions by considering previous cases, but the use of machine learning does not amount to legal reasoning in the classical sense of the term, which is a much more complex task.

Machine-learning algorithms can process gigantic databases and identify patterns in order to formulate predictions not only of legal decisions, but also of any type of human behaviour. But machine learning does not only allow prediction: algorithms can also suggest decision options by taking into account both the predictions and the foreseeable consequences of different possible actions.[6] This last stage, that of recommendation or prescription, opens the way to automation. Although automation is already well established in some sectors (pricing, targeted advertising, high-frequency trading) and expected to increase as more and more sophisticated algorithms are employed, it does not appear that judicial systems have yet opted for a full automation of judicial decision-making. On the contrary, it seems that most judicial systems use predictive techniques or recommendation algorithms with the sole objective of assisting and helping human judges in their decision-making.

It is still hard to say how much machine learning can or should replace humans in judicial decision-making. In some areas, machines have already largely taken over routine tasks. In many countries, automated tools are used to process tickets, such as parking tickets and speeding tickets. In France, the sanctioning of traffic offences is automated: radars take pictures of speeding vehicles and a software program matches the photographs with the national registration file, so that fine notices can automatically be sent (by post mail) to the address mentioned in the file.[7] However, these basic techniques do not involve AI as such. In 2020, the Australian authorities went further by installing AI-equipped cameras on public roads to detect, behind the windshield, whether the driver is on the phone.[8] In Europe, several countries (like Poland, Serbia or Slovakia) are using algorithms to allocate cases among the judges.[9] Nevertheless, such developments have nothing to do with entrusting a machine with the task of rendering justice. Only a very few countries seem, for the moment, to have taken that direction. In March 2019, the Estonian Ministry of Justice announced its decision to work on the creation of 'robot judges' to decide small claims disputes of less than €7,000.[10] The trial would take place exclusively online, the parties would communicate their elements by uploading them on a platform and the case would be decided by an AI tool. The project focuses on contract cases and especially litigation related to termination arrangements and unpaid claims. Its promoter, Estonia's Chief

[6] L. Kart, A. Linden and W. Schulte, *Extend Your Portfolio of Analytics Capabilities* (Gartner research report, 2013).

[7] The Centre Automatisé de Constatation des Infractions Routières was created in 2004.

[8] 'AI Cameras to Catch Texting Australian Drivers', BBC, 2 December 2019.

[9] ePanstwo Foundation, *alGOVrithms 2.0 – State of Play: Usage on Algorithms by the Governments in Czechia, Georgia, Hungary, Poland, Serbia and Slovakia* (2021).

[10] E. Niiler, 'Can AI Be a Fair Judge in Court? Estonia Thinks So', *Wired*, 25 March 2019.

Data Officer Ott Velsberg, declared that he wanted to 'eliminate the human element'.[11] Little information has leaked out, however, since the spring 2019 announcement and it is currently difficult to know the status of this project.

This chapter proceeds as follow. Section 23.2 is devoted to the use of AI tools by the courts. It is divided into three subsections. Section 23.2.1 deals with the use of risk assessment tools, which are widespread in the United States but highly regulated in Europe, particularly in France. Section 23.2.2 presents the possibilities opened by machine-learning algorithms trained on databases composed of judicial decisions, which are able to anticipate court decisions or recommend solutions to judges. Section 23.2.3 considers the very unlikely eventuality of full automation of judicial decision-making.

23.2 AI IN THE COURTROOM

At the present time, American and European courts are trying to take advantage of the predictive capabilities of AI tools, either by using risk assessment algorithms or by using predictive tools that analyse past court decisions.

23.2.1 *Use of Risk Assessment Tools*

Machine-learning models trained on large data sets can produce scores that represent predictions or likely outcomes, like the risk of a borrower's default or the risk of committing a criminal offence. While American courts make extensive use of risk assessment algorithms in criminal matters, this practice is highly regulated in Europe, especially in France.

23.2.1.1 *Use of Risk Assessment Tools in the USA*

It is now common practice in the United States to use scoring algorithms to assess the risk of a defendant committing an act of recidivism or not appearing for trial. These risk assessment tools can be found all over the USA and are not always based on machine learning.[12] These tools can be used to decide whether to release a prisoner before trial, instead of the traditional bail, or be considered in sentencing decisions.[13] The use of assessment tools is praised by its promoters for its efficiency. It is said they allow a better management of the occupation of prisons. For instance, some researchers have developed an algorithm that would help reduce by 24.8 per cent the number of offences committed in New York City or, alternatively, reduce the number of prisoners by 42 per cent while keeping the number of offences at the same level.[14] Other studies showed that algorithms clearly outperform humans in predicting recidivism,[15] which is

[11] T. Shelton, 'Estonia: From AI Judges to Robot Bartenders, Is the Post-Soviet State the Dark Horse of Digital Tech?', *NBC News* (15 June 2019).

[12] The most common ones are the Public Safety Assessment (PSA), the Virginia Pretrial Risk Assessment Instrument (VPRAI), the Ohio Risk Assessment System Pretrial Assessment Tool (ORAS-PAT) and Correctional Offender Management Profiling for Alternative Sanctions (COMPAS).

[13] D. A. Elyounes, 'Bail or Jail? Judicial versus Algorithmic Decision-Making in the Pretrial System' (2020) 21 *Science and Technology Law Review* 376.

[14] J. Kleinberg, H. Lakkaraju, J. Leskovec, J. Ludwig and S. Mullainathan, 'Human Decisions and Machine Predictions' (2017), NBER Working Paper No. 23180.

[15] Z. J. Lin, J. Jongbin, S. Goel and J. Skeem, 'The Limits of Human Predictions of Recidivism' (2020) 6 *Science Advances* 7.

consistent with the observation that a purely mathematical risk assessment is more effective and neutral than a human assessment of an individual's dangerousness.

OBJECTIONS RAISED AGAINST RISK ASSESSMENT TOOLS The use of algorithms in judicial decision-making raises various objections. First, the reliability of such algorithmic tools has been questioned. Not only can the algorithms be poorly designed but they are also dependent on the quality of data: it frequently happens that data is misclassified, incomplete, inaccurate or outdated, which leads to unreliable results. The COMPAS algorithm, which has a 65 per cent correct response rate, has been shown to be no more reliable than 400 individuals with no expertise in the area, who have a 63 per cent reliability rate, even when using only two variables, like the defendant's age and their number of previous convictions.[16] It was also alleged that the COMPAS score is unreliable in forecasting violent crime, since only 20 per cent of the people predicted to commit violent crimes actually went on to do so.[17] Nevertheless, when a full range of crimes are taken into account (including misdemeanours), 61 per cent of those deemed likely to reoffend were arrested for subsequent crimes within two years. Moreover, another study concluded that defendants assigned the highest risk score reoffended at almost four times the rate as those assigned the lowest score (81 per cent vs 22 per cent),[18] which argues in favour of the reliability of the algorithm.[19]

Second, like most AI tools, such algorithms can be biased and discriminatory. Poor quality data or questionable methodological choices not only affect the reliability of algorithms but can lead to frankly discriminatory results. Algorithms reflect the values and biases of the programmers and process data that is itself biased. It can even happen that an algorithm trained with well-selected and good quality data turns out to be unfair. The problem is well known.[20] The unfairness of an algorithm is particularly apparent when the errors it makes concern one social group more frequently than another. A few years ago, a study conducted on the COMPAS algorithm showed that the software had an ethnic bias against people of colour.[21] Based on a sample study, ProPublica concluded that black defendants who did not recidivate over a two-year period were nearly twice as likely to be misclassified as higher risk compared to their white counterparts (45 per cent vs 23 per cent) and that white defendants who reoffended within

[16] J. Dressel and H. Farid, 'The Accuracy, Fairness and Limits of Predicting Recidivism' (2018) 4 *Science Advances* 1. Another team showed that a basic set of rules based on a person's age, sex and prior convictions could predict recidivism as well as COMPAS: E. Angelino, N. Larus-Stone, D. Alabi, M. Seltzer and C. Rudin, 'Learning Certifiably Optimal Rule Lists for Categorical Data' (2018) 234 *Journal of Machine Learning Research* 1. Those findings were challenged: A. Holsinger, C. Lowenkamp, E. Latessa et al., 'A Rejoinder to Dressel and Farid: New Study Finds Computer Algorithm Is More Accurate Than Humans at Predicting Arrest and as Good as a Group of 20 Lay Experts' (2018) 82(2) *Federal Probation* 51.

[17] J. Angwin, J. Larson, S. Mattu and L. Kirchner, 'Machine Bias', *ProPublica*, 23 May 2016.

[18] A. Feller et al., 'A Computer Program Used for Bail and Sentencing Decisions Was Labeled Biased against Blacks. It's Actually Not That Clear', *The Washington Post*, 17 October 2016.

[19] A study showed that maching-learning models achieve better predictive power than a structured professional risk assessment tool at the expense of not satisfying relevant group fairness metrics: M. Miron, S. Tolan, E. Gómez et al., 'Evaluating Causes of Algorithmic Bias in Juvenile Criminal Recidivism' (2021) 29 *Artificial Intelligence and Law* 111.

[20] S. Barocas and A. Selbst, 'Big Data's Disparate Impact' (2016) 104 *California Law Review* 671; C. O'Neil, *Weapons of Math Destruction: How Big Data Increases Inequality and Threatens Democracy* (New York: Crown Publishers, 2016); V. Eubanks, *Automating Inequality, How High-Tech Tools Profile, Police, and Punish the Poor* (New York: St Martin's Press, 2018).

[21] Angwin et al., see fn 17.

the next two years were mistakenly labelled low risk almost twice as often as black reoffenders (48 per cent vs 28 per cent).

Third, it is indisputable that machine-learning techniques do not allow for a precise explanation of their results. The 'black box' effect of machine-learning algorithms is frequently noted.[22] Algorithms are not designed to provide humanly interpretable representations but to formulate, by induction, internal models that are expressed in a space specific to the machine.[23] A deep neural network can be trained on a large volume of data, which allows a large number of parameters to be identified that will guide future decisions. But these features do not make sense to humans and therefore cannot be used as explanations. This technical obstacle is coupled with a legal one: algorithms are generally proprietary tools, protected as trade secrets or intellectual property rights, which can prevent access to the methodology, the decision tree, the factors taken into account and their weight. And in the context of justice, it is not tolerable that decisions having a serious impact on human lives be made without the person concerned being able to understand the method used to reach such a result.

At the present time, the debate on the reliability and fairness of risk assessment tools is still raging in the USA. The aforementioned ProPublica study has been widely circulated, commented on and questioned.[24] In 2019, twenty-seven academics published an opinion statement to encourage the end of the use of pretrial risk assessment tools, on the grounds that actuarial pretrial risk assessments suffer from serious technical flaws that undermine their accuracy, validity and effectiveness.[25] In July 2020, the Pretrial Justice Institute – a non-profit advocacy group that has been, in the past, very favourable to pretrial risk assessment instruments – released a report alleging that risk assessment tools cannot accurately predict whether an individual represents a risk to the community.[26] In an open letter, a group of criminologists and law professors replied that a 'large body of social science evidence' shows that 'objective, reliable and valid risk assessment instruments are more accurate in assessing risk' than human judgments alone.[27] These experts added that the argument that assessment tools are racially biased is not sufficiently substantiated and is only based on the single ProPublica study, which focuses on a single risk assessment instrument, in only one jurisdiction.[28]

The very notion of fairness in algorithmic assessment has also been the subject of intense discussions.[29] Northpointe (now Equivant), the creator of COMPAS, contended the algorithm is fair because the number of defendants classified as 'high risk' that reoffended was the same whether they were black or white (around 60 per cent of high-risk defendants). But ProPublica argued that among defendants *who ultimately did not reoffend*, blacks were more than twice as

[22] F. Pasquale, *The Black Box Society: The Secret Algorithms That Control Money and Information* (Cambridge, MA: Harvard University Press, 2015); S. Wachter, B. Mittelstadt and C. Russell, 'Counterfactual Explanations without Opening the Black Box: Automated Decisions and the GDPR' (2018) 31(2) *Harvard Journal of Law and Technology*.

[23] J.-M. Deltorn, 'La protection des données personnelles face aux algorithmes prédictifs' (2017) 12 *Revue des Droits et Libertés Fondamentaux*.

[24] Feller et al., see fn 18; C. Rudin, C. Wang and B. Coker, 'The Age of Secrecy and Unfairness in Recidivism Prediction' (2020) 2 *Harvard Data Science Review* 1.

[25] M. Minow, J. Zittrain, J. Bowers et al., 'Technical Flaws of Pretrial Risk Assessments Raise Grave Concerns', *Berkman Klein Center Blog* (17 July 2019).

[26] Pretrial Justice Institute, 'The Case against Pretrial Risk Assessment Instruments' (November 2020), https://university.pretrial.org.

[27] J. Austin, S. L. Desmarais, J. Monahan et al., 'Open Letter to the Pretrial Justice Institute' (2020), jfa-associates.com.

[28] Ibid.

[29] A. Chouldechova, 'Fair Prediction with Disparate Impact: A Study of Bias in Recidivism Prediction Instruments' (2017) 5 *Big Data* 153; A. Završnik 'Algorithmic Justice: Algorithms and Big Data in Criminal Justice Settings' (2019) 18 *European Journal of Criminology* 623.

likely as whites to be classified as medium or high risk (42 per cent vs 22 per cent). In other words, COMPAS satisfies equal positive predictive values since among those called higher risk, the proportion of defendants who got rearrested is approximately the same regardless of race. But COMPAS does not satisfy equal false positive rates by race since among defendants who did not get rearrested, black defendants were twice as likely to be misclassified as high risk. The difficulty is that satisfying both fairness criteria at the same time would require either that there is no racial disparity in recidivism rates or that the model does not produce any false positives or false negatives, which is impossible.[30] In any case, these objections and debates show that the widespread adoption of these tools by the courts must be accompanied by significant safeguards.

LEGAL SAFEGUARDS FOR THE USE OF RISK ASSESSMENT TOOLS The use of risk assessment tools by the courts must be supervised and accompanied to preserve the rights and freedoms of those subject to trial. In particular, the persons concerned must be able to effectively contest the decisions taken. This is what emerges from the litigation on this subject, even if the law is not fixed on this point. In 2017, the Kansas Court of Appeals decided a case in which the defendant had been evaluated using the LSI-R (Level of Service Inventory-Revised) risk assessment tool and had only been given access to a cover page summarizing his general scores. He argued that the refusal to disclose the details of his LSI-R assessment violated his right to due process. The court ruled that denying the defendant access to his complete LSI-R assessment made it impossible for him to 'challenge the accuracy of the information' used in 'determining the conditions of his probation'.[31]

The same year, the Wisconsin Supreme Court[32] decided a case that involved COMPAS. The defendant, Eric Loomis, was charged with five criminal counts related to a drive-by shooting and pled guilty to two of the less severe charges. Loomis' COMPAS report indicated a high risk of recidivism. The trial court referred to the COMPAS assessment in its sentencing determination and, based in part on this assessment, sentenced Loomis to six years of imprisonment and five years of extended supervision. Loomis challenged the decision, arguing that the use of COMPAS in sentencing violated his right to due process and his right to be sentenced based on accurate information because the proprietary nature of the COMPAS software prevented him from assessing the accuracy of the score. He also asserted that his right to an individualized sentence was violated because COMPAS relied on information about the characteristics of a larger group to make an inference about his personal likelihood to commit future crimes. Loomis additionally argued that the court unconstitutionally considered gender at sentencing by relying on a risk assessment that took gender into account. The court replied that the use of gender as a factor in the risk assessment served the non-discriminatory purpose of promoting accuracy and added that Loomis could have verified the accuracy of the information used in sentencing, as COMPAS uses only publicly available data and data provided by the defendant. The court also recognized that COMPAS provides only aggregate data on recidivism risk for groups similar to the offender but insisted that COMPAS is not the sole basis for a decision. Therefore, as courts have the discretion and information necessary to disagree with the assessment when appropriate, sentencing is still sufficiently individualized. The Wisconsin Supreme Court ruled that COMPAS can be used as an additional source of information at sentencing on

[30] S. Mitchell, E. Potash, S. Barocas, A. D'Amour and K. Lum, 'Algorithmic Fairness: Choices, Assumptions, and Definitions' (2021) 8(1) *Annual Review of Statistics and Its Application* 141.

[31] *State of Kansas* v. *John Keith Walls*, No. 116,027 (2017).

[32] *State* v. *Loomis*, 881 NW 2d 749 (Wis. 2016), analysed in (2017) 130 *Harvard Law Review* 1530.

condition that courts list the other factors taken into consideration. The court added that pretrial assessments that incorporate a COMPAS assessment must include various written warnings for judges like the fact that the algorithm is confidential or the risk of discrimination.[33]

If the Loomis decision imposed restrictions by preventing judges from relying exclusively on the assessment produced by the algorithm, the Wisconsin judges did not seem particularly troubled by the fact that most of the COMPAS features are not disclosed. We can therefore find these guarantees very insufficient and regret that the US Supreme Court did not accept taking up the case. Since then, Idaho has adopted a new law providing that 'all pretrial risk assessment tools shall be transparent'.[34] In particular, all the elements used to build the algorithm (data, documents, records) 'shall be open to public inspection, auditing, and testing' and the defendant shall be entitled to review all calculations and data used to calculate their own risk score and no trade secret or other intellectual property protections can be invoked to refuse to disclose all elements. For the time being, the transparency imposed by the Idaho statute applies only in that state: elsewhere, the guarantees currently provided by positive law are very thin, even though the influence of scores is important – judges tend to lengthen sentences for defendants with higher scores and shorten sentences for those with lower scores.[35]

23.2.1.2 *Risk Assessment Tools in the EU*

The use of decision support tools is not widespread in European courts.[36] The situation varies according to national laws and the policies followed in the various countries. While French law prohibits the use of risk assessment algorithms by judges, European Union law merely regulates them.

FRENCH BAN ON THE USE OF ALGORITHMIC ASSESSMENT TOOLS In France, the use of assessment tools in judicial decision-making has been prohibited since the French Data Protection Act was adopted in 1978.[37] Article 47 para. 1 and Article 95 para. 1 of this law provide that 'no judicial decision involving an assessment of a person's behavior may be based on automated processing of personal data intended to evaluate certain aspects of that person's personality'.[38] This provision could maybe be interpreted as not fully prohibiting having knowledge of such scores but only prohibiting basing the decision on them. This last interpretation would be more consistent with Article 4-3 of the Law of 18 November 2016 that provides that online conciliation, mediation or arbitration services 'may not be based solely on an algorithmic or automated processing of personal data'.[39] Either way, the scope of the prohibition is limited, since only algorithms intended 'to evaluate certain aspects of the defendant's

[33] The following should be mentioned: the confidential nature of the algorithm, the fact that it uses data relating to groups of individuals, the fact that the data is collected and processed on a national scale (and not on a state scale), the possible discriminatory effect on minorities and the fact that COMPAS was initially developed to assist the administration in the application of sentences (and not their determination).

[34] ID Code §19-1910 (1) (2019).

[35] M. Stevenson and J. L. Doleac, 'Algorithmic Risk Assessment in the Hands of Humans', IZA Discussion Paper No. 12853.

[36] E. Chelioudakis, 'Risk Assessment Tools in Criminal Justice: Is There a Need for Such Tools in Europe and Would Their Use Comply with European Data Protection Law?' (2020) 1(2) *Australian National University Journal of Law & Technology* 72.

[37] Law No. 78-17 of 6 January 1978, *Informatique et Libertés*.

[38] 'Aucune décision de justice impliquant une appréciation sur le comportement d'une personne ne peut avoir pour fondement un traitement automatisé de données à caractère personnel destiné à évaluer certains aspects de sa personnalité.'

[39] Law No. 2016-1547 of 18 November 2016, on the Modernization of Justice in the 21st Century.

personality' are prohibited. It is, in any case, clear that the prohibition covers algorithms that attempt to assess the risk of recidivism. Such a general prohibition is not only to be regretted, given the insight that such tools can provide, but also incompatible with European law.

RELATIVE PROHIBITION OF RISK ASSESSMENT TOOLS IN EU LAW The use of risk assessment algorithms by the courts is not, as such, prohibited by EU law. Article 11 of the Directive 2016/680 (known as the Law Enforcement Directive-LED), which applies to 'the processing of personal data for the purposes of the prevention, investigation, detection or prosecution of criminal offences or the execution of criminal penalties' prohibits decisions 'based solely on automated processing, including profiling, which produces an adverse legal effect concerning the data subject or significantly affects him or her'. Similarly, Article 22 of the General Protection Regulation 2016/679 (GDPR), whose scope is more general and does not relate exclusively to criminal matters, protects the right not to be subject to a decision based solely on automated processing, including profiling, which produces 'legal effects concerning or significantly affecting them in a similar way'. Those provisions only prohibit decisions based 'solely' on automated processes. In other words, they merely prohibit fully automated decisions without human involvement in the decision process. And both the LED and the GDPR allow for exceptions, in particular where national laws so provide.

Of course, the fundamental rights of those subject to trial must be respected in such a way as to ensure privacy and data protection, the prohibition of discrimination and the right to a fair trial.[40] However, no provision in EU law is currently dealing specifically with the use of algorithmic decision support tools in the field of justice, even if the situation will change rapidly. In 2018, the Council of Europe's European Commission for the Efficiency of Justice (CEPEJ) adopted a 'European Ethical Charter on the Use of Artificial Intelligence in Judicial Systems and Their Environment',[41] which sets out five principles: respect for fundamental rights, non-discrimination, quality and security, transparency, impartiality and fairness (including accessibility and understandability) and the principle of 'under user control' (ensuring that users are informed actors and in control of their choices). More recently, the EU Commission has released a proposal for an Artificial Intelligence Act[42] that provides for new rules concerning the use of risk assessment tools. Algorithms used by law enforcement authorities and judges are included in the list of high-risk AI systems, which triggers the application of binding rules to protect the rights of the persons concerned. This includes extensive obligations in relation to data governance, transparency, human oversight, accuracy, robustness and cybersecurity. In particular, the Act provides that human oversight must be ensured and that providers of high-risk systems must realize conformity assessments. These AI systems will therefore be closely monitored, which is an important step that will affect all AI systems used by the courts.

23.2.2 *Algorithmic Prediction of Court Decisions*

Predicting the probability that an individual will engage in a certain behaviour, such as committing an offence, is one thing, but predicting the possibility that a formal institution will make a certain decision is quite another. French jurists have coined the term 'predictive justice'[43] to refer

[40] A. Završnik, 'Criminal Justice, Artificial Intelligence Systems, and Human Rights' (2020) 20 *ERA Forum* 567.

[41] CEPEJ, *European Ethical Charter on the Use of Artificial Intelligence in Judicial Systems* (Council of Europe, 2019).

[42] Artificial Intelligence Act, COM (2021) 206 final.

[43] S. Lebreton-Derrien, 'La justice prédictive. Introduction à une justice "simplement" virtuelle' (2018) 60 *Archives de Philosophie du droit* 14; Y. Méneceur, 'L'intelligence artificielle. Quel futur pour la justice prédictive?' (2018)

to the use of machine learning in order to provide statistical modelling based on the analysis of large volumes of past decisions. The term can be misleading because it is not, strictly speaking, 'predicting' what the court decision would be.[44] The aim is more modestly to evaluate the chances of success of a procedure, the quantum of a future conviction or even to develop models capable of reproducing the range of judicial decisions rendered on a given point. In France, the Open Data policy opens up many prospects for the development of algorithmic tools, even if this evolution raises the issue of regulation.

23.2.2.1 *French Open Data Policy on Judicial Decisions*

In France, the Law of 7 October 2016 (Law for a Digital Republic) launched the Open Data policy of the French administrations.[45] The law provided for unrestricted free access to all the available data emanating from public administrations, including decisions of all courts.[46] Up to now, French citizens have always had free access to the decisions rendered by higher courts, but not to decisions of lower courts. The new law provided that 'decisions rendered by the judicial courts are made available to the public free of charge while respecting the privacy of the persons concerned' (Article 21). However, this provision was never implemented because of the intense debate about the terms of application of the reform, especially concerning the conditions to be respected in order to protect the privacy of litigants. An academic report commissioned by the Ministry of Justice[47] noted that full anonymization is impossible to achieve and suggested that the requirements for pseudonymizing decisions be strengthened. Then another major issue was raised: should the names of judges be removed or not? The various organizations representing judges and legal professionals adopted completely opposite positions on that issue, some being in favour of deleting the names of judges before publication, others being against. But the mention of the names of judges in judicial decisions is related to the right to a fair trial set out in Article 6, para. 1, of the European Convention on Human Rights. In *Vernes* v. *France*,[48] the European Court of Human Rights specifically sanctioned France on the basis of Article 6 (1), in a case where the applicant had been sanctioned by an authority whose composition they did not know. The court underlined that the fact of not knowing the composition of the court does not allow the litigant to be assured that their case was judged in an impartial way. It was therefore finally decided to publish the decisions with the names of the judges who composed the court.

The principle of publishing all courts' decisions was thus reaffirmed in 2019[49] with various safeguards designed to protect litigants and judges. The law now provides that the name of any natural person mentioned in a decision should be removed before publication, and also that other elements should be removed as well if the disclosure of such elements is likely to jeopardize the safety or privacy of the person concerned or their relatives (Article L111-13 para. 2 of the Code of Judicial Organization). Moreover, although it was finally decided that the name of courts' members and clerks should appear in the published versions of the decisions, their

JurisClasseur Périodique 190; F. Rouvière, 'La justice prédictive : version moderne de la boule de cristal' (2017) *Revue Trimestrielle de Droit civil* 527; A. Garapon, 'Les enjeux de la justice prédictive' (2017) *JurisClasseur Périodique* 31.

44 For results of purely lexical analyses carried out on the only basis of keywords: N. Aletras, D. Tsarapatsanis, D. Preomiuc-Pietro and V. Lampos, 'Predicting Judicial Decisions of the European Court of Human Rights: A Natural Language Processing Perspective' (2016) *Peer J Computer Science* 2, e93.

45 Law No. 2016-1321 of 7 October 2016 for a Digital Republic.

46 Article L111-13 of the Code of the Organization of Justice and Article 10 of the Code of Administrative Justice.

47 L. Cadiet (ed.), *Open data des décisions de justice, Mission d'étude et de préfiguration de l'ouverture au public des décisions de justice* (Paris: Ministry of Justice, 2017).

48 ECHR, *Vernes* v. *France*, No. 30183/06.

49 Programming Law No. 2019-222 of 23 March 2019 for the reform of the justice system 2018–2022.

names can be removed in cases where such a disclosure would put their safety or privacy in jeopardy. The new policy is currently being implemented: all judicial decisions should be published by December 2025.[50]

23.2.2.2 *French Ban on Judicial Profiling*

While the dissemination of all court decisions is a sign of transparency, the fact that algorithms can reveal the particular characteristics and opinions of each judge is cause for concern. To prevent this risk, the new law provided that 'the identity data of judges and registry staff may not be reused for the purpose or effect of evaluating, analyzing, comparing or predicting their actual or supposed professional practices' (Article L111-13 para. 3 of the Code of Judicial Organization). Individuals who violate this provision are subject to severe criminal penalties. Although such a rule is extremely harsh, it should not be understood as completely prohibiting judicial analytics.[51] Under French law, criminal rules must be interpreted strictly (Article 111-4 of the Penal Code), which excludes reasoning by analogy.[52] In this case, the law only prohibits the reuse of 'identity data' of judges and clerks for a given purpose, namely the evaluation, analysis, comparison or prediction of the 'real or supposed professional practices' of the persons concerned. Yet the law does not prohibit the processing of other types of data: court decisions can easily be processed as long as the names of judges is excluded from the elements taken into account. Of course, in cases where the reidentification of judges is easy, in particular when they rule as a single judge, the reference to the court or chamber that ruled on the case may be problematic. But the most important point is to make sure that the analyses do not target the professional practices of a particular judge. The Constitutional Council specifically ruled that the new provision does not violate the right to a fair and equitable procedure and emphasized that the prohibition is meant to avoid strategies 'likely to alter the functioning of justice'.[53] The law aims to prohibit the nominative and personalized profiling of judges, in order to avoid pressure or destabilizing strategies aimed at a particular judge, such as systematic requests for recusal. But processing judicial decisions is authorized, as long as the identity of the judges is not taken into account and that they are not personally targeted.

Of course, the very principle of the ban could be criticized. It could be argued that transparency requires the production of personalized analyses that provide real visibility on the activity of judges. It could also be claimed that the right to a fair trial implies being able to ensure, through statistics, the impartiality of judges. However, the function of French judges has never been to render decisions or opinions in their own name. Judicial decisions are written in an impersonal manner and rendered in the name of the French people. In this context, the new law aims primarily to protect judges by ensuring that they are not personally questioned for their professional practices. An example from a few years ago illustrates this issue. A French start-up developed an algorithm analysing decisions made in the context of disputes relating to 'Obligations to Leave the French Territory' ('Obligations de quitter le territoire Français'). These deportation measures can be appealed before administrative courts. The algorithm calculated the rate of rejection of appeals by year, by court and by chamber. While some of them had rejection rates between 97 per cent and 100 per cent, others had rejection rates between 47 per cent and 60 per cent. The company that developed the algorithm concluded

[50] Decree No. 2020-797 of 29 June 2020 and Order (*arrêté*) of 29 April 2021.

[51] F. G'sell, 'Predicting Courts' Decisions Is Lawful in France and Will Remain So', *Actualités du droit*, 2 July 2019.

[52] Similarly, the European Court of Human Rights ruled that 'criminal law must not be extensively construed to an accused's detriment, for instance by analogy'. ECHR, 25 May 1993, *Kokkinakis* v. *Greece*, para. 52.

[53] Constitutional Council, 21 March 2019, No. 2019-778 DC, para. 93.

that these 'highly significant' statistics indicated that 'an apparent bias exists among some appeal judges'.[54] This conclusion was set out in an article published on Medium, which presented tables showing the names of the judges that had rendered the decisions. Not only were the statistics presented not sufficient, without further evidence, to justify the conclusion that the judges were biased and unfair, but the very fact of disclosing the names of the judges involved was questionable. Today, such statistics would be subject to the prohibition. On the other hand, it would certainly be possible to publish this information without mentioning the name of the judges and to exploit these informative and enlightening elements.

23.2.2.3 *Algorithmic Processing of Judicial Decisions*

Litigants and lawyers now have the possibility to use sophisticated AI tools that can provide an assessment of the possible outcome of a legal proceeding. The possibility for the parties to have an objective and reliable assessment of what they can hope to obtain in court should lead them to negotiate effectively.[55] There should be more and more disputes being settled, as the use of algorithmic tools develops among litigants, lawyers and judges, even though it is still very difficult, for the time being, to assess the impact of the use of algorithms on the way conflicts will be amicably settled in the future.[56] Moreover, the courts themselves should benefit from the insight given by machine-learning algorithms. Judges will be able to take advantage of algorithmic models that can reproduce the range of judicial decisions on a given issue and even suggest a solution consistent with what was already decided. Of course, such a perspective does not raise any impediment in legal systems based on the rule of precedent. But such a change is, on the other hand, less evident in civil law countries. While China has started using machine learning to ensure consistency in the law, this evolution is more controversial in France.

EXAMPLE OF CHINESE JUSTICE Since 2017, China has established three Internet Courts in Beijing, Guangzhou and Hangzhou to adjudicate primarily e-commerce disputes, product liability for online sales and copyrights. These fully digital courts are the most advanced of the 'smart courts' that the Chinese authorities have set up throughout the country since 2016,[57] as part of a proactive and effective strategy to digitize the judicial process.[58] Proceedings before the Internet Courts are held entirely remotely. Litigants can introduce and follow the proceedings directly through applications that are usually available on the popular WeChat platform. Most often, facial recognition is used to identify parties during the proceedings. AI tools assist court clerks and judges with most of the tasks: analysing documents, searching for precedents, collecting evidence, transcribing hearings, drafting pleadings, etc. In the Beijing court, which is one of the most advanced, AI is used to generate procedural documents, such as subpoenas, which are 100 per cent automated.[59] Some courts even employ 'robot judges' who are in fact

54 M. Benesty, 'L'impartialité de certains juges mise à mal par l'intelligence artificielle', *Medium*, 18 April 2016.

55 D. Stevenson and N. Wagoner, 'Bargaining in the Shadow of Big Data' (2016) 67 *Florida Law Review* 1337.

56 A. J. Casey and A. Niblett, 'Will Robot Judges Change Litigation and Settlement Outcomes?', *MIT Computational Law Report* (14 August 2020).

57 B. M. Chen and Z. Li, 'How Will Technology Change the Face of Chinese Justice?' (2020), Hong Kong Faculty of Law Research Paper No. 2020/058; M. Zou, '"Smart Courts" in China and the Future of Personal Injury Litigation' (2020) *Journal of Personal Injury Law* (forthcoming).

58 C. Shi, T. Sourdin and B. Li, 'The Smart Court – A New Pathway to Justice in China?' (2021) 12 *International Journal for Court Administration* 4; A. J. Schmitz, 'Expanding Access to Remedies through E-Court Initiatives' (2019) 67 *Buffalo Law Review* 89; S. Papagianneas, 'Smart Courts: Toward the Digitization and Automation of Justice', *The China Story*, 21 August 2020.

59 G. Du, 'Beijing Internet Court's First Year at a Glance: Inside China's Internet Courts Series -05', *China Observer*, 19 October 2019.

simply virtual agents with a voice and facial expressions, that can welcome the litigants on the virtual courtroom and assist them, in particular in the drafting of their request.[60] They can also assist judges in basic and repetitive tasks, answer the phone and make appointments.

AI is also involved in decision-making. It is intended to enable Chinese judges to consistently apply the new principle of 'similar rulings for similar cases' imposed by the Supreme People's Court of China since the latest round of judicial reforms (from 2014 to 2017).[61] Chinese judges are now bound by their own precedents and by higher courts' precedents. More specifically, they are required to systematically research precedents to ensure that similar cases are given the same solution. If they want to deviate from precedents, they must present their reasons and obtain the approval of a superior; otherwise, they are liable.[62] Chinese judges are thus encouraged to use AI in order to replicate the principles and criteria applied in previous decisions. In 2018, the Similar Case Intelligent Recommendation System, a search engine that selects previous decisions related to the case under consideration, was made available to judges and litigants.[63] The software makes recommendations by referring to previous similar cases, taking into account the facts, the nature of the dispute and the applicable laws. It is even possible, in some courts, to use applications that automatically draft judgments. In other courts, such as the Shanghai High People's Court, AI is used not to produce decisions but to correct inconsistencies and ensure that judges meet their obligations.[64] When a judgment is issued, the 'abnormal judgment warning'[65] program analyses it and issues a warning if the proposed judgment is not sufficiently consistent with previous decisions. The warning is sent to the judge's superiors. This tool is mainly used in criminal cases to determine whether the sentence proposed or handed down by the judge is consistent with previous sentences.

The algorithmic *stare decisis* policy implemented by the Chinese authorities is, for the time being, unique and subject to criticism in China. It has been argued that the AI tools used are not that effective and make many mistakes.[66] The software does not always manage to find cases that are close enough to the case under review. Automatically written judgments are sometimes hard to understand. In most cases, judgments produced automatically must be taken up manually by the judges: in the Beijing Court, half of a decision is produced by the machine, the other half being written manually by the judge.[67] Finally, some people emphasize the risk that the influence of algorithms and, indirectly, of those who developed them, weighs on the independence of judges.[68] The most experienced Chinese judges believe that their expertise is sufficient and that they do not need the tool.[69] In any case, these tools are not intended to replace judges but to support them: despite the massive use of virtual agents and recommendation algorithms, the Chinese system appears to maintain the principle of a human judicial decision.

60 J. Deng, 'Should the Common Law System Welcome Artificial Intelligence: A Case Study of China's Same-Type Case Reference System?' (2019) 3 *Georgetown Law Technology Review* 223 at 227.
61 Ibid.
62 M. Yu and G. Du, 'Why Are Chinese Courts Turning to AI?', *The Diplomat*, 19 January 2019.
63 Chen and Li, see fn 57.
64 Ibid.
65 Yu and Du, see fn 62.
66 Shi et al., see fn 58.
67 The exact figure is that judgments and transactions are 50.3 per cent machine-generated, while pleadings are 100 per cent automated. Du, see fn 59.
68 Ibid.
69 Ibid

USE OF MACHINE LEARNING BY FRENCH COURTS In the French legal system, the solution of a dispute is supposed to be reached by deductive reasoning from a written and general rule, even if all French lawyers, starting with judges, scrupulously study precedents. In this context, algorithms could provide the French judges with new insights into their own case law. They could make it possible to have a better idea of the practices of trial judges, which are hardly known, unlike the decisions of the Court of Cassation, which are published and scrupulously studied.[70] They could make judges aware of their own biases or possible mistakes[71] and encourage them to make better decisions. In so doing, they could contribute to harmonize the law and to achieve legal certainty, predictability and equal treatment of citizens.[72] In 2020, the Ministry of Justice launched the Datajust project for this very purpose.[73] The Datajust algorithm processes data extracted from appeal decisions rendered between 2017 and 2019 on personal injury compensation. The objective of the Datajust project is to provide litigants and judges with a non-mandatory benchmark. It is also to encourage litigants to settle out of court.[74]

There are objections to the deployment of machine-learning tools in the courts. Some French authors have highlighted the risk that judges would systematically align themselves with the results produced by the algorithms, falling into 'judicial conformism'[75] by reproducing the same solutions indefinitely.[76] Yet it could be argued that the most sophisticated algorithms focus primarily on the reasoning followed by judges in past decisions and are capable of proposing innovative solutions. Moreover, the risk of standardization of decisions must be tempered insofar as the analysis of mass data allows for a high degree of personalization. There remains a justified concern about the influence that algorithmic tools could have on judicial decisions and the prospect of judges abandoning their independence in favour of technology.

In any case, regulation seems necessary to ensure the quality and transparency of algorithms. Judges and litigants must, in particular, be fully informed of their methodology and the particularities of their design. In French law, decisions taken on the basis of algorithmic processing must include an explicit statement informing the person affected by the decision, who can obtain communication of the rules defining the software and the main characteristics of its implementation (Article L311-3-1 of the Code of Relations between the Public and the Administration). In July 2020, various French authorities (the vice-president of the Conseil d'État, the president of the National Bar Council and the president of the Ordre des avocats au Conseil d'État et à la Cour de cassation) signed a joint declaration affirming their commitment to the five principles stated in the aforementioned 'European Ethical Charter on the Use of Artificial Intelligence in Judicial Systems and Their Environment'.[77] They also called for the creation of a system to regulate and control the algorithms used for the exploitation of databases of court decisions, including the creation of a public authority in charge of this control. Such regulation will come from the adoption of the above-mentioned European Artificial Intelligence

[70] V. Vigneau, 'Le passé ne manque pas d'avenir. Libres propos d'un juge sur la justice prédictive' (2018) *Dalloz* 1095.

[71] A. Chen, 'How Artificial Intelligence Can Help Us Make Judges Less Biased', *The Verge*, 17 January 2019. On whether algorithms would make discrimination more obvious, see J. Kleinberg, J. Ludwig, S. Mullainathan and C. R. Sunstein, 'Discrimination in the Age of Algorithms' (2018) 10 *Journal of Legal Analysis* 113.

[72] Vigneau, see fn 70.

[73] Decree No. 2020-356 of 27 March 2020.

[74] See the presentation of the project on the Etalab website: https://entrepreneur-interet-general.etalab.gouv.fr/defis/2019/datajust.html.

[75] Vigneau, see fn 70.

[76] Garapon, see fn 43.

[77] See fn 41.

Act,[78] which qualifies the algorithms used in the field of justice as high-risk systems.[79] In particular, the transparency of these systems will be ensured by providing users with a certain amount of information. Human supervision will have to be guaranteed, in view of the tendency of professionals to rely on these systems (automation bias). The providers of such systems will have to take the necessary steps to ensure their accuracy, robustness and security. A supervisory authority will be designated in each Member State.

23.2.3 *Toward AI Judges?*

The more sophisticated algorithms become, the more they will produce recommendations that judges will be tempted to follow: this is why the total automation of the judicial decision seems to be inevitable. In Europe, the automation of judicial decisions is, for now, prohibited by both the GDPR (Article 22) and the Law Enforcement Directive (Article 11) that proscribe decisions based 'solely' on automated processes that significantly affect the people involved. However, this prohibition can be circumvented, since both the GDPR and the LED admit exceptions and allow national laws to derogate from it. However, even assuming that such automation is technically and legally possible, it would be necessary to establish that such a perspective is desirable.

23.2.3.1 *Is Full Automation of Judicial Decision-Making Possible?*

Technology allows some decisions to be automated, as is the case in many countries concerning traffic offences, which do not require very advanced software. AI also makes it possible to automate repetitive decisions in technical fields, such as tax matters.[80] Would it be possible in more complex cases? Algorithms are not only able to assess the chances of success of a procedure or the amount of compensation that the plaintiff can expect, they can also isolate the legal arguments and factual elements that were decisive in the adoption of past decisions, therefore they are a form of legal reasoning. In the United States, the Do Not Pay software, which uses IBM's Watson AI system, generates, in a fully automated manner, the complaint to be filed in court and is even able to produce the legal arguments that the plaintiff can read at the hearing. The machine is indeed capable of preparing in advance a legal strategy to respond to the defendant's predictable arguments.[81] Do Not Pay claims a 55 per cent success rate for actions brought with its tool.[82] However, the company itself emphasizes that the software is only designed for small, repetitive disputes, not for complex litigation.

Indeed, although machine-learning algorithms can deal with routine legal problems (traffic violations, uncovered cheques) for which the analysis of past decisions may be sufficient, they cannot handle cases with a certain degree of complexity or singularity, at least in the current state of technology.[83] Algorithms based on mathematical or algorithmic models can propose solutions within a precise framework and given limits. Yet understanding singular or unusual cases requires more general AI techniques, which are still beyond our reach.[84] Let us take the example of the interpretation of the French Law of 5 July 1985, which applies to car accidents involving 'motorized ground vehicles' (*véhicules terrestres à moteur*). Determining the scope of application of this law

78 See fn 42.
79 See Annex III point 8 of the proposed Regulation.
80 B. Alarie, A. Niblett and A. H. Yoon, 'Regulation by Machine' (2016), 30th Conference on Neural Information Processing Systems (NIPS 2016), Barcelona, Spain.
81 C. Haskins, 'New App Lets You "Sue Anyone by Pressing a Button"', *Vice* (10 October 2018).
82 Ibid.
83 Abiteboul and G'sell, see fn 5.
84 Ibid.

implies specifying what a 'motorized ground vehicle' is. The question has arisen as to whether or not a lawnmower is a 'motorized ground vehicle'. It was held that a 'self-propelled' lawnmower is a 'motorized ground vehicle' insofar as it is 'a motorized machine with four wheels enabling it to travel, equipped with a seat on which a person sits to drive it'.[85] On the other hand, a lawnmower driven by a person walking on foot is not considered a 'motorized ground vehicle'. Could an algorithm have done the reasoning that leads to such a distinction? In the absence of a previous decision on this specific question, it would have been necessary to refer to other decisions on lawnmowers and to reflect on the semantics of the word 'motorized ground vehicle'. In order to reach a relevant answer, the algorithm would have had to use other AI techniques than machine learning, such as general knowledge bases, semantic analysis and logical reasoning. However, using pure logical reasoning in the legal field is limited, since it is precisely not possible to translate all the law into precise rules that can be used by a machine.[86]

It appears that technology can help in simple cases, but not in the most complex ones. Machine learning can predict or propose solutions by considering previous decisions but these decisions are not always available. Even when they are, the data may be insufficient, incomplete, inaccurate or even contradictory, which is frequent in the law because judgments or laws often contradict each other. Then, if the examination of past decisions is not sufficient, it is necessary to call upon a wide range of techniques beyond the learning techniques currently considered. In any case, proposing a legal argument is a much more complex task than simply providing a solution based on machine learning.

23.2.3.2 *Is the Automation of Judicial Decision-Making Desirable?*

Even assuming that the above-mentioned limitations disappear over time and that AI systems are, more and more, able to deal satisfactorily with complex and unusual cases, it is not certain that automation would be desirable. Of course, AI advocates might be tempted to point out the flaws and limitations of human justice to conclude that algorithms are preferable to it.

First, they could argue that human judges are so partial and biased that the possible unfairness of algorithms is ultimately negligible. Various studies in the United States have shown that, under similar conditions, bail amounts are 25 per cent higher[87] and prison sentences are 12 per cent longer[88] for black defendants. In homicide cases, the death penalty is more likely to be imposed when the defendant is black, and sentences are more severe when the victim is white.[89] Litigants' gender is also a frequently noted bias.[90] In France, women are sentenced to an average of twenty days less than men, all other things being equal.[91] In general, political preferences, ethnic origin and certain demographic characteristics have an influence over judicial decisions.[92] Other circumstances may be listed, such as the reluctance to make several decisions in a

[85] Cass. 2e Civ. 24 June 2004, No. 02-20.208, *Bull. civ.* II, no. 308, 260.

[86] Abiteboul and G'sell, see fn 5; D. Bourcier, 'L'acte de juger est-il modélisable?', see fn 4.

[87] I. Ayres and J. Waldfogel, 'A Market Test for Race Discrimination in Bail Setting' (1994) 46 *Stanford Law Review* 987.

[88] D. B. Mustard, 'Racial, Ethnic, and Gender Disparities in Sentencing: Evidence from the U.S. Federal Courts' (2001) 44 *Journal of Law & Economics* 285 at 300.

[89] R. R. Banks et al., 'Discrimination and Implicit Bias in a Racially Unequal Society' (2006) 94 *California Law Review* 1169 at 1175; J. J. Rachlinski, S. L. Johnson, A. J. Wistrich and C. Guthrie, 'Does Unconscious Racial Bias Affect Trial Judges?' (2009) 84 *Notre Dame Law Review* 1195.

[90] A. L. Miller, 'Expertise Fails to Attenuate Gendered Biases in Judicial Decision-Making' (2019) 10(2) *Social Psychological and Personality Science* 227.

[91] A. Philippe, 'Vous jurez de n'écouter ni la haine, ni la méchanceté … Les biais affectant les décisions de justice' (2015) 4 *Les Cahiers de la Justice* 563.

[92] T. J. Miles and C. R. Sunstein, 'The New Legal Realism' (2008) 75 *University of Chicago Law Review* 831; C. Jolls and C. R. Sunstein, 'The Law of Implicit Bias' (2006) 94 *California Law Review* 969 (implicit biases relating to disadvantaged groups).

row in the same direction,[93] the context of an election campaign,[94] the media environment,[95] the performance of a local football team,[96] the defendant's birthday[97] or even physical attractiveness.[98] It has even been demonstrated that lenient judgment is more likely to be adopted at the beginning of the day or after a meal since the probability of a favourable ruling declines with the number of hours worked.[99] In the light of these studies, it is easy to conclude that an AI programmed to adopt decisions according to objective criteria, in a quasi-mathematical way, would ultimately prove to be more just and legitimate. An algorithmic assessment of the risk of recidivism of a defendant would be preferable to a subjective human perception of the dangerousness of the person concerned.[100]

Second, although the opacity of algorithms is considered problematic, human decisions themselves are opaque and difficult to explain. Even though judges must provide the legal arguments on which their decisions are based, these arguments do not always appear clear, precise and convincing. They might even mask other less avowed reasons or a certain subjectivity of the judge. Antonio Cassese, former president of the International Criminal Tribunal for the former Yugoslavia, wrote that judges are 'experts in manipulation'.[101] Indeed, one might sometimes wonder whether the reasons given by judges are not mainly intended to formally legitimize the decision. Moreover, while a judicial decision is not explained beyond its official motivation, the code of a software program and the data on which its choices were based can be made public.

In addition to the limitations of human justice, AI has its own advantages. AI tools make it possible to process cases quickly, efficiently and inexpensively. AI could thus guarantee better access to justice and efficiency. In Estonia, the government hopes that the use of AI tools will leave more time for human judges to solve more complex problems. Moreover, unlike humans who make biased decisions and have difficulty making progress, algorithms can be improved.[102] Data quality can be enhanced. The design of algorithms can be modified to make them fairer, more consistent and more transparent.[103] The quality of the algorithms can be evaluated and

93 D. L. Chen, T. J. Moskowitz and K. Shue, 'Decision-Making under the Gambler's Fallacy: Evidence from Asylum Judges, Loan Officers, and Baseball Umpires' (2016), NBER Working Paper No. 22026.

94 D. L. Chen, 'Priming Ideology: Why Presidential Elections Affect US Judges' (2016), TSE Working Paper No. 16-681.

95 A. Philippe and A. Ouss, '"No Hatred or Malice, Fear or Affection": Media and Sentencing' (2018) 126(5) *Journal of Political Economy* 2134.

96 O. Eren and N. Mocan, 'Emotional Judges and Unlucky Juveniles' (2016), NBER Working Paper No. 22611.

97 D. L. Chen and A. Philippe, 'Clash of Norms: Judicial Leniency on Defendant Birthdays' (2018), TSE Working Paper No. 18-934.

98 R. Hollier, 'Physical Attractiveness Bias in the Legal System' (2017), thelawproject.com.au.

99 S. Danziger, J. Levav and L. Avnaim-Pesso, 'Extraneous Factors in Judicial Decisions' (2011) 108(17) *PNAS* 6889.

100 J. Kleinberg, H. Lakkaraju, J. Leskovec, J. Ludwig and S. Mullainathan, 'Human Decisions and Machine Predictions' (2017), NBER Working Paper No. 23180.

101
> Nous vons tous rédigé des jugements. Nous savons que l'on pourrait considérer les juges comme des experts en manipulation. Les juges 'manient' habilement les lois, les critères, les principes d'interprétation dans le but, bien sûr, de rendre justice dans un cas d'espèce. En particulier dans la justice pénale, on sent intuitivement qu'un homme est coupable, que le sens commun devrait nous conduire à cette conclusion. La construction du magnifique raisonnement juridique qui le justifie est postérieure.
>
> R. Badinter and S. Breyer (eds.), *Les entretiens de Provence, Le juge dans la société contemporaine* (Paris: Fayard, 2003), p. 44.

102 Some authors argue that it is easier to demonstrate bias in an algorithm than human discrimination once you have the data or parameters used. J. Kleinberg, J. Ludwig, S. Mullainathan and C. R. Sunstein, 'Discrimination in the Age of Algorithms' (2019), NBER Working Paper No. 25548; J. Kleinberg, S. Mullainathan and M. Raghavan, 'Inherent Trade-offs in the Fair Determination of Risk Scores' (2017) 67 *Innovations in Theoretical Computer Science*; S. Tolan, 'Fair and Unbiased Algorithmic Decision Making: Current State and Future Challenges' (2018), JRC Digital Economy Working Paper No. 2018-10; C. R. Sunstein, 'Algorithms, Correcting Biases' (2019) 86(2) *Social Research: An International Quarterly* 499.

103 S. Mullainathan, 'Biased Algorithms Are Easier to Fix Than Biased People', *The New York Times* (6 December 2019).

controlled on a regular basis. Under these conditions, AI judges would be fairer than human judges and would avoid the inconsistencies and contradictions between judgments that are so common in the law,[104] not to mention the fact that algorithms make it possible to better detect discrimination.[105]

Nevertheless, these advantages of AI should not make us forget the limits and risks that have already been mentioned. Believing that algorithms are well-behaved by nature is a mistake. The efficiency and fairness of algorithms depend not only on the quality of the data but also on the way they are designed. The risk of error or discrimination is significant. In particular, machine-learning algorithms can perpetuate existing discrimination or reproduce past mistakes. Their opacity is a very real problem. Last but not least, it does not appear that technology can, at present, offer satisfactory solutions in cases that are not particularly basic and repetitive. Algorithms can certainly provide considerable support to judges, but they cannot apprehend complex and singular situations. Most cases present elements of singularity that justify their apprehension by humans endowed with the capacity to understand, in a general way, the entire situation that is submitted to them, including their human and emotional aspects. For all these reasons, it appears desirable that human judges retain full independence in their decision-making.

23.3 CONCLUSION

It appears that the technological tools currently being developed are capable of substantially assisting judges in their daily work. In particular, data analysis of widely available court decisions will evaluate, in an unprecedented way, the activity of the courts and the quality of justice. In doing so, it will allow for more efficient and faster dispute resolution, as well as cost reductions for litigants and society. On the other hand, the limits of AI are obvious as soon as complex decisions are envisaged. As current tools have relatively limited legal reasoning capabilities, there is a considerable distance between the functions of a judge and what algorithms can currently achieve. We should probably not conclude that this state of affairs will remain unchanged. Activities that in the past seemed unfeasible by algorithms, such as chess or translation, have become feasible. Given the speed of technological progress, it is difficult to imagine the capabilities of machines in the near or distant future. It is therefore hard to give a definitive answer to the question of whether algorithms could one day propose decisions that would be just as relevant as those of a judge. If it were ever possible, should we go down this path and relieve humans of the colossal responsibility to judge others in order to entrust it to software that makes fewer mistakes? Put in these terms, the question here seems quite radical. If it is difficult at present to pronounce on the future with certainty, one can certainly admit that the technological evolution will probably not cause the disappearance of humans from judicial adjudication but a new, progressive and subtle redistribution of tasks between men and machines.

[104] J. Park, 'Your Honor, AI' (2 April 2020) 41 *Harvard International Review* 46.
[105] Kleinberg, Ludwig et al., see fn 102.

24

Combating Bias in AI and Machine Learning in Consumer-Facing Services

Charlyn Ho with Contributing Authors: Marc Martin, Divya Taneja, and D. Sean West (Healthcare Case Study)Sam Boro and Coimbra Jackson (Consumer Finance Case Study)

24.1 INTRODUCTION

Artificial intelligence (AI) seeks to enable computers to imitate intelligent human behavior, and machine learning (ML), a subset of AI, involves systems that learn from data without relying on rules-based programming. ML techniques include supervised learning (a method of teaching ML algorithms to "learn" by example) and deep learning (a subset of ML that abstracts complex concepts through layers mimicking neural networks of biological systems).[1] AI has the promise to revolutionize practically every industry it touches and to significantly affect consumer interactions with companies that provide services to consumers. This chapter focuses on two industries that are related to sensitive consumer information – healthcare and consumer financial services – to highlight the potential of AI to transform traditional sectors and modernize the status quo of how healthcare and consumer financial services are provided in the United States and to flag the potential legal risks. For example, AI systems may be able to predict patient outcomes, speed up the drug discovery process, and personalize healthcare,[2] as well as transform credit underwriting practices to extend credit and other financial services to underserved individuals. However, despite its promise, the use of AI is not without legal risks that could generate significant liability for the developer and user of the ML algorithm.

One such risk is "algorithmic bias," which is when application of the ML algorithm results in discrimination, even if unintentional. More specifically, such algorithmic bias occurs when an ML algorithm makes decisions that treat similarly situated individuals differently where there is no justification for such differences, regardless of intent.[3] Use of ML algorithms can violate US antidiscrimination and other laws if it causes discrimination on the basis of a protected class. Absent strong policies and procedures to prevent and mitigate bias throughout the life cycle of an ML algorithm, it is possible that existing human biases can be embedded into the ML

[1] A. Wilson, "A Brief Introduction to Supervised Learning," *Towards Data Science* (September 29, 2019), www.towardsdatascience.com/a-brief-introduction-to-supervised-learning-54a3e3932590.

[2] As a further illustration of AI and ML's power to transform healthcare, "AI has the promise to revolutionize healthcare with machine learning (ML) techniques to predict patient outcomes and personalize patient care[.] . . . Trained ML algorithms can identify causes of diseases by detecting relationships between a set of inputs, such as weight, height, and blood pressure, and an output, such as the likelihood of developing heart disease." C. Ho, M. Martin, S. Ratican, D. Taneja, and D. S. West, "How to Mitigate Algorithmic Bias in Healthcare," *MedCity News* (August 31, 2020), www.medcitynews.com/2020/08/how-to-mitigating-algorithmic-bias-in-healthcare.

[3] N. Turner Lee, P. Resnick, and G. Barton, "Algorithmic Bias Detection and Mitigation: Best Practices and Policies to Reduce Consumer Harms," *Brookings* (May 22, 2019), www.brookings.edu/research/algorithmic-bias-detection-and-mitigation-best-practices-and-policies-to-reduce-consumer-harms.

algorithm with potentially serious consequences. This is particularly the case in the healthcare context, where life and death decisions are being made algorithmically, and in the consumer finance context, where algorithms draw connections based on information about countless aspects of consumers' lives to determine their eligibility for financial products and services.

This chapter is intended to provide companies with tips and tools to spot and mitigate the legal risk of algorithmic bias as well as highlight areas where the solution is not legal but rather technical. Effective risk mitigation requires close coordination between the legal team and the developers of the ML algorithms. Section 24.2 describes the legal landscape governing algorithmic bias in the United States generally and discusses emerging tools to combat algorithmic bias that build on existing recommended best practices, such as adversarial debiasing and use of synthetic data, Section 24.3 describes algorithmic bias in the healthcare context, Section 24.4 describes algorithmic bias in the consumer finance context, and Section 24.5 provides our conclusions.

24.2 RELEVANT UNITED STATES LAW GOVERNING AI AND ML

At present, there is no single comprehensive regulatory regime governing algorithmic bias. There is no federal law that expressly covers AI, including algorithmic bias, although several bills have been introduced. States and municipalities are starting (in the last few years) to propose and pass laws that specifically govern AI. As an example, Illinois passed a first-of-its-kind measure that would impose restrictions on employers' use of AI "interview bots" in hiring on May 29, 2019 (effective January 1, 2020), and several states and municipalities have passed laws regulating the use of facial recognition technologies.[4]

The California Privacy Rights Act (CPRA)[5] is the first state privacy law that expressly covers automated systems. This state law, which will be enforceable beginning July 1, 2023, with obligations beginning January 1, 2022, creates an opt-out right for consumers with regard to a business's use of automated decision-making technology. The CPRA defines profiling to mean "any form of automated processing of personal information ... to evaluate certain personal aspects relating to a natural person, and in particular to analyze or predict aspects concerning that natural person's performance at work, economic situation, health, personal preferences, interests, reliability, behavior, location or movements."[6] If a consumer wishes to opt out of the automated decision-making a business has implemented, the business will need to have a method to determine what process is automated and how to extract consumer's information per the consumer's request. Additionally, the CPRA requires that regulations be promulgated specifying a business's obligation to provide consumers with information about the logic involved in the automated decision-making and the likely effects of such automated decision-making on the consumer. On March 2, 2021, Virginia became the second state to enact a comprehensive consumer privacy law called the Consumer Data Protection Act (CDPA), which also includes conditions on automated decision-making. Virginia's CDPA provides consumers the right to opt out of "profiling in furtherance of decisions that produce legal or similarly significant effects concerning the consumer."[7]

[4] Artificial Intelligence Video Interview Act, Pub. Act No. 101-0260, 820 Ill. Comp. Stat. § 42 (eff. January 1, 2020).
[5] California Consumer Privacy Act of 2018, Cal. Civ. Code § 1798.100 (2018).
[6] CPRA § 1798.140(z).
[7] VA Code § 59.1-573(A)4-5.

Given the absence of a comprehensive regulatory regime governing algorithmic bias, we must look to how existing laws apply to this rapidly evolving and growing technology in everyday life. It is also important for legal practitioners working with AI and ML technologies to carefully monitor new legislation, because California is likely to be the first of many governments to pass legislation dealing with algorithmic decision-making.

24.2.1 *Summary of Current Best Practices for Combating Algorithmic Bias*

Developing ML algorithms often requires vast quantities of training data for the ML algorithm to "learn." For example, if a health insurer wants to use an ML algorithm to estimate healthcare insurance costs, data scientists can train the ML algorithm on historical healthcare claims data for the ML algorithm to "learn" what variables affect healthcare insurance premiums to predict healthcare insurance costs. In other words, ML algorithms use training data to learn how to recognize and apply patterns to make accurate predictions when presented with new data.

Current best practices for combating algorithmic bias center around avoiding the introduction of bias at each stage of the ML algorithm's development. For example, the Federal Trade Commission's (FTC) 2016 report titled "Big Data, A Tool for Inclusion or Exclusion?"[8] encourages companies to, among other things, consider four questions regarding their algorithms: (1) How representative is the data set? If data sets are missing information from populations, take appropriate steps to address the problem. This is more simply known as the "garbage in, garbage out" problem.[9] (2) Does your data model account for biases? Ensure that hidden bias is not having an unintended impact on certain populations.[10] (3) How accurate are your predictions based on big data? Correlation is not causation. Balance the risk of using the results from big data, especially where policies could negatively affect certain populations. Consider human oversight for important decisions, such as those implicating health, credit, and employment.[11] (4) Does your reliance on big data raise ethical or fairness concerns? Consider using big data to advance opportunities for underrepresented populations.[12]

Additionally, the FTC's April 2020 blog post titled "Using Artificial Intelligence and Algorithms"[13] recommends that companies (1) be transparent regarding their use of AI and ML,[14] (2) explain their decision to the consumer, (3) ensure their decisions are fair, (4) ensure that their data and models are robust and empirically sound, and (5) hold themselves accountable for compliance, ethics, fairness, and nondiscrimination.

[8] FTC Report, "Big Data: A Tool for Inclusion or Exclusion? Understanding the Issues," Federal Trade Commission (January 2016), www.ftc.gov/reports/big-data-tool-inclusion-or-exclusion-understanding-issues-ftc-report.

[9] Ibid., 27–28.

[10] Ibid., 28–29.

[11] Ibid., 29–31.

[12] Ibid., 31–32.

[13] A. Smith, "Using Artificial Intelligence and Algorithms," Federal Trade Commission, Business Blog (April 8, 2020), www.ftc.gov/news-events/blogs/business-blog/2020/04/using-artificial-intelligence-algorithms.

[14] It is important to prioritize transparency in deploying AI and ML. One example of a company's attempt to increase transparency is Microsoft's Transparency Notes. As explained by Microsoft's Chief Responsible AI Officer, "[W]e developed Transparency Notes to help teams communicate the purposes, capabilities and limitations of an AI system so our customers can understand when and how to deploy our platform technologies. Transparency Notes fill the gap between marketing and technical documentation, proactively communicating information that our customers need to know to deploy AI responsibly." N. Crampton, "The Building Blocks of Microsoft's Responsible AI Program," Microsoft On the Issues Blog (January 19, 2021), https://blogs.microsoft.com/on-the-issues/2021/01/19/microsoft-responsible-ai-program.

Although these recommended best practices may seem straightforward, implementing them is not a simple task. Data scientists cannot easily remove biases that human beings often inherently and unconsciously imbue into training data and, therefore, the ML algorithm. There are few practical solutions to eliminate such unintended bias from an ML algorithm without impairing its efficacy, although there are some industry best practices on how to avoid and combat bias.

Further, because algorithmic bias may be introduced into an ML algorithm at many different points in the development cycle, eliminating it requires constant vigilance throughout the development and deployment process. Training data can be infected by several types of bias, including historical bias (bias already existing in the world that is reflected in the data collection process even with perfect sampling and feature selection), representation bias (bias resulting from how the relevant population is defined and sampled), measurement bias (bias resulting from the way features are selected and measured), and coded bias (bias introduced by the people developing the algorithms).

Even when care is taken to root out bias from data sets by not relying on protected characteristics (race, color, sex or gender, religion, age, disability status, national origin, marital status, or genetic information), sometimes the algorithm uses variables that function as proxies for protected classes.[15] For example, zip codes and/or language may correlate closely with race. Additionally, while it may seem logical to "blind" the ML algorithm to protected characteristics by omitting this variable from the training data, this mitigation technique may in and of itself result in bias. Two data scientists observed in their research on AI-based sentencing algorithms that women are less likely to reoffend than men in many jurisdictions.[16] Therefore, blinding the ML algorithm to gender may result in judges being less likely to release female defendants before trial even though they have a lower chance of reoffending and may make it harder for companies to detect, prevent, and eliminate bias on exactly that criteria.

Because the data scientists who develop ML algorithms may not be attuned to the legal considerations of algorithmic bias, both developers and users of ML algorithms should partner closely with their legal teams to mitigate potential legal challenges arising from developing and/or using ML algorithms, particularly when data as sensitive as healthcare or financial data is involved.

24.2.2 *Emerging Tools to Combat Algorithmic Bias*

Based on our experience counseling businesses seeking to eliminate algorithmic bias, it is often challenging to eliminate bias from the training data for a variety of reasons. First, companies may not have policies and procedures to detect and test for algorithmic bias and may be unaware of such bias, particularly if they did not develop the ML algorithm in-house. Second, given the vast amounts of data needed to train ML algorithms, companies developing ML algorithms may need to source training data from third-party sources and therefore may not have control or influence over the initial collection of that training data. As a result, even if a company identifies that its training data contains bias, it is not clear how it can rectify this issue to avoid algorithmic bias. Third, US privacy and other laws may limit companies' ability to source representative data, whereas countries that have large populations and different privacy laws and norms (like China) may find it easier to develop and train ML algorithms on diverse training data. Finally, in the

[15] FTC Report, "Big Data," 25, note 8.

[16] S. Corbett-Davies, E. Pierson, A. Feller, S. Goel, and A. Huq, "Algorithmic Decision Making and the Cost of Fairness" (January 28, 2017), dl.acm.org/doi/10.1145/3097983.3098095.

absence of being able to rectify a biased ML algorithm, companies are faced with the unappealing choice of forging ahead with the ML algorithm, knowing there is a risk of liability as a result of the bias, or starting over with a different ML algorithm.

AI developers can attempt to remove bias in either the training data, in the trained model itself, or in the predictions (which are generally known as pre-processing, in-processing, and post-processing bias mitigation techniques).[17] Below, we describe nascent methods of mitigating, or even potentially eliminating, algorithmic bias that companies can consider deploying (1) in the trained model and (2) in the training data when it is impractical or impossible to remove bias from historical training data or inherent human bias introduced by the data scientists developing the ML algorithm.

24.2.2.1 *Adversarial Debiasing*

Adversarial debiasing is a supervised deep learning method whereby two algorithms are used to predict an output variable (e.g., organ transplant suitability) based on a given input (e.g., patient medical records) while remaining unbiased with respect to a particular protected variable (e.g., race). The first algorithm is known as the "predictor" and simply refers to the ML algorithm that uses inputs (X) to predict outcomes (Y), such as using an ML algorithm to predict a patient's suitability for an organ transplant based on medical records or an individual's creditworthiness based on credit card history. As discussed above, predictor algorithms can perpetuate bias; for example, an ML algorithm may not use gender as an input variable but may rely on proxy variables (such as shopping habits or income) that correlate (even unintentionally) with gender.[18]

In an ideal world, companies could still harness the power of AI trained on data that may contain bias (as it may be challenging, practically speaking, to source data absent bias for the reasons stated above), but train the AI not to base decisions on protected variables like race, age, gender, etc. (Z). This is where the "adversary" algorithm comes in. In adversarial debiasing, the "adversary" is an algorithm used in conjunction with the predictor algorithm that is trained to predict the association of the protected variable, Z, with the output, Y.[19] If the adversary is able to predict Z from Y (predict that an output like a patient's need for healthcare or an individual's creditworthiness is invalidly influenced by a protected variable, like race, age, or gender), with everything else being equal, then there may be bias in the model. The ML model can then be trained to rely less and less on the protected variable and gradually become "debiased." When the predictor and adversarial algorithms are trained over multiple iterations, they have the potential to yield an unbiased predictive algorithm that does not significantly sacrifice accuracy. In one study on adversarial debiasing, Google and Stanford researchers demonstrated the ability to train a demonstrably less biased algorithm that still performed the task nearly as well as the original algorithm.[20]

Algorithmic debiasing can be one in a series of bias mitigation techniques that build on each other. In a recent study, the *Harvard Business Review* outlined how financial services companies can reduce algorithmic bias by (1) removing bias from data before a model is built, (2) picking

[17] IBM Research Trusted AI, "AI Fairness 360 – Resources," IBM Research, aif360.mybluemix.net/resources#overview.

[18] See A. Klein, "Reducing Bias in AI-Based Financial Services," Brookings (July 10, 2020), www.brookings.edu/research/reducing-bias-in-ai-based-financial-services/ (describing how numerous variables can be closely correlated with the gender of an applicant even if gender is not specifically used for underwriting purposes).

[19] B. H. Zhang, B. Lemoine, and M. Mitchell, "Mitigating Unwanted Biases with Adversarial Learning," Association for the Advancement of Artificial Intelligence (January 22, 2018), dl.acm.org/doi/10.1145/3278721.3278779.

[20] Ibid.

better goals for models that discriminate, and (3) utilizing algorithmic debiasing by introducing an AI-driven adversary.[21] In this study, one bank recognized that, based on historical discrepancies, women were required to make 30 percent more than a man to be approved for the same size loan. Consequently, the bank used AI to reconstitute its training data and shift the female distribution that moved the proportion of loans previously made to women to be closer to the same amount as for men with an equivalent risk profile. However, even once the data is adjusted, an AI model can still present bias. An extra precaution the bank could take is to penalize an AI model that treats a protected class unequally and reward a model for positive actions. For example, using reinforcement learning (which is a method of training ML algorithms whereby the algorithm is rewarded at different decision points and programmed to maximize rewards) a bank could create an AI model that penalizes a system that does not give credit equally to older and younger applicants, all other factors being equal. Lastly, a financial services company can introduce an AI-driven adversary to root out decision-making based on a specific protected variable. An AI-driven adversary is effectively a self-check system, where a bank will create an AI model that predicts and detects any discriminatory effects of the original AI model. If the adversary AI model detects discriminatory effects, it can mitigate the bias in the original AI model using the methods described above. Adversarial debiasing is still a fairly new technique, but it provides a glimmer of hope for a pragmatic tool to combat bias in AI.

24.2.2.2 *Synthetic Data*

The use of synthetic data (i.e., artificially generated data that replicates real-world statistical components) is another tool to root out bias in AI. Synthetic data holds promise as a technique for augmenting, replacing, or correcting for biases in training data. Data synthesis is an emerging data augmentation technique that creates and enables access to realistic (albeit not real) data that retains the properties of an original, real data set. To create synthetic data, an artificial neural network or other ML process learns the characteristics and relationships of the real data to generate the synthetic, yet realistic, data. To date, the most common purposes of using synthetic data have been situations where real data is expensive to collect or unavailable or to preserve and protect data subject privacy. Synthetic data can also be useful as a cybersecurity enhancement technique since, by definition, synthetic data is not personal data and therefore if breached is not subject to the data breach notification laws that may be triggered if personal data is breached.

The process of creating a synthetic data set can also be leveraged for mitigating bias in the original, real data set. A team from IBM Research presented an illustration of how synthetic data could be employed to reduce bias in AI:[22] When bias in AI is the result of a data set involving a privileged and unprivileged group (for example, men and women), for every data point a new synthetic data point can be created that has the same features, except the synthetic data point would be labeled with the other gender. These new synthetic data points together with the original data points would make up the new data set, which ideally would equally weight men and women. So, rather than trying to remove discrimination from the data set, unlike some other approaches, synthetic data instead generates a new data set that is similar to the real one and aims to be debiased while preserving data utility. Although there may be risks associated with its

[21] S. Townson, "AI Can Make Bank Loans More Fair," *Harvard Business Review* (November 6, 2020), www.hbr.org/2020/11/ai-can-make-bank-loans-more-fair.

[22] B. Marr, "Does Synthetic Data Hold the Secret to Artificial Intelligence?," *Forbes* (November 5, 2018), www.forbes.com/sites/bernardmarr/2018/11/05/does-synthetic-data-hold-the-secret-to-artificial-intelligence/?sh=c9c3db842f84.

use, such as inaccurate or ineffectual algorithms, synthetic data holds promise as a tool to mitigate bias in AI.

24.2.2.3 *Other Practical Bias Mitigation Techniques*

As these solutions continue to be tested and refined, developers of AI solutions could consider other practical backstops, such as conducting regular audits of algorithms to check for bias,[23] increasing human involvement in the design and monitoring of algorithms, and relying on cross-functional teams to pressure test an algorithm from different perspectives.[24] Users of AI solutions that do not have the means to change the design or development of the ML algorithm could consider contractually mitigating their liability by requiring the AI developers from whom they purchase the ML algorithm to implement antibias techniques and bias mitigation best practices and indemnify for liability arising out of any unlawful discrimination or other claim caused by bias in the ML algorithm.

Note that current efforts to tackle algorithmic bias have largely focused on achieving parity across protected groups; for example, ensuring that sicker Black patients are not deprioritized for healthcare as compared to healthier White patients. However, within each grouping of individuals, including within classes protected by law, there are countless differences between the individuals within each group. As a result, it is challenging to provide equal outcomes to all similarly situated individuals. To address this issue of individual-level discrimination,[25] some researchers are now seeking individual fairness through a better understanding of how ML algorithms handle subgroupings of users (however, please see our commentary on fairness below). It is possible for an ML model to produce nonbiased results on average for groups that are better represented in the training data but still to discriminate against minority subgroups that are underrepresented in the training data. For example, an algorithm that has been corrected for gender bias on average may still discriminate at the subgroup level – such as transgender or gender-fluid individuals who are underrepresented in the data set.

In a recent paper,[26] researchers at the Massachusetts Institute of Technology (MIT) looked to create distributional robust fairness or individual-level fairness and to make it more likely that individuals within subgroups are treated fairly. Subgroup discrimination is a problem that could go unnoticed because the subgroup is small enough to meet optimal fairness metrics established by the ML algorithm developer. But the subgroup may be large enough to still create legal risk of discrimination. The authors suggest using methods to enhance individual fairness and to adjust for subgroup discrimination. The potential solution would involve starting with the developer's fairness metric and then generating a fictional set of all similar individuals to determine potential outcomes. The entity could then take the worst counterfactual position (i.e., the most unfair example) and update its model to account for this counterfactual. The entity would then repeat this process until distributional robust fairness is met.

[23] World Economic Forum, "How to Prevent Discriminatory Outcomes in Machine Learning" (March 2018), www3.weforum.org/docs/WEF_40065_White_Paper_How_to_Prevent_Discriminatory_Outcomes_in_Machine_Learning.pdf.

[24] Turner Lee et al., "Algorithmic Bias Detection and Mitigation," note 2.

[25] J. Duchi, T. Hashimoto, and H. Namkoong, "Distributionally Robust Losses against Mixture Covariate Shifts," Stanford University (2019), web.stanford.edu/~hnamk/papers/DuchiHaNa19.pdf.

[26] M. Weber, M. Yurochkin, S. Botros, and V. Markov, "Black Loans Matter: Fighting Bias for AI Fairness in Lending," MIT-IBM Watson AI Lab (November 27, 2020), mitibmwatsonailab.mit.edu/research/blog/black-loans-matter-fighting-bias-for-ai-fairness-in-lending.

24.2.3 *Achieving "Fairness" in AI*

The problem of how to combat unfair algorithmic decision-making has received much attention in computer science literature. Despite this academic scrutiny, little progress has been made on how to mitigate against the risk of unfairness by computational decision-makers. In part, this lack of progress is a result of there being no universal definition of fairness. Fairness is a multifaceted societal construct and often depends on individual perspective. Computer scientists have created antibias tool kits[27] that arguably do not allow ML algorithms to achieve societal "fairness" given its amorphous definition but rather aim to optimize accuracy of prediction while achieving statistical or mathematical "sameness." Despite the distinction between societal fairness and mathematical sameness, the term "fairness" is still used in computer science literature to describe antibias mitigation techniques and metrics. Several metrics for measuring computational fairness have been advanced, including demographic parity (also known as statistical parity), equality of odds, and equality of opportunity.

Under demographic parity,[28] the likelihood of a positive outcome should be the same regardless of whether a person is in a protected group or not. With this antibias method, the ML algorithm will make predictions that are not dependent on a protected variable ("Z" in our previous example). Under equality of odds,[29] the likelihood of true positives and false positives should be the same regardless of whether a person represents a protected variable or not. Therefore, equality of odds is satisfied if the accuracy of the ML algorithm is constant across all groups. Under equality of opportunity,[30] the likelihood of true positives should be the same regardless of whether a person is in a protected group or not. Therefore, under equality of opportunity, individuals who represent different protected variables should have an equal chance of being classified by the ML algorithm for a positive outcome.

Applying this to a hypothetical scenario where a race-blind ML algorithm seeks to classify individuals' need for healthcare or eligibility for financial services could result in a number of outcomes. First, if the ML algorithm achieves demographic parity, then the percentage of White individuals and Black individuals deemed to need healthcare is equal, regardless of whether one group on average needs more healthcare than the other group. Similarly, the percentage of White individuals and Black individuals deemed to be creditworthy is equal, regardless of whether one group on average has lower credit scores than the other group. Second, if the ML algorithm achieves equality of odds, then no matter whether a patient is White or Black, if they are sick, they have equal odds of being deemed to need healthcare, and if they are not sick, they have equal odds of being deemed to not need healthcare. Therefore, if a higher percentage of the Black patient population is sick, then a higher percentage of Black patients will be deemed to need healthcare. Note that if equality of odds is satisfied, demographic parity may not be satisfied because White patients and Black patients will be recommended to need healthcare at different levels. Similarly, no matter whether an individual is White or Black, if they have low credit, they have equal odds of being denied a loan, and if they have high credit they have equal

[27] IBM Research Trusted AI, "AI Fairness 360 – Resources," fn 17.

[28] "Machine Learning Glossary: Fairness, Demographic Parity," Google.com, developers.google.com/machine-learning/glossary/fairness#demographic-parity.

[29] "Machine Learning Glossary: Fairness, Equalized Odds," Google.com, developers.google.com/machine-learning/glossary/fairness#equalized-odds.

[30] "Machine Learning Glossary: Fairness, Equality of Opportunity," Google.com, developers.google.com/machine-learning/glossary/fairness#equality-of-opportunity.

odds of being approved for a loan. Therefore, if a higher percentage of Black people have lower credit, then a higher percentage of Black people will be denied financial services. Third, if the ML algorithm achieves equality of opportunity, individuals of different races should have an equal chance of being classified as needing healthcare or approved for a loan. Note that in contrast to equality of odds, equality of opportunity only requires nondiscrimination for positive predictions (one that yields a benefit to a person) but does not require nondiscrimination for negative outcomes (one that is disadvantageous to a person). As a result, the ML algorithm does not need to be nondiscriminatory in determining whether people who are not sick are deemed not to need healthcare at an equal rate.

These are all normative concepts of fairness seeking to define standards of fairness that ML algorithms should achieve. As such, they can exist in tension with antidiscrimination laws that do not utilize fairness as a legal standard.

24.2.4 *Unfairness versus Unlawful Discrimination*

Apart from the problem of there being a lack of widely held normative or legal concept of computational fairness, laws and regulations prohibiting discrimination in the United States are not aimed at promoting notions of fairness. Similarly, "bias" in an ML algorithm is not the same as "discrimination." Instead of seeking to optimize fairness, antidiscrimination laws operate as "side-constraints" – rules that limit the means by which other goals can be pursued. As side-constraints, antidiscrimination laws do not require or permit decisions based on protected classifications in the pursuit of fairness, rather they require decision-makers to provide adequate reasons for certain decisions that either involve disparate treatment of individuals based on protected classifications or have a disparate impact on groups sharing a protected trait.[31]

In the United States, discrimination claims are typically similarly evaluated regardless of the direction in which benefits flow, which means courts will not typically grant decision-makers deference when they are making decisions based on protected classifications in an attempt to correct for past discrimination. As a result, a healthcare or financial services provider that employs techniques such as adversarial debiasing to influence an AI system in an attempt to correct for historical, representation, or measurement bias impacting a group sharing a protected trait could be subject to a discrimination claim under a disparate treatment theory because the adversarial model employed by the provider would be making decisions on the basis of a protected classification.

Therefore, before engaging in debiasing or other activities that could give rise to a discrimination claim even if for a beneficial purpose, an organization should carefully consider and document why the debiasing or other activities are necessary to train the algorithm.

[31] Thomas Nachbar provides an overview of how antidiscrimination laws may apply to AI:

> The application of discrimination law to algorithmic discrimination presents a host of both challenges and opportunities .... [T]he systematization and reduction in cost of complex decisionmaking permitted by computerizing it is likely to lead to an explosion of outcomes, many of them likely to be disparate along historically important categories, such as race and sex. Those outcomes are only a starting place for discrimination law, which requires a deeper inquiry into the justification for practices that lead to disparate outcomes.

T. Nachbar, "Algorithmic Fairness, Algorithmic Discrimination," Virginia Public Law and Legal Theory Research Paper, University of Virginia School of Law (January 2020), 40, https://papers.ssrn.com/sol3/papers.cfm?abstract_id=3530053.

24.2.5 *Enforcement Actions and Apportionment of Legal Liability*

Regulators are beginning to bring actions against companies alleging discrimination caused by AI tools. Regardless of whether a company develops an AI model in-house or licenses it from a third party, the company may have liability exposure for unlawful discrimination resulting from the AI model. For example, the New York Department of Financial Services (DFS) recently announced an investigation into alleged algorithmic bias involving the underwriting of the Apple Card credit card issued by Goldman Sachs Bank USA. Prompted by a Twitter thread by a prominent fintech developer and entrepreneur alleging gender bias in credit limits, the DFS opened the investigation. According to the person's tweet, he was approved for a credit limit twenty times higher than his wife, despite filing taxes jointly and his wife having a higher credit score. DFS Superintendent Lacewell's announcement explained that this investigation into Goldman Sachs is not only about looking at this single algorithm. Rather, she said, the DFS wanted to engage with the tech community to ensure that algorithms increase consumer access to financial services and that they do not discriminate on prohibited bases. Goldman Sachs stated that it did not take into consideration protected classes when making its credit decisions and noted specifically that it did not know gender or marital status during the application process. On March 23, 2021, the DFS finally released the results of its investigation, finding that the bank did not violate any fair lending laws.[32] The DFS conducted statistical analysis of the bank's underwriting and found no disparate treatment or disparate impact caused by the algorithm used for underwriting purposes. However, the DFS explained in its report that the bank's underwriting should have been more explainable to its applicants so that the credit terms, offers, and decisioning were clearer. While no fair lending violation was found here, the investigation shows that regulators are sophisticated enough to analyze algorithmic biases.

Enforcement actions like the one brought by the DFS against Goldman Sachs illustrate the challenge in apportioning legal liability for algorithmic discrimination. It may be difficult to discern who is legally liable in cases of algorithmic bias given (1) the nascent state of the law in this space (i.e., whether AI itself can be considered "negligent" or "culpable")[33] and (2) the number of parties involved in the development, deployment, and use of AI tools can range from the financial services providers and healthcare providers utilizing the ML algorithm to the software developers creating the ML algorithm, the third-party data provider licensing the training data, and the end users who are being affected by the algorithm's decision-making. As a result, determining who caused the alleged discrimination is challenging, and even if it is clear who caused the alleged discrimination, determining liability can be difficult. Further complicating the issue of apportionment of liability is that ML algorithms often contain open source code (which is written by the open source code community) in addition to proprietary code. Many other factors can influence apportionment of liability; for example, whether the company that allegedly caused the algorithmic discrimination licensed or purchased the ML algorithm. Plaintiffs alleging harm caused by algorithmic discrimination can pursue claims against multiple parties involved in the development, deployment, and use of the ML algorithm and under

[32] New York Department of Financial Services, "DFS Issues Findings on the Apple Card and Its Underwriter Goldman Sachs Bank" (March 23, 2021), www.dfs.ny.gov/reports_and_publications/press_releases/pr202103231.

[33] Thomas Nachbar recognizes that antidiscrimination laws may require "adaptation" in the AI context: "It is not a question whether discrimination law will be applied to computational decisionmaking; it will be. The question is how discrimination law will have to adapt to computational decisionmaking and how computational decisionmaking will have to adapt to discrimination law." Nachbar, "Algorithmic Fairness, Algorithmic Discrimination," 40–41, fn 31.

multiple legal grounds, including tort and breach of contract. Given the complexity surrounding use of AI, companies should take a risk-based approach in the use of AI by determining which harms to avoid and who is best able to prevent those harms. As noted above, companies may be able to make their potential liability exposure more predictable by ensuring that they carefully review and negotiate contracts relating to AI systems and allocate liability contractually in advance, including adding appropriate representations, warranties and indemnities from the provider of the ML algorithm. Having described how AI and ML fit into the current legal regime in the United States generally and offered recommendations on how companies can mitigate the risk of algorithmic bias, we now explore, in Sections 24.3 and 24.4, the issue of algorithmic bias in two use cases that are of particular sensitivity for US consumers: healthcare and consumer finance.

24.3 AI AND ML IN HEALTHCARE

Trained ML algorithms can be used in a myriad of ways in the healthcare industry, including to identify causes of diseases by establishing relationships between a set of inputs (e.g., weight, height, blood pressure) and an output (e.g., the likelihood of developing heart disease). As an example of the power of training ML algorithms on large amounts of data, a group of scientists trained a highly accurate AI system using electronic medical records of nearly 600,000 patients to extract clinically relevant data from large data sets and associate common medical conditions with specific information.[34] The ML algorithm was able to assist physicians in reducing misdiagnosis in common childhood conditions by assessing patients' symptoms, history, lab results, and other clinical data.

ML algorithms developed in the healthcare context have already demonstrated the risk of algorithmic bias. In one prepandemic study,[35] an algorithm used by UnitedHealth to predict which patients would require extra medical care favored White patients over Black patients, moving up the White patients in the queue for special treatments over sicker Black patients who "suffered from far more chronic illnesses." Race was not a factor in the algorithm's decision-making, but race correlated with other factors that affected the outcome. The lead researcher of this study – which motivated the DFS and Department of Health (DOH) to write a letter to UnitedHealth inquiring about this alleged bias – stated that "[t]he algorithm's skew sprang from the way it used health costs as a proxy for a person's care requirements, making its predictions reflect economic inequality as much as health needs." The DFS and DOH were particularly troubled by the algorithm's reliance on historical spending to evaluate future healthcare needs and stated that this dependence posed a significant risk of conflicts of interest and also unconscious bias. The DFS and DOH cite studies documenting the barriers to receiving healthcare that Black patients suffer. Therefore, utilizing medical history in the algorithm, including healthcare expenditures, is unlikely to reflect the true medical needs of Black patients as they historically have had less access to, and therefore less opportunity to receive and pay for, medical treatment.

AI is being utilized in the fight against the COVID-19 pandemic, including to triage patients and expedite the discovery of a vaccine. For example, researchers have developed an AI-powered

[34] C. Metz, "A.I. Shows Promise Assisting Physicians," *New York Times* (February 11, 2019), www.nytimes.com/2019/02/11/health/artificial-intelligence-medical-diagnosis.html.

[35] Z. Obermeyer, B. Powers, C. Vogell, and S. Mullainathan, "Dissecting Racial Bias in an Algorithm Used to Manage the Health of Populations" 366 *Science* 6464 (October 25, 2019), 447–453, www.science.org/doi/10.1126/science.aax2342.

tool that predicts with 70–80 percent accuracy which newly infected COVID-19 patients are likely to develop severe lung disease.[36] The US Centers for Disease Control and Prevention has leveraged Microsoft's AI-powered bot service to create its own COVID-19 assessment bot[37] that can assess a user's symptoms and risk factors to suggest a next course of action, including whether to go to the hospital. While these advances will benefit many patients, they do not absolve the concerns relating to algorithmic bias and its repercussions for certain groups. Use of AI to triage COVID-19 patients based on symptoms and preexisting conditions can perpetuate well-researched and well-documented preexisting human prejudice against the pain and symptoms of people of color and women. Data on COVID-19 shows disparities based on race and socio-economic status,[38] including substantially higher mortality rates among certain racial groups. The risk of algorithmic bias in ML algorithms designed to combat COVID-19 is heightened because the data is not equally distributed across age groups, race, and other patient characteristics.[39] Without representative data, there is a higher risk of bias. However, as discussed in more detail in Section 24.3.1, if such AI tools were debiased using adversarial debiasing, synthetic data, or some other solution, an AI tool could triage patients more appropriately based on their symptoms so that they receive the healthcare they need.

24.3.1 *US Legal Landscape Relating to Algorithmic Bias in Healthcare*

While US laws that specifically address AI and ML are still sparse (although new AI- and ML-related laws have been introduced recently), existing federal and state laws may make algorithmic discrimination and bias unlawful, regardless of intent. For example, Section 1557 of the Affordable Care Act (ACA)[40] prohibits any healthcare provider from receiving federal funds to refuse to treat – or to otherwise discriminate against – an individual based on protected classifications such as race, national origin, or sex. In addition to healthcare-specific laws, several states specifically prohibit discrimination in hospitals or clinics based on protected classifications.[41]

Although different laws apply different standards for when unlawful discrimination exists, generally an antidiscrimination claim requires establishing either disparate treatment or disparate impact. Disparate treatment can be established by either facially disparate treatment (such as explicit race classifications) or intentional, but facially neutral, discrimination (such as zip code classification with the intent that zip codes serve as a rough proxy for race). Disparate impact can be established by showing a facially neutral policy or practice disproportionately affects a group sharing a protected trait, such as a religion.

36 X. Jiang, M. Coffee, A. Bari, et al., "Towards an Artificial Intelligence Framework for Data-Driven Prediction of Coronavirus Clinical Severity" 63 *Computers, Materials & Continua* 1 (March 30, 2020), 537–551, www.techscience.com/cmc/v63n1/38464.

37 H. Bitran and J. Gabarra, "Delivering Information and Eliminating Bottlenecks with CDC's COVID-19 Assessment Bot," Microsoft Blog (March 20, 2020), www.blogs.microsoft.com/blog/2020/03/20/delivering-information-and-eliminating-bottlenecks-with-cdcs-covid-19-assessment-bot.

38 M. Webb Hooper, A. M. Nápoles, and E. J. Pérez-Stable, "COVID-19 and Racial/Ethnic Disparities" 323 *JAMA* 24 (2020), 2466–2467, www.jamanetwork.com/journals/jama/fullarticle/2766098.

39 A. Burlacu, R. Crisan-Dabija, R. V. Popa, et al., "Curbing the AI-Induced Enthusiasm in Diagnosing COVID-19 on Chest X-Rays: The Present and the Near-Future," *medRxiv* (May 1, 2020), www.medrxiv.org/content/10.1101/2020.04.28.20082776v1.full.pdf.

40 Patient Protection & Affordable Care Act, Pub. L. No. 111-148, § 1557, 124 Stat. 119, 260 (2010), www.hhs.gov/civil-rights/for-individuals/section-1557/index.html.

41 *Doe* v. *BlueCross BlueShield of Tenn., Inc.*, 926 F 3d 235 (6th Cir. 2019).

We expect that it is more likely that AI developers working on healthcare-related ML algorithms would design a facially neutral algorithm that contains undetected biases that results in disparate impacts than an algorithm that intentionally treats people differently on an unlawful basis. In fact, a 2014 White House study on big data[42] concluded that it is very rare for algorithmic bias to arise from intentional disparate treatment; rather, the algorithmic bias is often caused by poor training data (either inaccurate, out of date, or nonrepresentative of the population) and unintentional perpetuation of historical biases. Therefore, it is important for AI developers and users to keep abreast of developments in this complex area of law.

Continuing to use the ACA as an example of how algorithmic bias may be treated under US law, at least some ACA Section 1557 claims can be established under a theory of disparate impact, but whether such claims can rely on disparate impact alone is not yet well-defined. Instead of providing its own rules on discrimination, Section 1557 applies four preexisting race, sex, age, and disability discrimination laws to federally subsidized health programs. Not all of these underlying laws allow plaintiffs to bring claims based on disparate impact, and courts are divided on whether a single standard should govern all Section 1557 claims or the differing standards from the underlying law should be applied. If the differing standards from the underlying law were applied, then different types of discrimination would be treated differently under Section 1557. Under such an interpretation, a Section 1557 race discrimination claim must allege disparate treatment, but a Section 1557 age, disability, or sex discrimination claim could allege disparate treatment or disparate impact. This reliance on differing standards appears to be the emerging majority position, but at least one federal court has ruled that Congress intended to create a new cause of action with a single standard by passing Section 1557.

In addition, establishing either disparate treatment or disparate impact alone is rarely enough to establish liability. After a prima facie discrimination analysis under either theory, the inquiry generally shifts to whether there is enough justification for the discriminatory practice. The standards for when a practice will be considered justified varies for different statutory schemes and by discrimination type, but even facially discriminatory practices are permissible if a justification is found to be sufficient. Only when the justification is insufficient is discrimination unlawful. Medical decision-making, algorithmic or otherwise, will often be based on certain protected classifications. However, such classifications would not constitute unlawful discrimination when the classifications are relevant to medical outcomes, such as the ways COVID-19 may affect men and women differently.[43]

Given the complexities of the antidiscrimination legal landscape and differing interpretations on how laws that predate the advent of AI and ML govern algorithmic bias, both AI developers and users are encouraged to work closely with their legal teams to evaluate the legal risks associated with their particular AI/ML use case.

24.4 AI AND ML IN CONSUMER FINANCIAL SERVICES

As with the healthcare industry and many others, AI and ML use in the consumer financial services industry is still nascent,[44] but adoption is accelerating. With technological advances,

[42] Exec. Office of the President, "Big Data: Seizing Opportunities, Preserving Values" (May 1, 2014), obamawhitehouse.archives.gov/sites/default/files/docs/big_data_privacy_report_may_1_2014.pdf.

[43] J.-M. Jin, P. Bai, W. He, et al., "Gender Differences in Patients with COVID-19: Focus on Severity and Mortality," *Frontiers in Public Health* (April 29, 2020), www.frontiersin.org/articles/10.3389/fpubh.2020.00152/full.

[44] T. C. W. Lin, "Artificial Intelligence, Finance, and the Law" 88 *Fordham Law Review* 2 (2019), 531–551, ir.lawnet.fordham.edu/cgi/viewcontent.cgi?article=5630&context=flr.

cybersecurity threats, and regulatory changes, there is a pressing need for financial institutions to rethink how technologies like AI and ML can improve data security, processes, and customer products and services. Financial institutions are now competing with a growing number of cloud-native industry disruptors, and as a result customer expectations are shifting. AI technology is gaining wider adoption across the financial services industry as businesses learn of the benefits AI offers to a whole host of processes. Fueled by the deluge of data created over the past decade and the meteoritic rise of computing power, AI is being adopted by the financial industry at an accelerated pace with a sharp increase in the number of future uses of AI technologies in the financial sector. Global spending on AI systems is forecast to reach $77.6 billion in 2022 with a compound annual growth rate for the 2017–2022 forecast period of 37.3 percent.[45] Today, only 24 percent of customers report that they believe their bank understands their current goals.[46] This is compounded by the risk of financial crime: In the last twenty-four months, 56 percent of financial institutions have experienced consumer fraud and 41 percent have experienced cybercrime.[47]

The most prominent use of AI models in consumer finance involves credit underwriting and decisioning. AI models assist creditors by taking in data points submitted in credit applications, as well as other factors, and providing outputs about the consumer's creditworthiness. By engaging this technology, creditors are able to conduct more efficient underwriting, enhance their credit decisioning practices, and in many cases expand access to credit for consumers who may be rejected under traditional credit scoring models.[48]

24.4.1 *Credit Scoring, Alternative Data, and Underwriting*

When making credit decisions, lenders evaluate an applicant's income, assets, liabilities, credit report, and credit score. An applicant's credit score is generally derived from one of the major consumer reporting agencies and comes in the form of the applicant's FICO score, but consumer information used in credit decisioning can come from many alternative sources, so long as it has a bearing on a consumer's creditworthiness. Whereas the FICO score is developed from valuing those items that appear on an applicant's credit report, nontraditional data points can include data from other sources that may serve as proxies for creditworthiness, including social media behavior, payment history of rent or utilities, online reviews, and educational history. These factors merely scratch the surface of the possibilities of AI credit or risk scoring models, as companies boast of evaluating many thousands of different data points to predict creditworthiness, broadening the scope of issues that can affect a consumer's creditworthiness such as data gleaned from an applicant's mobile device, including usage and location data.[49] Financial technology or fintech companies have capitalized on the availability of alternative

[45] IDC, "Worldwide Artificial Intelligence Spending Guide," www.idc.com/getdoc.jsp?containerId=IDC_P33198; M. Colangelo, "Mass Adoption of AI in Financial Services Expected within Two Years," *Forbes* (February 20, 2020), www.forbes.com/sites/cognitiveworld/2020/02/20/mass-adoption-of-ai-in-financial-services-expected-within-two-years/?sh=3b24a5277d71.

[46] NIIT Technologies, "At the Heart of Personalization" (2019), www.coforgetech.com/sites/default/files/2020-07/Whitepaper%20-%20BFS%20-%20Delivering%20Personalized%20Digital%20Banking%20Experience_ed. . .pdf.

[47] N. Robinson, "PwC's Global Economic Crime and Fraud Survey 2018," PwC (2018), www.pwc.com/m1/en/publications/economic-crime-fraud-survey-2018.html.

[48] P. A. Ficklin and P. Watkins, "An Update on Credit Access and the Bureau's First No-Action Letter," Consumer Financial Protection Bureau Blog (August 6, 2019), www.consumerfinance.gov/about-us/blog/update-credit-access-and-no-action-letter.

[49] AWS (Amazon Web Services), "Lenddo Case Study" (2015), aws.amazon.com/solutions/case-studies/lenddo/.

data and pioneered the alternative data approach to credit scoring and underwriting. Fintech companies are now relying on nontraditional methods to determine creditworthiness, such as evaluating data that falls outside the traditional factors influencing creditworthiness and/or combining alternative data with traditional factors to make a credit decision.

24.4.2 *Targeted Advertising for Financial Services*

Advertising platforms for consumer financial services are subject to federal and state antidiscrimination laws. Many advertising platforms utilize ML tools about the users on their platforms (social media platforms) to create pools of "lookalike" users for the purpose of evaluating users' likelihood of clicking on certain advertisements.

Platforms can be paid for engagement (or per click), so the platform has an incentive to pick advertisements that will be clicked and direct those advertisements to users who are more likely to click them. In general, when an advertiser places an advertisement on a platform, the advertiser chooses the audience that will receive the advertisement. Platforms offer categories to choose from for targeting advertisements, and then the platforms also offer lookalike audience tools. These lookalike audience tools involve the platform itself taking active steps to extend the advertiser's chosen audience. As a result, even if an advertiser targets a particular group of potential customers, the platform's advertisement delivery system may only show the advertisement to a more limited group of customers. Similarly, if an advertiser directs ads to an unrepresented group, the platform may not deliver ads to that group based on its algorithms. Some platforms' lookalike tools end up recreating groupings defined by their protected class and function like an advertiser that is intentionally targeting or excluding users based on their protected class.

Targeted advertising of financial services raises unique issues because a financial institution may design a compliant advertising strategy, place it on an advertising platform, and then the advertising platform enables filtering or exclusion that is discriminatory or algorithmically makes its own decisions to place the ad in a way that it is discriminating on prohibited bases. State and federal regulators are beginning to bring actions against these advertising platforms. In some of these actions, the advertising platforms have had to look at the inputs to their algorithms and create separate advertising portals for regulated advertisements. To date, regulators have focused on the advertising platforms' activities in targeting ads that result in discriminatory effects, but financial institutions may need to increase their diligence of their advertising partners to understand the platforms' practices, including their use of AI and ML processes to target advertising.

24.4.3 *US Legal Landscape Relating to Algorithmic Bias in Consumer Financial Services*

There is no specific law at the federal or state level in the United States that directly addresses the use of AI in consumer financial services. Despite the lack of regulatory precision, consumer financial regulators are applying existing laws to the use of AI. For purposes of AI models in consumer finance, regulators are taking a cautious approach to ensure that they are not imposing overly burdensome existing regulations on this technology and are encouraging innovation in the space to address consumer needs and expand access to consumer financial services.

In particular, two existing laws and their implementing regulations impose requirements on financial institutions regardless of the type of underwriting model used. The Equal Credit Opportunity Act (ECOA), implemented by Regulation B, and the Fair Credit Reporting Act (FCRA), implemented by Regulation V, both impose disclosure requirements on credit underwriting activities and prohibit discrimination.

Regulation B implements ECOA and has the purpose of "promot[ing] the availability of credit to all creditworthy applicants without regard to race, color, religion, national origin, sex, marital status, or age" or without regard to a person's income being derived from public assistance or a person's exercise of their rights under the Consumer Credit Protection Act.[50] Under Regulation B, the term "creditor" means a "person who, in the ordinary course of business, regularly participates in a credit decision, including setting the terms of the credit."[51] In general, this means that a person could be a creditor under Regulation B if they "accept applications and refer applicants to creditors, or select or offer to select creditors to whom credit requests can be made" or who "influence the credit decision by indicating whether or not it will purchase the obligation if the transaction is consummated."[52]

Creditors are prohibited from (1) discriminating against an applicant on a prohibited basis for any aspect of a credit transaction or (2) making any oral or written statement, including advertisements, to applicants or prospective applicants that would discourage, on a prohibited basis, a reasonable person from applying.[53] A credit transaction includes application procedures or criteria used to evaluate creditworthiness.

Looking at ECOA and Regulation B, it becomes clear that the regulations are intended to prohibit a creditor from using (1) discriminatory credit application and processing procedures and (2) any statements or advertisements that would discourage an applicant from pursuing a credit application on a prohibited basis. Targeting of particular consumers for certain credit advertisements is not prohibited, but actions that would actively or effectively discriminate against a consumer on a prohibited basis are a violation. However, a creditor is not prohibited, and is rather encouraged, to "affirmatively solicit or encourage members of traditionally disadvantaged groups to apply for credit."[54]

ECOA and Regulation B also impose adverse action notice requirements. An adverse action occurs when a creditor refuses to grant credit in substantially the amount or on substantially the terms requested by an applicant. An adverse action notice tells an applicant the reasons why the creditor took the adverse action, so the underwriting process is transparent to the applicant.

FCRA imposes disclosure and reporting requirements on companies that use consumer report information to make a credit decision. The definition of "consumer report" is very broad, encompassing all information that bears on the individual's creditworthiness, character, general reputation, personal characteristics, and similar issues. In short, a consumer report is far broader than a credit score and encompasses activities by data aggregators that may be providing information for FCRA purposes when that data is requested and provided for evaluating a credit application or other accounts. Many data aggregators may be covered by FCRA as consumer reporting agencies because they lack controls to prevent such usage of their information.

Like ECOA, FCRA also imposes adverse action notice requirements. FCRA requires that the creditor provide an adverse action notice to an applicant when negative information from the applicant's credit report was relied upon for the adverse action. Consumer finance companies that utilize AI models for credit underwriting may be pulling information from a multitude of sources, some of which are providing information in ways that make them a consumer reporting agency under FCRA.

[50] 12 CFR § 1002.1(b).

[51] Ibid., § 1002.2(l).

[52] Ibid., § 1002.2(l) cmt. 1.

[53] Ibid., § 1002.4.

[54] Ibid., § 1002.4(b) cmt. 2.

24.4.4 *Proxy Discrimination*

A disparate impact may occur in the context of consumer financial services through proxy discrimination, whereby a facially neutral practice disproportionately harms members of a protected class. Proxy discrimination takes a facially neutral practice a step further, wherein the entity is not impermissibly utilizing specific protected classes to evaluate creditworthiness, but is instead relying on proxies for those protected classes to produce a disparate impact. At times, the entity using the proxies may know that they are using proxies for prohibited classes, or it could happen without the entity knowing that the disparate impact occurs without direct action by the entity. Use of AI/ML processes could increase the chances of a disparate impact resulting without the entity knowing due to the entity's failure to test its systems and algorithms appropriately to determine that it is discriminating against protected classes through proxies.

In short, proxy discrimination often occurs through algorithmic redlining. Whereas in traditional redlining a financial institution may draw lines around specific zip codes or neighborhoods to limit lending to certain communities, proxy discrimination via algorithm can occur when an AI model finds patterns that already exist and exploits them or even creates discriminatory effects by "finding" patterns and limiting the availability of financial products to protected classes. Predictive AI models will digest thousands of data points and find correlations between that data and the end user's lending goals. For example, utilizing nontraditional data like social media activity could create disparate impact on the basis of race by negatively scoring social media interests that are primarily shared by members of a certain race. The same could occur for discrimination on the basis of sex by negatively scoring purchase activity for products or services that are primarily purchased by women.

With more data, AI models become more effective at making connections between seemingly unrelated and disconnected data points. As a result, as AI models mature, proxy discrimination is likely to increase without new regulatory and oversight approaches or industry self-regulation. Some advertising platforms (like social media platforms) utilize their vast troves of data and sophisticated models to enable advertisers to target ads to specific groups of people, subdivided by categories (created by the advertising platform directly or by users) that the advertising platform then enables for filtering and targeting purposes by the advertisers. As a result, advertising platforms, through filtering and directing advertising spend, may cause disparate impact in consumer financial services availability and become subject to credit regulations.

24.4.5 *Regulatory Flexibility*

Without specific laws, there is regulatory uncertainty about how consumer finance companies may utilize AI models. Regulators around the world are starting to step into the gap and begin the journey to understand and possibly regulate the use of AI models in consumer finance. In the final months of the last administration, the head of the Consumer Financial Protection Bureau's (CFPB) Office of Innovation published a blog post discussing how the CFPB viewed the use of AI models under ECOA and FCRA.[55] In short, the CFPB wanted creditors to understand that there is regulatory flexibility under these statutory schemes to use AI models, and to engage in using AI models that the industry has been slow to adopt.

[55] P. A. Ficklin, T. Pahl, and P. Watkins, "Innovation Spotlight: Providing Adverse Action Notices When Using AI/ML Models," CFPB Blog (July 7, 2020), www.consumerfinance.gov/about-us/blog/innovation-spotlight-providing-adverse-action-notices-when-using-ai-ml-models.

The CFPB explained that it sees AI models as having the potential to expand credit access to "credit invisibles" – those consumers that are non-scoreable with traditional underwriting techniques. Using AI models, creditors may be able to make credit decisions more efficiently for more types of borrowers at a lower cost. However, the CFPB recognized that AI models could create or amplify risks of unlawful discrimination, transparency in underwriting, and consumer privacy issues.

Under ECOA there is flexibility for a creditor because the law does not require a creditor to describe how or why a disclosed factor adversely affected the application or how the factor relates to creditworthiness. As a result, a creditor using an AI model may disclose a reason for the adverse action, even if the factor is not entirely clear to the applicant. Further, the CFPB noted that although the laws contain model forms for adverse action notices, the list of reasons for an adverse action are not exclusive, and a creditor can include additional reasons that reflect alternative data sources or different underwriting models.

The CFPB provided an example of how this could work by providing its first no-action letter to a company that uses AI in its credit underwriting model. The recipient of the no-action letter, Upstart,[56] uses a combination of alternative data and AI models to determine creditworthiness. In coordination with the CFPB, Upstart has found that its model approves over 25 percent more consumers and provides 16 percent lower average APRs for loans compared to traditional lending models. When the CFPB tested the Upstart model, it found no disparities in approval rate and APR for minority, female, or older applicants.

But Upstart's ability to expand credit access has been met with questions about its models and the factors it may use that could result in proxy discrimination. In February 2020, members of the Senate Banking Committee sent a letter to Upstart[57] and other student lenders seeking information about how the lenders used filters and categories that make credit decisions based on "educational characteristics" or "economic outcomes." The letter asked for explanations about how those characteristics are formulated and factored into the underwriting decisions. The senators' questions stemmed from a report that found evidence that lenders that considered the school the student borrower attends when making credit decisions could result in a disparate impact on minority borrowers by giving higher interest rates to students attending historically Black colleges and universities and Hispanic-serving institutions. Nevertheless, these past actions and guidance from the CFPB under the last administration could be short-lived if the new leadership of the CFPB under the Biden administration takes a different policy approach, as might be expected.

Other federal agencies have considered regulating algorithms in consumer finance in the future. Late in the last administration, the Department of Housing and Urban Development (HUD) issued a proposed rule that would modify the burden of proof for a disparate impact claim under the Fair Housing Act (FHA) and would include certain defenses for companies that use algorithms for making housing and credit decisions that are subject to the FHA. In the final rule,[58] the agency stepped back and decided not to provide a direct defense for algorithms, saying that to do so would be premature with the technology so new and rapidly changing. Although not providing a direct defense for algorithms, under the final rule a defendant can still

[56] "Upstart CEO Testifies about AI in Credit Underwriting," Upstart Blog, www.upstart.com/blog/upstart-ceo-dave-girouard-testifies-in-congress-about-ai-in-credit-underwriting.

[57] S. Brown, E. Warren, R. Menendez, C. Booker, and K. Harris, "Letter to D. Girouard," United States Senate (February 13, 2020), www.banking.senate.gov/newsroom/minority/brown-senate-democrats-press-upstart-lenders-for-answers-following-reports-of-higher-interest-rates-for-students-of-minority-serving-institutions.

[58] Department of Housing and Urban Development, Final Rule, 24 CFR § 100 (2020).

defend its risk assessment model (algorithmic or otherwise) by showing that its use of the model served a valid interest, such as by showing that the predictive analysis accurately assessed risk or that the model is not overly restrictive on members of a protected class. Although HUD found it premature to regulate in this space during the last administration, it would not be surprising if HUD under the Biden administration takes a more aggressive regulatory approach. In any event, it seems inevitable that more federal and state agencies will pursue regulating algorithmic processes. Legislators are also actively pursuing answers about regulatory oversight of algorithmic bias.[59]

24.5 CONCLUSION

Healthcare and financial technology are just a couple of industries among many that are being transformed by the power of AI and ML. In the context of personal decisions like those dealing with healthcare and personal finances, AI holds great potential to improve the quality and consistency of service. This promise, however, needs to be tempered with understanding and evaluating the potential risks and emerging best practices to eliminate algorithmic bias.

Data scientists cannot easily remove biases that human beings often inherently and unconsciously imbue into training data and, therefore, the ML algorithm. There are few practical solutions to actually eliminate such unintended bias from an ML algorithm without impairing its efficacy, although there are some industry best practices that offer suggestions on how to avoid and combat bias. If AI tools are debiased using adversarial debiasing, synthetic data, or some other solution, an AI tool could triage patients more appropriately based on their symptoms so that they receive the healthcare that they need. By engaging AI, creditors are able to conduct more efficient underwriting, enhance their credit decisioning practices, and in many cases expand access to credit for consumers that may be rejected under traditional credit scoring models.

Additionally, computer scientists have created antibias tool kits. These toolkits arguably do not allow ML algorithms to achieve societal "fairness" but rather aim to optimize accuracy of prediction while achieving statistical or mathematical "sameness." A few of the metrics used to measure computational fairness are equality of odds and equality of opportunity. Under equality of odds, the likelihood of true positives and false positives should be the same regardless of whether a person represents a protected variable or not. Under equality of opportunity, the likelihood of true positives should be the same regardless of whether a person is in a protected group or not. These are just a few ways in which a financial services provider or a healthcare institution can combat bias in AI technologies without losing the value of having AI systems. Companies in the financial services and healthcare industries should consider emerging antibias tools and recommended best practices to detect, avoid, and mitigate algorithmic bias.

59 "Senator Warren Asks Regulators about Discrimination Built Into Automated Lending Decisions," Press Release, Elizabeth Warren (June 12, 2019), www.warren.senate.gov/oversight/letters/senator-warren-asks-regulators-about-discrimination-built-into-automated-lending-decisions.

25

Keeping AI Legal

Migle Laukyte

25.1 INTRODUCTION

The chapter addresses the question of how to continue developing artificial intelligence (AI) without challenging and infringing legal norms, principles and values, represented by the current legal frameworks of liberal democratic societies. To answer this question, the chapter first of all briefly deals with the concept of legality (what it means to be legal in the age of disruptive technologies) and then relates it to two specific private law challenges. The first challenge is related to intellectual property law and is represented by the clash between trade secret protection of algorithms and increasing public need for algorithmic transparency and explicability; the second challenge is related to consumer protection where the questions of liability and shifting roles of the main stakeholders build the space for discussing who is who in building, developing and using AI.

The title of this chapter – 'Keeping AI Legal' – is built on two premises: first of all, that AI is legal and, second, that it is possible for it to remain so, regardless of the levels of its autonomy, intelligence, rationality, sociability and other features. Therefore, the goal of this chapter is to address the legal future of AI through its current threats to – or clashes with – the legal framework broadly construed. In particular, the chapter focuses on two clashes that as of today represent serious legal problems and most probably will become more urgent in the future; namely, these clashes are related to intellectual property law and consumer protection law.

The question is not as simple as it might sound. Anyone familiar with the topic of AI is very much aware of difficulties related to the unpredictable development of AI-based technologies, its threats and risks that go far beyond a legal void or incompatibility with existing legal categories.[1] It stands somewhere beyond the most urgent challenges for humanity, such as climate change, poverty, hunger and pandemics – it is not perceived as an issue that needs an immediate solution and, therefore, it is 'parked' on the shelf labelled 'questions to deal with later'. This chapter (and this book) are attempts to now take the label off and address some of the AI-related challenges to (private) law.[2]

The project leading to these results has received funding from 'la Caixa' Foundation (ID 100010434), under agreement LCF/PR/PR16/51110009.

[1] The literature on AI risks abounds. For more about these risks, see Eliezer Yudkowsky, 'Artificial Intelligence as a Positive and Negative Factor in Global Risk', in Nick Bostrom and Milan M. Circovic (eds.), *Global Catastrophic Risks* (New York: Oxford University Press, 2008), p. 308; James Barrat, *Our Final Invention: Artificial Intelligence and the End of Human Era* (New York: Thomas Dunne Books, 2015); see https://futureoflife.org/background/benefits-risks-of-artificial-intelligence (literature review).

[2] Changes can happen faster than we imagine, and National Public Radio (NPR)'s interview with Thomas Friedman is admonitory in this sense. He describes the world in 2004 in the following way: 'Facebook didn't exist; Twitter was a

The chapter is organized as follows: the second section briefly deals with the concept of legality (Section 25.2.1) and its intersection with the developments of AI (Section 25.2.2). The main argument is that to keep AI legal means to keep it within the current legal framework and, if that is not feasible (as seems likely), then the ethical framework should be a temporal guide, but not a permanent alternative.

In the third section, this theoretical analysis is adopted to the private law domain, represented by intellectual property law (Section 25.3.1) and consumer protection law (Section 25.3.2). This section identifies what the author considers to be two among many obstacles to the legality of AI. In particular, in Section 25.3.1, the focus is on the clash between trade secret protection and public interest for algorithmic transparency, and Section 25.3.2 deals with entangling and shifting roles, dilemmas and certainties between consumers and producers of AI. Section 25.4 is dedicated to presenting the concluding remarks and suggesting a few ideas on how to move forward.

A few considerations on the terminology are necessary. For the purposes of this chapter, AI is understood as a wide range of technologies, both virtual or embodied, that show significant levels of autonomy, intelligence and ability to meaningfully interact with humans. This means that the AI in this chapter refers to the most sophisticated AIs that we have today or those that show promising capabilities, that could lead to become such an AI. The companion robots or humanoid robots[3] that already understand human speech, can read emotions on a human face and can interact with a human, are examples of such AI. Such AI also represents a new concept of product, that is, a product that is no longer under complete human control, can make its own decisions or choose how to move around or fulfil certain tasks.[4] In this sense, this chapter refers to strong AI rather than to weak AI.[5]

This chapter does not provide a complete overview of private law–related problems that AI is currently facing or might face in the future. The overall goal of this chapter is to focus on what the author considers to be most important issues to ensure the legality of AI. Hopefully, it might lead to novel approaches and enrich the debate with fresh outlooks.

25.2 CONCEPT OF LEGALITY

25.2.1 *What Is Legality?*

Piero Calamandrei argues that legality conditions freedom because it is the only and least imperfect way to ensure the certainty of law, understood as the boundaries that separate one's

sound; the cloud was in the sky; 4G was a parking place; LinkedIn was a prison; applications were what you sent to college; and Skype for most people was [a] typo.' Obviously the change between the situation in 2004 and 2011 is enormous (interview with Thomas Friedman with NPR, www.npr.org/2011/09/06/140214150/thomas-friedman-on-how-america-fell-behind?t=1615287727229).

[3] For instance, Samsung's Bot Care, a companion and assistant, Softbank Robotics' Pepper and Hanson Robotics' Sophia are all examples of such robots that show a potential to bring us closer to (almost) fully autonomous and intelligent AI.

[4] To be sure, the question is whether such AI should be considered as a product in the first place or should constitute a new legal category, such as, for instance, a subcategory of 'autonomous products'. The idea of such products was advanced in Aidan Cunniffe, 'Autonomous Products' (2017), https://aidancunniffe.com/autonomous-products-aa7ae68be7bb (the author suggests that App Store and Google Search are autonomous products as they evolved without a direct intervention of engineers).

[5] Strong or general AI represents the kind of AI that is similar to human intelligence, whereas weak or narrow AI is represented by specific applications in well-defined domains that do not reach the levels of complexity and adaptability of strong AI. An example of a weak AI is Google Maps, whereas strong AI has not yet been built. Some robots – for example, the aforementioned robot Sophia – already show some promising features of such abilities. See Henry Alexander Wittke, *Artificial Intelligence: An Approach to Assess the Impact on the Information Economy* (Baden-Baden: Tectum, 2020), p. 9 (difference between strong and weak AI).

freedom from that of the others or a practical possibility to know before acting what is permitted and what is prohibited.[6] He also adds that to be able to know that there should be a pre-existing norm that would foresee possible actions. Such pre-existing norms can only be possible within the system of legality that regulates interpersonal behaviour *ex ante* and not *ex post*, thanks to the abstractly constructed rules that would be triggered by the specific cases, that is, cases with certain characteristics (or triggers).

Legality is hence understood as a 'a property of being law'[7] and basically means that the legislator establishes what is permitted – and to what extent – and what is not, 'by indicating the spatial, material, and subjective *boundaries* of behaviour'[8] that stem from legal traditions, culture, beliefs and values of that particular society. This is why many countries have excluded from the realms of legality those technological advancements that were considered to be incompatible with it (at least for a certain period of time), be it virtual private networks in Russia, Facebook in Bangladesh, or Google Street View in Austria.[9] The international treaties that establish the illegality of certain weapons show that on certain questions, many countries found some sort of agreement and therefore shared their idea of legality,[10] yet these are quite rare cases as finding an agreement on an international level is a challenging enterprise: the lack of support for an international prohibition of human cloning is exemplary.[11]

The next section applies these theoretical insights about legality to the specific case of AI: is there something special and particular about AI that makes its relationship with legal order different from the one that has been established in the case of other technologies?

25.2.2 *Legality of AI*

If we follow the argument of Calamandrei, we will need a pre-existing norm to make sure that the AI we develop is legal, yet the whole problem between AI and law is the difference in the speed at which they evolve – quite typical in the case of legal regulation of a majority of technologies – and consequential ontological dissimilarity of the worlds that law and AI create and represent. Indeed, what exists in the world that AI is creating cannot be easily subsumed under the existing legal categories, and this is why Calamandrei's pre-existing norm more often than not might not even exist or, if existing, is not able to cover the case (situation, scenario) represented by AI. Furthermore, the attempts of subsumption more often than not create tensions and conflicts between what is (law) and what is continuously evolving (AI).

AI is pervasive and all-inclusive, applicable to any activity, trade or interaction. There is not a single branch of law – at least, not to the author's knowledge – that would not or could not be

6 Paolo Calamandrei, *Sin legalidad no hay libertad* (Madrid: Editorial Trota, 2016).

7 Scott J. Shapiro, *Legality* (London: Belknap Press of Harvard University Press, 2011), p. 7. However, Shapiro also recognizes the ambiguities of the term, by highlighting that it might refer to something being legal or lawful, but also it can refer to the values of the Rule of Law. Furthermore, the concept of legality also depends on specific branches of law: see, for instance, the concept of legality in the international criminal law as explained by the European Court of Human Rights in Case 2312/08 and 34179/08, *Maktouf and Damjanovic* v. *Bosnia and Herzegovina* [2013], https://hudoc.echr.coe.int/eng#{%22appno%22:[%2234179/08%22],%22itemid%22:[%22001-122716%22]}.

8 Hans Lindahl, *Fault Lines of Globalization: Legal Order and the Politics of A-Legality* (Oxford: Oxford University Press, 2013), p. 24.

9 For more examples see www.pro-tech.co.uk/news/blogs-and-news/banned-technologies.

10 See, for example, 'The Protocol for the Prohibition of the Use in War of Asphyxiating, Poisonous or other Gases, and of Bacteriological Methods of Warfare' (1925), www.brad.ac.uk/acad/sbtwc/keytext/genprot.htm.

11 Adèle Langlois, 'The Global Governance of Human Cloning: The Case of UNESCO' (2017) 3 *Palgrave Communications*, www.nature.com/articles/palcomms201719.pdf.

affected by AI.[12] However, not all the branches of law have recognized the existence of AI; for many branches of law, the AI is still too underdeveloped to be taken into consideration and therefore does not represent an issue of legality. In this sense, the AI is many times a-legal, meaning that it is neither legal nor illegal, because 'it transgresses the boundaries on the basis of which behaviour is either legal or illegal, creating a situation of indeterminacy within the order as it stands'.[13] The question is whether this indeterminacy can be maintained for long. According to some authors, and in particular with reference to blockchain technology, a-legality also means that 'autonomous systems do not need to abide to existing rules and jurisdictional constraints; they can be designed to bypass or simply ignore the laws of particular jurisdiction'.[14] However, this is not a legally desirable outcome.

This is where the ethics comes into play. It is not a purpose of this work to address the links between law and ethics, although many would agree that there are overlaps and common history as well as very strong differences.[15] However, in the situations of a-legality, the importance of ethics is crucial. This is why, in the times of (legal) uncertainties related to AI, ethics offers some valuable insights on what kind of direction the AI research should take so as to be in line not only with ethical principles, but also with legal frameworks and social values.[16]

What needs to be kept in mind in case of AI (but not only) is that there is an inclination to foster self-adopted ethical commitments in business and industry settings. However – this is the main shortcoming of ethical regulation of AI – these commitments are insufficient and are usually instrumental to discourage any kind of intervention on the side of the legislator so as to mitigate risks and address abuses.[17] Indeed, the business stakeholders are more comfortable with the non-legally enforceable ethical rules that they could adhere to (or not), rather than with the normative framework that requires compliance and punishes if there is none.

What is particular about AI is that due to its pervasiveness and its impact on the quality of human lives, it cannot stay a-legal and its regulation is mandatory. In what follows, I address specific cases that illustrate how the future legality of AI might be seriously under threat. These cases indicate what problems we have today that – if left on their own – might end up hampering the development of AI or direct it towards undesired outcomes and inadmissible side effects.

25.3 LEGALITY OF AI IN PRIVATE LAW

In the previous section, we saw a short theoretical account of what we talk about when we talk about legality, what values it represents and why it is fundamental in developing AI. In this

[12] Even family law and, in particular, marriage has not escaped AI: for more about it, Margaret Ryznar, 'Robot Love' (2018) 49 *Seton Hall Law Review* 353 (discussing not only the possibility of marriage with, but also the eventuality of divorce from, the robot).

[13] Lindahl, *Fault Lines of Globalization*, p. 36.

[14] Primavera de Filippi and Aaron Wright, *Blockchain and the Law: The Rule of Code* (Cambridge, MA and London: Harvard University Press, 2018), p. 44.

[15] See, for example, Daniel W. Skubik, *At the Intersection of Legality and Morality: Hartian Law as Natural Law* (New York: Peter Lang, 1990); David Lyons, *Ethics and the Rule of Law* (New York: Cambridge University Press, 1984); Leon Petrazycki, *Law and Morality* (London and New York: Routledge, 2017); Gregorio Peces-Barba, *Ética, Poder y Derecho* (Mexico: Distribuciones Fontamara, 2000); Francisco Javier Ansuategui Roig, *Razón y Voluntad en el Estado de Derecho: Un Enfoque Filosófico-Jurídico* (Madrid: Dykinson, 2014).

[16] This ethical component is represented by numerous and continuous references to ethics in all the EU documents that deal with AI. Ethics is also established as one of the three components of trustworthy AI, together with robustness and lawfulness (which could be understood as a synonym to legality); see High Level Expert Group, *Ethics Guidelines for Trustworthy AI* (European Commission, 2019).

[17] Thilo Hagendorff, 'The Ethics of AI Ethics: An Evaluation of Guidelines' (2020) 30 *Minds & Machines* 99.

section, the focus is on legal issues of AI that are usually regulated by private law and, in particular, by intellectual property law and consumer protection law.[18] The question stands as follows: if our aim is to keep AI legal, what are the basic threats for this legality in the fields of intellectual property and consumer protection? This question triggers other questions, such as what to do about these threats, how to balance the variety of interests involved and many more. To be sure, there are no easy answers nor quick solutions and, furthermore, the following sections address enormous problems in a very succinct way and do not aim to be exhaustive. However, concretizing these legal problems might be helpful and provide novel insights. The two concrete legal problems are trade secrets as refers to intellectual property law and consumers as refers to consumer protection law.[19]

25.3.1 *Intellectual Property Law*

The first problem with keeping AI legal is represented by the following challenge: how to strike a balance between, on the one hand, the secrecy ensured by intellectual property law through trade secret protection and, on the other hand, the public interest in understanding, assessing and learning about the internal workings of AI.[20] In fact, it is a clash between the AI developer's interest in keeping its AI-related knowledge to itself so as to maintain a competitive advantage on the market and the social interest to know how the particular AI-based tools (processes, services, systems, etc.) function and whether they are really compliant with the legal framework, in particular, with the norms concerning privacy and personal data protection.[21]

Public opinion has become very much aware of the risks and price (literally and metaphorically) that people are paying for technological advancements in their everyday lives. The price, besides its monetary form, is also calculated in terms of loss of personal data, confidentiality, intimacy, safety and secrecy of communications and other fundamental human rights.[22] Furthermore, the big technological companies are no longer perceived just as business entities, but rather undertake the role of 'cultural leaders',[23] and therefore have a more profound and multilayered impact in the society.

[18] Undoubtedly, private law is not the only branch of law that deals with intellectual property and consumer protection: for example, public law – for instance, administrative law – has a lot to do with these issues as well. However, in this chapter, the focus is on private law only.

[19] Of course, there are much more concrete problems, but for the purposes of this chapter, I will address only these two.

[20] This chapter addresses trade secret protection and not patent protection, which is also an option to protect a company's intellectual assets. However, trade secret protection offers advantages, such as secrecy, no limitations for it in terms of time, freedom from long, expensive and complicated patentability procedures, etc. Furthermore, trade secrets are considered to be 'particularly suited to technologies that are not capable of independent discovery or reverse engineering, technologies that are rapidly replaced by new innovations, and technologies that cannot be described without expending significant effort, all of which are especially prevalent in AI', as argued by Jessica M. Meyers, 'Artificial Intelligence and Trade Secrets' (2019) 11 *Lanslide* 3, www.americanbar.org/groups. See also intellectual_property_law/publications/landslide/2018-19/january-february/artificial-intelligence-trade-secrets-webinar.

[21] See Council Regulation 2016/679 on the protection of natural persons with regard to the processing of personal data and on the free movement of such data, OJ 2016 No. L119, 27 April 2016.

[22] Among many, Mathias Rise, 'Human Rights and Artificial Intelligence: An Urgently Needed Agenda' (2018), *Carr Center for Human Rights Policy*, https://carrcenter.hks.harvard.edu/files/cchr/files/humanrightsai_designed.pdf; European Agency of Fundamental Rights, 'Getting the Future Right: Artificial Intelligence and Fundamental Rights', Report (2020), https://fra.europa.eu/%20sites/default/files/fra_uploads/fra-2020-artificial-intelligence_en.pdf; Filippo Raso, Hannah Hilligoss, V. Krishnamurthy, C. Bavitz and L. Kim, 'Artificial Intelligence & Human Rights: Opportunities & Risks' (2018), Berkman Klein Center Research Publication No. 2018-6, https://ssrn.com/abstract=3259344.

[23] *O'Grady* v. *Superior Court*, 139 Cal.App. 4th 1423 (2006), Case No. H028579, www.internetlibrary.com/pdf/OGrady-Apple-Cal-Crt-App.pdf (case dealing with the disclosure of Apple product to be released in the market).

This does not mean an easier life for technological companies that are engaged in a number of synchronized and distributed conflicts. Just to contextualize, one of such conflicts is endemic in the business environment and refers to the competition with other market players, some of which do not hesitate to use illegal means so as to access their competitors' trade secrets and know-how;[24] the second conflict refers to the aforementioned battle with the public that asks for transparency and accountability of algorithms and AI-based systems, whereas the third conflict is the one with the State that needs to balance these interests and find the right solution for all the stakeholders involved. And, all of this tries to keep up with the pace of technological discoveries, advancements and updates, regulations and compliance requirements, human resources management and other problems related to the company's life cycle.

In the area of trade secrets and AI, the courts have addressed this problem in relation to other technologies, and the history of the clash between public interest and trade secrets has been addressed repeatedly. For example, in the *O'Grady* v. *Superior Court* case, the court is adamant in evaluating Apple's claim that 'the public has no right to know a company's trade secrets'. Indeed, according to the court:

> Surely this statement [the public has no right to know a company's trade secrets] cannot stand as a categorical proposition. As recent history illustrates, business entities may adopt secret practices that threaten not only their own survival and the investments of their shareholders, but the welfare of a whole industry, sector, or community. Labeling such matters 'confidential' and 'proprietary' cannot drain them of compelling public interest. Timely disclosure might avert the infliction of unmeasured harm on many thousands of individuals, ... It therefore cannot be declared that publication of trade secrets is ipso facto outside the sphere of matters appropriately deemed of 'great public importance'.[25]

The EU does not seem to depart too much from the US approach. In fact, the EU Trade Secret Directive is aware of the importance of public interest and establishes limits to trade secret protection as concerns

> the application of Union or national rules that require the disclosure of information, including trade secrets, to the public or to public authorities. Nor should it affect the application of rules that allow public authorities to collect information for the performance of their duties, or rules that allow or require any subsequent disclosure by those public authorities of relevant information to the public. Such rules include, in particular, rules on the disclosure by the Union's institutions and bodies or national public authorities of business-related information they hold pursuant to [list of specific regulations] or pursuant to other rules on public access to documents or on the transparency obligations of national public authorities.[26]

[24] European Union Intellectual Property Office, 'The Baseline of Trade Secrets Litigation in the EU Member States' (2018), https://euipo.europa.eu/tunnel-web/secure/webdav/guest/document_library/observatory/documents/reports/2018_Baseline_of_Trade_Secrets_Litigations_in_EU_Member_States/2018_Baseline_of_Trade_Secrets_Litigations_in_EU_Member_States_EN.pdf.

[25] *O'Grady* v. *Superior Court*, 139 Cal.App. 4th 1423 (2006). The court continues its explanation of why public interest should prevail by denying the argument of Apple (namely, that social utility of trade secrets is endemic to their protection and therefore public interest cannot be used as an argument to violate this protection) by arguing that there is

> the more fundamental judgment, embodied in the state and federal guarantees of expressional freedom, that free and open disclosure of ideas and information serves the public good. When two public interests collide, it is no answer to simply point to one and ignore the other. . . . In the abstract, at least, it seems plain that where both cannot be accommodated, it is the statutory quasi-property right that must give way, not the deeply rooted constitutional right to share and acquire information.

[26] Council Directive 2016/943 on the protection of undisclosed know-how and business information (trade secrets) against their unlawful acquisition, use and disclosure, OJ 2016 No. L157, 15 June 2016.

Therefore, there is an effort to keep the balance between trade secret protection and public interest both in the USA and the EU, and this balance is threatened by the algorithmic turn that many businesses are taking advantage of. The European Commission has repeatedly expressed the need for transparency, explicability and accountability (besides other features) as concerns algorithms, AI, robotics and related fields.[27] The same approach and need has been highlighted by many practitioners, academics and legal scholars who see in the advancement of opaque and black-box AI, protected by trade secret law, a serious threat to democratic societies.[28] The companies might need either to look for a different protection of their AI – for example, choose patent protection – or to assume that the public sector is no longer willing to accept lack of transparency and accountability of AI.[29]

25.3.2 *Consumer Protection Law*

Consumer protection law is a legal means to mediate between consumers on the one hand, who are usually assumed to be a weaker party,[30] and businesses (producers, suppliers, manufacturers) on the other hand. This is not an easy task, even when we speak about such common goods as food or furniture. Obviously, the complicated issue of consumer protection turns into an enormously complex challenge in the case of AI and other emerging disruptive technologies.[31]

Where does the challenge come from in the case of AI? There are two main problems. One is related to the business perspective on AI and the other related to the consumers' perspective. Section 25.3.2.1 will address the business side of complexity, whereas Section 25.3.2.2 focuses on the consumer perspective. This section also introduces a few ideas on the changes that AI introduces to our understanding of the roles of consumer and producer.

25.3.2.1 *Business Side of AI: Liability Problem*

The liability problem of producers, manufacturers or suppliers of AI (whomever legally makes available the AI-based product to the consumer[32]) is that the growing autonomy, intelligence and complexity of AI is threatening to tear apart the EU strict liability regime applicable to the

[27] High Level Expert Group, *Ethics Guidelines for Trustworthy AI*; European Commission, 'White Paper on Artificial Intelligence – A European Approach to Excellence and Trust' (2020), https://ec.europa.eu/info/sites/info/files/commission-white-paper-artificial-intelligence-feb2020_en.pdf, among others.

[28] Rafael De Asis, *Una Mirada a la Robótica desde los Derechos Humanos* (Madrid: Dykinson, 2015); Andrew D. Selbst and Julia Powles, 'Meaningful Information and the Right to Explanation' (2017) 7 *International Data Privacy Law* 233; Karl M. Manheim and Lyric Kaplan, 'Artificial Intelligence: Risks to Privacy and Democracy' (2018) 21 *Yale Journal of Law and Technology* 106.

[29] For more on this, see Directorate-General for Parliamentary Research Services (European Parliament), 'A Governance Framework for Algorithmic Accountability and Transparency' (2019), https://op.%20europa.eu/en/publication-detail/-/publication/8ed84cfe-8e62–11e9–9369-01aa75ed71a1/language-en.

[30] Of course, if we believe in the model of perfect competition, the consumer is the ruler, yet we witness every day that this is not the case. For a general overview, see Geraint Howells and Stephen Weatherill, *Consumer Protection Law* (New York: Routledge, 2nd ed., 2005).

[31] Additional complexity comes from the fact that these technologies are mainly data-driven, and therefore data availability, quality and safety have to be taken into account. Furthermore, we can also observe the increasing emphasis not only on data protection and data security, but overall security of AI-based systems in terms of the cybersecurity threats they are subject to. See EU Agency for Cybersecurity's report 'Artificial Intelligence Cybersecurity Challenges' (2020), www.enisa.europa.eu/publications/%20artificial-intelligence-cybersecurity-challenges.

[32] For the sake of simplicity, I will refer to them all as *producers*, unless otherwise specified. The producer here is represented by the company and not by a human being.

producers of defective AI-based products offered to consumers.[33] Indeed, the current strict liability regime for defective products – the only liability regime that is harmonized on an EU level besides a few very specific exceptions[34] – is based on the idea of the producer's knowledge of the product it produces (manufactures, imports, distributes, etc.), of application of all the safety and security standards, measures and methodologies and on the predictability of the product itself. To be sure, the development of autonomous and intelligent machines clashes with this consumer protection framework in more than one way: indeed, how the machines – autonomous enough to take decisions on their own, unpredictable, able to learn on their own and from their own mistakes and consequently capable of reprogramming themselves – fit the idea of product as we know it?

This question leads us to speculations because, first of all, such autonomous and intelligent machines are still works in progress, and, secondly, the speculations about such machines, that may or may not come into being, are often useless. Yet, as this chapter is about keeping AI legal, we need to address these possibilities because the liability question in this scenario will be decisive in promoting or blocking the financial investments in AI. The same position is advanced by many other authors as well. Indeed, 'a speculative assessment is a precondition for informed decisions about the introduction and design of emerging technologies'[35] and what is at risk if we do not address this scenario is that we will end up in situations where 'the allocation of liability is unfair or inefficient'.[36]

Therefore, the question is how to keep AI legal by balancing, on the one hand, the liability threats, and uncertainties, for the AI producers and, on the other hand, motivate and incentivize their investment in AI? This is to say, the challenge for the future of AI lies in finding the right balance between the responsibility for it and freedom to advance its levels of autonomy, intelligence and other (human-like) features.[37] These questions indicate that perhaps there is a need to rethink the existing liability categories. According to the latest initiatives of the EU, the general idea is that what is needed are adjustments and specifications to the current liability regimes, but these regimes should work as they are.[38] In other words, for the time being, the existing liability

33 The consumer protection law in Europe is composed of numerous directives and regulations, such as Council Directive 85/374/EEC on the approximation of the laws, regulations and administrative provisions of the Member States concerning liability for defective products, OJ 1985 No. L210, 25 July 1985; Council Directive 2001/95/EC on general product safety, OJ 2002 No. L11, 15 January 2002; Council Directive 2019/771 on certain aspects concerning contracts for the sale of goods, OJ 2019 No. L136, 22 May 2019; etc. However, when we speak about the strict liability problem of producers of AI, we should also bear in mind that the problem of liability expands beyond consumer protection and is also relevant to contractual relations of B2B interactions, insurance calculations and other related questions that fall outside the scope of this chapter.

34 Expert Group on Liability and New Technologies – New Technologies Formation, 'Liability for Artificial Intelligence and Other Emerging Technologies' (2019), https://ec.europa.eu/transparency/regexpert/index.cfm?do=groupDetail.groupMeetingDoc&docid=36608.

35 Mireille Hildebrandt, 'Technology and the End of Law', in Eric Claes, Wouter Devroe and Bert Keirsbilck (eds.), *Facing the Limits of the Law* (Berlin: Springer, 2009), p. 447.

36 Expert Group, 'Liability for Artificial Intelligence', p. 3.

37 The conflict between these two sides – responsibility and freedom – of AI advancement is not limited to the private law domain, but is also addressed in public law, in particular as concerns the autonomous weapons and international law. For more about it, see Marcus Wagner, 'The Dehumanization of International Humanitarian Law: Legal, Ethical, and Political Implications of Autonomous Weapon Systems' (2014) 47 *Vanderbilt Journal of Transnational Law* 1371 (addressing the threat of organized irresponsibility that might be caused by autonomous weapons systems). As different as the private and public law approaches (to the AI and responsibility/liability problem) can be, there is also space for cross-fertilization of ideas and concerns, such as ethical issues, lack of standards or need for an international agreement.

38 See the European Parliament resolution of 20 October 2020 with recommendations to the Commission on a civil liability regime for artificial intelligence (2020/2014(INL)). The EU Parliament '[b]elieves that there is no need for a

regimes ensure the balance between liability and freedom to innovate, yet the question remains open and this balance might be too delicate to last.

There are many connected questions that need to be dealt with in making the current liability frameworks more apt to deal with AI. To start with, there is no common vocabulary nor terminology, and AI seems to be anything and everything; for example, the EU Parliament resolution (20202/2014 (INL)) defines AI as 'a large group of different technologies, including simple statistics, machine learning and deep learning', whereas the EU Commission focuses on AI – together with Internet of Things (IoT), advanced robotics and autonomous systems – as an example of emerging digital technologies,[39] thus referring to something more technologically sophisticated and advanced than mere statistics. Further pending questions are – or are likely to become – other specific definitions (such as AI autonomy or its levels[40]) and their limitations (for instance, what is predictable and what is not in case of autonomous AI?). Similar questions regard other features of AI, such as sociability, intelligence, rationality, reactivity and others.

What seems to be the way undertaken by the EU is to focus on the risk that a specific AI gives rise to rather than on AI itself. In particular, the distinction is being made between high-risk AI systems and other systems. That is, in the case of the former a strict liability regime applies; in the case of the latter, it is fault-based.[41] This distinction constitutes a risk-based approach to liability. If we cannot know nor predict how AI develops, we focus on the impact (or risk) that the AI could have.

Another possible approach could be human-centred. That is, we could not only require AI to be programmed in a way as to prioritize human well-being whenever possible, but could also classify – and consequently regulate – AI according to the control a person can exercise over it. This distinction is similar to the one established by the international community as concerns the autonomous weapons to measure the involvement of a human operator,[42] and the one that is used in the ethics debate to refer to the different levels of human oversight.[43] What makes it particularly complicated in terms of consumer protection is that the line between where a producer's control is substituted by (accompanied, supported, aligned with) a consumer's control is unclear and, more often than not, blurred, as this control can move between the two of them, be switched from one to another or any of them might erroneously think that the

complete revision of the well-functioning liability regimes, [but] considers that specific and coordinated adjustments to the liability regimes are necessary to avoid a situation in which persons who suffer harm or whose property is damaged end up without compensation'.

39 EU Commission staff working document 'Liability for emerging digital technologies Accompanying the document Communication from the Commission to the European Parliament, the European Council, the Council, the European Economic and Social Committee and the Committee of the Regions Artificial intelligence for Europe' (SWD/2018/137 final), https://eur-lex.europa.eu/legal-content/en/ALL/?uri=CELEX%3A52018SC0137.

40 Similar to the levels of autonomy that currently are applied to autonomous cars; see National Highway Traffic Safety Administration, 'Automated Vehicles for Safety', www.nhtsa.gov/technology-innovation/automated-vehicles-safety.

41 EU Parliament resolution (2020/2014(INL)). Art. 3 of this resolution defines high-risk AI as those systems that represent a significant potential in an autonomously operating AI-system to cause harm or damage to one or more persons in a manner that is random and goes beyond what can reasonably be expected; the significance of the potential depends on the interplay between the severity of possible harm or damage, the degree of autonomy of decision-making, the likelihood that the risk materializes and the manner and the context in which the AI-system is being used.

42 In this case, there are three categories: human-in-the-loop, human-on-the-loop and human-out-of-the-loop. Only the category human-out-of-the-loop does not involve human. For more, see Human Rights Watch, 'Losing Humanity: The Case against Killer Robots' (2012), www.hrw.org/report/2012/11/19/losing-humanity/case-against-killer-robots.

43 For example, in High Level Expert Group, *Ethics Guidelines for Trustworthy AI*, reference is made to human-in-the-loop, human-on-the-loop and human-in-command approaches.

other party is controlling specific functionalities. Let us move to the consumer side of the issue and address this and other questions in more detail.

25.3.2.2 *Consumer Side of AI: Vulnerable or Empowered?*

The further issue that concerns the problem of keeping AI legal not only today, but also in the future, is related to the position of consumers. In the previous section, we looked at the position of companies as producers of AI and some of the challenges they will probably meet to keep AI legal. In this section, the focus shifts to the consumers and the question – the challenge to the legality of future AI – is framed as follows: how to balance, on the one hand, the growing need for autonomous and intelligent machines in our everyday lives (to take care of and accompany the elderly, to assist the ill or incapacitated are just two of the possible scenarios where such machines could be game changers[44]) and, on the other hand, the vulnerability and lack of knowledge and understanding of the AI by consumers, in particular by those who have the biggest need for highly sophisticated AI-based assistance.[45] It is true that consumers have more choices today than they had just twenty years ago, but if the offer of products and services is growing, the understanding of that offer does not seem to follow the same vector.[46]

There is a deep literature research in the field of informational asymmetry, and in particular what it means in the field of (such complex) technologies, where still the majority of consumers were born before the almost complete digitalization of society and still find themselves lost when it comes to being aware and conscious of the decisions they are making as a consumer. Indeed, this is a common problem that applies to all consumers – AI could easily lead to one of the main negative effects on consumers, namely, a complete or partial destruction of their sense of autonomy.[47] It seems then that in the near future we are going to assist the downfall of human autonomy as consumers and the increase of artificial autonomy of machines. From this perspective it seems like machines do not empower, but on the contrary, make people more vulnerable.

Yet the complexity does not end with this shift of autonomy from humans to machines. Differently from traditional products, AI-based products and services are becoming not only passive objects for use and consumption, but also the active objects that change in accordance to the identified needs of a consumer. These needs might correspond to the real needs of the consumer, but can also be the outcome of consumer profiling that might not necessarily represent the reality of specific needs that a human might have. Therefore the AI-based products not only satisfy the current needs of a consumer, but also anticipate – what these tools imagine to be – the next human need.[48] Differently from the IoT or ambient intelligence, the AI-based and

[44] In this respect, a sector-based classification of AI products could be useful. For instance, AI products related to healthcare (representing primary necessity) should be treated differently to those related to domotics. This brings us back to the importance of terminology and the variety of applications that AI could be used for.

[45] It is true that not all consumers are interested in the workings of AI, but the point is that in case the consumer wants to know more about AI, they should be guaranteed with such a possibility.

[46] There are also further problems such as privacy and personal data protection, profiling threats, advertising, the role of consumer protection organizations and other open questions. As already mentioned, this chapter focuses only on a few selected issues and does not aim to address the consumer protection topic in relation to AI exhaustively.

[47] Quentin André, Ziv Carmon, Kurt Wertenbroch et al., 'Consumer Choice and Autonomy in the Age of Artificial Intelligence and Big Data' (2018) 5 *Consumer Needs and Solutions* 28.

[48] The majority of readers will know the platform Netflix. The Netflix algorithm makes it possible to offer consumers a variety of series and films on the basis of their history of using Netflix. But here comes the big paradox for consumers: we think that we have more to choose from, but is it really so? Who decides what we are going to watch: is it still us or is it the algorithm?

social interaction-oriented robotics aim to group these anticipatory and predictive features within a single tool and sooner or later will be able to offer a wide spectrum of capabilities that will enable the machine to predict and interpret human behaviour as if the machine itself had this human capacity to understand the mixture of information that we provide by talking, acting upon the environment and using body language.[49]

There is one more thing to have in mind as concerns consumer protection: 'technology in itself is neither good, nor bad, but it is never neutral',[50] in the sense that it always has an impact on our behaviour, whether encouraging certain kinds of behaviour (a mobile telephone invites us to interact with others more often, download apps and use other services) or discouraging other kinds of behaviour (knowledge of how many steps are lacking of our daily 10,000 steps threshold, discouraging us from taking a bus and pushing us to start walking instead). In the case of AI, the situation gets more intricate and therefore we should pay even more attention to this phenomenon. If we cannot completely predict machines' behaviour, how can we predict the effects the unpredictable behaviour could have on a human being? Furthermore, the ability to impact behaviour leads not only to the loss of individual autonomy and vulnerability, but also to the threats of manipulation and exclusion.

In the previous section, I mentioned that what makes a difference in the case of AI is that as autonomous, intelligent or social these machines become, the human oversight should be maintained over it. It might seem contradictory, because more autonomy usually comes with less control (this is what happens with children), but with AI it should not be the case. More autonomy should come with more control, and this control should come from both producers and consumers. In this sense, the goal is not to have a new kind of prosumer[51] – an AI prosumer or a consumer who acts as both the consumer and producer of AI – but to make the producer act as a producer and, most importantly, as a consumer (differently from a prosumer, the point in this change is that it is the producer and not consumer that changes perspective). It means that the producer is not building AI for someone else, but it builds it for its own use as a consumer. It does not mean that the producer should be forced to use its own products, but it does mean a change of mindset and approach to what one is producing and launching on the market. This change of mindset also means ethical commitment and could be extremely important in building trust-based relationship between AI and consumers.[52]

Change will be easier to bring about when the AI community has advanced more considerably in the AI standardization and certification processes. There are many international, national and private initiatives around, all of which, in one way or another, acknowledge that AI standards are not just technical requirements, but also represent cultural change and act for global governance tools.[53]

[49] See Pepper the social robot of Softbank Robotics, www.softbankrobotics.com/emea/en/pepper.

[50] Hildebrandt, 'Technology and the End of the Law', p. 451 (defines this lack of neutrality of technology as technological normativity).

[51] George Ritzer, 'Focusing on the Prosumer: On Correcting an Error in the History of Social Theory', in Birgit Blättel-Mink and Kai-Uwe Hellmann (eds.), *Prosumer Revisited* (Wiesbaden: Springer, 2010), pp. 61–79.

[52] Indeed, when Steve Jobs confessed that his children are not allowed to use an iPad, it made many consumers wonder about the iPad's (and other Apple products') impact on consumers. For more about this and other examples, see Eleanor Cummins, 'Industry Insiders Don't Use Their Products Like We Do. That Should Worry Us' (3 August 2018), www.popsci.com/industry-insiders-dont-use-their-products-like-we-do.

[53] Peter Cihon, 'Standards for AI Governance: International Standards to Enable Global Coordination in AI Research & Development' (2019), Technical Report, www.fhi.ox.ac.uk/wp-content/uploads/Standards_-FHI-Technical-Report.pdf.

25.4 CONCLUSION

This chapter deals with the legality of future AI and it aimed to address the theoretical background of legality, its challenges in regulating technological advancements and to connect it to the real problems that (private) law is likely to meet in relation to AI advancements. The challenges that AI pose reverberate to the ages-old questions related to our understanding of the world and its workings/ Indeed, 'we favour freedom, equality and the common good, but we are unclear about what these ideas mean . . .',[54] and less so in the age of AI.

There are many suggestions on how to move forward and there are many ideas around it from virtue ethics to new legal frameworks, from independent auditing to complaint institutions, from an expanded academic curriculum dedicated to make people aware of the ethics of technology.[55] Additional proposals range from the establishment of compensation funds,[56] the updates of insurance regimes,[57] codes of conduct,[58] to the idea of a micro directive, understood as a personalized indication of legal behaviour, empowered by predictive technologies.[59] All the proposals claim to put the human interest as a top priority. Along the same lines are further suggestions to make legal norms part of AI, as already done with privacy by design and by default. These approaches opened the door to further incorporations, such as transparency by design.[60] Very much related to them are the advancements towards explainable AI,[61] as a continuation of the right to explainability that EU citizens are entitled with thanks to the EU legislation on privacy and personal data protection.

Perhaps the idea that runs through this chapter is that transparency – either represented by explainability or other formulae, such as standardization and certification – might be the key feature for keeping AI legal. Consumers and citizens will ask to know more about AI and therefore trade secret protection will probably need to open up more than it actually does, and companies might be pushed to collaborate. That might first come in specific fields of use, such as public administration, and later on expand to the private sector as well, if not as a legal obligation, at least as a form of corporate social responsibility and ethical commitment. The consumer protection law will probably support this shift and applaud the ensuing merger between producer and consumer, not only in the sense that the consumer becomes a kind of producer of the product (as it is in the case of the prosumer), but also, and most importantly, that the producer makes a bigger effort to step into the shoes of the consumer.

This consideration leads us to see that the question of keeping AI legal, represented in this chapter as a puzzle of different questions coming from intellectual property law and consumer protection law domains, depends on how the ones who create AI frame their relationship with it and what they set as an overall goal of AI development. Putting humans at the centre of this development seems to be the best strategy to keep AI legal.

[54] Lyons, *Ethics and the Rule of Law*, p. 5.

[55] Hagendorff, 'The Ethics of AI Ethics', 113.

[56] Expert Group, 'Liability for Artificial Intelligence'.

[57] See Insurance Europe, 'Key Messages on Civil Liability and Artificial Intelligence' (2021), https://insuranceeurope.eu/sites/default/files/attachments/Key%20messages%20on%20civil%20liability%20and%20artificial%20intelligence.pdf.

[58] See, for example, 'A Guide to Good Practice for Digital and Data-Driven Health Technologies' issued by the National Health Service of the UK, www.gov.uk/government/publications/code-of-conduct-for-data-driven-health-and-care-technology/initial-code-of-conduct-for-data-driven-health-and-care-technology.

[59] Anthony J. Casey and Anthony Niblett, 'The Death of Rules and Standards' (2017) 92 *Indiana Law Journal* 1401.

[60] Heike Felzmann, Eduard Fosch-Villaronga, Christoph Lutz and Aurelia Tamo-Larrieux, 'Towards Transparency by Design for Artificial Intelligence' (2020) 26 *Science and Engineering Ethics* 3333.

[61] Alejandro Barredo Arrieta, Natalia Diaz-Rodriguez, Javier Del Ser et al., 'Explainable Artificial Intelligence (XAI): Concepts, Taxonomies, Opportunities and Challenges toward Responsible AI' (2020) 58 *Information Fusion* 82.

26

Colluding through Smart Technologies

Understanding Agreements in the Age of Algorithms

Giuseppe Colangelo and Francesco Mezzanotte

26.1 INTRODUCTION

There is a red thread that is of interest for antitrust experts, which links together the foundational elements of contracts, as comparatively detectable in modern systems of law, and the more specific notion of cartels or concerted practices. Both legal contracts and illegal networks of contracts aimed at controlling markets and market prices have as their basis some form of mutual understanding between parties aimed at coordinating the behaviour of two or more subjects according to a certain 'common meeting of the mind'.[1]

In dealing with juridical rules depending on the existence and on the nature of the psychic states of the agents, a modern approach to the juridical phenomenon starts from the recognized impossibility of scrutinizing the inner forum of single individuals and (even more clearly) legal entities, and therefore of grounding certain technical notions – such as that of agreement – on purely subjective and intellectual elements.[2]

In this regard, the abandonment of the nineteenth-century theories inspired by the dogma of the will goes hand in hand with the progressive emergence of an array of external indices on the basis of which legal systems have been prompted to consider the presence and the substantive content of a promise exchanged among the parties.[3] As a significant example, the standard rules on the formation of the contract offer a very effective representation of the close interdependence that exists between the legally binding manifestations of the will and the techniques available to legal subjects to mutually exchange information and communications.[4]

In this context, the most recent diffusion of digital technologies and automatized processes represents only the latest stage of an evolutionary path that has always called the interpreter to adapt the operational consequences of a pre-juridical notion, such as that of agreement, to the particular forms and tools available to the parties that mutually express their positions and, ultimately, their

[1] This can be explained in that freedom of contract is faciliatory in nature, allowing private parties to agree on the terms of their contracts, while at the same time some of those agreements are regulated by other areas of law, such as antitrust or competition law, leading to their invalidation. See C. Sunstein, 'Paradoxes of the Regulatory State' (1997) 57 *University of Chicago Law Review* 707.

[2] E. Peel, *Treitel on the Law of Contract* (14th ed., London: Thomson-Sweet & Maxwell, 2015), para. 1-002.

[3] See P. Sirena, *Introduction to Private Law* (3rd ed., Bologna: il Mulino, 2020), p. 315 (overview of the history of concepts); P. Ziegler, *Der subjektive Parteiwille. Ein Vergleich des deutschen und englischen Vertragsrechts* (Tübingen: Mohr Siebeck, 2018), pp. 25–30.

[4] R. B. Schlesinger (ed.), *Formation of Contracts: A Study for the Common Core of Legal Systems* (New York-London: Dobbs Ferry, 1968).

consent.[5] At the same time, the development of transactions based on the operation of algorithms, such as those that characterize smart contracts (especially when powered by blockchain technology), may appear so disconnected from human activity as to question the very premise of the discourse, namely that at the basis of a given legal effect there is an agreement between two or more subjects, inspired (at least indirectly) by their individual determination.[6]

In this framework, the intensive application of algorithmic technologies in entrepreneurial transactions has more recently been raising peculiar issues from the point of view of antitrust law, where some form of conscious coordination between undertakings is considered necessary in order to trigger the enforcement mechanisms meant to sanction anticompetitive practices. It then becomes crucial for legal theorists and public bodies to examine the relationship between the meeting of the mind and the meeting of algorithms, in order to clarify whether the latter is (or should be treated as) a modern substitute for the former, or whether there is still room to ground the results of an entrepreneurial activity based on the automation granted by digital processes on the free determination of market actors.

The chapter proceeds as follows: Section 26.2 sets the scene of the analysis by describing how digital technologies are currently challenging legal remedies commonly applied by antitrust authorities against anticompetitive cartels. Section 26.3 looks at the issue through the more traditional lens of contract theories, which allow to widen the investigation with a parallelism taken from the constitutive elements of agreement, commonly understood as an essential condition for a valid transaction. Section 26.4 concludes the analysis with a preliminary assessment of the main policy options that are currently animating, both at regulatory and academic level, the debate on a need to reform some of the foundational doctrines of antitrust law.

26.2 NEW CHALLENGES TO ANTITRUST LAW

Because antitrust rules have been designed to deal with human facilitation of coordination, they require some form of mutual understanding among firms looking at the means of communication used by players in order to coordinate, while mere interdependent conduct or collusion without communication (conscious parallelism) is lawful.

In particular, the case law has clarified that, irrespective of the form, the existence of an agreement requires 'a concurrence of wills' on the implementation of a policy, 'the pursuit of an objective, or the adoption of a given line of conduct on the market', the form in which it is manifested being unimportant so long as it constitutes the faithful expression of the parties' intention,[7] or a 'meeting of minds', 'a unity of purpose or a common design and understanding' as well as 'a conscious commitment to a common scheme'.[8]

[5] R. Weber, 'Smart Contracts: Do We Need New Legal Rules?', in A. De Franceschi and R. Schulze (eds.), *Digital Revolution: New Challenges for Law* (Munich-Baden-Baden: C. H. Beck-Nomos, 2019), pp. 299, 307; D. Defossez, 'Acceptance Sent through Email: Is the Postal Rule Applicable?' (2019) 11 *Law, State and Telecommunications Review* 23.

[6] See R. Janal, 'Fishing for an Agreement: Data Access and the Notion of Contract', in S. Lohsse, R. Schulze and D. Staudenmayer (eds.), *Trading Data in the Digital Economy: Legal Concepts and Tools* (Baden-Baden: Hart-Nomos, 2017), p. 271; compare A. U. Janssen, 'Demystifying Smart Contracts', in C. J. H. Jansen, B. A. Schuijling and I. V. Aronstein (eds.), *Onderneming en Digitalisering* (Deventer: Wolters Kluwer, 2019), p. 15.

[7] Case T-41/96, *Bayer AG* v. *Commission* [2000] ECR II-3383, paras. 69 and 173. See also Case T-208/01, *Volkswagen AG* v. *Commission* [2003] ECR II-5141.

[8] *Interstate Circuit Inc.* v. *US*, 306 US 208, 810 (1939); *American Tobacco Co.* v. *US*, 328 US 781, 809–10 (1946); *Monsanto Co.* v. *Spray-Rite Service Corp.*, 465 US 752, 768 (1984).

Further, the concept of concerted practices has been introduced in the EU; this is defined as any direct or indirect contacts intended to influence the conduct of other firms, with the aim of filling potential gaps by precluding coordination between firms that, 'without having reached the stage where an agreement, properly called, has been concluded, knowingly substitutes practical co-operation between them for the risks of competition'.[9] Moreover, in order to manage forms of coordination that are intermediate between agreements and conscious parallelism, courts have intervened to facilitate best practices (such as price announcements and information exchanges).

Given that, under certain conditions, oligopolists can coordinate their business behaviours without entering into an arrangement, antitrust authorities have traditionally struggled with tacit collusion. Therefore, the very notion of agreement has been questioned because it is deemed to be too formalistic, hard to make operational and disconnected from the modem theory of oligopoly. Notably, the suggestion has been made to reform the agreement requirement by interpreting it as applicable to all interdependent behaviour that is successful in producing oligopoly prices.[10] In this framework, the wide-scale use of algorithms and the emergence of blockchain technology is currently posing even growing challenges to antitrust practitioners and experts.

26.2.1 Collusion by Algorithms

Pricing algorithms are algorithms that use price as an input and/or use a computational procedure to determine price as an output.[11] They may make explicit collusive agreements more stable, by making it easier to monitor prices, thereby limiting the incentives to deviate or helping to detect deviations, and they may promote new forms of tacit collusion by triggering automatized coordination independently of any human intervention and even autonomously learning to play collusive strategies (so-called algorithmic collusion).

The main concern posed to regulatory bodies is that algorithms (in particular, self-learning algorithms) may amplify the oligopoly problem expanding the grey area between unlawful explicit collusion and lawful tacit collusion by coordinating independently of human intervention and even autonomously learning to collude without communicating with one another.[12]

Two approaches have emerged within the law and economics literature. According to a first strand, algorithmic collusion represents a realistic scenario and may eventually disrupt antitrust law.[13] In contrast, other scholars highlight the lack of evidence downplaying algorithmic

[9] Cases C-48, 49, 51-57/69, *ICI* v. *Commission* (Dyestuff) [1972] ECR 619.

[10] L. Kaplow, 'On the Meaning of Horizontal Agreements in Competition Law' (2011) 99 *California Law Review* 683.

[11] UK Competition and Markets Authority, 'Pricing Algorithms' (2018), p. 9, https://assets.publishing.service.gov.uk/government/uploads/system/uploads/attachment_data/file/746353/Algorithms_econ_report.pdf.

[12] OECD, 'Algorithms and Collusion: Competition Policy in the Digital Age' (2017), pp. 25 and 34–36, www.oecd.org/competition/algorithms-collusion-competition-policy-in-the-digital-age.htm.

[13] See, e.g., S. Assad, R. Clark, D. Ershov and L. Xu, 'Algorithmic Pricing and Competition: Empirical Evidence from the German Retail Gasoline Market' (2020), CESifo Working Paper No. 8521, www.cesifo.org/en/publikationen/2020/working-paper/algorithmic-pricing-and-competition-empirical-evidence-german; Z. Y. Brown and A. MacKay, 'Competition in Pricing Algorithms' (2020), Harvard Business School Working Paper No. 67, https://hbswk.hbs.edu/item/competition-in-pricing-algorithms; E. Calvano, G. Calzolari, V. Denicolò and S. Pastorello, 'Artificial Intelligence, Algorithmic Pricing and Collusion' (2020) 110 *American Economic Review* 3267; E. Calvano, G. Calzolari, V. Denicolò and S. Pastorello, 'Algorithmic Pricing: What Implications for Competition Policy?' (2019) 55 *Review of Industrial Organization* 1; A. Ezrachi and M. Stucke, *Virtual Competition: The Promise and Perils of the Algorithm-Driven Economy* (Cambridge, MA-London: Harvard University Press, 2016); J. E. Harrington, 'Developing Competition Law for Collusion by Autonomous Price-Setting Agents' (2018) 14 *Journal of Competition Law and*

collusion as merely speculative and further arguing that the expanding use of algorithms raises familiar issues to antitrust enforcers that are well within the existing canon.[14]

Policy makers and competition authorities have endorsed a wait-and-see approach so far. According to the UK Competition and Markets Authority (CMA), algorithmic pricing is more likely to exacerbate 'traditional' risk factors facilitating collusion in markets that are already susceptible to human coordination.[15] In a similar vein, the French and German antitrust authorities, as well as the UK Digital Competition Expert Panel, have concluded that, in the situations considered so far, the current legal framework is sufficient to tackle possible competitive concerns.[16]

The European Commission, instead, appeared ready to endorse a proactive approach. Indeed, it published an open public consultation on the need for a new competition tool that allows to intervene when a structural lack of competition prevents the market from functioning properly, such as oligopolistic market structures with an increased risk of tacit collusion, including markets featuring increased transparency due to algorithm-based technological solutions.[17] However, in the proposal presented in December 2020, the planned new competition tool has been folded into the Digital Markets Act and apparently watered down into market investigations that will allow the Commission to update the obligations for gatekeepers and design remedies to tackle systematic infringements of the Digital Markets Act rules.[18]

At this stage a complete reshaping of antitrust law has been deemed exaggerated. After all, antitrust authorities have already been able to tackle the algorithmic-facilitated coordination in some scenarios. Indeed, antitrust authorities have detected cartels implemented thanks to the use of dynamic pricing algorithms, that is, software designed to monitor market changes and automatically react adjusting conspirators' prices in order to avoid eventual undercuts.[19] Admittedly, in this scenario, algorithms play a secondary role serving as a mere tool to facilitate and enforce an explicit coordination already established between humans; hence, it is not

Economics 331; S. K. Mehra, 'Antitrust and the Robo-Seller: Competition in the Time of Algorithms' (2016) 100 *Minnesota Law Review* 1323.

14 See, e.g., L. Bernhardt and R. Dewenter, 'Collusion by Code or Algorithmic Collusion? When Pricing Algorithms Take Over' (2020) 16 *European Competition Journal* 312; A. Gautier, A. Ittoo and P. Van Cleynenbreugel, 'AI Algorithms, Price Discrimination and Collusion: A Technological, Economic and Legal Perspective' (2020) 50 *European Journal of Law and Economics* 405; A. Ittoo and N. Petit, 'Algorithmic Pricing Agents and Tacit Collusion: A Technological Perspective', in H. Jacquemin and A. De Streel (eds.), *L'intelligence artificielle et le droit* (Brussels: Larcier, 2017), p. 241; J. Johnson and D. Sokol, 'Understanding AI Collusion and Compliance', in D. Sokol and B. van Rooij (eds.), *Cambridge Handbook of Compliance* (Cambridge: Cambridge University Press, 2021), p. 881; M. K. Ohlhausen, 'Should We Fear the Things That Go Beep in the Night? Some Initial Thoughts on the Intersection of Antitrust Law and Algorithmic Pricing' (2017), p. 11, www.ftc.gov/public-statements/2017/05/should-we-fear-things-go-beep-night-some-initial-thoughts-intersection; U. Schwalbe, 'Algorithms, Machine Learning, and Collusion' (2019) 14 *Journal of Competition Law & Economics* 568.

15 UK Competition and Markets Authority, 'Pricing Algorithms', p. 48.

16 Autorité de la Concurrence and Bundeskartellamt, 'Algorithms and Competition' (2019), www.bundeskartellamt.de/SharedDocs/Meldung/EN/Pressemitteilungen/2019/06_11_2019_Algorithms_and_Competition.html; UK Digital Competition Expert Panel, 'Unlocking Digital Competition' (2019), https://assets.publishing.service.gov.uk/government/uploads/system/uploads/attachment_data/file/785547/unlocking_digital_competition_furman_review_web.pdf.

17 European Commission, 'New Competition Tool', Inception impact assessment (2020), ec.europa.eu/info/law/better-regulation/have-your-say/initiatives/12416-New-competition-tool.

18 European Commission, 'Proposal for a Regulation on contestable and fair markets in the digital sector (Digital Markets Act)', COM(2020) 842 final.

19 See European Commission, 24 July 2018, Case AT.40465 (Asus), AT.40469 (Denon & Marantz), AT.40181 (Philips), AT.40182 (Pioneer); UK Competition and Markets Authority, Case 5022 (12 August 2016) 3, Online sales of posters and frames; US Department of Justice, US v. *David Topkin* (6 April 2015).

problematic to evaluate these conducts within the standard definition of agreement and concerted practice.

As previously mentioned, pricing algorithms may also lead to tacit coordination and may extend tacit collusion beyond the boundary of oligopoly. In particular, the collusive outcome may be reached via third-party algorithms, companies could unilaterally use algorithms to facilitate conscious parallelism and finally self-learning algorithms may even autonomously collude.

Under the first hypothesis, competitors adopt the same algorithmic pricing model and third-party providers of algorithm services act as a hub in a so-called hub-and-spoke scenario, allowing coordination without the need of direct communication or contact between the companies. The CMA has considered this hypothesis of conspiracy as the most immediate risk.[20] Nonetheless, it poses competition issues that could be addressed under existing antitrust rules. Indeed, according to the case law, because it is the rim that connects the spokes, proof of a hub-and-spoke cartel requires evidence of a horizontal agreement among the spokes (the so-called rim requirement), showing awareness or foreseeability of anti-competitive effects.[21]

Two additional hypotheses appear more troublesome from the perspective of the antitrust enforcement. Notably, companies may unilaterally design pricing algorithms to react to rivals' pricing or may rely on algorithms that, learning by themselves, may arrive at tacit coordination, without the need for any human intervention and without communicating with one another. In the former case, because algorithms have been designed to respond intelligently to the conduct of competitors, the mere interaction of algorithms increases the likelihood of reaching a conscious parallelism, without requiring companies to engage in any communication.[22] Hence, the question for antitrust enforcers is whether this algorithmic interaction may constitute a form of coordination (algorithmic communication), facilitated for instance by signalling practices. In the latter case, because there is no human intervention and no communication between algorithms, it may be difficult to attribute their conduct to a firm. Against this backdrop, the growing use of algorithms in business decision-making has reinvigorated the debate about the need to revisit the antitrust notion of agreement.

26.2.2 *Collusion by Blockchain*

Rather than debating algorithmic collusion, a recent strand of literature urges investigation of the potential anticompetitive use of blockchain technology.[23] Indeed, the antitrust enforcement is designed to tackle issues where market power is centralized, which consequently appears at odds with decentralization.[24]

[20] UK Competition and Markets Authority, 'Pricing Algorithms', p. 31.

[21] See, e.g., Case C-74/14, *Eturas UAB and others* v. *Lietuvos Respublikos konkurencijos taryba* [2016] 4 CMLR 19; *United States* v. *Apple, Inc.* (The eBook Case), 791 F 3d 290 (2nd Cir. 2015).

[22] M. Vestager, 'Algorithms and Competition' (2017), Remarks at the Bundeskartellamt 18th Conference on Competition, https://ec.europa.eu/competition/speeches/index_theme_17.html.

[23] See J. Abadi and M. Brunnermeier, 'Blockchain Economics' (2018), NBER Working Paper No. 25407, www.nber.org/papers/w25407; C. Catalini and C. Tucker, 'Antitrust and Costless Verification: An Optimistic and a Pessimistic View of Blockchain Technology' (2019) 82 *Antitrust Law Journal* 861; L. W. Cong and Z. He, 'Blockchain Disruption and Smart Contacts' (2018), NBER Working Paper No. 24399, www.nber.org/papers/w24399; A. Deng, 'Smart Contracts and Blockchains: Steroid for Collusion?' (2018), https://papers.ssrn.com/sol3/papers.cfm?abstract_id=3187010; T. Schrepel, 'Collusion by Blockchain and Smart Contracts' (2019) 33 *Harvard Journal of Law & Technology* 117.

[24] Catalini and Tucker, 'Antitrust and Costless Verification'.

While algorithmic collusion seems just another way of implementing well-known anti-competitive practices, blockchain-based collusion, especially involving the use of smart contracts, changes the nature of collusion creating an almost infinite number of possibilities for antitrust infringement.[25] Further, by allowing the implementation of agreements whose constraint stems from cryptographic rules, blockchain and smart contracts transform collusion into a cooperative game strengthening trust and stability among colluders. Therefore, blockchain solutions may create fundamental issues for antitrust facilitating both the sharing of sensitive information and the implementation of anticompetitive agreements. This perspective has caught the attention of the US antitrust enforcers. As recently acknowledged by Makan Delrahim, former chief of the Antitrust Division at the US Department of Justice, even though blockchain technology offers tremendous potential value, there is potential for misuse of well-crafted blockchain solutions.[26]

In contrast, some scholars call for a cautionary approach pointing out that, although the blockchain may create additional possibilities to reach and protect collusive outcomes, the underlying theories are not new nor is the technology itself illegal but rather the use that the parties make of it.[27]

In order to assess the potential anticompetitive risks brought by the blockchain technology, it is useful to distinguish the case in which a collusive outcome is reached or facilitated due to the participation of a blockchain consortium from the case in which users of the blockchain codify their collusive agreement in a smart contract.

The former scenario reflects the traditional concerns about horizontal co-operation agreements that may lead to the sharing of sensitive information; hence, it should be tackled by antitrust authorities pursuant to the general principles for the assessment of the exchange of information.[28] In this regard, it has been noted that private/permissioned blockchains require more attention than public/permission-less blockchains.[29] Although a public blockchain offers enhanced data visibility, at the same time it is open to everyone's participation, which lowers the risk of collusion. Instead, a private blockchain allows participants to get exclusive and secure access to potentially relevant information. Nonetheless, in both hypotheses, a blockchain consortium would merely represent a new technological means to facilitate collusion by exchanging information. Against this backdrop, the added value of the blockchain technology is represented by the possibility of ensuring the authenticity of the information, hence reinforcing confidence among colluding parties, and to allow better monitoring of the collusive agreement thanks to the real-time recording of transactions.

[25] Schrepel, 'Collusion by Blockchain and Smart Contracts'.

[26] M. Delrahim, 'Never Break the Chain: Pursuing Antifragility in Antitrust Enforcement' (2020), Remarks at the Thirteenth Annual Conference on Innovation Economics, www.justice.gov/opa/speech/assistant-attorney-general-makan-delrahim-delivers-remarks-thirteenth-annual-conference.

[27] R. Nazzini, 'The Blockchain (R)evolution and the Role of Antitrust' (2019), https://papers.ssrn.com/sol3/papers.cfm?abstract_id=3256728. See also, OECD, 'Blockchain Technology and Competition Policy' (2018), https://one.oecd.org/document/DAF/COMP/WD(2018)47/en/pdf.

[28] See European Commission, 'Guidelines on the applicability of Article 101 of the Treaty on the Functioning of the European Union to horizontal co-operation agreements Text with EEA relevance', (2011) OJ C 11/1; Federal Trade Commission and US Department of Justice, 'Antitrust Guidelines for Collaboration among Competitors' (2000), www.ftc.gov/sites/default/files/documents/public_events/joint-venture-hearings-antitrust-guidelines-collaboration-among-competitors/ftcdojguidelines-2.pdf.

[29] I. Lianos, 'Blockchain Competition – Gaining Competitive Advantage in the Digital Economy: Competition Law Implications', in P. Hacker, I. Lianos, G. Dimitropoulos and S. Eich (eds.), *Regulating Blockchain: Political and Legal Challenges* (Oxford: Oxford University Press, 2019), p. 329; C. Pike and A. Capobianco, 'Antitrust and the Trust Machine' (2020), OECD Blockchain Policy Series, www.oecd.org/daf/competition/antitrust-and-the-trust-machine-2020.pdf.

More problematic from the antitrust enforcement perspective appears the use of blockchain coupled with smart contracts. Indeed, this combination may sustain the collusive outcome and improve its stability by making the terms of the agreement immutable without the consent of all the users and by automating the execution of the collusion, that is, automatically activating side payments when certain conditions are met and punishments upon deviations.

The combination of blockchain and smart contracts is not only able to sustain an explicit collusion by efficiently enforcing an agreement, but may also facilitate tacit collusion.[30] Notably, in order to execute the smart contract under certain conditions, the parties need to feed it with external data that allow the provisions of the contract to be triggered and that are provided by 'oracles', programs that retrieve and verify external data through methods such as web application programming interfaces or market data feeds. The members of a blockchain consortium may choose to rely on each other as record keepers for the oracle service, hence improving the monitoring of participants' behaviour. Therefore, by generating decentralized consensus, the blockchain may lead to greater knowledge of aggregate business conditions, which can foster tacit collusion among sellers .[31]

26.3 LOOKING FOR A LEGALLY RELEVANT AGREEMENT: SKETCHES FROM CONTRACT LAW

The fundamental question remains of under what conditions can a tacit or factual understanding among two or more market actors be said to exist and to be legally relevant? After all, those advocating for a necessary revision of traditional antitrust remedies start from the difficulty of framing the concept of agreement as it relates to smart technologies (sophisticated forms of inter-individual coordination facilitated by an automatized, and thus depersonalized, meeting of algorithms).[32]

General private law theories may offer a contribution to the discussion, considering in particular that the element represented by the parties' common intention is the requirement for the validity and efficacy of bilateral and multilateral legal transactions, to the point of being frequently presented as inherently connected to the very definition of what a 'contract', in juridical terms, is.[33]

A comparative analysis of national laws is not provided here,[34] instead the focus is on model laws.[35] Starting from the common core of European systems, Article 2:101, para. 1, of the Principles of European Contract Law (PECL) is particularly clear in stating that '[a] contract is concluded if: (*a*) the parties intend to be legally bound, and (*b*) they reach a sufficient agreement', with this latter element identified in presence of terms that 'have been sufficiently defined by the parties so that the contract can be enforced, or can be [otherwise] determined'

30 Deng, 'Smart Contracts and Blockchains: Steroid for Collusion?'.

31 Cong and He, 'Blockchain Disruption and Smart Contacts'.

32 OECD, 'Algorithms and Collusion: Competition Policy in the Digital Age', p. 39.

33 H. Kötz, 'Comparative Contract Law', in M. Reimann and R. Zimmermann (eds.), *The Oxford Handbook of Comparative Law* (2nd ed., Oxford: Oxford University Press, 2019), p. 902. See also, Peel, *Treitel on the Law of Contract*, p. 1 (describing the contract as an agreement giving rise to obligations that are enforced or recognized by the law).

34 See H. Beale, B. Fauvarque-Cosson, J. Rutgers and S. Vogenauer, *Cases, Materials and Texts on Contract Law* (3rd ed., Oxford: Hart Publishing, 2019), Part 2 (general reference for basic comparative materials).

35 For methodological remarks on the value of uniform law models see N. Jansen and R. Zimmermann, 'European Contract Laws: Foundations, Commentaries, Synthesis', in N. Jansen and R. Zimmermann (eds.), *Commentaries on European Contract Laws* (Oxford: Oxford University Press, 2018), p. 1; P. Sirena, 'Die Rolle wissenschaftlicher Entwürfe im europäischen Privatrecht' (2018) *Zeitschrift für Europäisches Privatrecht* 838.

(Article 2:103).[36] The substantial identification of the notion of contract with the requirement of agreement is even more explicit in the text of the Draft Common Frame of Reference (DCFR), according to which '[a] contract is an agreement which is intended to give rise to a binding legal relationship or to have some other legal effect' (Article 1:101).[37] The American Restatement (Second) of the Law of Contracts issued by the American Law Institute,[38] though clarifying that the notion of agreement (i.e. a 'manifestation of mutual assent on the part of two or more persons') 'has in some respects a wider meaning than contract' (§3),[39] defines this latter concept as 'a promise or a set of promises for the breach of which the law gives a remedy, or the performance of which the law in some way recognizes as a duty' (§1), in this way giving relevance to the 'manifestation of intention to act or refrain from acting in a specified way' as expressed by the promisor and addressed to the promisee (§2.1–3).[40] In a similar vein, the Uniform Commercial Code (UCC) defines the 'Contract' as 'the total legal obligation that results from the parties' agreement' (§1–201(12)), considering this latter element as 'the bargain of the parties in fact, as found in their language or inferred from other circumstances, including course of performance, course of dealing, or usage of trade' (§1–201(3)).[41]

While these introductory notes confirm that the legal validity of a contract ubiquitously mandates a series of declarations (or expressions) of will communicated, and eventually shared, by the contractors, it must nonetheless be stressed that the approach taken by legal systems in the application of these agreement-related requirements operates without any considerations of their concrete understanding and of the actual intentions of the parties.[42] Indeed, irrespective of the way in which each single jurisdiction formalizes this point in its blackletter rules, the test adopted by courts and contractual interpreters to ascertain the presence of a binding juridical act and to identify its relevant terms rests on a merely external standard, based on the indications ascribable to materialized expressions, or other conducts of the would-be parties, and without the need (and even the abstract possibility) of giving weight to their subjective states of mind.[43]

Lord Clarke stated that '[w]hether there is a binding contract depends not upon [the parties'] subjective state of mind, but upon a consideration of what was communicated between them by words or conduct, and whether that leads objectively to a conclusion that they intended to create legal relations.'[44] In more general terms, this is the core idea detectable at the bottom of the guiding principle of the 'objective theory of contract': '[T]he intentions of the parties to a contract or alleged contract are to be ascertained from their words and conduct rather than

36 O. Lando and H. Beale (eds.), *Principles of European Contract Law* (PECL), Parts I and II (Le Hague-London-Boston: Kluwer Law International, 2000).

37 C. von Bar, E. Clive and H. Schulte-Nölke (eds.), *Principles, Definitions and Model Rules of European Private Law: Draft Common Frame of Reference* (Outline ed.; Munich: Sellier, 2009).

38 American Law Institute, *Restatement of The Law Second, Contracts* (1981).

39 Ibid., §3 and Comment (a), where it is explicated that '[t]he word "agreement" contains no implication that legal consequences are or are not produced'.

40 Ibid., §2 and Comment (a), where it is explicated that

> [i]f by virtue of other operative facts there is a legal duty to perform, the promise is a contract; but the word 'promise' is not limited to acts having legal effect. Like 'contract,' however, the word 'promise' is commonly and quite properly also used to refer to the complex of human relations which results from the promisor's words or acts of assurance, including the justified expectations of the promisee and any moral or legal duty which arises to make good the assurance by performance.

41 UCC, Art. 1. General Provisions, Part II.

42 See G. Christandl, 'Formation of Contracts', in Jansen and Zimmermann *Commentaries*, p. 231.

43 Peel, *Treitel on The Law of Contract*, para. 1-002 (defines a purely subjective approach as simply 'unworkable').

44 *RTS Flexible Systems Ltd* v. *Molkerei Alois Müller GmbH & Co* KG4, [2010] UKSC 14, 45.

their unexpressed intentions.'[45] Transposed to the notion of agreement, this approach 'necessarily dictates that there is no absolute requirement of a subjective meeting of the minds',[46] that agreement is to be determined by a third-party arbiter through the fabrication of the meaning of a reasonable person.[47] These general points have concrete impacts on several operational aspects of contract regulation, starting from the fundamental issue of its conclusion: at what condition is it possible to treat a mutual understanding of two or more individuals as a valid and binding contract?

26.3.1 *Objective Approach to Contractual Agreement: Applications in Contract Formation*

The more traditional way through which the juridical analysis materializes the requirement of the consent applies a conventional procedure that links together the exchange of an offer (where the offeror unequivocally indicates its intention to be bound to definite contractual conditions), with the correlative acceptance on behalf of the offeree.[48] This offer–acceptance model for discovering the existence and content of an agreement is not always consistent with modern commercial contracting dynamics,[49] but it has proved in case law to be a flexible and reliable model[50] capable of being adapted to the technological changes of the twentieth century (telex, fax, the Internet and email).[51]

A closer look at the operational rules that inspire the concrete application of this procedural test shows that, while its historical origins were inextricably connected with the ambition to identify an actual meeting of the minds of the contracting parties, modern systems of laws assign substantial importance to practical and equitable considerations.[52] Examples of the modern approach include (a) the postal rule, according to which English law considers the acceptance valid and binding at the moment of its shipment, and thus treats the contract as validly concluded even in the absence of knowledge by the offeror of the acceptance[53] and (b) limitations on the power of revocation of the offer, aimed at safeguarding the reliance of the offeree, but inconceivable from a purely subjective perspective (rooted on the intention of the offeror).[54]

[45] J. M. Perillo, 'The Origins of the Objective Theory of Contract Formation and Interpretation' (2000) 69 *Fordham Law Review* 427.

[46] In these exact terms, M. Furmston and G. Tolhurst, *Contract Formation: Law and Practice* (2nd ed., Oxford: Oxford University Press, 2016), p. 6.

[47] *Norwich Union Fire Insurance Society Ltd* v. *WM H Price Ltd* [1934] AC 455, 463.

[48] See as a relevant formalization of these rules, DCFR, Art. II-4:201 to II-4:211.

[49] S. J. Bayern, 'The Nature and Timing of Contract Formation', in L. A. DiMatteo and M. Hogg (eds.), *Comparative Contract Law: British and American Perspectives* (Oxford: Oxford University Press, 2015), p. 77; M. Siems, 'Unevenly Formed Contracts: Ignoring the Mirror of Offer and Acceptance' (2004) *European Review of Private Law* 771.

[50] Furmston and Tolhurst, *Contract Formation*, p. 7.

[51] D. Nolan, 'Offer and Acceptance in the Electronic Age', in A. Burrows and E. Peel (eds.), *Contract Formation and Parties* (Oxford: Oxford University Press, 2010), p. 61; A. M. Benedetti and F. P. Patti, 'La revoca della proposta: atto finale? La regola migliore, tra storia e comparazione' (2017) *Rivista di diritto civile* 1293, 1334 (an in-depth comparative analysis).

[52] A. T. von Mehren, 'The Formation of Contracts', in *International Encyclopedia of Comparative Law, Vol. VII: Contracts in General* (Tübingen-Leiden-Boston: Mohr Siebeck, 2008), p. 82: 'In the early 19th century this issue – along with many others that arise in connection with the formation of contracts – was approached not in terms of practical and equitable considerations but of "meeting of the minds".'

[53] *Adams* v. *Lindsell* [1818] 1 B&Ald 681; *Dunlop* v. *Higgins* [1848] 1 HLX 381. See E. McKendrick, *Contract Law: Text, Cases, and Materials* (7th ed., Oxford: Oxford University Press, 2016), p. 106.

[54] S. Gardner, 'Trashing with Trollope: A Deconstruction of the Postal Rules in Contract' (1992) 12 *Oxford Journal of Legal Studies* 170.

Consistent with this line of reasoning, it is today widely accepted that the presence of a consent among two or more individuals may be identified and evidenced not only through the formal exchange of explicit statements, but, among other means, by any form of conduct that is capable of showing agreement.[55] The rule has been traditionally applied in commercial contexts, as in cases of a prompt acceptance implied in the immediate performance rendered by the offeree, or in scenarios of prolonged negotiations resulting in mutual performance, even in the absence of an identifiable formal meeting of offer and acceptance.[56]

When transposed to modern negotiation settings, the application of this latter rule appears potentially apt to coordinate the traditional juridical approach to contract formation with more problematic issues recently discussed in the light of the growing diffusion of computerized transaction protocols capable of automatically executing the terms of a contract.[57]

26.3.2 *Objective Approach to the Agreement Requirement and the Smart Contract*

Confronted with the increasing number of digitally automatized transactions concluded on daily bases in a heterogeneous series of market contexts, legal scholars have started questioning the compatibility of these innovative forms of 'contracts' with the traditional private law doctrines.[58]

The idea of a contract whose terms are encoded in algorithmic language and that is capable of being 'smartly' (automatically) executed at the mere objective detection of a predefined triggering factor (operating as a kind of 'digital condition precedent')[59] might deprive of its traditional value a standard requirement such as that of a meeting of the minds, that would be no longer effectively shared by the interested individuals.[60] Specifying this argument through an exemplary remark, one may wonder whether the programming code through which the smart contract is designed may actually represent an 'understandable language' supporting, in credible terms, a mutual understanding between the contracting parties.[61]

At the present stage of development, these digital tools do not seem to greatly differ from old-fashioned analogical contracts, at least as for what concerns the legally relevant elements mandated for their valid formation (such as 'offer and acceptance procedures, consideration, intention to create legal relations, and capacity').[62]

55 See Art. 2:204 PECL and Art. II-4:204 DCFR, which identically state that '[a]ny form of statement or conduct by the offeree is an acceptance if it indicates assent to the offer'. On the same note, see Unidroit Principles on International Commercial Contracts (2016), Art. 2.1.1; *Restatement* §19; UCC, §2–204 ('A contract for sale of goods may be made in any manner sufficient to show agreement, including conduct by both parties which recognizes the existence of such a contract').

56 See Unidroit Principles on International Commercial Contracts (2016), Art. 2.1.1, Comment 2.

57 According to the well-known definition of 'smart contract' elaborated by Nick Szabo with specific reference to the case of the vending machine. See N. Szabo, 'Smart Contracts' (1994), www.fon.hum.uva.nl/rob/Courses/InformationInSpeech/CDROM/Literature/LOTwinterschool2006/szabo.best.vwh.net/smart.contracts.html.

58 See J. Lingwall and R. Mogallapu, 'Should Code Be Law: Smart Contracts, Blockchain, and Boilerplate' (2019) 88 *University of Missouri-Kansas City Law Review* 285; P. De Filippi and A. Wright, *Blockchain and the Law: The Rule of Code* (Cambridge, MA-London: Harvard University Press, 2018), p. 74.

59 P. Paech, 'The Governance of Blockchain Financial Networks' (2017) 80 *Modern Law Review* 1073, 1082.

60 R. O'Shields, 'Smart Contracts: Legal Agreements for the Blockchain' (2017) 21 *North Carolina Banking Institute* 177.

61 Weber, 'Smart Contracts', pp. 304–305, who, though observing that '[i]n real life, parties do indeed not often fully understand the programming language of a smart contract (and thereby its contents)', is nonetheless willing to conclude that '[p]ersons who enter into a smart contract accept the binding force of the technical conditions even if they do not really understand all details of the technology'.

62 In explicit terms, referring to English contract law, M. Durovic and A. U. Janssen, 'The Formation of Blockchain-Based Smart Contracts in the Light of Contract Law' (2018) 26 *European Review of Private Law* 753; see P. Sirena and

The academic debate has more recently focused on the future development of systems capable of autonomously conducting negotiations, using big data to draft contract clauses and constantly adapting their content through machine learning technologies.[63] The current state of smart contracts is not associated with artificial intelligence,[64] but rather operates in a strictly deterministic way, including the automatic fulfilment of the specific obligations correlated to the set of conditions encoded in the software.[65] In more explicit terms, this implies that the automatized process through which the operating system executes a digital performance (smart contract code) does not affect the juridical characters of the underlying agreement that binds the legal subjects ('smart legal contract').[66]

A large group of legal scholars see the benefits of smart contracts in their 'self-execution' and 'self-enforcement' of contracts.[67] Other doctrines of the law of contract – and in particular those concerning the element of the agreement, and of the process of detection of a binding 'meeting of the minds' among its parties – appear to be largely less affected by the impact of digital technologies.[68]

An example of this line of reasoning is found in the model rules on contract formation provided in the Unidroit Principles on International Commercial Contracts, updated in 2016. In line with the general approach detectable in modern legal systems, this soft law instrument not only considers it possible to ascertain the presence of mutual consent 'by conduct of the parties that is sufficient to show agreement' (Article 2.1.1), but then explicitly refers the notion of 'parties' conduct' to cases 'where the parties agree to use a system capable of setting in motion self-executing electronic actions leading to the conclusion of a contract without the intervention of a natural person'.[69] With these considerations in mind, it is possible to turn back to the

F. P. Patti, 'Smart Contracts and Automation of Private Relationships' (2020), Bocconi Legal Studies Research Paper Series (extended to continental legal systems), https://papers.ssrn.com/sol3/papers.cfm?abstract_id=3662402.

63 L. H. Scholz, 'Algorithmic Contracts' (2017) 20 *Stanford Technology Law Review* 128, 164; S. Williams, 'Predictive Contracting' (2019) 1 *Columbia Business Law Review* 621.

64 J. M. Lipshaw, 'The Persistence of "Dumb" Contracts' (2019) 2 *Stanford Journal of Blockchain Law & Policy* 1; S. A. McKinney, R. Landy and R. Wilka, 'Smart Contracts, Blockchain, and the Next Frontier of Transactional Law' (2018) 13 *Washington Journal of Law, Technology & Arts* 313, 322; V. Gatteschi. F. Lamberti and C. Demartini, 'Technology of Smart Contracts', in L. A. Di Matteo, M. Cannarsa and C. Poncibò (eds.), *The Cambridge Handbook of Smart Contracts, Blockchain Technology and Digital Platforms* (Cambridge: Cambridge University Press, 2019), p. 37.

65 See M. Cannarsa, 'Interpretation of Contracts and Smart Contracts: Smart Interpretation or Interpretation of Smart Contracts?' (2018) 26 *European Review of Private Law* 773. This latter aspect is at the bottom of the often cited statement that challenges the 'smartness' of a smart contract, focusing on its rigid operation according to the IF-THEN parameter, incapable of adapting the programmed performance to relevant contextual circumstances. See E. Mik, 'Smart Contracts: Terminology, Technical Limitations and Real World Complexity' (2017) 9 *Law Innovation & Technology* 269.

66 See J. Stark, 'Making Sense of Blockchain Smart Contracts' (2016), www.coindesk.com/making-sense-smart-contracts/ ; B. Carron and V. Botteron, 'How Smart Can a Contract Be?', in D. Kraus, T. Obrist and O. Hari (eds.), *Blockchains, Smart Contracts, Decentralised Autonomous Organisations and the Law* (Cheltenham-Northampton: Edward Elgar, 2019), p. 101, 111–114; M. Durovic and F. Lech, 'The Enforceability of Smart Contracts' (2019) 5 *Italian Law Journal* 493, 499.

67 K. Werbach and N. Cornell, 'Contracts Ex Machina' (2017) 67 *Duke Law Journal* 313, 318.

68 See generally, E. Mik, 'The Resilience of Contract Law in Light of Technological Change', in M. Furmston (ed.), *The Future of the Law of Contract* (Oxon-New York: Routledge, 2020), p. 112; G. Gitti, 'Robotic Transactional Decisions' (2018) *Osservatorio del diritto civile e commerciale* 619, 622 (observation that in the praxis of smart contracts it is still frequently possible to detect the standard sequence of exchange of offer and acceptance among the parties).

69 Unidroit Principles on International Commercial Contracts (2016), Art. 2.1.1, Comment 3 and Illustration:

> Automobile manufacturer A and components supplier B set up an electronic data interchange system which, as soon as A's stocks of components fall below a certain level, automatically generates orders for the components and executes such orders. The fact that A and B have agreed on the operation of such a system makes the orders and performances binding on A and B, even though they have been generated without the personal intervention of A and B.

implications of digital contracts and, more in general, algorithmic-based transactions, in the sector of antitrust law.

26.4 SO WHAT ABOUT ANTITRUST LAW?

From an antitrust law perspective, the main concern posed by the growing application of smart technologies regards the possibility of increasing the achievement of tacit collusion. Indeed, even if smart technologies were able to better support explicit collusive outcomes, these scenarios can be still scrutinized under current antitrust provisions. In those cases, algorithms and blockchains merely represent new tools that allow undertakings to efficiently reach and protect a coordination that however is established between humans and belongs to them. Hence, the challenge for the authorities is to detect and prove elements showing a coordination among firms, but relevant theories and notions are not threatened by the emergence of new technologies as such. On the other hand, whether these technologies are fit for fostering tacit collusion or even generating new forms of conscious parallelism, they would critically expand the blind spot of antitrust enforcement. Indeed, as illustrated, competition law challenges the means used by market players to reach a collusive outcome, rather than prohibiting collusion as such. Against this backdrop, the debate in antitrust circles crucially depends on the reliability of the evolutions of algorithmic collusion as a realistic scenario and the eventual remedies to deploy.

As far as the technological substance of smart contracts and blockchains will continue to operate according to the deterministic logic that inspires it today (under the IF-THEN parameter of execution, stimulated by a digitalized triggering factor), settled hermeneutical tools nowadays available to the interpreter, analysed in this chapter also from a purely contract law perspective, do not seem to be qualitatively altered. Rather, standard factors commonly applied for the detection of a binding agreement appear still suited to identify cases where the collusive intention of the parties may be ascertained, even in the absence of an explicit intention, as an objective evidence implicitly derivable by their conducts (such as the deliberate reliance of two or more market actors on a certain common software or program, applied as a shared pricing-strategy tool).

The wait-and-see approach that has been up to now assumed by national antitrust authorities (and ultimately by the EU Commission) in the evaluation of possible amendments to existing competition rules and doctrines stands as a logic corollary of the observation that algorithmic pricing, as we currently know it, is more likely to exacerbate traditional risk factors, than to have a disruptive impact on competition law.[70]

Margrethe Vestager suggested, in 2017, that all the previous considerations should not be understood as an invitation to disregard possible future technological developments, underestimating the importance of being ready to tackle innovative issues raised by algorithms that, rather than working as mere tools in the hands of humans, will be instead capable of autonomously coordinating among themselves, and learning over time to collude.[71] At the same time, even assuming that science fiction scenario as a credible future reality, it appears highly questionable that the main focus of a perspective reform of antitrust law should then be put on the legal notions of agreement, and on a necessary extension of its scope capable of encompassing not just 'meeting of the minds' but also 'meeting of algorithms'. As our analysis has shown, such a radical

[70] UK Competition and Markets Authority, 'Pricing Algorithms', p. 48.
[71] Vestager, 'Algorithms and Competition'.

revision would be inconsistent with current operational aspects of agreement-related requirements (which, even in a traditional approach to contract law, cannot be intended in a strictly subjective way), and would also prove unhelpful to keep the practice at stake within traditional antitrust boundaries. Instead, it should be investigated whether, and under what conditions, the conduct of deep learning systems could be ascribed to firms or natural persons.[72]

In sum, if algorithmic collusion emerges as a real concern, tacit collusion will become a business standard practice; hence, its very lawfulness will be questioned. Therefore, rather than wrestling on the notion of agreement, the debate should be focused on the appropriateness of a regulatory intervention aimed at forbidding collusive outcomes as such, regardless of the means used and of a finding of mutual understanding. However, the age of digital smart collusion has not arrived yet and is even not foreseeable in the near future. In the meantime, collusive attempts through smart technologies appropriately belong to the regular business-as-usual antitrust enforcement; hence, they do not require any reshaping of current rules and theories.

[72] This point raises a series of foundational issues that clearly go beyond the scope of the present research, up to the question of the true legal nature of artificial intelligence, and of the forms and conditions of its possible subjectivization. See, G. Teubner, 'Digital Personhood? The Status of Autonomous Software Agents in Private Law' (2018), https://ssrn.com/abstract=3177096; G. Wagner, 'Robot Liability', in S. Lohsse, R. Schulze and D. Staudenmayer (eds.), *Liability for Artificial Intelligence and the Internet of Things* (Baden-Baden: Hart-Nomos, 2019), p. 27.

27

The Folly of Regulating against AI's Existential Threat

John O. McGinnis

27.1 INTRODUCTION

Artificial intelligence (AI) continues to make substantial progress. But with that progress has come the concern that AI may become the master rather than the servant of human destiny.[1] For instance, Elon Musk, one the world's greatest entrepreneurs and richest men, has recently joined the chorus of those warning against its potentially existential threat to humanity.[2] This chapter will consider the costs and benefits of regulation of AI to prevent such dangers.

It proceeds by a cost-benefit analysis. Two different kind of arguments suggest that we should sway either in favor of or against regulation of AI because of its existential risks. First, it might be argued that the precautionary principle in its strong form requires that government should regulate or even prohibit activity whenever that activity causes a substantial potential threat. But this version of the precautionary principle in general and particularly in the case of AI is incoherent. Failing to develop AI as quickly as possible exposes society to substantial potential threats, including existential ones. Second, on the other hand, it might be argued that since most of the existential threats from AI are likely decades in the future, we should largely ignore those threats given the economic discount rate. But that view unfairly treats the lives of subsequent generations as less valuable than our own.

If we consider regulation of AI without any thumb on the scale, we must first consider all the benefits AI brings. Already we are witnessing a wide range of great benefits from AI, of which I treat the very substantial aid in addressing the Covid epidemic and reducing the costs of legal services as exemplary. We can expect more of such benefits in the future. Because it is difficult to know what direction successful AI research will take, any substantive regulation is likely to tamp down on those benefits.

In contrast to the concrete and predictable benefits of AI, its harms are speculative. Currently, we are a very long way from Strong AI. Indeed, AI lacks the ability to register itself as part of our world, which would seem a prerequisite to taking action that was autonomous from its creator and thus independently harmful.

In any event, there is no prospect of international verification of any regulation of AI. In the absence of such verification, rogue regimes would likely benefit from the domestic regulation of AI by well-functioning democratic nations, like the United States. Empowering human

[1] See, e.g., Bill Joy, "Why the Future Doesn't Need Us," *Wired* (April 1, 2000), www.wired.com/2000/04/joy-2/.

[2] Kelsey Piper, "Why Elon Musk Fears Artificial Intelligence," *Vox* (November 2, 2018), www.vox.com/future-perfect/2018/11/2/18053418/elon-musk-artificial-intelligence-google-deepmind-openai.

malevolence through restricting democratic societies from enjoying greater AI capacity is far more likely to cause harm than uncontrolled AI acting on its own. Instead of regulation, governments, like the United States, should engage in subsidizing the kind of AI research that they think least likely to lead to harms. This approach – promoting so-called Friendly AI – would have the advantage of accelerating the benefits of AI in general, while creating the kind of AI that is best positioned to forestall the dangers of a runaway AI.

27.2 THUMBS ON THE SCALE OF COST-BENEFIT ANALYSIS?

Cost-benefit analysis for regulating AI faces the threshold issues of both the precautionary principle and the discount rate. The precautionary principle reflects a controversial set of ideas that include requiring the government to take preventive action in the face of uncertainty and shifting the burden of proof to those who want to undertake an innovation to show it does not cause harm. A strong form holds that regulation is required whenever an activity creates a substantial possible risk to health, safety, or the environment, even if the supporting evidence is speculative and even if the economic costs of regulation are high.[3]

But the strong form of the precautionary principle has been rightly criticized because it does not sufficiently consider the benefits of innovation that the regulation will prevent.[4] Why should these be discounted more than the risks of harm? Doing so creates obstacles to progress and may create harm itself. If the principle is applied to the regulation it requires, it is self-refuting because the regulation itself creates a possible risk by decreasing innovation and thereby reducing the wealth that helps us avoid harm.

The precautionary principle as applied to AI's existential risk of slipping the leash of human control seems particularly problematic. Progress in AI, as will be discussed in Section 27.3, is delivering widespread benefits. Some of the benefits counter very serious risks to humanity, like pandemics. Other advances may temper existential risks, like climate change or the danger of asteroids hitting the earth. Still other advances are improving economic efficiency and access to justice. Any regulation that slows AI down thus has serious downsides.

The kernel of truth in the precautionary principle – its weaker form – is that regulators should not ignore dangers, even if they are uncertain.[5] But regulators should discount the risk of such dangers based upon the probability of their occurrence. Again, this requirement applies to regulation of AI, because, as I discuss in Section 27.4, there are reasons to doubt that this risk is substantial – certainly not as substantial as the risks, including the existential risks, it may counter.

The strength of the precautionary principle rationale in favoring the regulation of AI is weakened the greater the discount rate attached to future dangers. If it is high, any risk from future AI imposes less cost, because the threat is almost certainly a generation or more distant.[6] But ethicists have persuasively argued that discounting the future so radically and comprehensively violates a requirement of intergenerational neutrality.[7] Intergenerational neutrality seems

[3] Richard B. Stewart, "Environmental Regulatory Decision Making under Uncertainty," in Timothy Swanson (ed.), *Research in Law and Economics, Vol. 20: An Introduction to the Law and Economics of Environmental Policy – Issues in Institutional Design* (Bingley: Emerald, 2002), p. 71 (discussing the prohibitory version of precautionary revolution).

[4] Cass R. Sunstein, *Laws of Fear: Beyond the Precautionary Principle* (Cambridge: Cambridge University Press, 2005), pp. 14–18.

[5] Ibid. at p. 76 (considering the nonpreclusion precautionary principle).

[6] David Weisbach and Cass R. Sunstein, "Climate Change and Discounting the Future: A Guide for the Perplexed" (2008) 27 *Yale & Law Policy Review* 433, 436.

[7] Ibid.

the more attractive stance under an original position type of analysis, because no one chooses the generation in which they are born.[8]

As with the precautionary principle, a requirement that the future be discounted contains a kernel of truth: One may want to evaluate different public projects for their efficiency under discounting. The timing of the stream of income an innovation produces or the regulation that reduces a stream of income will affect the wealth of future generations. Greater wealth provides a benefit to future generation, because it will provide them with greater flexibility in adapting to their situation – in this case addressing the existential risks of AI.[9] The one present exaction that I recommend – spending money to encourage Friendly AI – is justified even in light of discounting because it is likely to speed research into fundamental computer science and related fields, thus boosting the wealth of future generations.

27.3 AI'S EXTRAORDINARY BENEFITS

One concern about regulating AI in any way is that it will get in the way of continued progress in AI that delivers extraordinary benefits. In this section, I discuss those benefits, which guard against very great, sometimes existential, risks to humanity, as well as the improvement of everyday life, including for citizens of modest means. While I touch on many such benefits, I focus on only two as examples to demonstrate their pervasiveness – the enormous importance of AI in combating the pandemic and its improvement in the delivery of legal services.

27.3.1 *AI and the Pandemic*

AI has been crucial in every aspect of the pandemic – in discovering vaccines that may end it, in improving projections of its courses for establishing better policy, in developing medical treatments to save lives, and in creating ways of living that keep up productivity during the time of crisis. If Covid had happened just twenty years ago before the intervening progress in AI, vaccines would not have been deployed within anything like the short time they have been, and treatments would not have been improved as rapidly. Without access to virtual ways of living society would have been forced to the bitter choice of losing far more productivity or enduring many more deaths. AI has been almost entirely responsible for the improvement.

AI helps find patterns in information and those discoveries were crucial in developing vaccines. The basic idea behind a vaccine is to expose the body to a part of the virus so that our immune system is primed to defeat the full version without getting sick from the shot that delivers the vaccine. But there are thousands of subcomponents of a virus that could be targeted. Machine learning can help predict based on experience with past viruses which of these subcomponents is best to target. In the case of Covid, computer scientists moved quickly to find the optimal targets.[10]

Machine intelligence has also been useful in many facets of treatment as well. For instance, it has helped to predict outcomes for classes of patients, showing which patients can be sent home

[8] On the attractiveness of the original position, see John Rawls, *A Theory of Justice* (Cambridge, MA: Harvard University Press, 1971), p. 12.

[9] Ibid. at p. 437.

[10] Arash Keshvarzi Arshadi, Julia Webb, Milad Salem, et al., "Artificial Intelligence for COVID-19 Drug Discovery and Development" (August 18, 2020) *Frontiers in Artificial Intelligence*, doi.org/10.3389/frai.2020.00065.

safely.[11] Other machine learning programs have sifted through approved drugs to discover ones that would speed recovery from the disease.[12]

Machine intelligence also helped in mapping the disease. That mapping function assisted nations in deploying resources to test even asymptomatic individuals coming from nation predicted to have spikes in disease.[13] It has also foretold the spread of the disease in many jurisdictions as when a model based on machine intelligence provided a continuous projection of the future incidence of infections, deaths, and hospitalization from the disease in the various states of the United States and countries of the world.[14]

More generally, computational progress was at the heart of the algorithms that allowed the development of the many services that permitted people to work virtually and shop online throughout the pandemic.[15] These services permitted far more distancing and less loss of productivity than would have occurred even a decade before. It is not too much to say that developments in computer science and AI were the single most important defense against the pandemic.

AI can be expected to improve on all these dimensions in the future. Machine intelligence as it progresses may provide even earlier warning of outbreaks, saving lives and reducing social costs.[16] Continued progress is particularly important as future pandemics will potentially be even more deadly than Covid, posing existential threats to humanity.

Beyond addressing the pandemic there is every reason to expect that progress in AI will aid in improving health. For instance, recent developments in AI are solving the protein folding problem.[17] Although the amino acid sequence dictates the shape of the protection it encodes, it has been very difficult to predict the shape from the sequence. A new algorithm based on sophisticated neural networks predicts these shapes with far greater accuracy than before. This development promises faster discoveries of drugs. These kinds of breakthroughs are essential to help humans ward off death, which at least for the individual is a kind of existential threat.

Pandemics are not the only more general existential threat that AI will help humanity escape. Since addressing any existential threat requires organizing information, AI will help avoid them all. For instance, AI helps us project the effects of climate change by predicting the results of changing temperatures on the earth. It also helps people to adapt to climate change as when it recommends strategies to make agricultural production more efficient in light of changing weather. It helps environmentally friendly energy production become more efficient, forestalling further climate change.[18]

[11] Kat Jercich, "NYU Combines AI and EHR Data to Assess Clinic Outcomes," *HealthCare IT News* (October 7, 2020), www.healthcareitnews.com/news/nyu-combines-ai-and-ehr-data-assess-covid-19-outcomes.

[12] Joel Kowalewski and Anandasankar Ray, "Predicting Novel Drugs for SARS-CoV-2 Using Machine Learning from a >10 Million Chemical Space" (2020) 6(8) *Helion* e04369.

[13] Hamsa Bastani, "How Artificial Intelligence Can Slow the Spread of Covid," *Knowledge@Wharton* (March 2, 2020), https://knowledge.wharton.upenn.edu/article/how-artificial-intelligence-can-slow-the-spread-of-covid-19/.

[14] Ashlee Vance, "The 27 Year Old Who Became a Covid Data Superstar," *Bloomberg* (February 19, 2021), www.bloomberg.com/news/articles/2021-02-19/covid-pandemic-how-youyang-gu-used-ai-and-data-to-make-most-accurate-prediction.

[15] Alan Shen, "The Growing Role of Artificial Intelligence in Unified Communications," *Unify Square*, www.unifysquare.com/blog/artificial-intelligence-in-unified-communications (undated Webinar).

[16] Sathian Dananjayan and Gerald Marshall Raj, "Artificial Intelligence during a Pandemic: The Covid-19 Example" (2020) 35(5) *International Journal of Health Planning and Management* 1260.

[17] Ewen Callaway, "'It Will Change Everything': Deep Mind's AI Makes Gigantic Leap in Solving Protein Structures" (November 30, 2020) *Nature*, www.nature.com/articles/d41586-020-03348-4

[18] Renee Cho, "Artificial Intelligence – A Game Changer for Climate Change," *State of the Planet* (June 5, 2018), https://blogs-dev.ei.columbia.edu/2018/06/05/artificial-intelligence-climate-environment.

AI also helps other less well-known existential threats. For instance, asteroid strikes on the planet could kill millions of people. Neural nets are being developed to predict them.[19] The relatively inexpensive aid that AI can provide to forestalling dangers, like those from asteroids, is particularly important, because governments do not pay enough attention to low-probability risks that would nevertheless result in large-scale catastrophes.[20]

27.3.2 *Benefits for Everyday Life*

Besides helping society respond to existential and particularly serious threats, AI improves efficiency and economic growth more generally. Some have estimated that in the next few decades, advances in AI will lead to over US$10,000 in additional per capita income.[21] AI is involved in almost every sector of the economy, from manufacturing to services, from distribution among companies to sales to consumers.

Given the legal focus of this volume, this section focuses on the benefits to the efficiency of legal services and the broadening of access to these services. AI is involved in improving efficiency at every stage of law, including the discovery in litigation, search for relevant cases, generation of transactional documents, and prediction of legal outcomes.[22] To summarize: High-level research in computational models of legal reasoning that when combined with the greater capacity to extract information from legal documents will lead to more autonomous forms of legal reasoning. By lowering the cost of finding and litigating about the law, these changes will not only make the law more efficient but also improve access to justice. While the organized bar has various rules that attempt to prevent many of these developments, it will not succeed in preventing these innovations from making legal services more efficient.[23]

Machine intelligence is most advanced in legal discovery.[24] Predictive coding is the practice by which lawyers look at a sample set of documents discoverable in a case. Algorithms are then constructed to predict which documents are relevant. Predictive coding has transformed legal discovery with the law firms setting up e-discovery units within their firms and independent businesses offering innovative services. It has been estimated that this industry is already worth US$10 billion. It improves efficiency by radically reducing the time that lawyers must devote to searching for relevant documents.

Computerized search has been available in rudimentary form since the 1960s.[25] But it is improving as computation improves.[26] First, search is improving in finding cases by algorithms that are better at finding the relevant cases. Second, firms are using network analysis to assess which cases are the most important. Third, cases may be connected to the legal briefs that cite cases, better assessing the value of citing particular cases based on outcomes. While much of

[19] John D. Hefele, Francesco Bortolussi, and Simon Portegies Zwart, "Identifying Earth-Impacting Asteroids Using an Artificial Neural Network" (2020) 634 *Astronomy and Astrophysics*, Article A45.

[20] Richard A. Posner, *Catastrophe: Risk and Response* (Oxford: Oxford University Press, 2004), p. 8.

[21] Catherine Clifford, "OpenAI's Sam Altman: Artificial Intelligence Will Generate Enough Wealth to Pay Each Adult $13,500 a Year," *CNBC* (March 17, 2021), www.cnbc.com/2021/03/17/openais-altman-ai-will-make-wealth-to-pay-all-adults-13500-a-year.html.

[22] John O. McGinnis and Russell Pearce, "The Great Disruption: How Machine Intelligence Will Transform the Role of Lawyers in the Delivery of Legal Services" (2014) 82(6) *Fordham Law Review* 3041.

[23] See, e.g., Marketers Media, "E-Discovery Market Is Expected to Reach USD 24 Billion Forecast by 2023" (February 2021), https://marketersmedia.com/e-discovery-market-is-expected-to-reach-a-usd-24-billion-by-forecast-to-2023/230074.

[24] McGinnis and Pearce, at 3047.

[25] F. Allan Hanson, "From Key Numbers to Keywords: How Automation Has Transformed the Law" (2002) 94 *Law Library Journal* 563, 573.

[26] McGinnis and Pearce, at 3048.

commercial search still depends on keywords, there has been progress in so-called semantic search, where legal documents are tagged to reflect higher-level semantic meaning.

AI will also improve the production of transaction documents.[27] It is already well known that firms like Legal Zoom have generated forms for wills and trusts, broadening access to rudimentary legal services.[28] But other firms are using computers to produce more complex documents for a wider variety of transactions. One advantage of such production is that the differences between varieties of transactional documents will be able to be traced and their results in litigation assessed.

AI will also improve predictions in the legal field.[29] Much of lawyering consists of predicting outcomes, like whether a patent is valid. AI can use big data to help make such predictions, increasing efficiency and reducing likely litigation, because parties will be more likely to settle if they can agree on a predicted outcome. Already, companies are offering predictive services in discrete areas of the law, like patents.[30] As AI improves, it should be able to offer these services in more legal areas. Efficient predictions of case outcomes would broaden access to law.

Ultimately, the holy grail of the intersection of AI and law is the creation of machines that can engage in reasoning, not just predict the reasoning of others. Progress is being made here as well. Programs like Watson allow for information extraction from legal texts. This information can then be placed within computational models of legal reasoning to yield legal argument based on facts and circumstances.[31]

It is true that the organized bar often opposes the provision of legal services by nonlawyers, and professional responsibility rules, often encoded in state law, prohibit such provision. But these rules will be ineffective to prevent the efficiencies and broader access afforded by AI.[32] First, all these services can be used as inputs into the lawyers' work, making that work more efficient without triggering the prohibition. Second, legal services produced without lawyers provide greater access to the law for those who cannot afford to pay a lawyer. This type of broadened access is likely to win over the less than plausible argument that it is an illegal practice of law.

While the attention here has been on AI's development in law because of the general focus of this volume, further progress in AI will speed economic growth throughout the economy.[33] The same kind of progress in law will improve business by making it easier to find relevant information, analyze data, and use it to improve decision-making.

Information analysis through sensors will move outside the office. For instance, developments in self-driving cars will make transportation more efficient.[34] Weather forecasts will continue to improve, making agriculture more efficient and saving lives in extreme weather events.[35] Indeed,

27 Ibid. at 3050–3051.

28 Benjamin H. Barton, "A Glass Half Full Look at the Changes in the American Legal Market," University of Tennessee Legal Studies Research Paper No. 210 (2013), 17, http://papers.ssrn.com/sol3/papers.cfm?abstract_id=2054857.

29 McGinnis and Pearce, at 3052–3053.

30 Tam Harbert, "Lex Machina Arms Corporate Leaders and Patent Attorneys with Predictive Analytics," *Data Informed* (2012), http://data-informed.com/lex-machina-arms-corporate-leaders-and-patent-attorneys-with-predictive-analytics.

31 Kevin D. Ashley, *Artificial Intelligence and Legal Analytics: New Tools for Law Practice in the Digital Age* (Cambridge: Cambridge University Press, 2017), pp. 1–34.

32 Benjamin H. Barton, "Lawyers' Monopoly: What Goes and What Stays" (2014) 82(6) *Fordham Law Review* 3068.

33 Irving Wladawsky-Berger, "The Impact of Artificial Intelligence on the World Economy," *Wall Street Journal* (November 16, 2018), www.wsj.com/articles/the-impact-of-artificial-intelligence-on-the-world-economy-1542398991.

34 Michael Wooldridge, *A Brief History of Artificial Intelligence* (New York: Flatiron Books, 2021), pp. 146–156.

35 Ted Alcorn, "How AI Can Make Weather Forecasts Less Cloudy," *Wall Street Journal* (April 4, 2021), www.wsj.com/articles/how-ai-can-make-weather-forecasting-less-cloudy-11617566400.

it is hard to think of many areas that will not be continually improved by developments in AI. Thus, the benefits for everyday life as well as warding off existential risks are large, certain, and immediate.

27.4 EXISTENTIAL RISKS FROM AI

In contrast to the certainty of substantial benefits there is no consensus that we face existential risks from AI. Indeed, the consensus of technology thinkers doubts that we face an existential threat from AI.[36] Both the likelihood and imminence are relevant to the benefits of contemporary regulation. Threats must be discounted by the likelihood that we will face them. To be sure, an existential threat is a large one, but even so it is subject to discounting if it is of low probability.

Besides the consensus, there are some good reasons to doubt an existential threat from AI. We can divide these threats into malevolence and indifference. A malevolent AI would seek to destroy humanity or subjugate it. But it is hard to understand why it would have such a motiveless malignancy. Positing a will to power, as Stephen Pinker notes, confuses intelligence with dominance.[37] To be sure, humans have some of these traits but these emerged from an evolutionary process not rational design. Intelligence and dominance appear together in humans, but there is logical reason that they be conjoined. Even stranger is the idea of a blundering, indifferent AI that wipes out humanity. How could an AI simultaneously have a superintelligence and yet be so clueless?[38]

Perhaps even more important is the fact that that threat is not imminent. The temporal distance is not a reason to discount an existential threat. We owe equal concern to subsequent generations – they are our children and grandchildren. But distance compounds the problems of regulation, discussed in Section 27.5. If an existing threatening AI is not imminent, the mechanisms that will lead to it are not imminent either. Given that those future mechanisms are opaque to contemporary regulators, they will not be able to figure out how to prohibit them. Moreover, we are likely to have a better idea of what lines of our research are likely to lead to an AI that is an existential threat closer in time to that threat's existence. Thus, any regulation focused on this threat should be postponed to a time when regulators would enjoy greater knowledge.

And there are also good reasons to believe in the accuracy of the consensus that rejects the imminence kind of general AI most likely to lead to an existential threat. First, currently research is far from creating or even focusing on creating a general AI that has the breath of interests and capabilities that could be threatening. Instead, research focuses on narrow AI, that is, in generating machine capabilities that can reproduce and sometimes outstrip human capabilities in discrete areas.[39] As one leading computer scientist notes, even discussion of general AI occurs in bars after the formal conference is over, not on the panels themselves.[40]

36 Eva Hamrud, "AI Is Not Actually a Threat to Humanity, Scientists Say," *Metafact* (April 11, 2021), www.sciencealert.com/here-s-why-ai-is-not-an-existential-threat-to-humanity.

37 Steven Pinker, "AI Won't Takeover the World, and What Our Fears of the Robopocalypse Reveal," *Big Think* (n.d.), https://bigthink.com/videos/steven-pinker-on-artificial-intelligence-apocalypse (notes that alpha males fear the rise of AI).

38 Ibid.

39 Wooldridge, at p. 32.

40 Ibid.

Moreover, currently, all AI can do is engage in "automated reckoning."[41] Thus, AI possesses tremendous skills at calculation. The scope of this calculation grows ever broader from calculating with numbers to performing mathematical functions to calculating pixels to recognize shapes and objects. And this growing power is transforming the world, but it is doing so under human control. Some of these calculative capacities bump up against other social concerns, just as they can when done by humans. Thus, if the enterprises they facilitate empower discrimination, or lead to accidents, they should be regulated, but that should be the focus of regulation, not diffuse malevolence or uncontrolled activity.

For malevolence, an AI needs judgment about the world. Such judgment requires the AI to understand itself as part of the world and thus make decisions about what ought to be done and assign itself responsibility.[42] Of course, the ability to operate ethically with good judgment likely also implies the ability to operate unethically with bad judgment. But until AIs get this capacity, they are unlikely to create a serious existential risk. And that capacity is nowhere near being realized, thus pushing the need for current regulation into the future.

27.5 REGULATION

27.5.1 *Dilemmas or Regulating AI, Particularly for Existential Threats*

Another problem to be weighed in any cost-benefit analysis is the difficulty of regulation in this area. If it were possible to regulate against the existential threats of AI without harming innovation, regulation might be warranted even if the dangers of the existential threat appear low. But the existential threat could only come from fundamental progress in AI and it is that progress that is generating innovation.

The government can regulate specific downsides of AI. Privacy can be protected from algorithms that might invade it.[43] Existing algorithms, like the people who create them, should be prevented from engaging in discrimination.[44] If AI mechanisms put people out work, they can be subject to special taxes to pay for retraining the displaced workers.[45] But all of these regulations focus on the actual applications and effects of AI in the current world. Regulation of the existential threats would have to focus on preventing a form of AI that does not yet exist and that has no current consequences. That is a much more difficult regulatory enterprise. It is certainly not clear which research program is going to lead to such threats, even if such threats exist.

Moreover, any regulation in this field faces several crippling dilemmas. Given the speed and unpredictability of regulations in this field, it would be impossible to regulate AI research with a complex code.[46] The code would be rapidly outdated. But if the regulation takes the form of a standard, the necessary vagueness of the standard – to prevent any research that will lead to

[41] Brian Cantwell Smith, *The Promise of Artificial Intelligence: Reckoning and Judgement* (Cambridge, MA: MIT Press, 2019), p. xvii.

[42] Ibid., at pp. 110–114.

[43] Charlotte A. Tschider, "Regulating the Internet of Things: Discrimination, Privacy, and Cybersecurity in the Artificial Intelligence Age" (2018) 96(1) *Denver Law Review* 87.

[44] Nizan Packin and Yafit Lev-Aretz, "Learning Algorithms and Discrimination," in Woodrow Barfield and Ugo Pagallo (eds.), *Research Handbook on the Law of Artificial Intelligence* (Cheltenham: Elgar, 2018), p. 88.

[45] Uwe Thuemmel, "Optimal Taxation of Robots," CESifo, Working Paper No. 7317 (2018) (studying the optimal taxation of robots and labor income).

[46] Jay P. Kesan and Rajiv C. Shah, "Shaping Code" (2005) 18(2) *Harvard Journal of Law & Technology* 319, 334.

existential threats – will provide enormous discretion to regulators.[47] It will thus also deter research and investment in AI, from the fear that lines of research may be unpredictably shut down.

A second dilemma lies in the bureaucracy that would enforce the regulation. A common problem of enforcement is the difficulty that a centralized bureaucracy has in obtaining the information to impose good regulations.[48] But this common problem would be substantially exacerbated in regulating AI for existential threats. First, the matter to be regulated would be changing very fast, requiring continuous updating. Second, it would be particularly hard for the government to get experts to be regulators comparable to those working in the field. First, the remuneration in the field of AI is very high, making it hard to find regulators at a government salary.[49] Second, knowledge becomes rapidly outdated, creating a mismatch between the long tenure of government bureaucrats and their mission of updating regulation to make it effective.

27.5.2 *Internationalizing Regulation*

Yet another problem is that any regulation would have to be done at the international level. Regulating at the national regulation would have two enormous problems. First, it would simply displace prohibited lines of research from the regulating nation and cause them to go elsewhere. Second, assuming that well-functioning democracies, like the United States, imposed regulations on themselves, the displacement would benefit totalitarian nations and rogue states. But international regulation would be difficult to negotiate and impossible to verify. It could not even prevent displacement to nations that would use research to improve their own threats to world order.

National regulation always creates the problem of displacement to other nations. But that displacement may not be a problem if the threat being regulated imposes costs only within national borders. But, of course, the existential threat that AI imposes is transnational by its very nature. And any potentially successful line of AI research is also potentially very lucrative. It is thus impossible to contain without international agreement on regulations.

A potential successful line of AI research also may enhance both offensive and defensive weaponry.[50] As a result, AI research is an essential matter of national security and geopolitics. Thus, international regulation would be needed, because no state would be willing to constrain only its own research for fear that such constraint would ultimately redound to the detriment of its national security.

But while international regulation is necessary, effective international regulation is impossible. First, the problems of national regulation, as discussed in Section 27.5.2, would be exacerbated in the international context. Creating an international bureaucracy is always difficult because of the competing national demands for jobs.[51] In an area of computer science where expertise of the highest level is demanded and would need to be constantly renewed, the

[47] Seth C. Oranburg, "Encouraging Entrepreneurship and Innovation through Regulatory Democratization" (2020) 57 *San Diego Law Review* 757, 792.

[48] Cf. Roberta Romano, "Regulating in the Dark and a Postscript Assessment of the Iron Law of Financial Regulating" (2014) 43(1) *Hofstra Law Review* 25, 47.

[49] Cade Metz, "Tech Giants Are Paying Huge Salaries for Scarce AI Talent," *The New York Times* (October 22, 2017), www.nytimes.com/2017/10/22/technology/artificial-intelligence-experts-salaries.html.

[50] Daniel S. Hoadley and Kelley M. Sayler, "Artificial Intelligence and National Security," *Congressional Research Service* (2019), R45178.

[51] Anu Bradford, "Unintended Agency Problems: How International Bureaucracies Are Built and Empowered" (2018) 57 *Virginia Journal of International Law* 159, 216. For a more general discussion of the geopolitics of regulating AI, see

parochialism of demands for appointment by nationality would prove to be an obstacle to effectiveness.

A more substantial problem is the need for verifying compliance with any international accord. In the absence of verification, some nations could take up lines of research that were either banned or regulated and pursue them. Given the importance of AI to national security, that certain effort would endanger the security of the nations that abided by the regulations. And, of course, it would not be a random group of nations that would not abide by the regulations. Rogue nations, like North Korea, would either not sign an agreement or not abide by its strictures if they could avoid doing so. Nations that do not have a strong record of adherence to the rule of law might sign agreements and not abide by the rules.

Nor could there be a system that would verify compliance with rules about AI research and development. Verifying compliance is a problem even for nuclear arms control treaties[52] where there is at least substantial infrastructure that can be used to determine compliance. But research into AI generally requires no such infrastructure. Even a treaty's authorization to send inspectors around the nation would be futile. Thus, given the substantial returns to the national interest from violating the treaty and the impossibility of verifying compliance, it would be hardly rational for states to agree to an international treaty in the first place. If they could not make such an agreement, it would not be rational to regulate AI to prevent possible existential harms.

These problems apply to any effort to regulate AI for existential risks. Thus, legislation requiring administrative certification of AI safety will be no more effective than any other kind of national regulation.[53] All forms of national regulation by a democracy like the United States would impede its own national security without doing anything substantial to ward off existential threats.

27.6 SUBSIDIZATION OF AI THAT WILL DO NO HARM

One possible response to ward off existential AI is for the government to subsidize AI research and require those getting subsidies to avoid the dangers insofar as they can be avoided. Because subsidies do not prevent any beneficial research, they will not have the costs of preventing innovation. Moreover, subsidies for fundamental research into AI rather than applications are warranted anyway because industry underproduces fundamental research as opposed to that which may immediately lead to a product because it will be hard to capture all the benefits.[54]

It might be argued that, however, that subsidization, however valuable to progress in AI, will not help against existential threats because regulators will not know which lines to subsidize and which to not subsidize for the same reasons that they will fail to be able to figure out which lines of research to regulate because of existential threat. But with subsidization, at least at first, government agencies do not have to make those decisions themselves. Instead, as a condition of gaining the grant, they can ask the researchers to deliberate about the problem and describe in writing why they see no substantial prospect of existential threat from their own line of research

John O. McGinnis, *Accelerating Democracy: Transforming Governance Through Technology* (Princeton, NJ, Princeton, University Press) pp. 100–101.

52 Roger Fritzel, *Nuclear Testing and National Security* (Washington, DC: National Defense University Press, 1981), p. 27 (discussing imperfects of comprehensive and limited nuclear test ban treaties).

53 Matthew V. Scherer, "Regulating Artificial Intelligence: Risk Challenges, Competencies and Strategies" (2016) 29(2) *Harvard Journal of Law and Technology* 354 (arguing for agency certification of AI safety).

54 Nathan Myhrvold, "Basic Science Cannot Survive without Government Funding," *Scientific American* (February 1, 2016), www.scientificamerican.com/article/basic-science-can-t-survive-without-government-funding/.

together with any emerging threats they can identify. This deliberation is likely to generate a body of knowledge about what would constitute a threat if there were one. Second, these reports might offer an early warning about when such threats would be imminent. It would have these advantages without putting a nation's national security at risk. Finally, insofar as a safe AI – sometimes dubbed Friendly AI – is developed, the AI may help humans better identify any existential threats.[55]

27.7 CONCLUSION

There is an overwhelming case against the current regulation of AI for existential risks. The regulation would compromise the progress in AI because regulators could not tell which lines of research make existential threats. Part of the reason is that these risks are not imminent and are not probable, thus making identification even harder. Finally, regulating at the national level might empower rogue nations to threaten the national security of well-functioning democracies. But international regulation is not possible, because it is difficult, if not impossible, to verify that prohibited lines of research are not occurring within another nation's territory. Encouraging with subsidies the development of AI that is not an existential threat is the best way forward, because it will build up knowledge of potential dangers.

[55] Eliezer Yudkowsky, "Creating Friendly AI 1.0: The Analysis and Design of Benevolent Goal Architectures," Machine Intelligence Research Institute (June 15, 2001).

28

AI and the Law

Interdisciplinary Challenges and Comparative Perspectives

Cristina Poncibò and Michel Cannarsa

28.1 INTERDISCIPLINARY AND COMPARATIVE EXPLORATION OF AI AND LAW

There are numerous definitions of artificial intelligence (AI) offered by technologists and others. Chapters 1 and 2 offer some definitions and introduce the reader to technological 'buzzwords'.[1] Among the many definitions offered, Stanford professor John McCarthy's description serves our purposes: AI is 'the science and engineering of making intelligent machines, especially intelligent computer programmes; it is related to the similar task of using computers to understand human intelligence'.[2] McCarthy also observes that the leap from AI to human intelligence may be impossible – 'cognitive sciences still have not succeeded in determining exactly what the human abilities are. Very likely the organization of the intellectual mechanisms for AI can usefully be different from that in people.' Thus, AI may fall short of human intelligence, but its acceleration is expected to continue with an equal acceleration in its applications. This is the context for the current undertaking. What do the current and what will future applications of AI say to societal structures (law, ethics) and how will these structures respond?

The chapters of this book offer an interdisciplinary and comparative analysis of the impact of AI technologies on the understanding and practice of the law. The book analyses the rise of AI and its impact on the law and its different categories, in theory and practice, by relying on the expertise of leading scholars from different legal systems, approaching AI technologies according to their disciplines (public law, private law, consumer law, intellectual property law, ethics, technology and law). In the area of public law, the book covers the issues of data protection, data security (Chapter 10), consumer (Chapter 19) and competition law and policy (Chapter 26). The book explores the role of government *through* AI. Governments and human beings behind AI are not disinterested ideologically, and they aim at anticipating behaviours and to steer them in a predetermined direction.[3] The book discusses the potentialities of AI technologies as

[1] S. Samioli, M. López Cobo, E. Gómez, G. De Prato, F. Martínez-Plumed and B. Delipetrev, *AI Watch: Defining Artificial Intelligence* (Publications Office of the European Union, 2020) (definition of AI), https://publications.jrc.ec.europa.eu/repository/bitstream/JRC118163/jrc118163_ai_watch._defining_artificial_intelligence_1.pdf; The European Commission's High Level Expert Group on Artificial Intelligence, 'A Definition of AI: Main Capabilities and Disciplines' (April 2019), https://ec.europa.eu/newsroom/dae/document.cfm?doc_id=56341; S. J. Russell and P. Norvig, *Artificial Intelligence: A Modern Approach* (London: Pearson, 3rd ed., 2011).

[2] J. McCarthy, 'What Is AI?', http://jmc.stanford.edu/artificial-intelligence/what-is-ai.

[3] D. Freeman Engstrom, D. E. Ho, C. M. Sharkey and M.-F. Cuéllar, 'Government by Algorithm: Artificial Intelligence in Federal Administrative Agencies', Report submitted to the Administrative Conference of the United States (2020), www-cdn.law.stanford.edu/wp-content/uploads/2020/02/ACUS-AI-Report.pdf.

instruments of governance with respect to selected areas of intervention, such as company law (Chapter 6), competition law (Chapter 26) and data protection (Chapter 10). Other chapters deal with private law issues concerning AI personhood (Chapter 20), contracts (Chapters 4–6), torts (Chapters 7 and 8 on tort theories) and Chapter 12 is about autonomous vehicles. These issues are viewed from the perspective of the constitutional principles and ethical concerns raised by this technology.

The group of scholars and practitioners come from various jurisdictions (Europe, the USA and China) and provide an extensive comparative overview. The results of their works show how technology challenges the legal traditions of the world in their implementation of the law (see Chapter 1).[4] The book analyses the impact of AI from the lens of different disciplines to provide the basis of a better understanding of new technology and its impact on law and ethics from a global perspective.[5] It examines the potential of AI to enhance, compete and replace law. It contributes to the international research and debate in the field of law and AI[6] that are deeply related to the current and future advancement of AI technologies in society.[7]

Some authors rely on case studies by providing their views on practical problems raised by AI with respect, for example, to liability issues for vehicles and robots, and in relation to the Internet of Things in public and private law (Chapters 12, 13 and 14). The purpose of the book is to help bridge legal and ethical discourses that, while having different rationales and goals, are complementary in approaching technological power and the promise of hyper-automation and consequent efficiency gains.

This new area of legal and technological research has many branches that the book examines by considering specific cases, with many significant interconnections and commonalities among them. The most important fields of technology with an impact on the law are currently machine learning, including deep learning and predictive analytics, natural language processing, comprising translation, classification and clustering, and information extraction. The variety of these technologies, including machine learning and robotics (Chapter 14), makes it difficult for scientists and regulators, as well as legal scholars, to agree on a single definition of AI.[8] The definitional problem impacts the academic discussion about AI's legal personality (Chapter 20).

AI technologies may offer an alternative paradigm of normativity across borders and jurisdictions. Such a function impacts the regulation of AI where the technology shapes regulation, such as when it is paired with the personalisation and factualisation of norms that lead to the emergence of self-regulation grounded in the technology itself. Then, we still must agree to

[4] P. Glenn, *Legal Traditions of the World: Sustainable Diversity in Law* (Oxford: Oxford University Press, 2014).

[5] Proposal for a Regulation of the European Parliament and of the Council Regulation laying down harmonized rules on artificial intelligence (Artificial Intelligence Act), COM(2021) 206 final; European Commission, Communication, 'Fostering a European Approach to Artificial Intelligence', COM(2021) 205 final (examples of an interdisciplinary projects and the need for interdisciplinarity approach to regulating AI).

[6] W. Barfield, *The Cambridge Handbook of the Law of Algorithms* (Cambridge: Cambridge University Press, 2021); M. Ebers and S. Navas *Algorithms and Law* (Cambridge: Cambridge University Press, 2020).

[7] About new applications, see R. Vinuesa, H. Azizpour, I. Leite et al., 'The Role of Artificial Intelligence in Achieving the Sustainable Development Goals' (2020) 11 *Nature Communications* 233, doi.org/10.1038/s41467-019-14108-y and M. Kritikos, 'Ten Technologies to Fight Coronavirus', European Parliamentary Research Service (EPRS), PE 641.543 (2020), 1–2.

[8] If the use of AI in law is discussed, it is important to bear one distinction between 'weak' and 'strong' AI in mind. AI used in the legal industry is commonly referred to as 'weak' (or 'shallow') AI. It seems intelligent, but it still has defined functions. It has no self-awareness. Weak AI has to be distinguished from 'strong' AI, also known as artificial general intelligence or 'deep' AI. Strong AI would match or exceed human intelligence that is often defined as the ability 'to reason, represent knowledge, plan, learn, communicate in natural language and integrate all these skills toward a common goal'. In order to achieve strong AI status, a system has to be able to carry out these abilities. Whether or when strong AI will emerge is highly contested in the scientific community.

qualify this normativity as legal, or legally relevant, which is essential if we want to make it an object of study by jurists and not abandon it to other social and hard sciences. This is the case of AI entering binding contracts as discussed in Chapters 4 and 5. From a theoretical point of view, the normative capacity of algorithms is essentially based on effectiveness, systematicity and flawlessness, which makes it vulnerable to criticism with respect to ethics and public policy. On the reverse side, this legitimation process carries with it the limitation of the role of humans in making decisions based on free will.

Eventually, AI regulation will be entrusted to technology-based private powers hopefully monitored by the state. The book discusses these fundamental issues (particularly Chapters 23–27) and develops an analysis that brings together law and ethics for a critical and forward-looking assessment of AI technologies. The central issue is whether it will be possible and feasible for public and private actors to systematically include ethical values, principles, legal requirements and procedures in the design and development of AI technologies. This incorporation by design will preserve the capacity of governments to shape technology according to the core principles of law and democracy.[9]

This chapter examines two fundamental research questions concerning AI normativity, on the one hand, and AI regulation and ethics by design, on the other. The aim is to flesh out the main challenges posed by AI and discuss the future directions of research in the field.

28.2 AI NORMATIVITY

AI technologies offer a different paradigm to rule society. They also provide new modes in execution and enforcement of individual rights and obligations. The investigation conducted in this book confirms that emerging technologies, particularly AI, have normative effects and produce technology-based norms that coexist, interface, cooperate and compete with traditional legal orders. Technological normativity must be shaped to cooperate with the values and norms of human society. Societal norms will compete with AI to form a new type of normativity that will best regulate or standardise automated, autonomous and evolutive systems.

In theory, technology, as a system of logic, schemes and codes, seems refractory to *juridification*, introducing a spontaneous order and, in the end, highlighting the false promise of an independent digital environment, based on efficient and global norms, from the physical world (and its inefficient and state-based laws).[10] The question is whether self-regulation in technological environments would risk making the ethics of the machine hegemonic and result in juridical nihilism. This is the concern enunciated by Irti and Severino in their critical assessment of the impersonal domain of technology governed by its own logic devoid of human morality and ethics.[11]

The analyses presented in this book show that AI normativity has unique characteristics. They stress how technology is faster, efficient and global compared to state laws and legal systems. Algorithms can rule globally through the Internet and offer a new paradigm for social regulation, which may compete with state law. This book should be of interest to comparative lawyers tasked

[9] V. Dignum, M. Baldoni, C. Baroglio et al., 'Ethics by Design: Necessity or Curse?' in *Proceedings of the 2018 AAAI/ACM Conference on AI, Ethics, and Society* (AIES '18) (New York: Association for Computing Machinery), pp. 60–66, doi.org/10.1145/3278721.3278745.

[10] C. Poncibò, 'Blockchain in Comparative Law' in B. Cappiello and G. Carullo (eds.), *Blockchain, Law and Governance* (Berlin: Springer, 2020), p. 137 (describing blockchain networks as transnational private regimes based on coding).

[11] N. Irti and E. Severino, *Dialogo su diritto e tecnica* (Bari: Laterza, 2001).

with understanding the interaction of global technology with state law. Currently, the normative structure of AI is in the hands of private entities from big tech to AI start-up companies. In practice, because of the pervasiveness of AI numerous normative perspectives are needed to establish standards for creating algorithms that are used to influence and guide human actions.[12]

First, algorithms reproduce the trends that are most present in their training data. This creates a normalised view of the problem they are programmed to solve. The level of details that algorithms can discern is enormous, as for instance, in automated image pattern recognition or autonomous driving. This first form of digital power will encourage humans to rely on algorithmic recommendations. The automatic and objective processing of large datasets produces trends and best practices, whether ethically good or bad.

A second form of digital normativity arises from the use of predictive algorithms trained on objective observational data without accounting for the process through which this data has been generated. For instance, algorithms that provide a customer with purchasing suggestions only rely on previous purchases made by the same and other customers, without access to the personal reasons underlying these purchases. This form of automatic data processing diminishes the inherent subjectivity of customer preferences: the individual is objectivised (normalised) by the algorithm. This second form of normativity is a recursive and dynamic process – algorithmic recommendations emanating from previous human actions in turn influence their next actions.

Third, the normative role of algorithms takes another form when their efficiency outperforms that of humans. If, for a given application, an algorithm has a higher predictive power than human experts, it may be reasonable to rely solely on this algorithm to make decisions. The algorithm then creates the norm by imposing its efficiency. With efficiency becoming the norm, the question becomes whether humans will be willing or able to judge for themselves if the outcomes of this efficiency are sufficient to meet their needs. The book examines the rise of AI normativity and its effect on the role of facts in designing norms and the personalisation that AI tools may grant to individuals and social groups.

28.2.1 *Factualisation*

The primacy of AI is also indicative of the factualisation of law. One of the roles that law serves is to usher citizens on the path to facts and, in a democracy, citizens vote to collectively choose the direction of society. In civil law jurisdictions, the facts guide and shape the law. In this way, the law passes from normative causality to practical correlation. The reality of the facts prevails over the fiction of the legal texts. It follows that legality is modified through its reconstruction of facts, which reflect the evolving interests and values in a community and their consequent validation. Law is thus reversible, circumstantial and not absolute as it is subject to contextualisation. There is no room for static norms; legality will be tested by the evolution of AI, which will expand in various ways by modelling itself on the specificity of a new basket of facts generated by AI's application to larger datasets.

The relationship between facts and norms (*ex facto oritur jus*) has long been pondered by philosophers.[13] However, the emergence of technology that produces social norms based on facts is new and deserves attention. As AI normativity evolves it will lead to the creation of immanent and spontaneous norms, internally generated (human–AI interface) far from any

[12] E. Fourneret and B. Yvert, 'Digital Normativity: A Challenge for Human Subjectivation', *Frontiers in Artificial Intelligence* (28 April 2020), doi.org/10.3389/frai.2020.00027.

[13] J. Habermas, *Between Facts and Norms* (Cambridge, MA: MIT Press, 1996).

legal deliberation and evaluation. The self-learning machine by repetitive analyses identifies new correlations and creates new standards.[14] The outcome of self-learning processes are new rules based on the findings of AI analytics that work outside of existing legal frameworks. Consequently, the rule, with a potential normative dimension, tends to be reduced to the outcomes of AI applications to data. Like the notion of 'code is law',[15] an AI-generated law is produced outside of traditional democratic, parliamentary and constitutional processes. Consequently, the distinction between fact and norm is destined to recompose itself in the unfolding of real processes managed by technologies. If this is the case, then the existing conceptualisation of law will need to be changed to include the normative and factual expressions of technologies.

28.2.2 *Personalisation*

The autonomous and spontaneous nature of this new form of law is associated with personalisation as well as factualisation. Algorithms process individualised facts without considering any broader human ethical or moral concerns (Chapters 21 and 22). In theory, the law has a general and impersonal scope that ensures the absence of any discrimination among humans and, for the sake of impartiality, it takes very little account of individual situations. There is no such equality in the age of AI technologies given its statistical power to individualise the rules of engagement.[16] This individualisation will be replicated in the law: 'the emergence of superhuman capacities of information-processing through artificial intelligence could make it possible to personalize the law and achieve a level of granularity that has hitherto been unprecedented on a large scale. Granular legal norms could increase individual fairness without reducing legal certainty.'[17]

Since the French Revolution of 1789, the law of the parliament has prevailed over rules of social groups, such as the medieval guild system. The hyper-personalisation made possible by AI may result in recreating 'personal laws'. At the same time, the risks of discrimination among humans based on certain characteristics, such as age, gender, social class, race or religion, may increase. AI's purpose is to treat people differently, for example by processing personalised content of consumers and users available on the Internet. AI can then target individuals with customised content and marketing to influence their purchasing decisions and manipulate their behaviours on the Internet and in the physical world. Human engagement with AI systems may lead to a new form of law centred on micro-directives that 'will emerge to provide all of the benefits of both rules and standards without the costs of either. These micro-directives will provide *ex ante* behavioral prescriptions finely tailored to every possible scenario.'[18] Even minor contractual relationships will be tailored to the individual. Micro-directives allow for certain

[14] American National Standards Institute, 'Comments from the American National Standards Institute on National Institute of Standards and Technology, Request for Information on Artificial Intelligence Standards' (Docket Number 190312229-01), 3.

[15] See Lawrence Lessig, 'Code Is Law' (January 1, 2000), *Harvard Magazine*, www.harvardmagazine.com/2000/01/code-is-law-html#.

[16] C. Busch and A. De Franceschi (eds.), *Algorithmic Regulation and Personalized Law: A Handbook* (Oxford: Hart, 2020). See also, A. J. Casey and A. Niblett, 'Framework for the New Personalization of Law' (2019) 86(2) *University of Chicago Law Review* 333; A. J. Casey and A. Niblett, 'Self-Driving Laws' (2016) 66(4) *University of Toronto Law Journal* 429.

[17] C. Busch and A. De Franceschi, 'Granular Legal Norms: Big Data and the Personalization of Private Law' in V. Mak, E. Tjong Tjin Taj and A. Berlee (eds.), *Research Handbook on Data Science and Law* (Cheltenham-Northampton: Edward Elgar, 2018), pp. 408–424 (quotation from abstract).

[18] A. J. Casey and A. Niblett, 'The Death of Rules and Standards' (2017) 92(4) *Indiana Law Journal* 1401–1402.

benefits, such as allowing for individual negotiation of specific terms and conditions. But it can also perpetuate structural imbalances as is the case in B2C and in contract relationships between large and small and medium-sized enterprises. Lawyers and regulators will have to be fully aware of the systemic consequences of the pervasive dimension of AI technologies and protect against their negative effects on legal rules, especially harm to human rights.

28.3 AI REGULATION

The rise of AI technologies has become an issue of power not of technology, whether directly connected to AI or companies that implement such technologies. This power may challenge state power and its sovereignty over the rule of law. State law and traditional notions of justice, including due process rights, may become second-best options that are bound to be progressively replaced by scientific and mathematical modes of regulation.

The clash of state and technological powers will be felt in the administration of justice (Chapter 23). Deliberative processes will be affected by AI-generated predictive or quantitative justice (statistical justice).[19] The use of AI in the court system will have a direct impact on the legal profession as the judiciary increasingly relies on AI and, to the extreme, replaces human judges with AI ones. AI may be seen, by governments, as the solution to the high costs of justice and to increase access to justice. The book's authors argue that the humanity of justice makes it essential that human judges be maintained with AI being limited to a supporting role.

The issues related to the regulation of AI is a common theme throughout the book. In this respect, the difficulty of individual states' ability to regulate AI is discussed and the need for an internationally recognised regulation of algorithms is noted. These difficulties become more pronounced if technology advances to superintelligence (see Chapter 27).[20] Global phenomena, such as the Internet and AI, question the state's ability to govern numerous areas of society. Accordingly, the book considers forms of autonomous self-regulation, regulatory rules incorporated into the design of AI and other rules implemented by network operators. These types of self-regulation cannot be left to AI tech companies alone. A better model would be one of co-regulation involving public-private regulatory cooperation. In this respect, the EU Commission is assessing the potential of European standardisation bodies to lead the regulatory effort as espoused in its proposed 'Artificial Intelligence Act' (Chapter 22).[21]

The difficulty of public institutions in governing AI is resulting in a sort of *delegation of power* from the government to private or semi-private actors (international and European standardisation bodies). This approach relies on these bodies to embed legal and ethical principles into the standards for the design, manufacture and programming of these technologies. The idea of *regulation by design* has been criticised as not adequate for data protection and privacy.[22] Standardising bodies lack the ability to systematically ensure that legal rules are respected. In addition, these actors are far from immune from sectorial and economic interests. It is therefore

[19] J. Ulenaers, 'The Impact of Artificial Intelligence on the Right to a Fair Trial: Towards a Robot Judge?' (2020) 11(2) *Asian Journal of Law and Economics* 8.

[20] See Chapter 27's argument that the existential threat of AI is exaggerated; see N. Bostrom, *Superintelligence: Paths, Dangers, Strategies* (Oxford: Oxford University Press, 2014).

[21] European Commission, Proposal for a Regulation laying down harmonised rules on artificial intelligence ('Artificial Intelligence Act'), COM(2021) 206 final.

[22] A. E. Waldman, 'Data Protection by Design? A Critique of Article 25 of the GDPR' (2021) 53 *Cornell International Law Journal* 147. See generally, K. Yeung, 'Towards an Understanding of Regulation by Design' in R. Brownsword and K. Yeung (eds.), *Regulating Technologies: Legal Futures, Regulatory Frames and Technological Fixes* (Oxford: Hart, 2008), chapter 4.

fair to say that such delegation to standardisation helps public authorities to avoid taking the legal and political responsibility for regulating new and fast-growing technologies. However, it produces a system into which technology shapes regulation and not the opposite. Philosopher of science E. Severino asserts that the risks of technology continue to gain momentum with respect to the law.[23]

Implicit in the concept of public-private co-regulation is the ability of law to adapt and change to cope with these innovations. The analyses presented in this book indicate that the driving force of this process is based on three principles of accountability, responsibility and transparency (ART), as discussed in the areas of liability for autonomous vehicles, contractual liability, product liability, and so forth. The first (*accountability*) refers to a system's need to explain and justify decisions and actions to its partners, users and others with whom it interacts. To ensure accountability, decisions must be derivable from, and explained by, the decision-making algorithms used. This includes the need for representation of the moral values and societal norms in the context of the operation of AI.[24] The second (*responsibility*) refers both to the capability of AI systems and people interacting with them. The AI, as well as its creator and operator-user, must be responsible for AI-generated decisions, diagnosing errors and unexpected results. The chain of responsibility includes those that create datasets to ensure the fair use of data. The third principle is *transparency* and refers to the need to describe, inspect and reproduce the mechanisms through which an AI system uses data to make decisions and learns to adapt to its environment. Current AI algorithms are essentially 'black boxes', which runs counter to transparency. However, regulators and users demand explanation and clarity. Methods are needed to inspect algorithms and their results and to manage data provenance and dynamics. In this respect, some contributions make clear how AI systems are particularly risky for the most vulnerable, such as consumers. Thus, the three ART principles need to be strongly applied when AI technologies are impacting the rights of the vulnerable.

28.4 ETHICS BY DESIGN

In addressing different disciplines and case studies, the contributions in the book converge in noting that, in the end, the central issues are identifying those that write algorithms and how.[25] Is the informed consent of users enough to solve problems of abuse or overreaching? The answer is in the negative unless the workings of AI are transparent, and the creators and operators of AI systems are held to be accountable and responsible. Moreover, the ability to access the algorithm is insufficient for the understanding of ordinary citizens. Consumers are subject to manipulation by programmers that increases their propensity to spend or subjects them to other forms of abuse.[26]

[23] Irti and Severino, *Dialogo su diritto e tecnica*.

[24] Accountability in AI requires both functionality for guiding action (by forming beliefs and making decisions) and for explanation (by placing decisions in a broader context and by classifying them along moral values).

[25] According to the Stanford AI Index 2019, the ethical challenges most mentioned across fifty-nine ethical AI framework documents were: fairness; interpretability and explainability; transparency and accountability; data privacy, reliability, robustness and security; R. Perrault, Y. Shoham, E. Brynjolfsson et al., *The AI Index 2019 Annual Report* (AI Index Steering Committee, Human-Centered AI Institute, Stanford University, Stanford, December 2019), 149, https://hai.stanford.edu/sites/default/files/ai_index_2019_report.pdf.

[26] Council of Europe, 'Algorithms and Human Rights, Study on the Human rights dimensions of automated data processing techniques and possible regulatory implications', Council of Europe study, DGI(2017)12, prepared by the Committee of Experts on Internet Intermediaries (MSI-NET), 2018; Berkman Klein Center, 'Artificial Intelligence & Human Rights: Opportunities and Risks' (25 September 2018), doi.org/10.2139/ssrn.3259344.

The best starting point is to acknowledge that AI technologies are not neutral or apolitical as one might imagine at first glance. A properly drawn algorithm has the advantage of being a priori fairer than decisions rooted in human decision subjectivity. On the surface, the mathematical rigour and logic of algorithms promise less biased decision-making.[27] However, regulators must continue to monitor the development of new and advanced AI to prevent the covert abuse of power that these new technologies allow. The criteria, parameters and the accessible data behind AI are determined by humans. Algorithmic logic may act as a facade for the intentions and trade-offs made by humans.

The current analysis confirms that ethical challenges remain in protecting core values and human dignity from rapid technological change.[28] Ethics by design methodology consists, first, in identifying the system of values to be incorporated into new technologies and how they can best be protected. Scientific and societal anchoring of pragmatic ethics is required to preserve human free will.[29]

28.5 PERSPECTIVES

The hope is that legal rules relating to AI technologies can frame their progress and limit the risks of abuse. This hope is tentative as technology seriously challenges the theory and practice of the law across legal traditions. The use of interdisciplinary and comparative methodologies in this book makes clear that AI is currently impacting our understanding of the law. The degree of this impact and law's response is unclear currently. The book claims that AI can be understood as a regulatory technology and confirms that AI can produce normative effects some of which may be contrary to public laws and regulations. The book notes the growing importance of establishing algorithmic normativity (AI-specific norms) as opposed to public law normativity, which is based upon more general and abstract norms. The fear is that public and transparent law will be eroded insidiously by private opaque and subconscious standards.

In concluding, we underline that AI's normativity is solely dependent on its effectiveness. The effectiveness and ubiquity of AI is disassociated with norms developed by democratic deliberation by public institutions. This dependence on its effectiveness makes it fragile. Humans will remain in control despite their often unconscious and involuntary reception of the effectiveness of AI. They can free themselves from it, provided they want to. Such a decision is only possible if information about AI systems and how they work is made accessible and understandable. Without informed consent, the fear of Italian philosopher Norberto Bobbio may be realised that instead of a future based on human rights the world will be ruled by a dictatorial presence aided by an all-controlling AI.[30]

In a way, ethics becomes more important than formal law in the future world of advanced AI. In the words of Hans Jonas, it is the ethical approach that will (and should) preserve human dignity.[31] The goal is to ensure that the machine, devoid of conscience, is always at the service of humans. Algorithm ethics is mostly a replication of human ethics prior to the age of AI.

[27] The European Commission's High Level Expert Group on Artificial Intelligence, 'Ethics Guidelines for Trustworthy AI' (8 April 2019). See also, The European Commission's High Level Expert Group on Artificial Intelligence, 'Policy and Investment Recommendations for Trustworthy AI' (26 June 2019).

[28] P. Verbeek, *Moralizing Technology* (Chicago: University of Chicago Press, 2011).

[29] E. Mik, 'Contracts in Code?' (2021) 13(2) *Law, Innovation and Technology* 1.

[30] N. Bobbio, *L'età dei diritti* (Turin: Einaudi, 1990).

[31] A. Jonas, *The Imperative of Responsibility: In Search of an Ethics for the Technological Age* (Chicago: University of Chicago Press, 1985).

The chapters of this book show that profound change in society, and by necessity in the law, is underway. The idea of robot judges (Chapter 23) represents the enormity of the change. In fact, the degree that AI reshapes the substance of law will increase. Will this invite jurists to rethink the object of study away from state law? The answer is that the jurist and lawyer[32] of the future will need expanded skill sets including traditional knowledge of law as well as technical knowledge of how AI systems are created and applied.

It is our hope that this book will help readers to decipher the impact of technologies on the law and vice versa. The rise of AI has created ethical, sociological and philosophical problems. Because of this, governments and jurists must continue to write the rules to preserve social life and democratic institutions.

[32] L. DiMatteo, A. Janssen, P. Ortolani, F. de Elizalde, M. Cannarsa and M. Durovic (eds.), *Lawyering in the Digital Age* (New York: Cambridge University Press, 2021).